by the same author

COMANCHES

T. R. FEHRENBACH

COMANCHES
THE DESTRUCTION
OF A PEOPLE

DA CAPO PRESS

Library of Congress Cataloging in Publication Data

Fehrenbach, T. R.
  Comanches: the destruction of a people / T. R. Fehrenbach.—1st Da
Capo Press ed.
     p.   cm.
  Originally published: New York: Knopf, 1974.
  Includes bibliographical references and index.
  ISBN 0-306-80586-3 (pbk.)
  1. Comanche Indians—History. I. Title.
E99.C85F44   1994   94-12128
973′ .04974—dc20   CIP

First Da Capo Press edition 1994

This Da Capo Press paperback edition of *Comanches* is an
unabridged republication of the edition originally published in
New York in 1974. It is here reprinted by arrangement with
Alfred A. Knopf and the author.

01 02 03 EBC 10 9 8 7 6 5

Published by Da Capo Press, Inc.

A member of the Perseus Books Group

Grateful acknowledgment is made to the following for permission
to reprint the illustrations listed on pages ix–xii: Museum of the
American Indian, New York, New York, Heye Foundation; Rare Book
Division, The New York Public Library, Astor, Lenox and Tilden
Foundations; The New-York Historical Society, New York City;
The Smithsonian Institution National Anthropological Archives,
Bureau of American Ethnology Collection; The University of Texas
Press, Austin; Western History Collections, University of Oklahoma
Library; The U.S. Army Field Artillery Center and Fort Sill Museum,
Fort Sill, Oklahoma; The National Collection of Fine Arts,
Smithsonian Institution.

*To those who have seldom been too cold, hot, or wet,
never really hungry, and confidently expect to see many to-
morrows, a people who had none of these advantages come
as something of a shock. . . . Yet, they survived, even thrived,
and were happy with their ways.
To Europeans and Texans it was astonishing and insufferable
that such a people should prefer their own gods,
food, and customs to civilization's blessings.
But they did, and they clung to these ancestral ways.
And for this they perished.
To persevere to such ultimate tragedy
is a highway to continuing remembrance.*

—W. W. NEWCOMB, JR.

CONTENTS

ILLUSTRATIONS

xii

MAPS

PREFACE

THIS IS THE STORY OF THE NERMERNUH OR PEOPLE, A FEW THOUSAND North American Indians, from their prehistoric beginnings to their destruction as an independent people. In one sense the passage of the People was of little importance, a minor footnote to American history. But in another sense, these few thousands who lived and died on the plains shaped the continent in ways that few modern Americans have seen or understood.

It is actually impossible to reconstruct the full history of this people. The Nermernuh, the True Human Beings, had no writing or records, not even the crude but effective "calendars" of their Kiowa allies. They rode into modern history peculiarly poor in lore and legend, and because their days of power were ephemeral, they enjoyed no long autumn in which to remember and record their greatness. They passed out of history as quickly as they entered it.

And significantly, Europeans never learned much about them while they still roamed the continent. The Nermernuh were never easily penetrable; they were a race apart. They destroyed the ancient dream of Spanish empire in North America; they shredded the Mexican frontier; they blocked the French advance into the Southwest; and they delayed the advance of the Anglo-American conquest of the continent for almost sixty years. Yet their enemies knew little about them. The Spaniards never quite grasped the realities of their northern frontier; the Mexicans failed to meet them. The French presence proved transitory. The Anglo-Americans who finally mastered the entire inner continent by the advance of an industrial civilization never saw the People as people. They had no interest in Indians, as Indians. The Nermernuh were an obstacle that could not be fitted into any American scheme of things, and therefore had to be destroyed, removed like other predators from the plains.

Consequently, no genuine study of the Nermernuh was made until the 1930s, much too late. Long before an ethnologist arrived among them, the survivors of the People had been reduced to confused and apathetic remnants, shot through with diffusions and contradictions from whites and other Amerindians. Their folk consciousness, like their folk pride, was broken, the essence of their folk memory lost. The old men no longer understood what their fathers had believed or thought; even the legends had become garbled. And by this time so much well-meaning mythology had been absorbed into the conventional knowledge of the American Indian that many essential truths were obscured.

The People were scattered bands of wanderers, never a nation, and in the strict sense, not even a tribe. No set of Europeans or Anglo-Americans ever came into contact with all of them at one time. Therefore, even the written records of the People's enemies are splintered and confused. This fragmentary evidence, however, combined with scattered native legends and illumined by modern scholarship, can be woven into a reasonably complete whole. The details are missing but the design is clear—and history, or at least the meaning to be found in history, lies in designs, not details.

Any history of the People, no matter who writes it, must suffer from the fact that records were kept only by the People's enemies. Although time has provided perspective, historical vision can also be lost. Most writers on American Indian subjects are bothered by changing intellectual trends and fashions, which dictate new mythologies. Anglo-Americans, above all, have been troubled by guilt feelings, morality, and hypocrisy, whether direct or in reverse. Any ideology tends to obscure perspectives and reality.

The life and death of the People on the plains was and remains a human story, and like so much human history, it is tragic in its essence. The fact that Americans, for the most part, tend to reject a tragic view of human existence is probably the greatest source of American difficulty in understanding Amerindian history. The People were entirely true to themselves from first to last, and this faithfulness destroyed them. Their destroyers were also true to themselves, and could not have been otherwise.

History is brutal; only future peril lies in omitting or obscuring man's continuing brutalities. Generations that have been sheltered from the brutalities of the past are poorly equipped to cope with those of their own times. The story of the People is a brutal story, and its judgments must be brutal. These judgments may offend those who would have man be a different kind of being, and the world a different sort of place.

Finally, this book requires a linguistic note.

American Indian names, words, and concepts have been much confused in translation or transliteration. The North American tongues, whether highly inflected dialects like the Nahuatl of the Mexicans or merely agglutinative ones like most Algonquian idioms, derived from roots alien to all Indo-European languages. Most American Indian languages were extremely symbolic and require two translations into Spanish, French, or English: the literal and the conventional. And most American Indian dialects created sounds that Anglo-Americans simply cannot pronounce easily. The European ear always heard something different from what the Indian mouth uttered. Many inconsistencies became standardized.

Early penetrators of Indian country often employed a crudely effective system in writing down Indian words—they spelled them phonetically in their contemporary language. Thus the Lewis and Clark expedition recorded *Kiowa* as *Cay-au-wa*. But scholarly conventions soon rendered this as Kiowa (Webster: *Kâ'-i-gwŭ*), which few modern Americans can pronounce even with a dictionary. The conventions that spelled *Kiowa* (KAY-uh-wuh), *Tonkawa* (TONK-away), and *Karankawa* (Kah-RAHNK-away) so they look alike are too strong to ignore. To avoid confusion, I have often indicated an approximate contemporary American English phonetic spelling of an Amerindian word, and I have used this form of spelling for most obscure, not yet conventionalized Amerindian names.

General readers, for whom this book is intended, would certainly be alienated by such usages as Webster's phonetics, or the International Phonetics System, struggling with spellings like *hïtän, puhakʌt, or Nɜmɜnə.*

The Shoshone language of the People is utterly different from English and most Indo-European tongues. It is sonorous, with irregular vowel sounds, some long drawn out, and some drawled sounds that do not exist in English. It has the rolled or flapped *r* (r) and certain explosive consonants such as *v* (β) and *t* (t̬). A Shoshone oration sounds like a chant punctuated with minor explosions to American ears.

This may be unimportant. However, language shapes and is shaped by human consciousness, and something of the nature of a people is lost when the flavor of their language is gone. This applies to all races and tongues. Something happened to the memory, and even the dignity, of the Athapaskan warrior whose Mexican name, *Heh-ROHN-ee-moh,* was once widely used throughout the Southwest by people who had never seen it in print, when he became Geronimo on TV.

I
DEATH IN THE HIGH COUNTRY

THE PEOPLE AND THE AMERICAN INDIANS

1

THE AMERINDIANS

As far back as history can scrutinize,
man's intellectual and spiritual potentialities
have not changed.
    —J. Frank Dobie

THOUSANDS OF YEARS AGO, NOT LONG AFTER MEN BEGAN FORGING INTO a still subarctic Europe out of central Asia, other men marched east on an incredible trek into the Americas.

The origin of man on earth is still a mystery, and what physical and psychic circuitry was imprinted on man by his long evolution on this planet is far from scientifically established. No one knows where or when Homo sapiens, man in his present form, appeared or how he became separated into subspecies or races and diffused across the globe. The evidence of old bones suggests that the game-rich savannas of Ice Age Africa were the human birthplace, but the evidence is fragmentary and not decisive. Whether Homo sapiens evolved once in a single region, or whether there were parallel evolutions of protohuman stocks in several places—thus accounting for distinctive racial differences—is not clear. One thing does seem to be clear, however: man did not originate in the New World.

No evidence has ever been found of the remains of high apes, hominids, or half-men such as the Neanderthals in the Americas. The oldest manlike relics in the Western Hemisphere are perfectly human, and they show that the creatures who scattered them had both tools and fire. The most ancient human skulls unearthed from American limestone are distinctly those of Homo sapiens, men and

3

women whose physical characteristics and, presumably, mental potential were not markedly different from present-day man. Other things about these bones and long-extinguished campfires are unclear—they seem to have been left by a dolichocephalic or long-headed race with heavy jaws and flat, curved leg bones, perhaps an early Australoid or proto-Caucasoid people. This race, which hunted the hairy monsters of the last Ice Age, the woolly mammoth, the giant sloth, and the great mastodon on the High Plains, was in North America at least fifteen thousand years ago. It either vanished with the massive Pleistocene animals it lived on, owing to dramatic climatic changes as the glacial ice retreated north, or else it was exterminated or absorbed by newer waves of invaders out of Asia.

But all men entered the Americas as invaders, and as true men: erect, gregarious, possessing a basic technology of weapons, tools, and fire, with speech and symbolism. These invaders almost certainly came from Asia, perhaps out of the Altai, over a land bridge that rose between Siberia and Alaska when so much of the world's surface water was trapped in shining ice. Even at the worst of the last Ice Age, this land route was passable by people on foot; the southern shores were ice-free and there were always a few unglaciated corridors leading south. Small streams of human beings, wearing animal skins and furs and carrying their infants and flint-tipped spears, trekked across the land bridge for several millennia before it sank again into the icy Bering Strait. Some stayed in the gloomy northland; others scattered across the immensity of the North American continent until they reached the ocean; others pushed their way through the cordilleras and the rain forests of Middle America and their campfires burned in the rare, chill air of the Andes. This invasion must have begun between 10,000 and 7000 B.C.; by 5000 B.C. it was in full swing—a great *Völkerwanderung* that still had not ended when European explorers burst upon America.

The race that appropriated what was then a manless, primordial wilderness was a small, tough, dark, almost incredibly hardy breed. It came equipped to conquer the continents for humankind, with its knowledge of fire, its flint spears and picks, axes, pipes, and drills made out of stone or animal bone. It brought domesticated dogs and, probably, the bow and arrow in the last migrations out of Asia.

But even these tough, persistent travelers who braved Siberian ice were at the mercy of the American environment. This was a hunting people, who ate seeds and fruits and roots and berries when they could find them but mainly lived on fresh meat. Their life was the endless pursuit and slaughter of other living creatures. Such men could reap little beyond immediate subsistence from the earth and they must be forever on the move, since even their tiny numbers and crude weaponry soon exhausted or frightened off the game upon which they lived.

Still, gripping their bows and spears, shivering in their crudely fashioned animal skins, carrying their helpless infants on their backs, living in caves and brush arbors according to the season, gorging on bloody, half-charred flesh or going hungry when the hunters failed, spanning only a short, brutish existence that probably only rarely lasted thirty years, these wanderers were human— as fully human as any men and women alive today. Forced into cunning and cultural plasticity by their physical limitations and by their prolonged infancy and childhood, which separated man from the other Pleistocene creatures, they had begun to think and plan and organize, to learn painful lessons, and to pass the acquired knowledge across the generations. They were blood-banded, the hunting ten-groups with trains of females and infants, already aware of the need for interband cooperation and the dread necessity of the oldest human taboo, the prohibition of incest. They were already a genetically select species with at least a million years of biological and cultural development behind them. They had not marched innocent out of Eden: they were man the hunter, man the killer, then and now the most dangerous and formidable creature ever to appear on a four-billion-year-old earth.

Grubbing, hunting, killing, feasting, mating, dying and giving birth, exulting in the new moon of spring, browning under the harsh wind and brazen summer sun, moaning beneath the hungry winter snows, they were different from modern man only in circumstance. Their knowledge of the world and their acquired artifacts were primitive, but their human culture was already enormously complex—far more complete and complex than civilized men thought even a hundred years ago. The structures of their bodies and minds were already permanently shaped into the human form. They knew hope, fear, ecstasy, love, disillusion, and despair, and occasionally they found time for wonder. They were not free creatures: they were hounded by a hundred dark dreads and fearful taboos. They sensed mystery in their existence and in the universe and they tried desperately to find some meaning in it all; they strove to see and understand the cosmic forces that ruled the physical world so that they might bend them to their needs and wishes, the basis of all human religion. Their speech was already highly symbolic and complex, far richer in conception than scholars once believed. The evidence of primitive North American languages, which apparently passed unchanged through millennia of Stone Age existence into modern times, shows that the earliest Americans could express, sometimes clumsily but more often in symbols of singing beauty, almost any concept or thought or feeling expressed by modern man. Then as now the fundamental things applied: the pain of birth and death, the joy of mating, the instinct of motherhood, the thrill of the chase, the exultation of the kill, the hunger for security. Their basic consciousness was not fundamentally different from the basic consciousness of any other men. Seeing the sun rise, the moon set, the red fire throw giant black shadows on their cavern walls, at bay or in exaltation, these men and women felt the same things felt by modern man. In the truest sense—against the earth clock—they *were* modern men.

They entered America and survived.

This people was Mongoloid, as the human species is presently subclassified. They were Mongoloid or Asian by skin shade, head shape, hair and eye color, and form. Thousands of years after the last migration, the infants of this race were still born with the characteristic Mongoloid eye fold, though in many adults this tended to disappear. The people, however, did change somewhat in the New World because of changed environment, and because of long inbreeding in small, isolated groups.

Predatory man traveled in small bands, and the bands arrived in America widely separated by time and distance. Although all human beings had long since learned the genetic horrors of incest, circumstance still forced Stone Age hunters to inbreeding. Among the isolated groups of hunters in America the mating of first cousins was a norm. This, and certainly climatic or environmental factors, caused the emigrants from Asia to change from the peoples they left behind, and also to vary slightly among themselves from region to region and band to kinship band in height, in skin pigmentation, and in facial features. Some were short, others grew quite tall; some had round faces and others aquiline; and skin shades varied from yellowish to deep brown, with a reddish copper tone predominating throughout North America. All retained the dark hair and eyes, the deep chests and bandy, almost delicate legs, and the relatively hairless bodies of their Mongolian ancestry. Collectively they formed a new race, a new subspecies in the New World.

Columbus, thinking he had reached the Orient in 1492, called this people *indios* or Indians. Other Spaniards described them as *colorados* or red men. They entered history as American Indians, or Amerindians. In their tongues they were never anything but men, or people, or human beings.

The Amerindians survived and prevailed in the Americas. But whatever face is put on it, the Americas did not prove a hospitable region for the advancement of primitive mankind. The reasons were not completely geographical, since the hemisphere held every kind of climate and region. Nor is there any indication that there was some limitation in the race itself. All men seem to have the same potentialities, and all men have struggled equally valiantly against their environments. The Amerindians were tough and valiant and intelligent, but they were probably robbed of their full potential by a combination of circumstances.

The nature of the American invasion was not auspicious. A very small number of human beings entered the Americas in widely scattered, predatory bands. They crossed the continents by myriad routes. The same isolation that caused inbreeding and minor physical differences among Amerindians created something vastly more important. Life was too hard for Stone Age man for weak physical characteristics to survive, but there was a vast cultural inbreeding among the separate bands and tribes, which resulted over millennia in an almost fantastic cultural splintering. By the time of the birth of Christ there was more cultural differentiation among the Amerindians than among human beings descended from a common stock anywhere else on earth. The Amerindians had evolved into hundreds, perhaps thousands, of distinct and separate peoples.

Once the land bridge sank into the Bering Strait, the Amerindians were cut off from the major currents and cultural diffusions that swept periodically over the unitary Eurasian continent—but for crucial ages they also remained isolated from each other in the wooded vastnesses of the American land masses. They were separated from the Old World and from each other until at last the struggling bands had grown into clans, and the strengthened clans into tribes, and the larger tribes into primitive confederacies that once again came into close contact with neighboring peoples. Unlimited territorial space did not free the Amerindians in the broadest sense; it wreaked something rather terrible upon them. Space and mobility sparked countless forms of experimentation within the limitations of a Stone Age technology; but these hardened into frozen cultural patterns. Some of these differences were essentially meaningless, such as the fact that some peoples cut arrow shafts with two grooves, others with three or four. But many of them were fundamental, striking to the heart of human behavior in moral codes, taboos, and kinship and sexual practices. Most Amerindian peoples created utterly different ways of recognizing kinship, different laws, and different social orders. Inevitably, the taboos of one tribe sometimes became the imperatives of another and the cherished customs of one people anathema to another. For centuries the cultural, like the genetic base, was cribbed and confined; then, when at last the peoples of the Americas numbered in the millions and impinged upon each other and strong cultural diffusions might have taken place, it was too late.

No human beings can be quite so culturally conservative as those living close to the survival level, always on the thin edge of ethnic extinction. While the Amerindians tended to be gregarious, they were also ethnocentric. Every people believed its own ways were best. Each was convinced its own customs and laws were more "natural" and "human."

One evidence of the fantastic cultural separation of the Amerindian invaders was the near-improbable splintering of language that occurred among them. Their tongues underwent a shattering proliferation, in marked contrast to what occurred in Eurasia: All the ancient and modern tongues of Europe, with the exception of the Finnish-Magyar enclaves, stem from a common Indo-European root, and carry through the centuries certain basic psychic unities and world-views. Greek, Latin, German, and Russian, though mutually unintelligible even in prehistoric times, form one great linguistic stock. The Amerindians, however, had devised at least 140 such stocks when Europeans found them living side by side, and all of these language groups apparently developed independently, with no two of them having a common root. They shared no common word for "father" or "mother"; each had entirely different sounds and structures. And within the great stocks, such as Uto-Aztekan, Siouan, Caddoan, Algonquian, and others, there were hundreds of distinct dialects. The vast migrations of the Amerindian *Völkerwanderung* also muddied the linguistic map. Enclaves were thrust in with enclaves; Athapaskan speakers were surrounded by Uto-Aztekans, and Uto-Aztekan-speaking peoples imposed on older stocks. The Shoshone dialects of the Great Western Basin were akin to the Nahuatl of the Toltec artisans of Mexico, but the Utes, Paiutes, and Shoshone of the Rocky Mountain system had lost all cultural contact with their onetime kinsmen who migrated south and formed the seven Nahua-speaking tribes of ancient Mexico. All told, the Amerindians spoke thousands of different languages and dialects. The situation in Europe would have been analogous to that in America only if tribes speaking Latin, Hittite, Aramaic, Egyptian, Gaelic, German, and Chinese had all settled side by side and maintained their cultural identity within the confines of medieval France.

When the Europeans arrived in the Americas, they, like each Amerindian tribe, were convinced that all human behavior had evolved along certain "natural" lines in obedience to "natural" laws. Their philosophy and religion taught this. When Western values were called into question and proved parochial, the tendency then became one of searching for earlier, perhaps biological but still universal, patterns imprinted onto all mankind. But natural behavior, among Amerindians, was natural only within the confines of one people or tribe. Some tribes were matrilineal, i.e., tracing blood descent through the mother, the oldest way; most had become patrilineal like the Indo-Europeans. Basic sexual practices varied widely from tribe to tribe. Some peoples shared females among siblings; some were totally promiscuous. Among other tribes, even the notion of such behavior led to bloodshed. The Amerindian peoples were as culturally diverse, even on similar material levels, as English and Chinese, or Nigerians and Danes.

The apparent fusion among twentieth-century Amerindians is

reservation-bred. It came from their being thrown together under a common conquest and oppression, and from intermarriages and diffusions among themselves after the destruction of their independence. Ironically, unity among modern Amerindians is possible only because of the diffusion through them of the common language and civilization of the white man. The struggle of the surviving Amerindians, even more ironically, has evolved into a process of using the white man's own morality and law.

The Amerindian peoples, however, universally shared one common trait: a roughly similar world-view that ran from the Arctic Circle to the Andes and transcended all languages and cultural levels. This cosmic vision of the world, which they brought out of Asia, did not seek to connect cause with effect, made magic a surrogate for science, and substituted subjective experience for empirical observation. It was a world-view probably once shared by all mankind, and emanations are still found among all the races and cultures of man. It began to crack in Europe with the Hellenic civilization, when the Greeks, however dimly, began to discern the principles of cause and effect, and left traditions upon which later men could substitute scientific rationalism for soul-satisfying superstition.

The pre-Columbian Amerindians were not only culturally diverse at the most primitive level, they were also widely separated by their degree of cultural development. There was the enormous gulf between the pyramid-building Meso-American civilization and Pame-speaking primitives of the northern Mexican deserts, and between the architects and inhabitants of magnificent Palenque and Copán in Chiapas and Guatemala, and the blowgun-using peoples of the rain forest. But there were also enormous gulfs in acquired culture between many of the Amerindians of North America, where no true civilization rose: between the Seneca of the Atlantic seaboard and the miserable Diggers of the western mountains; between the splendid Cherokees and the grubbing Coahuiltecans of the south Texas coastal plains.

The popular image still sees the race as quite similar from sea to sea. The image was and is false, even though all the Amerindians were in a stone artifact culture and everywhere *looked* much the same. The Spanish were the first to fabricate indestructible images, partly by accident, partly for their own purposes. From their early experience in the Indies they branded the *indios* as *gente sin razón*, that is, primitives apparently impervious to European rationales. They stubbornly held, into the twentieth century in Mexico and in other places, that Indians were incapable of managing their own affairs, even with the evidence of the Aztecs and the Incas lying all about them. The fact that all the inhabitants of the Americas were Indians branded them in the European mind.

The image most vividly retained in the United States is that of the mounted Plains tribes, the last peoples who valiantly resisted the final conquest of the continent. Yet the so-called Plains culture represented only a tiny segment of Amerindian America, and the Plains Indians were not the most numerous, most accomplished, or even the most warlike. They were simply the tribes last known and most widely publicized. And even these tribes did not share a common culture. There were differences between Cheyennes and Comanches that transcended those between Italians and Swedes—who themselves tended to appear homogeneous to the Amerindians.

The main thing that distinguished the Amerindian branch of mankind was that some time after the Siberian invasions of the Americas ended, the two worlds came to run on different cultural clocks. By 5000 B.C. an enormous cultural gulf was widening between the continents.

There is no evidence that the Amerindian wanderers possessed any less mental or physical or psychological equipment than any other race of man when they passed through primeval Alaska. When the spear-carrying, fur-wearing Asian-Amerindians marched east into endless space, men everywhere had fire, tools, and garments, and had begun to domesticate certain beasts. But no man, anywhere, so far as is now known, had ever planted a seed, baked bread, or erected a temple, let alone envisioned a city that would begin the process of human civilization. When the Amerindians entered America all men were hunters and gatherers, everywhere living similar cycles of passage from birth to death.

But about 6500 B.C., perhaps through sheer accident, the primitive peoples of the Middle East, probably in the Anatolian highlands, learned to save and sow the seeds of wild cereal grasses. They soon domesticated several varieties of natural cereal grains, and thus began to shape vegetable life to their needs and purposes as they had begun to control certain animals. Soon afterward, as prehistory

Nerm woman, twentieth century.
Photograph by Edward S. Curtis.

can be measured, a similar breakthrough was made in the monsoon belt of Asia, with the planting of rice shoots. Within two thousand years this agricultural revolution—against which the so-called Industrial Revolution seems only a change of phase—had exploded across most of Eurasia. Wherever soils and rainfall were sufficient, men and women began to save seeds and lay out fields.

The agricultural revolution was the first decisive event in human history. For the first time, farming gave human beings some power over their environment; they were no longer entirely at the mercy of nature; they had begun to shape the earth. There was still the tyranny of the seasons, and a vast number of cosmic forces beyond any man's understanding or control. However, men and women had created a process that allowed them to remain in one place, to congregate and increase their numbers beyond anything that predatory life could possibly support, and to plan for the future with a reasonable hope of success. The poor, stunted oat and barley and wheat plants that sprouted uncertainly in the periodic rainfall of the eastern Mediterranean basin, and the rice shoots that began to green the carved-out hillsides of East Asia with the sure arrival of the monsoon rains, did far more for human beings than ease their hunger and increase their numbers. They fundamentally changed man's place in the nature of things on earth.

Just as all mammalian life rests on water and grass, all human organization beyond the hunting band had to rest on the cultivation of some cereal grain. Mankind had gone as far as it could without the creation of some reasonably dependable, nutritious, storable food supply. No hunter or herdsman, however intelligent and hardy, could hope to achieve civilization; he could only create variations of barbaric life styles. No hunting or herding society could possibly develop a complex social system with a true differentiation of labor that would free some men from primary jobs. Above all else, no predators could ever build a city, because they had to move with their game or herds. Only with the assurance of a steady food supply year after year, and, eventually, of a surplus beyond immediate needs, could men begin to organize, observe, and experiment, and think beyond the present perils of existence.

The Hebrew Bible shows that urban civilization was long suspected and resisted by still barbaric tribes. But agriculture was power, and no new technique creating power has ever long been successfully resisted by mankind. Fields were scratched out in the then lush regions of the Middle East. Farmers, agonizing over their precious seeds, had to learn the calendar, and, further, they yearned to propitiate or control the mysterious forces that ordered the sun and rain and frost. They sought gods, made sacrifices, and erected temples of mud brick. Communities congregated around the temples, beside the great rivers whose waters fertilized the fields. Soon the surplus that the fields produced permitted social specialization. It was no longer necessary for everyone to help produce food; artisans and priesthoods rose. The population began to divide into hereditary castes, which reflected their economic functions. Leisure from primary labor gave the priest-engineer class the opportunity to observe and to plan, and towns slowly surrounded the important temples. By the fourth millennium before Christ, on the ruins of an even earlier culture on the edge of the Arabian desert, the people of Mesopotamia had created a genuine agrarian civilization around an awesome organized religion. This civilization had a complex social order, writing, philosophy, and exquisite art. More important, the people of ancient Sumer began to understand a certain mathematical order to the world, where formerly all men had seen only random chaos.

The essence of civilization, however, was neither art nor order, but power: power over the human environment, power to command men. Even high art was a form of power. Only organized, civilized populations could maintain any element of control over the environment by assuring crops and food supply and by disciplining themselves—and every intelligent leader of barbarians, no matter how much he might emotionally reject all other values of civilization, in some way understood this fact. For this reason, no matter how many times Cain slew Abel, or the barbarians sacked Babylon, or dark ages descended, little that had been learned was ever irretrievably lost. The Indo-European barbarians who destroyed the first Minoan Mediterranean civilization were fertilized by it and made Greece; the later barbarians who brought down Rome inevitably spent a thousand years trying to resurrect it. As archaeologists continually discover, more things that we still live by emerged from the distant Babylons than modern man has dreamed, or perhaps has been willing to admit.

The Amerindians traveled this same road and at a comparable

pace, but their start was late. In the beginning they were hampered by the smallness of their breeding stock, their enormous isolation from the Old World and from each other within the New, and the fact that in America certain useful animals—the horse and the ox— did not exist. The progenitors of such species did not survive the Ice Age in the Western Hemisphere. Most important of all, the Amerindians made the vital breakthrough to agriculture at least several thousands of years after the farming revolution had swept Eurasia.

Agriculture was known by 2500 B.C.; stored maize or corn seeds found in New Mexico have been dated that far back by the radiocarbon process. There are many theories about diffusions of men and culture between the prehistoric worlds, but no hard evidence of it. There were definite similarities between the earliest American and Afro-Asian civilizations in artwork, religious practices, and pyramids.

It appears there were two independent discoveries of agriculture in the Americas: one in the Gulf regions of Middle America, the other on the Pacific slopes of the Andes, paralleling the apparent twin discoveries in Eurasia. American development roughly followed the patterns of the Old World. Hunters settled down to raise crops; they developed calendars and priesthoods to keep them. Populations congregated in fertile areas and had to organize themselves. Cities rose around massive temples dedicated to the cosmic forces that were seen as demon-gods. Remaining savagery and barbarism struggled bitterly with advancing civilization. Development was uneven, diffusions erratic and uncertain, even among peoples speaking the same language and living in similar regions. At every period, peoples with enormous variations in material culture lived almost side by side. The patterns that were expressed in the pyramids of America and of Egypt were roughly the same.

The great difference was on the clock: the Americas had started up the spiral road perhaps as much as four thousand years behind the Eurasian populations. This was a tiny time gulf in comparison to at least a million years of human evolution and development, but agricultural revolution enormously accelerated cultural development; the Americas were too-long static, and fell irretrievably behind.

The Amerindians burned fields out of the tropic jungle of Middle America and dug planting holes with sticks; they dropped the seeds of the indigenous teosinte plant, the god-given Indian maize or corn, and prayed for rain. They built permanent shelters and became sedentary in small, cribbed, and filthy villages; their numbers grew. Trying to control the seasonal, climatic tyranny that dominated their life, they invented awesome cults which in turn came to rule their actions and consciousness. From them emerged priests and magicians and engineers and hereditary clans and castes, and the elite classes began to create exotic civilizations. The Amerindians built pyramids around which sprang up large temple communities, in the same general and more fertile latitudes as in the Old World. They envisioned similar demon-gods and propitiated them with obeisance and sacrifice, with dances, music, rites, and human blood. Peaceful, ceremonial civilizations took root, faced various human and natural disasters, withered, then were rebuilt. In an inexorable human pattern, warrior elites replaced or else joined the ruling priestly classes. Finally, the Amerindian civilizations, on the northern and the southern continents, began to forge a series of universal states or empires under a succession of imperial peoples, of which the Incas and the Aztecs were but the last.

The Amerindian civilizations, the Meso-American with its Maya and Mexic subcultures and the South American Incas high in the Andes, were remarkable human achievements. They were in no sense inferior to those that first rose in Afro-Asia. But they must be seen against the global calendar. At their brave beginnings, they were millennia behind in development.

When Abraham departed Ur of the Chaldees, all Amerindians were savage hunters. When the hosts of Sargon of Akkad forged bronze swords and spears and marched in disciplined cadence behind their captains, the Amerindians were still pursuing animals in small bands with flint-tipped sticks. When Greek-speaking Indo-European barbarians were pouring out of the Balkans into Achaia, battling and merging with the civilization of decadent thalassocracies, or sea empires, and when the Egyptian pyramids were already very old, only a few struggling mud villages had sprouted around the marshy shores of Mexican lakes. When the Israelites were carried off to Babylon and the Athenians were creating the aristocratic beginnings of classic Hellenic civilization, the villagers of Middle America were dominated by strange magicians who wore masks and practiced weird rites; they were slaughtering virgins and fertilizing their maize fields with smoking human blood. When the first Amerindian pyramids were put together from mud bricks, Rome and Han China were already aging empires. Mexico and Peru achieved a genuine civilization only about the time Rome fell, and when the pattern of brilliant civilizations and recurrent dark ages in the Old World was already millennia old.

Nor could the gap be closed, because in both worlds civilizations went through similar cycles. Great Teotihuacán on the once lush and verdant Mexican plateau endured its *Götterdämmerung;* it was razed and burned and buried like once-mighty Nineveh. The rain forest engulfed splendid Palenque and Copán, while their builders vanished like the creators of the deserted Indus civilization. In both worlds, barbarians pressed down from the north, killed and destroyed, then settled down and piled new stones on old. Nothing was lost in the violent interregna, but because of the pattern of decline and fall, followed by rebirth, the development gap could not be closed. The Amerindian civilizations enjoyed only a little more than one millennium before final disaster unexpectedly overtook them. They had risen to tremendous accomplishments. They had organized large, immensely disciplined populations that numbered millions, articulated by impressive hierarchies ruling complex and diverse societies. They threw up wise men and brilliant artisans and engineers. They had discovered mathematics and devised a calendar superior to the Gregorian. They had writing and had begun a literature; they raised huge palaces and splendid monuments. They did all these things without the horse or cow, without the wheel, and without metal tools of any kind. The last of a series of imperial peoples—the Mexica or Aztecs in Middle America and the Incas in Peru—had forged vast states by the time the Spaniards came. Again, however, these magnificent accomplishments and human triumphs must be placed in full perspective against the rest of the world. It was not the sixteenth Christian century in New World cultural time when Europeans burst into the Western Hemisphere.

The most advanced of the Amerindians were far closer in cultural parity to long-vanished Sumer on the Mesopotamian plain. Like all humankind in the fourth millennium before Christ, they still sacrificed human beings to their demon-gods. The warlike Tarasca, northwest of Mexico, had just begun to pound out copper implements. The Amerindian civilizations in culturally relevant time were caught somewhere between ancient Sumer and Sargon of Akkad. This doomed them when Europeans discovered them.

These civilizations would have been doomed even had the Europeans come bearing gifts instead of sword and Cross. The culture shock would probably have been as great if the Chinese had been the new arrivals. They were isolated and fragile cultures, still proceeding along uncertain lines. They had not been subjected to the constant shocks and collisions and diffusions that had nurtured civilization across Eurasia since the earliest times. They were brittle, so brittle that the very coming of the Spaniards confused their rulers and destroyed their worlds. Cortés and Pizarro conquered millions with mere handfuls of mounted and iron-armed men. Their destruction was a total tragedy for the Amerindians, and from the Amerindian viewpoint should never have been seen as anything else. But from the viewpoint of the rest of the world, everything they had achieved had already been achieved before. Their great contributions to the world of the natural products—tobacco, chocolate, tubers, maize, beans, and other crops—that eventually came to comprise most of the agricultural production of the world were resources that almost certainly would have been found out by any men who entered the Americas, then or later.

CERTAIN REFLECTIONS OF THE MESO-AMERICAN CULTURE SPREAD FAR beyond the exotic blood-stained temples of the Aztecs. Agricultural techniques crept up the spine of Mexico, along the cordilleras into what is now the southwestern United States. The planting of the teosinte seed somehow leaped over the arid wastes and cultural void of northern Mexico and southern Texas; corn and squash and beans changed the life styles of the Amerindian hunters in the southern Rocky Mountain system and from the southern Gulf coastal plain to the cold taigas of the far eastern Atlantic slopes. The planting of Indian corn, in fact, had reached its geographical limits in North America before the white men came.

The Caddoan, Algonquian-speaking, and other great tribal groups from the southern pine forests through New England had become largely sedentary and agricultural some time after the birth of Christ. They took the first turn on the road—the forest tribes had begun to congregate in settled villages, expand their numbers, and rely primarily upon their fields for food. They still hunted in the tangled woodlands, where the prevalence of predators, both human and animal, kept the game supply small, but this hunting only supplemented their diet. With planted fields, the eastern tribes began to carve out fixed territories. They felled trees and built permanent shelters: large, well-timbered houses and lodges set in clan centers or towns. As small kinship bands expanded into clans and tribes, they evolved established lineages and even political organization. The agricultural Amerindians had both civil and military leadership, hereditary priesthoods, and the greater stocks, such as the Caddoans and the Algonquians, even formed the nucleus of nations with widespread tribal confederacies.

The tribal system of the Iroquois was as intricate and as vital to their life style as the clan system of the Scots. The general cultural level of the woodland Amerindians of the eastern and southern regions was probably hardly inferior to that of the Germanic tribes of the Russian plain before they came into close contact with the Romans. However, the Amerindians never worked bronze or ferrous metals, and they lacked the horse, two assets that civilization had diffused throughout the Eurasian steppes. But the Iroquois, a confederation of several tribes, had nonetheless begun to hack out an abortive Amerindian empire in the Middle Atlantic region. Creeks and Chickasaws, Caddoans and Cherokees, living comfortably in great airy lodges, sitting on great councils, were no longer predatory savages. They were high barbarians.

There were other barbaric peoples in the far Southwest. The so-called Puebloan culture (from the Spanish *pueblo,* village or town) took deep root among the Uto-Aztekan-speaking holders of the high plateaus of modern Arizona, Colorado, and New Mexico. The Puebloans were not one people, but rather a succession of different tribes who in different times and places built spacious houses from stone slabs, chinked them with the native adobe, and provided them with ladders and thatched roofs. The various Pueblo dwellers planted corn, cotton, tobacco, squash, and beans; they also cultivated and ate sunflower seeds. They wove cloth for garments, fashioned excellent pottery, and created superior ornaments. Men and women worked in the fields in disciplined endeavor, and they developed splendid and impressive rituals and ceremonies. Their rain dances and other festivals were performed in a blaze of color, feathers, capes, and jewels. The Puebloans lived well on the surplus of their sun-drenched fields; they even sometimes traded with the distant Caddos. Like the Caddoans on the other side of Texas, they were not particularly belligerent. The Puebloans were in that first stage of agricultural organization in which their great energies were turned toward their crops.

By approximately the year 1000, this Puebloan culture apparently was spreading widely throughout the North American Southwest. Pueblos were built high in Colorado, and others were founded far out on the Great Plains; one large ruin has been unearthed along the Canadian River in the Texas Panhandle. Other offshoots of this culture seeped into the trans-Pecos basin. The incipient civilization, however, struggled against great, and finally fatal, odds. It developed in a region that had been lush and fertile during the last Ice Age, but that had become progressively hotter and drier as the Ice Age passed, a feature of the fraying Pleistocene in both the Old and New Worlds. In the Old World, some thousands of years earlier, the rich North African plains had turned into deadly Saharan deserts; the rains that had made the hillsides of ancient Greece and Italy green with tall stands of trees in early historic times gradually ceased. Once-rich plains parched and eroded, and the Pleistocene timbers of the Mediterranean region, once cut down by men, could never grow again. In North America, this same process caused cyclical drought. Long periods of ample rainfall were followed, in the Southwest and Mexico, by decades of disastrous drought. In the East, cold-demanding birch trees retreated northward toward the Arctic, but on the high mesas of the Rocky Mountain system the climatic change was more dramatic. The birthplace of the Puebloan protocivilization turned into a near-desert, forcing the culture to contract back to the reaches of the upper Rio Grande. Even beside the great river, the Puebloan farmers struggled against cyclic drought and creeping desert. Lack of rainfall drove the Puebloans from their defensible high mesas, making their future uncertain even had they not been beset by human enemies long before the Europeans came.

Far beyond the splendid palaces and cities of the Mexic civilization, between the sun-drenched farms of the Puebloans and the smoky lodges of the forest Amerindians, rose the huge, high heartland of the North American continent. This was the center of the continental land mass: a vast, rising series of prairies and plateaus that stretched between the timberlands that fringed the Mississippi basin and the foothills of the Rockies, and reached from Canada deep into Texas. It was an enormous, varied, but almost formless land with few dividing boundaries. But these boundaries and landmarks were sharp: rare river bottoms, with shallow, muddy flows but carved deeply into the land and lined with trees; distant scarps and buttes thrusting their crumbling limestone up from the dusty mesa; mesquite-studded landscapes vanishing suddenly into the high, thin air of blue-mountained desert; and perhaps most dramatic to the human eye, the border region where the trees and rain ran out and the landscapes turned to unmeasurable miles of bending, soughing grass. It was a country of great subregions, of stark bluffs and rolling ridges, of island clumps of lonely trees, of occasional vast canyons cut deep beneath the prairie floor. In its primordial state it invariably startled and amazed the Western European mind and eye. Men from the parochial viewscapes of the Atlantic regions could never quite explain the effect of this land upon them when they saw it for the first time. It exalted some; it oppressed many more. Lewis and Clark, crossing these regions, called them the Great Plains; other Europeans likened the vast, rising prairies to an ocean, and termed them the sea of grass. They were lands that for millennia lay as uncharted as the oceans; they were not fully penetrated by Caucasians until less than a hundred years ago.

In world terms this region resembled more than anywhere else the vast plains and steppes of central Asia, once a camping ground for the Western peoples on their march, in more historic times the cradle of successive waves of wild barbarians. Over it all the rain fell less and less from east to west—the huge limestone plateaus became arid beyond the ninety-eighth meridian. And the rain was eccentric in its patterns, falling here and there year by year. From high in the cold Canadian forest to the cedar brakes of the central Texas hills, there was nothing to impede the winds. They blew free, now south, now north, in constant warfare that set off great electrical displays and generated black funnel clouds, tornadoes that sometimes dipped and tore the earth. The winds brought moisture from the south in spring that blanketed the plains of central North America with wild flower glory, like the poppies of central Asia;

they also dried and burned the sere, rustling grass; they brought ice rains and in winter layered snow on snow. It was a country of terrible meteorological change, blazing in deep summer under a brazen sun that made the distant bluff sides dance in shimmering heat, shivering in winter under the ice storms that howled off the roof of the world and froze the earth under scudding clouds and the low-slung moon. Like the center of all vast continental land masses, it lay far from tempering seas or currents; unlike some which lay far south, it was not shielded by sheltering mountains.

The land was hard on man and beast; it made all life upon it volatile and restless, cruel but hardy, ever-moving. In this kind of country human civilization did not easily sprout or take root—the kind of country out of which the Huns and their savage counterparts continually rode into history. The Amerindians who chose the vast heartland, or were pushed into it by circumstance, remained predatory, primitive hunters for thousands of years. They were tough, energetic, intelligent, and wholly valiant people, but they were men on foot, armed only with flint-tipped wooden darts and spears. They were able to equip themselves to cope with this land and to live on it, but not to shape it.

They had little opportunity to pause or wonder, to chart the heavens or to think about the sum of things. The bands had to be eternally on the move as they exhausted the feeble resources at their command—the roots and berries and the nervous game of each tree-lined river bottom or sheltered canyon. Home was where they camped, in the canyons or the foothills, in the mountain meadows or, rarely, far out on the limitless sea of grass.

These grasslands were one of the world's original great repositories of animal life. The midcontinent swarmed with wild flesh, surpassing even ancient Africa, far more meat and bone and blood than lived in the milder but more tangled and gloomy woodlands, where abundant great cats and other predators diminished the herbivorous populations. Millions upon millions of great beasts roamed the plains: the *Bison bison* or American buffalo, frequent bands of antelope, and a large variety of deer, large and small. There were also bear along the bottoms and in the high canyons and many sorts of lesser game and birds. This country was a hunter's paradise in one sense—but it provided no easy meat for primitively armed men.

The deer were keen-eyed and keen-scented in the open country, fleet and hard to kill with weapons of extremely limited range. The bear was no simple target for crude spears. And the countless bison, however stupid in their shaggy herds, were difficult to approach on the open prairie. The buffalo would stand in confused bewilderment while a whole band was killed one by one provided the animals neither smelled nor saw the source of danger, but the Amerindian hunters had no means to slaughter them at a distance. The most successful way to hunt was to stampede a herd into muddy bottoms or over a cliff by setting fires or some other means. If hunters could surround a clump or trap a herd they had meat—too much meat, most of which went to waste. And the herds, millions of great horned grazing beasts, were continually on the move. They followed the erratic rain patterns and the green grass; thus, they also migrated randomly, often far out on the open plains, where they stayed for months or even years. Hunters on foot, their women bearing babies on their backs, could not follow the migrating bison easily.

During the warm months when the earth provided many forms of food—roots, berries, tubers, wild fruits, grubs, and turtles—and when the small animal populations were thick with spring increase, the hunting parties lived well enough by eating anything and everything that the human stomach could digest. When howling blizzards drove them off the plains and when the canyons were piled with frozen snows, then came the hungry moons. Late winter, in the stark symbolism of the Plains Amerindian languages, was the "Time our babies cry for food."

The infants sickened and old people died. The most ancient campsites around the North American plains have revealed, along with shaped flints and the remains of long-extinguished fires and slaughtered animals, the cracked and charred bones of human beings. Many of the hunting bands certainly practiced cannibalism, breaking the second oldest human taboo. This was an ancient practice that survived in ritual cannibalism among many Amerindians into modern times. The Mexica or Aztecs ceremonially ate parts or organs of slain enemies, as did many native peoples of the entire Southwest. Moctezuma's people had grown civilized in Mexico, but somewhere, millennia in their Uto-Aztekan past along the continental divide, the lords of Mexico had eaten human meat. This unhappy practice was not peculiarly Amerindian, and the ancient cannibalism was forced by circumstance. In the nineteenth century there were several recorded instances in which Europeans trapped in winter in this same vast wasteland ate one another.

Throughout many thousands of years of existence in North America, the Plains and mountain Amerindians never rose culturally above savagery. The geophysical odds against them were too great, just as the odds against most of the Amerindians in the American rain forests and desert regions were too great for civilization. Yet even against such odds, the people who lived as hunters and grubbers in the earth retained their essential humanity. They maintained a culture that, if it did not advance, did not regress. They kept fire and tools and language, and therefore exercised intelligence. They understood blood kinship and evolved complex ways of recognizing and expressing it. They had the small but effective band organization that allowed the race to survive and even prevail. They had learned much about survival in an almost totally hostile world, and they had learned to pass all acquired understanding on to each succeeding generation. Forced to move continually in a desperate search for food and shelter, and to carry everything they owned upon their backs, they could develop only crude, animal hide abodes and brush arbors, and only a handful of portable artifacts. They could develop no large populations nor philosophy nor high art nor politics. Over the millennia in America the hunting tribes remained what they had been—true men, vastly evolved physically and mentally, but men who had not yet taken a single step on the road toward the seed and civilization. When the Christian era was beginning in the Old World, their culture had not changed materially in perhaps forty thousand years.

Thus North America presented a complex, varied, and restless human landscape in the thousand years before Europeans came. From the impressive halls of Moctezuma to the great lodges of the Iroquois, from the stone-slab pueblos of the Southwest to smoky animal hide shelters of the Plains and mountain bands, there was no single Amerindian culture. There were myriad cultural levels that we may identify as the "high civilization" of central Mexico, with writing, astronomy, astrology, and sculptured art, with men organized into disciplined armies and waging vast imperial wars; the "high barbarians" in the deep woodlands between the Mississippi basin and the eastern ocean, people with clan chiefs and classes and sacred totems erecting timbered palisades along their rivers; the peaceful, "proto-civilized" agriculturists on the southwestern mesas, eating sunflower seeds and living colorful, ceremonial lives; and in between, among the danker forests, deep in the mountain deserts, and high on the fringes of the awesome plains, the "aboriginal" savage hunters who scorned all other ways.

Nor was this world static, as so many modern Americans have believed. It was alive with restless, brutal, dramatic change. The empires of the Mexicans and Incas were on the march. The Algonquian confederacies were raising intertribal warfare into a hideous art. The savage tribes were still volatile, unsettled, always poised to desert ancient hunting grounds in search of fresher lands. The Mexica only entered the Valley of Mexico in the thirteenth century, perhaps pushed out of the arid north by drought, perhaps by other savage tribes; and new tribes were gathering on their own northern frontiers when Cortés's caravels appeared.

Athapaskan-speaking peoples, who had lived for thousands of years high in the fern-filled forests of the Pacific north, pushed into the Rocky Mountain system of the arid Southwest sometime after the year 1000. They burst through the Uto-Aztekan tribes, harassing the peaceful Puebloan culture unmercifully, perhaps giving it a fatal push toward extinction. Millennia earlier, the Uto-Aztekans had themselves split and sundered primitive Hokan-speaking tribes, driving the survivors into deserts east and west—the despised Coahuiltecs and Yumas. Everywhere, as the lords of the conquered Mexica admitted to Cortés, it was the way of life for men to seize new lands with shield and spear. The Amerindian world of North America was rent with ancient, festering hatreds. The reverberations of the Athapaskan invasion into the Southwest had far from subsided when Coronado rode along the upper Rio Grande. It was an ancient story, common to all humankind. One people, one culture, continually supplanted another as the Mexica destroyed Azcapotzalco and made the Xochimilca slaves; peoples superior in numbers, organization, or sometimes nothing more than sheer will or savage desperation exterminated, expelled, or subdued hapless enemies. If the losers survived, they survived on marginal lands or poorer hunting grounds unwanted by the conquerors. North America was a world of constant, brutal change long before Europeans impinged on it.

Yet this North American continent was static on another plane.

Amerindian wanderers had perhaps lived for too many centuries intoxicated with the opportunities of unlimited space. The thousands of years they had passed as hunters before the first seed was planted still strongly affected even the most advanced Amerindian peoples, establishing patterns that a few centuries of civilization or high barbarism could not remove from Mexicans or Mohawks. The Amerindians had made all their advances within a primordial world-view that saw all events as accident or happenstance and that relied on magic to deter or promote the course of the world. They treated hallucinations as truth, and trusted visions over empirical observation, instinct above reason. All Amerindians—Revered Speakers on the Mexic throne or Stone Age savages in the southwestern deserts —believed in magic and shared a common religiosity. The only real difference was that between a savage faith that was inchoate, personal, and primitive in its expression, and a civilized superstition that was highly sophisticated in its structure, integral to an organized and disciplined society, and that expressed itself in art.

Shaped by thousands of years of brutal struggle on harsh continents, when the margin of survival was always thin, all Amerindians were deeply, passionately conservative, with the true conservatism of received patterns of thought. There was no contradiction in the fact that the Amerindians seized upon and adopted new artifacts and inventions easily. They could and did adopt the bow, the horse, firearms, and iron—but in every case they adapted such artifacts and the techniques that came with them to existing culture. The Athapaskan wanderers on the high mesas who learned the techniques of growing corn from the Puebloans did not adopt Puebloan culture—they adapted maize into their own patterns. This was the Amerindian reaction: new techniques and artifacts enlarged their opportunities; they rarely altered the tribal behavior patterns in a radical manner. Each Amerindian people had become as assured of the *rightness*, not just the success, of its ways as fully civilized people were assured of their own superiority. This was what the Spanish meant when they branded the *indio* as *gente sin razón*.

The conquering Mexica, forging vast hegemonies with obsidian-edged swords and spears, could not rise above their tribalism any more than they dared invent a newer world-view. Their empire was brittle because the minds of the Mexica were rigid and impervious to certain forms of reality. There was such arrogance in their world-view, and the common world-view of almost all Amerindians, that the race preferred to die by the millions rather than surrender its ancient grasp of things. The Mexican Amerindians were the most civilized and flexible on the continent; they had undergone the most development and change. And in the end, many of them were able to adapt and survive, despite the cruelties of the conq ·e: ors and the ravages of Old World disease. Other Amerindians to the north, still barbaric and savage, were far less able to cast off their necessary vanities and illusions. Human beings wh)se essential belief is in happenstance and magic do not easily learn from defeat.

The tragedy of the Amerindians was that their long experience in America had caused them to do *everything* according to certain fetishes and ways. They were practical only on one level—adapting themselves to the environment. No more than the jaguars of the jungles did they consider adapting the world to themselves. The Amerindian tribes learned to survive in the wilderness—they proved again and again they had adapted far better than Europeans would to their own conditions. But the cost of that very survival was too great when the Amerindian was confronted with total change.

The Mexic people believed that the sun would not rise unless the gods were fed with smoking human hearts, and the corn would not grow unless the fields were sprayed with symbolic human blood. Thus Moctezuma the Younger sent wizards out against Cortés when he had hundreds of battalions at his command. Most Amerindians substituted human will—medicine or magic—for rational observation and reaction. Moctezuma read doom in oracles, and other valiant men rode into battle believing that cosmic forces could turn bullets from their breasts. When all failed, they blamed their magic, refusing to the last to accept the tyranny of cause and effect over human dreams and hopes. Such men, always bewildered in the world, ride the crest of exultant, exuberant, magical luck or divine favor, or, thwarted, sink into a manic-depressive abyss. *They* do not fail; the spirits turn against them.

The Amerindians could make war, exterminate each other, or make each other slaves without destroying the Amerindian world. All operated within a common context. The Indo-Europeans, however, destroyed the Amerindian world completely. It was not just by bullets against crude bows, or by the diseases of the Old World against which the isolated Americans had no acquired immunity. Nor was it by intoxicants: many Amerindians had potent drugs long before the Europeans brought rum or whiskey. The tribes used intoxicants or hallucinogens sparingly, and for magical purposes, until their world began to disintegrate. Then, the miserable descendants of the Aztecs retreated into pulque-soaked escape; other Amerindians found solace in peyote.

The Indo-Europeans did more than defeat the Amerindians. From the time of the great explorations, Westerners embarked on the conquest of many lands and peoples; but when the western tide retreated, most ancient cultures reemerged, altered but still constituting essential elements of the structure and thought of post-colonial societies. Only the Amerindians, and a few isolated island folk, were psychically if not physically destroyed. Their world-view was shattered, and their deepest beliefs and cherished ways were proven not only insufficient, but *wrong*. The conquerors never quite understood the ultimate cruelty of this destruction, which went beyond the pain of mere death and conquest. The Westerners no more understood the Amerindians than the Amerindians, in turn, could cope with the sudden shock of the far future impinging on their present world.

The Amerindian was not inferior to his enemies in brain or physique. He was desperately inferior in culture, the acquired culture of thousands of years of experience. Moctezuma II was no uncouth savage; he had lore and learning and even a human dignity beyond Cortés's ken. But Cortés, like all white men, arrived with vast reserves beyond the grasp of any Indian. He was cool and confident, implacable in his sustained determination. He invoked his own God, but in his heart never quite confused His favor with the efficacy of guns and brigantines, of disciplined steel and clever diplomacy. Cortés was certain of his share of the glory that Heaven reserved to mortals for their own efforts, and before him the brilliant Moctezuma was a superstitious savage, valiant but helpless in a collapsing world.

The Amerindian was inferior in terms of wielding power in all its manifold forms, which is, at bottom, the story of civilized man's march across the earth. The Amerindian powerfully developed and projected his magic into a consuming religiosity. He lived by this as much as he lived off nature. Forty thousand years back, probably all mankind had shared this same religiosity. Even four thousand years back, Amerindians and Eurasians might have met on almost equal terms. But when the Amerindians veered off from the rest of mankind on their heroic trek into hidden continents, they were trapped by circumstance. They survived, and clung to a quality of heart and mind that stayed close to the human dawn. It was valiant; all the races of man are equally valiant, if not equally successful, in their struggle against adversity. It was admirable, because it was human. It should be remembered even in destruction with respect.

2

THE PEOPLE

Their arrows are broken and their springs are dried up. . . .
Their council fires have long since gone out . . .
and their war cry is fast dying away. . . .
They will live only in the songs
and chronicles of their exterminators.
Let these be true to their rude virtues as men,
and pay tribute to their unhappy fate as a people.
—Charles Sprague

IN THE SIXTEENTH CENTURY OF THE CHRISTIAN ERA, WHEN MEN WERE setting out from the stormy promontory of Western Europe in cockleshell ships to reunite the world with guns and trade and steel, the Amerindian people who were to bar the advance of European empires most ferociously and successfully lived high in the eastern Rockies above the headwaters of the Arkansas, in the country now called Wyoming.

This was a land of breathtaking beauty, of majestic snow-capped peaks and dark, timbered canyons and broad mountain meadows. But it was also a brutal homeland, a harsh mountain habitat in which food was hard to find and the winters howled along the continental divide. In this country the Amerindians had survived. They had not prospered nor prevailed. They had erected no temples nor great lodges. They were still mostly hunters and gatherers, trapped in a bitter cultural stasis that had endured since Amerindian man entered the continent. Unlike the civilized, urban Mexicans or the barbaric Algonquian clansmen of the East, the Amerindians in the mountains remained as aboriginal inhabitants.

They had only the culture and consciousness that their ancient ancestors had carried out of Asia. They were Stone Age hunters who had never felled a timber, raised a house, or planted a seed. They had flint tools and arrows and spears, and they made a number of basic artifacts from animal parts or stone. They cured animal hides for garments and shelters. They fashioned their picks, pipes, arrows, and drills with skill and even a certain artistry, but neither their techniques nor their life styles had changed for millennia. They had devised hide drums and bone rattles and reed flutes and made monotonous music, and they practiced a startling cosmetology, with garish face paints, fetishistically worked hair, and tattooed breasts, to express something in their makeup as old as man himself. They were primitives, hunters and grubbers across the land, a nomadic people who like other Amerindian tribes eternally roamed the face of North America.

This people, however, had a powerful human consciousness. They were Nermernuh, "People," from the root word of their ancient Uto-Aztekan dialect, *Nerm*, "Human Being." They called themselves People, not "the People." During their long separation and isolated wanderings in America, the Asian hunting bands had come to look upon themselves as unique, and each people believed itself to be the most human of all men. This was not modern racism; the Nermernuh or People had no racial dogmas, nor for that matter, dogmas of any kind. Their feeling, however, sprang from the human instincts upon which all human racism rests. The Nermernuh were all alike; they spoke one language; they followed the same life styles; they shared the same taboos. All other men were demonstrably different. The Nermernuh did not deny the biological humanity of other men, but it was obvious that other human beings were not quite People like themselves.

They held together, the greatest of all human strengths against the world; they held apart, the greatest of all man's failings toward humanity.

They were not quite Jews among Gentiles, but rather Hebrews in the desert before finding their Law and God. In their world it was Them and Us and had been since the beginning, no different in the American wilderness from what it had been in the Arabian desert, though the Nermernuh collected hair instead of the dried foreskins of their enemies.

The other Amerindians of the North American heartland did not call them People; each tribe reserved that term for itself. The Cheyennes called them *Shishin-ohts-hit-ahn-ay-oh* in their own sonorous language, "Snake People." The Athapaskan-speaking tribes called them *Idahi*. The Siouan-speaking peoples of the western river valleys knew them as *Pah-dooh-kah* or *Pádoucas*. The mountain Utes, close cousins who had become alienated through the centuries, called them *Koh-mahts:* "Those Against Us," "Enemy." Like most Amerindian peoples, the Nermernuh had many names, their own and those they acquired secondhand from enemies.

They were Shoshone-speaking, part of a great Amerindian language group, the Uto-Aztekan, that reached from western Canada deep through Sonora into central Mexico, and after the Algonquian and Athapaskan was the most widespread Amerindian linguistic family. At various times, men who spoke Shoshone hunted in almost every one of the western United States, from Oregon to New Mexico. Shoshone was a tongue of the western mountains. It was also a tongue of many cultures, from the Diggers of the Great Basin to the Hopi.

The Nermernuh themselves descended from wanderers who had ranged from the headwaters of the Green and Snake rivers eastward into Kansas, through Utah, Idaho, Colorado, and Wyoming. They had traveled the upper reaches of the Missouri and the Platte. The legends of the Arikari stated that the Crows knew the Nermernuh or People in the Snake River country in very ancient times. Perhaps significantly, most other northern Amerindians identified the Shoshone-speaking People with the Snake. The Nermernuh themselves, so far as their legends ran, could recall no time beyond that which found them in the eastern Rockies above the headsprings of the Arkansas.

As a people they had only the vaguest notions of their origin. They had no institutional records, only human memory, passed down from generation to generation by word of mouth. The memories were familial, and soon grew dim—but then, few civilized people know their family histories beyond several generations. The People believed that in the beginning they had somehow sprung from a magical mating of the animals, for they could see the animal in themselves. They revered the wolf, not exactly as a totem but as a possible ancestor, and respected the wolf's cousin, the coyote, and thus did not eat the coyote's relative, the dog. This was a splendid, if accidental, symbology, for the People resembled wolves. They were wild creatures with a strong sense of family responsibility, and among their own kind knew warmth and dignity and love—yet they ran in packs, cunning as the coyote, and they were feral on the blood trail.

Very little will ever be known about the lives or collective history of the Nermernuh while they were west of Kansas. Other peoples and tribes had rich stores of legend and folklore, and they made up many songs. The Nermernuh, when they rode into history, had little legend and fewer songs. In fact, the cupboard of folk memory was so bare that the People were suspected of consciously wanting to forget their past. Almost certainly there was no greatness in it, before the People left the mountains. And the mountains had shaped the People brutally.

They were a small, dark race, shorter, darker, and more squat than the Amerindians to the east and those living along the rivers that cut through the plains, though not those of the mountains or of Mexico. The hunting males appeared darker than the women, because the men wore less clothing and were more exposed to the elements. The People had the deep, wide chests of all Amerindians, but they were not handsomely proportioned. They were heavy-muscled, with short, squat legs. They were made for and by the mountains; they were not the tall, graceful Amerindians of the prairies.

The males rarely exceeded five and one-half feet in height; the females averaged six inches less.

The skin tones of the People ranged from a faint copper red to weather-beaten brown. They all had black or deep brown eyes, with bloodshot sclera. Their Asian ancestry showed in their straight black hair, their relatively hairless bodies and beardless faces, and in their slant-eyed infants. The People had broad faces and large, round heads. They were a brachycephalic race, with an index of eighty-three, one of the broad-headed peoples that emerged from Asia after the Cro-Magnons. Their facial features were heavy and massive.

Their age-old existence was dominated by the constant search for food. Their hunting grounds were hardly a reservoir of vulnerable game. The deer were fleet and wary; the mountain elk were huge;

and the bear that lived in the bottoms and canyons was a dangerous animal for men to wound with arrows or to approach with spears. The People lived mostly from much less splendid prey: rabbits, reptiles, and the smaller rodents. They snared small animals and charred the carcasses in their fires, started laboriously with wooden drills. They cooked birds with the feathers on and roasted rodents, often undrawn, in the skin. They tossed squirming turtles onto the coals, steaming them alive in the shell; they considered spring terrapins a delicacy. They scorned fowl as the food of cowards and had an ancient, ancestral taboo against water creatures such as frogs and fish. But if they were starving, the Nermernuh would eat anything: fish, fowl, lizards, snakes, and grubs.

It was a glorious occasion in the camp when some sturdy hunter brought down an elk or killed a bear, a bloody triumph of human skill and spirit. Best of all were the times when bison entered the territory of the People and bands of cooperative hunters could surround and stampede a herd. The Nermernuh, like all prehorse Amerindians, hunted buffalo by setting the prairies and meadows afire, and they often destroyed an entire area in the search for meat. When the maddened, snorting animals stampeded over cliffs, fell into pits, or were bogged down in the river bottoms, spears struck home and flint knives bit deep, and the women and children, shrieking, ran to rejoice and share in the kill.

The People sucked up warm blood; they carved out the hot livers, savoring exploded gall bladder salts. They gobbled raw entrails, drawing the greasy guts through their teeth to strip out the last, mysterious delight. They loved the taste of blood and milk drawn from slashed cow udders and, especially, the curdled milk they sometimes found in the belly of a calf or fawn.

With the keen edge of their appetite removed, the men did the heavy butchering and skinning, which was beyond the females' strength. Then the women hacked out bloody steaks, some to be roasted upon sticks, some to be sun-cured. They removed the stomachs of other buffalo, cooking the whole sac over coals. Horns and hoofs and hide were carefully preserved to make useful artifacts and instruments. The great stampedes were wasteful of animal flesh, but the People made the utmost use of what they had to the limits of their abilities.

There was never enough meat. The folk sometimes gorged in the fat months and hungered through the winter, since no store of imperfectly preserved jerky strips could last through the snows. Then the People endured stoically, like the beasts upon which they preyed.

A Nermernuh feast would have appalled the sensibilities of more civilized men—but because the People ate and used the whole animal, they got the vital nutrients that for ages had allowed the race to survive. If the Nermernuh had eaten only lean meat, they would soon have sickened and died. The Amerindians had no scientific understanding of their need for minerals and salts; their tastes derived from instinct.

Through endless years of trial and error, the People had also learned to use a vast store of natural vegetable foods. They gathered wild plums and grapes, currants and berries in season, eating till their stomachs swelled; they ate acorns and other native nuts. They considered as edible plants things that Anglo-American pioneers hardly recognized as food: sego lilies and sumac, wild bitter onions, mesquite beans, cactus tunas, hackberries, Jerusalem artichokes, and yap roots. The Nermernuh in all had smelled out some thirty varieties of natural plants for food, and it was also because they ate all these things that they survived.

But because they rapidly stripped the land of the meager resources they could extract, the People could not congregate, and their numbers could not increase. Few babies were born, and fewer survived the snows. Since all the Amerindians of North America had followed this life style until a few centuries before the Europeans found them—corn planting seems to have been diffused across the continent after about A.D. 500—there were probably no more than one million North American Indians in all in the sixteenth century. The People, who never learned to plant a seed, numbered fewer than five thousand, and their hunting bands seldom included more than a few hundred individuals. Any increase would in itself have been a collective form of suicide. The prime directive of the People was the eternal hunt for food.

They were hardy—they had to be, to succeed in the struggle for existence. But they were hardy without being healthy. Both sexes could endure enormous suffering and discomfort without complaint. With little food or water the hunters ranged far on their powerful, bandy legs; the women could give birth and immediately resume the trail. However, the People had physical bodies inherently no different from modern men and women, and if they had been hardened by adversity, they were still vulnerable to all of mankind's ills. Hunger, constant exposure, and an utter lack of sanitation took terrible tolls. The People died easily from pneumonia during the winter snows. They suffered hideously from rheumatism as they began to age, and at all ages they were ravaged by intestinal disease. Living in the open made them arthritic, and blindness was not uncommon. Pursuing a rough, dangerous existence, in which a thorn scratch could prove fatal, they perished quickly from wounds, snake bites, and badly broken bones.

They did have a crude but often efficacious medicine. Like the civilized Mexic Amerindians, who developed empirical healing techniques totally outside the magic of their religion, and whose medicine in many ways was superior to contemporary European forms of treatment, the North American tribes had learned many medicinal, mechanical, and thermal cures for obvious maladies. The People practiced rough surgery and could set simple fractures adequately. They knew how to suck out snake-bite poisons and to pack wounds with grass. They used poultices made from the prickly pear, and salves derived from animal fats and oils. They treated toothache with tree fungus, filled tooth cavities with dried mushrooms, and had discovered that willow bark was a powerful laxative. They also devised a "sweat lodge," an animal hide tent turned into a steam room. Thus many Amerindian remedies were as practical as the tribes' grim survival techniques in the hunt and war, and these simple cures, together with the heroic endurance of powerful constitutions, sometimes permitted People with terrible injuries to recover.

Yet more died. The People had no more understanding of infections and diseases without visible external causes than Europeans. They attributed these to malignant spirits, and here their medicine became mixed with religiosity. In fact, the division between practical remedies, learned from observation, and magic was never clearcut. Herb pastes and poultices had to be painted on in certain magical patterns, such as dog tracks, and also to be painted on the patient's dog, for full effect. The People believed that no cures were effective without particular secret rites and incantations, and without the acceptance by the sufferer of certain taboos. There were cases in which people preferred to die rather than accept the penance of the cure. The People believed that the gigantic mammoth bones they found across their hunting grounds were the remains of their ancient bogey, the great Cannibal Owl, and thus had magic properties. They made powders from these huge fossils to sprinkle wounds, or else placed the bones themselves upon sufferers in the trust that this sucked out evil spirits. Even simple surgery required spells and incantations. Each family had its own, preferred magic; there was no "body of knowledge." While such cures could only be psychological, it was a magic not to be entirely despised. Buffalo cures and mammoth bones were no less helpful, and far less damaging, than eighteenth-century European remedies such as medicinal bleeding.

Women had difficulty in conceiving, and infection killed many in childbirth. The awful exposure and constant hunger and labor turned Nermernuh women into crones at twenty-five, while the men's powers frequently failed by thirty. The vast majority of the People who reached the age of forty already carried the seeds and signs of imminent death, although the People, like most Asian stock, did not turn gray.

The aging patterns of their lives were hardly different from those of the crowded, hungry agrarian populations of parts of present Asia, where men and women also age and die by thirty. The great difference, however, between primitive predatory and primitive agrarian man was that hunting man could not increase his numbers. Always moving, always running short of food, the hunting Amerindians could not spawn the millions that began to cover the earth in the Old World and in maize-growing Mexico. These teeming populations also frequently went hungry, but they had far more control over their environment.

Even the small mastery that the People had achieved over nature required enormous effort. They made their tools and artifacts with terrible, time-consuming labor. It was a hard, laborious process for the women to cure and tan deer hides and bison skins, and to sew buckskin shirts and skirts with bone picks and awls and animal sinews. The making of weapons—reserved for men—was enormously difficult for a race with only fire and flints: the fashioning of true-flying arrows from seasoned ash or dogwood; glue boiled down from horns and hoofs to fasten carefully selected turkey, owl, or buzzard feathers; strings stretched out of buffalo sinew or bear gut;

shields patiently put together with convex layers of weathered, hardened hides. The primitive tools, buffalo robes, tents, and moccasins the Nermernuh made represented investments far greater in real terms than the artifacts and wardrobes of civilized men. Each family had to make its own.

All that the People made had to be fashioned in temporary camps, then taken with them on the move. They had no time to weave or to make clay pots, any more than they had time to put up permanent shelters. They lived in brush arbors in the warm months, and in portable bison-hide tents or tipis in the cold. Tents and their pine or cedar poles had to be carried from camp to camp. The People could devise nothing heavy or elaborate. The women strapped the infants on their backs and carried all other burdens on the march, aided only by the muscle power of travois-pulling dogs. The men had to be free to scout and find fresh meat, and to protect the column from ever-present human enemies. Thus the People could afford few possessions; they were trapped in an endless cultural cycle, gorging or starving according to season and circumstance.

Mercifully, few grew old. The image the Nermernuh had of old age was malevolent, for there was no place for a female who could not work or keep up, or for a pain-wracked, dim-eyed hunter who could not take the trail. There was no way for the People to prepare for old age. Life was such that most died young, but suicide and euthanasia were widespread throughout the bands. A man or woman who could no longer make the march, or who would starve before the thaws, walked off to die in privacy like a proud animal. The obviously fatally ill were usually abandoned to their fate, partly out of sheer pragmatism, partly out of fear of the hostile spirits believed to surround the stricken or unfortunate. The deformed were destroyed; women caught in incest were executed; twins were killed because they appeared to be unnatural; in bad times, and in very ancient times, girl infants were exposed. The People showed very little concern for such anticipated death. The Nermernuh knew man had little time upon the earth.

But they were not inhuman. They cherished children, more, probably, than peoples not threatened with imminent extinction. There were never enough births to assure the future—a fundamental fact that caused orphaned children to be freely adopted by all North American tribes. Infants were cradled for ten months, swaddled securely against a carrying board in skins and furs, through which a urination hole was cut. They were packed in mosses that were daily changed; they were bathed and oiled in animal fats. Infants lived a messy but comfortable, secure existence. They were crooned over and given pet names. When they were old enough, they ran free in exuberant packs, playing games, the boys nude, the girls in breechclouts. Their rearing was tolerant but pragmatic. Children were not instructed in "right" and "wrong," but they learned the ways of the People quickly in a society in which all persons, according to sex and age, followed exactly the same life style. Children learned from the approval or disapproval of their parents and their kin, and there was rarely any need to punish them. In a hunting society no child, no individual, could ever be a secluded individualist, or ever be independent of the ways of the People or his family—though predatory man as a supreme individualist is an illusion that persists among more civilized societies.

And because the People were human, they believed in an afterlife, as apparently did all primitive men. They buried their dead, the corpses ritually painted and dressed, sitting upright in a cave or crevice or open wash, facing the rising sun. The People feared the dead, but more emotionally than systematically; they had no belief that the dead could harm them. The possessions of the dead, while the People were in the harsh mountains, were buried with them.

The mourning rites for young hunter-warriors struck down in the prime or promise of life invariably startled later European observers. The horror and desperate mourning that the unanticipated death of a young male provoked among the People was common to most American Indians. The howls and shrieks, the withdrawal and long-drawn-out grief that wracked close kin, the despair that convulsed whole camps when several warriors died and the lamentations that might continue for months, derived from Amerindian history. Among hunting peoples the death of a young hunter presaged the destruction of the family group: his mate, his parents, and his aging in-laws, who by custom looked to him to provide meat. The extinction of too many hunters doomed an entire band, for it would be left without protection. The wails and lamentations of relatives were not just for the dead—they were mourning their own destruction. The Shoshones of the mountain regions immolated wives upon their husbands' graves, along with their possessions. The children of the hunter might be adopted; the old folks, if they had no other sons-in-law or sons, might starve if they had reached old age. The death of the young and vigorous male was the greatest of all tragedies among the isolated, atomistic societies of Stone Age hunting men.

IN THE MOUNTAINS THE NERMERNUH WERE GROUPED IN PATRILINEAL bands, in which close relatives usually camped together. Since men and young females had to work, the training and care of children was often left to aunts or grandparents, and the older men who might once have been great hunter-warriors, but who now were more respected for their arrow-making skills. Thus, there were the seeds of social differentiation within the Nermernuh, though this was confined within the family group. No man could yet earn his meat only by making weapons or by providing services of any kind. The bands, however, were no longer strictly groupings of blood relatives, as they once had been. They were groupings of convenience, for hunting and protection, and any person of the Nermernuh was usually welcome in any band, for the differences between the widely separated hunting groups were minimal—the accentuation of some words, a few quirks or traits, nothing more.

The bands did not form a genuine society. They were merely convenient, gregarious groups in which each family head was supreme. The bands often did not even congregate; one might be scattered along a river or stream for several miles. Kinship was recognized within the bands and People in general so far as it could be recalled, but as among all the very primitive Amerindians, memory was inexact and dim. Nomadic hunters could not keep track of extensive genealogies; these were the concerns of sedentary peoples, or of "high barbarians" like the eastern Algonquians. Consequently, the Nermernuh had not evolved clans, those powerful organizations that ruled the lives of more advanced Amerindians. They had no clan chiefs, just as they had no totems, another invention of barbarian man. The Nermernuh, in fact, had no organization beyond the hunting band, for each band was autonomous. In strict terms, then, the People did not even form a tribe, as Indo-Europeans and other Amerindians defined the term.

Close intermarriage was common within each band. There were several reasons. Interband mating was difficult, though hunters might seek out a wife in a different band, because the bands might be separated by hundreds of miles for many years. The exact relationship between the bands is not known; they were all of the People, and recognized as such. Unlike other human tribes, the Nermernuh bands never fought each other, for any reason whatever. The People seemed to operate according to some ancient instinct: the different bands, which might form or dissolve from time to time, never impinged on each other; they were migratory, but each kept to a defined territory. After many centuries, when they were being crowded in upon one another, the separate bands of the Nermernuh were enormously, almost instinctively, reluctant to trespass on the territory of another band. Boundaries were recognized and traditional, but they were as mysterious in their origin as those carved out in the desert by Arabian tribes.

Furthermore, the Nermernuh were reluctant to permit daughters to take mates outside the band. The husband of a daughter took on certain ancient obligations to her parents; he was their provider and defender, as well as hers. They were also reluctant to see a young male mate outside the group, because his services were often lost; he might even join his wife's parents' band. Therefore, there was much close intermixture—cousin mating with cousin—within each band. The People had no taboo against this, although they made great efforts to avoid true incest.

To avoid the risk of incest, boys and girls were separated early. Brothers and sisters did not share the same tipi. Custom demanded that a male who was touched or sometimes even approached by his nubile sister should kill the girl. Boy children began to avoid girl children at a very early age, for both absorbed the tribal taboos almost with their mothers' milk.

However, there was no other sex taboo among the People. Nonincestuous exploration and experimentation were permitted and even approved, as sex was neither clothed in nor prevented by morality. Female frigidity seems to have been rare among the Nermernuh; the nineteenth-century descendants of the People do not appear to have understood the concept. It was normal for older, still unmarried girls to initiate younger boys in sexual play—a pattern that persisted throughout the tribe's independent existence. Mating was done without ceremony among the mountain Shoshones. Couples began sleeping with each other, and the husband—who first must have passed his rites of manhood—became a new family head. The girls had no puberty rites, although they were instructed in female duties, usually by their aunts.

In this era there were no courting ceremonies, no dowries or bride prices, and probably little romance. The mating was a recognized marriage, an economic and reproductive institution that allowed the People to survive. There was little adultery and no rape within the band, because no need or opportunity for such acts arose. Polygamy was permitted, and the Nermernuh practiced both levirate and sororate marriage, that is, men normally took their brothers' widows as wives, and sisters frec;. ently married the same husband. The roots of such customs were of course empirical in both the Old and New Worlds, and they were common among many primitive societies. The People, however, practiced also an anticipatory levirate, in that brothers were expected to share wives. Husbands permitted· unmarried younger brothers to use their wives, in full expectation of later reciprocity. This may have made for tighter family groups, but it further confused the People's genealogy.

In a hunting economy, few males could afford multiple wives, and in the Rocky Mountain era polygamy was rare. Its practice was usually the fulfillment of family obligations, for there could be no unattached females. All the sexual customs of the People began to change when they emerged onto the plains—a problem that has confused later ethnologists, and the Nermernuh themselves, in the ways that all societies are confused when ancient customs erode and become altered under changing circumstances.

There was homosexuality among the Nermernuh, but almost nothing is known about it in ancient times. Certainly it was a luxury that the brutal existence of a hunting society hardly afforded, and it ran deeply counter to the survival instincts of the Amerindian bands.

The individual family groups were ruled by a tyranny of biology and circumstance. Only males had the power to hunt and fight, the two roles that ensured immediate survival. All other work logically fell to females, with one symbolic exception—men made weapons. The males being stronger, though not necessarily more aggressive, they could enforce their dominion over females and family. The male-female roles had long been set in hardening custom-cement. Females had become inferior and subordinate. Among the Nermernuh as among most other Amerindians, women had become almost chattels, as the ancient practice of wife-immolation revealed. The "squaw concept" was deeply rooted, and it had nowhere disappeared even among Amerindians on higher cultural levels, except among the industrious Puebloans, who were in the throes of a great cultural transition when calamity dispersed them. Puebloan men and women did the same kind of work in irrigated fields, and this led to a measure of equality between the sexes. But in hunting societies there was no possible way for women's status to improve, and it did not improve over thousands of years.

Female status was complicated by another factor: the uneasiness with which the Nermernuh, like most primitive peoples, regarded menstruation. Bleeding females were held to be unclean and cursed. They had to remain apart, and could not be touched by men until their period ended, and then only after bathing and other rites of purification. Female menstruation was believed to nullify all magic or medicine; its very awesomeness reinforced the social inferiority of women. No woman could appear in council unless summoned, nor could any woman, until she had passed the menopause, become a priestess or shaman. However, the curse was considered lifted with the menopause, if a Nermernuh woman lived that long.

There is no evidence that the women of the People felt their position to be unfair or oppressive. Conditioned by millennia of experience, they could envision no other order of things.

Beyond the family, which the male hunter family head ruled absolutely, the People had only the sketchiest of social or civil organization. Family heads were equals, though they of course varied enormously in esteem and prestige in the eyes of others within the band. Some hunters were splendid providers, others barely got by. The People, however, did have certain leaders, for even the most primitive and homogeneous human society could not quite exist without them.

They selected leaders for war, though the authority of the war chief never extended beyond the war trail. Here the man rarely sought the office; the office sought the man, usually some intelligent, experienced, or lucky warrior. The war chief received total obedience, because every member of an Amerindian war band was a volunteer whose discipline was implicit in his following the war trail. This discipline was so ingrained as to be almost instinctive— like the discipline each warrior invariably exhibited in eating and drinking sparingly and enduring heroically while at war. Hunter-warriors cooperated like a pack of wolves, running behind a crafty leader. But failure, or even pure bad luck, quickly destroyed any war chief's prestige and authority, and war leaders rose and fell continually.

The so-called peace chief, or band headman, was not a chief in any modern meaning of the word. The Nermernuh, like virtually all Amerindians, surprisingly had always separated military and civil government. Each band had its civil chief, almost always a powerful family head who had exhibited courage and wisdom in the hunt and in war, and a man whose counsel had proven good. Again, the office found the man, and the man made the office, because chieftainship was not wrapped in legal or traditional authority but was charismatic in nature. The position was what the wisdom and personality of the accepted leader made it. His powers, such as they were, were those of a mediator rather than a magistrate. The peace chief could move the camp, since he was always the most prominent tribesman in it, but he could not give orders to any family head, prevent injustice or enforce justice, punish, or make peace or war. He was merely a recognized first among equals whose advice was often sought, and whose suggestions were usually followed. The success of such chiefs depended upon their being able to understand the tribal mood and to solve disputes in a way that impressed the collective band as being fair. The post was more one of honor than true authority.

On the surface, hunting band society was a pure democracy of adult males, who made all the great decisions—peace, war, alliance, migration—around the council fire. The councils of the Nermernuh, like those of virtually all the North American peoples, were extremely important affairs. Their procedure was ruled far more rigidly by centuries of custom than any modern parliament is governed by rules of order. Here the males gathered and smoked the ceremonial pipe, then spoke according to a hierarchy of age and experience. Younger warrior-hunters rarely spoke up, and women were barred unless they were called upon to testify. Nermernuh traditions did not allow debate in council. The reasons were buried in ancestral memory, but they may be explained as rooted in the fact that, among a primitive people whose males were independent and aggressive by nature, direct debate had led to bloodshed.

Council meetings were a series of speeches or orations. Europeans and Anglo-Americans who took part in such councils in later centuries were often stunned by the brilliance of Amerindian oratory, and the striking imagery of the indigenous languages. Few Europeans then understood that it was possible for a society to have a rich language and an enormous body of tradition without possessing writing, and few Europeans knew that because of the importance of the council in Amerindian life, the orators invariably practiced and rehearsed their speeches before rising among their equals. The council was ruled by inflexible courtesy: no oration was ever interrupted, for any reason. On one recorded occasion, a respected speaker halted in the midst of his peroration to contemplate. No one departed or spoke before he resumed—although his contemplation required several hours.

No speaker's honor or intentions might be impugned in council, though counterarguments could be offered in succeeding orations. The councils of the People, whom Europeans considered to be anarchic savages, were invariably impressive to white men, who were perhaps painfully aware that few civilized conventions from Rome to Washington had ever quite attained the dignity and decorum of these squatting primitives, inhaling sumac smoke and chanting sonorous arguments by firelight and drum.

Decisions were almost always made by acclamation, when one or more speakers had moved the council. Unless the decision was unanimous, there was none. This meant that decisions were almost always drawn from experience or folk wisdom, that they rarely followed radical or novel advice. Once the decision had been reached, it was announced through the encampment by criers. And here occurred another phenomenon that invariably impressed later European observers: although the council had no means of enforcing its decisions, they were always honored and carried out. On the rare occasions when some family head could not agree, he was obliged to leave the jurisdiction by separating from the band.

The problem was that Europeans failed to understand the People's form of society and government. The Nermernuh had no "law" or "government" because they needed none—they were still a people. The apparently loose-knit and anarchic hunting society was utterly homogeneous. The People actually had the oldest and most effective of all governments: the tyranny of custom. Every Nerm or Human Being absorbed the customs of his People from birth. Europeans insisted upon thinking of the People in their own terms, and therefore could never comprehend the unwritten codes by which the People's writ ran through countless scattered tipis and encampments.

The People's law was not a complex, rationalized thing, which could be changed by the decisions of emperors, judges, or parliaments at will, and which at times could be understood fully only by trained elites. The People's law consisted of their conventional wisdom, accreted by painful experience. No individual or council could set such custom-law aside; every chief or council made decisions that all the People immediately understood.

The People and the Europeans were never to comprehend one another's laws and government. To the People, so far as they understood European arguments, the white men were slaves, always fearful of superiors and bowing to some distant authority, demanding that the red men do the same. But many Europeans misunderstood the People; in fact, came to consider them splendidly free barbarians living in a pure democracy. They never quite grasped the crushing rule of custom among the People, a tyranny so pervasive and so ancient that few Nermernuh ever consciously thought about it or could articulate it.

No Nerm really had much option to choose freely. Custom, convention, and scores of accrued taboos had long destroyed all possible individuality. Observers recorded a fact that some students of the People have overlooked: in almost every similar situation, every Nerm acted or reacted in almost exactly the same way. In a tribal society there was no right or wrong, and never any individualists. There was simply one accepted manner of doing things. Compared to Europeans, the Nerm consciously believed he was free, because he never quite recognized that while he could spurn all human orders, he could not break any established pattern without the severest psychic penalties.

This mountain hunter was not a "noble savage." Such concepts were always illusions of highly organized, overbureaucratized societies, wanting desperately to believe that man's nature was to be

free, and that somehow civilization had tyrannized him. The Shoshone hunter was hardly a joyous creature of nature. The People
were not clean, not "good," not "noble," not merciful, nor, hard as
their life was, were they industrious. They were a people surviving
by the skin of their teeth, beset by forces they could not comprehend. They were desperate not to offend these forces, which they
saw as spirits. Over their history they had acquired a certain dignity, but it was more the instinctive dignity of a prime animal,
accepting stoically the hurts of nature, than the achieved dignity of
rational men. It was splendid in one way, because Nerm dignity
allowed no self-pity or sentimentality. The People affirmed to the
death, and with dignity, their way of life—not only because they
knew no other way, but because they had come to believe it was
ordained and sacred.

Men who lived so dangerously were and had to be deeply religious, although their beliefs were primitive and, according to their
cosmogony, entirely practical. The thrust of the Nermernuh religion was to find the pattern for securing supernatural power and
favor, the gift they called *puha* ("poohah"), or "medicine." The
People never had time for abstract thought. Each individual was
raised understanding what and who he was—a Human Being of the
People—and never wondered why he was. His religion, which
every person took with desperate seriousness, was an attempt to
understand the spirit forces so he might manipulate them, in order
to survive and prosper.

It was an individual search, without group rituals, and therefore
many Old World invaders neither understood it as religion, nor saw
it as the primitive root of their own religious inventions. European
man and the Amerindians were divided not by religion but by science. The Europeans who arrived in America had already separated
their magic or spiritual world from the world of cause and effect,
however they might light candles or refuse to face the fact. The
Amerindian still combined science and religion, while the People
pursued their religion with the fervor of dedicated scientists. The
Nermernuh had no Hebrew acceptance of a remote God's will.
They were determined to smell out and ensnare the spirits that
lived in the rocks and rills and animal life, to gain the *puha* or
power that would bring the buffalo down before their spears, that
would overcome sickness and make them victorious in war. There

was great fear behind and within each search, but also great comfort. The Nerm believed in *his* magic—though he believed the
world was run by magic—only when it worked for him. If it did
not, he knew he had failed and sought new magic. But if the magic
appeared to bring success, the *puhakut* or maker of strong medicine
became caught up in an intoxication and belief in his personal invulnerability that Europeans, who had come to believe in an impersonal operation of the universe, could hardly comprehend. Once
such men had found their medicine they faced the future unafraid.

This religion had no ethic, or concept of moral elevation, or
notion of reward and punishment. The People's ethic was strictly
social; magic or religion was secret and personal. The spirits gave
aid because they favored some individual, and the award had no
moral or social strings attached. The Nermernuh had no concept of
man in nature, or of a covenant between man and God. But they
believed that the spirits, which could be merciful, were also capricious. The magic-maker lived eternally in fear of offending them. As
he developed his magic—according to the same patterns that children devise personal signs and some men seek to break a jinx or
improve their luck—he became trammeled in countless intricate
actions and taboos. Almost from childhood, the Nerm was forced to
do everything in a certain consistent way. To break any pattern was
to destroy the magic and ensure ill luck or even destruction.

Although such a personal, magic-based religion could have no
group dogma or ritual—each individual had a hundred pressing
dogmas and rituals constantly on his mind—every hunter's beliefs
fitted into a definite social context. The Nermernuh understood
each other's secret incantations and personal taboos and respected
them without ever attempting to correlate them into a coherent
body of belief.

Since the People saw the universe as random, without mathematical or natural order, their only means to scientific manipulation
was through visions that revealed the way to magical powers. The
Shoshone peoples of the high mountains had once believed only in
spontaneous visions or psychic revelations, but in the eastern
Rockies the Nermernuh had learned from the more advanced tribes
of the plains that visions might be induced. Thus they learned
method for their magic. While the People continued to accept the
spontaneous visions that came in blinding psychic experiences, they
had begun to seek them also in socially recognized ways.

Every male at puberty, before he took his first hunt or war trail, sought his personal *puha* or medicine. Its revelation or selection would be the most important event in his life. He must find it, and interpret it properly, for this was his basic medicine, which would guide him throughout life. Of course, he would later seek specific medicine for all the great happenings of his career—preparations for hunts and war, during mourning, at mating, or for the birth of children. There had to be medicine for every occasion, or else, without a serving magic, the warrior believed he would walk helplessly through the world like a menstruating woman.

The youth sought his magic visions through vigils. He retired to some lonely spot which was believed to have some special aura. He made careful preparation, usually assisted by an older person who had made strong medicine himself. He prayed, smoked tobacco or sumac leaves, fasted, sang, and sometimes employed self-mutilation to induce pain. The People knew the usefulness of hunger, pain, and purgatives like willow bark to make the mind have visions. They had no intoxicants or hallucinogens, like the southwestern peoples and the Mexicans. The vigilant tried to disorient his mind and senses, sometimes working himself up into a frenzy, because the People thought that minds that saw inwardly saw most true. Unlike many peoples to the east, however, the Nermernuh never abased themselves before the spirit world. The Siouans wallowed in humility before the spirits and begged for mercy. The People had more dignity in their vigils; they expected the spirit world to be benevolent.

The puberty vigil was like the knighthood vigil of medieval Europe, which was not Christian but war-barbarian in origin. If necessary, the young male stood vigil for four nights and days. And he usually had his vision: a high wind, a storm, the passage of some great bird, a wolf call, a shooting star. Either a psychic experience or an observed physical phenomenon would do; the People did not distinguish between the two in their magic-ordered universe. The manifestation told him his magic, and which spirit was to be his guardian. The experience would be socially recognized by all his tribe.

Having found his power, the Nerm believed in it with such ferocity that European minds always called it arrogance. One did not question medicine—to "trust God but keep your powder dry" to the Amerindian was to nullify all magic through lack of faith. But with the *puha* granted by the spirit world, the owner also acquired a series of complex taboos. Some of these were his own inventions, like the hexes and charms of children, others were established and socially recognized. No outsider, and certainly no non-Amerindian, ever completely understood the imperatives and proscriptions that went with *puha*. The hunter with an eagle sign—very powerful—must take on the idiosyncrasies of the great bird, such as permitting no one to pass behind him while he ate. Those with wolf, coyote, bear, deer, or buffalo medicine must be careful never to offend the guardian spirits of those animals. And the deepest part of the magic was secret; it lost its power if it was spoken.

Magic frequently failed to work, either because the holder had violated a taboo, nullified it with a female, or else had weak faith. The taboo violation was serious. No Nerm scoffed at it; in fact, sometimes hunters refused powerful medicine because of the taboos they believed it would impose. Although the People had no concept of reward or punishment from the spirit world, they saw a kind of balance that probably is instinctive within the human consciousness. Everything had its price; every power required some onerous duty or forced observance of a difficult taboo. Guardian spirits gave altruistically, but they also took away. The violation of taboos could cause a Nerm intense psychosomatic pain, even death, and the fear of taboo violation constantly caused hysteric tension. The average Nerm lived in something very close to a manic-depressive cycle, horror following close upon exultation as his magic worked or failed.

Since magic had no group ritual or group dogma, the People had no priests. Some men, however, had more powerful visions than others, and made stronger medicine. These *puhakut* were shamans, or medicine men. Usually a *puhakut* had originated an impressive set of cabals and rites that had proven successful under test, satisfying all observers of their power. The shamans were forceful mystics who believed in their *puha*, though a few in historic times were obviously charlatans. Medicine men were not especially healers, for magic ranged into every field, but they did offer cures. Since the *puha* was given, not earned, no holder could refuse a request for help. Shamans did have considerable success in curing psychosomatic ills, very little with wounds and fevers. They could not be accused of malpractice, since their medicine was only as good as the faith of the sufferer made it.

There was more than one story, however, of shamans destroyed because they became drunk with power or sour with age and frightened the People with malevolent spells. Such old men were dangerous. Medicine men did not form a class, though they did accept gifts for services. They were only hunter-warriors considered to have a little more insight into, or favor from, the guardian spirits that ruled the world. Women could also become *puhakut*, but only after the female menopause.

It is a truism that only those who are born or converted into a religious view can fully comprehend it. The magic-cosmos of the People must always remain a mystery to nonbelievers, because it was shattered and destroyed along with the People. The Nermernuh survivors of the twentieth century no longer understood exactly what their forefathers had truly believed. They no longer believed it themselves. Most had become at least nominal Christians, and their belief in most, if not all, magic was shattered. Even before this, the People's beliefs had become shot through with diffusions from other peoples. During their last century on the plains the Nermernuh had acquired the "spirit seance" from the Algonquian Cheyennes, complete with the mysterious shaking of the tipi, the eagle dance and others from the northern tribes, and the beaver ceremony from the Pawnees. They had also absorbed the thunderbird myth from the southwestern tribes. The first Europeans who came into contact with the Nermernuh further confused understanding by writing down much nonsense concerning their religious views.

The eighteenth- and nineteenth-century travelers who examined the People's beliefs or discussed such questions with them were convinced that European myths were universal, and that the Amerindians must merely have different versions of them. It did not occur to Europeans and Anglo-Americans to examine the indigenous cosmology independently; they either tried to correlate it with their own or to impose their own upon it. Here they perpetrated lasting illusions and misconceptions.

The People never saw God in the rain, wind, or thunder. They had no notion of an Hebraic Yahweh, or even a Mexic sun god, and in fact they had no pressing interest in the overall nature of the universe. Europeans, however, strained to find a "Sure Enough Father" or a "Great Spirit" among the Nermernuh, and created this concept for them. It was true that some Amerindians had such concepts, but not the People. They could indeed envision such a spirit, which might have created them and the cosmos, but they failed to take such a creator seriously. To their minds, such a deity obviously could not be particularly active or effective. Like Father-Sun, Mother-Earth, and also the Mother-Moon, which looked down coldly on the affairs of men, and all of which the People venerated as forces, such a god was too remote to serve as a guardian spirit. The magic-seekers had no use for remote gods who rode the heavens and endured forever while men died. These spirits might well have nurtured man, but none had ever shown him the personal consideration they desired and expected from animistic guardians.

The gods of the Nermernuh were protective spirits who dwelt in the rocks and thunder, and above all in the animals. The People were animists, with a world-view that was old in Asia long before their ancestors trekked into America. They prayed to the eagle spirit for soaring strength, to the deer spirit for agility, to the wolf spirit for wise ferocity; they were wary of the crow spirit, for he was malicious. They revered the buffalo spirit, saying prayers that it might send the bison to be slaughtered. This was both their science and their religion. When they made good medicine, the spirits answered; when they offended, or the spirits were capricious, men died and women went hungry, and their wailing infants perished beneath the snows.

It was white men who confused the wolf with God, the sun with the Great Spirit, and benevolent or malicious guardians with Manichaean notions of Good and Evil. Europeans probably could not help projecting their own cosmology on the Indians, though they had very little effect in changing them. The People understood such concepts, and the suspicion must be strong that they often gave the white men affirmation, either from courtesy or sheer weariness, of beliefs and myths that were foreign to the red man, and in which he had no lasting interest.

Men with buffalo medicine prayed to the great beasts to come into their valleys, making buffalo magic with horns, flutes, rattles, and drums. When the bison came and were killed, they scrupulously left the heart intact within the skeleton, so that with it the buffalo spirit might live and replenish the plains. They broke no buffalo taboo. Those with strong magic lived their allotted time on

Bear claw charm with feathers.

earth, then, painted and set to face the rising sun, they were mysteriously carried into that shadow land beyond the sun whose name symbolized the only paradise a hunting people knew, the Happy Hunting Ground. This was not a land of milk and honey, but a verdant valley filled with grazing beasts. There, People were never cold or hungry, and they knew no sorrow or pain.

This belief in an afterlife, and the equally universal legend of a time when continents sank in a catastrophic flood, were the only beliefs the People shared with European man.

They had never developed a true mechanics of salvation, any more than a coherent theology. There was no set means of getting to the Happy Hunting Ground. It was not reserved for males—all sexes and ages went there when they died—and it was not a reward for a good life on earth. The People believed that all Human Beings were equalized by death. They did expect—and this was a social rather than a religious view—that warriors who died defending the People or women who perished in childbirth might have especial consideration in heaven because of their services to the human race. The idea that lazy, evil, murderous, or cowardly people went to their reward in a Bad Hunting Ground, where footsore hunters pursued shadowy animals in vain and women wailed all night from hunger —a place worse than life on earth—never existed among the mountain Nermernuh. Hell was projected into the Shoshone mind by nineteenth-century Christian missionaries.

Heaven, however, could be denied men. The human mind probably had to devise a way. Those whose hair was cut off after death could not enter paradise. The People, like almost all Amerindians, had an ancient hair fetish, probably as old as man himself upon the Asian continent. Males combed, decorated, greased, and never cut their hair, except perhaps a patch to show the deepest mourning. They believed that scalping annihilated the human spirit thing, or soul. Strangling also throttled the soul, and death by night made it dubious whether the shade could find the land beyond the sun. Mutilation of the dead was an act of terrible vengeance, because it was supposed that the dead took the damage into their afterlife. The people whose corpses were scalped or horribly mutilated were destroyed. They became ghosts, ominous shades who came out with the rising moon.

The primordial meanness and cruelty of the human spirit had

thus found ways to rob enemies of strength and dignity and carry vengeance beyond the grave. The scalps that the People tore from their slain foes were originally not trophies but totems—they were symbols of the everlasting inhumanity of man to man. The most ancient totem of the People was the grisly scalp pole, which they carried everywhere and set before their tents, and their most ancient—and almost only—socializing ritual was the scalp dance. Both practices were so old among the People, and so universal among all North American Indians, that it is certain that they came out of central Asia with the first invaders. There is solid evidence of this. Modern archaeologists have found scalped corpses in frozen grave sites in the Altai, some with their hair recovered and re-stitched to their torn heads. The People always tried to preserve the hair of their own in war, standing over fallen comrades to the death, ferociously defending their passage to paradise as bitterly as they tried to keep heaven from being populated with other breeds of men.

The ghosts the People caused made them uneasy, though they did not actually fear harm from them. The ghost image was of scalped, bloody specters who walked by night, or of bare-boned skeletons that rose with the swollen moon. Nermernuh avoided sites where they knew that men had died.

They had two other bogeys. One was the Cannibal Owl, which descended in the dark to devour men. They believed the monstrous mammoth bones that still dotted the plains were the remains of this horrible creature. There were also *nenuhpee,* or manlike things no more than a foot high, which shot arrows that always killed. It was possible to have ghost magic, or be favored by the spirits of the Little Men, but these medicines were so powerful, and therefore so dangerous to the holder, that the Nermernuh avoided them.

THIS WAS THE WORLD OF MOUNTAIN PEOPLE: A BRUTAL UNIVERSE OF strenuous effort and ever-present hunger, of splendid but also dangerous magic, in which most brave men consciously hoped they would die young. The People were wary of spirits and uneasy about most things, but they were rarely afraid of death itself. Death too often came as release.

It was not all hunger and hardship and primordial cruelty and pain. The People had the ephemeral joys of childhood, for boys and girls played and romped until about the age of nine or ten, free from the fears and dangers of adult life or medicine. The child grew up soon enough, learned the duties and burdens of People, and assumed them. The boy child learned to hunt and kill, the girl was taken as a mate. No child had to be forced into these roles; there was neither option nor escape.

The People had good, well-fed times, when they lolled about their summer arbors. They had—despite much false writing to the contrary—a keen sense of humor. They could laugh at each other and themselves. Inured to a brutal existence, they also laughed at things that would have made civilized men weep. And it was a brave world, for despite the constant hardship, the constant pressure of hunger and imminent death, the small, dark People were creatures of enormous courage. They risked destruction daily, and bore hurts without self-pity.

They were not the shapers, organizers, and destroyers of a mathematically ordered universe, but they had fire and tools and skills and magic; they had a rich, expressive language and a deep, ancient human consciousness, and therefore they were not animals. They were man the hunter, man the killer, man as he lived for eight hundred generations across the earth, a life style difficult and dangerous, but one without conflict between ideals and action, between necessity and right. Perhaps it was because the People collectively possessed so little power that these weathered, hungry, stunted, dirty, and painfully ignorant people possessed such individual dignity. Each man stood alone, and in the loneliness of his power-magic created his own universe.

His world-view, however, had become unassailable, and his life style had become not merely good, but sacred. This was the total sureness that either so angered or so bewildered white men, to whom few things were sacred except their own concept of civilization. To the Nerm all his concepts, all his ways, were as sacred as his magic or medicine bag, filled with secret, personal things, that hung between his loins. The male Nerm wore a breechclout neither for modesty nor for convenience, but to protect his medicine with secret knots and magical herbs tied fast beside his penis, his most magic and important organ. He had a world-view that would die

Nerm man, twentieth century.
Photograph by Edward S. Curtis.

very hard, however it might be shattered by superior powers and adversity. Some magic, perhaps, can never be utterly conquered: survivors of the People, in later centuries, still wore symbolic clouts or horsehide strings to protect their genitals inside their modern, mass-made trousers.

In their world and against their world the People were not powerful, however. Even among the surrounding tribes of other Amerindians, the Nermernuh of the mountains were a despised people. There were only a scattered few of them, wandering in isolated bands. They were scorned and hardly feared by other peoples in the midcontinental heartland, many of whom had planted corn, cured tobacco, and raised thatch-roofed houses in the vast Missouri drainage for a thousand years.

These peoples had seized the sheltered valleys and driven their pine and cedar posts deep along the rivers. They had carved out extensive fields, and they stored maize ears against the winters, while in the summer they ate their vegetables and squash. They hunted when it suited them, for meat or for pelts for robes, or when the periodic dry spells parched their fields. They rarely knew the hunger or the exposure that was the People's normal lot. There were more of them, and they had pressed the People back to the bitter mountains, on lands they themselves did not want. These peoples, proud Siouans, a great Siouan-speaking arc of Omahas and Missouris, Iowas, Kansanses, and Poncas, their southern Osage cousins, and the Caddoan Wichitas, had songs and rich rituals that bespoke their barbaric approach to civilization. They had invented great socializing events—the dances, ceremonies, and culture that men whose future seems assured have leisure to invent.

High in the Wyoming country the People had few songs and hardly any dances. They had been ringed in, perhaps for a thousand years. There appeared to be no escape for them. A European observer who was empowered to see this primitive America would have agreed with the Iowas and Poncas, and certainly with the Senecas and Mexica, that the People were an ignorant race who had made the worst of all possible uses of their environment. It would have appeared to any sensible observer that the barbarians owned the future, and that the still savage tribes would be hard put even to survive.

Yet those more numerous and potentially powerful peoples of the

North American heartland were to be brushed easily from the earth. Their rich stores of song and story were to be forgotten. No historian would record their legends; their passing would be briefly noted. These tribes vanished, even their memory destroyed. They would be recalled only by the rivers and valleys to which they gave their names, and even then the vast majority of the usurpers of their lands would never realize that Omaha, Missouri, Iowa, and Kansas were not mere place names—that they had once stood for peoples.

The Nermernuh would also vanish like the rest, but not before they rode into history like the whirlwind. If they had no songs, they would cause songs and legends that probably would not die so long as men lived upon the continent. For the People were to fight the most relentlessly, successfully, and valiantly of all the tribes around the plains, not to secure a homeland but to preserve their sacred life styles. They would fight from plateau to high plateau and cover the high country with countless graves, until at last the continent took their bones, and their shades perhaps passed, as they believed, to the land beyond the sun.

3

THE BLOOD TRAIL

*War was a state of mind among the Indians,
and therefore never terminated.*
—Alfred L. Kroeber

THE FIRST DRIVE OF THE AMERINDIANS WAS A BIOLOGICAL IMPERATIVE: the hunt for food in the struggle to survive. Their one great social imperative, however, was war.

The second imperative may have grown out of the first, but there is no clear-cut evidence to prove that it did. The theories for the origins of war and violence among the Amerindian peoples are no more than hypotheses; modern opinion is divided as to whether warfare between men derives from instinctive aggressions or from social factors. The weight of evidence would appear to lie with instinct—the weight of argument, elsewhere. Confusions surrounding Amerindian war and violence were and are inherent in the confusions surrounding European civilization's own concepts of warfare and aggression. Still, it is reasonably certain that warfare and killing between men is as old as the symbolic story of Cain and Abel, and that the Amerindian war ethic, like the scalp pole, came with the race from the Old World.

There is simply no conclusive, noncontradictory, or established evidence to explicate the logic of Amerindian warfare. It varied as greatly from place to place and time to time as the tribal cultures. The myth that agrarian or more highly civilized peoples tended to be less warlike than predatory, savage tribes is totally contrary to fact, though this was true in certain times and circumstances, as the

Cain legend was probably composed to attest. Many of the most primitive hunting and gathering cultures, such as the Arawakan of the islands and the Coahuiltecan of south Texas and northern Mexico, were exceedingly peaceful. Columbus wrote truthfully of gentle, timid *indios*. But the two most advanced, agrarian, organized, and secure peoples in North America, the Iroquois confederacy of the eastern woodlands and the Mexica or Aztecs of Mexico, were the most bloodthirsty and savage warmakers upon the continent. This might be explained by the fact that both tribes were relatively recently risen from savagery, the Mexica being recent conquerors of an ancient civilization. But the Maya, whose ancestors had been urban and agrarian for a millennium, were extremely belligerent. Mayan warfare was internecine, not intertribal, and possibly more bitter for that reason. It virtually destroyed Mayan civilization in Yucatán before the Spanish came, and the decadent descendants of that civilization were not completely subdued until 1901, by a Mexican army.

Neither the Mexica nor the Iroquois had anything to fear from the surrounding Amerindians. Both had seized all the territory they could possibly hold or use. Neither had any shortage of land or food. Both were the strongest peoples in their respective regions. Both, however, waged unremitting war against their neighbors. Both mounted long-range expeditions, unmercifully harassing tribes that were hundreds of miles distant. The Iroquois enjoyed—there can be no other description for it—falling upon and massacring other tribes. Infusing warfare with religion, the Mexica dedicated the male child to the Sun-God at birth, with prayers that he might fall in battle, and he was trained to take his rank and place in the Mexic battalions at an early age. The Aztecs slaughtered thousands in battle and other thousands in sacrifice to their war-demon, Huitzilopochtli. They even, uniquely, preserved some close enemies, so that they would always have a source of victims and a convenient training ground for war.

The Mexica raised organized belligerence to an extreme art, and the Algonquian confederacy lagged behind only in prolonged drive; barbarian clans lacked the organization and resources of a high civilization to sustain war. Against the sheer violence of these two peoples, the Amerindian wars of the North American plains seem ceremonial and almost harmless.

On the other hand, the highly ritual barbarism of the Puebloan culture was essentially peaceable. The industrious farmers and pottery-makers of the high southwestern mesas, male and female, had no time to study war. The similarly advanced Caddoans of the southern pine forests lived well from their corn and bean fields, built temples and houses, and exhibited no drive to battle with their neighbors. In its early stages, the Mexican agrarian culture and rising civilization appears to have been quite peaceful. Villagers put aside their weapons for seeds and digging sticks, and continued a quiet, communal life for almost a thousand years, before they became organized under vast bureaucracies and warrior kings.

The Amerindian history of warfare seems every bit as varied and complex as the progress of the differentiated peoples toward barbarism and civilization. Probably, all Amerindians possessed a similar human potential for violence and war, whether social or instinctive, just as they shared with all human beings, everywhere, the same potential for intelligence, progress, and civilization. Degrees of difference are called forth merely by circumstance.

The pattern of Amerindian warfare suggests that it was not totally irrational or intentionally suicidal. Smaller and weaker peoples, such as the Coahuiltecans of south Texas, the Shoshones of the Great Northern Basin, some Caribbean tribes, and others who had been pushed onto poor, arid, or marginal lands, were rarely warlike to the extent of seeking conflict with more powerful neighbors. All such peoples feared reprisals.

Formerly powerful tribes like the Tarahumares of Chihuahua, almost exterminated by the Spanish in the seventeenth century, became "cowardly" skulkers after their near-destruction. When the Mexica or Aztecs were a small tribe living, only on sufferance, on mud islands in Lake Texcoco, they paid tribute and avoided provoking the powerful city communities around them. There were many such patterns from Mexico to the High Plains, where Lewis and Clark found "peaceful" Mandans and others living in constant dread of the stronger Sioux.

On the other hand, the most numerous and powerful peoples usually appropriated the richest hunting or farming grounds, and these wealthy tribes tended to be the most warlike on the continent. It is, of course, unprovable whether such peoples were warlike because they were strong and numerous, or were rich and numerous because they were warlike and seized choice territories. The Mexica, for instance, discovered fresh belligerence with new-found power, and so did the Shoshones who adopted the horse. Whichever, there *was* a corollary between holding rich territory, thus enjoying economic security, and the ability to make war. Small, hungry, or poorly organized peoples could not afford deadly conflicts and tried to avoid them—a pattern no different from that which prevailed in Eurasia, or in the vast power struggles between twentieth-century nations.

Many Amerindian wars surely began as territorial disputes, struggles to seize or hold desirable lands. Frequently, tribes were driven by some natural disaster such as drought to invade more fertile territories. These invasions and displacements caused endemic wars and lasting hatreds. Conflicts crystallized: when the white men arrived, there were enmities so old among many peoples that Amerindians no longer remembered their beginning. Anglo-Americans reported how the very hair rose on the necks of Crow allies when they saw the mark of a Dakota. Athapaskans and Shoshones hated each other with a feral fury. Europeans who entered virgin Amerindian country and made contact with the tribes usually did so peacefully at first, while they were warned of the deadly or pernicious nature of other, neighboring peoples. This too followed a pattern. It was the nature of primitive men not to fear total strangers and even to offer them hospitality; true hatred was reserved for familiar peoples close at hand with whom there had long been war.

The ancient, ineradicable hatreds made conquest infinitely easier for invading Europeans. Cortés could never have conquered Mexico without his hordes of Nahua allies. Large numbers of Amerindians marched with every Spanish expedition as eager volunteers, while the United States Army recruited Amerindian scouts. Until the very twilight of their independent existence, the western Amerindians continued to kill each other more than they killed white soldiers; there was no stage of the European-Indian wars in which the whites lacked willing, bloodthirsty native allies. It would be anachronistic to see this as ethnic treason, however. It no more occurred to the North American Indians that they were of one single race, or were brothers of any kind, than it had to

Europeans during the previous thousand years or through the great wars of the twentieth century.

ARMED, WANDERING, CONSTANTLY IMPINGING, UTTERLY DIFFERENT IN tongue and customs, the tribes made war. There were no unarmed or completely peaceful Amerindians. Even the weakest and most degraded of tribes would fight to avoid extermination, or would kill enemies who fell into their hands. The scrounging Coahuiltecans frequently fought each other for a water hole; the Puebloans threw up a pitiful shower of arrows at Coronado's mailed horsemen, and, in 1680, drove the Spanish out of New Mexico by fire and blood. The great difference was that Puebloans and Coahuiltecans could not afford the luxury of regular war; this was reserved for Mexica, Dakotas, and Iroquois. But all tribes had an ethos of violence—there were no Amerindian pacifists.

As with most primitive folk, this violence was usually directed entirely outside the band or tribe. Either instinctively or consciously, the homogeneous tribal hunting peoples like the Nermernuh did not allow internal violence or bloodshed. There was rarely any rape, robbery, murder, or other crime inside any Amerindian society. The prohibition was not formalized, but it was total in the Amerindian mind. Such things offended the whole tribe or band. When murder, adultery, or other injuries did occur, the oldest human law, the *lex talionis*, prevailed. Every family head was considered supreme; the warrior could punish or even kill his females or his children for disobedience or crimes. The adulteress might be slain. More often, among the People, she would be disfigured, usually by cutting off her nose. The offended male carried out this punishment, and often also sought satisfaction from his cuckolder. Very rarely, however, did such affairs create actual bloodshed between males. Primitive warriors did not fight to the death over women.

For one thing, tribal custom threw an enervating moral cloud over the trespasser. A show of force was usually enough to secure the cuckold both his woman and his honor, with a sort of payment for damages. Many warriors were reluctant to mutilate desirable females to satisfy honor; a beating was often enough. The codes that governed Nermernuh society were similar to those that ruled behavior among higher animals. The males were aggressive toward outsiders and they frequently made a show of force within the band. They threatened and bullied—but almost always stopped short of actually shedding the blood of their own kind.

When a killing that could not be justified under tribal custom did occur, justice took a simple course: the victim's close kin hunted down the murderer and killed him. This was far more a form of execution than a reprisal since a murderer's own kin never involved themselves in the quarrel, and never tried to avenge his death. Justice did not lead to blood feuds within the bands. Such feuds could occur only within more highly socialized societies, which had developed clans and assigned them functions, just as murder became commonplace only in human society with the rise of heterogeneous civilizations, where different bloodlines and tribes and classes came to live under common jurisdictions, and rigid custom no longer prevailed.

Within the tribe or camp, there was a strict moral code, but this never went beyond the ethnic boundary. The People, like all Amerindians and most human beings, clearly distinguished between the murder of one's own kind and the killing of outsiders. This was a universal morality that became confused only when scribes translated Moses' sensible camp order, *Thou shalt do no murder*, into the humanly impossible dictum, *Thou shalt not kill*.

The only code that protected the outsider was the ancient one of hospitality to a complete stranger. Distant travelers, of any race, could usually move among Amerindians in peace. Propinquity usually bred the opposite of understanding among Amerindians. And a highly significant number of European-Amerindian hostilities came about through an accidental European involvement in ancient feuds. Thus the French fostered the enmity of the terrible Iroquois when a Frenchman shot two warriors who attacked the Indians he was among. In the same way, it was not possible for whites to be friends and allies of both Crows and Sioux, or of Ottawas and Senecas, or of Comanches and Apaches. The whites proved singularly stupid in not recognizing this salient fact.

As anthropology shows, the internal morality of any people does not easily cross ethnic lines. The relations between different Amerindian peoples were determined solely by their relative strength or weakness, and their different natures, whether static, aggressive, or dynamic. The alien tribe was fair game for all the aggressions forbidden against one's blood kin.

Long before Columbus opened the New World, Amerindian warfare had become institutionalized. War was so deeply imbedded in the Amerindian ethos that its rationale was self-sustaining. It was part of existence, and life was unthinkable without it. Among the People, like all surrounding peoples, every male was a warrior as well as a hunter. The terms were synonymous in most Amerindian tongues. And manhood as the Amerindians understood it was not merely a biological state. It required rites of passage, through violence.

The pubescent male had to seek his magic or medicine, but he was not a man until he had been blooded in both the hunt and war. The boy-child was taken on hunts when he was big enough to participate. Here he proved his strength, courage, and skill, preferably in close battle with some large animal. Just as the African warrior sought to kill a lion, the Nerm boy who was daring and lucky enough to kill a bear and survive earned great respect. And only the youngster tested in the hunt could become eligible to take up the supreme business of the Nerm male: the war trail.

Such courage tests and violence rites obviously arose because of sheer necessity in the predatory stage of human development. Hunting man lived in blood and by blood for hundreds of generations. The man who could not kill had no hope of survival, much less of propagation of his race. A man who could not defend his hearthfire was socially useless. The enormous value placed on human courage by the hunting Amerindians was not accidental or artificial, for bravery and killing ability were a social value fundamental to survival. But because the Nermernuh were human, and had created a human if primitive society, courage had acquired cultural values also.

Demonstrated valor had become the main road of the male Nerm to prestige, the esteem of his family and his peers. Even a society made up of primitive hunters and gatherers had such things as social rank and pride and honors. If the courage and blood skills of the warrior determined the survival of his women and offspring and the collective existence of his band, they also determined his status in the world he knew. The powerful warrior was esteemed and

Warrior in medicine paint, c. 1884.
Posed reservation photograph.

made to feel a great man among his People, the coward was not tolerated, and the marginal fighting man despised.

Until the boy warrior had fought the enemy and proven himself in combat, he could not know the companionship of the warpath or hunting trail. He would not be accepted as a man by his elders or his peers. No one would admire him, ask his advice, or, perhaps the greatest of all human satisfactions, obey his orders. The women would scorn him and the children laugh at him. No unproven male dared speak in council, or risked shame by trying to take a mate. Without a string of universally recognized feats and war honors, he would never become a camp headman or war chief. The lordly warrior, who did no menial work, bore no burdens, and had his females at his beck and call, earned his position not from the fact of maleness but from blood courage.

The war honors system was almost universal among American Indians, and it obviously survived intact among tribes that rose with agriculture to barbarism or even civilization. Thus the secure Mohawks were compelled to trot hundreds of miles to seek enemies upon whom to make war, and the Mexica mounted annual expeditions. The Aztecs were entirely agrarian, with a very high degree of civilization, yet they assiduously trained every boy in arms, sent him as an auxiliary with the armies after puberty, and allowed him to rise in status within his clan only through honors gained in war. Only the proven warrior might become a teacher, a judge, a clan chief, or a priest. War provided plunder, lands, captives, security, revenge, excitement, and the secret joys of sating bloodlust and inflicting pain. Its prestige factor meant that Amerindian societies as they existed could never eradicate it.

Amerindian warfare, however, did not resemble European conflicts, in the main. With the possible exception of Middle Americans, Amerindian peoples never became territorial in the way the settled Indo-European tribes became fixed to their conquered soil. The North American Indians, even the newly agrarian barbarians, were still dominated by the hunters' concept of the land. Like the Nermernuh, they had no concept of hallowed, ancestral ground. They had always moved; they avoided burial sites as unlucky or unhealthy. They had never put down solid roots. While one people often tried to seize another's hunting grounds, beyond civilized Middle America no group had any real concept of even tribal ownership of the soil.

A million Amerindians thinly scattered across the sheer immensity of North America almost inevitably came to look on the land as Europeans might look upon the air or sea. Their concept was of tribal or, rather, band ranges. On these ranges they harvested the natural produce of the land, just as fishermen netted the resources of the oceans. To the Indians, some tribe or people *ruled* the land, as among Europeans some nation frequently ruled the sea. No one owned clear title. Therefore, the Amerindians rarely fought over land as such, or defended soil to the death.

Amerindian warfare was fought guerrilla style, with raids and counterraids; it was not a series of petty Thermopylaes and disputed barricades at which Indo-Europeans died so stubbornly and yet so readily. The Nermernuh and other Amerindians had sacred places, but never any sacred soil. Because Europeans and Amerindians never really grasped each other's concept of land tenure, they also misunderstood each other's way of making war. Trading blood for ground was hard for the Amerindian mind to understand; the stand at Thermopylae would have struck even the bravest warrior as a sort of madness. A race of very limited numbers, always on the thin edge of survival, found little honor in death, however heroic. What Amerindians honored was success in war, and they mourned every casualty as a folk tragedy. The purpose of war was to kill the enemy, loot his camps, mutilate his corpse and so deny him eternity, rape his women, and steal his children. The great value of war honors was wasted if the earner was not alive to enjoy them.

The Amerindian warrior thus never knew the "civilized," haunted cast of mind that paid tribute to an Alamo or an Antietam, where brave men stood and battered each other to the death, and, dying, considered themselves victors. Among the Amerindians, this heroic myth emerged only in Mexico, where the culture had devised its own Valhalla myth. Trapped, the Nerm warrior and any Indian would fight for his life as valiantly as any on earth, and with a peculiar ferocity to kill his enemy even while dying. Yet no Nerm would accept an Alamo or imitate Horatio by choice. The Amerindian concept of the soil not only made it relatively easy for many tribes to be displaced, it also created among many Europeans a notion of Indian cowardice. Any sensible warrior faced with great pressures would sacrifice his heritage of ancestral soil. He was to experience great bewilderment and terrible frustration when he came up against a race that stood its ground and honored the memory of massacres of its own kind.

Among a people so traditional, so rigidly custom-bound, and so ruled by magic, warfare had to be traditional and magic-dominated. Every step in war was governed by custom, fetish, or taboo. Europeans sometimes believed that all Indian warfare was ceremonial in nature, some sort of game. Nothing was further from the truth. Indian warfare *was* ceremonial, because the Amerindians were a race ceremonial in all things, but it was no game—except in the sense that all men, everywhere, in some ways have made war into a game.

Since war had a preexisting rationale, the first step in the beginning of a campaign was the securing of the proper magic. This medicine was sought in visions, which were rarely spontaneous. The Nermernuh pursued them the way men in other societies sought oracles or horoscopes. Since the war society of the Nermernuh was fluid, and there was no permanent military rank or privilege of leading men at war, any proven warrior might lead a war party if he presented the proper medicine. A warrior became trail chief by convincing his potential followers, through his explanations of his visions, that he had made powerful medicine. It was, of course, easier for a great warrior to convince others than for a new man—but when times were ripe, there were warriors ready to follow any suitable medicine against the enemy.

A warrior who prayed to the eagle spirit and afterward saw the eagle seize its prey could bring this vision before the council, or perhaps a smaller body of restless young males. This, and countless other possible manifestations, might be discussed and interpreted amid growing excitement: if the People sent out warriors, they would fall on the enemy like the eagle on the rabbit. The war party was authorized.

The man with the *puha* or power became war chief, a rank held only during the life of the mission. All who went on the war party agreed to follow his orders. Again, experienced leaders raised war parties more readily than young men, but every war leader originated in this way. The key was the magic, and how convincingly it was portrayed. It was no accident that all great Amerindian leaders were also powerful orators. However, more than oratory was required for successful chieftainship; war chiefs were both visionary and practical. The chief had to be capable of organization and command, for Nermernuh war parties were carefully planned. After the unfolding of the initial magic, another shaman or *puhakut* might be consulted for buttressing opinions. But this ended the uses of medicine. The People did not carry shamans along on war parties; they had no "owl" or "buffalo" doctors for prophecy or healing, like some tribes.

Once the band council authorized the war party, the news was spread through the camp. Any warrior might join or not, according to his own disposition and medicine. Every individual on the war trail needed his individual magic and read his personal portents. The news always caused hubbub and excitement among the whole band. War was the one great socializing event the People had, since they never congregated for other ceremonials, not even the hunt. The warriors were sent off with an elaborate, emotional ceremony: the war dance.

The dance itself was an individualistic rite, chaotic in the extreme. Warriors who were going on the raid made medicine by leaping, stomping, chanting, and howling to the sound of a hide drum around a blazing bonfire. The dance was both medicinal and emotional, serving the same purposes that still provoke political rallies and pep sessions before athletic contests. The women performed the same duties as girls at football rallies, encouraging the future combatants with their screeching, screams, and frenzied leaping from the sidelines. The Nerm woman was not a passive participant or a solemn wife or mother at the moment of preparation for war. She accepted and even gloried in the ways of the People. She took huge pride in the exploits of her menfolk, for these enhanced her own prestige.

The women, old and young, whooped to honor the brave words and deeds of the warriors. The strident *yee-yee-yee* of their voices from beyond the circle of dancers spurred the energies of the men going against the enemy. Women at this time did not go out to war. Females could not keep up on foot on the war trail. But the People's women were fighters, and they would battle ferociously if they were attacked in camp. The mothers defended their babies to the death, and fought as viciously as warriors, for women and children were not spared in Amerindian warfare. Women were raped and mutilated; infants were either slaughtered or carried away. The best a captured female could hope for was secondary status as a wife among the enemy. Knowing this, women were always dangerous when attacked, and they inflicted the most hideous torments on captured enemy warriors.

The war party painted their faces black, the color of death, and danced and departed during darkness. Because an ancient war party that prepared and marched in daylight had met disaster, every war party of the People left by night. The first night, however, the warriors were exhausted from the dance, and they might go only a little way before making camp.

The discipline and organization of Amerindian war parties, measured against the whole tenor of Amerindian life and culture, always surprised Europeans. But war was a serious business, and its practice had taught all Indians the value of tight discipline, careful planning, and control. The war chief was a complete dictator whose every order was obeyed. If a follower could not agree with a command, he was duty-bound to leave the party.

The trail chief determined the mission—that was inherent in his vision and medicine—and decided how it was to be carried out. He chose the times and routes of march, selected the scouts who ranged far ahead of the main body, and set the watches for the sleeping camp. He detailed warriors for logistic duties. He planned the strategy and the tactics for attack. He alone could order a withdrawal or accede to a truce. Theoretically, all honors and spoils fell exclusively to him, but in practice, every successful war chief awarded honors freely and gave away most of the captured booty. This pragmatism not only increased his popularity, but greatly enhanced his prestige.

His command and authority, however, could quickly collapse if some event or omen seemed to contravene his medicine. In a magic-dominated universe any unexpected disaster, or sheer bad luck, could ruin a war chief as thoroughly as demonstrated incompetence. Despite the enormous valor and discipline and effort warriors put into a raid, most Amerindians were easily demoralized by strange omens or startling setbacks. The Nermernuh fighting men had few genuine beliefs, and therefore no dogmas to sustain them against adversity. The magic-oriented mind was filled with fears and doubts that bubbled just beneath the surface. Convinced of strong medicine, the Nermernuh war band took the trail at the crest of a manic wave, fearsome as ravening wolves. But anything that smacked of countervailing magic snapped their confidence and threw them into the wallows of near-hysteria. Bad luck, casualties, the death of the leader made warriors who could endure any expected difficulty quail and even flee in panic.

The war party moved across wide stretches of unpopulated country; in the vastness of the continent the Amerindian camps were widely separated. Whether the purpose of the war party was revenge, booty, or sport, it usually operated in essentially the same way. A revenge raid might be called off if a single enemy were encountered and killed, provided this satisfied the leader's medicine. More often, the object of a war party was to seek out and ambush a larger body of some neighboring enemy, without being ambushed in turn. No Amerindian sought open battle openly arrived at, for the reason that the hunting peoples could not afford casualties. The fear of casualties did not dampen the ardor for war, however; it merely gave warfare peculiar patterns. A successful raid consisted of a stealthy approach, surprise, and massacre.

The war band marched with great care to avoid detection by enemy hunters. Whether the party knew where the enemy camped, from recent scouting, or had to search him out, it had to cross miles of rough, open, potentially dangerous country. Under such conditions, Amerindian warriors were really hunters, stalking their prey. And they retained a full range of hunting skills that had long disappeared in the agrarian world. The Nermernuh and similar Amerindians were not more keen-eyed than civilized men—in fact, many had poor sight and eye defects were common—but the Nerm knew what to look for on the ground, and he could read signs with an uncanny accuracy. He had that sharp sense of his surroundings that only creatures who lived always in the open could develop. In a wilderness where the dust and vegetation of centuries were still little disturbed by man, every human passage left its mark. The Nerm hunter-warrior could read in the dust, the soft earth, and in crushed grasses that men had passed; a crushed leaf, a moccasin print, or an old camp fire told him when, sometimes who, and in what strength. Coming into enemy country, the war party became a band of wolves, sniffing out a trail.

Meanwhile, the warriors made every effort to move undetected. They tried to leave no sign of their own by making cold camps, eating dried meat, enduring heat and cold and sometimes punishing thirst with stoic discipline. The Nermernuh preferred to march in daylight, but to avoid discovery they would move by the light of the moon, often holing up in woods or rocks by day. No European army marched, or could march, with such wilderness skills, such personal discipline, or for that matter, such implicit deadliness.

In this sense, Amerindian warfare was far less a game than the ritual combats Europeans staged on open fields, where ranks of mailed men flailed at each other to the death, or carried out vast slaughters by concentrated musketry at close range. For while Amerindian life was ringed about with taboos, the race had no rules for war. Anything was fair, in a process whose goal was surprise and massacre. The Amerindian was totally practical in war, trying to kill without being killed.

Ironically, early Europeans considered the Amerindians cowardly because of their tactics, not realizing that their own warfare had grown ceremonial and stylized. In time, the Amerindian pattern was to reshape the tactics of warfare across the world, and civilized armies would no longer march with banners and trumpets and engage in ritual combats, but move with scouts reconnoitering, making every effort to blend into the terrain.

Discovery, which destroyed the element of surprise, frequently aborted the whole mission. No competent war leader ever accepted combat on equal terms if he had another option. It was no disgrace, only a disappointment, to retreat, blaming bad medicine. In fact, a true battle between opposing Amerindians usually developed only when two war parties met by accident, or an attacked band reacted swiftly and successfully against surprise.

This trait, based on Amerindian culture and logic, made war parties confusing and unpredictable to most Europeans in America. Whites frequently saw hostile Indians break off an attack for what seemed to Europeans no cause at all, aborting a mission just at the point where European instincts would have pressed the attack home. The Nermernuh and their cultural kin completely lacked that implacable determination to stand their ground that allowed Europeans to be slaughtered by the millions. But they also lacked the European will to press forward against all odds, snatching victory from defeat through sheer tenacity and force of purpose. This erratic conduct, so marked among the Nermernuh and their neighbors, such as the Dakotas and Cheyennes, was regarded by most whites with both bewilderment and contempt. Thus, the Amerindians would rarely win decisive, hard-fought victories, but, then, such victories never entered into the Amerindian logic of war.

Battles between opposing warriors, once begun, usually quickly deteriorated into a series of feints and skirmishes, as both sides tried to use cover and concealment to take individual warriors in the rear, or to loose arrows at each other. If the engagement took place in brush or timber, there might not be any sign of combat at all: merely a waving bush or limb here and there, the whisper of a passing arrow, or a grunt or scream as some missile struck home. Such a "battle" might cover a wide area, run for many miles, and go on for hours or even days, as one side retreated and the other pursued, but not too closely. Mortality in Amerindian battles, by European standards, was extremely low. The low casualty rates were the result of the tactics used, not the primitive stone weapons, because axes, arrows, and flint spears in strong hands could do fearful execution.

Precisely because close combat and bloody stands were not the norm, hand-to-hand fighting was considered the epitome of courage. The warrior who accepted personal combat gained great prestige, because he was risking his life. Since all Amerindians tried strenuously to prevent the capture or mutilation of comrades, close fighting sometimes erupted around the bodies of the fallen. A warrior who prevented the capture or mutilation of a comrade gained special honor, and any warrior who actually landed a blow by hand, or touched a living enemy, won the highest war honor of all. The French named this practice of seeking to touch the enemy "counting coup" in the seventeenth century. It was a common custom of all the midcontinental tribes.

The coup or blow counted only if it was delivered by hand, using spear, knife, or hand ax. Given the reflexes of Amerindian hunter-warriors, and the fact that even a warrior dying of ghastly wounds was dangerous to the last gasp, coup was never counted with impunity. Because it was dangerous and difficult to kill an enemy by hand, or to take the scalp of a living warrior, a coup earned far more prestige than a death inflicted by arrow from ambush, or a scalp ripped from a corpse. The coup-seeker usually risked his life.

Originally, the practice must have risen from a useful courage rite, since the willingness to stand up against an armed warrior in personal combat, like the willingness to attack a powerful beast with ax or spear, was a survival value for the Amerindian band. A band that had such warriors defended its hearths successfully. But the custom was eventually, like many human behaviors, so encrusted with mystical social values as to become counterproductive to its original purpose. Warriors risked their lives merely to gain social recognition, and no few men lost their lives in a vain pursuit of glory. Thus Europeans were often bewildered by the phenomenon of a whole war party refusing to stand and fight, while a few foolhardy individuals might charge, in effect committing suicide.

The coup required witnesses. Any warrior landing a blow immediately screamed *Aaa-hey!* ("I claim it!")—not a victory shout, but a demand for recognition. It was possible to claim an unwitnessed coup through solemn oaths, but like the kills claimed by military pilots, confirmation normally required testimonials. The People had a rigid code for counting coup—only two warriors might claim a blow against a single enemy. The Cheyennes, however, permitted three, and the Dog Eaters or Arapahos recognized four coups against one fallen foe.

The successful war party was not seen or surprised, but sneaked through the enemy territory and scouted an enemy encampment. If the attack could be launched with complete surprise, the result was rout and massacre. The surprised enemy rarely tried to fight; men, women, and children ran for their lives. The shrieking attackers ran amok, sparing no one in the melee.

Old men and women too feeble to fight or flee were butchered. Often infants were destroyed ruthlessly, axed, dashed to death against rocks or trees, tossed bloodily on jagged spears. Wounded or captured females were usually raped; if there was no time for that, they were dispatched and scalped immediately. Boys and girls of the right age, old enough not to become a nuisance or have a poor chance for survival, but too young to escape or carry hatreds, were often made captive. They would be adopted into the family of their captor, and eventually be accepted as full members of the tribe. There was no real pattern to the slaughter, rape, or seizure, just as there were no rules. The blood-mad warriors were ruled by whim, and the completeness of victory. Counterattacked or hard pressed, they slew and ran. With more time, they allowed themselves the luxury of taking captives for adoption, and prisoners for sport. And warriors who had no sons, or who had lost children of their own, often captured and protected enemy children against the ravages of their own kind. One warrior might rape and kill a small girl, his comrade protect and cherish another of the same age as his own.

There was no stigma against such adopted people, but again there was only the pattern of individual needs and whim. Some boy captives were made slaves, and the Nermernuh, particularly, castrated many boy prisoners. If the passage out of enemy country was difficult, few captives survived. The Nermernuh war bands began raping and killing their prisoners on the trail, leaving the grisly relics behind to enrage the enemy. They were proud of leaving such sign behind.

The dead were mutilated horribly. Arms and legs were severed, genitals invariably smashed or amputated. Female breasts were sliced off, and corpses of both sexes were eviscerated and decapitated. Bloody entrails were burned if there was time. All this crippled the enemy dead for eternity. Above all, the scalp of every age and sex was taken, by drawing a deep cut around the hair line, then popping off the top of the head. Sometimes the whole scalp, sometimes only a centerpiece was retained, to be tanned carefully and stretched and preserved as a permanent trophy.

The worst fate was reserved for captured males. Women were raped and killed, but rarely systematically tortured, because torture was part of the male courage rite. The People took extreme care against any warrior captive escaping, and it was almost impossible to escape from Amerindian captors. Those who did so were mostly boys who pretended to accept their fate and bided their time until they were trusted by their adoptive families. But grown men and women were bound cruelly with rawhide thongs, arms outstretched on cross-stakes; they were trussed down, spread-eagled, at night. If the treatment crippled the captives, they were promptly killed. But if torture was intended, reasonable effort was made to keep the victims alive.

Unfortunately, the only records and observations of Amerindian tortures were left by white men, usually French travelers and traders. Every people or tribe had its especial haters and also its apologists. The Abenakis, French allies, were blackened forever in the memories of New Englanders; while the English-oriented Iroquois were painted by the French, who were frequent victims, in the worst terms of all. The Athapaskans or Apaches of the Southwest received more written publicity concerning their torture practices than perhaps all other tribes, but, as a number of nineteenth-century soldier authorities suggested, the Apaches were maligned: they were no worse than any other savage tribe. There was always a tendency among whites friendly to any particular Amerindian people to deny or discount its tortures of enemies. But this hardly fitted the facts; the torture of captives was as universal among Amerindians in North America as the custom of taking scalps. Torture rites were imbedded in the culture, as old as the race itself.

Like every other custom, torture practices varied widely, according to whim and also circumstance. Some kinds required leisure and security. It was believed by some that the Nermernuh did not torture, unlike the Kiowas, Apaches, Cheyennes, and Sioux, who all had fearsome reputations. But the evidence was mostly taken in the period when the People were primarily long-distance raiders, operating deep in hostile country, or from survivors of the People in the twentieth century. The Nermernuh did torture captives. They were, however, not particularly adept, because they had neither the time nor the patience for the torments devised by agrarian Amerindians, and their tortures were often carried out on the trail.

Hard pressed, they tore open young girls and left them, bleeding, to die. They sometimes staked captives to the earth, facing the sun, without eyelids, and moved on. Modern writers tend to overlook some older evidence. Seventeenth- and eighteenth-century accounts show that those Amerindians with the richest cultural and ritual traditions, almost always the settled "barbarians" and not the "savages," possessed the greatest repertory of imaginative torments. The "peaceful" Caddoans were far more skilled at keeping hapless captives in exquisite agony for days than Apaches or the nomadic Nermernuh. The Kiowas, who took a far richer culture than the People onto the plains, were much cleverer torturers. This pattern should have surprised no one. Civilization raised judicial torture in France to a fine art, and the French and Spanish scribes who described Indian tortures wreaked on whites and other Indians with indignant horror came from societies that subjected women and children to protracted inquisitions beyond the practical understanding of any American aborigine. They killed human beings on the wheel and rack and at the stake, amid scenes of festive sadism no different from the Nermernuh's deep, instinctive delight in inflicting agony.

The protracted rape, humiliation, and murder of female captives began on the homeward journey, leaving a bloody trail behind the war party. This began when the warriors believed they had put enough distance behind them for security, and they could make a camp and light fires. There was no taboo against tormenting women, but this rarely went beyond sexual assault, though Amerindians were known to impale women on rough-cut stakes, or cut their heel tendons and leave them in the wilderness. Purely sexual sadism seems to have been almost unknown, because there was little sexual frustration to feed it. More often than not, the captive female brought back to camp had more to fear from the jealousy of the Nermernuh women, who heaped abuse and even physical punishment on them.

If there were male prisoners, the normal practice was to try to bring them back for the pleasure of the women. When this was impractical, they were killed on the trail. Since bravery was the supreme virtue among Amerindians, torture was the supreme test. The tormentors got the same psychic satisfaction from breaking a victim's spirit while they destroyed his nerves and body as they derived from mutilating the dead. However, because valor was so respected in this war culture, the tortured captive who died bravely gained honor even in the eyes of enemies, a nicety most European minds failed to grasp. The victim who was defiant to the last even won a sort of triumph: he made bad magic for his killers. There is one documented case of a nameless white man on the plains who laughed in the faces of his Nermernuh captors with complete coolness as they graphically threatened his genitals with fire and steel. Abashed, a war chief ordered him released unharmed, as having a magic too powerful to challenge.

A Spanish-recorded description of the mass torture of a number of captured Tonkawas is enough to show why the subject of torture was always close to the minds of whites on the Amerindian frontier. In this case, the Nermernuh warriors staked out their victims, and began applying fire to each captive's hands and feet until the nerves had been destroyed in each extremity. Then, they amputated the ruined extremities and began the fire torture again against the sensitive, bleeding flesh. All of the victims were scalped alive, so that they would know the full extent of their degradation. Finally, tiring of the business, the Nermernuh tore out the Tonkawas' tongues to silence their cries, and heaped the writhing victims' scrota and bellies with blazing coals. The Nermernuh then went to sleep around the torture fire.

Even worse fates could befall warriors brought back alive to Nermernuh encampments. Here, especially once the victim's screams established that his medicine was broken, the work was left to the women. Most observers reported that the women were far more patient and vicious tormentors than the males. It may have been the exercise of vengeance against their lot in life, but at any rate, the females destroyed the captive by the most drawn-out and hideous means they could devise. They cut off his fingers and peeled his eyes; they stretched his tongue and charred his soles, and they invariably devoted fiendish attention to his penis and testicles. The torture went on for hours, even days, so long as the body survived.

Meanwhile, if the war party had come back with glory and with captives and booty—and without losses—the whole band erupted in frenzied celebration. Warriors recounted their deeds to the thump of drums and the admiring whoops of women. Great men honored others and themselves. Coups were claimed, and reputations established—or destroyed. The returned warriors then danced themselves into exhaustion while their bloody trophies hung drying on the scalp poles.

If the war party came back reporting disaster or with any dead, the hysteria was reversed. Lamentation swelled through the night, and might go on for days. Bereaved families mourned for months; women cut their breasts and severed fingers in despair. Councils and *puhakut* sought medicine for revenge. And thus the cycle would go on, war and reprisal without end.

WARFARE DID ERASE SOME AMERINDIAN PEOPLES BEFORE THE EUROpeans arrived, but since Amerindian wars and campaigns were rarely sustained, the result was seldom extermination. Weaker peoples were displaced and driven into marginal lands, as the Uto-Aztekans had displaced the Hokans, and the Nahuas succeeded the Otomíes; the powerful Siouans and Algonquians would later drive the northern Shoshones deeper into the barren Northern Basin, and the Nermernuh themselves would disperse the T'Inde, or southern Athapaskans. If there were no Waterloos, there were a hundred minor Punic wars across the continent, each one determining some Amerindian destiny. The pattern was one of perpetual struggle for cultural life and death in the mountains and across the plains.

The warfare was supportable, and not so destructive as it might have been, because the quarter-million Amerindians across the middle of the American continent had so much room that they were not driven to stand and die upon any one spot. Most of the warring tribes were nearly equal in war skills: many potential victims escaped. The truly bloody massacres were few and far between. In sum, for all the glory and exultation and prestige the Amerindians found in war, neither their world-view nor their resources permitted sustained conflict. War was random and sporadic, if endemic. It was almost impossible for a great leader to rise and command except ephemerally, and no people could devise or maintain a grand plan or strategy for conquest.

These limitations—not some inherent restraint or racial discipline or ethos—kept the Amerindians from destroying themselves. The culture endowed even the brutal cycle of birth, hunting, war, rape, torture, and slaughter with poetry and ceremony. The emotional outlook of the late twentieth century, in which more and more human beings have come to see all life on the planet as endangered, and, perhaps not too late, to realize the importance of all living things and to believe that all life styles may be worthy of respect, was entirely absent in prehistoric America. The Nermernuh did not understand nature, or man in nature, or even, man against nature, any more than animals did. It was simply beyond their minds and resources to envision the wasteland-peace of utter victory over either man or environment.

This world might have gone on for thousands more years, had not the New World been subjected to remorseless change by the Old.

4

THE HORSE BARBARIANS

It is by no means certain
that the possession of the horse has bettered their condition.
Indeed, by facilitating the capture of buffalo,
previously taken perhaps by stratagem,
by introducing a medium by which at least
the wealthy may always purchase supplies,
as well as by rendering practicable
long migrations for food or trade,
the horse may have contributed somewhat
to their present spirit of improvidence.
　　　　—Hubert Howe Bancroft, 1883

No historian knows exactly how, where, or when the great change in the life of the Nermernuh came about. This change was the introduction of the horse across the North American midcontinent, which ran far ahead of actual European penetration. The People lacked even legends about the appearance of the horse in later times; it was as if they had had horses always.

Another mystery surrounds the division of the People into two distinct, though linguistically identical, cultures: northern Shoshones and southwestern Comanches. Like the date of the introduction of the horse, the precise year or years of this event is obscure. The horse must have played a part in it, because without the horse no part of the People could have moved out onto the plains. The Nermernuh possessed contradictory tales and legends of how they split apart. Probably, neither decisive happening took place suddenly. The People discovered the horse, adopted the horse and buffalo culture, and separated over a period of years. This occurred, almost certainly, toward the close of the seventeenth century, when the very existence of the Shoshone people was still unknown to the European world.

The origin of the horse on the Great Plains of North America is no mystery. The horse came from the Spanish, who in the sixteenth century conquered almost all of Mexico and pushed up into the present southwestern states.

The horse was especially important to the Spanish conquest and explorations. Early conquistadores gave as much credit to their steeds for their successes as to their God. Cortés' expedition was saved by his horsemen in several crucial battles in Mexico, and after the fall of the Mexic empire, horses carried the Spaniards everywhere. Steel-armed and -armored riders possessed an immense military advantage over flint-armed warriors on foot. Across northern Mexico, and far into the plateaus and high mesas of the southwestern United States, small parties of mounted soldiery could cut their way through any hostile Amerindians alive. Coronado in 1540 scattered and butchered the pitiful array of Hopi and Zuñi bowmen who tried to bar him from the pueblos. His and the contemporary de Soto expedition were usually in far more danger from the hostile environment than from the natives. Even then, only mounted Spaniards could have ranged so thoroughly through the arid *tierra despoblada* or virtually uninhabited regions of the North American Southwest.

The Spanish horse itself was peculiarly fitted for its role. The Iberian mustang (from the Spanish *mesteño*) was not the huge, heavy, grain-fed animal of northwestern Europe and the British Isles; it was a desert-bred mount that was actually a relict of the long Moorish occupation of Spain. It had a dash of pure Arabian blood, crossed with hardy North African barb. The Spanish horse was extremely tough, wiry, and mobile. It had been bred to live entirely off grass, and to cover vast distances between water holes. It could and did carry men in armor over countless leagues of burning desert and high, harsh plateaus, grazing on whatever pasture lay at hand, where larger, more impressive mounts would have foundered without corn.

This Afro-Asian Spanish horse was a small, unlovely beast, rarely standing more than fourteen hands high. It was shaggy, unkempt, and often appeared ungainly and ill-proportioned to horsemen accustomed to other breeds. But no horseflesh on earth could have been better suited to the arid and semiarid mesas and grasslands of North America. Here, the mustang thrived under conditions that killed more delicately bred animals. The mustang required no special care or handling; it multiplied as readily in the wild as on sheltered ranges. Because it was not impressive or beautiful in European horsemen's eyes, then and later many men discounted the Spanish mustang's performance, not understanding the breed's almost perfect symbiosis with its new environment. More than any other horse, the mustang was suited to the great bison range that ran from Canada to Texas, for the Iberian animal flourished in this land as well as the native buffalo.

The horse, finally, was also particularly important to Spanish culture, for reasons that long preceded its performance in the conquest of America. Spaniards were horsemen. Most of the true conquistador types came out of Extremadura and Salamanca, a high, harsh, arid, stock-raising country, which had few large rivers and had been devoid of trees since the Middle Ages. Castilians from the high mesa or great inner plateau of Spain were accustomed to ride, just as they were accustomed to country such as they found in northern Mexico and the North American Southwest. Coronado reported to his king that the plains were a fertile country, not inferior to Spain, though unfortunately lacking in precious metals; later Anglo-Saxon travelers were at first appalled by this land and mistermed it desert, because Englishmen normally went on foot, and had no experience with country lacking abundant water and timber. The conquistadores rode easily through arid regions that other Europeans could cross only painfully, if at all, on foot with oxen. And the horse had still deeper values for the Spaniard: in Castilian, *caballero,* horseman, was the only common word for gentleman. It was no accident that the early conquerors of New Spain or Mexico began to raise huge horse herds. They soon made Mexico a land famed for the quality of both its horseflesh and its riders.

The laws of the *virreinato,* the viceregency, of New Spain, that forbade the conquered *indios* to use horses or firearms, for military reasons, were soon ignored in the case of horses. Spanish *encomenderos* and *hacendados,* owning vast herds of livestock, could not operate without mounted Indian servants. They taught Amerindians to groom, saddle, bridle, and break horses; it was impossible to keep Amerindian serfs or slaves from learning how to ride. There is no question that in sixteenth-century Mexico the knowledge of horses and horsemanship passed into the heads and hands of pacified *indios,* and from them to some still wild tribes. After 1550, Spanish expeditions frequently encountered mounted Amerindians in parts of northern Mexico, though these posed no military threat to them.

Earlier writers, romanticizing, held that the Spanish horse was transmitted to the North American Indians through the early *entradas,* such as Coronado's expedition. Coronado and his successors surely lost mounts on the plains, but many of these were geldings, and most were probably eaten by predators or wild Amerindians. The evidence is overwhelming that the many Spanish parties that entered the country above the Rio Grande through the middle seventeenth century never encountered Amerindians on horseback. The indigenes did not learn horsemanship from passing conquistadores, for the evidence is also overwhelming that not only the Spanish horse, but a Spanish horse culture, was transmitted with the animal—and this could have been diffused through the Amerindians only by long observation and experience. This happened long after the Spanish had established permanent horse-raising settlements north of the Rio Grande.

The beginning was the entry in 1598 of the *Adelantado* Don Juan de Oñate, future governor and captain-general of the Province of New Mexico, into the country along the upper Rio Grande. Oñate named New Mexico as he crossed the Rio Bravo at El Paso del Norte. The name was symbolic: New Spain, with its New Leons and New Galicias, was largely pacified, and now Spaniards were pouring northward from old Mexico to make new colonies. Oñate came to seize, subdue, and settle the regions that Coronado had ravaged and abandoned nearly sixty years before. He brought four-hundred soldiers and many priests, and more important, 130 soldier families marched with him as colonists. More important still, though Oñate and his people could not have known it, were the seven thousand domestic animals, including three-hundred Spanish colts and mares, that came with his train. These animals were to play a more decisive role in American history than the colonists who created a sterile and struggling version of the Hispanic-Mexican culture along the upper Rio Grande.

The Spanish subdued the agricultural, Puebloan-culture natives of the region, and, in effect, enslaved them. They founded Santa Fe and a sprinkling of missions and ranches and villages. Both the Spanish colonists and the missionary friars needed Puebloan labor for their projects, to build the mud-brick forts, missionary compounds, and churches, and to care for the conquerors' immense herds. *Indio* youths had to be taught horse care and horsemanship on Spanish *ranchos*. Unquestionably, some Amerindian slaves escaped with horses into the countryside. Meanwhile, the Spanish in New Mexico had planted a horse culture in close proximity to the High Plains of North America. It was inevitable that something so inherently useful to the hunting savages of the western mountains would be closely observed and imitated.

The gardening Puebloans had no use for horses, except to tend for their Spanish masters. However, the surrounding warlike Athapaskan or Apache peoples did. The horse allowed them to hunt more freely on the plains, and also to range more widely on their raids. The horse was not the basic cause of Spanish-Apache wars; the Spanish conquerors inherited that animosity when they assumed the rule, and therefore the protection, of the agrarian Puebloans. But the horse intensified and focused these wars. By the 1650s, Spanish accounts show that mounted Apaches were raiding Spanish-Amerindian settlements in New Mexico, running off with cattle and horses. One such raid, in 1659, carried off three hundred horses.

The aggressive Apache tribes never bothered to learn horse breeding; they preferred to raid the Spanish settlements for their mounts. This led to unmerciful harassment of the peaceable Puebloans—whom, ominously, the Spanish could not adequately defend against mounted Amerindians. For the Apaches could strike quickly and fade back into the mountains to the north and west, or vanish into the endless prairies and mesas to the east.

The inability of the Spanish governors to prevent such raids upon the Puebloan communities was the major factor behind the great revolt of the New Mexico Amerindians in 1680. Subdued into forced labor by Spanish colonists and friars, their ancient rites and religions suppressed by Catholic missionaries, and now harried constantly by the surrounding Apaches eager to seize horses, the Puebloan people finally rose in desperation. They drove the Spanish out amid scenes of massacre and horror; only some two thousand Europeans escaped the uprising. And for ten years the Puebloans held their independence and tried to reassume their old life styles, until the Spaniards, beginning in 1690, finally reconquered the province.

Fleeing Spaniards left behind immense herds of livestock, including thousands of horses. The Puebloans and Apaches ate the sheep and cattle, but since the rebels had little need for horses, they either allowed these to run wild into the deserts and mountains—forming the nucleus of the great mustang herds of the Southwest—or let them be driven off by raiding Amerindians. This was the great "horse dispersal" that forever changed the history of the American West.

Prior to 1650, there was never any mention in Spanish accounts of Indians with horses north of Sonora. Through 1680, only the neighboring Apaches had acquired horses in any quantity. As late as 1675, Spanish expeditions marching through Texas and other parts of the Southwest had seen neither wild horses nor mounted *indios*. But in 1681, the Mendoza-López *entrada* into Texas struck mounted Apaches along the Rio Pecos, and also lost some horses to Amerindian raiders.

The constant raiding between the indigenes of North America obviously spread horseflesh widely and rapidly. There was also trade, as the existence of Puebloan pottery as far east as the Gulf coast attests. The knowledge of the horse burst through the Amerindian midcontinent like prairie fire before the wind. The fame of the Spanish mustang also acted like a magnet, drawing distant peoples toward the Southwest from the northern Rockies. The great horse dispersal was one of the most rapid and widespread technological diffusions in human history. By 1700, all the Texas tribes, including the Caddoans deep in the eastern pine woods, had horses and knew how to use them. The technology also went north as fast as horses' hoofs could carry it. By 1750, the tribes east of the Canadian Rockies were riding horseback, and the Spanish horse and horse culture were deeply rooted in regions where no conquistador had trod.

It is clear, however, that the horse meant different things to different Amerindian peoples, according to their former level of culture. The horse had meant mainly trouble to the Puebloans, by exposing them to Apache and other Amerindian raids. The highly advanced barbarian culture of the agrarian Caddoans, a forest-dwelling, gardening tribe, was affected very little by the horse. The Caddoans found the horse useful in the hunt, but they were not strongly attracted to the bison plains to their west. Spanish travelers in the eighteenth century found the Caddoans willing to trade horses cheaply, and from this drew erroneous conclusions—that the Caddo confederacies had large quantities of horseflesh. Rather, they did not value the animals so highly as did other Amerindians or the Spanish. Forest-dwelling Indians were no more likely to develop a true horse culture than forest-dwelling Anglo-Saxons, or their emigrant descendants who in these same years were forging into the timbered Atlantic slopes of North America.

The horse was of greater use to the peoples who lived on the fringes of the Great Plains. Most of these tribes had come to live both by hunting and by agriculture in the last thousand years. The horse was a valuable tool; it allowed these tribes to hunt more easily on the vast bison range. It added to their mobility for both the hunt and war—as the Spanish sorrowfully learned in New Mexico—but it did not make a decisive revolution in their lives or culture.

The Athapaskan invaders of the Southwest are a case in point. Moving into the country of the Puebloans, they had remained warlike and primitive, but centuries of close proximity to the Hopis, Zuñis, and other such peoples had allowed them to learn a crude agriculture. One Athapaskan band, the Navajo, had separated from the others and remained nomadic and predatory, but all the Athapaskans east of the Rockies had begun to plant maize in the river valleys beside their camps. They soon acquired a taste for corn. When they found the horse, they used it aggressively for hunting and raiding, but they had one foot too firmly imbedded in the agrarian world for the horse to make a profound change in their life style. They continued to be semisedentary and grow crops. Many peoples scattered through the great Missouri watershed, the more advanced tribes, did likewise.

The horse did not have a decisive impact, either, on some of the most primitive hunters and gatherers. Amerindians in the mountains, and on the plains and deserts of southern Texas and northern Mexico, had a limited use for mounts. They were beyond the bison range, and too weak to be interested in raiding other tribes. The Coahuiltecans and similar peoples were more likely to eat any horse that fell into their hands than to try breeding it. Part of this was of course cultural conservatism; the major factor was environment.

But some peoples on the fringes of the buffalo range found enormous opportunity in learning to ride. The horse was a beast of burden to carry the infants and meager impedimenta of the camp out on the trackless plains, and it offered the means for men armed with flint weapons to pursue and kill the great animals on superior terms. Mounted, they could begin to harry the bison for the first time on its own terms and grounds. They could follow the aimless, endless peregrinations of the huge herds. The hunter on horseback was more than a match for the buffalo. While the agrarian and semiagrarian tribes felt no need to desert their fields in order to track the herds, many of the purely predatory peoples, who lived by meat, were drawn irresistibly to the horse and the plains. By making the buffalo their staff of life, they had much to gain and nothing to lose.

There were some thirty of these tribes, a dozen of whom were to become major peoples. They learned to exploit the technology of the Spanish horse completely in terms of their environment and former culture. They made a major advance, creating what is sometimes called the Plains culture. They were generally the least culturally advanced of the Amerindians, but this was no anomaly. New techniques have often been exploited most fully by cultures with little or no vested interest in a former way of life. Tribes went out with the horse onto the plains because it increased their security, comfort, wealth, and power.

Still, this was far more a technological revolution than a cultural one. In fact, there was no real cultural revolution at all, as when the Uto-Aztekan Puebloans took up farming. The hunting tribes who seized the horse and followed the bison on the plains remained hunters, and remained nomadic. They only increased their range and their food supply. The advance was on a single plane, and it was in no sense an advance toward civilization. In fact, as Bancroft noted in the nineteenth century, the diffusion of the horse across the Great Plains actually may have worked a cultural regression. It halted any normal progress toward agriculture, organization, and diversification. The mounted hunter who now could usually find sufficient meat reaffirmed his ancient, predatory culture. The horse did less to free such peoples than to trap them.

The buffalo was the centerpiece of the new-old Great Plains

culture. It provided meat, shelter, clothing, weapons, tools, rope, bedding, glue, cosmetics, fuel, and drink (blood)—everything peoples in a stone-artifact, hunting culture required. The adaptation was ingenious, but too complete. Tribes came to depend upon the buffalo so completely that they stultified the culture, while the opportunities offered by the horse-buffalo complex were strictly limited.

Evidence is very clear that the horse merely provided more mobility in hunting and that nothing else in the Plains culture was new. The Spanish in the sixteenth century had found the Apaches and other tribes on the edge of the bison plains using buffalo-hide tipis, buffalo robes and garments, and all other artifacts of buffalo hide, horn, and sinew. The travois was already an ancient device, perhaps even brought from Asia, pulled by dogs. Hodge and other historians and anthropologists read the wrong signposts in considering that the horse, bison, tipis, sun dance, and soldier societies were inventions of the Plains culture. Everything else antedated the arrival of the horse; each so-called "Plains tribe" carried its own ancient cultural baggage out onto the sea of grass, adapting old ways and nomadism to horseback, though there was now some diffusion and cross-fertilization between the tribes.

The most evident revolution was in a change of power structures and relationships. This came first between Amerindians who successfully mastered horses and those who used the horse in only limited ways. The mounted peoples rapidly became efficient hunters and much more powerful militarily. Suddenly, by adopting the horse, small or obscure tribes found new riches and security; they grew in numbers and deadliness. Eventually, this revolution also worked against the encroaching Europeans, as Amerindians on horseback began to overturn the power balance on the Spanish frontier.

In the year 1705, a small party of short, dark, squat Amerindians appeared in New Mexico, traveling with a band of mountain Utes. The Spanish had never seen or identified either of these peoples. They were able to communicate with the Utes through other Indians, and the Utes described their companions as *Koh-mahts*, "Those Who Are Always Against Us." Although historic enemies, they were ethnic cousins of the Utes, traveling together because they had made a truce in this strange country. Such a truce was not unusual among the hostile tribes, nor was it any more illogical than the frequent truces that held between hostile European nations: the tribes forged them for convenience. Now, both the Utes and Kohmahts were banded against Athapaskans while looking for Spanish mounts.

The Spanish wrote down the name as *Komántcia*. They considered this a true tribal name, just as most Europeans took Amerindian descriptions of other peoples as tribal names. The name was also written as *Comantz* and *Commanche*, gradually becoming conventionalized as *Comanche*. Like the Puebloan term *Apache*—"Enemy"—for Athapaskans, the name was to be symbolic. It would pass into English through Mexicans in Texas, but oddly, no American knew the origin of the name until the 1920s, when an anthropologist working among the Colorado Utes suddenly correlated the two words.

The Utes' cousins were Nermernuh, Rocky Mountain Shoshones. They were not able to make a deal for horses but, significantly, the party stole a few and rode them away. This fact alone shows that the People had at least some familiarity with the Spanish horse by 1705. Even more conclusive evidence is the fact that La Sever's map of 1701 indicated Pádouca—the Siouan name for Nermernuh—near the headwaters of the Arkansas River, in the "Cansez" country. The People had horses before 1700 because some of them had already moved southeastward onto the Colorado-Kansas plateaus. The two great events in the life of the People, the horse revolution and their migration to the bison plains, had begun before the eighteenth century.

There could have been no mass, concerted movement. This was not the Shoshone way. The Nermernuh must have seized the horse and gone out after the buffalo in small hunting groups, probably at first consisting of only a few families. Later, the cultural choice seems to have been made by larger autonomous bands, who grouped together for mutual convenience and protection on the prairie. It seems that this decisive choice—to debouch across the meat-rich, but windswept and dangerous plains rather than to remain in the bitter but sheltering mountains—provoked much discussion and heated argument in band councils. For while there are no legends whatever concerning how the People acquired the horse, there are several differing fables as to how they separated.

According to one tale, a band broke apart due to the death of a boy in a violent children's game, and some of the band moved away to the plains. Another legend tells how two powerful warriors became embittered over the division of a bear carcass and splintered a band. Both stories are probably based on fact, because it was the nature of the atomistic Shoshone hunters to act this way, continually breaking up and re-forming new kinship bands. Yet there had to be deeper reasons behind the separation, since large numbers of the People soon joined the dissidents who had come down from the Rockies.

Many Nermernuh obviously saw the advantages of hunting bison on horseback and realized that, to hunt successfully, it was easier to move entire encampments to the buffalo stamping grounds. Now their food could never escape them when it moved away. The Great Plains were wild and forbidding, burning in summer, icy with blizzard winds in winter, a barren boundless landscape of buttes and rippling grasses. Still, widely separated river bottoms gave shelter, and the horse-magic was very strong. Hunger was a greater force than cultural conservatism; some People embraced the new technology and let it carry them with the sweeping wind. Seeking to exploit the opportunity in full, they rode into a newer cultural trap. Other mountain Shoshones, just as surely, refused to move or do anything differently. Perhaps they saw the choice and rejected it; perhaps horses were not available to these bands. So the People dissolved, band by band, forming new associations. Some stayed behind; others rode into history.

The separation took many winters. The first bands who ventured onto the plains became widely separated, not only from the mountain People, but from the later bands who followed them. The early bands may have been those that eventually pushed farthest south; this is not certain, because horse Indians were extremely volatile. But it is fact that the bands that moved far south, eventually to the cedar hills and brakes of central Texas, lost all contact with and even knowledge of both the mountain Shoshones and the northernmost horse bands. The Shoshones who stayed behind, meanwhile, knew only their horse cousins who lived close beside the Arkansas, whom they came to call *Yampahreekuh,* or Eaters of the Yap Root.

In their Plains adaptation the People remained true to themselves. Their band organization was still atomistic, with large family or, basically, kinship groupings, without clans or tribal government. The bands had little contact with one another. They were united only in language, common culture, and a consciousness that they, and only they, were People. They did not fight among themselves. A century later, when a northern and far southern band encountered each other in Mexico, to their mutual surprise, they immediately recognized and accepted each other as People. When the bands moved out onto the plains, none of them had a sun dance, a tribal council, police or soldier societies, paramount chiefs or medicine men, or much in the way of songs, ceremonies, or legends. Nor did they ever acquire any of these things. But they were true Plains Indians, whose whole life style revolved around the economic-military complex erected on the horse and buffalo.

Some authorities mistakenly assumed that such attributes as sun dances and warrior societies were definitive to the Plains culture, which caused Anglo-Americans to think that the northern tribes, especially the Algonquian Cheyennes and Siouan Dakotas, were the prime exemplars and possibly even the prototypes of the horse Indians. Unfortunately, Americans made contact with these peoples before they knew the Nermernuh. The belief was strengthened by subtle prejudice. The proud, handsome, aquiline-faced Algonquians and Siouans, representing lighter and larger Amerindian stocks, were always held in great respect by both whites and other Amerindians. The northern tribes had splendid qualities which even Europeans recognized. They threw up great leaders. Though great warriors, they lacked the feral quality of the thoroughly intractable Nermernuh. Even in their final destruction, the northern tribes stole the stage. Nothing could surpass Custer's reckless last stand in drama, or the massacre at Wounded Knee in traumatic tragedy. But the Siouan and Algonquian Plains Amerindians were not a standard by which to judge the Plains culture, or its roots.

By any such standard, the Nermernuh who became Comanches were an anomaly on the plains. They did not fit Hodge's definitions. Yet it is far more probable that the Comanches were the true prototype of the horse Indian in North America. There can be little real argument, if it is understood that the so-called Plains tribes did not develop a new culture on the Great Plains, but took their cultures with them in the pursuit of buffalo.

The Nermernuh were not the first people to make contact with the Spanish horse culture, but they may well have been the first to exploit it fully. Comanches unquestionably had horses and were breeding horseflesh when the animals were still a curiosity to the northernmost North American tribes. The Spanish Southwest from first to last remained the center of the horse complex, and the prime source of the animals. The Nermernuh quickly moved south, adjacent to Spanish New Mexico's horse lode, which proved a never-failing source of riches and power. It is significant that Nermernuh seized both the commanding position athwart the routes to New Mexico, and—at the same time—the richest portion of the North American bison plains, the southern stretches below the Arkansas.

The cold High Plains offered no such riches, either in horses or buffalo. One reason the Comanches had no dog soldiers or hunt organization was that they needed none on the southern range. All Comanches had horses, and there was a fantastic plenty of game.

The fact that the Nermernuh or Comanches possessed more horses and greater horse knowledge than any other people is well attested. Dodge stated that they were the finest, and in fact only successful, horse breeders on the entire Great Plains. They were the most skilled horse stealers, also, and as Dodge wrote, this was not a palm awarded lightly among horse Indians. All authorities agree that the Nermernuh had vast horse herds by the nineteenth century. One band of only two thousand People had a horse herd of fifteen thousand animals, not including four hundred mules. This was wealth beyond the imagining of Osages or Pawnees. Ordinary warriors of the Nermernuh often owned 250 horses, and war chiefs might have as many as fifteen hundred, while among the Dakotas, a paramount chief might own no more than fifty head. On occasion, when the tribes met in peace for talk or trade, the Nermernuh gave horse gifts to Cheyennes and Arapahos that left their chiefs stunned with both envy and appreciation of the Comanches' careless largesse. It was natural that the Shoshone dialect became the trade language of the entire plains—a fact not always mentioned in histories. Eventually, most other tribes came to procure their mounts through the Comanches.

Finally, contemporary authorities agreed that the People made the finest horsemen of them all. The artist Catlin, who had sketched both Dakotas and Comanches, admired the Sioux but wrote that the Dakotas were no match for the squat Comanches on horseback. The

German Möllhausen flatly stated the same opinion. Other Europeans said that while other Indians rode, Comanches—man, woman, and child—had learned to live on horseback. The United States soldiers who called the northern tribes the "finest light cavalry in the world" made two errors: mounted Indians were never "cavalry" in the European sense, and these soldiers had not yet met mounted Comanches.

The Nermernuh, the once poor and despised Shoshones of the mountains, were the People who blazed a horse trail across the midcontinent. They may have learned their own lore from the Spanish through Apaches, but other tribes learned from them. And it was inevitable that in a technology based on hunting bison from horseback, those who rode best on the finest horses would forge military and economic power on the plains.

The Comanches were consistent in their adoption of the horse culture and horsemanship; they invented nothing. Everything was copied slavishly from the Spaniards: bridles, saddles, lances, the way they mounted from the right side, a habit the Spanish inherited from the Moors. The Comanche war bridle was made of horsehide or hair, half-hitched about the horse's jaw. The saddle was a pad with short stirrup strips, weighing about three pounds. While Comanches imitated heavy Mexican saddles, building seats from bison bone and hide, they preferred the lighter rig, which resembled modern racing gear. It was perfect for agile, lightly encumbered riders. The lightness of Comanche equipment, and the smallness of the squat riders, allowed the small Spanish mustangs, rarely weigh-

Warriors practicing mounted maneuvers.
Drawing by George Catlin, c. 1836.

ing over seven hundred pounds, to outrace European military horses, especially over short distances. The only innovation the Comanches made was the use of a loop or thong slipped around the horse's neck from which a rider could hang over the horse's side, shielding himself from hostile bullets or arrows. Only the most skilled horsemen could use this trick, but the Comanches quickly became some of the most superb riders who ever lived.

The horse that gave the Nermernuh freedom to move about and follow the buffalo also gave the bands an enormous exuberance and exhilaration. Before the invention of machines, horsemanship was one of the most intoxicating techniques men could know. The mounted Amerindian got the same sense of power and freedom at the gallop that modern men have felt behind powerful engines. The horse did work some changes in Nermernuh psychology. Now the hunter never needed to trap or grub; he was a superior being while thundering after fleeing animals on his pony. He could race past running buffalo, selecting prime beasts for his kill. All the Plains Indians got this same sense of power, pride, and superiority on horseback, but the Nermernuh, who had come up from nothing, seem to have been most affected. They had always been warlike. Mounted, free as the winds that stirred the dust, they developed a peculiar arrogance. They rejoiced in the life they had come to lead —their magic had been totally affirmed.

The tiny bands soon reveled in new riches: fresh meat in every buffalo-hide lodge, a plethora of horns, hoofs, and skins. There was no need to practice female immolation or infanticide, and these virtually disappeared. The bands grew larger. The Nermernuh had always had a strong band consciousness, and easier circumstances gave this greater play. The aged and orphaned did not starve because the stronger hunters always made special provision for them now. And the same great men who had once struggled to feed a single female and brood on foot could now support several wives. The greatest hunter-warriors could take two or three wives and additional female slaves. The sex ratio in such small groupings made wholesale polygamy impossible, of course, and the majority of men still took only a single mate; but there was a form of natural selection as the strongest came to breed most prolifically. There were still hungry times in the worst winter storms, but more infants lived. The first generation on the plains experienced a small population explosion.

The old dozen-groups became large parties of mounted hunters. Bands that had rarely numbered more than sixty in all swelled to two hundred, five hundred, and then into the thousands, until their camps strung out for miles. This gregariousness now created no problem, for the ponies bred also and the buffalo seemed endless. One band, two bands, then a dozen different Nerm bands scattered across the High Plains. The larger of the bands soon mounted five hundred riders for the hunt or war.

The actual numbers of the Nermernuh can only be estimated. The Spanish believed that there could not have been more than seven thousand in 1690. Less than a century later, a governor of New Mexico claimed there were thirty thousand Comanches east of the Spanish settlements. This last figure, like the first, may have been too high, but it showed what was happening.

There was, however, a definite limit to the population growth. For all the exhilaration and new joy the Amerindians found, life was still desperately hard, short, and stultifying. Fewer People starved, but the death rate from all other causes remained perilously high. And birth rates were extremely low, especially considering the sexual habits of Plains Indians.

The female's lot had been improved by horse power. She had more to eat, and animals to carry her infants. And plural marriages, where they occurred, divided the crushing labor. But the women's work—they did everything except hunt and butcher—was still impossibly difficult. The women rode constantly beside the men on the nomadic wanderings, and the life on horseback seems to have caused countless miscarriages. A very high proportion of Nerm women were barren; few bore more than two children. A family of more than three was remarkable. While many warriors were killed in battle, even more females died in childbirth or from miscarriages. After a couple of generations, the population again apparently stabilized.

For all its efflorescence, the horse revolution did not begin a new dynamism that fed upon itself, like the Industrial Revolution. Yet the horse did introduce certain new factors into Nermernuh society. If the buffalo had become the centerpiece of the whole economy, the horse—the means to hunting buffalo and a powerful aid in waging war—acquired a central place in Comanche society.

It played very much the same role as the horse among primitive Arabs. Understandably, Nermernuh warriors began to cherish their steeds like desert nomads; and they came to love their war ponies and were not ashamed of expressing that love. The cruelest warrior had a very human quirk: he could take delight from the terminal convulsions of a human enemy, but few Comanches were capable of whipping or mistreating horses. And the beasts responded; they gave their owners speed, constancy, and courage. Comanche ponies could be directed with a touch, a word; the best-trained, most intelligent horses responded to the needs of their riders without instruction. In the hunt or war, the warrior's life depended upon the reactions of his mount, and warriors raised their horses so that they could fearlessly entrust them with it.

This did not mean that Comanches could not be brutal to horses. The criterion was necessity. When required, Comanches killed their ponies ruthlessly with hard riding, spurring them to final efforts with methods beyond the knowledge and certainly the stomachs of more civilized peoples. An Amerindian could take a horse abandoned by whites as blown and make it carry him wherever he was going. At times the people also used horses for food, but only in cases of dire necessity, and then they saved the brood mares to the last. Of course, all warriors rode their ponies into danger and caused them to suffer wounds and mutilation in war, but this was no different from European practice. Millions of beautiful, pampered, cherished steeds perished on a thousand European battlefields from Agincourt to Waterloo and beyond.

Comanche children handled horses from the time they were big enough to leap astride. Boys looked forward to owning their own war horse with the keenest anticipation, for the horse rapidly acquired symbolic values in the Comanche system of war honors, status, and prestige. The prime source of new horseflesh, even for the horse-breeding Comanches, lay in raiding and war, either against other Amerindians or Europeans.

The People had a preference for paints or pinto ponies. They especially revered a white horse, but pure whites were rare. They learned to breed for spotted ponies. Most Comanche stallions were gelded, a trick the People learned from the Spanish, but good paint stock was preserved for breeding.

As the horse became wrapped in symbolic prestige, it took on values beyond its actual use for hunting and war. No Comanche could acquire too many horses, just as some men can never get enough money—the horse, on the plains, inevitably became Comanche wealth, and a liquid form of riches. It was a medium of exchange in a society that was not equipped by custom or tradition to cope with that elusive concept, money.

The Nermernuh had never had wealth or goods beyond the self-made artifacts of each family. The horse as property created problems for them. It was customary for a warrior's personal belongings to be either destroyed with him or given away when he died, and for a time horses were immolated on their owners' graves. But the practice became scandalous, even while custom demanded it, for destroying horses was like burning money. Soon, relatives of dead chiefs and horse-rich warriors merely shaved the tails of the departed's horses, and they also grew very reluctant, despite much surly criticism, to bestow them throughout the band. Horse inheritance began to raise as many problems among the Comanches as estate inheritance did in Europe. They remained chronically uneasy about these problems, with which they had no institutional or legal means of coping.

The horse as disposable wealth or currency also subtly changed Comanche mating customs. Marriage had been a union of convenience for economic and biological survival. The Comanches, like all Plains Amerindians, were never sexually chaste by European standards, but they lived according to intricate relationships and patterns. While there was no marriage ceremony, there was still a recognized marriage relationship. There were no restrictions on premarital sex, and no special aura surrounded the sex act. Comanches regarded early sex play with rough good humor. Pubescent boys normally set up their own tipis, although neither sex went through recognized puberty rites. It was perfectly proper for pubescent boys to be initiated into sex by slightly older girls, who slipped into their tents at night, privately but rarely secretly. Comanches knew who was lying with whom and were usually amused by the knowledge.

There was no privacy between brothers, either adoptive or by blood. The custom of brothers' sharing wives was particularly abhorrent to European observers—who also rarely understood such sharing of white female captives. Brothers expected and got full reciprocity. The People did not consider this immoral but, conversely, highly moral, symbolic of the brotherhood bond; the women had no choice in the matter. However, the Nermernuh did not follow the practices of some tribes on the plains: they never sold or offered women to outsiders or European visitors—there were never any white "squaw men" among the Comanches.

The Nermernuh had no bride prices or dowries when they moved out onto the prairie, though sons-in-law took on certain obligations to wives' parents. Horse wealth changed the status of females from semichattel partners in marriage, for warriors with horses began buying wives. A splendid gift of a horse herd could not help but influence the choice of parents or brothers toward acceptance of a mate, and it was perhaps inevitable that fathers and brothers and uncles began to sell nubile females. The accepted way of acquiring a wife was to offer horses, which were not accepted unless a deal was consummated. Families turned into hard, greedy bargainers, and this gave the greater, richer warriors the advantage in acquiring wives. As time passed, Comanche males could not easily purchase a good wife until they were twenty-five or even thirty and possessed many horses. Since such warriors invariably chose much younger women in Amerindian terms—girls of sixteen or younger—this changed the marriage relationship, and for the worse.

The warrior now more than ever saw his women as his property, and the generation gap and wife buying put romantic, sexual love outside the boundaries of recognized marriage. Women had no say whatever in the matter, but they could and did respond ever more frequently with covert rebellion. Adultery, wife stealing, and desertion by wives for other males became increasingly common on the plains. Here again, Comanche society was not prepared to cope.

Young people were still permitted much private courting, but these adventures no longer led to formal mating. Marriage could only take place after a suitor had won consent from a girl's father or guardian males. Approaches varied widely; they could be either crude or very subtle and still fall within socially acceptable practice. Great warriors often presented a suit in grand or grossly spectacular ways, such as driving a horse herd to the lodge of the prospective bride's father. The presents were never delivered directly—bad form—but simply left. It was also bad form for a warrior ever to make a direct advance to any female. If the gift was refused, nothing more was said; that was the end of it. But if the family took the horses, the rest of the business consisted of hammering out a contract between the bridegroom and his intended's family.

Marriage now was a contract between males rather than between man and wife. In addition to the bride gift, the suitor usually had to promise services, such as providing meat for a specified time, and during the father's old age. The woman could and did make her wishes known yet she rarely prevailed against a handsome gift or a powerful connection. Poorer warriors might aspire through hints, usually made first to a brother. The casual use of the term *nermerar-rah*—"Brother of my children's mother"—was an open hint. Such indirect approaches averted possible embarrassment.

Thus horse wealth was beginning to create problems of inheritance and property, certain class distinctions, and loveless matings between young girls and relatively old men. And here there was trouble, because married women were not permitted to indulge in extramarital sex, or to continue to see previous suitors. When adultery, desertion, or elopement occurred, it was an affront and disgrace to the husband or girl's family. If a girl eloped, her family almost always sought some kind of satisfaction. Cuckolded warriors did likewise.

Amazingly, however, these aberrations from accepted codes still rarely resulted in actual bloodshed, just as they had been settled peacefully prior to the advent of the horse culture. After all, adultery or wife stealing or eloping with a girl was the unauthorized use or misappropriation of property. Such matters could be adjudicated. The normal course was for the offended parties to accost the male offender and demand redress. Cuckolders were called out, not for mortal combat but for some hard bargaining. Custom recognized the injury, and conventional wisdom usually forced the offender to offer justice in the form of services or horses. Ironically (but only for alien ears), the cuckolded male addressed the wife-stealer as "brother"—perfectly proper, since woman-sharing had forged a recognized bond. This fact by itself shows why blood was rarely shed. The bargaining was carried on by intermediaries, usually kinfolk. If the offender was an eloper, frequently the family had to make restitution, to clear the family name.

As some men acquired vast herds, and these were usually the strongest, most aggressive, and bravest warriors, they became nearly invulnerable to Comanche justice. Such men could laugh at the complaints of weak fathers or poor husbands who lacked prestige. The same held true of a man with many brothers, all of whom were prepared to back him. Beyond all adjudication lay the implied threat of force, and offended parties who could not bring power to bear got no more justice in Comanche camps than they received in civilized courts of law. Bargaining thus was one-sided, but custom was so strong that the offender, however sneeringly, was forced by convention to grant some measure of redress. Society held together. But, on the plains, a major worry among aging males was the conduct of their child-brides.

It was possible for offenders to transgress so flagrantly that there could be no hope of peaceful adjudication. Such people were forced to flee. Unless they could find refuge with another band of Comanches, ostracism meant a precarious existence and early death. Significantly, such exile was far more feared by the Nermernuh than death, because for all its apparent lack of cohesion and government, the society was much more tightly knit than civilized communities.

If males still did not battle over errant wives, female blood continued to be shed. As in the mountain culture, an offended husband was empowered by custom to punish his wife, even to kill her.

Just as the slaughter of a warrior's horses over his bier had been transmuted into shearing horse tails, the immolation of widows and daughters had been reduced to symbolic mutilation. After the horse helped to provide sufficient food for everyone in the band, there was no longer any reason to do away with warriorless females. Old custom, however, died hard. Surviving females immolated themselves symbolically, by slashing arms, faces, and breasts, slicing off fingers or ears. The wounds were painful, disfiguring, and often accidentally fatal. Although they expressed grief, they were primarily a social convention.

Males did not mutilate themselves for any cause. However, in deep mourning, they did shear their hair. While this rite rarely impressed Europeans of the time, it had deep significance. Like many other primitives, the People's males possessed a profound hair fetish. Male hair was otherwise never cut or trimmed, and hair was second in male significance only to the sexual organ. Therefore, the disparity between male and female sacrifice in mourning only seemed unbalanced—though it cannot be discounted that horses and men were considered more valuable than females. Also indicative of the status of women is the fact that while many Comanches stole females, none ever stole another Comanche's horse. The act was apparently unthinkable.

There was a definite hierarchy among women, reflecting the hierarchy among the Plains Comanches, that the men themselves at least theoretically denied. The wives of strong men lived better and were envied and admired. Females in plural households also lived much more comfortably, by dividing up the crushing labor of sewing, cooking, caring for infants, preparing meat, and bearing the household burdens. In such households there was always a pecking order: one wife was first, and was respected as such. Newer wives, and especially captive females, were often abused by the older or established, while the lordly male pretended not to notice such rivalries. The wives of great men usually had their private tipis, in which they lived with their own children. These were never far away, however, and were connected to the sleeping robes of the male by rawhide thongs. Wives were summoned by peremptory pulling.

The Nermernuh always wanted more babies. Children were welcomed, and there were no illegitimates. Pregnant females were considered highly desirable and quickly married; some man would always take them in preference to a possibly barren wife. Childbirth was surrounded with taboos. The husband was banished from the presence. Midwives assisted, while the grandfather, if there was one, waited ceremoniously outside the tipi. If the child emerged alive, and if it was a boy, he was told, "You have a close friend"—a cause for much rejoicing. Less welcome was the ritual statement: "It is a girl."

In either case, grandparents, if still living, otherwise uncles and aunts, took over child training. The parents were much too busy with the primary labors of living. Older men, who were not so eager for the hunt or war, taught boys all they knew, while the older women instructed girls about their lot. In all this there was much that was practical, including the fact that fathers never had to discipline their sons. Stern uncles were the villains, and fathers emerged as friends and idols. No ethnologist ever recorded a case of a boy resenting his father, or rebelling against his authority.

A birth of twins caused as much consternation on the plains as it had in the mountains. Such unlucky omens were still destroyed, and as in every other case, the mother had nothing to say about it.

The horse, therefore, no more freed the Nerm female than it

freed the Comanche hunter-warrior. Whatever reduction in labor and increase in food it brought about was offset by the increased assertiveness of the male. Old patterns were intensified: the dominant male on foot became the lordly male on horseback, making females more than ever his property. The question of whether women were content with this lot in life is meaningless in human or social terms; they knew no other. And history records that Comanche women defended their life style to its end just as eagerly and ferociously as the men.

WHILE IT WILL NEVER BE KNOWN EXACTLY WHERE OR WHEN THE SHOshones who became Comanches got the horse and set out after the buffalo on the prairies, it is certain that shortly after the turn of the eighteenth century they had become full "horse barbarians." By 1701, at least some Nermernuh were out on the Great Plains where Europeans came to know them, as revealed by French-drawn maps. French trader-agents had begun to come across them athwart what was later known as the Santa Fe Trail, between New Mexico and Missouri. Perhaps more significant, there is no apparent difference between Bourgemond's description of the Pádouca he visited in 1724 in Kansas and the descriptions of Colonel Dodge and Randolph Marcy, written more than a century later. Thus, the complete Plains culture of the Comanches had taken its permanent form a few years after they rode out of the Wyoming mountains. The horse culture solidified before they came south of the Arkansas.

The bison—the American buffalo—that the Nermernuh were seeking out was a shaggy-coated relic of the decaying Pleistocene, essentially a northern mammal that had extended its range far south during the last Ice Age and failed to retreat or disappear with the vanishing ice. The bison, however, was a beast unfitted by nature to survive. A sluggish, mild-tempered, and unintelligent herbivore, it was obstinate and even stupid compared to other animals. The sight or smell of the death of its own kind rarely disturbed it. Yet the bison was erratic. If some random phenomenon, a sudden wind or lightning flash, stampeded the herd, it moved like a tidal wave, impossible to stop or turn, short of exhaustion or death.

The beasts had survived and multiplied primarily because they had no natural enemies. Cougars and wolves might snatch a calf or cripple a cow, but nothing on the plains could bring down a full-grown bull. The only dangerous predator of the buffalo in North America was man, and until man had the horse, the buffalo were safe from destruction.

Despite certain myths, the Amerindians were prodigal with buffalo. Their early modes of hunting—stampedes and fires—turned hundreds and even thousands of buffalo into meat that rotted on the fringes of the plains. The horse made the slaughter more selective, and probably reduced the actual numbers killed, but the Amerindians still wasted buffalo, because this was the way of all men on earth.

The bison was still in no danger of extermination when thousands of mounted Amerindians began to hunt them on the plains. By the eighteenth century, it is estimated that at least sixty million animals lived across a range that covered the midcontinent. This range was then much wider than is commonly realized. Bison grazed almost to the Gulf of Mexico, near present Houston, and from the Rockies to Kentucky. The greatest number, however, moved in a vast stream east of the Rockies that arched from high in Canada through Kansas deep into Texas, ending near modern Austin and San Antonio at the curving Balcones escarpment. The largest concentration lived on the southern plains, that portion of the Great Plains south of the Arkansas; the greatest herds roamed the Texas Panhandle. Into historic times, this was the part of North America least hospitable to man, and the whole region of the bison range was inhabited by no more than a quarter-million Amerindians. With horses or without them, armed with crude weapons, this number of Stone Age primitives could hardly dent the massive herds. Natural causes destroyed more buffalo than hunters. Since Amerindian numbers did not increase substantially even after the horse was introduced, the race could not foreseeably have ever exterminated the buffalo. Logically, Amerindians did not conceive of an end to the bison. To them it was part of nature, mysterious but as inevitable as the wind and rain.

The horse tribes learned that the best time for hunting came in late summer or fall, after the molting season. The buffalo grew a dark brown fur pelt in the fall, best for robes, and put on its winter fat. At this time, whole bands of Amerindians broke camp along their streams and valleys and moved out on the open plains, killing buffalo until November and early December, or the first deep snow. Even among the atomistic Nermernuh, the hunt was something of a cooperative venture. Every man, woman, and child went along and took part, each performing a role suited to sex and strength.

The hunter scouts rode out to locate the stands. The main body of hunters followed, with the entire camp, mounted, close behind. Flocks of ravens usually pointed out the herds, as these birds ate parasites from bison hides. On the northern ranges, the hunts were very tightly organized, like war parties, with hunt chiefs and hunt police. The Comanches, however, never hunted the far northern ranges where there were fewer buffalo; on their ranges there were so many beasts the hunts required little regulation. The bands appointed hunt leaders to make the broad decisions, such as when and where to hunt, and when to move the main encampment. Beyond that, the individual hunting parties organized things for themselves. The hunters were allowed to ride helter-skelter and shoot bison at random, since there was no shortage.

The Nerm hunter liked to run his horse alongside a heaving bison, shooting his arrows just behind the short rib. He made hunting sport as well as work. His bow, on the plains fashioned out of *bois d'arc* or Osage orange, driving an ash or mulberry shaft with a broad flint point, was a powerful weapon at short range. Between thirty and fifty yards this weapon was highly accurate, and the arrows had such force that they drove entirely through a giant bull at fifteen yards. A well-placed shaft was fatal, and since both hunter and his train were mounted, it did not matter how far the dying animal ran in its death throes.

The ponies understood their part in the hunt. Running free, guided only by words or knee pressure, the trained hunting horse leaped away from the buffalo at the twang of the bow string. Wounded animals sometimes turned in rage to butt and gore, and if a stampeding bull collapsed suddenly, it could crash into a close-running horse and rider.

Some hunters found the bow too tame. They preferred to use the fourteen-foot Plains lance, a weapon copied from the conquistadores. It took more strength and daring to spear a buffalo, and to carry only a lance on the hunt was a mark of pride. Any type of mounted hunting could be dangerous. Riders running through a herd could be thrown, or their horses horned, or their ponies could snap legs in prairie dog holes. Many hunters were trampled, or died from broken bones. Yet the very danger made the hunt more exciting.

If their other work was done, and the men permitted, women and girls liked to chase after the fleeing beasts with bow and spear. They often dispatched single confused or wounded animals. Women were almost as skillful with bows as warriors; they lacked only the same strength. Small children, meanwhile, screamed in excitement, dreaming of the time when they would be big enough to wield lance or bow. They rode yip-yipping in play hunts, pretending to be great warriors, while the real killing went on.

As the snorting, arrow-studded bison finally came down, the last gouts of blood pouring from foaming mouths, the women descended upon them with flint knives. The carcass belonged to the man who killed it, easily identified by the markings on his shafts. But in the great fall hunts, skinning and butchering were a community affair; families pitched in to process each carcass in turn. The men did the first, hard work of skinning and quartering, leaving the rest for women and girls. When this was done, the hunt leader always set aside meat and hides for the aged, the ailing, or the orphaned. The hunters always killed a few extra beasts; no one starved. While the People butchered, the ponies stood guard. Out on the plains the Comanches were always wary when on foot; they watched for a telltale twitch of pony ears that foretold possible danger.

There was usually a rush to be the first to reach a fresh carcass, to enjoy the first fruits of the hunt. These were the hot and smoking delicacies: livers smeared with the salty juices of gall bladders, warm blood, raw brains from the cracked skull, and fresh bone marrow. These were eaten on the spot. Another favorite was the warm gut, stripped between the teeth. The women cut these viands out, while children begged with outstretched hands.

Later, while bison steaks were roasting, the long-drawn-out, laborious work of tanning hides began. Meat was usually cooked on pointed sticks over either hot coals or open fires, emerging charred outside and red within. Such meat was breakfast, lunch, or dinner; Comanches ate whenever they were hungry. Soon after they came on the plains, the People began to acquire metal pots from the New

Mexicans. They boiled or stewed flesh in these, warming the water with heated stones. Sometimes women stewed buffalo paunches instead of cooking them over coals. The pot made meal preparation easier, but since the People had no concept of sanitation, it caused many digestive problems. A hunt camp quickly resembled an open abattoir. Nermernuh never washed, except during ceremonial purifications; they threw bones and scraps of food about, and littered the surroundings of their tipis. When the camp smelled too much, they moved.

There was no ceremony to meals; food was consumed when ready. On certain occasions, a bit of meat might be sliced off, held to the spirits, then buried in symbolic oblation—a variation of a custom widespread among all primitive peoples. In eating, the Comanches were gluttonous. While they had meat, they never ate sparingly, and as a race they had a tendency to grow paunchy even on their limited diet.

Other animals were hunted besides the buffalo: skittering antelope, great elk, and smaller varieties of deer, and even small game such as rabbits and hares. The great quantities of sun-cured bison flesh prepared in the fall were usually sufficient for the winter, however, and other meats, and the fruits, berries, nuts, and roots the Comanches ate, were supplements. The old taboos against eating dogs and frogs and water creatures, and the prejudice against turkeys and other birds, persisted on the plains. Faced with starvation, though, Comanches threw taboo to the winds and ate anything and everything, just as their forebears had done. Children also loved a sort of Comanche candy made with mesquite beans and bone marrow, and dried meat strips flavored with crushed nuts, fruits, or berries, called pemmican.

With the first bad winter weather, or earlier if the band had all the hides and dried meat it needed for the winter, the hunters sought shelter in a canyon or along a protected river bottom. Here the bands spread out along flowing water. The Nermernuh on the plains camped beside running water when possible, and they spread out widely, sometimes for miles. Groups of kinfolk camped together, in small clumps. There were clusters of tipis, but no compact village as such.

The tipi provided excellent shelter. It was made of tanned bison hides sewn together with the flesh side out, fitted over a framework of slender pine or cedar poles. The People always made them in the same pattern: twenty-two poles to a frame. The poles, between ten and twenty feet in length, were carefully peeled to a slender suppleness. Tipi construction revealed the mountain origin of the Shoshone Nermernuh; they made a four-pole base like the Utes, and unlike all other so-called Plains tribes. Twenty bison skins fitted over this frame, making a shelter twelve to fifteen feet in diameter.

The tents, cleverly put together, were flapped and ditched, and had the strength to withstand the most violent winds and blizzards. They were warm and comfortable because fires could be banked inside them. Plains tipis were generally superior in comfort to all the sod dugouts, cabins, and shanties that Anglo-Americans erected on this frontier. A tipi was put up in fifteen minutes by the women, and could be taken down and packed on horseback in five. Skins and poles were easily carried in the horse travois. An ingenious invention, the tipi was completely mobile and immensely practical in this terrain. The Comanches lived in tents, however, only in cold weather. In the summer they still preferred brush arbors and slept on light bedding under the stars.

By the time the People were erecting their tipis along the north fork of the Platte, where the French found them and fixed Pádouca in Cansez Territory, they fitted the lasting image of the Plains Indian. No more than a quarter of all North American Indians looked like this or lived in this way, but it was the "horse barbarians" who

Tipis. Late nineteenth century.
Photograph by William S. Soule, c. 1867–74.

burned their image most deeply and ineradicably into American memory.

They were a copper-toned race dressed in buckskins. The People never bothered with as many clothes as the northern Siouans and Cheyennes; warriors normally went about only in breechclout and moccasins. As in centuries before, the breechclout protected the sacred medicine bag that hung between the loins, and the Plains moccasins were of soft, chewed deerskin, sewn with tougher buffalo-hide soles. These were not the moccasins of the timberlands but were made for horsemen; they were in fact a sort of boot that reached from foot to hip. The foot covering and legging were usually painted blue, and often ornamented with beads—later, with silver from New Mexico. For the coldest weather, women sewed an arctic boot out of bison wool, and both sexes dressed in heavy buffalo robes.

These robes, sewn together with animal sinews, were made from prime winter pelts and were very warm. Whites later estimated that one good buffalo robe was the equal of four woolen blankets in protection against chill. Comanches also made bearskin and wolf- and skunk-hide robes, and rabbit furs were popular for small children. The Comanches only began to wear decorated and ornamented buckskin shirts after they became friendly with the southern Cheyennes in the nineteenth century, and then only for ceremonial occasions.

The women were more fully and more colorfully attired. They wore shirts, and also buckskin skirts—long, full, fringed, and highly decorated. Only young girls went naked in breechclouts; nudity among grown females was uncommon. The women lavished great care on their garments, sewing beautiful beaded shirts, skirts, and moccasins from yellow- or buff-colored skins. The clothing was put together with crude materials and tools and great labor, but it was both practical and decorative. The People also made rawhide cases to carry extra wardrobes.

Men and women wore no hats or headgear in the summer but everyone used fur hats in cold weather. Headgear was important to Comanches only in war. They devised the grimmest and most striking war helmet on the plains: a headdress made from the bison scalp, in which the great, thrusting horns of the bull buffalo were retained. The stark horns gave the mounted warriors a frightening

Woman's beaded buckskin dress, with painted decoration. Nine-teenth century.

and unforgettable appearance which no enemy forgot. Comanches in feathers were a cinema invention. Wissler never found any evidence that the Nermernuh ever wore the spectacular, streaming feather warbonnets of the northern tribes until the reservation period. Then, when Comanche culture was crumbling, the People adopted bandannas from the whites and feathers from the Cheyennes. In their last years on the plains, some Comanches took to drooping eagle feathers in their hair to show important deeds—but this was copied from the northern Amerindians, and the feathers never had the symbolic meaning for Comanches that they had for Algonquians and Sioux.

Instead, Comanches carried their war honors and war status on their shields. The war shield was considered to have magical powers. Each warrior made his own shield, carefully laminating layers of the toughest bison hide, which were shaped to present a convex surface and packed in between with furs. Such shields would deflect lance or arrow, and, at ranges beyond fifty yards, stop or turn a musket ball. The shield was painted with magic markings, and the warrior took it up with all the ceremony and symbolism of the Spartan soldier. He decorated it with bear teeth, human hair, or horse tails, signifying he was a great hunter, deadly warrior, or mighty horse thief.

War shields were carried in rawhide covers when not in use and were never taken inside tipis. Especially, no unclean females could be permitted to touch them, or even come near them, lest their magic properties be destroyed. Shields were often stored beyond the camp to prevent such sullying. Comanche warriors, whose lives depended upon their war shields' strength and medicine, took this business very seriously.

Although they did not wear war feathers in their hair, the men exercised great care in its dressing. Since they were not shorn, long and straggly locks were greased with bear fat or buffalo dung. Warriors parted their greasy strands along the top of the scalp and braided the locks on each side. They then decorated the braids according to individual taste, with whatever means were at hand. Silver bits, colored cloth, beads, glass, tin, and certain kinds of feathers became popular in the eighteenth century. A single yellow feather worn in the scalp lock was fashionable, though totally lacking in any symbolic meaning. The men brushed their hair regularly

Horse hide war shield, decorated with feathers and medicine symbols. Nineteenth century.

with porcupine quill brushes. Hair was a source of male vanity, and observers reported that warriors spent much time at this toilet.

At the same time, like most Asian peoples, the Nermernuh retained an ancient horror of facial hair. The Shoshones, like many Amerindians, were never completely beardless. The myth that Amerindians lacked facial hair arose from the fact that warriors carefully plucked their beards. After French traders introduced mirrors to them, the Comanches would give almost anything to get one. A small hand mirror was worth a horse, a pile of buffalo skins, almost anything, in the service of male vanity.

Female hair, however, was not considered to have any special power or meaning. Comanche women cropped their hair short for convenience and comfort, rarely even combing it. Since neither sex washed, except for certain purifications, parasites were a continual presence and problem, which the People stoically ignored.

Both sexes shared a paint fetish. From the most ancient times, Amerindians had made paints: reds, blacks, blues, yellows, and ocher from clays and combinations of berry juices. Later, they acquired vermilion from traders. Face painting was as old and almost as universal a custom as male hair fetishes. For the People, face paint had social, ceremonial, magic, and psychic importance. Much as European clowns designed individual makeup, each person designed a special decoration that became peculiarly his or her own. Face paint was applied for all important occasions.

Comanche war paint was black, the color of death. The normal war markings consisted of broad black stripes daubed across the face and forehead. Women did not paint for war and used gayer colors, such as reds and yellows. They also liked to redden their ears and put on orange cheek rouge, sometimes painting the entire face in a mélange of colors that defied description. Each Comanche always had his or her cosmetics bag close at hand, ready for every occasion, whether dance or council.

The People had also learned tattooing, probably from the Wichitas and Pawnees to the east who had raised this practice to a fine art. Both sexes drew patterns on their chests, the women sometimes ringing their breasts to the nipples. Warriors often tattooed battle scars, to make them more conspicuous.

By most civilized standards, Comanche tastes were grotesque, from the grim buffalo-skull war helmets to face paints and dangling ornaments. Increasing contacts with Europeans, French trader-agents out of Canada and the Missouri country, and Spaniards in New Mexico gave these tastes full play. The traders brought all sorts of baubles and gaudy ornaments, bangles of silver and tin, glass beads, copper bracelets, and large earrings as well as mirrors and vermilion. In the eyes of many Europeans, the Comanche thirst for the gaudy contrasted oddly with their innate Amerindian bearing and dignity, and Europeans and Anglo-Americans were to remark on this at every meeting. The Comanches neither knew nor cared what the white men thought.

THERE WERE NEVER VERY MANY OF THESE "HORSE BARBARIANS," whether Comanches, Cheyennes, or Sioux. Early in the twentieth century, Wissler estimated that there had been a hundred thousand plains people in all prior to the European invasions. Later guesses have tended to double this figure, to a top figure of 250,000. The Plains Indians were divided into thirty ethnic groups, of which eleven in the United States and Canada could be considered major tribes. And of these, only two peoples, the Dakotas and the Comanches, who were to emerge respectively as the lords of the northern and southern plains, ever numbered as many as twenty thousand. Even these great peoples, acknowledged as the most fearsome by all Amerindians around them, never mounted more than a few thousand hunter-warriors. The Shoshones who became Comanches perhaps threw five thousand warriors over the plains, but never more than a small fraction of this number at any one place or time.

Yet this handful of savages on their shaggy, many-colored ponies, in grotesque warbonnets, and with feathered lances and garish war shields, whose tents and camps were mere dots in a primordial wilderness, created the dominant image and memory of a vanished culture. The horse lifted them to riches as they understood riches and made them the most dangerous predators on the continent. The horse exalted them and reaffirmed them. The horse made them powerful in their time and place, but it also made them static, inflexible, and dangerously self-satisfied. The Amerindians who found the European horse and adapted it to their needs were to be those Amerindians most intransigent toward further change.

The Nermernuh, like all their horse-riding neighbors, were still the People, encased within all their ancient customs, traditions, and taboos. The horse changed nothing of their magic-oriented universe or their world-view. They accepted the horse as they accepted the sun and moon, as something added to their sacred and eternal life style. The horse made them prouder and deadlier, but changed no basis for their pride in themselves. The horse made them question nothing. Thus the horse did both great service and great damage to the race.

The names of the horse peoples, however, may be those longest remembered on the continent: Dakota, Cheyenne, Kiowa, Comanche.

They stood for violence, cruelty, and blood courage—values that civilization professes to abhor. They were neither noble nor free. Yet, they will be remembered and recalled with a certain pride and nostalgia, because they also represented freedoms and values denied civilized mankind: freedom from subordination and slavery —men who took no orders except by choice, lordly creatures living as they pleased across the land. These dark-eyed hunter-killers must be remembered as long as men remain men.

For something in their lives—the hot thrill of the chase, the horses running in the wind, the lance and shield and war whoop brandished against man's fate, their defiance to the bitter end—will always pull at powerful blood memories buried in all of us.

5

DEATH IN THE HIGH COUNTRY

*All the evidence that we have
from French and Spanish sources and from Indian tradition
indicates that the period from 1660 to 1700 in the lands
west of the Mississippi was one of frightful raiding,
the aggressors being those tribes that had obtained
metal knives, hatchets, firearms, and horses,
the victims being the Indians
who still had only flint weapons.*
—George E. Hyde, *Mystery of the Arikaras*

THE FIRST EFFECT OF EUROPEAN PENETRATION OF THE NORTH AMERI-
can continent was a series of vast upheavals and massacres among
the native peoples: not Europeans against Amerindians, but Indians
killing and displacing Indians.

The reason was the introduction of European artifacts and technologies—the horse, firearms, metal weapons—to tribes engaged in
endemic warfare and with crystallized feuds and hatreds. The diffusion spread unequally and created great imbalances. Certain
tribes, with access to horses or to weapons, gained an enormous
military advantage and exploited this at the expense of surrounding
peoples. The advantage was both material and psychological and,
like most great power imbalances, ushered in a period of bloody
and decisive conflicts.

The late seventeenth and early eighteenth centuries were a time
of vast movements and battles among the midcontinental Amerindians. However, these events took place beyond the then existing
boundaries of European power and influence, and they were only

dimly perceived by Europeans. They had nothing to do with direct European aggression against Amerindians; but they were partly the result of intra-European rivalries beyond the line of the Azores—the great struggle for control of North American empires.

What happened in inner North America resembled the effects of certain European penetrations of the coasts of Africa and Asia. Here, as there, some peoples in contact with Europeans gained technical superiority over more remote tribes in the interior. And the massacres that took place made as little impression on the European consciousness, then or later, as the massacres and destructive slave raids that shaped modern Africa.

Disaster for the Amerindians did not come just from European settlement and displacement. It came from any sort of European contact, including the peaceful penetrations of French merchants. This fact tended to be obscured, because the very different but equally imperial drives of the Spanish and English determined the final course of American development. The largely ignored seventeenth-century experience of white men in North America is most instructive in demonstrating the effects of any civilized European contact with native savages and barbarians. And the events between 1650 and 1750 show clearly that Amerindian warfare was never the game of horse raiding and coup counting that some later authorities insisted.

Frank Gilbert Roe's concept of Indian wars as horse raids, and J. Frank Dobie and Martin S. Garretson's agreement that Indians were not murderous when they met no resistance does have some validity when applied to later times, particularly the nineteenth century. After 1807, and especially after 1840, the power balances between the Plains tribes had again stabilized, and warfare reflected this stabilization, just as the striking of a balance of power has always been reflected in the nature of European conflicts. But even in these years, a deadly residue of earlier events remained, reflected in the murderous feuds that the encroaching whites saw and recorded—and exploited. If the threat of mutual destruction by a more powerful enemy could not forge an alliance, nothing could bring together Athapaskans and Comanches, or Comanches and Tonkawas, or Dakotas and Crows.

In the late seventeenth century, two enormous forces for change were working among the midcontinental Amerindians. One was the horse technology diffusing out of the Southwest. The other, concurrently, was the introduction of French firearms and an iron-weapon technology through the Missouri watershed from the north and east. Both diffusions created power revolutions on the Great Plains.

While the Spanish were unwittingly and unwillingly transmitting the horse to the plains, the French, from their enclave in Quebec, were deliberately making other revolutionary means available to Indians. The French had vast imperial schemes, but their efforts were much less focused than those of the Spanish or English. The English were rarely consciously imperial; they were represented mostly by dissidents, refugees, and a few more respectable colonists on the Atlantic slopes, who had already established ineradicable ethnic enclaves. The Spanish were consciously erecting a Hispanic empire upon and out of the native races. The French did envision a time when the fleur-de-lis would fly over most of North America, but France lacked the available colonists of the English and the civilizing mission, enthusiasm, and institutions of the Spaniards. Their thrust was primarily mercantile. Pursuing trade with the natives, the French made extensive contacts and penetrations far beyond the range of the other Europeans, with plans of consolidating their sphere of influence into a vast trading empire.

Precisely because the French did not approach the Amerindians as land-hungry colonists or enslaving *encomenderos* and friars, they tended to be far more successful in their early contacts. The French ranged far afield of their actual limit of settlement in Canada. Traders, trappers, and agents crossed the Great Lakes region and traversed the Mississippi-Missouri drainage. The nature of the French imperial vision allowed these advance agents liberties denied both the English and the Spanish, who always had settlements to defend from hostile natives. Operating beyond the borders of actual French territory, trader-agents had no qualms about trading guns, metals, and liquor to the Amerindians; in fact, their entire policy was based upon winning friends and influence by such means.

The policy served two purposes. First, it was aimed at allying the natives with the French, which would turn them against other Europeans and give them the means to resist Spanish or English penetrations. Second, it was highly profitable for the limited number of men engaged. European goods, primarily Caribbean rum and iron weapons, could be exchanged with the tribes for many times their European value in animal furs and skins. The French were the first in a long line of trader-trappers that eventually included Scots, Anglo-Americans, and New Mexicans, all exchanging modern muskets, knives, mirrors, axes, and metal arrowheads for valuable furs. The policy was fully understood and bitterly resented by both Spaniards and Englishmen in America. All the powers observed the fact that there was no peace "beyond the line" and that North America was the scene of a struggle for empire—but the French, peculiarly, seemed to ally themselves with Indians against other Europeans. The fact that French weapons and policy were turned against other white men created fears, and deep hatreds, from New England to New Mexico.

Just as the horse reaffirmed the profoundly conservative culture of the hunting tribes, French muskets and iron opened new opportunities for developing the old patterns of hunting and warfare. They seem to have made no other cultural change. One of the peculiarities of the Amerindian was that he seized upon such introductions eagerly but gave them only limited use. The warrior who acquired a new musket or steel-edged ax never seems to have wondered what lay behind such tools; he merely rejoiced in the new powers they afforded him. He turned them to his own magic and put them to uses he understood. As Wissler and almost all authorities now agree, the net result of these European infusions was to reinforce the essentially static culture of the Amerindians. The only change was that now the Amerindians could do with guns and iron warheads what they had done from time immemorial with flints, and now they were more dangerous and effective.

In waves beginning at each end of the midcontinent, the horse and the new weapons began to tear the old Amerindian structures and relationships apart. The people who mastered the horse at one end, and those who got iron and muskets at the other, carried their ancient wars to newer, bloodier plateaus. What resulted was that from Missouri to the Rockies, and from British Columbia to the Rio Grande, an intensified warfare brought dramatic changes to the plains. There was a newer, greater collision of mobile and armed peoples exploiting horses and steel.

Significantly for the history of the continent, the same peoples did not acquire both horses and iron weapons at the same time. The

French way was to pass gradually through the tribes, trading with and arming those with whom they came in contact. By this policy the French unwittingly made a terrible mistake: they armed the enemies of the two Amerindian peoples who were to exploit most fully the Spanish mustang, and they thus unwittingly incurred the hostility of the eventual lords of the northern and southern plains. French penetrations were to be fatally delayed by the two great tribes of horse Indians, Dakotas and Comanches.

This was not evident in the early stages. The French armed the semisedentary peoples around the Great Lakes and along the Missouri drainage, and these tribes, powerful and exultant with steel and firearms, wreaked a fearful punishment on the weaker, purely predatory bands of Indians. The Caddoans in the south, and the Crows and Blackfeet in the north, became very powerful—with their power precariously based on a supply of French weapons.

In the late seventeenth century the French-allied and -armed peoples began to exert terrible pressures on their neighbors beyond the French range of influence and penetration. The numerous Dakotas were able to survive the onslaughts, though many were pushed westward toward the barren plains. Here, they found their salvation in the horse that in these same years was spreading like a prairie fire toward the Canadian border. But some tribes were beyond the range of both the horse and French weapons, or for some reason were not able to exploit the horse. The Shoshones of the Rocky Mountains were a case in point, though they were only one Amerindian tribe among many who suffered the same fate.

The eastern Shoshone bands were savagely mauled by Crows and Blackfeet with iron axes and firearms. They were entirely displaced, being driven northward into even more inhospitable country, where they became the despised Diggers of the Northern Basin. Here, those who survived were living a precarious existence when Lewis and Clark crossed the continental divide. They were eating roots and tubers and starving through the harsh winters, complaining bitterly that if only they had had muskets, they could have held richer hunting grounds.

Meanwhile, those Shoshones who went with the horse and moved out on the Great Plains enjoyed an entirely different fate. Quite possibly, although there is no record, the pressure of mountain enemies had something to do with the movement of so many proto-

Comanches toward the plains. And the horse culture did more than solve the Shoshone economic problem with a wealth of bison meat. The mounted tribes quickly gained a great advantage over those still largely on foot, even though armed with muskets. They could strike harder and elude most pursuit. While it cannot be proved that the Comanches were the prototype of the Plains horse Indians, their thorough mastery of the horse compared to that of other tribes immediately gave them a peculiar deadliness—the savagery of a new people, long abused and now raised to new heights of power. For all its inherent traps, it is impossible to say that the Comanche-Shoshones, or the Cheyennes and Dakotas who imitated them, made the wrong choice. They made a virtue of necessity; if they had not found the horse they would have been overwhelmed, massacred, and probably dispersed.

Moving southeastward, away from the Blackfeet and Crows, the Nermernuh retained some old enmities, since they never moved beyond the range of the Colorado Utes. And they quickly found new enemies on the Great Plains. More and more peoples were getting horses and taking to the buffalo range. Despite its immensity, they began to collide and fight over their new territory. For the first fifty years of the horse culture, no bison ranges or hunting grounds were fixed. The Nermernuh had bloody brushes

Pawnees capturing and breaking wild ponies.
Drawing by George Catlin, c. 1836.

with a score of tribes, and a continual, running warfare with the Pawnees along the Platte. This plains warfare, however, was skirmishing compared to the savage exterminations among the mountain and the Missouri Valley peoples. The tribes were mobile, and, above all, they had room to maneuver, and to hunt and increase. And noticeably, the Plains peoples did not turn their full fury against each other, but against those tribes who did not or could not master the horse culture quickly.

Thus the brunt, and the horror, of Amerindian warfare descended upon the valley tribes such as Mandans and Crows, despite their former access to French weapons. As the Anglo-Americans reported in many accounts during the early nineteenth century, these peoples lost the wars and never dared venture fully out on the plains. To the end they huddled in miserable villages for protection, hungry, but too fearful of the better riders to follow the bison herds.

The French muskets and axes were murderously effective in mountains and timbered regions, but far less so in open country. The weapons were cumbersome, close-range arms. It was contrary to Amerindian instincts to employ musketry like Europeans. The warriors fought individually; therefore, these single-shot, short-range, highly inaccurate firearms were primarily useful in terrain where the gunner could find cover to reload, or concealment from which to spring with his hand ax, or tomahawk. There is, in fact, much evidence to show that the European flintlock at first conferred more of a psychological advantage on its Amerindian user than a practical one, with its frightening flash and bang, and its missile that sped too swiftly for the eye to see, and thus killed mysteriously. The timber country tribes did adapt the flintlock musket to their tactics splendidly, as a number of Europeans and Anglo-Americans from Braddock to St. Clair could have testified. And while it had certain superiorities over the spear and arrow in timber or brush, neither the musket nor the more accurate flintlock rifle was ever designed for effective mounted warfare. European cavalry, in fact, relied upon the lance and saber.

Thus the horse Indians suffered no real handicap by being deprived of firearms. And while the psychological hunger for muskets lingered through the eighteenth century and a musket was long a status symbol among the Comanches, the plains hunters actually had at hand a far more effective weapons system in the bow and arrow. European tastes in tactics and weaponry had never run to mounted archers, for all the historic damage done to European armies by Asian horsemen advancing under clouds of arrows—yet for one last time, on the Great Plains of North America, this ancient central Asian technique of warfare was to prove its deadliness, against both Amerindians and white men.

The warrior who rode best shot best, and if the Comanches were acknowledged as the superior horsemen on the plains, it followed that they became the deadliest bowmen. Training in hunting sharpened these skills. Every Comanche boy learned to gallop beside a fleeing bison, holding his seat with his knees on a charging, swerving pony, loosing his shafts with pinpoint accuracy. Although the musket had a greater killing range than the short Comanche *bois d'arc* bow, the Comanche arrow was infinitely more accurate, even from horseback. The disparity was greater in the rate of fire. A Comanche warrior could loose twenty shafts at the gallop, closing in on the prey, while a musket-armed man could get off one shot and reload.

The Comanches, along with the Wichitas, had the reputation of making the best arrows on the plains. It required enormous labor and infinite patience to fashion a dogwood, mulberry, or ash shaft that would fly true. The carefully seasoned shafts were feathered with turkey, owl, or buzzard, never the hawk or eagle used by some tribes, since blood ruined hawk and eagle feathers. Every arrow was a considerable investment and was recovered whenever possible.

Another French diffusion was as important to the culture as the musket and steel ax head. This was a crude knowledge of forging iron. Along with knives and hatchets, traders gave the Amerindians some simple metal-working techniques. The Comanches, like the other peoples, never had the slightest idea where iron came from or any interest in learning to smelt ores, but they quickly learned to beat metals into weapons. They used scraps—pieces of barrel hoops, frying pans, files, and other relics of the alien civilization that reached the frontier. They heated these cherry-red over blazing coals, then tempered the glowing metal by plunging it in cold water, and hammered out crude but effective points for their shafts and spears.

The Amerindians had always made two kinds of points, hunting heads and warheads. The hunting head was broad and flat, designed for maximum destruction of animal blood vessels and tissue, and also for easy withdrawal. The flint warhead was ingeniously cruel: smaller and narrower but chipped with crudely barbed edges. It could not be pulled from a wound without inflicting hideous further damage to the flesh. War arrows made ghastly wounds, and warheads could normally be removed only by pushing the point and shaft entirely through the body. This technique was carried over into metal warheads, which were often barbed.

Toward the close of the eighteenth century, and particularly after new industrial techniques made iron artifacts cheaper in the European civilization, a vast trade in metal arrowheads was carried on all across the Amerindian frontier. Largely overlooked, this trade continued far into the nineteenth century. Low-grade iron arrow points turned out in quantity by forges were greatly sought after by all the tribes; they took a deadly edge and even soft iron was more than adequate for the Amerindian purpose. These points were produced so cheaply by crude industries that trading companies could supply a packet of one dozen to the Indians at a cost of a *medio real*, a sixteenth of a Spanish dollar, half a bit, or some six cents. The same packet cost the Amerindians a prime fur, or at least a buffalo robe worth many dollars in the civilized marketplace. Over two centuries, millions of these iron arrowheads were sold to the Amerindians, and they killed more human beings of both races than all the guns traded to Indians combined, though this trade never attracted a tenth of the attention of the traffic in firearms.

It was no longer strictly correct to describe the eighteenth-century Plains Amerindians as Stone Age hunters. Although their culture was basically unchanged, most Indians now used metal weapons and artifacts. Such weapons made the tribes, already mounted, the most formidable fighters Europeans had yet encountered in America. And unlike some other peoples, the Comanches seem to have grasped the fact that their own weapons, improved with iron edges, were superior to the muzzle-loading firearms of white men. After a century on the plains, and noticeably after about 1800, most Comanches began to discard muskets and pistols and to rely on their older weapons. European firearms, then, for all the damage they caused in the timberlands, were not decisive on the plains in the seventeenth and eighteenth centuries.

What was decisive in warfare in the open was the horse. Here again, however, a whole new military technology was unequally exploited. All the Plains tribes rode, and all of the peoples powerful enough to be secure out on the Great Plains became horse nomads, ranging after the buffalo. All used the horse in war—but with marked differences.

The Pawnees, the Crows, the Wichitas, and even the mighty Dakotas or Sioux used the horse primarily for transportation and mobility. Only in the cinema did the Sioux or the southwestern Apaches attack on horseback. In actuality, they rode to the vicinity of the enemy, dismounted, and then fought on foot. They sneaked into enemy encampments on foot and attempted to steal horses on foot. Plains Indians were more dragoons—mounted infantry—than true cavalry.

The Comanches, however, had become a people on horseback, and they spurned doing anything on foot. Preferring to fight from horseback, they developed tactics to fit. In one respect the Nermernuh were unique: they were the only people who staged mounted horse raids, whether after a single pony or an entire remuda.

The Plains Shoshones apparently experimented with several forms of tactics and weapons systems in their first years on the bison range. Early French accounts of the Pádouca describe the People as fighting on horseback, but wielding long-shafted, stone-headed axes. Other reports describe Pádouca horses swathed in a stiff, bison-hide armor. This armor was apparently soon discarded, as it turned neither iron arrowheads nor musket balls. The evolution of the Nerm warrior to mounted ax-man was perfectly logical, given the mountain origins of the tribe. Before the horse, the Amerindian hand ax or tomahawk was the principal weapon for close combat, and it did terrifying execution in the West as well as the East. But while the hand ax was to remain a valuable adjunct and subsidiary weapon, it was not suitable for true mounted warfare. For this the bow was needed.

Comanche horse archers, however, were not quite cavalry in the European sense. They never developed mass tactics like Persians or Huns, nor used shock action like European knights. They rode and fought very much as individuals, and they never pressed a charge home. At the same time, a war party of mounted Comanches fought in a manner that was marvelously synchronized. Just when they developed and perfected their final tactics on horseback is not known, but this probably came during the eighteenth-century skirmishing for the buffalo plains. They developed a cavalry system that Europeans always had trouble understanding, and even describing, though in time all Europeans came to view it with respect, if not awe.

Comanches approached an enemy, whether mounted or on foot, galloping, circling, weaving, each warrior apparently taking no orders from the war chief. The horsemen were never a solid line. They formed a swirling, breaking, dissolving, and grouping mass of separate horses and riders thundering across the prairie, making difficult moving targets. The horsemen charged, broke off before contact, dodged, and weaved. Cannon, which Europeans often used so effectively against massed primitives, was of limited usefulness against such a charge—and so was massed musketry. Such tactics could only be performed by magnificent horsemen, and the net effect sometimes mesmerized the waiting enemy. Often, the Com-

Plains metal hand axes or tomahawks. The top ax is Comanche, the bottom two Osage, identified by distinctive markings.

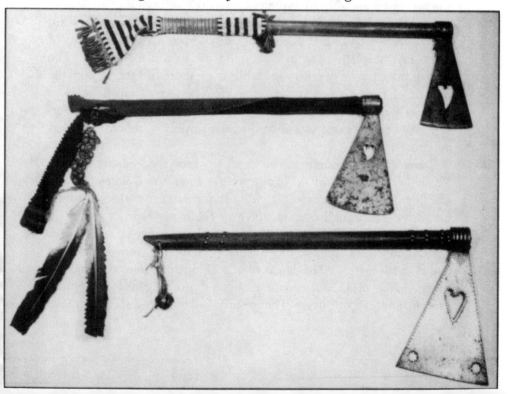

anches tried to encircle the enemy. This circle had magic power in the Comanche mind, and probably derived from the buffalo "surround" or stand. But it was also a practical maneuver. Circling the enemy, the rapidly moving horsemen held the foe at bay, under attack from every side, while they themselves presented only fleeting individual targets. The Comanches also had the trick, already mentioned, of hanging over the far side of their ponies, supported by a strap or thong, thus almost fully protected from ball or arrow.

The swirling circle closed to within arrow distance, hurled thrumming shafts, then danced back out of enemy range. Warriors trained to bring down a charging bison at the gallop were deadly archers at fifty yards. What seemed a light brush, the merest battle contact, often drew deep blood and inflicted considerable casualties. But the swarming, whooping horse barbarians, gesticulating obscenely, seemingly almost playing at war, failed to impress disciplined soldiers drawn up to meet an onslaught. The charge never came. The Comanches rode around and through, filling the air with arrows—and while the charge never struck home, somehow the Comanches stampeded the enemy horse strings, and sometimes even broke up European defensive formations.

If the enemy formation dissolved, or showed a weakness, the Comanches were able to exploit it instantly, riding close and sending arrows in clouds. If an enemy tried to flee, the Comanches did charge. And as Colonel Richard Dodge wrote, the surest form of death on the plains was to turn one's back on a Comanche. The Amerindian ponies were unbeatable over short distances, and the pursuit of running targets was the kind of sport Comanche boys were weaned on. After a few such brushes, better-armed and better-organized white cavalry tendered a vast respect to mounted Amerindians.

Comanches, of course, never stood to receive an enemy charge. Their own ranks dissolved even more at such times, wheeling and swirling individually, while tight-knit formations rushed through uselessly. Occasionally, some brave or foolhardy warrior, eager to count coup, might ride to seek hand-to-hand combat with ax or lance; the others simply raced about, peppering the floundering enemy with arrows. The lance attack of Spanish horsemen or the saber charge of U.S. dragoons dissipated itself against the empty prairie, and it cost lives. The scruffy-looking Amerindian horses were incredibly quick and agile compared to heavier cavalry mounts, more accurately polo ponies than war horses. Comanche riders could turn rapidly, strike, and retreat, cutting a confused enemy formation on blown horses to pieces before it could regroup.

As most historians came to acknowledge, the Comanches were superior in mounted combat to any European or Anglo-American soldiery until the advent of repeating firearms changed the balance. Foot troops were helpless against mounted Comanches in open country, and heavy cavalry could not match, meet, or break them. The Europeans had no light cavalry in America that could compare.

Comanche warfare did not result in so many slaughters as might be expected from this superiority for the same reasons that casualties in ancient native warfare remained relatively low. The Amerindians rarely tried to wipe out the enemy if this would cost them additional casualties. Such victory was meaningless to Comanches. When an enemy pursued them, they never gave battle by choice, unless they pulled the enemy into difficult terrain, or held overwhelming advantages in numbers, or were trapped themselves. The Amerindian way was to scout and strike from ambush.

The Comanches emerged as the most cunning warriors on the plains, as Dodge said, the "most mischievously artful of all the United States' Indians." They knew most tricks and stratagems used from Cannae to Senlac Hill. They tried to draw an enemy out of cover by pretending to flee; they would even play dead in order to deceive an enemy into coming close. They gave no quarter and expected none. There was, as the Texas historian Rupert N. Richardson described it, a peculiarly deadly quality about the Comanche, even compared to other warlike Amerindians.

It was a deadliness the Nermernuh or Comanches had learned in war, had perfected on the prairies, long before Spaniards, Frenchmen, or Anglo-Americans came fully into contact with them.

HUNTING, EATING, BREEDING, GROWING STRONGER EVERY MOON, THE mounted bands of Nermernuh were pulled southeastward along the great arc of the Rockies. They were skirmishing and sometimes fighting with the other new horse Indians, Wichitas and Pawnees; they kept up old acquaintance with the Utes and Crows. While no exact timetable exists and the Comanches left few trail marks, they began to move south from the Platte country about 1700, and a few years later spilled southward over the Arkansas River.

Hodge proposed, and many others agreed, that the Nermernuh or Comanches were pushed south of the Arkansas by the expanding power of the Dakotas to the north. Some Pádoucas were driven off the plains by Sioux, as well as by pressures from Crows and Blackfeet—but these were northern Shoshones, never Shoshone horse Indians. As Richardson stated, there is absolutely no evidence that the Comanches rode south to escape the Sioux, or for that matter, that Comanches ever came in contact with the Dakotas in the seventeenth or eighteenth century. The assertion is a calumny, in fact, against the Comanches. The People had horses before either the Sioux or Cheyennes, and they made room for no one on the plains. They rode south by choice.

Their reasons were obvious. The greatest concentration of bison was on the southern plains, especially the high plateaus of Texas. The regions along the Platte and the Black Hills were barren compared to the lands south of the Arkansas. Furthermore, and perhaps the primary reason why the Comanches were drawn south, the southern bison range lay adjacent to the major source of Spanish horseflesh in New Mexico. Also, the winters there were milder than on the High Plains, and the land was not yet teeming with horse Indians. It took no peculiar Amerindian logic to see the riches and the strategic value of the southern plains.

But while this vast, bison-rich empire was barren of true horse Amerindians in the late seventeenth century, it was hardly unclaimed. It was patrolled by large bands of transplanted Athapaskans, those same peoples who had—centuries earlier—moved from the far Pacific Northwest and marched along the Rockies, causing great displacements and reverberations among the Uto-Aztekan stocks. These Athapaskans were fierce, extremely warlike, predatory peoples, with a culture and organization very similar to the mountain Shoshones. Moving onto the mesas and the fringes of the Great Plains in the Southwest, they had ravaged the Puebloan culture savagely; they probably had as much to do with the retardation of that peaceable culture as the cyclic droughts.

Like all Amerindians, the Athapaskans called themselves People, *T'Inde,* or by variants of the term *Náizhan* (NICE-hahn), "Our

Kind." The Puebloan Zuñis identified them to the Spaniards as *Apaches* or enemies, and the Spanish, with some justice, recorded them for posterity as enemies of mankind.

In the Southwest, the Apaches fragmented and took on local characteristics. The Spanish divided the bands into western and eastern Apaches according to their location in relation to the settlements in New Mexico, and gave them a great number of arbitrary band names. The western Apaches, such as Chiricahuas, Navajos, and San Carlos, were migratory hunting peoples on the southwestern mesas, each band almost a separate tribe, aloof and clannish. The eastern Apaches were more important and numerous. These bands ranged from the Dismal River in Nebraska through central Texas, where they had pushed the fierce Tonkawas almost off the plains. They were typical of the prehorse Amerindian Plains culture; they raised their red and white bison-hide tipis from the Red River between Texas and present Oklahoma to the Colorado plateaus; they used the dog travois, and they hunted buffalo along the fringes of the Great Plains as best they could. They were divided and unorganized, like the Shoshones, but collectively they were a powerful race. By the seventeenth century they had extirpated the Puebloan culture completely in the trans-Pecos region of Texas, and, during the great revolt of 1680–90 against the Spanish, almost exterminated some Puebloan peoples in New Mexico.

These bands, whom the Spanish called *Palomas* ("Doves"), *Faraones* ("Pharaohs"), *Jicarillas* ("Basket-Makers"), *Carlanas,* and other names, were recognized by the early explorers as the lords of the Texas plains. The Spanish called their great, straggling encampments *rancherías,* and one explorer claimed he saw a *ranchería* of "five thousand souls" along the upper Arkansas—doubtless an exaggeration. But there were thousands of Apaches in scattered, semipermanent settlements along the river valleys from Nebraska deep into Texas.

The eastern Apaches had also learned from the Puebloans, for they had begun to plant maize, squash, pumpkins, and beans in straggling fields beside the streams. Since they had to pause while these crops ripened, the eastern Apaches had become less migratory and more settled. Some bands, like the Jicarillas, were quite advanced toward an agrarian barbarism. Collectively, the eastern groups had made the best possible adjustment in the prehorse age of dividing their efforts between seasonal hunting and agriculture. Yet, ironically, it was this very taste for corn that killed them, when their lands were invaded by true savages on horseback.

The Apaches were the first warlike people to acquire the horse from the Spanish, but, already partly agrarian, they never became great horsemen. They never bothered to learn horse breeding. And they saw the horse primarily as a useful tool in their raids against the Spanish-Puebloan settlements. Thus, while riding Apaches had begun to harass New Mexico brutally in the 1650s—Navajos out of the west, many bands from the east—no Apaches were lured by the buffalo onto the plains. They preferred their fields to the harvest of the herds.

Farming also further fragmented the Athapaskans. The advanced Jicarillas, who used irrigation techniques and wove baskets, considered themselves a different folk from the more predatory bands. While Apaches did not make war on each other, they would not assist each other, either. Thus, the lords of the southern plains, scattered, separated, living beside strung-out fields, and fixed to the soil for long periods of time, were particularly vulnerable to the new form of warfare that the horse Shoshones developed on the prairies. They were the losers in a great struggle for cultural life and death that engulfed the southern plains at the beginning of the eighteenth century.

THERE WAS NO CONCERTED COMANCHE MOVEMENT SOUTH OF THE Arkansas, just as there had been no mass movement of the horse Shoshones out onto the Great Plains. The Comanches seem to have begun raiding Apache country long before the bands began to migrate. Just when, where, and how the Nermernuh and T'Inde came into contact east of the Rockies is no more known than other facts about the great events of prehistoric Amerindian times. The first contacts, and clashes, may have been casual. On the other hand, the Athapaskans may very well have retained ancestral memories of the people they called *Idahi*, "Snakes," from the far north, and the horse Shoshones recalled old hatreds of the men they knew as *Neepan,* or *Na-vohnuh.* One thing is certain: the renewed acquaintance resulted in one of the bitterest, bloodiest, and most lasting Amerindian feuds of all time.

Amerindian wars, like Old World wars and hatreds, were alleviated by truces and remissions from time to time, and enemies sometimes even became allies. This never happened between Apache and Comanche. All Comanches, everywhere, became the foes of all Apaches, and the final tragedy was that both peoples, in the twilight of their existence, willingly and remorselessly helped the white man exterminate each other. It was war to the knife and beyond the grave. The mutual hatred of the two peoples, the great warrior tribes of the Southwest, was a hair-raising phenomenon, transcending any ephemeral hatred they conceived for Europeans.

However begun, the Comanche-Apache war was no Amerindian game, no joyous horse raid, no courage rite. It was a fundamental part of the great western upheaval caused by European weapons and horses entering the midcontinent. It only ended when a new balance had been achieved by the Apaches being driven entirely from the plains.

When Comanches discovered Apaches south of the Arkansas late in the seventeenth century, the horse had already greatly deepened the dimension of Amerindian war. By 1700, the normal hunting or migrating range of a Plains tribe extended about eight hundred miles. Whereas before, a hundred-mile war raid was an extended operation, the radius of the normal raid was now between three and four hundred miles in any direction from a band encampment.

Such striking distances long seemed absolutely incredible to Europeans, especially those who tended to think in European scales. Yet Amerindian war parties had little trouble covering such distances on horseback: the Indian ponies foraged off the native grass, and the warriors carried dried meat and water in animal-gut canteens. Both horses and men were able to endure extreme hardships, while the Amerindians' discipline and stoic indifference to suffering on the war trail were proverbial.

The long striking distances did require certain refinements and innovations. There were greater logistical preparations, pack horses carrying stores of meat and mesquite-bean meal. Also, the war parties carried along several mounts for each warrior. It was extremely important to have fresh ponies, and more than one pony, in case of close pursuit. Women began to ride along with war parties, especially on extended operations. They normally did not fight, but erected base camps where they stayed to provide logistical support and the comforts of home.

Married women liked to be taken on war parties, and some single girls, wild spirits, ran off with warriors going raiding, despite the scandal to their families. Women could fight if necessary. Sometimes they formed a second line of battle, sniping from cover with arrows, killing enemy wounded while a larger battle still raged. They were always prepared to torture any captives that were brought back to the base camp.

All warriors, and especially war chiefs, had to become more skillful at remembering terrain as raids extended into country that was increasingly unfamiliar. Most Comanches became good at mapping. From memory, a warrior who had traversed a territory could sketch on the ground with a pointed stick a map that accurately pointed out significant land features, laid out marches, and showed distances to scale. Comanches who memorized such crude maps often followed them on the ground for as much as a thousand miles; once a Comanche had ridden anywhere, the others could always retrace his hoof prints.

Since war raids now covered many miles and took many days, the best war leaders had to become capable of excellent staff planning. Warfare might still be random, irrational, magic-dominated, and lacking sustained purpose by civilized standards, but, by the same measure, war party planning and organization were phenomenal. Marches and routes were carefully laid out and scouted; duties were painstakingly assigned. No Comanche ever rode blindly into strange or hostile territory. Comanches were rarely ambushed, and never ran out of food or water, or found themselves lost on the endless prairie, all of which happened regularly to white expeditions.

Extended operations also called for new means of communication. Scouts now often rode as much as a day ahead of the main body in open country. The Comanches and other Plains peoples soon devised the smoke signal telegraph. This was never universal; it was used only by the Plains horse Indians. When scouts wanted to communicate intelligence, they lit fires on buttes or high mesas, and shaped the greasewood smoke with a buffalo robe or blanket. The signals were simple and easily read: *discovery—enemy in sight—buffalo—alarm, danger—come—stop—friends—coast clear.* Smoke signals had handicaps: they could not be used at night, and they were hardly secure, since they alerted both friend and enemy.

But in the hot, clear air of the Southwest, Amerindians could communicate over many miles.

Meanwhile, the vast extensions of ranges had brought wandering tribes into new contacts with each other. These were not invariably hostile. One great problem among the Amerindians was that of communication, since each tribe had its own language. The solution, adopted for both peace and war, was the devising of a sign language. Like the smoke signal, this was purely a Great Plains phenomenon; it was used only on the horse and bison range. The language used only one identical set of signs and symbols from Canada to the Rio Grande.

By the eighteenth century, Dakotas and Blackfeet were able to talk to Comanches or Wichitas through this medium, wherever they might meet. The sign talk was almost as fast as speech. The language was like the culture from which it sprang, highly ceremonial and even poetic, but also conceptual. Since more white men on the plains learned the sign talk than the spoken dialects, sign-language concepts strongly affected white notions of how Amerindians thought and spoke. "Winters" did not necessarily stand for years in every tongue as they did in sign talk, but such conceptions became firmly imbedded in the white consciousness.

The diffusion of this universal language over such a huge area between peoples who had never seen each other was remarkable. It indicates that there must have been more contact and communication between the tribes than is otherwise revealed. The development followed recognizable patterns. The Nermernuh, who became powerful but remained highly parochial on their own ranges, were not adept at sign talk. The Kiowas, a much smaller, very wide-ranging, and mobile clan, were the acknowledged experts, just as the citizens of small nations are usually better linguists than those of great empires.

In the universal symbol language, the designation for Comanches was a rapid, backward, wavy movement of the index finger drawn across the breast, signifying "snake." This did not have certain significances whites gave it, however, concerning Comanche characteristics. It was merely the ancient designation of the Idahi, the Snake People, the Shoshone-speakers who had once dwelt on the bends of the Snake River in Idaho.

Horse warfare taught the Comanches new tricks. One was that

the best time to stage raids was the period of the full moon. Rising late, the full moon gave light to travel by, especially on the return trail when raiders might have to ride by night. They avoided striking during a crescent moon, since they believed that this time presaged rain, which slowed war parties. In addition, mud caused them to leave telltale tracks. The optimum time for war was between the coming of the new spring grass, providing forage, and the start of the fall hunt, when all the tribes were too busy with the meat harvest to fight.

There was still a thin line between a "war" and a "raid." The only real difference lay in the purpose determined by the leader's medicine. If the mission was horse stealing, the raiders might still massacre if they got the chance; but if the mission was to kill or avenge an injury, then it was pursued with single-minded seriousness until sufficient blood was shed. The pattern was again random. At times, the war chief might be satisfied with a single scalp; others would often require wholesale vengeance.

THE COMANCHES BEGAN TO MOUNT LONG-DISTANCE WAR RAIDS AGAINST the Navonuh or Athapaskans soon after they encountered them below the Arkansas, exactly as they carried on expeditions against the adjacent Pawnees and Utes to the east and west. They had a great incentive, because the eastern Apaches were rich in horseflesh taken from the Spanish in New Mexico. The first strikes were doubtless sporting horse raids. However, the Nermernuh soon discovered that the Apaches were especially vulnerable to their mode of warfare, compared to Utes or other plains tribes. The Utes were ensconced in mountains, while the Pawnees and Wichitas were as mobile as Comanches. The Eastern Apaches, husbanding their crops in spring and summer, were easy to locate, surround, and attack on horseback—and the Apaches were not given to bloody pursuit back across the trackless plains.

Since the Comanches moved regularly, never camping in the same spot, the Athapaskans found their lodges very hard to locate, and Apache war bands, who used horses only for transportation, were never comfortable out on the sea of grass.

The Nermernuh struck one Apache camp, then another, at widely separated spots. Sometimes they ran off all the horses, leaving the enemy warriors raging and helpless; when conditions were right, they massacred the whole camp. The Nermernuh did not consciously commit genocide; this was simply warfare as they knew it. Frequently, they carried off women and small children to be trained as Comanches, because their biases were cultural, never racial. Some authorities have asserted that the southwestern Indians only began to keep captive servants or slaves after they had picked up the practice from the Spanish, but the evidence is dubious. Slavery was endemic in Amerindian Mexico centuries before Cortés, and the earliest Spanish explorers left records of finding captive aliens among all the tribes.

Warfare between Apaches and Comanches was never organized on a tribal basis; it could not be, since neither formed extensive tribes. It was between band and band, enemies by a mutual cultural antipathy, institutionalized by ancient custom and new trauma. It soon became decisive, for all its randomness, particularly as more and more Comanche bands debouched below the Arkansas—bringing their women and children along on extended raids, seeing the country, enjoying its richness in limitless space and endless herds. There was really no difference between a Comanche "village" and a war base camp. Wherever a Comanche rode and erected his tipi was home. Thousands of the Nermernuh spilled south through the southern plains, striking in every direction at the Apache *rancherías*. The result was near-extermination of the advanced eastern Apaches. The sum of a hundred raids was the same as the sum of a hundred pitched battles on the soil of Europe during the *Völkerwanderung*. Apache camps were destroyed one by one, and the whole people began to be displaced.

This great war, or rather, vast series of petty raids and massacres, went largely unseen and unreported, even by the adjacent Spanish in New Mexico. The Spaniards had only vague conceptions of what was happening beyond their sphere of influence in those days. They were still consolidating their reconquest of the upper Rio Grande, and were largely ignorant about "wild" Indians. Shortly after 1700, the New Mexican authorities realized that something had happened to their old enemies, the Apaches, but they knew none of the details. In 1705, they made the first known contact with the *Komántcia* or Comanches, and by 1706, the Spanish governor was able to connect the appearance of this new tribe of *indios* with the disasters befalling the eastern Apaches.

In this same year, the men at Santa Fe knew that the Apaches had been decisively beaten to the north and east of New Mexico, because Apache refugees were fleeing into or across Spanish territory, moving from the edge of the eastern plains into the arid western mountains. To the delight of the authorities, the Jicarilla band agreed to embrace Christianity and begged for Spanish protection. The Jicarillas were allowed to migrate westward into New Mexico and settle under Spanish guns.

Other Apaches were retreating to the west without permission. The Mescaleros (makers of *tizwin,* an intoxicant the Mexicans called *mescal*) moved further west and deeper into the Rocky Mountains. In fact, all the Apaches of whom the Spanish kept track moved southwest, into the dry mesas of New Mexico and Arizona. Other bands they had recorded simply vanished from the earth. The Faraones, Carlanas, Palomas, and others disappeared from history.

Some eastern Apaches apparently formed themselves into a new group—probably survivors of decimated bands—and called themselves the *Ipa'Nde,* or "Ipa's People," followers of a great war chief. The Spanish named them *Lipanes,* and the Comanches, *Nipan.* The chief Ipa did not prove to be a savior of his people. The Spaniards heard rumors of a "great battle" fought between the Comanches and Lipanes on the Red River to the east, in which the Apaches were completely routed.

In the end, the Apaches were entirely driven off the southern plains. Those remnants that were not pushed west, into the southern Rockies, fled into the barren trans-Pecos region of Texas, or into the country of the Tonkawas, along the San Saba and upper Nueces rivers, and through the valleys of the Guadalupe and Llano. These eastern survivors, now known as Lipanes or Lipan Apaches, were often confused with the New Mexico Mescaleros, for they ceased to be Plains Indians. Like the western bands, they reverted to mountain and desert hunters and gatherers, skulkers in the Spanish-Mexican borderlands. They no longer farmed or even tried to hunt buffalo. The Lipans had begun their long descent into the status of a despised, though still dangerous, predatory border tribe, doomed to eventual extinction between two superior forces.

The evidence is that the losers in this Amerindian warfare turned even more predatory and hostile. The Apaches were the greatest victims of the Comanches; they were driven into inhospitable borderlands, and it is understandable that from this time forward they were implacably hostile to all other Amerindians as well as to the Spanish-Mexicans. They made the borderlands suffer terribly from both their poverty and their proximity. They could make no peace with the Spanish, because the Apaches could not accept Spanish dominion and life styles. The Comanches killed them whenever they caught them on the plains. They were safe only in their mountain-desert fastnesses, from which they emerged to raid and plunder —not their destroyers but the more vulnerable Spaniards and Amerindians close at hand.

BY 1725, MOST OF THOSE LANDS EAST OF THE SOUTHERN ROCKIES THAT the Spaniards had called *Apachería* had become *Comanchería*, the domain of the Comanches. The terrible, buffalo-horned warriors on horseback had seized an enormous new empire. This territory was comprised of all the lands between the Spanish frontier and the Arkansas River, lying between the Grand Cordillera and the Cross Timbers of Texas. Its core covered six hundred miles from north to south, four hundred miles from east to west, lying entirely on the southern portions of the Great Plains from the ninety-eighth meridian to the foothills of the Rockies. It was an empire to make any people proud, and the influence and the fear inspired by the invading Nermernuh extended far beyond the lands the war bands patrolled. All camps and settlements within a thousand miles of *Comanchería* were within the riding range of the horse barbarians.

The heart of *Comanchería* consisted of the most ancient land mass on the North American continent. This was high but relatively level country, a series of vast limestone plateaus sloping gradually eastward. It was an ocean of waving grasses, broken only by buttes and infrequent streams, with scattered high escarpments, deep canyons, and hidden arroyos. The rivers that cut across these high plains were shallow, low-banked, sandy-bottomed streams, heavily salted with gypsum, lined by clumps of trees. In places, through the eons, they had carved deep chasms below the surface of the prairie, providing secure shelters from the storms that seasonally swept over them.

This was the general nature of the land, but a country so vast had to have many local variations. In the west, up against the sands of New Mexico, rose the great palisaded plain Coronado's soldiers had named the Llano Estacado, which unfortunately became translated into English not in its true meaning of a barrier rising like a fortress, but as "Staked Plains." The great, high, barren Llano Estacado walled off *Comanchería* from the south and west. It rose in what is now called the Texas Panhandle south of the Canadian River, and ran north and east, ending in another natural phenomenon, the Texas Cap Rock.

From these high escarpments the mesa merged almost imperceptibly into another gently sloping plain to the southeast, the Edwards Plateau. The broad limestone formations of the Edwards country marched grandly eastward for hundreds of miles, ending in the broken, cedar-studded hills above the Balcones Scarp, north and west of modern Austin and San Antonio. The lower regions of the plateau were less broad plains than limestone hills and canyons, dotted with oaks, grassy meadows, and cedar brakes—a land of small, clear streams and gentle beauty, resembling portions of the Appalachians. In the far southwest, the Edwards ended sharply at the mountains of the Big Bend country, a separated segment of the southern Rockies. North, between the massive Cap Rock and the Cross Timbers—then a great stand of trees standing starkly against the beginning plains—lay huge stretches of dark-soiled prairie, which rose in the western high country and gradually vanished in the oak clumps that appeared like floating islands on the eastern fringes of the grasslands.

These high plains stood between the eastern timbers and the blue-shadowed western mountains, unchanged since the earth emerged from the last Ice Age. This was high, dry, late-Pleistocene terrain, where the rain rarely exceeded twenty inches annually, and where even that was random. The climate was cyclic: wet years covered the soil with deep, matted grasses, which in dry years burned brown or disappeared. Spring was the wettest season, the prairies burning dry and sere by fall. This land was in no sense a desert. It only appeared to be desert to the first Anglo-Saxons who entered it, for they had no understanding or experience of country with erratic rains and no timber. And because they failed to understand the nature of the land, the Anglo-Saxons did their best, in later years, to turn it into desert, by plowing and denuding the soil.

During the spring rains the entire southern plains blazed with an ephemeral beauty, a riot of wild flowers gleaming in deep, green grass. In this season even the treeless mesa of the Llano Estacado was dotted with shallow, brimming playa lakes. Then, as the rains ceased and the southern midcontinental sun sucked the earth, the ponds dried into sand and mud, and the lush buffalo, bunchflower, needle, and other native grasses yellowed and withered. By late summer the plains did appear desertlike; but this "desert" was almost as ephemeral as the lush spring, for the grass and flowers only awaited a random rain to come again in glory. The earth was matted with the accumulation of generations of resurrected vegetation and seeds. While some sections burned dry, and might stay arid for months and even years, there was always rain and grass somewhere on the prairie, and the native life, unchecked by boundaries or fences, moved to find it. Even the winters, despite their icy blizzards, were relatively mild. The earth never froze beneath the snows, and somewhere, always, there were water and grass for nomadic wildlife.

The infrequent rivers—the Arkansas, Cimarron, Canadian, Washita, Red, Pease, Brazos, Colorado, Pecos—and their canyons, and the more frequent springs in the arroyos, made fertile oases. They gave life to great cottonwood trees, and their sandy banks were covered with wild plums and mustang grapevines. To the east, downstream, appeared thickening stands of pecans and walnuts, interspersed with ash, elm, chinaberry, hackberry, *bois d'arc* or Osage orange, willows, and oaks. Redbud and haws and persimmon bushes sprouted. The land was not barren anywhere; even in the driest portions, clumps of mesquite struggled to suck sustenance from the soil.

The proof of richness was the teeming wildlife, the greatest concentration of animals on the North American continent.

Coronado found the Llano Estacado swarming with buffalo, in "numbers impossible to estimate," as he wrote to his king. The Spanish, disillusioned at not finding the Seven Cities of Cíbola on the plains, named the native herbivores *cíbolos.* Some Spaniards guessed that individual herds numbered in the millions. There were also hundreds of thousands of pronghorn antelope, and bear and cats and great elk in the canyons. There were peccaries and hares and rabbits and, soon, wild horses, with wolves and coyotes to prey on them. The high plateaus of Texas lacked the variety of animals in Africa, but because the great predators were fewer, these grasslands held more game.

In this vast territory, Comanches found everything they required for their way of life. The grazing beasts provided meat and horn and hides. The river banks offered wood, forage and fruits, nuts and berries, food and raw materials. The bears gave up fat, fur, and sinews. The canyon brakes made superb, protected camp sites.

The winter blizzards were passing things; here, the sun shone in all seasons. The deep winter months were seldom hungry ones, as so often in the north, for the bison massed on the southern ranges in cold weather. The Comanches had found, and seized, a natural hunter's paradise for horse Amerindians. And compared to most Amerindian peoples, they were now highly secure upon their new territories. Their vast striking range, and their new and fearsome reputation, made all other tribes give *Comanchería* a wide berth. Buffalo-hungry Caddoans in the east and starving Apaches and Tonkawas in the south rarely dared to venture onto the Comanche range.

True to their ancient fashion, the Comanches who entered this country remained in scattered, widely separated bands. The bands might join briefly for war against Apaches, but otherwise each operated independently. Each remained autonomous, virtually a tribe in itself. Each came to hunt, and patrol, in a recognized band territory.

Thirteen different bands of Comanches were identified in historic times. There were undoubtedly others, for small bands coalesced and broke apart from time to time. Neither the Spanish nor Anglo-Americans ever identified all the bands; some were known only to the People themselves. And some recognized bands disappeared a few years later. Five major bands had appeared on the southern plains in the eighteenth century. These five played the greatest role in Comanche history, and only these survived into the late 1800s.

The largest band, which may have been the first to follow the bison southward on the plains, were called *Pehnahterkuh* (Penateka) or "Honey-Eaters." They were also known as *Pehnahner,*

"Wasps," or *Hoh'ees*, "Timber People." The Spanish eventually identified this band as southern Comanches. They pushed the farthest south, taking up a range entirely within the present borders of Texas. Their domain was the broad Edwards Plateau, both its high mesas in the west and its southern and eastern timbered fringes, where they found the trees and honey that gave them their Comanche name. The name, however, like certain others, was misleading. The principal food of the Pehnahterkuh, as of all Comanches, was buffalo.

On the north, Pehnahterkuh country merged into the territory of the *Nawyehkuh* or *Nawkohnee* (Nokoni), "Those Who Turn Back." This was the most nomadic and farthest ranging of the bands. Nawkohnee moved often and far, covering great distances in a few days. They roamed principally between the Cross Timbers west of modern Fort Worth and the New Mexican mountains. Nawkohnee might be spotted on the Red River, then riding near Santa Fe, and a month later the same group might camp on the Colorado plateau. The Spanish found this movement hard to credit, and always believed that there were very many Nawkohnee on the plains.

Later, this band changed its name to *Dertsahnaw-yehkuh*, "Wanderers," because of the death of a band headman called Nawkohnee. This confused white identification of the band. Several smaller, offshoot bands shared its general range. The most important were the *Tahneemuh*, "Liver-Eaters," and the *Tehnahwah*, "Those Who Stay Downstream." The Spanish at Santa Fe lumped all these bands together as eastern Comanches.

North of the Nawkohnee country lay *Kuhtsoo-ehkuh* territory. The Kuhtsoo-ehkuh (Kotsoteka), "Buffalo-Eaters," hunted mostly through western Oklahoma, making their winter camps along the Canadian.

Higher still on the southern plains, with a range that extended north to the Arkansas, were the *Yampahreekuh* or *Yahp-paheenuh*, "Eaters of the Yap Root," the ancient Shoshone staple. Again, while the northern band might have retained a taste for tubers, it ate as much meat as the Kuhtsoo-ehkuh, and lived by hunting buffalo.

There was one more important band: the *Kwerhar-rehnuh*, or "Antelopes." Kwerhar-rehnuh rode the windswept, barren-looking ranges of the Llano Estacado west of all the other bands. They were often called *Kwah-heeher kehnuh* (Kwahadi) by other Comanches,

"Sun Shades on Their Backs," because they made bison-hide parasols. The Antelopes were actually the smallest of the larger bands, never numbering more than two thousand, but they were considered the most remote, aloof, and fierce of all the bands. Their own people considered them the most conservative of all Comanches. It was probably no accident that they held the richest hunting grounds of all, and were not disturbed in their camps deep in the Palo Duro and Tule canyons by their own kind.

The five major bands—Pehnahterkuh, Nawkohnee, Kuhtsooehkuh, Yampahreekuh, and Kwerhar-rehnuh—could each mount at least five hundred warriors. The many smaller bands that appeared and vanished included the *Eeh-tahtah-oh*, "Burnt Meat," and the "Upstream," "Midstream," "Underbank," and "Water-Horse" Comanches. Some of these were identified only in Comanche legend. One particularly fascinated both the other bands and white men. This was the *Nahmah-er-er-nuh*, an obscene term usually rendered as "Fornicators," or *Waw-ah-hees*, "Those with Maggots on the Penis." These Comanches were said to be incestuous.

The bands were large enough to provide sufficient human breeding stock, and they had little regular contact with each other. The southern and northern bands had no contact at all in the eighteenth century. Living far apart, each band developed different interests. The northern and eastern bands fought with mountain Utes and other plains tribes; the Pehnahterkuh rooted out Lipan Apaches and Tonkawas. All, however, retained an ancestral hatred for all Apaches. Cultural conservatism was so strong, also, that the bands developed few if any differences. From north to south there was some variance in dances and such ceremonies, and a certain difference in accents. Comanches could recognize a member of another band, but white men were rarely able to distinguish between Comanches—or, for that matter, many different kinds of horse Indians.

The victory over the Apaches was so complete, and the new Comanche lands so broad and rich and deep, that this had certain dangerous consequences. One was an enormous Comanche sense of band security. By 1750, few if any surrounding peoples dared set foot in Comanche country. The northern horse Indians, Cheyennes and Pawnees, stayed above the Arkansas. The Apaches and Tonkawas were dispersed along and below the Balcones Scarp or skulking in the Big Bend mountains. The Utes rarely came east of the

Rockies. The Wichitas disputed the eastern fringes of *Comanchería,* but the Wichitas were not powerful enough to raid deeply.

With all the bison they could use at hand, never pressed by external enemies, there was no reason for the Comanches to develop a tribal discipline. They soon got all the horses they needed from New Mexico. Comanches did not even bother to organize for the fall hunts—in fact, they could hunt all year on the southern plains —and, depending upon vast distances and the fearsome reputation of their raiders, they made very careless camps in the depths of their territory.

They erected their tipis in open timber along flowing streams. Tents were usually set up in family groups, and it was usual for a band camp to extend laterally beside a river, sometimes over as much as fifteen miles. The only reason the Comanches camped together at all was the human need for social intercourse. Camps afforded no protection or security, and the only sentinels were the ever-present dogs. This was quite different from the practices of the Dakotas and other tribes on the northern plains, who made tight camps on ground especially selected for concealment and security. While the Comanches had become the finest mounted warriors in North America, their encampments were probably the most vulnerable of all those among the warlike Plains Indians.

The other dangerous consequence of the Apache wars was that during their course the whole Comanche society became attuned to continual, long-distance raiding. The movement into *Apachería* was made up of a series of extended campaigns that lasted several generations in terms of Comanche life spans. Comanches had transformed Apache-raiding into a way of life, and this search for scalps and horses and war honors not only finally displaced the Athapaskans from the plains, it raised the whole concept of war among Comanches to a greater intensity. This pattern, and the fact that the southern ranges were so rich in buffalo, changed the prime directive of Comanche existence from hunting meat to making war.

Much as the horse affirmed the hunting life style, the extermination and displacement of the Apaches affirmed the Comanche style of warfare. After 1750, when the new range was completely won, the Comanche bands were never again satisfied with mere bison hunting. The society, such as existed, had developed a liking and even a hunger for war, and the Comanches were not to become settled or tractable neighbors in the Southwest.

The sullen hatred of the Apaches was understandable, and their incessant raiding of the borderlands was economically justified. Apaches had become poor by Amerindian standards. The Comanches, however, were rich, the *nouveaux riches* of the plains—and also the *enfants terribles*. Their war drives were not economically motivated. They bred horses, and so had all the mounts they needed to hunt buffalo. They continued raiding, however, because, for all its apparent looseness and male democracy, Comanche society had turned into a tightening hierarchy of prestige. Men gained prestige only through war exploits, and, above all, by leading other men in battle. It was not accidental that by this time Comanche war chiefs always gave away the booty that fell to them from war raids. Most chiefs already held hundreds of fine horses—but no chief ever had enough prestige. With all the meat the bands would ever need grazing stupidly beside the camps, male life increasingly became wrapped up in a search for war. A Comanche band at peace was composed of males without purpose, and men with no hope of gaining honor or advancement.

The band image, and self-image, of the Comanche man was that of a bold, aggressive warrior. The boy passed into manhood through blood rites, killing, and he grew in stature and remained a man only by a continual, public affirmation of his skills and courage. In this ethos, any weakness became sin. Thus, what had developed as a

Comanche encampment.
Drawing by George Catlin, c. 1836.

necessary drive among primitive hunters grew into a perversion, which no longer preserved life but increasingly endangered it. With bodily hungers satisfied, the urge to violence in such an ethos was extreme.

The evidence is that from the eighteenth century onward, violence within the camp was only precariously avoided. Comanche lore records that confrontations and standoffs between warriors, sometimes over women, always involving individual prestige, became more and more common. Murder became more prevalent on the southern plains, and murder was almost always the result of some great warrior's arrogance or refusal to back down when in the wrong. Two things alone prevented increasing violence between touchy, arrogant, violence-oriented warriors with too little to do in camp: one, the ancient, almost sacrosanct taboo against killing one's own People; the other, the fact that aggressions could be turned outside the tribe into war.

The ethos and self-image of the Comanche warrior tended to make old age a horror psychologically. The infirmities that early beset primitive men—the toothaches, the rheumatism and arthritis, the failing vision and digestion that, despite the mythology of the strong, healthy savage, afflicted the Comanches terribly—were bad enough and made all the People dread the aging process. But age created a special, agonizing problem for the great warrior as his powers failed. He was unable to maintain his public image, and his vital personal prestige.

Most Plains Indians had a similar warrior ethos, but most tribes also provided a more secure place for the aging male. The accepted image of the old man across most of mid-America was that of a respected elder, who turned to making straight arrows, instructing young warriors, and offering wise and mild arguments in council. The Cheyennes and Kiowas, with richer cultural traditions than the Nermernuh, gave the old respect and even security. They were honored in council for accumulated wisdom and had their own social organization, the elders' smoke lodge. The Comanches in fact had all these conventions and institutions, but now they honored none of them. The warrior who could no longer maintain his prowess on the war trail was an object of scorn, not always subtly expressed. He often lost control of his younger wives, and his counsel drew no respect.

Band wisdom held that old bulls should accept this changing status gracefully. Yet most could not adjust, for they were offered nothing to ease the transition, nothing that would help them resign themselves to the situation. The image of old age, always pejorative, now became positively malignant among Comanches. Old men were considered unnatural, arguing for peace, trying to hold on to females they did not deserve, and denying the youthful their full place in the sun. Clashes in council had something of the nature of a class war—for an older warrior, counseling against a raid or war, was in fact preserving the status quo, while new warriors were always eager to emerge and tarnish ancient prestige with fresher deeds. "The brave die young" became the most universal and widely repeated of all Comanche proverbs, and the saying itself was a denigration of the old.

The young men saw to it that their elders did not starve, but they never allowed them the useful place for which they hungered most. Increasingly, there arose Comanche legends about evil old men, using spells and sorcery against the young. Many suspected medicine men were killed, and suicides, rare among postmenstrual women, were common among aging males.

Thus, there was everything to push the Comanches into eternal repetition of the ancient death cycle on the plains, and nothing, not even a conventional wisdom or the counsel of experienced men, to prevent it. In one sense, the Nermernuh had made a splendid, valiant adaptation to a new environment; but at the same time they had grown into a death-oriented people. And in this lay the seeds of their destruction.

II

FAILED EMPIRES

THE PEOPLE AND THE
FRENCH AND SPANIARDS

Spain's frontier institutions were made
in the West Indies and further developed
in the fertile Mesa Central around Mexico City,
where the Indians were civilized, sedentary, agricultural,
and, as compared with the nomads of the Plains,
as docile as sheep . . .
  The labors of the holy fathers were at best
wholly negligible for the Indians and often disastrous to the missionaries.
The wild Comanche and Apache were not amenable
to the gentle philosophy of Christ nor were they tamed
by the mysteries and elaborate ceremonials of the church.
The warwhoop was sweeter to them than evening vespers;
the crescent bow was a better symbol
of their desires than the holy cross;
and it was far more joyful, in their eyes,
to chase the shaggy buffalo on pinto ponies
than to practice the art of dry-farming
under the direction of a black-robed priest.
            —Walter Prescott Webb

1

THE FORGOTTEN FRONTIER

. . . For a century the faith has been planted
in these provinces and nothing has prospered . . .
if we had only expended the money
that we spent fighting Indians,
since God took them to be an instrument
to punish our sins, in building new establishments,
where would not be raised the standard of the holy cross?
　　　—Diary of a Spanish missionary priest

THE SPANISH ENTERED THE NEW WORLD VIOLENTLY AND RUTHLESSLY
in the early sixteenth century. They were a people who had just
completed a great crusade, the reconquest of their peninsula from
the Muslim Moors, and they were at the apogee of their power and
élan. In a very real sense, the conquest of the New World was an
extension of their Iberian crusades. The Spanish applied many of
the same principles and practices to the conquest of the Amerindians
that they had applied to Jews and Moors in southern Spain. Like all
successful conquerors, they suffered from no self-doubt where alien
cultures were concerned.

The first inhabitants the Spanish found in the Americas were
ineluctably heathen and often primitive, and the Spaniards branded
them *gente sin razón,* a race unfit to determine its own destiny or
affairs. They granted them no sovereignty over American soil, and
no right to follow their own life styles, whether they were simple
"aborigines" or civilized beings organized into complex empires (although individual Spaniards were impressed by the exotic Mexic
civilization and preserved the only records of it that survived). All

153

indigenous cultures were considered pagan, inferior to the European in all respects, and subject to extirpation. Relations between the natives and the encroaching Europeans resolved themselves into a contest of power. The Spanish, incomparably stronger in organization, technology, and sustained willpower, struck down the Amerindian cultures where they could and seized both lands and peoples. They treated with the indigenes only when they were forced to do so by temporary or local weaknesses, and they always understood the advantages of using Amerindian pawns and allies. They tried to remake the Amerindians in the European mold, anxious to incorporate them without granting the race true equality.

The Spanish were not unique, to be sure; they set precedents that every other European invader of the Americas followed in some fashion. All Europeans believed that the Americas had to enter the European world on European terms. Nonetheless, the fact that it was Spaniards, and not English, Dutch, or Portuguese, who first burst into the advanced regions of America is historically significant. For the dominant Castilians were neither maritime nor mercantile; among Europeans, they were distinctively imperial. They did not see the New World as virgin territory, but as non-Christian kingdoms to be conquered, annexed, and consolidated within a Spanish empire. They crossed the ocean only to seize and conquer, and while they looted and destroyed like advancing Romans, they also, like Romans, remained to assimilate their conquests and plant their presence ineradicably in the land. And still again like the Romans, their conquests were not transitory; their diffusions of civilization survived the collapse of their hegemonies and world power.

If it had been the maritime powers that first chanced across Moctezuma's kingdom and the Inca empire, history might well have proceeded differently. These maritime nations would likely have operated as they did in Asia, where they erected fortified trading posts, gradually became involved in local politics, and bit by bit extended their influence and control. They would have raised forces of native soldiery and exacted tribute. They would, however, have found no successful means of incorporating overseas colonies under their constitutions, nor would they have had much interest in replacing the indigenous cults and cultures with their own. It is not inconceivable, therefore, that had the English looted Moctezuma's empire, by the twentieth century a new Mexic nation would have reemerged—headed, perhaps, by a pureblood Amerindian Prime Minister educated at Oxford, directed by a Marxist-inclined, indigenous elite, while in the teeming valleys of south-central Mexico, Nahuatl-speaking villages would have followed traditional life styles and even practiced their ancient religions (without, of course, recourse to human sacrifice, which any European rulers must have outlawed as they did suttee in India). Surrounded by relics of ancient grandeur, the Amerindian consciousness of the Americas might have been preserved.

The relics survived to be unearthed and admired, but the Amerindian consciousness did not, because the Spanish conquests, like the Roman, were true diffusions of a dominant civilization. The Spanish were the great destroyers of the Amerindians, in both body and soul, and even though millions of Amerindians survived the destruction in Central and South America, their modern descendants can only decry their peoples' fate in terms of Spanish-Catholic reference and, many of them, only in thought patterns formed by the Spanish tongue. They can no more revive what has been before than Muslim Egyptians can return to Pharaoh and Isis.

Notwithstanding the cruel and callous destruction of millions in the early years, the Spanish church-state never intended to exterminate the Indians. The determined policies were those of stifling alien cultures, not genocide. For the Spanish vision of American empire not only included the Amerindians, it needed them. From first to last, only a relative handful of Spaniards were free or willing to emigrate to the Americas, and those who came sailed as conquerors and rulers, not colonists; not only the Spanish vision, but the Spanish form of incorporation of the American empire was dependent upon subdued, exploitable Amerindians. The Spanish erected their empire not merely over the dead bodies of Amerindians, but upon their sweating backs, all the while germinating newer kingdoms within Amerindian wombs.

There was a deep dichotomy between Spanish theory and practice in America; this was inherent in the conflicting imperatives of expanding European civilization. The Crown wanted to treat the Amerindians as free subjects, not enslaved peoples, while the Church, that second arm of state, recognized them as true human beings, with souls capable of salvation. Appalled by the depopulation of the Indies, Crown and Church together, after Cortés' conquest of Mexico, determined to protect and preserve the American natives. But the Crown could not protect them against the exploitation of the conquistadores, and the Church was destroying the indigenous cultures. Spanish law and social theory presupposed that the Amerindians, converted and Hispanicized, were to be incorporated into Hispanic society as full citizens, but the very nature of the institutions created by the conquest made this impossible. The Spanish conquerors could maintain themselves only by exploiting Amerindians, and the descendants of the conquistadores quickly became a privileged elite, the conquered remaining supporting castes and classes. The Crown itself, fatally enmeshed in the dynastic wars of the Hapsburgs, found its American revenues dependent upon forced Indian labor. The desires of the conquistadores to remain masters and the fiscal needs of the Crown crystallized the socioeconomic patterns of the conquest. It was impractical, however enlightened the authority, to raise the conquered peoples above serfdom, in a system that was based on necessity, socialized by use and wont, and buttressed by Spanish racial arrogance.

In this there was nothing whatever historically unusual or surprising. What was different was the striking success of certain aspects of the assimilation. The Church took a deep, proprietary, and paternal interest in the indigenes. The Crown and Church together developed in New Spain, or Mexico, a remarkable system or process called "reducing." Conquered natives, both those entrusted as bonded serfs to the feudal *encomenderos* and those retained as vassals of the Crown, were further entrusted to the missionary and recivilizing efforts of the Spanish religious orders.

These orders—Franciscans, Dominicans, and Augustinians—had been recently disciplined and purified by the reforms of Isabella the Catholic. They were formed, in the sixteenth century, of zealous, energetic, and surprisingly humanistic friars. These men were not so much bigots, in the modern sense, as Europeans entirely certain of their own beliefs and values. They were sent, in small numbers and as hardy, courageous individuals, among the Amerindians. Within a generation, they had built convents on the sites of demolished cult centers, destroyed the old religions, and instructed millions of Amerindians in the Spanish language and rudimentary European civilization. While they ruthlessly extirpated old forms, these men also replaced them with their own. They could not have succeeded so extensively had they lacked a genuine concern for the entrusted Amerindians.

Much of the program was tailored to the recommendations of the *encomendero* turned friar, Bartolomé de Las Casas, whose brief description of the destruction of the "aborigines" in the Indies had appalled Iberian society. Las Casas argued that brutal enslavement of the indigenes killed them. He believed that the necessary labor to support the Spanish presence should be performed by imported African slaves—another deadly Spanish precedent that was widely imitated—while the Amerindians were gradually reoriented toward an economic role within the Hispanic civilization. They had to be taught the value of labor with love, careful patience, and instruction, not with the whip and branding iron. Las Casas recognized the profound culture shock that enveloped more primitive people suddenly conquered by a greater civilization, and in this he saw deeply —yet Las Casas and his followers did not see deeply enough: they believed the "reducing" could be done within a few generations.

In the broadest perspective, what the Spanish did in the early conquests of the Indies was not utterly reprehensible in world terms. Conquered and enslaved by superior power, millions of Europeans, Asians, and Africans had bowed their necks, endured, and survived. What gave the conquest of Spanish America its particular horror was the inability of the natives to survive their changed circumstances. The Amerindians refused to work under whip and gun; they ran away to die in swamps and mountains or rose in hopeless rebellion; the examples of torture and execution had no salutary effect on them. Totally demoralized, they sank into a deep apathy, failed to breed, and died out within a generation. The Spanish exterminations were cruel and careless, but carried out more in exasperation than by calculated policy.

Thus, the missionary policy was partly humanitarian, partly practical. Its purpose was to preserve the *indios* to take their appointed place as a supporting class within the American dominions. If it solidified both a spiritual and a temporal tyranny over the Amerindians, substituting new cults and masters for the old, it at least envisioned a place for Indians.

In the historical sense, the Spanish policy was immensely successful among the sedentary, civilized, and already highly organized Amerindian populations of south-central Mexico. These peoples had long been broken to incessant labor, paying tribute to native princes, and making great sacrifices in the observance of a pervasive, crushing religion. The Spanish priests restamped them in a Hispanic-Catholic mold, and the reduction was so complete that the *reducidos,* despite oppression, never rose in serious rebellion during three centuries.

The great depopulation of civilized Mexico marred this success, yet it was no part of Spanish policy. All Amerindians proved fatally susceptible to Old World diseases. Smallpox and something resembling typhus killed millions; even what were normal childhood maladies for Europeans often proved lethal to Amerindians. The indigenous population of south-central Mexico sank from possibly eleven million in 1520 to about one million by 1650, when the curve turned upward again. These deaths profoundly affected the course of the Spanish empire: they forced heavier burdens on the Amerindian survivors, who still had to support the Spanish presence, and thus further enslaved the indigenes; they caused a century of economic stagnation and depression, and turned the economy from crops to labor-saving stock-raising; and they paralyzed society, as a falling population often does. The shrinking numbers of Indians raised the proportion of *mestizos* or mixed bloods, who were less vulnerable to infection, starting the blended Spanish-Amerindian race toward its eventual domination. More important than all of this for the advance of the Spanish-American empire beyond the borders of the pre-Columbian civilization, the dearth of people halted the extension of Spanish Mexico.

If a converted, largely Hispanicized Amerindian population had enjoyed a normal growth, the older regions of New Spain would soon have sent streams of excess people northward behind the Spanish explorers. Instead, there was no one to seize and settle the northern lands protected by the Spanish flag. The Spanish had to seek out new Amerindian peoples in the north to repeat their colonization process—and their great and unsolved problem was that the precivilized tribes who inhabited the north were entirely unsuited for this role.

Although the Spanish no longer attempted to employ the feudal *encomienda,* transforming the natives into serfs under private landlords, but rather tried to reduce the *indios* through the missionary friars, what happened was very much a repetition of the destruction of the Indies. The empire advanced less upon the backs of the scattered indigenous tribes of northern Mexico than over their dead bodies.

The Spaniards seem never to have recognized the problem, at least officially. They insisted upon considering all *indios* alike, ignoring the immense relics of the Meso-American civilization that lay all about them in Mexico. They refused to concede the severe culture shock that Spanish conquest produced among true savages or barbarians. For two centuries the Spanish kept trying to reduce and incorporate wild *indios* who had never sown a seed and who were resistant to all forms of civilization, and for two centuries, under a policy of concern that cost millions, they kept killing Indians. This was partly a triumph of ideology over experience, because the idea of incorporating Amerindians never entirely died in Spanish-Catholic hearts, and partly the result of cultural bankruptcy, because the Spanish church-state was unable to come up with any other policy. The northern empire had to be peopled with reduced Amerindians—or not peopled at all. And so the European passage north beyond the lava flows became a trail of tragedy for the primitive Mexican Indians, and a doomed road of empire for Spain.

The troubles began in the Bajío, the semiarid region that lay between the cordilleras a few leagues beyond the Valley of Mexico. The Spaniards were drawn through this region by the discovery of rich silver lodes farther north, in the forbidding central bowl. All these central plateaus were inhabited by thinly scattered nomadic hunting tribes, whom the Aztecs or Mexica knew as *Chichimecs* (the Nahuatl word *chichimeca* meant "bloody meat" or "savages"). The Chichimec peoples were warlike aborigines with about the same cultural equipment as the Apaches of the North American Southwest.

The Chichimec war followed a pattern that all modern Americans would recognize. It was a classic "Western," "Indian" warfare. The Chichimecs camped in high, remote country, beyond the range of Spanish cavalry; they skulked near the roads and ridges, emerging now and then to raid and burn. They preyed continually on the parties of Europeans and their Amerindian servants going to and from the northern silver mines. The civilized Amerindians—and remember how heavily the Spanish depended upon Indian allies—

were no better at fighting Chichimecs than were the Spaniards. The gangs of impressed laborers, Tarascas and others, journeying north left their bones along the trails. The Chichimecs also raided mining camps, killing Spaniards and eating their horses and mules.

The war went on for fifty years. The Spanish tried to make peace, besides trying to conquer the Chichimecs, but peace was hard to forge with the scattered, independent tribes, and none of them wanted peace on Spanish terms, which required them to change their entire way of life. The war resolved into mutual butchery— and what was a nuisance for the Spanish was a disaster for the Indians. Hunted, harried, and massacred from time to time, always pursued, the Chichimecs at last wearied utterly of this unequal war. Their own losses were irreplaceable, while more silver seekers showed up yearly. Finally, at the close of the sixteenth century, and to the surprise of the Spanish, the Chichimecs at last gave up fighting. Survivors of the war permitted themselves to be gathered around the forts and way stations, some of which had grown into Spanish towns. The time was past when such rebels were branded and sold as slaves in Spanish Mexico; the Chichimecs were not punished. But neither did they turn into peaceful, useful agrarian subjects. Huddled miserably about the Spanish-Mexican settlements, they quickly died out in the early seventeenth century from a combination of disease, drink, and sheer despair.

Neither the Crown nor the Church learned from this experience with wild tribes, or from the fact that it appeared necessary to destroy such Amerindians to save them from savagery. Yet Spanish policy was never entirely unchanging or inflexible, and the missionary process was constantly modified. Better-organized religious orders were now sent into the wilder country of the arid north under military protection. Where single friars had walked unarmed among whole valleys of pacified southern Indians, the northern missions had to be fortified with high walls, and further protected by soldiers, who also rounded up wild *indios* for the friars and brought them back to the mission compounds if they ran away.

By the seventeenth century the dual fort-mission complex had become the normal Spanish stance beyond the borders of settled Mexico. The Crown maintained the forts, or presidios, at great expense, while the regular religious orders supplied the missions with hundreds of hard-working volunteers. The Spanish soon found that the forts and missions could not be combined, since the soldiery wreaked havoc among the Amerindian women. After a while, the soldiers erected their presidios a few miles from the convents. Such complexes sprang up across much of north-northwestern New Spain, trying to find, round up, and reduce the wild tribes that wandered the northern deserts and mountains, to save souls and also to populate the far frontier.

It was a romantic, humanitarian concept. It did not succeed, not because the Spanish failed to spend millions of pesos or invested too little effort, but because it failed to come to grips with the nature of primitive Amerindians. The theory was that the forts and missions would rapidly become self-supporting—or rather, be supported by the labors of congregated, converted Indians—but this rarely happened. The missions in fact rarely produced reduced Amerindians, whether in Chihuahua, Durango, Sonora, or Nuevo León, wherever wild tribes were found and made to undergo instruction. The system was implemented year after year at tremendous cost, and with a great deal of bitter infighting, jealousy, and controversy between the ecclesiastics and the Crown, between the military and the missionaries, and between the orders themselves.

The presidial soldiery disliked the dirty, boring, often dangerous duty, for which they were poorly paid and economically exploited by their officers, who served as commissaries. The cruelties they inflicted upon the Amerindians hindered the efforts of the friars, who constantly criticized their conduct. The military captains reported that the clerics were naïve, and by no means above reproach themselves. Such tensions were never resolved during the system's lifetime.

The mission compounds themselves were scenes of tension. Some Amerindians were lured or coerced into becoming mission Indians. The padres made promises, but what the *indio* got for protection, lodging in a barracks, and food was a demand for his incessant labors. This, and the sexual morality the friars enforced among their uncomprehending charges, quickly disillusioned most primitives with the reducing process. But if they refused to work, or ran away, they were caught and punished. Many priests, fearless, stubbornly dedicated to civilizing Indians, were also inflexible moralists and taskmasters. They came to believe the Spanish-Mexican proverb that the *indio*'s attention was best caught by the lash across his back, and many mission whipping posts were both busy and bloody. This sometimes resulted in violent rebellions.

About the middle of the seventeenth century, the Tarahumare Amerindians of Chihuahua, who had allowed the Spanish to build missions among them, revolted. The Tarahumares were then the dominant tribe across Chihuahua and Sonora, a numerous and powerful people. They burned down the missions, sometimes with the priests inside, and besieged the presidios. As in the Chichimec country farther south, the result was another classic "Indian war."

Pacification of the Tarahumares occupied the attention of several viceroys. In their deep mountains, the savages defied Spanish cavalry; the war lasted decades. The Tarahumare war finally ended in a classic Amerindian tragedy: a native girl led the Spanish horsemen to a secret stronghold, where the tribe was trapped and massacred. Some women and children were carried off as slaves, but the Tarahumares as a people were dispersed and almost exterminated. The remnants were never assimilated into Spanish-Mexican civilization. They fled into the most remote and barren regions of the northern Mexican deserts and mountains. Here, the pitiful, skulking survivors of a once-powerful tribe degenerated into the Tarahumares of the twentieth century, primitive "aborigines" slowly dying out, still stubbornly clinging to their culture and still hating all things Hispanic or civilized.

The overall success ratio of the presidial system was low. Many mission complexes failed to recruit any Amerindians. Others began auspiciously, but their populations were destroyed by disease and subsequent desertions. Also, even the less warlike peoples, such as the Coahuiltecans, showed the same alarming tendency as the fiercer, subjugated tribes to become apathetic in their enclosures and to die out within a generation. Although there were limited successes in some regions—among the Coahuiltecans for a while, and especially among the partly agrarian Pimas of the high northwest— and a few northern Mexican Amerindians were reduced and disappeared into the mass of the Spanish-Mexican, Indian-blooded population, most primitives found the missions prisons, and reacted to them like wild animals to incarceration. The Spanish experiments north of Aztec Mexico did not produce a healthy Hispanic-Amerindian population, but a trail of tragedy and extermination.

This experience should have been instructive, not only to the

Spanish authorities but to all Europeans confronting primitive Amerindians. However, the real nature of the problem was never understood, not even into the twentieth century. The Spanish never penetrated all of northern Mexico, and many small Amerindian enclaves survived in inaccessible places in Sonora, Nayarit, Durango, Chihuahua, and other regions, but the majority of the native peoples were exterminated or displaced. The Mexican Republic was still waging bloody campaigns against Apaches and Yaquis in the last quarter of the nineteenth century, suppressing the final, independent existence of these tribes. And the destruction continues, no longer carried out by black-robed priests and armored soldiers, but by secular postrevolutionary schools and the pervasive march of Mexican civilization. The cultures were incompatible, and there was and is no future for Indians, as Indians, even in Amerindian-blooded Mexico.

Thus, the Spanish conquest of the Mexican northland, the so-called *tierra despoblada* or uninhabited regions, did not at all resemble the Spanish incorporation of the civilized areas of Mexico and Peru. The process was much closer to the experience of the Anglo-Saxons in North America than has usually been seen, for all its differences in form and intent.

The Mexican north did not remain Amerindian. It was gradually peopled by colonists generated within New Spain. The leaders and the great landowners who seized the north were usually men out of Spain, while the supporting classes who settled the north—the soldiers and *rancheros* or small landholders, the cowmen or *vaqueros* who carved out cattle domains in wild country, the miners and merchants and even lawyers—were predominantly Spanish-Indian half-castes, or *mestizos*. Beginning at the Bajío just beyond the capital, the frontier of New Spain attracted vigorous *mestizos,* who were a despised caste in the Spanish cities, but who found genuine opportunity on the raw frontier. In the north many of them were accepted as Spanish or white, and pureblood Amerindians who adopted the Hispanic-Mexican culture were accredited as *mestizos.* Significantly, this Hispanic frontier population did not have an Amerindian consciousness, for the wild *indios* from first to last were enemies. Eventually, a certain dichotomy, which remains today, developed between the Hispanic-Mexican north and the heavily Amerindian-blooded south, not so much in culture as in outlook.

The north, beginning at the Bajío, became the cradle of the blended Mexican race and blended Mexican culture, the cradle of all significant Mexican social revolutions, and in a real sense, the birthplace of the truly Mexican nation.

While the foundations of a Mexican nation were being laid, the Spanish frontier advanced with glacial slowness toward the empty regions of North America. There were never enough colonists, either born in Mexico or emigrated from Spain. Except for the mining camps, which grew into towns, and the forts and missions and a few way stations, the Mexican north was a region of great cattle ranches or haciendas, for centuries thinly populated by the germinating Mexican race. The progress north was a trail of endemic Indian wars and displacements and exterminations—a pattern that later was obscured by the fact that Mexicans with native blood displaced the original inhabitants. Not until the middle of the eighteenth century was there a population growth in the Bajío to support a colonization of the far northeast. Then, large parties of colonists organized at Querétaro carried the Mexican cattle culture to the Bravo, or Rio Grande, forming struggling settlements from Laredo to the Gulf.

The lack of suitable Indians, and the delays caused by wild Indians, allowed the Hispanic empire to reach the Rio Grande only after a full two hundred years. The delay decided the fate of the Spanish empire in North America. There were always forts and outposts and missions far ahead of this settlement line of native Mexicans, but forts and flags did not forge a true empire—only a tenuous presence upon a hostile land.

Spain, through these two centuries, claimed all North America. There was nothing but Amerindians—or the dearth of them—to halt the Spanish march below the Arctic Circle. The claim could not be exploited. However, it was not one that proud Spaniards, the greatest explorers and conquerors of the modern world, were prepared to surrender easily.

They never did surrender it, in fact. Shortly, even before the Spanish empire and Spanish world power entirely collapsed, the Spanish were to be defeated in North America—not by distances, deserts, or other European peoples and powers—but by Amerindians on horseback such as Cortés and Pizarro never faced.

2

THE SPANISH
AND THE HORSE AMERINDIANS

Seeing the great barbarity of our enemies . . .
and that they were not to be frightened
and would not turn their backs,
the men were ordered to retreat.

—Report of the *Adelantado* Don Juan de Oñate
to King Philip III of Spain, 1601

THE PROVINCE OF NEW MEXICO, STRUNG OUT ALONG THE REACHES OF
the upper Rio Grande, was an anomaly on the Spanish North American frontier, like the Puebloan peoples upon whose farms and backs
the colony was based. The Spanish had leaped over a thousand
leagues of *tierra despoblada* to fasten their hold on New Mexico,
and the true Spanish-Mexican frontier never caught up with this
final, sixteenth-century conquest.

At the start of the eighteenth century, Santa Fe was still terribly
remote. The northern outpost of Monterrey, also founded at the
close of the sixteenth century, was virtually in another world, and
the viceregal capital at Mexico could have been in another universe.
Old and New Mexico were connected by vague trails, over which
communication took months at best. Just as the Puebloan culture
had been a dim reflection of the Mexic glory in the south, Spanish
New Mexico was a pale version of the culture and forms and institutions of New Spain. In one way, the Spaniards made a good life
along the upper Rio Grande, with plenty of horses and cattle and
sheep and maize and beans. Their adobes were comfortable beside
the hospitable waters, and between the mountains and the desert
Spanish arms had carved out a considerable empire, lying in the

sun. But it had become a somnolent empire, soon stultified. Two thousand Europeans and Hispanic Mexicans, ruling over a scattered barbarian population, separated from all the great currents of the eighteenth-century world, created neither a vibrant colony nor a vigorous culture. They simply put down roots and clung.

After the bloody rebellion of 1680–91 the servitude of the Puebloan Amerindians became more bearable, because the missionaries, now more pragmatic, stopped trying to erase all native culture. The authorities permitted the Puebloans to practice their ancient pagan rain dances and other customs alongside the Roman Mass, and this relaxation did much to ease the tensions among the conquered peoples. However, it also prevented the province from becoming completely Mexicanized. While in the eighteenth century much of the Amerindian population sank indistinguishably into the broad Mexican-Spanish mass, adopting the general Mexican *mestizo* culture, great numbers of Amerindians remained half-Catholic, half-pagan. The true Hispanic population grew slowly, from a few hundred in 1700, to a few thousand during the century. It would only reach about seven thousand after two hundred years.

The colony was uneconomic in governmental eyes. It produced no revenues for the Crown; rather, it provided a continual drain to support the local authorities and soldiers. Unlike the profitable, peaceful establishment in south-central New Spain, the frontier required military garrisons. No gold or silver mines were discovered to lure fresh hordes of Europeans north. A few hardy Iberian peasants were settled in the northern portions; the scattered, primitive Puebloans simply could not support a large body of conquerors. Santa Fe could not become a glittering, if parasitic, Hispanic center like Lima or the City of Mexico. It remained an adobe-brick outpost on a bleak and remote frontier.

The conquest of New Mexico was a logical extension of the Spanish dominions beyond Mexico. This seemed to give the Spaniards a firm foothold in North America, from which Spanish rule could be expanded throughout the Southwest. But this did not happen, first because the geography of the region was limiting for Spanish development beyond the area watered by the Rio Grande, second, because the determining factor was the presence of hostile, unconquerable Amerindians.

Almost from the beginning, the Spanish met great difficulties with North American Indians beyond the New Mexican pueblos. The officer Oñate explored the adjacent Great Plains beyond the Arkansas River, and he turned up an ominous portent for the future. While comparisons are difficult, it soon became evident that the Spanish faced greater problems with the Plains tribes than they had with the Chichimecs and other, similar peoples in Mexico. Oñate and many of his soldiers were experienced Indian fighters, but the armored Spanish cavalry met its match in Kansas. He found the Wichitas hostile. They attacked Oñate's camp to rescue a prisoner. Then, Oñate's party was forced to retreat from the plains after a savage battle with the neighboring Cansa or Kansas tribe.

The Plains tribes showed no superstitious fear of white men or their horses. They rejected Spanish assertions of sovereignty with showers of arrows. The warriors also fought with a personal ferocity that seemed to exceed anything the Spanish had met in the south. Their individualistic way of fighting—running to cover, striking swiftly with missiles, flowing around the Spanish flanks—was hard for the heavy, armored Spanish horsemen to counter. The shock effect of Spanish lances was dissipated against the endless ridges and prairies, while skirmishes inflicted serious casualties on the Europeans. Horses and steel eventually allowed the Spanish to cut through enemies still on foot—though Oñate soon withdrew from the Kansas-Wichita country.

The Spaniards were impressed with the fighting qualities of these *indios*. They refused to quit or surrender even when brought down or wounded to the death; they still tried to kill one last enemy. The Spanish did not then comprehend the North American conduct of warfare, which subjected captive warriors to the torture stake.

The Indians seem to have quickly smelled out Spanish treachery and understood that the Spanish did not come as friends but as conquerors. They were impressed only with European arms and horses. They were contemptuous of Spanish blandishments and the arguments of the friars, since all the nomadic, hunting peoples despised the life styles of the Puebloans. Against this culture block, the missionaries were helpless, because the Spanish process of conversion was coupled with agrarian reduction.

The priests did make valiant efforts to penetrate the wild tribes. Many ventured at various times into the wilderness, and some of these lost their lives. The soldiery, meanwhile, had little success in rounding up the Indians by force, for this was patently impossible. The Church and the authorities did not give up hope—in fact, officially, they never gave up their goal of Christianizing the savage tribes and reducing them to Spanish sovereignty—but the actual effort faltered almost at once.

In effect, the Spanish abandoned the Great Plains to the east and concentrated on New Mexico, and on the Ute and Apache bands in this region and in Colorado. The Apaches at first were not hostile. They had no reason to fear the strange white men, and Oñate, in one of the most erroneous reports in history, claimed to have subjected them. What soon happened, however, was that the Spanish, by extending rule and protection to the Puebloans, inevitably inherited the Puebloans' blood feuds with the surrounding Athapaskans. Navajos and Apaches intended to go on raiding the pueblos whether the Spanish came or went. Until the Apaches became at least limited horse Indians, their hostility and pressure was not serious. Then, mounted attacks threatened all the scattered towns, ranches, and settlements. Spanish reaction and pursuit was ineffective, since Apaches struck stealthily and retreated rapidly.

The helplessness of the Spanish to stop these bloody raids was the precipitating factor behind the great Puebloan rebellion of 1680 —though Spanish reconquest was made easier by the fact that during the Spanish absence of ten years the Athapaskans harried the agrarians unmercifully. Some villages were displaced and some peoples eliminated in New Mexico and in the trans-Pecos region east of El Paso. The peaceful, agrarian Amerindians were no match for mounted Apaches.

The Spanish reconquest of the province did little to remedy the situation. With the horse dispersal after 1680, the balance of power began to swing strongly toward the horse Amerindians. In a premechanical, preindustrial age, when battles were still decided by the hot rush of men on men, mounted warriors were the equal of Spanish cavalry in most respects. The Apaches waged the hit-and-run Amerindian style of raiding warfare; afterward, they rode back into the limitless territory surrounding the Spanish-Puebloan settlements. The nature of the Spanish economy—based on scattered towns, villages, and ranches, with grazing stock and open fields strung out along the river—made it terribly vulnerable to such guerrilla tactics. Conversely, the nomadic, predatory nature of the

Apaches geared the savages to constant marauding. Thus the Amerindians enjoyed sanctuary, while the Europeans were forced to defend their lives and property in place. And the horse gave Athapaskan warfare the thrust and dimension that Chichimec, Tarahumare, and Yaqui warfare in Mexico always lacked.

In a reversal of all previous trends, the momentum of war began to run against the Europeans. The wild bands had acquired a taste for Spanish horses and cattle, sheep and goats. They were positively drawn to raid the settlements. Soon, the Spanish became the hunted on this frontier, and now faced an Amerindian conflict on Amerindian terms. The weapons systems of the antagonists were roughly equal, and Spanish cruelty and treachery often matched the murderous joy Apaches found in raiding. However, even in decline the Spanish were superior to the surrounding indigenes in organization and sustained purpose, although they no longer wanted war; they wanted to dominate the land and rule it in peace. This produced a stalemate, a centuries-long standoff.

Only with a very large army and through a series of large-scale, sustained campaigns could the Spanish have destroyed the Apaches. The frontier could not support these, and Spain was unwilling to pay the price, especially once it was evident that such wars would produce no immediate profits. They would also have become, by necessity, wars of extermination, and the distant authorities in Madrid and Mexico City rejected such policies. The authorities, despite continual reversals, still clung to the notion of converting and incorporating the *indios*. The Church hierarchy fought powerfully against purely military measures, demanding that money spent on soldiers should instead be invested in missionary efforts. The priests wanted the soldiers to do no more than guard the missions.

Meanwhile, a few thousand Apache warriors, could they have acted in conjunction and held to the purpose, might have eradicated the Europeans entirely. Any prolonged Apache campaign could have destroyed the ranches and pueblos and subjected the towns to intolerable siege. But this, of course, was alien to the Amerindian culture and concept of war. The Athapaskans raided when necessity or the spirit-medicine moved them. Just as decisively, they lacked the stomach for the kind of losses that strategic warfare to drive out the Europeans would have demanded. The war chiefs, who were splendid tacticians, had little strategic sense. Even had some Apache leaders possessed such vision, the Apache social structure would have defeated them. In fact, it seems quite dubious that the Apaches had any desire to destroy the Spanish— the Spanish afforded them marvelous opportunities for war and glory.

Thus while a handful of rampaging Apaches or Navajos periodically kept the whole province in turmoil, bloodshed was random and sporadic. At times months or even years went by without raids. The colony suffered but survived, in a standoff between marauders and a now static outpost of civilization. New Mexicans recorded their history according to a pattern that would become common along all white frontiers in North America: there were "good" and "bad" Indian years.

This kind of stalemate between armed marauders and a civilized frontier was not unusual. It had happened many times across Eurasia. A static imperial frontier lost the initiative to warlike barbarians who were drawn to the loot and glory offered by raiding, and the frontier could not be made entirely safe. On the other hand, so long as the organization of the civilized communities remained superior and their will held, the higher culture was not in mortal danger. And the Spanish will to hold New Mexico was always sufficient to sustain the losses incurred from marauding Apaches. The Crown was determined to retain all the American territories, real or claimed. There was more vanity behind this determination than economic interest or strategic vision, particularly as Spanish power gradually declined vis-à-vis the other European nations.

New Mexico was the high-water mark of Spanish sixteenth-century expansion, and in the following century the society that supported Santa Fe sank dramatically in drive, effectiveness, and morale. However, the effect of the overall Spanish decline on the American empire can too easily be exaggerated. New Spain never felt the savage disillusionment of Castile, and Mexico lagged behind Iberia in degeneracy. What happened in the New World was not so much a Spanish decline as a Spanish failure to grow and change. All structures crystallized. Spanish administration was no better in 1700 than it had been in 1550; in fact, it was worse, because it had become more bureaucratized and stultified. Spanish forces were no better equipped or organized in the early eighteenth century than two hundred years earlier. There was certainly some loss of will—but the Spanish in America still reacted vigorously according to their interests, as they saw those interests. The reconquest of New Mexico showed this, and the efforts and sums expended on the northern frontier after 1690 were far from negligible.

Overall, the Spanish approach to its frontier has been despised too much. There is little evidence that the relative decline of Spanish world power against the rising maritime states affected New Mexico. The Spanish empire had already long reached and outrun the natural limits under which it was devised. The Spanish had explored most of the continent around them. They proceeded no farther because advance was impractical.

In this age, it would have been equally impractical, if not impossible, for any other European power to have done any more in the arid Southwest. In European terms, the region was uneconomic, and the rising Europeans were, above all, economic men. The geography of the area presented problems no northern European technology could solve. English colonists could hardly have coped with a region of erratic rainfall and little timber, totally unfitted for freehold farms. Dutch mercantilists must have avoided it. The French would have done less than the Spanish to plant a colony, since the French never believed in incorporating Amerindians. And the mounted Apaches presented Europeans with a problem that subsequent Anglo-American history showed they were not yet prepared to face.

Only the Spanish, with their peculiarly Roman dream and scheme of empire, would have made the effort, and that effort must always be judged against the fact that there was no population pressure behind the Spanish frontier, and no hope of gaining profit from it. The effort was not niggardly in terms of a preindustrial, nonmercantile society. Church and Crown spent millions of pesos throughout the eighteenth century on the Texas–New Mexico frontiers.

The stagnation of Hispanic society and state affected the frontier most seriously where defense was concerned. Here, Spanish organization not only was inadequate to meet the actual needs of the frontier, but also policy caused the frontier people to suffer needlessly.

The Spanish state was absolutist in theory and highly centralized.

All military, fiscal, civic, judicial, and religious powers had come to reside in the Crown, which appointed all officers and magistrates and controlled the patronage of the Church. This might have given great coherence to a worldwide empire, but while Spanish theory was often superb, Spanish practice tended to be disastrous. Whether a strong monarch or a degenerate's favorites manipulated the Crown, its powers were articulated through a bureaucracy that had become almost completely ossified and autonomous. The system could have been operated efficiently only by a powerful ruler and officers at all levels infused with an overriding purpose and élan. By the seventeenth century, both had disappeared from Spanish government, and the bureaucracy proved beyond Spanish powers to rationalize or control. This bureaucratic despotism could not be implemented effectively across the ocean and could not bridge the vast communications gaps between Madrid and Mexico, and New Spain and Santa Fe.

If the system had not grown venal and corrupt it could not have worked at all. The Spanish had a late Roman passion for regulation, which was often unrealistic and unreasonable. Corruption allowed men to avoid sensible laws and orders, but it also permitted them to cut through an absolutely stifling bureaucratic structure. All Spanish administration, given the absolutist, centralizing theory and the complete impossibility of rationalizing an effective Spanish bureaucracy, moved through a labyrinthine maze, beset by convoluted internal politics. Action was haphazard, sporadic, marked by incredible indecision, and even more incredible delays. Law was often splendid as enunciated by Spanish jurists, and instruction of higher authority eminently sensible, but in the bureaucratic maze, the whole effect was lost. It took years to process simple papers, and decades to implement major decisions, if they were implemented at all. The Bourbon kings began to reform the system after 1700, but it was not until the last quarter of the eighteenth century that any real change was felt.

Spanish society was also corporate, with different guilds and castes enjoying a degree of autonomy. While this added to the social stagnation, it also allowed men to resist the total despotism of the state. Without the privileges of the clergy, the military, the guilds and other craftsmen, there would have been no buffer against the naked absolutism of the Crown and its heavy-handed minions in the bureaucracy.

Spanish officers, meanwhile, possessed enormous powers, but no authority to make laws or policy. The viceroys were petty autocrats so far as the subjects in the New World were concerned, but they themselves were utterly subservient to the councils at Seville. All great officers were short-tenured and insecure, shackled with countless checks and balances, with little chance to achieve much. Logically, many officials devoted their short time in office to becoming rich. The governors at Santa Fe were political appointees with hordes of enemies and few options. It is almost incredible, against the backdrop of the system, that so many viceroys of New Spain and governors of the frontier provinces were good-humored, able men, who worked energetically, if ineffectively.

The men in Madrid rarely saw the Spanish borderlands in terms of lands and peoples living within Hispanic civilization. By the late seventeenth century, when Spain's power was challenged everywhere, Spanish governments saw American territories only in terms of French or other foreign ambitions. Distant authority had no real interest in the welfare of the frontier people, whether Spanish, *criollo, mestizo,* or Indian. They were mere pawns in a much greater game played out in European terms of reference and thinking. This orientation made it impossible for the government to solve the primary problem of New Mexico, which was never the French king's ambitions or agents in the Mississippi-Missouri drainage, but marauding Apaches.

Distant authority, in fact, rarely fully understood the Indian problem. To believe that a few bands of horse barbarians posed a danger to the Spanish flag was demeaning to the race of Pizarro and Cortés, and to the immense pride acquired in the conquests. Officialdom had the fine contempt of any civilized bureaucracy for "naked savages." The notion that Apache aborigines might outride and outsmart and outfight Spanish cavaliers was untenable. Understandably, few Spanish officers dared praise the wild *indios* too much or disillusion higher authority. The pride and reputation of every Spanish officer on the frontier were at stake, and there were times when it was better for an officer's career to let the frontier settlements suffer than to risk a futile expedition or a possible defeat. Explanations of the true situation crashed into a wall of disbelief and contempt.

Meanwhile, on the bloody ground, lessons were learned and forgotten, and had continually to be relearned as officials came and went. Some officers passed on valuable knowledge—some Spanish documents reveal that certain Spanish leaders learned everything there was to be learned by any European about fighting Apache Indians. Others wrote nothing, but demonstrated their experience by their actions. Yet the hard lessons were never collectively learned, because the Hispanic empire was unreceptive to them.

While the infrastructure of the Spanish state gave frontier governors insurmountable problems, the Spanish soldiery had become a ragged band of cavaliers. Individual soldiers, who were also considered colonists, were poorly and irregularly paid. Few maintained families, as they were supposed to do. Spanish captains were entrusted with the commissariat, and too many devoted more time to extorting money from their men than fighting *indios*. The troops were also supposed to be made up of pureblood Spaniards of good character. This was patently impossible, on the North American frontier or anywhere else in the eighteenth-century world. Presidial posts had to be filled with a poor quality of men.

The rank and file were increasingly made up of *mestizos* and Hispanicized Amerindians who were accepted as *mestizos*. Many were wife-deserters, drunkards, or fugitives from the hangman. Just as so many of the much more motivated and disciplined clergy lost their enthusiasm and grew lax from a repeated experience of futility, the garrisons became indolent on the rough frontier. The soldiery was arrogant toward settlers, priests, and Indians, who all responded in kind. Spanish borderlands seethed with undying tensions between soldiers and missionaries, *rancheros* and mission Indians, presidials and settlers.

The state of the arms and equipment of the garrisons was appalling. Uniforms rotted away and were rarely replaced. Firearms were ancient. Standard muskets were snaphances or miquelet-locks rather than the more modern flintlock guns. By the eighteenth century, there were no longer many firearms in service, since they were not regularly replaced when lost or destroyed by wear and tear. The average fort possessed fewer guns than Cortés had carried into Mexico. The standard armament of the Spanish frontier soldier had become the lance and buckler. He was a living European anachronism, and one that startled Anglo-American travelers in the early nineteenth century when they first visited New Mexico.

The few companies of this soldiery provided no effective defense against murderous, hard-riding horse Indians. Logically, the Spanish settlements might have provided self-defense forces, and, actually, all Spanish subjects were organized into local militias by law, but the quality of the militia was deliberately kept low—in fact, the forming of a militia, its possession of firearms, and its effective organization and training were discouraged when not actually forbidden. The Crown and all officialdom were highly suspicious of local forces, owing to a history filled with separatist feelings and countless regional rebellions. Then and later, officialdom in Mexico preferred to leave the frontier helpless rather than support local self-defense forces that might someday oppose authority. Such policies had tragic consequences for generations of men on the Spanish-Mexican frontiers.

Various Amerindian auxiliaries and allies were denied guns and horses by law. These regulations could not be enforced against those temporary allies who were not subject to Spanish control, and the Spanish were frequently dependent upon the services of such Indians. The native contingents that formed the greater part of all "Spanish" expeditions carried their own weapons and fought their own way, not always under firm command. They left much to be desired, especially when such contingents were composed of tamed or broken *indios* like Puebloans. But the truth was that Amerindian allies, induced by promises of loot or motivated by ancient hatreds of other Indians, won most of the famous Spanish victories. A Spanish-Amerindian force was often more effective than a hostile warband, because the Europeans provided a cutting core of steel-armed men, and Spanish officers drove the Amerindians to sustained campaigns they would not have undertaken themselves.

Spanish organization and arms, for all their glaring faults, were enough to conquer and pacify Amerindian Mexico, and to subjugate peoples such as the Puebloans. They were much less effective against the great spaces and far more formidable primitives above the Rio Bravo. The Spanish made no headway against the Apaches —and the Athapaskans, as the Comanche-Apache wars proved, were not horse Indians.

Thus, while the Spanish planted their red and gold flag high in North America, and in the year 1700 there seemed to be no human power or principality to bar their advance to the north pole, the flag was planted in shaky sand. The North American provinces were founded on two great fallacies: that Indians could not pose a serious threat to European arms, and that North American Indians could be assimilated into a Hispanic society within a few generations.

These delusions, not its internal failures and contradictions, brought the Spanish empire to its final tragedy north of the Rio Grande.

3

THE COMANCHE BARRIER

The purposes of the French enemy
seem to be to penetrate little by little inland . . .
　　　　—Report of Don Antonio de Valverde Cosina,
　　　　　　governor of New Mexico, to the viceroy of New Spain

THE SPANISH GOVERNORS OF NEW MEXICO, MOSTLY POLITICAL AP-
pointees who came and went, sometimes with honor, as often in
disgrace, never had much information about what was happening
beyond the Spanish frontier. After 1706, with vast changes and continual turmoil taking place out on the eastern plains, the Spanish
understood even less. The Spanish incursions into this hostile country were few and far between; they depended on normally unreliable information from passing *indios* under truce or at the Taos
trade fairs, and their information was almost always out of date.
Spaniards were very slow to grasp the fact that the Comanches had
seized the plains and virtually destroyed the eastern Apaches.

The Spanish had been battling raiding Apaches and Utes for
many years, and around the turn of the eighteenth century, Apache
raids from the west were particularly troubling. The western
Apaches were killing travelers and burning homes and ranches,
sometimes whole villages, with their priests and Puebloans. They
drove off thousands of horses and often carried away small children.
They caught Spaniards and Puebloans and *mestizos* and tortured
them over slow fires, or staked them out naked for the ants and
buzzards, or buried them to face a burning sun with peeled eyelids.
They raped women and girls and left them with hanging entrails to
die in agony. The people of New Mexico had come to bear the

177

Apache curse as they bore the other scourges of life—drought, poverty, and smallpox. From the Apaches they wanted only peace, and when the eastern Apaches gave it to them, the major reaction was a tired relief. The rulers seem to have known that some sort of disaster was overtaking the Apaches, but not for many years did they realize its full extent.

Warfare between the Apaches and the new "Horse People," as the Pawnees now called Comanches, was not dramatic. The Athapaskans suffered more of a slow slaughter than a sudden cataclysm, as their warriors, who preferred to fight on foot, were continually searched out and ridden down by fast-moving Comanches. Throughout the first quarter of the eighteenth century, although the Apaches were already beaten north and east of New Mexico, there were still a great many Apache bands roaming east of the Rockies—the peoples the Spanish knew as Palomas, Lemitas, Ochos, Quartelejos, and by many other names. Palomas appeared as far north as Denver in these years, and Navajos still went eastward seeking wars with the *Parikis*, whom the French named *Panis* or Pawnees. Only in the 1720s did these bands begin to vanish, and by the fourth decade of the century there were no Apaches on the plains. The Spanish in New Mexico only slowly adjusted to this fact.

They had little exact knowledge of events in what they still considered *Apachería*, and, in any case, the authorities had a different perspective from the people, who wanted only relief. In the same months that Comanches first appeared at Santa Fe demanding horses, French goods had also arrived in the New Mexican settlements. Amerindians on the frontier never worried the Spanish powers nearly as much as did the threat of European encroachments on the Hispanic domain.

The Spanish, of course, had long been aware that French trader-agents were passing across the entire midcontinent, dominating the European fur trade, everywhere making friends and influencing Indians. The French deliberately passed out guns and steel blades around cheerful, rum-soaked councils, angering the Spanish who denied the *indios* arms, and also filling men with fear as far away as Madrid.

Spanish policy on the frontier is understandable only in the light of this apprehension of the French. The authorities were intransigently set against the idea of French penetration, even of lands they had never conquered. The arrival of a Bourbon prince in the Escurial in 1700 had no effect on a great Spanish-French rivalry for the Southwest, which had already begun. In the seventeenth century, the Crown decreed the death penalty for any foreigner captured in Spanish territories—though Charles II ameliorated this policy somewhat when the authorities at Santa Fe refused to ransom purported European captives from the Navajos, and the Amerindians subsequently decapitated them. However, toward the close of the seventeenth century, Spanish power in the Gulf region was in rapid decline, as were Spanish fortunes in Europe. The Gulf was no longer a Spanish lake, and the Southwest could not remain a Spanish preserve. A great, extended rivalry and struggle now dominated all Europeans in the Southwest.

An air of unreality still hangs over this struggle for empire, since the land was then in the hands of powerful Amerindian tribes, and it remained in Amerindian hands long after the struggle had passed. It was a rivalry of dreams and claims.

During the Spanish debacle in New Mexico which began in 1680, a New Mexican renegade, Peñalosa, excited the French court with the prospect of a French southwestern empire. Peñalosa wildly exaggerated the mineral wealth of the region but also clearly pinpointed Spanish weakness. In 1684, La Salle, the greatest explorer of North America the French produced, was commissioned to sail to the mouth of the Mississippi, to build forts, and to "advance the cause of God among the Indians and make great conquests for the glory of the King, by seizures of provinces rich in silver and defended only by a few indolent and enervated Spaniards."

La Salle's navigation was fatally inaccurate, and he landed on the Texas coast, where his expedition was destroyed by a combination of unpreparedness, internal dissension, and Karankawa Indians. The Spanish governor of Coahuila marched into Texas and burned the ruins of La Salle's rotting fort on Matagorda Bay in 1689. Soon afterward, the Spanish tried to plant a mission among the Caddoans of east Texas, but this isolated post failed by 1692 and was withdrawn. The Spanish were extremely jealous of Texas, which they called the New Philippines, but they were not equipped to man a frontier a thousand miles north of their true frontier line in Mexico.

The French, therefore, continued to penetrate. By the early eighteenth century, d'Iberville had planted the French flag permanently along the upper Gulf from the mouth of the Mississippi to Mobile. They created the new province of Louisiana and were moving inland along the waterways, with the ultimate aim of connecting the Gulf territories with a French empire expanding through the midcontinent from Quebec.

Despite grandiose commissions issued by Louis XIV, the French scheme of North American empire remained mercantile. The Sieur de Cadillac, governor of Louisiana, and his principal lieutenants had little interest in advancing the cause of God—or, for that matter, of the king—among the Amerindians. They were in the pay of Crozat, the French merchant who held the trading monopoly for the Louisiana territory. The French colors waved over fortified trading posts rather than over imperial strongholds with civilizing missions. Louisiana was not a French colony, but a French trading enterprise. It became a colony of sorts only by accident a few years later, when French settlers displaced by the English in Acadia, or Nova Scotia, found refuge there.

Since the time of La Salle, the French had claimed the Mississippi-Missouri watershed, including Texas. The Spanish had reluctantly begun to recognize the Mississippi claim and a boundary between the Red and Sabine rivers. But they refuted the Texas claim. Therefore, when Cadillac sent agents up the Red to build forts, he encroached upon Spanish territory. Meanwhile, French trader-agents out of Canada were still traversing the Missouri waterways and the Great Plains to the west.

By 1713, Cadillac and his lieutenant, the Québecois Louis Juchereau de St. Denis, had destroyed any Spanish hope of planting missions among the numerous and powerful Caddoans of the east Texas Hasinai confederacy. Furthermore they supplied the Caddoans with muskets to resist the Spaniards. The French followed the same policy as they penetrated overland to the west. They supplied arms to the Wichitas far up the Red River on the Texas-Oklahoma border, and to the Pawnees along the Platte. French muskets even reached the eastern Apaches on the borders of New Mexico, wreaking havoc among the Spanish settlements, and French goods arrived as contraband in Santa Fe and Taos, causing consternation among the authorities. There is considerable evidence in the reports that the authorities were far more worried about

French smugglers than French arms agents selling guns to Indians. The latter killed colonists indirectly, but the former destroyed the exorbitant profits of the Spanish monopolists supplying the frontier.

These French activities alarmed and enraged the Spanish as much as similar French machinations in the East worried the English along the Atlantic seaboard. They were almost impossible for the Spanish to counter, because the French had seemingly discovered the magic way to win over the Amerindians. The French offered the natives what they most wanted, without offending their sovereignty or settling colonists among them.

The French explorer-trader-trapper-agents were on the whole a remarkable breed of Europeans: they had a quality of blending both into the forests of North America and into Amerindian society; they seemed to live comfortably in the wilderness among "savage" peoples; they adopted Indian ways and took Indian wives. It was perhaps surprising that so many Frenchmen "went native" so easily, since many were educated and wellborn members of the bourgeoisie and even the gentility. Some were certainly rebellious spirits, alienated from their own world, and there is little question that the most effective of them, like the Canadian St. Denis, worked far more for their personal interests than for the interests of France or the French king.

St. Denis, very early, realized that he could make greater profits on the Louisiana frontier if he could open trading relations with the Spanish. To this end, he actually worked out several schemes to induce the Spanish in Mexico to put garrisons and settlers in east Texas; he had more to do with drawing the Spanish back into the New Philippines than any Spanish cleric or imperialist. Both he and his superior, Cadillac, stood to make profits from a lucrative if illegal trade with permanent Spanish garrisons in Texas.

The French never had more than a handful of soldiers in this part of the world. Their power came entirely from the influence they held over the native Amerindians. They could go where no other Europeans, English or Spanish, dared go, making maps and seemingly strategic alliances. It appeared that they were forging a powerful French network across the entire inner continent, from the Ohio Valley to the Rockies, and from Canada to the Gulf of Mexico. There is no question that they created enormous troubles for the other European empires, both by selling guns and by instigating Amerindian resistance. From the viewpoint of other Europeans, they were directly responsible for frustrating the advance of civilization, and indirectly responsible for the torture and death of thousands of European settlers on the continent. And it is true that civilized Frenchmen, moving among the savages, often incited wars they could not control, and were present when European victims were burned.

In retrospect, these strategic activities worried the other powers unduly. The French infrastructure, except in Quebec and along the Louisiana coast, did not include powerful military forces or large contingents of colonists. French agents caused trouble, but the French "empire" rested on a loose, volatile series of alliances with primitive tribes. And despite the damage French machinations did the Spanish and New England frontiers, the French actually did far more damage to the Indians themselves.

French weapons set off the vast convulsions that racked Amerindian western America in the seventeenth century, and ironically, wherever the French set up permanent outposts among the Amerindians to carry on their trade, they destroyed almost as many friendly natives with their transmitted diseases and traded guns and rum as the other Europeans with their aggressive wars. French contacts accidentally wiped out the numerous Natchez people along the Mississippi and several other Missouri country tribes. Their protection of the Caddoan Hasinai confederacy pushed that empire toward oblivion with smallpox. Unwittingly, the French were annihilating the very peoples upon whom their continued presence in America depended. What was left was a frail structure easily blown away by a few soldiers and a few thousand advancing colonists. Except in Quebec and in parts of Louisiana, the French presence would prove ephemeral.

This, however, was little comfort to Spaniards, who had their own problems with colonization. The viceroys of New Spain were haunted by nightmares of French encroachments into a territory they had far from secured. In 1716, the Spanish established four new presidios in east Texas, along the Louisiana frontier, and drew up a comprehensive plan for proselytizing and incorporating all the Texas Amerindians. They were equally worried about the New Mexico frontier, for French trader-agents were moving freely across what would a century later be known as the Santa Fe Trail.

Spanish New Mexico was the focal point of the Southwest, the only permanent European community above the Rio Bravo. It drew the French traders the same way it drew Indian raiders. The French moved out of the Mississippi valley and made contact with the Siouan and Caddoan peoples all along the eastern fringes of the Great Plains—Osages and Pawnees and Wichitas. La Harpe and Du Tisne penetrated into the territory of the true Plains Indians, and other Frenchmen visited and mapped the locations of the Comanches. The Spanish followed French movements as closely as they could, angry and fearful at French successes among the *indios*, aware that French muskets had reached the hostile Wichitas and Apaches.

While Spanish-Catholic ideology toward Indians was inflexible, Spanish policy could be influenced by events. When Comanches began appearing in New Mexico, the authorities, already fighting Apaches and Utes, might have resisted them. Almost from the first, however, Spanish governments determined to make peace with the new horse Indians, and, if possible, to use them as a buffer against French encroachments.

The Comanches came into the Southwest without any grudges toward the New Mexicans. They did desire Spanish horses. The first contacts were Comanche attempts to trade, which the Spanish rebuffed. This was a mistake, because within a few seasons the Comanches began great, sweeping horse raids into New Mexico. So long as the Spanish had goods and animals the Comanches wanted, there had either to be peaceful contacts, or war and raiding. Although Spanish policy tended to be erratic and confused, with contradictory men running things according to contradictory orders, from 1716 through the end of the century, the broad aim of Spanish policy was to hammer out some sort of peace with the Comanches.

Thus, when the Comanches staged a great raid against Taos in 1716, Don Juan de Padellano rode with an unusually powerful punitive expedition after the marauders. This was standard, though usually ineffective, policy, but Padellano also had a second ploy in mind. He was successful in striking a Comanche camp and winning a local victory. After this impressive show of force, he released captives and broadcast that the Spanish preferred peace and trade to war. Again, in 1719, Captain Cristóbal de la Serna, who was also a settler in the province, rode against raiding Comanches, defeated a war band, and made the offer: peace and trade, or pursuit and war.

More than a century before the Anglo-Americans arrived on these plains and mountains, the Spaniards had begun to involve the Comanches in a great game that the People never fully understood. Truces were called, and Spaniards and members of several roaming bands sat down in council to negotiate. The Spanish were dealing from weakness, and their motives were clear—but not, however, to the Amerindians.

All surviving Comanche lore reveals that from first to last the People felt a deep unease in dealing with Europeans, whether Spanish, French, or Anglo-Americans. They had no fear of whites; in fact, they were rather in contempt of them. The problem for Comanches was that they could not read the white man's mind. Raised in their own conventional wisdom and sacred truths, they were bewildered by white motivations, and, above all, by European concepts totally foreign to their own mentality.

The People understood certain forms of diplomacy. Their own band councils were powerful exercises in diplomatic debate, where equals hammered out hard decisions. They understood such things

Warriors in council, with brass ceremonial pipes.
Drawing by George Catlin, c. 1836.

as truces, border arrangements, and trading relations, for the tribes and bands worked these out with each other constantly. As the spread of horses and the sign language showed, the Amerindian bands were not islands on the plains; they mixed incessant war with frequent diplomacy. But Europeans approached diplomacy differently.

The Spanish insisted upon treating with a Comanche nation and making agreements in treaty form, as Europeans carried on their relations with each other. Apparently, the band organization of the People was incomprehensible to most European minds, especially to the high leadership that came and went in the Southwest. The Spanish, and those who followed them, could not understand a folk society, or organization that did not go beyond the hunting group. All Comanches looked and talked alike; they never fought among themselves; and almost all Comanches invariably reacted to similar circumstances in the same way. To Europeans, who regularly killed each other in murders and internecine wars, who were intensely separatist individuals held together only by powerful, pervasive, imposed despotisms, the Comanches seemed to be excellently organized. The Spanish wrote ignorantly of a "Comanche nation" and the "great chief of all the Comanches" whom they sought assiduously, but could never quite find. Spanish approaches to the Comanches were therefore flawed from the start.

But while the Europeans revealed their ignorance in every report, the People knew even less concerning white men. European forms and policies made no sense to them. Obviously powerful European war chiefs in command of hundreds of armed men spoke of their own subservience to some distant chief no man ever saw, and they demanded commitments in this chief's name that no Comanche chief could make or enforce. A Comanche leader who gave his word rarely broke it, because bad faith was a breach of custom, a far more powerful deterrent than any European law. But his word had no force of law for other men; the war chief's authority to make a truce normally did not extend beyond a single war party, or the conclusion of a single war trail.

The Comanches grasped the fact that Spaniards and Frenchmen were different from one another, and enemies; this fitted into their own world. What confused them badly was the Spanish system of organization. It was impossible for a Comanche to credit the notion that the settlements in New Mexico, the communities just coming into being in south Texas, and the Hispanic establishment in distant New Spain were subject to a single authority. Comanches considered each Spanish officer his own man, and Spanish-speaking communities separated by great distances as autonomous. From the first, intelligent Comanches were made uneasy by emissaries who prated meaningless concepts and made impossible demands.

The Comanches were ignorant but not stupid, a distinction many Europeans failed to make. They could see through the hypocrisy upon which civilized forms seemed to depend. The Europeans, even when motivated by the best intentions, said one thing and did another, and, understandably, the more direct "primitives" were made wary.

If the whites were contemptuous of the simple savage, the ignorant child of nature, the *gente sin razón*, the evidence is that the Amerindians were at least consistent. They did not change, while Europeans changed continually from the stimulus of shifting power relationships or some distant politics. The ability of the European to change his mind and stance, depending upon circumstance, bewildered the Indian, yet it was a source of power, however much bad faith it demonstrated to the Amerindian. The Comanche's inability to adjust, his need to be direct and repeat what was in his heart and mind, over the long run was a weakness that helped destroy him.

Padellano's and Serna's ploys were successful in the main. The Spanish held councils with Comanches, professed their eternal friendship in the name of the king, and proffered gifts and promises of trade. The Spanish were able to make peace with the bands plaguing New Mexico, though not with all Comanches—they were never in contact or council with more than a handful. So long as the Comanches adjacent to New Mexico could get horses from the Spanish, they had no real need to make war on them. They had plenty of other enemies.

They were still pursuing Apaches in the east, driving the Lipans farther and farther south into the San Saba country. The Comanches north of New Mexico soon began a long-drawn-out war with the Colorado Utes, a bloody raiding that continued without a truce for sixty years. The bands east of New Mexico who would have been tempted to raid Spanish settlements found themselves in joyous plains warfare with the Wichita peoples along the Red River. And the Comanches were beginning to ride deep into Texas, to the Balcones Scarp, massacring scattered groups of Tonkawas and Lipans where they found them.

The Spanish-Comanche truce was uneasy and left much to be desired by the New Mexicans. The Comanches did not help the Spanish with the Apache problem, since the raiders now came from the western mountains beyond Comanche range. The peace did not end Comanche raiding, either, for individuals and whole bands were never party to the agreement. The Spanish had to learn slowly and painfully the true nature of Comanche society. And, frequently, there was little to choose between Comanche trading parleys and Comanche horse raids. Warriors rode up to Spanish settlements in great force and soon discovered that the white men had little stomach for hard bargaining. On every sweep the Comanches drove away large horse herds, on one occasion netting at least fifteen hundred. It was after 1720 that the Comanches built up the fabulous store of horseflesh that was the envy of all Plains Amerindians.

The other aim of Spanish policy, to interpose the Plains Indians as a barrier to the French traders, came closer to accomplishment. The Spanish did not achieve this, for they were never very good at winning friends among the Indians. The French themselves alienated the Comanches.

The People, like many primitives, took a narrow view of neutrality. Like most Amerindians, they accepted true neutrality—that is, they had no hostility toward complete strangers who had never harmed them and who took no part in their affairs. Trouble began when the French started doing business with separate, mutually hostile tribes.

This was a touchy course to steer among the long-standing, crystallized Amerindian hatreds. The wisest policy was for the French to try to patch up truces among all the tribes they wanted to influence before the trading began. The French understood Amerindians and generally they made excellent intermediaries, because they were trusted as neutrals, but no policy of forging peace among the tribes could be completely successful in a society as warlike as the Amerindian. Further, the French found it impossible to make concurrent contacts with all warring tribes. Before the French were really aware that the Comanches had emerged on the plains as a dominant people, they had already supplied guns and steel to Pawnees, Wichitas, and Apaches. All the Shoshone stock, punished by French-armed Crows and Blackfeet, were inclined to distrust the white men who had armed their enemies.

Having hammered out peace, as they thought, with the Comanches, the Spanish authorities hoped to repeat this success with the more distant Pawnees. The governors at Santa Fe were agitated by persistent rumors, brought back by raiding Navajos and confirmed by Comanches, that the French were building forts or permanent colonies on the Platte River. There were tales of white women in Nebraska, and men in white and scarlet coats. The Spanish believed they must end this menace, either by destroying the suspected French outposts or by making an alliance with the Pawnees.

In the summer of 1720, Santa Fe sent a well-armed and splendidly mounted expedition north through Colorado to the Kansas-Nebraska territory. There were 120 men, Spaniards and Amerindian allies, under the command of Don Pedro de Villasur, lieutenant-general of New Mexico. The party also carried along a large quantity of trade goods, to win the goodwill of the Pawnees, since its mission included either peace or war. A priest accompanied the expedition—the Spanish were always hopeful of a breakthrough to Christian conversion, and at every opportunity built chapels among the Indians.

Villasur had two experienced Spanish frontiersmen, Captains Tomás Olguín and Serna, under his command. However, he himself was a political appointee, arrogant and contemptuous of advice. He was the sort of European who made no concessions to the frontier: he carried along his personal servants and private silver plate, campaigning as a Spanish gentleman. His plan was to make contact with the Pawnees through a Pawnee slave who had been stolen as a child by the Apaches and sold to the Spanish. Completely confident of his ability to overawe Indians, Villasur blundered badly in the wilderness.

Coming at last upon a great Pawnee mound-village on the plains, the Spanish tried to open communications through the slave. First, the messenger was rebuffed because he wore European clothing; then the man discarded these and deserted, presumably taking up his old life among his people. Finally, the Spanish party went through a ridiculous charade of sending written messages, some in

French, to the Pawnees. Villasur was certain that Frenchmen were among the Pawnees, and that the Europeans would be in command. The Pawnees may or may not have been under the direction or influence of French agents, but it is certain that they were hostile to the Spanish and loyal to their French friends. The Spanish expedition made no headway. Over the protests of Serna and Olguín, Villasur camped in an exposed position surrounded by tall grass on the open prairie. Security was lax, entrusted to Amerindian auxiliaries. The Pawnees enveloped the Spanish camp during darkness, then at dawn some five hundred warriors charged in among the startled soldiers.

The horse herd was stampeded, the soldiers cut down by clouds of arrows. The musket fire was also heavy, for the Pawnees were either assisted by Frenchmen, or else had many French guns. The Spanish party was slaughtered in the grass. Villasur, Olguín, Serna, and the priest were killed, along with fifty-odd others. Most of the Amerindian allies deserted, and only fourteen Spaniards escaped the battle to make it back to Santa Fe.

For years afterward the Spanish insisted that this fight was instigated and directed by the French, and that the surprise ambush was contrary to the rules of war. In any case, the outcome was a terrible setback for the Spaniards. It was to be the last *entrada* of the plains—the Spanish never again risked such an expedition out of New Mexico.

The battle on the Platte was seemingly a great victory for the French in the Southwest, whether they directed it or not. But while Villasur's defeat and death checked the Spanish, it produced no gains for France. Like the Spanish, the Comanches now considered the French allies of the Pawnees, their enemies. And the French could not prevent their trade muskets from being used against Comanches in the continual brush wars of the Indians.

The word spread through *Comanchería* that the French were untrustworthy, and the Comanches tended to avoid them. The French were not unaware of this problem. In 1724, the governor of Louisiana sent the Sieur de Bourgemond up the Missouri and across to Kansas to negotiate with the Comanches. Bourgemond, who camped among and observed different bands of Comanches, was able to forge a truce between them and certain tribes, such as the Missouri, Osages, Iowas, and Kansas. But he did not reconcile Comanches with Pawnees and Wichitas. However, before he departed, Bourgemond promised to send traders with guns for the Comanches.

These never arrived because the French got caught up in a Sauk-Fox war to the east, which closed the Missouri to them for several years. By 1725, the French had become *personae non gratae* in Comanche country, and the plains between the Arkansas and the Cross Timbers and New Mexico were no longer safe for travelers. The French came westward along the Red and armed the Wichitas, and this again did not improve relations with the Comanches.

Ironically, the French, the greatest European penetrators of the Amerindians, continually succeeded in alienating many of the most powerful and strategically situated tribes. They became enemies of the Iroquois confederacy, the Sauk and Fox peoples, the Dakotas, and the Comanches. In each case the alienation was accidental, and it arose from French friendship or assistance to these peoples' enemies. In every instance the hostility was extremely damaging to French interests and ambitions. The alliance of the Iroquois with the English frustrated the French in the East, and that of the Dakotas and Comanches halted French expansion westward across the Great Plains. French traders could not get beyond the Platte, and the rich profits to be made in New Mexico remained beyond their grasp. For twenty years, Comanche hatred imposed an impassable barrier across the southern plains.

A trading party did get through in 1739, and was allowed to sell its goods in New Mexico. Toward the middle of the century, French agents were able to patch together a peace between the Wichitas and Comanches, and thus between the Comanches and themselves. But this came too late, and when several trading parties reached Santa Fe, they were arrested and deported by Spanish officials.

The Comanche hostility toward the French had two historic effects. First, it saved the Spanish empire in the Southwest from French penetration and from the organization of powerful Amerindian alliances directed against its frontiers. More important, it saved the Comanches themselves. There were never any permanent trading posts in Comanche country, no white visitors to sell guns and rum and demoralize the Comanche culture; there were never any squaw men in Comanche lodges, and there was no infusion of fatal European maladies. Thus the People remained strong in their aloofness, avoiding the fate of the Caddoans and the Natchez and a hundred other peoples wiped out by disease.

Impinged upon by white men on two sides, understanding and liking neither group, the Comanches grew wary in these years. The People were ignorant of the great currents passing over their world, but they were hardly fools. They saw the state of the *indios* under Spanish rule, and they also recognized the deterioration and destruction of many neighbors who were brought into the French sphere. In these years the Nermernuh adopted what was to become the historic stance of all subsequent Comanche bands. They remained proud, savage, and aloof, determined to deal with Europeans on their own terms.

Whether the stance was conscious or instinctive, the People had become a powerful barrier to all future movement across the plains.

4

TRAGEDY IN TEXAS

*. . . The memory of this event remains today
on the Taovayases frontier as a disgrace
to the Spanish race.*
　　　　—Eighteenth-century Spanish report
　　　　　on the Parilla expedition, 1759

THE SPANISH HAD EXPLORED THE VAST SPACES OF TEXAS, OR THE NEW Philippines, in the sixteenth and seventeenth centuries, and found the region lacking in wealth and charm. The climate of the central portions was salubrious and appealing, but, unfortunately, the province held neither silver nor easily conquerable *indios*. It was an extension of the Sonoran plain, suitable for reduction only through the slow, grinding process of the presidial system, and it lay far beyond the then-limits of the presidial frontier in New Spain. Sensibly, the Spanish abandoned the region above the stream the French called the River of Palms, and which they knew as the Bravo or Rio Grande.

The French seizure of Louisiana changed this attitude. That transformation is one aspect of the story of the Chevalier de St. Denis, the charming, enigmatic Québecois who commanded the French fort at Natchitoches, sold guns freely throughout the tribes, wielded enormous power and influence over the Caddoans and other Amerindians, married a Spanish officer's daughter, and engaged in great smuggling schemes with his father-in-law; who kept the governments of New Spain in fear and turmoil year after year; and who died at last rich and honored in his bed. St. Denis did more than any Spaniard to plant the Spanish flag in Texas and to bring

the Spanish into contact with the Pehnahterkuh or southern Comanches, for his fantastic career vastly accelerated the Spanish
timetable for colonizing the New Philippines.

The Spanish effort began in 1716, soon after the French erected
forts along the Red River. This was no spasmodic, reflex action,
quickly entered on and quickly abandoned, like the abortive effort
to plant a mission among the Caddoans in eastern Texas twenty-six
years earlier. The enterprise had the full backing of the Crown, and
the full attention of the viceroy of New Spain, the Marqués de
Valero. It was a great project of the Spanish church-state: the
Crown furnished soldiers and money, while the ecclesiastical
councils in Mexico supplied priests and friars. The reduction of the
New Philippines was carefully planned and organized. The Spanish
envisioned a string of presidios and mission compounds placed in a
great arc across central Texas, running from the Rio Bravo at
Laredo to the Sabine, the French-Spanish frontier. In general, the
missions would avoid the coast, which experience in Mexico had
proven to be unhealthy, and the arid plains beyond the Balcones
Scarp. The plan incorporated all the known Texas Amerindians
with whom the Spanish had some contact.

Three of the initial four missions were located in the Caddoan
country near the Sabine. Although these would be far distant from
the supporting civilization in New Spain, separated by leagues of
northern Mexican and southern Texas near-desert, strategy demanded a major effort in this region. The Caddoans of the Hasinai
confederacy were sedentary, unwarlike agrarians who had arrived
at a high degree of barbarism, comparable in many ways to that of
the Puebloans. Of all the *indios* of the New Philippines, they were
most suitable for reduction, and the most strategically placed, since
their lands overlapped the French frontier. The Spanish knew these
indios as Tejas, from the Caddoan word *teychas* or *tejas* meaning
"friend" or "ally." The fourth mission was sited at the mouth of the
Lavaca River on the Texas coast. It was to serve the Karankawas—
tall, fish-oil-smeared savages who practiced ritual cannibalism, and
whose constant mistreatment at the hands of European explorers
had made them surly toward white men. Although this mission
was supposed also to provide an outlet to the Gulf, it was soon
moved further inland, out of the fever-ridden coastal marshes.

Other mission-presidios were designated at strategic locations in the coastal bend of Texas. These, Rosario and Refugio, were in the range of both Karankawas and the southern Coahuiltecans. A mission was also sited to serve the Tancoas, or Tonkawas, a warlike people who lived on the fringes of the bison plains and whose culture was similar to that of the prehorse Comanches. Finally, in 1718, a mission was established near the headwaters of the San Antonio, about midway between the Bravo at Laredo and the east Texas settlements. This site, San Antonio de Valero, was intended as a way station and feeder point for the other projects, and it was near the camping grounds of several Coahuiltecan bands.

The effort, which was carried on for two full generations, was hardly negligible. Hundreds of Spaniards, devout priests and hard-bitten soldiery, devoted their lives to it. Millions of good silver pesos were spent on it. It failed not because of a lack of faith or effort, but because the whole Spanish premise that North American Indians could be civilized by such methods was false.

The east Texas missions never attracted the Caddoans, since they were under French influence and supplied with French firearms. The Caddoans refused to convert or serve the Spanish voluntarily, and the Spanish garrisons did not dare to use force to coerce them. The Tonkawa mission failed to interest any of that tribe. Again, the soldiers were unable and unwilling to round up these warriors by force. The Karankawa mission, Espiritú Santo, lured a few tribesmen with food and gifts. But almost immediately the Spanish transmitted measles to the converts, wreaking havoc through the entire tribe. The Karankawas fled the mission area and soon avoided all contacts; they attacked the soldiers sent after them. They retreated into the coastal swamps and islands, where they remained hostile.

In fact, the major result of the missionary effort was to exterminate the Amerindians. French and Spanish measles and smallpox together decimated the Caddoan confederacies. The peaceful Coahuiltecans in the south suffered a similar fate. Many hundreds of these Indians were coerced and congregated in the coastal bend missions and at San Antonio, which soon grew into a larger complex. Unwittingly, the friars practiced two generations of genocide. The gentle Coahuiltecans perished from disease, and from that even more frustrating phenomenon the missionaries could never understand—profound cultural demoralization. Only a handful of the Coahuiltecans survived to become lower-class Hispanic citizens.

Thus, the great effort totally failed to establish a Spanish-speaking population.

The Spanish persisted in the face of failure. A few Spanish inhabitants were settled in Texas. Tiny Spanish-Mexican communities did take root around the eastern forts, but without an infusion of Hispanicized Amerindians, and economically isolated, these could not grow. The Spanish government denied these settlements contacts with their natural trading partners, the French in Louisiana, and ruled them from New Spain. They existed, but were even more stagnant than the settlements on the New Mexican frontier.

There was a strictly limited colonial success with the complex at San Antonio, founded in the same year as the French established New Orleans. San Antonio was only some three hundred miles from the nearest outposts in New Spain, and in other respects it was a lucky location. The surrounding region rose like an oasis from the dusty, cactus-studded southern plains. There was water, good level lands, and plentiful timber and building stone. The climate was mild and dry, similar to parts of Spain. Best of all, it was within the hunting grounds of several wandering Coahuiltecan bands, but beyond the range of any powerful, dangerous Amerindian tribe.

For all these reasons, San Antonio became the only successful Spanish mission complex above the Rio Grande. The Franciscans brought related Coahuiltecan mission Indians, the easiest people to keep herded together, north from Mexico, and used these as a nucleus to attract the native bands. The early results were so encouraging that it was believed that San Antonio would fulfill the initial ten-year plan for colonizing Texas. In 1721, the viceroy of New Spain incorporated the site into the province of Coahuila and stationed a permanent garrison, the Presidio San Antonio de Béxar, and the area gradually collected about two hundred Hispanic settlers, excluding Indians. With this base, the missionary order decided that San Antonio was ready to support a larger population and requested the Crown to send out colonists. In 1731, fifty-six Canary Islanders were transported at a cost to the Crown of eighty thousand pesos. By the middle of the century, four missions had been added to the complex, which all together comprised about one thousand Amerindians.

Nonetheless, the early promise was soon blasted. Although more and more Coahuiltecans were gathered, there never was a second generation of mission Indians. The five missions fed upon the steady destruction of the remaining free-wandering Coahuiltecans. Meanwhile, although several hundred Hispanic colonists settled around San Antonio de Béxar, the settlement was as economically unviable as New Mexico. It was isolated. The settlers failed to carve out a flourishing community; like the New Mexicans, they tended to regress toward a semibarbarism. In the warm climate and fertile soil, the colonists easily raised corn and beans and cattle, but they built no schools, practiced no arts, and showed none of the manifestations of higher civilization.

The community attracted neither doctors nor lawyers, nor any professional men. There were learned men among the missionaries, but their efforts were reserved for Indians and their skills were dissipated in futile labors. The Texas frontier was illiterate and economically and socially stagnant. The same tensions among the orders, the soldiery, and civilian settlers that weakened the entire Mexican-Spanish frontier also plagued Texas. Each segment of the Hispanic society hated the other and protested every favor another received from the Crown. A handful of Coahuiltecans were reduced and sank into the general *mestizo* population. The census at the end of the century showed that only seventeen hundred people lived in San Antonio, the capital of the province of Texas, and of these fewer than four hundred were Spaniards.

By 1750, the frontier had again stagnated. The missions' original ten-year schedules had been extended again and again by an authoritarian bureaucracy that refused to admit reality, and now they were collapsing. The failure of the missions in Texas, however, was only part of the story. If there had been no other factors, the history of Spanish Texas might very well have proceeded much like that of northern Mexico—a land thinly but in the end firmly held by a scattered Spanish and *mestizo* population. The settlements in east Texas, at the coastal bend missions, and at San Antonio de Béxar were nuclei, and, if Mexico were the model, they should have diffused a Hispanic culture over a wider area. They did not, for the same reason the Hispanic culture in New Mexico remained confined to the valley of the Rio Grande. The Texas frontier settlements were soon beset and besieged by warlike, mounted Amerindians.

The Spanish in Texas were no more equipped to deal with this Indian trouble than they had been in New Mexico, although they did devote a greater military effort to the province because of French proximity. By 1720, the Crown maintained more soldiers in Texas than had been employed throughout the conquest and subjugation of the Aztec and Inca empires. The fact that these troops could not solve a growing Indian problem was extremely difficult to admit. Officialdom would not face the fact, or even the problem. The Spanish were as unrealistic in their attitude toward the presidial system as they were toward the missions. The authorities in distant Spain and Mexico expected a ragged, ill-paid, and poorly equipped soldiery, commanded by corrupt officers, to protect an extended frontier against vastly superior numbers of horse Indians. The fact was that the Spanish form of colonization could not cope with North American Indians.

THE LATE SEVENTEENTH CENTURY HAD BEEN A TIME OF MOVEMENT and bloodshed on the High Plains, and this turmoil extended into Texas during the next century. Among other tribes on the move, the Comanches triggered an era of violent displacements when they passed south of the Arkansas. The Spanish were generally ignorant of such events. Most of the reports they filed were confused and incorrect. The French agents penetrating along the Red knew more, of course, but the Frenchmen operating on the American frontier were free spirits. They seldom penned the voluminous and argumentative reports that clogged the Spanish bureaucracy, and, therefore, Southwest history has always had a largely Spanish cast.

By 1700, the Wichita peoples began drifting out of south-central Kansas toward the south and east. The movement of the Wichitas south was a violent homecoming. They probably began migrating out of Kansas about 1700 because of Comanche pressures. On their return across the Red, they came as enemies of their Hasinai kinsmen and the Osages on the east, contesters with the Comanches for the plains. After many migrations and wars, the vanguard Tawakonis and Wacos seized lands along the Brazos and Trinity rivers, deep in Texas, near the present Waco and Palestine. The Taovayas were northwest of these bands, along the Red above the Cross Timbers.

Here the French, moving up the river, made alliances and armed them with trade muskets, incurring the wrath of their Comanche enemies. The French traders quickly realized their mistake. They strove to correct it in the only way possible, by trying to reconcile the Wichitas and Comanches. As always, the French had to expend more diplomatic effort in patching truces between the tribes than in making friends themselves. Frenchmen pursued this project for years, working out of their bases among the Taovayas.

The focal point of French influence in the region was a great stronghold on the Red River that, incongruously, entered history as the "Spanish Fort." It is unclear whether the French erected this stockade as a trading post, or it was a great lodge of the Wichitas, who certainly had the capability to build such a timbered fort. Travelers did report that they had seen the French flag above its walls, and the Spanish in Texas and New Mexico and Madrid always believed the worst. Whoever it belonged to, the Spanish Fort was a center for French operations.

It was easier to convince the Wichitas to become friends of the Comanches than the other way around. However, the French finally managed this, in about 1747. The eastern Comanche bands accepted French gifts of muskets and made a truce with the Wichitas, for whom they did have respect. This was never so much an alliance as a pact of mutual toleration; the two peoples agreed to cease making war on each other, and the Taovayas were allowed limited hunting rights on the edges of the plains.

This was only a partial triumph for the French, whose great aim was to turn the Comanches solidly against the Spanish in America, and to induce them to make war on the Spanish frontier. Unlike the Wichitas, who had been Spanish foes for centuries, the Comanches now had trading rights and relationships with New Mexico. In these same years Comanches were admitted to the Taos trade fairs, and the New Mexicans pursued a desperate peace policy. The Comanches were wary of the glib-tongued French, and not inclined to join them in a general war. They were aloof and neutral where white men were concerned.

The Spanish in Texas soon changed this, by one of the great miscalculations of the century.

Through the early decades, all of the Spanish settlements in Texas were beyond the normal ranges of the two most dangerous tribes, the Apaches and the Comanches, who were driving them deeper into Texas. Mounted Comanches did pass by San Antonio soon after it was founded; they were more curious than hostile. The padres had few horses and the missions did not interest them, and the boundaries of the Comanche range were still far to the northwest, above the Edwards Plateau.

But the borders of *Apachería* had been drastically altered. Parties of Lipan Apaches were moving down the valleys of the Nueces and Guadalupe from the San Saba. These remnants of the eastern Apaches were divided into three main war bands, and collectively they could mount more than a thousand warriors. They soon sniffed out the settlements at San Antonio, which were now attracting farmers, ranchers, and a considerable horde of Coahuiltecan Indians. Almost by reflex action, the Lipans took to raiding San Antonio, as they had once raided New Mexico.

In the 1720s, Apaches killed many of the Coahuiltecans huddled about the San Antonio River, and this action undoubtedly had much to do with the early willingness of the bands to join the Spanish. In the year 1730, a large Apache war party attacked the garrison, which had not yet built its presidio, killed or wounded fifteen soldiers, and drove the rest to cover in the town. The Apaches then drove off sixty head of cattle and butchered them, like buffalo.

This affront to the power and dignity of Spain demanded a punitive expedition. The commandant, Bustillo y Cevallos, marched west of San Antonio to the San Saba, a tributary of the Colorado. Here, he surprised an Indian encampment, which may or may not have consisted of Lipans, and claimed to have killed two hundred Apaches of all ages and sexes. The Franciscan padres at San Antonio disparaged this victory as exaggerated, and also deplored the action of the soldiers.

One of the persistent patterns that ran through Spanish history on the frontier was this type of punitive expedition. While mounted to prove the power of Spain and to punish marauders, it was in reality an acceptance of the Amerindian mode of warfare. Many expeditions were also aimless. The Spaniards did not know their way through the trackless wastes, and very few commanders knew one kind of *indio* from the next. The evidence is clear that few cared about the difference; the harassed troops marched to find and kill Indians, and any they came across would serve that purpose.

Despite numerous punitive raids which did capture a few Apache women and children, the Lipans continually worried San Antonio. Horses and cattle were lost each year, and individual colonists were frequently killed in the environs. This warfare went on for twenty years.

Then, one day a party of Lipans entered the settlement boldly, asking to speak to the "brown robes," the friars. The priests accepted the parley eagerly, and barred the soldiers. Many of the Apaches spoke pidgin Spanish, and the two races could usually communicate through Amerindians the Spanish had taken and made slaves. The Lipans expressed a desire for peace. They asked to be allowed to buy back the women and children who had been captured and placed in the missions for reduction, with the priests' good services. And they also asked that a mission be located in the Lipan country, which they said was beside the San Saba.

The Franciscan fathers became excited and hopeful. No religious order had ever planted a mission among Apaches; this seemed to be a breakthrough of the first order. They petitioned their superiors in New Spain, who negotiated with the Crown. Although the frontier soldiery argued, and the bureaucracy as usual took years to act, at last a viceregal command came through: Colonel Don Diego Ortiz de Parilla was to escort five padres to the San Saba to erect a mission for the Lipans, which was to be guarded by a new fort, to be called San Luis de las Amarillas.

The new project was expected to serve several purposes. If the mission could reduce the Apaches in west-central Texas (as the province was now beginning to be called), this would remove the constant peril to the complex at San Antonio. Further, the fort, San Luis, would be a buffer pushed deeper into Indian country to serve the same purpose. Finally, persistent rumors had reached all the way to New Spain concerning silver mines in the San Saba country.

A group of Lipans meekly guided the Spanish expedition to the San Saba. The Spanish soldiers and priests, with Indian servants, began erecting a palisaded log mission, with the fort nearby. However, they saw few Apaches, and none came to settle. Lipan spokesmen explained to the *padre presidente*, Alonso Giraldo Terreros, that it was the hunting season. Later, there were new excuses to explain the absence of Lipans. The priests decided to be patient.

Across the sweep of years, it seems quite certain that the Lipan Apaches played a devious, cunning game. In this year, 1757, they had lured the Spanish far beyond the actual limits of the Lipan Apache range. The Spanish had entered *Comanchería,* country claimed and patrolled by hard-riding Pehnahterkuh bands, often visited by Nawkohnee. The Apaches, driven from this country by the Comanche enemy, obviously hoped to engage the enemies between whom they were caught in a mutually destructive war. The Lipans must have awaited the Comanche reaction with keen anticipation.

It is understandable that the Spanish made this error, for they had no knowledge of Amerindian ranges, or the Indian situation north of San Antonio. Neither in Texas nor New Mexico did the authorities then realize that the Apaches had been driven so far south. They merely knew that Apaches had been displaced from the region north and east of New Mexico.

There was never any evidence that the French played a part in this scheme, at least initially. They certainly became involved once the Spanish fort was erected on the San Saba. Within weeks or months, for news traveled fast across the apparently uninhabited country, the French on the Red River were apprised, and French agents assisted—if they did not organize—the counteraction of the northwestern Texas Indians.

In the summer of 1757, a friendly *indio* warned the Spanish in San Antonio to expect a great calamity; there was war talk beyond the frontier. Colonel Parilla took this seriously enough to alert all the Spanish in Texas. But as fall fell into winter and nothing happened, he resumed the relaxed and lazy garrison duties of the frontier.

The priests on the San Saba still had not gathered in any Apaches when the spring grass began to come up. But they were cheered by the March rains and impressed with the ephemeral loveliness of the surrounding plains. The moon grew full, rising bright over a riot of wild flowers on the prairie, and they had high hopes for success in the summer of 1758. Had they known they were near Comanche country, or known anything at all about Comanches, they would have been terrified. They were saying their evening prayers by the light of what soon all the Spaniards in Texas would know as a "Comanche moon."

The grass was thick and green, and under a full moon the Comanches could ride a hundred leagues.

One morning, the priests noted that all the Apaches in the vicinity of the fort and mission had vanished. They were startled by a screaming clamor beyond their gates. Several *indios* on horseback swooped down on the mission horse herd, which grazed between the mission and the log presidio. All the horses were lost.

Parilla, who was at the fort, threw his company on the walls. He sent a messenger to Terreros, requesting that the padres leave the separate mission and repair to the presidio. Terreros refused either to show fear or to accept the protection of the soldiers. Parilla then went personally to the mission and begged the *padre presidente* for the sake of God to seek safety in the fort, and to bring all the sacred articles with him.

Terreros answered that Indians he had never harmed would not wish him harm. Parilla then left seventeen soldiers with the priests and returned to the presidio.

As priest in charge, Padre Terreros insisted that routine be followed. The next morning, March 16, Mass was said as usual. But in the middle of the ceremony, the priests gathered in the chapel heard deep, booming yells from beyond the palisades.

The soldiers ran to the walls and cocked their miquelets. Terreros, with Padre Molina, climbed the parapet. Molina, who was to live beyond this morning, was made speechless by what he saw. Two thousand Indians, all mounted warriors, were slowly riding around the walls. Although the Spaniards did not recognize them, these warriors were Comanches and Wichitas—the first knowledge the Spanish had of the French-forged truce and alliance, which even then they did not understand.

Padre Molina at last found his tongue and told Terreros he feared for their lives. His superior, although stammering, replied that these people must be friendly. The noncommissioned officer in charge of the soldiers, who had been put under Terreros' orders, asked permission to open fire. Terreros refused to give the order. As Molina wrote later, the *padre presidente* was not calm, but seemingly hypnotized.

The savages were a breathtaking, barbaric spectacle—Plains Amerindians in the full panoply of war. The long lines of riders wore fantastic headdresses of plumes, deer antlers, and bison horns. Their faces were painted red and black—the color of death, had Molina known it. Every warrior carried a bow and lance or spear. The soldiers noticed that at least a hundred had new muskets.

One warrior rode to the mission palisade, dismounted, and boldly opened the gate. It was now too late to fire, for a horde of riders pushed inside the walls. Terreros ordered the priests to bring out gifts, and the Spanish began handing out tobacco pouches and beads with shaking hands.

The Comanche leader spoke peremptorily in the sign language. The mission priests had *indio* servants who understood these signs and translated for Terreros. The Comanches demanded that the gates of the nearby fort also be opened to them. Terreros agreed to write out such a message and let the Comanches deliver it to Colonel Parilla.

Parilla, meanwhile, had been alerted by another mission Indian. He had some horses inside the fort, and he mounted soldiers on these and ordered them to reinforce the mission. This party of soldiers rode directly into the Comanches pounding toward the fort with Terreros' message. Shots were fired; there was a brief, bloody melee. The Spaniards were shot or lanced to a man. Only one, badly wounded, was able to crawl to cover.

And back at the mission, the impatient Amerindians had begun to break down doors and loot the storerooms, without waiting for more gifts. The Europeans, priests and soldiers, gathered fearfully in a knot in the middle of the mission compound.

Then the Comanches who had ridden for the fort returned, shrieking and waving bloody scalps. The milling warriors immediately turned on the huddled Spaniards. The soldiers were filled with arrows before they could raise their muskets. A priest was stabbed by a lance; another Comanche decapitated him. Several warriors seized Terreros alive. He was probably saved from torture when a Comanche, eager with blood lust, shot him dead.

Molina ran blindly from this slaughter, and with several other survivors sought shelter in Terreros' private quarters. This proved no refuge, for the Comanches had set fire to the mission. Molina was hurt, but the fire and smoke of the burning walls drove him once again into the compound. Miraculously, the Comanches were too busy looting and mutilating to notice him in the fire and confusion. He slipped inside the mission chapel, which was made of logs too green to burn. Here he knelt, praying, until the Comanches were driven outside the mission by flames and smoke.

Molina and three others crawled to the presidio after midnight.

The Comanche horde prowled about the vicinity for three days, but the Indians did not attack the fort and soldiers. At last, after scouts reported all had gone, Parilla and Molina went back to the San Saba mission. They gave Padre Terreros and the other dead Europeans Christian burial. After that, there was nothing to be done but remain in the fort of San Luis while Parilla dispatched a messenger for assistance.

THE DESTRUCTION OF THE SAN SABA MISSION AND THE KILLING OF priests aroused consternation at San Antonio and Spanish fury in Mexico. Now, both the government and the ecclesiastics agreed that strong measures were demanded. When Comanches again appeared at San Luis in 1758, it was decided that these raiders must be taught a lesson. The provincial authorities at San Antonio planned a punitive expedition beyond any effort mounted till this time.

All the garrisons in Texas were called on to furnish troops. A large body of Indian auxiliaries was raised, mostly Coahuiltecans. Lipans appeared, offering to fight Comanches, and 134 Apaches were accepted for the force. In all, Parilla was placed in command of six hundred men, with two field guns and a large supply train. By eighteenth-century American standards, this was an enormous force, as large as the armies with which Cortés and Pizarro had conquered empires. It was considered more than enough to sweep the arrogant savages from the plains. And these were Parilla's orders: to march as far as necessary on an extended campaign, to teach the *indios* a lesson they would not forget.

The preparation took time, and required the final approval of the viceroy in distant Mexico. Parilla did not march until August 1759.

The Indian allies knew where Comanche country lay. However, Parilla was reluctant to march across the western plains; too many Spanish expeditions had met death or disaster in such arid regions. He kept to a route almost due north of San Antonio, hugging the fringes of the Great Plains. For many days the expedition encountered no Amerindians, traveling through broad, virgin country. Then Parilla's scouts reported an encampment to the north. These were Tonkawas, and Parilla certainly knew it, but he now exhibited a trait common to many frontier captains, then and later—he did not choose to distinguish between different kinds of *indios*. His army surrounded the unsuspecting Tonkawa village and attacked it. Threescore Tonkawa warriors, according to his report, were killed, and 150 women and children taken for forcible reduction. The army rested and went on.

By October 1759, Parilla was nearing the Red River, which by general agreement marked the end of the Spanish province of Texas and the beginning of "French" territory. And here, drawn up by the thousands to meet him, he suddenly found Indians.

Amerindians had blocked his path with breastworks, and horsemen swirled all around the Spanish army's flanks. There were Comanches, Wichitas, Red River Caddoans, probably Osages, and a number of other tribes. This was a coming together of several thousand warriors, and it must have been French inspired, for only the agents at the Spanish Fort could have effected such an ephemeral alliance of hostile tribes.

Parilla was no more awed than Villasur, although his Indian auxiliaries were agitated and his officers expressed concern. He gave the order to attack, as befitted a Spanish commander. The Spanish core of the army charged—but now it became clear that Parilla did not command a force of Cortes' caliber. The Lipan allies vanished; the Mexican militia hesitated; and the Coahuiltecans, never warlike even before their reduction, ran for their lives. Parilla's army suddenly melted away, and the panic was infectious. He avoided the fate of Villasur, but only by wholesale flight.

The retreat was a complete rout. The cannon were abandoned; the supply train was lost. Strangely, the enemy made no effort to pursue or destroy the Spanish host, and the Spanish suffered only minor losses, something that became very difficult to explain away when at last Parilla's bedraggled soldiers reappeared in San Antonio.

For all the lack of bloodshed, this was the greatest military catastrophe the Spanish suffered in the Americas, for it turned out to be decisive. The effects can hardly be exaggerated. Parilla's *entrada* had been a major effort, the greatest that the Spanish frontier could mount, and its humiliating failure was to weave a profound impression on both the Spanish and the Amerindian mind. The Spanish in Texas were left without resources and with badly shaken morale, whatever front they put on it. The Plains peoples, Comanches and

Wichitas, now thoroughly hostile from the Spanish incursions, had also become contemptuous of Spanish prowess and military power.

Parilla was sent in disgrace to New Spain for court-martial. In his defense, he claimed that he had been beset by six thousand armed Indians, which was surely an exaggeration, who were commanded by French officers under the French flag. Many Spanish soldiers swore that they had seen French coats and the fleur-de-lis in the *indio* van, and, whether true or not, they preferred to believe this. A French-engineered defeat was much more acceptable to Spanish pride than a humiliation at the hands of naked Indians.

In disgracing Don Diego de Parilla, the court found no evidence of French soldiers or officers along the Red River boundary. It was accepted that Frenchmen were present, and that they may have shown the flag—but defeat at the hands of a few *coureurs de bois* was as despicable as a humiliation by Amerindians. The memory, as a Spanish historian recounted, lingered bitterly on the frontier.

The ill-fated San Saba mission-fort and the Parilla expedition were the high-water marks of Spanish pride and power in Texas. Never again was a presidio authorized to be set amid warlike Indians, and never again was a serious effort proposed against the dread Comanches, whose reputation for bloodthirsty savagery now transcended that of the more familiar Apaches. Here, both in the minds and on the maps of the peoples on both sides of the Amerindian-Spanish frontier, the balance of power forever turned in Spanish Texas.

Once again, however, whatever their responsibility, the French were robbed of the opportunity to exploit the changed situation. The French no longer had any chance to take advantage of Spanish decay in the Southwest, for they themselves were being enveloped by the English in the East, and the French empire was then being demolished by English sea power all across the world. British troops and Anglo-American auxiliaries overran Quebec, extinguishing the French base in Canada; British warships dominated the approaches to America, isolating Louisiana.

Now far more apprehensive of British power than the old enmity of the French, the new Spanish king, Charles III, made an alliance with France, the so-called "Family Pact." Behind this lay less a feeling of Bourbon solidarity than a shared realization that the

Anglo-Saxons were a common danger. The English had long been as envious of the Spanish empire as the French, and they were emerging as vastly more powerful. In 1761, Spain entered the worldwide Seven Years War as an ally of France—a considerable error. It did not prevent English victory, while Spain was badly mauled, losing Florida permanently and the Philippines for a time, along with much treasure and shipping. The only compensation was the gain of the Louisiana territory, which France ceded to Spain in 1762 to prevent it from falling into English hands. The Spanish were permitted to keep this at the peace table, coming off better, perhaps, than Charles III had any right to expect.

The French empire in North America ended. Spain no longer had a European enemy on her frontiers—the English were yet behind the Appalachians. Spain had gained a vast new territory for which she had the necessary Hispanic colonists. The population of New Spain had grown; the millions in Mexico were at least twice as numerous as the Anglo-Saxons clinging to the Atlantic seaboard. In the last half of the century, these Mexican subjects were rapidly colonizing the northern reaches of New Spain, seeding lasting settlements south of the Bravo. Streams of ranchers came into the new province of Nuevo Santander, between Laredo and the Gulf, where new town sites were laid out—but no streams swept across the Rio Grande and on into the fertile regions higher in Texas, where the Spanish flag had gone centuries before. The time had passed when Spain could advance up the continent toward the Northern Lights.

The reason was no longer lack of men, but hostile *indios*. The Spanish frontier had become a disaster region. It had not advanced to the Red River and beyond to the old trading posts of the French entrepreneurs. It had stopped at Santa Fe and San Antonio. Worse, in between and around these distant outposts, the true frontier, the real line of permanent settlement, had begun to falter and retreat. The reason was swarms of horse Indians, such as the Crown could not contain and the Church could not convert.

In the borderlands, the western Apaches and eastern Lipans went on skulking and killing as before. They were always lurking on the fringes of Spanish settlements, picking off men and livestock, carrying off women and babes. They alone made the entire frontier unsafe, and hampered all development.

But a far worse terror now loomed out of the trackless plains of the north, the vast sweep of territory between Santa Fe and San Antonio. What happened was almost inevitable: *Comanchería* had reached its natural borders, impinging on the Spanish frontier, and *Comanchería*, true to its nature, was exporting war.

Two very different kinds of empires had found each other out, and though the Spanish never quite saw it in these terms, a great struggle for cultural life and death across the Southwest had begun. The nature of the two empires was such that once in close contact they could not live in peace, and only one could survive. It hardly mattered where and when the issue was provoked; bloodshed must have come in any case. The Europeans, running with the tide of arrogance and power, had carried the war, with their flag and settlements, to the Amerindians. But when the Spanish tide faltered, this could not bring peace. For the People, whose lives were a search for blood-glory and war prestige, smelled out Spanish weakness.

Gaining confidence, slowly at first but surely, Nermernuh warriors scouted and rode through the Spanish borderlands. From trading in New Mexico in the 1740s, they began to turn to raiding in Texas in the 1760s. A long terror descended over the entire frontier, because Spanish organization and institutions were totally unable to cope with war parties of long-striking, swiftly moving Comanches.

The garrisons of soldiers, never effective against Apaches, were helpless against real horse Amerindians. With devastating effectiveness the Comanches turned the lessons and tactics they had perfected on Apaches against the Spanish settlements. The bands remained high on the Texas-Oklahoma-Kansas plateaus, hundreds of leagues beyond the frontier. Here, economically secure among the vast herds of buffalo, protected by huge distances, they were invulnerable to what power the Spanish had to exert against them. Because they were mobile as few peoples in history had ever been —each warrior with his many mounts, needing no supply trains or great panoply of war—the scattered Hispanic settlements were always prey to them.

The Comanches, eternally poised for war, could strike when and where they chose. They struck deliberately, riding hundreds of leagues to do so. They mounted extended campaigns into Spanish territory. They avoided forts and concentrated soldiery, because

Warrior in winter dress, with fur hat, buckskin shirt, and buffalo robe.
Posed reservation photograph by William S. Soule, c. 1867–74.

fighting battles was not their way of war; they sought out soft places—villages and isolated dwellings in the Spanish rear. They harassed the ranches above the Rio Grande; then, unlike the Apaches, they made long rides far below the Bravo. Searching, scouting, striking, they found fabulous opportunities. The Spanish-Mexican frontier was ripe for raiding for a thousand miles.

Warriors made successful forays and drew maps in the dust for other warriors to follow under the full moon. They committed incredible stretches of terrain to memory—there were warriors who could ride confidently from the Red River to Durango. Soon, large parties of Comanches raided through Nuevo León and Nuevo Santander, through Coahuila and into Chihuahua. They scoured Sonora and Durango; some reached Jalisco. They rampaged across mountains and deserts, scattering to avoid detection, laying up by day when their dust might be seen, surrounding peaceful villages of peasants for dawn raids. They waylaid travelers, ravaged isolated ranches, destroyed whole villages along with their inhabitants. They spared neither age nor sex. They left pillars of rising smoke and circling vultures, and, as a Mexican official wrote, whole communities clothed in black and filled with tears.

All of the arid regions of northern Mexico were thinly populated, with great distances in between settlements. This was and still is largely barren country, splendid for Comanche operations. The inhabitants were sturdy but peaceable, whether Mexican or reduced Indian. They were unarmed and unorganized for defense or war, and no form of organization they knew was molded for Comanche raiding. The *vaqueros* were superb horsemen themselves, quick with rope and lance; they could fight *indios* but they could rarely find or catch them. The scattered *jacales* and haciendas could not be defended everywhere. The Comanches rode stealthily and struck, taking horses, leaving behind mutilated corpses and survivors in despair.

Pursuit, either by soldiers or assembled horsemen, was futile. The war bands merely divided into groups that took different trails. Since the Comanches took many excellent ponies on the war trail, changing from mount to mount to keep the whole string fresh, they could almost always outdistance pursuing cavalry. And while the Comanches could track Mexicans, reading everything in the dust of the trails, the Mexicans could not easily trail Indians. If the pursuers themselves split up, to follow the diverging trails, they might suddenly run into ambush. The Comanches communicated by smoke signals, and could quickly come together again.

Their war did not descend on colonial Mexico like a thunderbolt; it was the sting of a swarm of ferocious insects, who ripped and bit and tore. But the cumulative effect blighted the whole land. The raiding increased in intensity, building up through the last half of the century. Raids went unpunished, and it soon became apparent to the Comanches that they had little to fear if they avoided towns and close places where they might be trapped by superior forces. The time came when they rode boldly along the roads and through the valleys, dragging along captives openly, dividing loot beside smoldering ruins.

The People were vulnerable only in their homeland, and there they were almost as vulnerable as the Spanish, had the Spanish understood it. But the Spanish no longer had a taste for plunging into the unknown. They avoided *Comanchería*. Commanders recalled the fate of Don Diego de Parilla, and none would pursue too far. After 1759, no Spanish soldier ventured north or west of San Antonio. Thus the Comanches enjoyed privileged sanctuary, the *sine qua non* of all guerrilla warfare.

The frontier—which now in real terms had retreated far back into old Mexico—endured, with that enormous Mexican capacity for survival that sustained the villages against all the myriad horrors of existence. But all men on the northern frontier came to dread the green grass and the coming of the summer moon.

The Spanish maps, drawn in Europe, now showed the Spanish flag waving high across North America, through the far Missouri country. The true state of affairs was shown by the routes that travelers, even companies of Spanish cavalry, took when going from San Antonio to that other outpost of empire, Santa Fe. From San Antonio the route ran south to Laredo, from there across Coahuila to the borders of Durango, then through Chihuahua upward to El Paso del Norte, and thence clung to the valley of the upper Rio Grande. The northern outposts did not connect an empire—each was isolated in a hostile sea of *indios*. And where soldiers moved cautiously, ordinary men lived in perpetual fear.

To the Spanish-Mexicans, perhaps the most hideous aspect of the endemic Indian raids was the constant carrying off of captives. This was, of course, only a turnabout, for the Spanish had always seized *indio* slaves, and whenever they could, took the women and children of the Apaches and Comanches to be reduced by the friars. Captive Indian boys were often trained to be horse herders and house servants, once broken with the whip and properly instructed in Christianity. But because they represented, as they felt, a superior civilization, the Hispanic peoples fiercely resented the capture of Christians. It had always been Spanish policy to rescue or ransom captives of the Indians, and now the Comanches, who took many prisoners, found that they could profitably sell those they did not want for adoption, slaves, or sport. After extended raids far below the Rio Grande, Comanche bands appeared with their wretched captives in New Mexico, where the tenuous trading truce still held. They sold them for horses, tobacco, and other artifacts they desired.

The trading enraged most Spaniards. The Comanches, whom they regarded as savages, carried it out arrogantly and cruelly, sometimes abusing the captives in the hope of raising the Spanish price. Women were always returned raped, sometimes with child; even small children frequently bore the marks of careless torture. In 1761, the governor of New Mexico, raging at Comanche insolence during such a ransoming session, loosed his soldiers on an encampment near Santa Fe. Sixty Comanche lodges were destroyed, and the inhabitants massacred.

The Comanches may have understood this kind of reasoning, but the governor's superiors in New Spain did not. From 1759 onward, the government had adopted a policy of restraint toward Comanches, believing them to be too powerful to be handled except through patient diplomacy. The governor was disciplined for making war on "peaceful" Indians. The governmental theory was admirable, but it did fail to take true conditions into account. More than a few incidents had driven the Comanche bands to warfare against the Spanish, and it would take more than gestures of goodwill to make them stop. Comanche warriors, well aware of Spanish weaknesses, did not make truces except when it suited them with men they neither respected nor feared.

The ransoming was necessary to save Spanish-Mexican captives from death and worse. However, the government soon made a serious mistake. To prove friendship and goodwill, it authorized the distribution of gifts whenever contacts could be made with passing Comanches. In return, the Indians were expected to promise peace. The Comanches were not fooled: they took the gifts for what they were, tribute, and constantly demanded more. The Spanish failed to buy peace, at what became a considerable cost.

The authorities, then as earlier, were willing to let all the frontier communities suffer in the interest of their broader, long-range schemes. If a diplomatic plan for winning the confidence of Comanches was impractical, it was even less practical to propose the expenditures necessary for a prolonged Indian war, employing large numbers of men and much matériel on the unproductive frontier. The Indians did not interfere with what the authorities considered the true business of the American empire—providing revenues for Spain. The silver mines and great plantations of New Spain were beyond their range. For long years, then, the frontiers of New Spain were forced to endure the worst of all worlds. They were forbidden to defend themselves, while being denied adequate protection.

At bottom, there could be no right or wrong in this great struggle, though faith breaking and cruelty scarred each side, since it was not a war between men who professed the same values. It was a clash between two alien, impinging cultures. Either the semibarbarous, stultified Spanish-Mexican civilization or the ancient, primitive Amerindian culture would in the end prevail and dominate. In the vast perspective of human history, there was no other issue, because all history was and would be a record of power struggles and the success or failure of constant cultural diffusions.

The advantage no longer lay with the Hispanic civilization. The border could not be held by a culture that had become stagnant and fearful against bands of vigorous, powerful, armed Comanches. The more aggressive culture, in terms of power and dominance, had become superior. The Nermernuh, not the French or Spanish, had emerged as the true lords of the southwestern frontier.

5

FAILED EMPIRE

The country [above the Rio Grande]
should be given back to Nature and the Indians.
—Report of the inspector general,
the Marqués de Rubí

THE SPANISH GOVERNMENT REACTED SLUGGISHLY TO THE DISASTROUS
conditions on the North American frontier. The problem did not lie
with the Crown, for Charles III, eccentric but able, was the best of
the Spanish Bourbons, and he brought in ministers and officers determined to reform and revitalize the empire, to increase the revenue
and improve military defense. The fact that these officers, for the
most part capable, rational, and energetic men of the eighteenth-
century Enlightenment, accomplished very little over many years
was not their fault. The Crown and its servants presided over a
society and bureaucracy caught up in paralyzing contradictions and
sunk in deep decay. The best the Bourbons could do was to paper a
façade of modernity over this ruin. The officials Charles III sent to
America were primarily military men who sought military solutions,
but they were defeated by the deeper problems of Spanish-American
society. They were a handful of well-meaning aristocrats, authoritarian to the bone, battling against the fall of night across the Spanish empire.

In 1766, the king sent *Visitador* or Inspector General Marqués de
Rubí to investigate and evaluate conditions across the entire frontier from Louisiana to Baja California. Rubí covered seven thousand dusty miles, visiting every post and settlement, making maps,
and like the typical Bourbon official of his time, looking into every-

thing. He saw and recorded appalling conditions with utmost clarity.

Rubí quickly realized that the far-flung presidio-mission system was in a state of collapse. Apaches had destroyed the Candelario and San Lorenzo missions; the Texas presidios at San Luis on the San Saba, Orcoquisac on the Trinity, and El Cañón on the upper Nueces were in a virtual state of siege; even the garrison at San Antonio de Béxar hardly dared venture beyond the range of its guarding cannon. The soldiers were masters of the ground only within their walls. Spanish settlements were continually harassed, and the reduced Coahuiltecans at San Antonio lived in constant danger from raiding Lipans and Comanches. Under such conditions the missionary priests accomplished nothing.

Rubí also knew that the missions were failing for other reasons. The population of reduced *indios* was falling radically; many of the older missions were already deserted. The Marqués instinctively took the side of the military against the ecclesiastical arguments, but the evidence that the missions had failed in Texas was overwhelming. They were not producing a Hispanic population.

However, the inspector general was anything but impressed with the frontier system of defense. He was disgusted with the presidial soldiery, now almost wholly comprised of *mestizo* outcasts from Mexico, and the corruption of their officers, who acted as paymasters, quartermasters, and commissaries on the northern frontier. Corrupt practices kept the troops ragged, poorly mounted and equipped, and badly disciplined. Officers sold their labor to private landowners. They did little policing of the *indios*.

Rubí summed up his findings in a series of clear and scathing reports. His major conclusion was that the frontier in Texas was "imaginary": the presidios and missions did not give Spain control of the vast northern territories over the hordes of warlike Indians; and worse, they were so exposed that they afforded no protection to the "real" Spanish frontier, which still lay below the Rio Grande. Traveling through Texas, he was fully aware that the Indian problem was primary. The northern regions could never be secured until some means of controlling the wild *indios* was found.

Rubí's investigations convinced him that most of the southern and eastern Texas Indians presented no great problem. The Caddoans, Karankawas, Tonkawas, and several minor tribes were declining in numbers, and they could be controlled either by the present military force or through diplomacy. The trouble came from Wichitas, Comanches, and Apaches. Here, however, Rubí made a tremendous error; he was convinced by the conventional Spanish wisdom on the frontier that the Apaches were the greatest menace. The error was understandable. Apaches had terrorized Spanish settlements for more than a hundred years, and when the Comanches had driven them into the borderlands their depredations had intensified. The Spanish still knew very little about Comanches. They believed that the Comanche homeland lay far to the north, and undoubtedly they blamed many Comanche raids upon the Apaches.

Understanding almost nothing of Comanche organization and ethos, almost all Spanish officials believed that the Comanche trouble stemmed mainly from Spanish proximity to the eastern Apaches. Few Spaniards saw that by now Comanches were drawn to the settlements more for Spanish horses than in pursuit of Amerindian enemies, and it was an article of faith that peace could be made with the Comanches if the Spanish could somehow ally themselves with them in warfare against the Lipans.

Rubí's recommendations were almost entirely a military response to the Indian situation, as he understood it. They were clear-cut and radical:

1. The missions and forts in Texas, except La Bahía, which was beyond Comanche-Apache range and provided a strategic outlet to the Gulf, and San Antonio de Béxar should be abandoned.
2. San Antonio should be retained along with Santa Fe as a flag outpost, and strengthened by removing other Spanish settlements in Texas to its vicinity.
3. Fifteen new forts should be erected along the "real" frontier, on a general line between Laredo and the Sea of Cortés (Gulf of California) to protect New Spain against the northern Indians.
4. Alliances should be sought among the Comanches, Wichitas, and other far-northern tribes by the use of "French methods," winning the friendship of these peoples by leaving the territory and by fostering a common enmity against all Apaches.
5. A "war of extermination" should be waged against the Apaches in the borderlands, the surviving women and children to be carried off to Mexico as slaves.

These proposals were radical in three respects: they recognized the failure of the previous frontier policies and Spanish military weakness vis-à-vis the mounted Indians; they advocated the temporary abandonment of claimed territory; and, for the first time, they recommended an official policy of extermination against an Amerindian people. The Spanish were the greatest of all European destroyers of Amerindians, but they had never adopted a rationale of dispersal and extermination.

Most of what Rubí reported had been written by others earlier, but the Marqués had the ear and confidence of the king. Charles III incorporated all his recommendations into an edict called the "New Regulation of the Presidios," issued in 1772.

In Texas, the governor, the Baron de Ripperdá, closed the eastern missions that same year. The presidios on the Louisiana border were stripped and set afire. However, Ripperdá and his soldiers met unexpected difficulties with the five-hundred-odd Spanish colonists who had carved out small farms and pastures in the Texas pine forests. These settlers were at peace with the declining Caddoans, living comfortably in a fertile region, and far outside the horse Indians' range. Ripperdá understood the error of removing them to San Antonio but could not change his orders; the weeping colonists were marched away, their fields and houses burned.

At San Antonio, the resettled Spaniards found the best lands already taken, and themselves in constant danger from raiding Lipans and Comanches. As Ripperdá continually complained to higher authority, the Indian situation was bad; outlying ranches and farms were in constant peril. The transported colonists refused to remain at San Antonio, and Ripperdá finally compromised: they could not return to their old homes, but they were permitted to make a new settlement far to the east, on the Trinity. It was believed that this location, called Bucareli, might be safe, because it lay below a buffer region of Tonkawa and Wichita ranges.

For several years Bucareli thrived. But the Comanches finally smelled it out, and the Tonkawas and Wichitas further up the river proved no protection. In the spring of 1778, Comanche raiders stole some horses, and several Comanche warriors were killed in a battle with the settlers. Later that year, a large war party ran off 276 horses. The situation became so dangerous, the Bucareli priest wrote, that the men did not dare leave the settlement, even to hunt or to plant their fields.

After one year of constant fear, the Bucarelians decided not to risk another season of the spring grass and Comanche moons. They defied the distant government and returned to their old homes in the pine woods, establishing a new settlement near the old presidio of Nacogdoches. The governor accepted the *fait accompli*, the little colony survived, and its descendants still lived in east Texas two hundred years afterward. This was a happy ending, rare on the Spanish frontier. Other communities were less resourceful—and they had nowhere to go.

The simplest part of the New Regulations was the withdrawal from the north and the reestablishment of garrisons below the Rio Bravo. The parts of the strategy that called for alliances with the Texas Indians and a war against the Apaches proceeded much more slowly. The vast distances involved, the meager resources allotted, and the eternal dawdling of Spanish officialdom—which the highest officers tried to circumvent but which they could never quite escape —caused massive delays in implementing Rubí's recommendations.

For a few years "French methods" seemed to work well with the northern tribes, primarily because the Spanish could now call on the services of Frenchmen. When Louisiana fell to Spain, the great majority of officials and professional men returned to France, leaving behind a leaderless peasantry in the southern parishes and a few frontiersmen too accustomed to the wilderness ever to readjust to Europe. But a few capable agents remained, and these were enlisted by the Spanish Crown. One of these was Athanase de Mezières, son-in-law of Louis de St. Denis, who had spent thirty years on the Amerindian frontier.

Mezières was one of the best Indian agents who ever lived. Now a Spanish subject, he was appointed commandant of the Natchitoches district along the Red River in 1769. In conformity with Rubí's plan, he began to penetrate the northern Texas tribes, traveling far up the Red and Brazos Rivers into territory no Spaniard dared go. By 1771, he had forged alliances between the Spanish and all the Wichita subtribes—Tawehash, Wacos, and Tawakonis. In 1772, he recovered the cannon Parilla had lost at the Spanish Fort, sending them down the Trinity to Bucareli. By 1774, he had sat down with and convinced the council of at least one Comanche band to join the white men against the Apaches.

Mezières agreed with Rubí's concepts that the southern, coastal, and eastern inland tribes could be safely ignored; they were neither useful nor dangerous to the Spanish. Two of the Caddoan confederacies had already been wiped out by French-transmitted disease by the 1770s; the remaining one was not warlike. He concentrated on turning the Tonkawas, Wichitas, and Comanches toward a Spanish alliance, and by 1774 only the Comanches were still actively hostile.

He might possibly have eventually employed all these warlike tribes successfully against the Apaches in Texas. The Spanish were so impressed with Mezières' efforts that they transferred him to Texas as governor—but he died before taking office, and with his death all his work fell apart. He was the last of the great French Indian agents; there was no one left to carry on.

Teodoro de Croix, who became commandant general of the interior (frontier) provinces of New Spain in 1776, nevertheless proceeded with the master plan. During 1777–78 he called three great conferences, at San Antonio, Monclova in Coahuila, and at his headquarters in Chihuahua. These were war councils that all the important military and civil officials attended. De Croix put sixteen questions before each gathering, and received substantially the same answers. The conclusions of these councils summed up Spanish knowledge and thinking on the Apaches.

The Apache problem had existed on the frontier since the Spanish entered the country, and every year it grew worse. The Apaches had five thousand warriors, armed with bows, lances, and firearms. They attacked only by surprise and only when they had the advantage. There were not enough soldiers on the frontier for either offense or defense. It was imperative that the eastern Apaches be destroyed, but this campaign would require at least three thousand troops, far more than the Spanish had in New Spain.

The Comanches were enemies of the Apaches; therefore, an alliance should be made with them. With such an alliance, "by God's grace" the Apaches could be destroyed. Peace must be made with the Comanches, and the war should proceed.

From these conclusions, the commandant general drew up a plan of operations, revealing a simple but grandiose strategy. All the Spanish forces in northern New Spain, and all the soldiers and settlers and local militia that could be scraped together in New Mexico, were to advance toward the tenuous boundaries of *Apachería* from the south and west. Meanwhile, the Texas garrison, allied with a much greater force of Wichitas, Comanches, and other warlike northern Indians, was to advance to the south and west. The two forces would compress the Apaches along the Rio Grande, and the savages would be hunted down and destroyed band by band.

The plan required the element of surprise. To ensure that the *indios* would be lulled, the Spanish now sent protestations of peace and friendship to all the Apaches with whom they could make contact. De Croix was hoping to achieve the greatest Indian ambush of all time.

De Croix did not really believe that a single, three-thousand-man campaign could exterminate the Apache tribes, but he did consider the plan a master stroke that would ensure peace and "the happiness of the province." Many Apaches would be destroyed and the survivors demoralized by the tremendous show of force; they would be too fearful of Spanish power to wage more war. His vision actually leaped far beyond relief from Apache terror in Texas, New Mexico, and the northern provinces of New Spain. Removal of the Indian danger would return the "real" frontier to the Red River. The new border would still be a "war frontier" against Plains Indians, but the true Spanish boundary would run directly from Louisiana to Santa Fe, and behind this line Hispanic settlement must eventually fill the vacuum. Spain would have at last secured a gigantic North American empire.

The strategy was sound; its implementation was predicated on hopeless fantasies. The grand alliance with the northern *indios* was never consummated. Combined operations such as the Spanish conceived were impossible, given the organization of the Indians. Without the Comanches, the campaign could not be successful.

In fact, it was never begun. De Croix never found the money or men to implement the Spanish half of the plan. At every step he met bureaucratic delays and obfuscation. More important, the government never provided the money or men to mount an effective campaign against the Indians. The viceroys, in this era capable men, were more worried about the English than the Amerindians, never seeming to realize that the two problems were connected—the northern provinces would never be secure until they were safe from Amerindian attack and settled with a Spanish-speaking population. No Spanish administration believed that it was feasible to raise, equip, or pay three thousand soldiers to fight Apaches. Like so many great Spanish dreams, the pacification of Texas was never officially abandoned; it was merely allowed to fade away. Frontier communities in Texas, New Mexico, and across northern New Spain were thrown increasingly upon their own resources to deal with marauding *indios*.

In 1780, Domingo Cabello, the Texas governor, wrote from San Antonio: "There is no instant day or night when reports of barbarities and disorders do not arrive from the ranches. . . . Totally unprotected as we are, this can only result in the complete destruction and loss of this province." Sometimes a few soldiers were sent, or shifted, from place to place. They were rarely any more effective than before. A litany of protest, led by governors and commandants, swelled by colonists and priests, ascended constantly to the viceregal chair. It had no effect. The thinly populated northern provinces were unimportant economically, and they possessed no political influence or power. The best they could hope for was sympathy, and an occasional brilliant officer sent to command.

Attempts to make peace and forge an alliance with Comanches, begun in 1772, were continued over the years. The results were negligible; successes were local and proved transitory, although officials in New Mexico worked as hard for peace as had Mezieres in Texas. The Spanish suffered countless provocations, while handing out handsome presents and begging for peace when Comanches came in to ransom captives. These tactics failed.

However, a new Spanish officer, Don Juan Bautista de Anza, posted to New Mexico in 1779, probably saved the Spanish presence in that province during the years when Cabello's Texas was sinking to degradation and destruction. De Anza was a rarity among Spanish officialdom: a leader who understood the Amerindians, who saw clearly to the root of problems, and who dared to act upon his own convictions and authority. He believed that the Comanche problem could not be solved unless the Spanish first gained the Amerindians' respect.

Ordered to seek peace, he was convinced that the surest route to an understanding lay through war. He resolved to fight the horse *indios* with their own methods. In the fall of 1779, he gathered a great force of lancers and armed civilians, an army of six hundred men, including 259 Amerindian auxiliaries. Moving cautiously behind a screen of Amerindian scouts, taking devious routes, and making every effort to avoid detection, de Anza marched north onto the eastern Colorado plateau, deep in Comanche country. Here he came across the camp of a great Kuhtsoo-ehkuh war chief, known to the Spaniards as Cuerno Verde, or Green Horn.

The chief and most of the warriors were absent; they were off raiding Taos at that very time. De Anza attacked the camp and destroyed the lodges and the Comanche women and children. Then, leading his blooded force south of the Arkansas, he laid an ambush for the returning Cuerno Verde.

The battle, near the site still known as Greenhorn Peak, was a massacre of Comanches. Cuerno Verde and his close relatives were cut down; only a few warriors escaped, fleeing for their lives. The reverberations of this expedition rocked *Comanchería*, while de Anza and his army rode back to Santa Fe in triumph.

De Anza was in no sense a bloody militarist or hater of Amerindians; he used the only methods he believed would be successful against Comanches. He had no intention or hope of destroying the Nermernuh, because his own inflated estimate was that there were thirty thousand Comanches on the southern plains. His aim was to teach the raiders bitter lessons, hammer out a form of coexistence, and, eventually, turn them into friends and allies of Spain. After his first successes, however, all operations were delayed because Spain went to war with Great Britain, and de Anza was not able to campaign again until 1783.

During 1783–84, he and his lancers worked minor miracles. They rode the warpath like Amerindians, striking deep into Comanche country, surprising and killing isolated bands wherever they found them. Drawing upon the lessons learned from Serna and earlier frontiersmen, ruthlessness was mixed with tact and restraint—the Comanches were informed through released captives that they could have both peace and trade whenever they proved that they wanted them. These campaigns were of extreme significance. They showed that a European force, operating with native allies, could use the Indians' own tactics against them, and that the horse Indians deep in their own country were terribly vulnerable to sustained military operations. Evidence is clear that the surrounding Comanche bands soon grew weary of this game and acquired vast respect for de Anza. In July 1785, warriors appeared in New Mexico under a flag of truce, offering to make peace.

Now, de Anza revealed the true depth of his understanding of the Comanche situation. He refused to talk peace until *all* the bands that impinged on New Mexico had entered into the councils. He stated that there would be no peace with any Comanche until all Comanches agreed to it. He insisted that he, as the great chief of all the Spaniards, would meet only with a Comanche chief who was empowered to speak for all the Comanches. Unable to use European diplomacy successfully against a fragmented tribe, de Anza hit upon nothing less than a scheme to create a tribal government among the Comanches.

How much the Comanches understood of this, or what crises it caused, can only be surmised. It is known that virtually all the Yampahreekuh and Kuhtsoo-ehkuh Comanches sent representatives to a great council held at Taos. Here the assembled chiefs chose a leader, called Cuera (Leather Jacket), or sometimes Cota de Malla (Coat of Mail), to be their paramount spokesman. This was done only over violent protest among the Comanches themselves; in one altercation a chief known as Toro Blanco (White Bull) opposed Cuera and was killed.

There is little evidence that the Comanche motivation was fear of being destroyed. De Anza carefully refrained from threatening their hunting grounds, or trying to declare sovereignty over them. He simply offered the bands a choice between attractive trading terms and the bloody lance in war. These were terms all Comanches could understand and accept without humiliation. De Anza had won respect, impressing the Comanches as no white man had done in a hundred years. He behaved in ways they understood: with great dignity and confidence and with murderous ability in the field, yet with tact and intelligence, treating Comanche warriors as equals in council. De Anza was wrapped in impervious medicine, too powerful to fight. The Spanish accounts reported that six hundred, separate Comanche *rancherías* or "hordes" came to the Taos council.

De Anza welcomed Cuera with impressive ceremony, presenting him with a sword and banner as symbols of Spanish recognition of his dignity. The Spanish had begun the practice, which the British copied, of giving Amerindian chiefs medals and uniforms, titles and insignia, empty honors that pretended an Amerindian equality, and often pleased the "primitive" mind. But at Taos, solemn vows were also exchanged. The Comanches promised to war no more on New Mexico, and de Anza adroitly included the Utes and Indians under Spanish protection in the pledge. They agreed to assist the Spanish against the hated Apaches. In return, de Anza swore that the trade fairs of New Mexico would be open to the bands, and that they could buy goods and horses for meat, tallow, and hides.

These were promises that the Comanches did not make lightly in council, and that they would honor without hypocrisy. Thus Juan de Anza, who was worth a regiment to Spain on the frontier, won lasting peace from the Comanche danger for New Mexico. The peace became part of Comanche custom, a conventional wisdom that even the Kwerhar-rehnuh, who were not party to it, respected and maintained.

The 1786 truce was the beginning of a special relationship between the Spanish-Mexicans of New Mexico and the adjacent Comanche bands. The Comanches could now ride openly into Spanish settlements, dickering for horses; New Mexican traders could move safely on the Comanche plains. These traders and ranchers were the only civilized men who were allowed in Comanche camps with their goods and wagons, and they became known as Comancheros.

Nineteenth-century Anglo-Americans did not fully understand the role of the Comancheros, because they did not understand the nature of this peace. It was a treaty of coexistence between the bands and New Mexico. It did *not* include all Spaniards (the then-universal Amerindian term for white men) or extend to all Spanish settlements. Comanches did not grasp the concept that all these Europeans formed one nation, and it is improbable that they would have accepted a peace on such a basis. Their deal was with de Anza's people, no other Spaniards. Under its terms (which de Anza understood and had to accept), Texas and the provinces of northern New Spain were still fair game for the Kuhtsoo-ehkuh and Yampahreekuh. The Comancheros traded firearms and iron that was used against their fellow Mexicans to the Comanches, and continued to ransom Mexican captives. Anglo-American accounts invariably described the Comancheros as "renegades" and "half-breeds": the first from a lack of understanding that in the absence of protection by the Crown the frontier communities now protected themselves in any way they could; the second epithet one that confused later Americans by implying that Comancheros had Comanche blood. It meant nothing of the kind. In the eighteenth and nineteenth centuries, all but a handful of the Hispanic population of New Mexico was composed of half-breeds—people with mixed Amerindian and Spanish blood—by contemporary European or Anglo-American standards.

The peace saved New Mexico, still punished severely by the Apaches, from the devastation that was wreaked on Texas and northern Mexico. In the first flush of success, de Anza believed that the ramifications would be much greater than they proved. Comanches joined him in several expeditions against the Apaches, and the Spanish hoped that under leaders whose loyalty they bought, the Comanches would eventually become subjects of Spain. Ugarte, who took de Croix's post as commandant general of the interior provinces, wanted to appoint a Comanche "lieutenant general," with the king's commission and an annual salary of one hundred pesos, to serve as Spanish liaison with all the bands. The mission formula of reducing having failed, the king's soldiers hoped to introduce a military hierarchy to Europeanize the savages. Ugarte, however, did not fully trust *indios*. When some of the allied Comanches indicated that they desired to learn Spanish and asked for teachers, Ugarte argued that only children, whose minds could be influenced early, should be taught the language; warriors might learn too much about the Europeans.

Still, de Anza tried one ambitious project. In council after council, he encouraged the Comanches to "take the white man's road"— the closest that the sign language could come to expressing the idea that the Amerindians should become farmers. One band, called *Jupes* (*Hoo-payss*) agreed to try. The government at Santa Fe invested seven hundred dollars (then the equivalent of at least twenty-five thousand) in constructing a village for the Jupes near present Pueblo, Colorado.

The first result was predictable: unrest among the jealous Utes who had received no favors from the Crown. The second result was equally inevitable, though more mystifying to the Spanish mind. Several of the Jupes died of disease, and the whole band immediately abandoned the village site as taboo, returning to their old life pursuing the buffalo. Not even the miracle-worker Juan de Anza could reorder the Comanches' life styles or change their most ancient customs and beliefs.

The truce between the Comanches and the Utes was eventually broken, but the peace with New Mexico held. The Comancheros moved among the wild bands for a hundred years, and in the last years of the Spanish rule in America, Comanches from the Texas plains still occasionally joined with Spanish lancers in forays against Apaches along the upper Rio Grande. Whatever white men thought of him, the Comanches honored de Anza's memory and remained friendly with his "people."

NO PEACE HAD BEEN MADE WITH THE PEHNAHTERKUH, THE LARGEST of all the Comanche bands. Their southern range did not impinge upon New Mexico, but yearly it was extended farther south, toward San Antonio de Béxar and the lower Rio Grande. In the 1750s, the Pehnahterkuh, though they had appeared at San Antonio, still hunted north and west of the San Saba; but in later years, war parties coursed around San Antonio and beyond. In 1771, Comanches drove the new community of Laredo from the north bank of the Rio Grande. The town was rebuilt, as Nuevo Laredo, on the southern side, where the river afforded some protection. But here, as at San Antonio and all the localities scattered across the far northern provinces of Mexico, the Spanish-Mexican was a ranching culture, dependent upon outlying stock ranges and farms. Raiding Comanches could not easily capture the adobe towns—though they rode through them boldly at times—but they made life intolerable for the ranchers. In the familiar pattern, war parties avoided contact with armed *vaqueros*, unless they had an overwhelming advantage, but they attacked cattle and horse and goat ranches when the men were away, burning houses and *jacales*, raping and eviscerating women, murdering infants and carrying children away. The Comanche terror did not burst over this far-flung frontier in a day, a season, or even a decade. Because it was sporadic, some hundreds of isolated communities were permitted to survive from year to year; yet it was a slowly growing horror that steadily grew worse.

There were no officers in the eastern interior provinces with de Anza's energy or genius. Although the garrison at San Antonio was steadily increased in the 1770s—it eventually stood at eight full companies of soldiers—no effective military measures were ever taken against the Comanches. The winter camps of the Pehnah-terkuh still lay far north and west of San Antonio and the Rio Grande, in country no Spanish commander dared penetrate. None of the lessons learned in New Mexico seem to have been trans-mitted to the soldiery in Texas.

Domingo Cabello, the Texas governor, dispensed large quantities of trade goods—tobacco, cloth, vermilion, beads, and tools—to any Comanche or Lipan chief who would ride in to get them. War chiefs were plied with medals, uniforms, and staffs. These payoffs put a new burden on the impoverished frontier, for by the 1780s they cost five thousand dollars a year—a huge sum in that place and time. But the goods and gimmicks were to no avail. Some chiefs agreed to local truces that lasted a few years. But the fragmented Nermernuh were riding in hundreds of minor war bands, and no chief willing to make peace could control them. The Comanches made war when they felt like it or found the proper portents, and their medicine was almost always good. Some bands, who in all honesty never understood the Spanish political structure, accepted payment at San Antonio, then rode on to pillage at Laredo. The peace treaties that were sometimes jubilantly reported had no last-ing results.

What the Comanches did not destroy, the Lipans came out of the western mountains and river borderlands to scout and steal. Spanish records and reports, almost always inaccurate and confused about the true state of Amerindian affairs, still blamed far too much of the Indian terror on the Lipan Apaches. Lipan strength was declining year by year, since the Lipans' own ranges were being devastated by Comanches. They were a perennial nuisance, but not a primary threat to Spanish-American existence.

Nor were the other Texas Amerindians prospering. Rubí's and Mezières' predictions proved true. The Caddoan Hasinai, a century earlier the most numerous of all the Texas peoples, like the more primitive coastal Karankawas were fighting a losing battle against extinction from the endemic European diseases loosed among them. The Caddoans were dwindling rapidly, while the Karankawas, pushed into the Gulf marshes and islands, had already passed the biological point of no return. The Tonkawas, whom earlier mission-aries had described as a great and warlike nation, were hardly in better shape.

The Spanish merely surveyed these minor Amerindian peoples, constantly trying to recruit allies for various military expeditions, wooing amenable chiefs, assassinating suspected troublemakers.

Ironically the Spanish finally achieved their ambition of destroying the eastern Apaches. In 1790, Brigadier General Ugalde, commandant of the eastern interior provinces, seemed to achieve what de Anza had succeeded in doing in New Mexico. Ugalde put together a powerful horde of Wichitas and Comanches, who had entered Spanish territory for the express purpose of joining the Spaniards against the Apaches. Riding with this force, Ugalde's lancers trapped the major band of Lipans in a canyon on the Nueces west of San Antonio. Several hundred Apaches were slaughtered in a cul-de-sac, which afterward became known as the Cañón de Ugalde, near the later town that Anglo-Americans transliterated as Uvalde. The Apaches were never afterward a serious menace, though perhaps a thousand males survived throughout all the borderlands.

Spanish euphoria was short-lived, though enough premature reports of the end of the Indian menace were made to confuse future historians. The truce with the Wichitas and Comanches was ephemeral. Comanches still marauded, and at last Spanish authorities realized the true nature of the problem—distant raiders from *Comanchería* rather than *indios* from the borderlands.

In 1792, Manuel Muñoz, the new governor of Texas, reported bitterly that supposed peace treaties and the lavish disbursement of gifts had had no effect. That year was terrible for the entire border; more raids, burnings, killings, and torturings were reported than ever before. A crescendo of complaints rose to the viceregal government. The viceroy, the Conde de Revillagigedo, sent large contingents of troops to Texas. Of the four thousand Spanish-speaking people in that province, one thousand were now soldiers.

Revillagigedo, appointed by Charles III's ministers after the king's death in 1788, was the last capable viceroy of New Spain, and Ugalde was Spain's last great frontier general. Charles IV turned the Spanish government over to his wife's lover, the twenty-five-year-old guardsman Manuel Godoy. The administration of the empire sank into bottomless decadence and corruption; under the feeble Charles IV, government reflected society. Many of the good officers in America were recalled—many, as so often happened in the twisted morass of Spanish politics, in disgrace. The troops at

San Antonio, ordered to form powerful mobile units and pursue the Indians like de Anza and Ugalde, spent their time fortifying the presidio. When war broke out in Europe in 1793, they too were recalled.

The missions in Texas either fell into disrepair or were officially secularized. The principal mission at San Antonio contained only forty-three reduced Amerindians in 1793, when it was taken over by the military, and no other mission had any more. The total Texas Hispanic population fell to less than three thousand, including garrisons and converted *indios*.

After 1793, Spain no longer possessed an administration in New Spain with the will or energy to maintain the North American frontier. Under Charles III, Spain had briefly behaved as a great power; under Charles IV, she was becoming a pawn of other powers. In 1800, Napoleon wrested the recession of the Louisiana territory from Spain, but with a proviso that it would never be ceded to the Anglo-Saxons. Napoleon betrayed this trust in 1803, by selling the entire region to the United States. This once again placed a vigorous, expanding power on the borders of Spain's unpopulated northern territories, while doubling the size of the United States at the expense of Spain's failing empire.

Disaster continued to rain on Spain. In 1808, Napoleon seized the entire peninsula and drove the Bourbon dynasty from the throne. Its American empire never recovered from this shock, which created a severe constitutional and psychological crisis throughout the Hispanic-American world. While Spain was caught up in disorganized guerrilla warfare against the French invaders, Mexico erupted in social and anticolonial revolution. Hidalgo began his revolt in 1810, and his insurgency spread like wildfire across the northern provinces and territories of New Spain, which were liberal in politics and anti-Spanish in sentiment. The northern provinces were too weak and thinly populated to play more than a symbolic role in the uprising, but this still drew large Spanish forces back toward the north.

Also, North American adventurers, the peculiar breed that became known as "filibusters," joined Mexican and Spanish republicans in armed ventures to seize Texas. One such expedition seized San Antonio in 1813 after defeating a Spanish army. Joaquín de Arredondo, commandant of the eastern interior provinces, smashed this raid on the Medina, deporting the North American survivors back across the Sabine. These campaigns further weakened the frontier. Arredondo executed three hundred republicans at San Antonio; the royalist terror set the population back to the level of twenty years before. There was another filibustering expedition out of Louisiana a few years later. However, the Spanish secured a firm commitment to the Sabine boundary in the treaty that ceded Florida to the United States in 1819. Spanish authorities were not so sanguine as to believe that this treaty would solve the problem, because the rich lands of eastern Texas were empty and inviting to the hordes of North Americans pushing westward in these years.

Meanwhile, though the royalist authorities held firm control of the Hispanic communities in the frontier provinces by force, these communities were thrown upon their own resources to combat the Amerindians. From 1792 onward, the Amerindian peril grew steadily worse. All of the eastern interior provinces were within Comanche raiding range, and the bands now exercised their form of warfare upon an enemy totally unable to cope with it. Texas, Nuevo León, Nuevo Santander, Coahuila, Chihuahua, and even distant Durango suffered yearly from Comanche terror. Every report from the north indicated that the Comanches steadily grew more hostile and contemptuous. They ripped and shredded the entire frontier at will.

The extreme terror and helplessness of the far-flung Hispanic communities reflected the fact that this culture had no traditions of local defense. The population was not legally permitted firearms, and in the revolutionary atmosphere that pervaded New Spain after 1810, the authorities were even more hostile to local self-defense forces except under direct control of Spanish commanders. The towns from San Antonio to Laredo and, all across the Mexican provinces, the isolated villages and ranches were as vulnerable to raiding Comanches as the Romans of the late empire had been to small bands of ravaging barbarians after the departure of the legions.

The universal reaction of these communities was a frantic effort to buy peace at almost any price. Comanches were offered presents whenever they appeared, in desperate attempts to ransom individual towns and ranches. This was no longer an officially sponsored program inspired by the hope of forging treaties and alliances with the northern *indios*. It was the payment of local tribute to avoid massacre.

Ransom was sometimes successful, sometimes not, depending on the war parties' whims. Peace held universally only in New Mexico, where, as late as 1810, some Comanches joined the Spanish in fighting the western Apaches. New Mexico remained at peace primarily because an ironic pattern had evolved: the bands adjacent to that province raided through Texas into Mexico, and found the Comancheros a convenient market for plunder and captives. Some New Mexicans thus profited from the agony of the other regions.

In these years, large stretches of the northern territories were becoming desolate. Settlement regressed to what it had been many years earlier. Missions and villages were reduced to smoking ruins, or abandoned by their terrified inhabitants. Travelers dared not take the roads in the Comanche season, for the horse Indians now rode boldly through the entire region, often driving their stolen horses and unfortunate captives away by broad daylight. Punitive expeditions were no longer mounted against them by an army that was primarily concerned with holding down the civilized population for the Crown.

Under these circumstances, the royalist authorities were more amenable to a colonization scheme proposed by Moses Austin at San Antonio in 1820 than they would have been in earlier years. Austin had been a good Spanish subject in the Missouri country before that territory was ceded to France, and then to the United States. Many North Americans had entered Louisiana after 1763, and like the French population, most of these immigrants had proven loyal, useful citizens. Austin, vouched for by the Baron de Bastrop, a loyal royalist, petitioned to be allowed to settle North American colonists in Texas. In addition to Austin's ideas for economic development, Bastrop advanced three telling arguments to Commandant General Arredondo and the provincial council at Monterrey in favor of the scheme. These were that the Indian peril would never be ended until a civilized population was firmly settled between San Antonio and the Sabine; that no Hispanic colonists had succeeded in three hundred years; and that the North Americans might prove as useful to the Spanish as the Louisiana French had been in former years.

Arredondo—a ruthless general who was extremely powerful because of his successes against insurgents and filibusters and who reported directly to the Crown—was impressed by these considerations. His viewpoint was primarily military. He believed that a

North American colony would create a buffer between the Comanches and the borderlands and, if nothing else, at least relieve the pressure by diluting it. He also visualized that if the colony were restricted to the "right sort" of settlers—slave owners with substantial land grants—it might provide a European population in Texas that would uphold the Spanish Crown not only against wild *indios*, but from future filibustering North Americans and the predominantly liberal and *mestizo* inhabitants of the Mexican frontier, whom the Spanish rulers no longer trusted. Thus Arredondo grasped at a new solution to the old problem and pressured the civil authorities to grant Moses Austin's commission. It was approved early in 1821.

The opening of Texas to Anglo-Saxon colonists was Spain's last legacy to the southwestern frontier. A few weeks later, a military coup turned the viceregal armies against the Crown and toward Mexican independence. The consequent Mexican empire, and its rapidly succeeding republic, confirmed the Austin grant, carried on by Moses' son Stephen, and approved other grants with the similar hope of creating a buffer against the Comanches. A few hundred North American settlers trickled into east Texas, a stream that soon swelled to thousands. They generally settled east of the Colorado.

Meanwhile, with the lowering of the Spanish flag, virtually all of the professional garrison was withdrawn. In 1821, only fifty-nine soldiers remained in Texas, and there were hardly any more anywhere on the northern frontier. There were still fewer than four thousand Spanish-speaking people in the province, and only about fifteen thousand in all in the regions immediately below the Rio Grande.

The Comanches, who had frustrated French ambitions on the southern plains, had thrown up an impassable barrier to Hispanic settlement. In the cultural conflict, the horse Amerindians had become the full aggressors and emerged as the complete victors. The Pehnahterkuh now rode arrogantly into San Antonio, which they claimed as "their" town, taking what they wanted from a frightened citizenry that barred its doors. Comanche chiefs boasted that they permitted the Spanish to live on the edges of *Comanchería* only so that they might raise horses for them.

By the 1820s, the Comanches had extended their hunting ranges from the Arkansas to the Balcones Scarp, and their raiding range from Colorado to Durango. Everywhere on these ranges they were secure. They had killed Spanish-Mexicans at a ratio of two to one. The value of the property they had looted or destroyed ran into the millions. They had cost Hispanic civilization a major province, if not an empire.

The People, however, had also paid a price for this successful defense and expansion of their territory. They could not become sated, because Comanche warfare fed upon itself. The Yampah-reekuh bands had no economic necessity for war—everything they needed came from the buffalo or from New Mexico. Yet the Yam-pahreekuh every year rode a thousand miles to wreak relentless havoc on the Mexican frontier, in search of scalps, horse herds, and captives to maintain their warriors' social prestige. By 1820, the pattern had crystallized. The Comanches beyond the Red River had come to consider it as normal and as right to raid through Texas as to pursue the buffalo.

They had also acquired false and dangerous assumptions from their limited contacts with the Mexican civilization. As the scattered, helpless communities each tried to ransom themselves with presents, Comanches came to consider all civilized communities autonomous—organized like themselves. When Comanches accepted tribute in one region, devastated in another, then traded abused Spanish-Mexican captives in a third, they began to think that one civilized community had no interest in the fate of the next. They were gratified by the presents and goods they received for their capricious truces, and came to expect such tribute as their due. Out of their experience in these years the Comanches acquired the habits that were later to infuriate Anglo-Americans: the belief that they might make war on white men in one locality and trade peacefully in others, and that they should be rendered tribute at every encounter.

Their assumptions and their arrogance confirmed by victory, the People had cemented patterns for disaster.

III
SMOKE
AND TEARS
THE PEOPLE
AND THE MEXICANS

The Supreme Government simply must understand
that the Comanches, Apaches, Wichitas, and other small bands
of savages have not only hindered the settlement . . .
but for two centuries have laid waste to the villages
and committed thousands of murders and other crimes . . .
These depredations have dressed whole communities in black,
and filled their eyes with tears.
    The Government must realize that, with utterly baseless hope
and with paralyzing fears,
the cowardly governors and ecclesiastical councils
have presided over enormous crimes,
under the deliberate and infantile notion
that some day these barbarians will be converted to the faith,
and reduced to their dominions.
To this perverse view and policy, countless victims
have been and are still being sacrificed.
        —Report of Mexican official Tadeo Ortiz

COMANCHE WARFARE WITH THE MEXICANS WAS A CONTINUATION OF the bloody patterns that had evolved in the eighteenth century. The only change was that conditions became more chaotic and desperate in the northern provinces, because for the first three decades of independence the Supreme Government of Mexico did not concern itself with defense against the frontier Amerindians. In a war that did not deeply impress the Mexican national consciousness and that remained almost unknown to North Americans, the Mexicans became the principal victims of the Comanches in the nineteenth century. Comanche raiders killed thousands more Mexican soldiers, ranchers, and peasants south of the Rio Grande than they destroyed on the Anglo-American frontier.

237

Such conditions were permitted to continue in the north because independent Mexico was not a homogeneous or cohesive nation, and until the last quarter of the century, it never possessed a government stable or powerful enough to mount sustained campaigns against the Amerindians. The new republic, although it inherited the North American territories and boundaries of the Spanish empire, was unable to impose any effective rule over them. Spain's crumbling institutions and failed policies were continued unchanged until the 1830s, when the missions were finally closed. In effect, the outlying provinces had been abandoned earlier, by the withdrawal of Spanish soldiery and centralized administration.

Along with unmanageable frontiers, the republic inherited insuperable social, economic, and political problems from three hundred years of Spanish colonialism. The ten years of insurgent warfare that preceded independence reduced many of the richest provinces to economic ruin. The population was sharply divided by region, race, class, and caste. Only approximately 18 percent consisted of people of European descent, and these formed the property-holding, professional, and educated classes. Another 22 percent were *castas* or *mestizos,* the mixed bloods who had gained legal equality but who remained a largely despised caste and supporting class. The great majority, 60 percent, were reduced Amerindians, confined to hard-scrabble, communal *ejidos* or bound by peonage or debt slavery to the enormous estates that sprawled across the south-central provinces. The overwhelming mass of Mexicans was illiterate and impoverished, conscious of enormous grievances. The elites were bitterly polarized between conflicting conservative-centralist, reformist-federalist ideologies. Conservatives, supported by the great landholders and the institutions of the Church and military, preferred to continue the forms and traditions handed down from Spain; the reformers, impelled by the misery and frustrations of the *mestizos* and Amerindians, were determined to break the old patterns of society. None of the elite—the new custodians of Mexican civilization—of whatever ideology had any experience with public affairs or government, since they had been rigidly excluded from these during Spanish rule. Under these circumstances, Mexico, which far more resembled an Oriental empire than a modern nation, faced an enormous crisis of order. The republic's struggle was to emerge as a modern nation, and during that struggle for survival the rulers of Mexico were unprepared to cope with barbarians beyond the gates.

The ruling elites rarely perceived Mexico as a nation that extended beyond the outlines of the sixteenth-century Spanish conquest. Their Mexico was the Mexico of the central highlands, with its Spanish cities and vast estates. While they inherited all the pride of possession of the Spaniards in the northern empire and were emotionally and intellectually opposed to its alienation, members of the Creole society of the south had little consciousness of the frontier. Custodians of the republic, battling among themselves, failed to grasp either its challenges or its realities. The Amerindian problem remained only a minor historical footnote to Mexicans; they never quite understood that it was the principal reason why the territories above the Bravo had been lost.

After the removal of Spanish authoritarianism, the internal administration became vastly more inefficient and anarchic. Outlying states and territories became virtually separate fiefdoms, controlled by *caciques*—political chiefs who were inherently hostile to the pretensions of any central government. The capital, whether held by conservatives or reformers, seldom exerted its authority beyond the major cities of the core regions. It could not collect taxes or customs nor control such local militias as existed. Lacking even authority in the north, the Supreme Government could obviously not afford that region protection.

Ironically, the republic possessed a huge military force—an army of eighty thousand men, which continually bankrupted the treasury by annual budgets that exceeded the total national revenues. This army, a creation of the revolutionary decade, quickly emerged as a dominant incubus, destroying government after government. It was commanded by cynical praetorian generals, who rose to high positions through regular political treason. While the army drained revenues, corruption kept it ill equipped and badly disciplined. It was fully occupied by continual coups and palace revolutions, or engaged against the foreign interventions triggered by Mexican weakness and financial irresponsibility. Regularly employed against the people of Mexico, it was never used to defend the frontier against raiding Amerindians.

The result was the final, complete collapse of the mission-presidio system in the north, and a horrendous savaging of the entire Amerindian frontier. In the absence of effective government and sustained military campaigns, the Comanches were permitted to ride roughshod over the eastern provinces, and the western Apaches extended their depredations. A few thousand regular troops, properly led in a series of sustained campaigns, could certainly have ended the Indian danger. All of *Comanchería* lay within or immediately adjacent to the purported boundaries of Mexico, and the evidence of the previous century showed that the horse Indians were not invulnerable to determined operations. But in an era when the shape and even the continued existence of the emerging nation was at stake, the leaders of seven million Mexicans had neither the vision nor the resources to cope with the frontier.

The final outcome was more than the thousands of Mexican corpses bloating and purpling under the desert sun, the countless burnt-out hovels of goatherds in Chihuahua and ruined villages in Nuevo León, the isolation and impoverishment of frontier towns, or the screams of the hundreds of "Christian girls and boys carried off to slavery and worse" by the barbarians. It was more than the sense of desperation and humiliation that pervaded the northern regions, *mestizo* and more "Mexican" than the Creole haciendas and cities of the south, and turned them bitterly against the capital. The eventual result was the loss of half the territory drawn on the first, official maps of independent Mexico.

THE CONCEPT OF ARREDONDO AND THE SPANISH GOVERNMENT THAT Texas might be successfully colonized with Anglo-Americans was not mistaken. Stephen F. Austin located his colony in the rich river bottoms along the Gulf between the Colorado and the Brazos. The first years were difficult, but as the settlers brought in crops of corn and cotton, the colony began to thrive. In ten years, Austin settled fifteen hundred families on the land, and other developers who received Mexican land commissions brought in thousands more. And in this decade the Anglo-American colony cleared more timber, broke more soil, built more towns, and raised more crops and children than the Hispanic culture had in two hundred years.

The Texas colonists, however, did nothing to relieve the Mexican frontier from Indian pressures. Austin located his settlements east of the bison range, with a buffer of Wichitas between his people and the Comanches. He made effective treaties with the Tawakonis and Wacos higher on the Brazos. The truce between the Comanches and Wichitas held, and the bands paid little attention to Texas east of San Antonio. During its crucial formative years, the Anglo-American colony was secure.

The Karankawas attacked and killed a number of immigrants, since the Texans' outlets to the Gulf ran through Karankawa country, but Anglo-American frontiersmen did not supinely suffer Amerindian raids: Austin organized an effective militia and began a virtual war of extermination against the remaining Karankawas along the coast. Their lands were so thoroughly scoured that the survivors sought the protection of the padres at the La Bahía mission, who completed their destruction with disease. The tribe, despised for its cannibalism, became extinct, unnoticed and unlamented by either the whites or other Amerindians. And the Tonkawas were fearful of the Comanches and also enemies of the Lipans. They tried to maintain peace and friendship with the Texans, for their numbers were declining rapidly.

Thus the hopes of the Spanish and Mexican authorities for an Anglo-American buffer against the horse Indians were frustrated during the early years of the Texas settlement. Meanwhile, the authorities, or at least a large body of influential Mexican opinion, had become more concerned about another problem. The very success of the Anglo-American colony frightened them.

The Texan colony was generally east and north of all the old Hispanic settlements, and it did not become integrated into either Hispanic Texas or Mexico. The farms along the Brazos were separated from the civilized regions of Mexico by hundreds of miles of barren country; they were much closer to the United States. The Texans had only minimal contact with Mexicans. No assimilation took place, and their economic, cultural, and emotional ties remained completely with their kinfolk east of the Sabine. The utter neglect of the Mexican republic for the northern territories, which was more the result of political anarchy than of benign policy, had a predictable result. Provided with nothing from the Mexicans, the colonists were turning east Texas into a cultural and economic extension of the United States beyond the Mexican border.

The seeds of serious trouble lay in the increasing Mexican dread of the North American republic. While the United States government scrupulously respected the letter of the 1819 treaty and the

Sabine boundary inherited from Spain, hordes of Anglo-American frontiersmen were pushing west toward the northern territories that the Hispanic civilization had never settled or developed. In 1825, the United States government proposed to purchase Texas, an offer that was emotionally offensive to the Mexican elite. This fear of North American expansion, and the determination to keep it out of the Hispanic Southwest, now colored all Mexican relations with the Anglo-American colony in Texas. Official Mexico began to see it as a potential Trojan horse.

In 1828, General Manuel Mier y Terán inspected the province on behalf of the Supreme Government. His report was disturbing: Northeast of San Antonio the province had become Anglo-Saxon. The *norteamericanos* in Texas already outnumbered the Spanish-speaking population ten to one. They maintained their cultural and economic ties with the United States; they had their own schools (the Mexicans provided none for their own people); they were better educated and organized. Mier y Terán advised that unless action were taken the North Americans would dominate the province; he feared its loss to Mexico.

Mexico and the United States had inherited the old imperial rivalries of the European powers for North America, but now there was one immense difference. The northern republic was a vigorous, well-governed, dynamic nation, with a rapidly expanding population. The southern empire was a static society caught up in increasing anarchy, with most of its institutions in decay. The two countries were natural rivals and inevitable enemies until the question of dominance of the continent was determined and a stable boundary delineated along a line where the two distinct populations met. Mexico held title to the Southwest from the Sabine to the Pacific, but it held these territories so tenuously that the title was not secure. The United States, meanwhile, could not feel itself strategically secure upon the northern continent until it reached the Pacific and barred the possible encroachment of all European powers. The contest was unequal, but inevitable.

Inspired by fear, the Mexican government halted all Anglo-American immigration by "emergency" decree and forbade Negro slavery, both enormous irritants to the Texan colonists. The government also adopted other policies: the settlement of Mexican convicts and the introduction of Swiss, German, and other immigrants to dilute the Anglo influence; the strict enforcement of customs and other regulations to halt Texan trade with the United States; the sending of intelligence agents and military garrisons to place the province under the direct control of the central government. But when these policies could be implemented at all they could not be fully enforced, and the arrival of Mexican soldiers, a virtual army of occupation in the eyes of the colonists, caused serious frictions. By 1830, relations between the Supreme Government and the formerly self-governing colony were rapidly deteriorating, leading to the eventual revolt in 1835, by which the colonists wrested Texas from Mexico.

That revolt was by no means inevitable. Almost until the very end, the great majority of Texans were loyal Mexican citizens. Mexico had treated them munificently in the early years, with generous land grants and freedom from duties and taxes, and had allowed them self-government. If the colony had developed under the flag of a powerful, stable Hispanic nation that had no overpowering fear of the adjacent United States, Texas could well have become what Arredondo visualized: a prosperous, expanding buffer zone. A strong, stable government, also, could have taken measures to integrate the colony into the nation. However, the very inability of the Mexicans to form any kind of stable government after 1821 caused the immigrants to feel growing contempt, and to resist the belated efforts to control the province by the imposition of an authoritarian tyranny. Finally, Mexican weakness allowed a province inhabited by thirty thousand Anglo-American immigrants to win independence by arms from a nation of seven million.

The root cause of these historic events, which decisively determined the shape and future of the Hispanic Southwest, was not the machinations or greed of North Americans. The horse Amerindians —who played no direct part in these great events and had only the dimmest understanding of them—had first halted the penetration of the French, then barred significant Hispanic settlement. Cultures unable to cope with the horse Amerindians could not colonize the North American Southwest.

THE PEOPLE, IN THE EARLY NINETEENTH CENTURY, WERE IGNORANT OF the historic confrontation between two diverse European civilizations and were indifferent to its outcome. This was the age of greatest Comanche prestige and power. The bands that ranged from southern Texas to the Arkansas in Kansas had reached the greatest strength they would attain; there were probably between twenty and thirty thousand Comanches in all. They were secure as few savage peoples had ever appeared to be secure. They were living their finest hour.

They had defeated all European penetrations, and their domain was not threatened by any dangerous Amerindian enemies. They had mastery over their universe, so far as their way of life could ever master it. The patterns of their culture had crystallized, and if the hunt and war kept their numbers small, they were hardly in danger of extinction. The People, warriors and women, lived a short, perilous, brutish existence, full of pain and sorrow, but also filled with marvelous exhilaration and exultation. The patterns of their life, with the male population kept low by hunting and warfare and the females kept barren by constant riding and heavy labors, assured that they would never overpopulate the plains. The Comanches could not have destroyed the buffalo, their staff of life, in a million years of this closed cycle. They lived, or seemed to live, in a world without end, and it was the only world they knew or wanted to know.

The Amerindian situation on the plains could never be entirely constant, but by the close of the eighteenth century it had again been temporarily stabilized. Some tribes had emerged to dominance; others starved in bitterness on the fringes of the rich range or had already been pushed toward extinction. The successful peoples had hammered out certain patterns of coexistence, which did not always preclude wars. But these wars were more haphazard horse raids than the murderous onslaughts of the previous century.

The Comanches remained at peace with the Tawehash along the Red. The bands coexisted with the Wichitas in the Cross Timbers country. They had fought beside the Wichitas, and the French had somehow instilled the notion of a mutual tolerance. This was made easier by the fact that the tattooed warriors were fierce fighters whom the bands respected, and there were not too many of them, perhaps 2,600 in all. Amerindian truces and alliances were no more nor less logical than the arrangements worked out between civilized nations. Some were arrived at by accident, some came through necessity. Wichitas and Comanches did not impinge on each other, and their brief warfare had not hardened into historic hatred, such as the People had for the Utes and Athapaskans.

The war with the Utes continued despite de Anza's attempts at peace, but these no longer had the intensity of the years before 1786. One reason was that Comanche attention was heavily diverted to Texas and Mexico; raiding was far easier and more profitable to the south. The Utes sometimes raided out of the Rockies, and Comanches frequently pursued them. It was enjoyable enmity that threatened neither tribe's existence.

After 1790, the Lipan Apaches virtually vanished from the fringes of *Comanchería*. They had retreated below the Nueces. The Tonkawas, like the Lipans, were too reduced in number to dispute Comanche range. Meanwhile, the People had found a new ally.

In the 1780s, a new tribe, the Kiowas, appeared between the North Platte and the Arkansas. The Kiowas ("First" or "Principal People") were an anomaly on the bison plains. Their language was Tanoan, a tongue of the Puebloan culture of New Mexico. Their background was vastly different from the Nermernuh and from most other Plains tribes. In the seventeenth century, the Kiowas had abandoned their adobe dwellings and agrarian way of life when they adopted the horse and began to pursue the buffalo on the High Plains. They rode north in the era when the Nermernuh were moving south. The Spanish had no record of them until 1732, when they were already identifiable Plains horse Indians. Like the Comanches, the Kiowas seemed to prefer to forget whatever disasters had turned them from their former life. The only legends they possessed of their past told of an origin somewhere near the headwaters of the Missouri and along the upper Yellowstone, where they were friends of the Crows. But there was much more than this in their past, for the Kiowas carried the richest tribal culture of any of the peoples on the plains.

They worshiped the sun, in a total religion filled with supernatural pageantry and folklore. Their tongue held concepts, unique among horse Amerindians, that could hardly have originated in a nomadic, predatory culture. The Kiowas had sacred objects, the so-called *taime* dolls or idols—painted and dressed stone images, some two feet high. The keepers of these sacred images were more priests than medicine men. The Kiowas had "owl" and "buffalo" doctors, and they took skilled medicine men along to war. Their rituals were complex, and their dances elaborate and colorful, with hints of the "barbarian" grandeur of the Pueblos. They made an honored place for the aged at their fires, and the old men kept "calendars"—rolled, tanned hides painted with pictographs and mnemonic signs, which recorded the memorable events of many years. The Kiowas expressed art in paint, dance, and ritual, pointing to Mexic influences in their history.

Their sun dance was an elaborate event, for which all twelve circles of the tribe congregated annually. The dance was performed before the Sun Doll. Possibly, the Kiowas introduced this pageant to the other Plains tribes.

The tribal circle was small and tightly knit, arising from a people who had once formed a single community. Kiowas married within the tribe, and they had the beginnings of lineages and hierarchy. The *Koh-eet-senko*, a warrior society composed of the ten greatest warriors, formed a genuine military aristocracy.

These manifestations of higher culture did not impress the first Europeans who encountered Kiowas. They saw a dark, stocky people, horse Indians who quickly and possibly deservedly gained the reputation of being the most accomplished torturers on the plains. In all other aspects the Kiowas appeared no different from Comanches, for in dress, weapons, hunting, lodging, and war they made the common adaptation to the buffalo range.

There was, however, another anomaly within the tribal circle, a small, exclusive band who were Kiowas in everything but language. This group spoke an Athapaskan dialect. They were the *Naheeshandeenah* ("Our Kind") whom the other circles referred to as "The Thieves." They communicated with the others by sign talk, at which all Kiowas were peculiarly adept. The French called this band *Gattacka*, from the Pawnee, and around 1681, La Salle in the Illinois country wrote that the Gattacka stole horses from the Spanish—though the source of his information was not identified. They were an offshoot of the Athapaskan peoples of the Mackenzie River basin, who had somehow joined the Kiowas, themselves a small band, on their northern wanderings.

Anglo-Americans insisted upon calling them "Kiowa Apaches," because they spoke "Apache." The Kiowa Apaches, however, did not know that the other Apaches existed until the nineteenth century, and when they met, they were enemies. The two peoples only became friendly, and finally intermarried, when they discovered their similar dialects on the white man's reservations.

For a century, Kiowa life had been a heroic tour de force on the High Plains. They made a successful transition probably because they became extremely free-ranging and warlike. They clashed with many tribes, moving too rapidly to be crushed or exterminated. However, by 1780, the Dakota pressure in the Black Hills had become too strong. The few thousand Kiowas could not stand against Sioux numbers; they rode south, following the old trail of the Comanches.

They began to meet and fight the Nermernuh along the Arkansas. Even these fierce warriors would probably have been driven off the bison range except for a historic accident. About 1790, Kiowas and Comanches both appeared at a trading station in New Mexico, where a frightened Comanchero desperately arranged a truce in order to prevent a holocaust and to save his own hair. Representatives of the two peoples sat down in neutral territory and agreed to ride away in peace. The advantages of a lasting truce to the Kiowas were obvious, while the idea of making truces, by this time, had entered the conventional Comanche wisdom. Band councils debated the issue for many months. The northern Comanches finally agreed to accept the Kiowas as equals on their range, and the peace was honored by the southern bands. The peace quickly became cemented into a firm alliance when the Yampahreekuh introduced the Kiowas to the joys of riding south to Mexico.

The Kiowas became the longest-ranging raiders on the plains. They rarely camped below the Red, and they never formally allied with the Pehnahterkuh. But with the Yampahreekuh, they ravaged Mexico, and they penetrated that country deeper than any Comanche. Kiowas rode to Durango and beyond, where they were usually confused with Comanches. One war band went on a fantastic trek, which carried it to the borders of Guatemala and Yucatán. The warriors returned with tales of strange animals in trees and birds with brilliant plumage, of monkeys and parrots. The Kiowas also quickly emerged as the deadliest of the southwestern Amerindians. In proportion to their numbers, they killed more Anglo-Americans on the Texas-Kansas frontier than the Comanches.

Perhaps because the Kiowas were small in number and their males were eternally off on distant raids, their camps above the Red were often vulnerable to Amerindian enemies. By 1802, the Osages, southern Siouans from the Neosho River region, were raiding into Comanche-Kiowa territory. The Osages were being pushed west by Anglo-American pressures—the beginning of a long, tragic displacement that would soon affect the plains—but they were also well-armed with Anglo-American firearms. The Osages accomplished at least one historic massacre of a Kiowa encampment, slaughtering women and children and carrying off three of the sacred *taime* idols. The Utes captured the two remaining images in 1868; none were recovered.

The horse-poor Osages were not the only people driven toward *Comanchería*. The fame of the Comanche horse herds reached the entire High Plains, and between 1800 and 1807 many of the distant peoples tried to establish commercial relations. Very little was recorded of this, but it is clear that a considerable commerce did develop among the Plains Indians.

Comanches controlled the approaches to the major horse supply in the Spanish borderlands. They were also the only really successful horse breeders among the Amerindians—and they were too powerful to be raided with impunity. All this led other peoples to enter *Comanchería* asking peace in the sign language, and respectfully offering to trade for ponies. The Comanches were amenable to bargaining, especially with warriors from distant tribes with whom they had no historic enmity. They were incredibly rich in horseflesh by Amerindian standards, and such trading was one way of showing off their wealth.

Strangers, once accepted in peace, moved without danger in the Comanche camp. Hospitality was not violated on either side. The accounts indicate that the other Plains peoples not only envied the Comanches but admired their dash and spirit and their prowess in war. When they informed white men that the Comanches were the most cunning of all people, and the greatest horse thieves, these were meant as accolades. The other Amerindians also considered the Comanches excellent horse traders, but generous, and with a high sense of honor. Rich and powerful, the Comanche warriors assumed an almost aristocratic stance before the representatives of other tribes.

They loved to boast and to race their mounts against those of other warriors. The Comanches had become inveterate, almost reckless gamblers. They wagered on horse races and archery contests, and on rough games like the primitive "kick the ball" that the children played. They had also acquired dice, presumably out of New Mexico. Their random concept of the universe and belief in medicine made all games of chance irresistible. Uniquely among their neighbors, the Comanches would not sell or offer women to visitors—but warriors were known to bet, and lose, their horses, blankets, weapons, even their daughters and wives on a race or roll of dice. The men would wager everything except their medicine bags. They were, however, not above a certain cunning even in their gambling. It was a Comanche practice to train extremely scruffy and poor-looking ponies to race, and with such unimpressive horseflesh they won great wagers from overconfident strangers.

As Hodge reported, most of the adjacent Plains peoples spoke some of the Nermernuh tongue, because in these years it emerged as the trading language of the plains. This position of the Comanche dialect was unique, and it points strongly to the existence of a widespread, steady trade.

The broad patterns of the Amerindian relationships did not change over the first three decades of the century. The Kiowas and Comanches fought Utes and Osages, traded with New Mexico and the tribes above the Arkansas, and raided every year deep into Mexico. The Amerindian wars of this era more and more had settled

Comanches on the move.
Drawing by George Catlin, c. 1836.

down to relatively bloodless horse raids between tribes—though there were occasional grisly massacres that destroyed whole camps, especially by the Osages. Domains had been established, and the Plains tribes were nomadic only within these ranges. At times, there was even peace between the Comanches and the Utes and Osages.

During these years the Comanches made their first contacts with Anglo-American traders, who had begun to filter along the Santa Fe Trail. The Bent brothers were operating in Comanche country by 1829, and William Bent and Ceran St. Vrain built trading posts for Comanches and Kiowas. William Bent was skilled in dealings with the different Amerindians, understanding much of their psychology and using this knowledge for his business purposes. The northern bands did not exactly welcome such white traders, but Comanches had learned that there were different "tribes" of white men, and they accepted Bent and other traders once they clearly understood that the Anglo-Americans were not Mexicans, much the same as they accepted the Comancheros. The traders, on their side, recorded that they had less trouble with the Comanches than with Osages, who had already had trouble with Americans to the east. Much of what is known about Comanche life emerged from these contacts between 1825 and 1840, when a number of Anglo-Americans and Europeans were able to enjoy Comanche hospitality.

The relative stabilization of the plains in this period is shown by the course of the conflict that erupted between the Comanches and Kiowas on one side, and the Cheyennes and Arapahos on the other. By 1820, the two northern tribes were appearing on the borders of *Comancheria* in larger numbers. This was not yet part of the forced migrations of the eastern Amerindians that caused such turmoil in the 1830s and led to the destruction of so many peoples. This conflict was containable.

The Yampahreekuh, Kuhtsoo-ehkuh, Nawkohnee, and Kiowas began fighting with allied Arapahos and Cheyennes about 1830. Despite reports of "battles," this warfare was mostly a widespread feinting and skirmishing. However, it proved decisive. After ten years of fighting, it became apparent that the southern tribes could not dislodge the intruders along the Arkansas, but also that the northerners posed no real threat to the major Comanche ranges. Although William Bent played the major role in arranging a truce between the tribes, the solution accepted by the Amerindians would have done credit to the most civilized of statesmen.

In 1840 the principal warriors of all four peoples met in council and hammered out a treaty that was called the Great Peace. The terms provided that the impinging tribes would never again raid each other, and that they would henceforth engage in amicable horse trading. To cement the peace, the Comanches presented the northerners with thousands of ponies.

This made the Cheyennes and Arapahos rich in a day, and stunned by Comanche grandeur and generosity. This was a gesture the Comanches afforded easily, and whose effect they fully appreciated and enjoyed, for it raised their prestige on the plains enormously. And still, the purposes of the Great Peace were pragmatic and strategic. It did not mark a retreat of the participants from war in any sense; it was a practical realization that the powerful horse tribes could not profitably fight each other, and that in fact their separate, historic interests lay in other directions. The thrust of Comanche raiding was south, west, and east; the traditional enemies of the Cheyennes and Arapahos were to the north. The Great Peace secured each tribe's rear. It was not an alliance, rather an arrangement that allowed all the participants to pursue their older enemies and victims with full attention and even greater fury.

ALL THE EVIDENCE INDICATES THAT THE COMANCHE TERROR INTENSIfied in the 1840s. The pattern had become standardized; the raiders had even established regular routes into Mexico. A few miles north of the Rio Grande, near the present city of Del Rio, many trails out of *Comanchería* converged into a broad roadway, beaten by the passage of thousands of unshod Amerindian ponies. This trail, called the Comanche Trace, was a distinct landmark. It ran for some miles south of the river, gradually disappearing as the war bands dispersed across northern Mexico. Another broad trace led across the Rio Grande farther west, through the Santa Elena canyon. The trails ran through barren, almost desert country, debouching into the Mexican states of Tamaulipas, Coahuila, Nuevo León, and Chihuahua. They lay far west of the line of Anglo-American settlement, and the Comanches and Kiowas rode them boldly, driving back thousands of stolen horses.

All the Comanche bands joined in the raiding; the far northern Yampahreekuh and the southern Pehnahterkuh were the most active. The Pehnahterkuh never rode with Kiowas, but they tolerated them.

The raiders went south in entire family groups, taking along their women and children. Loosely allied, they set up base camps, usually in the eastern cordillera. These camps became collecting points for loot and captives. They were located about halfway up the mountainsides, in rough country close to Mexican settlements. From them, small war parties ranged widely, and often ravaged one region for months or even years. It has been incredible to some historians that the presence of Comanches did not arouse the whole Mexican countryside. But, communications were very poor, and the isolated communities had no history of, nor capacity for, collective action. Many, if not most, of the small depredations and killings were not even reported; sometimes the Comanches ravaged for many days before the surrounding territory was even alerted.

The raided regions included provinces that had been pacified by the Spaniards in the sixteenth century, as well as the towns and ranches established in the middle 1700s. Comanches regularly rode near large settlements such as Monclova and Monterrey, but they skirted the actual towns. Confined spaces and protecting walls were alien to the horse Amerindian. The urban nature of the Mexican culture permitted the civilization to survive, although fearful punishment was wreaked upon the outlying districts of what was essentially a stock-raising economy.

The new appearance of raiding *indios* in the long-settled, long-pacified regions of Coahuila and Nuevo León confused many Mexicans, who believed that the attackers originated in the blue-shadowed sierra. Mexicans found it hard to believe that the raiders came from north of the Red River, and continued to confuse Comanches with Apaches, who were also extending their depredations through Sonora and Chihuahua in these years. By the 1840s, the situation was worse than it had been during the preceding hundred years.

The Mexicans kept few official records and made no summation of the destruction. Some localities, such as some of the great *estancias,* maintained accounts of losses. One large hacienda claimed that the horses they lost numbered into the hundreds of thousands. There was never any general recapitulation of the loss of life, but hundreds of families suffered. Mexican dead ran in the thousands, and many hundreds of captives were carried away, most never to be heard from again.

The damage was not suffered in silence. Litanies of protest rose continually, but these were useless because of the internal condition of the nation. The army, occupied by the power struggles in the south, also soon became engaged in the north, when Mexico and the United States finally went to war over Texas. During this war the army was virtually destroyed. For three decades there was no effective federal force on the frontiers, and while local authorities tried to meet defense needs, their efforts were never coordinated and were always inadequate. The government did at least recognize the problem. When Mexico ceded the lands between the Sabine and the Pacific to the United States by the Treaty of Guadalupe Hidalgo in 1848, one clause the Mexicans demanded was the prevention of Indian raiding from the territories that now became part of the United States.

Although the Mexican frontier was vital to the emergence of the modern *mestizo* nation, the frontier never significantly intruded upon the consciousness of Mexican intellectuals and elite. For them, Indian troubles—beyond halting the advance of Mexican culture along the Rio Grande—did not pose a serious threat, but were merely another, minor problem of an era filled with despair and humiliations. The brunt of Comanche terror fell mainly upon a helpless, already oppressed peasantry which was not integrated into the urban civilization. That fact alone tells much about the state of health of that civilization, which was slowly moving toward the cataclysm of twentieth-century revolution.

The Comanches fought by their own codes, and this, as with almost all Amerindian warfare, makes any recounting seem a series of hideous atrocities by any civilized standard. The details, however, if seen in full perspective, reveal much of Comanche culture as well as Mexican, since cultures always reveal their essential natures in warfare. The story told by one survivor, who related her account many years later on an Oklahoma reservation, was typical of the Comanche warfare against the Mexicans.

This was a Mexican girl, carried away at about the age of seven. She did not remember her name, or who her parents were, except that they all lived near the "highest mountain in Mexico." The Comanches raided through the locality during the summer, riding down from that mountain where they had their base. They had already captured some of the little girl's friends. Surrounding a school on horseback, the warriors set the building afire with torches. They killed the teacher when he ran out, and then seized all the children. The girl herself was taken from her own house, where she was held in her grandmother's arms, by a warrior who was himself a Mexican reared by Comanches and adopted into the tribe. This warrior rode through the fence, seized the girl, and threw her behind him on his horse. She did not remember what happened to her grandmother. The Indian took her away.

Other Comanches joined them, warriors returning from individual operations. About dark, the band came upon a boy sheep herder; they killed him and ate the food in his knapsack. Then the party rode for the distant mountain, about four days' journey. They ran out of food before they got there, and killed and cooked a horse. When they arrived, the Comanche women in the camp snatched off the little girl's earrings and clothes. She was wet, exhausted, and terrified, but the other captive children in the camp told her that the Indians would not "really hurt" her.

The following morning, the Comanches heard the sounds of a wagon moving near the base of the mountain. Several warriors investigated. The captives heard shots, then the Comanches returned with food and blankets. They had killed a party of carters.

This was a large camp, where the raiders were assembling a vast store of goods and captives. The Comanches were totally unafraid; they rode out and returned regularly, raiding. The captive girls were not abused, but they were not allowed to eat near the men lest they destroy their medicine. Finally, probably in September of that year, all the Comanches in the camp, including the many women, rode off on one last raid. They left the captives, who were all small children about the girl's age, in the care of a Mexican slave. The children were very hungry, and this man killed and roasted a whole horse for them, which they ate greedily.

The Comanches came back with many horses. Now, most of the families in the camp wanted to go home. The lodges began to leave. The girl's captor wanted more horses, and planned to make more raids. He also intended to kill the little girl, because, as he told another warrior who was leaving the camp, she would get in the way.

This companion warrior felt sorry for the little girl, naked, alone, and frightened in the camp. He gave her captor a few arrows in exchange for her. This man's wife was dead, and his children were cared for by his niece, who ran his lodge for him. He put her on a mule and took her along with his own family band on the return to Texas.

The Comanches moved boldly and openly; no one bothered them. On the trail they passed one of the little girl's friends, bleeding in the dust. She had been raped and left to die. They saw another child, a boy, dead. The girl's new owner told her not to worry; he would not let harm come to her. By this time, almost all Comanches spoke a little Spanish from their regular contacts with New Mexico and the slaves in their camps. He also told her that when she grew up, she would be his wife. He ordered his niece to be kind to her, for sometimes the women were cruel to captives.

One night in camp, while her master was away checking his herd, a young warrior seized the girl and pulled her into the bushes. He exposed himself, and she saw that his scrotum was diseased. Before anything else could happen, her master ran up and threatened the other warrior. He took the girl back to camp and, after that, always kept her with him. He tied her ankles together beneath a horse so that she would not fall off when they rode together.

Still on the trail, the band met Kiowas. The girl's master, who was called Wahaawmaw, dressed her in a blanket and daubed her face with paint, and sent her with his niece to beg food from the Kiowas, as the Comanches were running low. The Kiowas gave them much dried meat and directed them to a nearby Comanche camp. The band was now far north, in *Comanchería*. On the following day, the girl and her captor arrived at a main camp, which included his dead wife's parents and his kinfolk.

Here, the women of the family struck her with whips, which was the custom when a new captive was brought into camp. The girl's job was to care for her master's children. One was crippled and had to be carried on her back. She was kept very busy. The master of the lodge was kind to her and never abused her, but he took a new wife, the younger sister of his dead one, who was named Poohkee. Poohkee did not like the little Mexican girl, and she sometimes poked her with blazing sticks from the fire, to make her cry. However, all the stepchildren stuck together, and protected her.

The winter was hard, with heavy snows and little meat. The horses ate cottonwood bark, and the warriors tried to hunt on snowshoes. Captive boys with the band dug frozen horses out of the snow for food. But spring came early, and Wahaawmaw taught the girl to ride and hunt. By the next fall she knew the language and all the customs of the Comanches. She bore her first child before she was fifteen.

This abduction of children angered the Mexicans more than the murders, rapes, and robberies. But while the Spanish Crown had always attempted to rescue or ransom captives—even *indios* who were under Spanish protection—the Mexican republic had neither a coherent ransom policy nor the money to fund one. The Comancheros of New Mexico were prepared to try to ransom captives, but this was tricky business, and they would undertake it only if their expenses were assured. Most captives came from the obscure peasantry, and their families were frequently killed at the time of seizure. Few carried off into *Comanchería* were ever seen again.

By the nineteenth century, every Comanche camp held Mexican captives—women, boys, and girls. There was no standard practice in the taking or keeping of captives; as always, this depended upon individual whim or need, since custom-law did not extend to captives unless they had been formally inducted into the tribe. Some warriors gelded Mexican boys and kept them as slaves to manage their horse herds. One Comanche was known to crucify a captive who angered him, a practice he undoubtedly learned in Mexico, for in the eighteenth century the Spanish authorities crucified captured highwaymen. Some girls and women were sold to other Amerindians. The same warrior who might pin a squirming baby with a lance, laughing at its feeble agonies, could also treat a captive with kindness, or even set him free. One Mexican was released because his captor found it too troublesome to teach him the Comanche language and way of doing things.

The experience was often a terrible one for child captives. Comanches liked to test the courage of boys. Young male captives were sometimes made to fight each other, supposedly to the death, to see how they behaved in such ordeals. They were threatened with torture, tied to stakes, and menaced with fire or sharp knives. Captives who failed to live up to Comanche standards might be killed in disgust; cowardly boys were sometimes castrated.

Most captives who survived became slaves, doing menial work about the camp. The boys tended horses; the girls were put to woman's work. The warriors could not have maintained their huge horse herds without the help of numerous Mexican slaves. The Comanches, however, admired courage in any race, and the boy who won their admiration did not have to remain a slave. There were always families that had lost children or women who were barren, and a valiant, useful child captive was frequently adopted.

Once adopted into a family, the captive gained all the rights and recognition of a born Comanche, and could rise to any honor. Several of the most famous Comanche war chiefs were captives, or the sons of captive women. Unlike the Kiowas, the Comanches had no prejudices regarding race or birth. It was frequently observed, by both Comanches and Europeans, that adopted boys who became full warriors were usually more cruel to their own people, and even more warlike than their foster parents, a normal consequence in situations of this kind.

Significantly, captive children adapted very quickly to the life. The age at which a boy was taken tended to be crucial. A very young boy rarely survived, or was killed if he became a nuisance on the trail. Older boys sometimes pretended to become Comanches, then ran away once they had become trusted to tend horses. The girls at any age were more amenable, quickly learning what was expected of them.

Such children quickly forgot their native language and old associations and strove to become accepted Comanches. The girls looked forward to becoming the wives of great warriors. The boys dreamed of the day when they would become an honored member of the warriors' circle, or lead their own war band. The children absorbed the beliefs and drives of the People, and many who returned or were rescued admitted candidly that they had learned to love the wild life on the plains, with its thrills, raw dangers, exaltations, and leisure that no civilized existence could match. Once children adjusted to Comanche life they were almost never able to readjust again to civilization. They became as culturally wild and stubborn as born Comanches. The process seemingly could not be reversed.

Despite the extreme cruelty with which some captives entered Comanche life, there is no question that many captives, even those never fully adopted, came to have affection for their captors. The feeling was mutual. Comanche foster parents mourned the loss of adopted children as violently as the loss of their own; adopted boys honored their fathers according to the strict Comanche custom. Slaves were not denied this feeling of belonging and affection. There are many recorded instances in which a Mexican slave died defending a Comanche camp. And most slaves were not held by force or fear. They were trusted to tend the horse herds, to make saddles, and to repair guns.

The seizure of women and children as captives and their adoption into the bands was so ancient and universal a custom among the Amerindians that they never fully understood the deep cultural, religious, and racial-sexual antagonisms this aroused among Europeans. It was a survival measure for the bands, but for the victimized peoples it was the worst affront of all.

The warfare of the Mexican republic against the northern *indios* itself soon degenerated into barbarism. This reaction was hardly unique to Mexicans; the same phenomenon occurred wherever Europeans were exposed to and brutalized by contact with Amerindian warfare. Significantly, this had not occurred while the Spanish Crown was maintaining soldiers to enforce order on the frontier. While Spanish authorities had always permitted the use of force to reduce *indios* and had employed selective, judicious murder to rid themselves of troublesome chiefs, only once had Crown officers embraced a policy of planned extermination, during the proposed campaign against the Apaches. And this policy had met powerful opposition from the missionary orders, which to the very end hoped for a successful reduction and conversion.

By the 1830s, however, the northern communities had suffered so terribly from raiding that the Mexican leadership could no longer see the horse Indians in terms of Catholic theology. Along with the suffering communities, more and more local authorities complained about the "cowardly" policies that produced no progress and that left the frontier exposed to continual danger. The northern states could not expect the effective intervention of the Mexican army; therefore, in many localities the political chiefs adopted de facto policies of *indio* extermination.

The authorities placed bounties on dead Amerindians, paying out silver pesos for *indio* scalps. The straight, coarse, Asian-Amerindian hair was readily identifiable—but unfortunately, such hair did not reveal the age, sex, or tribe of the slain Indian. There were many peaceable, inoffensive Amerindians, and also many Mexicans whose ancestry was largely or wholly Indian. There is no question that unscrupulous bounty hunters slaughtered hundreds of innocent parties and passed off their locks as Apache or Comanche. The authorities redeemed many scalps, but they soon recognized that few wild *indios* were being killed for profit. The program proved a bloody failure.

Other desperate expedients were tried. When possible, Apaches or Comanches were lured into Mexican settlements with the promise of parleys and gifts; then they were either shot down from ambush, or fed poisoned food and drink. A number of Apaches were killed in this fashion, but this policy also was a dismal failure. The *indios* quickly became wary of Mexican treachery, and the murders caused long-standing blood feuds that provoked wars far beyond the former random raids. For every Apache or Comanche slain by such methods, far more hapless Mexican peasants or *vaqueros* were cut down in vengeful strikes, or died screaming in the desert, staked out naked on live anthills.

The Mexicans' most effective retaliation against the Comanches, ironically, was involuntary. Nineteenth-century Mexico was still scourged by epidemics of all kinds, and the more the People penetrated south the more exposed they became to the diseases of civilization. For the first time, smallpox, measles, and cholera appeared among the Nermernuh; in 1816, and again in 1839, smallpox wiped out whole bands. Furthermore, venereal disease was rampant among the *mestizo* population, and now this plague too was visited on Comanches. Syphilis became endemic, and Comanche sexual habits spread it like a conflagration through some bands. Thus the warriors who raped across northern Mexico, carrying off children and women to their camps, unknowingly loosed frightful consequences on their own people. By the 1830s and 1840s, there was frequent evidence of epidemic disease and venereal maladies north of the Red River.

The Comanches had remained numerous and powerful through the eighteenth century by their very aloofness, while the Texas Hasinai, Tonkawas, and other tribes had been decimated by Spanish smallpox. The People still did not accept permanent contacts with Mexicans or Europeans, but their raids into Mexico spread Old World diseases among them as surely as if they had gathered around the towns or allowed trading posts or "squaw men."

This, however, was relatively slow-working retribution. Through the 1840s, the balance of blood and destruction heavily favored the horse Amerindians. An expanding area of northern Mexico lay in ruin. Crumbling missions stood abandoned, forts deserted, towns and villages returned to the desert; the ruins sometimes puzzled later travelers. Black smoke rose from charred ranch houses, sweetened with the charnel smell of burning flesh. The population was largely confined to the isolated towns and cities. Travelers who saw smoke rise or the swirling pillars of vultures in the high, clear sky crossed themselves and fled to safety. The stubborn, patient *campesinos* clinging to the mountainous countryside buried their dead, wept, and endured.

Over a broad region, settlement and civilization were set back more than a hundred years.

IV
BLOOD
ON THE MOON
THE PEOPLE AND THE TEXANS

Though armed with the guns of civilized workshops,
European frontiersmen sloughed off nearly all
the legal and cultural restraints of civilized society.
　　　—William H. McNeill, *The Rise of the West*

1

THE ANGLO-AMERICANS
AND THE NORTH AMERICAN INDIANS

We have set our lodges in these groves
and swung our children from these boughs from time immemorial.
When the game beats away from us,
we pull down our lodges and move away,
leaving no trace to frighten it, and in a while it comes back.
But the white man comes and cuts down the trees,
building houses and fences, and the buffaloes
get frightened and leave and never come back,
and the Indians are left to starve,
or if we follow the game,
we trespass on the hunting grounds
of other tribes and war ensues.
　　　　—Speech of the Pehnahterkuh civil chief Mook-war-ruh,
　　　　reported by the emissary Noah Smithwick, 1837

WHILE THE OTHER EUROPEAN EMPIRES WERE FAILING IN THE SOUTH-
west, the British approach to North America had been radically
different from that of the French and Spanish. The English-speaking
colonization of America was peculiarly unimperial. Early colonists
along the Atlantic came in successive waves of dissidents from the
British Isles, and they came in family groups without help or hin-
drance, or even much notice, from the home government. Men and
women who braved the ocean had no conscious intention of planting flags, creating British outposts, developing a native commerce,
or conquering and ruling a native population. The vast majority
represented philosophies, ethics, cults, and life styles that had failed
to win acceptance at home, but that they hoped to transport successfully to the New World. They found no precious metals and no

resources except the land, which they exploited according to the dictates of their conscience and culture.

From New England to the southern plantations, the English-speaking colonists were remarkably homogeneous despite apparent diversity. The great majority were Protestant, with the puritan ethos of the British lower-middle ranks of the time. They were journeymen and mechanics and the sons of small merchants and yeomen farmers in the main, with strikingly common drives and views. If they were rebels against the established religious, social, and political order, they were in no sense true utopians, but one of the most empirical and pragmatic peoples in world history. The real thrust of their Protestant ethic was expressed far less in sexual puritanism than in a massive will to power, with a willingness to seize all the means to that end. For better or for worse, these were people determined to shape their lives and environments, dour and inflexible in goals, but almost infinitely malleable and adaptable in working toward those goals. The English emigrants at first erected only a few cities in America, and their general culture remained primitive for many years—but, as de Tocqueville saw, they were civilized men and civilizers in the most fundamental sense. They put down roots and shaped the earth to their use, gaining control over themselves and their environment as few peoples had in history. Their ethos and society in world terms were immensely dynamic, restless, reaching from power to acquired power.

This immensely flexible society easily absorbed other northern European strains, assimilating them into a genuine British-American branch of civilization. It was fed both by constant immigration and by a phenomenal natural increase. For more than two centuries, the Anglo-American birth and infant survival rate exceeded that of any region in the world, and indeed all parts of the twentieth-century world. What had been small enclaves along the Atlantic inevitably began to expand into what seemed to be limitless territorial space. It was thought by contemporaries in the eighteenth century that Anglo-America would require a thousand years to settle the Mississippi Valley; it was colonized from behind the Appalachians in two generations. This dynamic growth, the despair of the Latin empires in America, decided the cultural fate of the continent. By the middle of the eighteenth century, there were already more English-speaking people in North America than all other Europeans and Amerindians combined. These numbers, and their aggressive dynamism, in the end prevailed over Spanish claims and rights by exploration, French forts and flags and Amerindian alliances, and the resistance of countless tribes. The battles, land purchases, and treaties that ceded North America to the English-speaking civilization were only ratifications of the fact that a horde of dissidents from the British Isles had carried out the only successful European colonization of the continent.

Like the arrival of all Europeans, the coming of the English was tragic for the native Amerindians. The English, however, brought about the destruction of the natives—"aborigines" and "high barbarians" alike—in different ways. The English, who came to create new communities, a transplanted society, had no use for Amerindians in their scheme of things. Because the colonists brought their families, the early settlers never needed the natives sexually; in fact, the presence of white females in early British America made impossible any large-scale mixing between the races, as had occurred in parts of French Canada and colonial Mexico. Women created a true society, and the society threw up impassable barriers. The English, like all Indo-Europeans, believed in principle in the subordination and exploitation of weaker or inferior peoples, but the primitive Indians, as the Spanish discovered, were totally unfitted to be subordinated for labor. They could not be induced to work by any means. The endemic labor shortages that plagued the North American frontier were solved by the transportation of bond servants, and the importation of African slaves. And the English who arrived in the seventeenth century and later had no experience with or interest in conquering, converting, or incorporating strange peoples.

The type of colonists who dared the Atlantic and the wilderness saw America only in terms of land—endless, open, empty lands, put before them by Providence for their purpose and design. The natives' use of the land seemed to the English no use at all, or else so wasteful as to be utterly immoral. A thousand hard-working Europeans could live from the same acreage that supported a handful of indolent hunting Indians.

However, it is certain that the British did not envision the extermination of the natives. For a very long time, the dominant belief was that there was more than enough room on the continent for both races, and that the Indians must make room. English settlement always began on empty or loosely held Amerindian territories, for the few Indians were very widely scattered over immense regions. There was rarely any immediate dispossession; settlement came by treaty or sale. The agreements, of course, were classic ploys in European-style diplomacy. When few in numbers, weak, and fearful of powerful confederacies, the colonists asked for very little. As their numbers and power grew, the newcomers increased their demands—a process so natural in the European scheme of things that it was rarely questioned or even articulated. The Amerindians were naturally bewildered by the "faithless" diplomacy of unilaterally changing treaties to meet changed conditions, since the Amerindian world was static, and based on static principles. At the same time, the English failed to recognize their own explosive dynamism or else consistently underestimated it, for almost to the last the British immigrants pretended that it was possible to carve out permanent lines of demarcation—this land for whites, this reserved "forever" for the Amerindians. Further, the whites were under the tragic illusion that the two races could live side by side in peace, still failing to understand, perhaps willfully, the violent effects of their own impingement on the tribes. As these illusions were exploded over two centuries, another one replaced them, which clung to the bitter end: that the primitive peoples would accept what circumstance demanded, take the white man's road, and prepare themselves to take a place in the white man's civilization.

All these were impossible dreams, leading to trauma and tragedy for both races and cultures.

The Anglo-Americans, like other Europeans, did not comprehend the roots of the tragedy, for they never grasped the complexity, diversity, religiosity, and utter conservatism of the fragile native cultures. They understood the Amerindian cultures only on the technical or physical plane. They persisted in equating Amerindians with Indo-European barbarians, comparing Creeks and Cherokees to Germanic tribes of the second Christian century just because they lived on apparently similar technical levels. And the heirs of the Judeo-Christian, Hellenic, and Germanic European civilization did not then understand the profound depths and power of primitive cultures, nor the enormous gulfs that cultures opened between the various branches of mankind.

Ancient Greeks were close to ancient Slavs, and Gauls to technically superior, disciplined Romans, because both shared a common
Indo-European cultural consciousness. Their heritage included
concepts of private property, hierarchy and aristocracy, moral dual-
ism, and forms of serfdom, slavery, or similar subordination. The
differences between the Indo-European peoples came primarily
from acquired ideologies, disciplines, and techniques. Thus, grand-
sons of Gauls crucified by Caesar could and did become Roman
senators, because the great difference between the civilized Medi-
terraneans and the barbaric northerners lay in acquired sophisti-
cation. The Greeks and Romans, and the Franks who pushed
Christendom to the Elbe and Danube, were themselves only a
few centuries removed from the common barbarian base.

But the Amerindians were isolated from all Europeans by world-
views and cultural divergences that had been widening for at least
four thousand years. To become "civilized" like Anglo-Americans
(or Spaniards), the truly primitive tribesman had to do more than
learn a new language and pick up a few new techniques. He had to
betray his whole concept of the world and man's role in it, and
destroy all his cultural instincts and laws and beliefs—everything
that to him seemed natural or sacred. The Amerindian spirit world
and the European universe of cause and effect did not just exist on
higher and lower technical planes. They were utterly disparate and
innately hostile; the freedoms of one were the abject tyrannies of
the other, and vice versa. The Amerindian adjusted and attuned to
nature, gaining an enormous spiritual intoxication but little power
over the real or physical world. The Indo-Europeans who reached
America eschewed spiritual intoxication and even spiritual peace
while mastering the physical world—even if they had to destroy
it—by appalling, incessant labor. Even in the hungriest bands, no
Amerindian warrior accepted such crushing tyranny. The Indian, as
an Indian, could not go very far down any white man's road to
civilization.

It was quite impossible, for centuries, for Europeans to grasp this
fact. Because the ways of life and mastery of the universe of the
Indians proved them brutish, ignorant, and ineffective in European
power terms, the Europeans granted the Amerindians no real culture or religion. The whites saw the brutality and fearfulness and
fragility of native existence without understanding its spirituality,

for it plumbed heights and depths Europeans rejected or of which they remained ignorant. European vision was linear and practical, like its languages. When they did comprehend something of the Amerindians' mental universe, Europeans rejected it with the same psychic violence that the Indians threw up against interminable labor. In the manipulative Anglo-American universe, the Amerindian preferences were worse than ignorant, they were grossly immoral.

Conflict was inevitable when such world-views collided.

The immediate cause of conflict, however, was more mundane. It rose from utterly disparate forms of land use. Almost all North American Indians, whether true savages or high barbarians, lived in a fragile symbiosis with the native wilderness. Europeans, out of a process that went back to the prehistoric deforestations of Greece and Italy, were compelled to advance their causes and civilizations by remaking nature. Before entering America, the British had had no experience with a primeval wilderness. The first settlers could not have survived had they not learned agronomy and woods lore from the tribes that received them with the hospitality reserved for distant travelers. Once ensconced, the planters and Pilgrims were compelled to attack and destroy the wilderness in order to create civilization as they knew it. They felled trees, made roads, put up fences, and erected permanent structures; they carved out fields and made smoke rise from a thousand raw clearings. A mere handful of industrious white men in a region soon utterly changed the face and nature of the land forever, ruining it for the ancient uses of the Amerindians.

The whites exulted in each crashing timber, each painfully cleared field, each laboriously raised roof. The Amerindians, seeing what was being done, were oppressed and demoralized by the destruction of the whole panoply of their cultural existence. White land use to the Amerindians was like fencing the air or sea. What encroaching civilization created was as appalling to the Amerindian as a howling wilderness to the Anglo-American-European mentality.

To have expected the invading civilization to have choked off its own dynamic growth required far too much from human nature and the nature of expanding cultures. No tribe, race, society, or culture possessed immutable title to the planet, though time might lend legitimacy; such matters, historically, were adjudicated by power or force. Faced with destruction, the Amerindians had two choices. They could defend their lands and life by war, or they could adapt to the encroaching culture. The ultimate tragedy of the race was that the separated Amerindian cultures on the continent could do neither successfully.

If the struggle had been only for the land, the Indian wars fought over North America would have been no less bloody, but ultimately no more tragic than the wars that periodically readjusted the maps, governments, and land titles of Europe. The great mass of the population always survived such wars, and sometimes even benefited by them, as the Saxons in the end benefited by the Norman conquest. But this was a struggle for cultural life or death. In conquering, Anglo-American civilization necessarily had to destroy the natives, by a process that even Thomas Jefferson understood no better than generations of Spanish priests and educators.

The pattern that began in seventeenth-century Virginia and Massachusetts unfolded remorselessly, with only local variations from coast to coast.

First contacts between the strangers were usually peaceful. The Indians lacked hatred for strangers; their energies were engaged in enmities with neighboring tribes. The first whites, few and weak, anxiously avoided trouble while making arrangements to use Indian lands. The poor sense of territoriality of the Amerindians made alienation of such lands easy through agreement. Many first settlers were sincere; some failed to think beyond the day and their own desires; some made treaties with hypocrisy in their hearts, knowing full well that future demands would be presented to the Indians.

The newcomers provoked all wars, by moving into or up against Amerindian country. But the Amerindians, as often as not, actually precipitated hostilities. In the seventeenth and eighteenth centuries, few Anglo-American frontier people ever sought an "Indian war." They instead pursued the impossible dream of somehow civilizing the wilderness without taking account of the existence of the Amerindians. It was not quite true that the Pilgrim Fathers fell first upon their knees and then upon the nearest Indians. They would have accepted friendship with the Amerindians had the natives been willing to become puritan Englishmen, and when the Pilgrims began to change the landscape and oppress the Indian mind, it was the Indians who fell upon the Pilgrims.

The bloodiest Indian wars were actually fought along the Atlantic seaboard in the seventeenth century, never on the western plains. Here, the whites suffered their greatest losses in proportion to total numbers. Thousands of English colonists were killed from the Virginia tidewater to New England when at last the various eastern confederacies took the war trail in despair, to throw the encroaching newcomers back into the ocean.

The nature of the British settlement in America and the nature of Amerindian warfare must be taken into full account in understanding the development of the relations between the races.

English colonists arrived in small groups of people, seeking either refuge or opportunity in virgin wilderness. The English frontier was always essentially civilian, undefended by troops or fortifications. The colonists filtered into thinly populated Amerindian territories, creating small, isolated settlements. When war broke out between the races and cultures, the full fury of Amerindian warfare thus fell first upon small farms and lonely cabins.

The native warfare was essentially the same all across the continent. Amerindians made war by stealth, surprise, ambush, massacre of noncombatants, and the ferocious torment of prisoners. By European standards, it was not war, but murder. Furthermore, the early description of Indian wars as "uprisings" or "conspiracies" was not entirely self-serving. The angry tribes did not send ambassadors to declare war, then meet the Europeans man to man on some selected field. They rose in sudden, secret hysteria, enflamed by portents, visions, and medicine, and descended upon unsuspecting settlements with fire and slaughter.

Survivors of Indian raids—who practiced mercy killing on men who had been left staked out with eyes, tongues, and genitals cut or burned away, who found wives and daughters impaled on sharpened fence stakes, and who buried disemboweled or decapitated infants—were unable to rationalize a brotherhood of man that included American Indians. There were whites who had lived among the tribes and knew them intimately, who understood the Amerindian sense of honor and dignity and poetic grasp of the world, and recognized their essential humanity as people capable of warmth, love, pride, humor, and despair, with aggressions the more terrible for being entirely turned outward. In the main, however, little of the humanity of the Amerindians came across the cultural blocks and distances between the races. The dominant view óf

Amerindians among the English became one of inhuman savages who were unpredictable and dangerous predators—a sort of human vermin who stood as a barrier to the kind of civilized refuge the British immigrants hoped to build in North America. Since the whole frontier population—not a protecting line of soldiers—became involved in endemic Indian wars, the entire population was predictably brutalized. Suffering terrible wrongs themselves, the frontier people inflicted terrible wrongs upon the Amerindians.

As often happened in such confrontations, the civilized people adopted many of the barbaric practices of their foes. In turn, they made war on Amerindian villages, and the scalping of dead Indians was almost a universal custom on the Anglo-American frontier. And as the entire race became more and more dehumanized in the white mind, the killing of Indians—any Indians—took on little more importance than the removal of any other potentially dangerous marauders, such as the cougars and bears that infested the dense forests.

The seventeenth-century colony of Massachusetts Bay paid bounties for Indian hair as for the pelts of wolves, and no regret was expressed until both species were almost extinct in the region. One of the marked characteristics of the expansion of Anglo-America was the fact that sympathy for the Amerindians came to exist in direct proportion to the distance in time or territory from an Indian frontier—and in the beginning, every region of British America was in some sense an Indian frontier. The violent, brutal attitudes of New England and Virginia colonists toward the natives were reflected in the next century by frontiersmen in the Mohawk Valley and in Pennsylvania, then in Kentucky and the Trans-Appalachian West. The Indian wars became unintelligible and regrettable along the eastern seaboard only when the great majority of the population had no direct memory of them, and when, in fact, only a tiny minority was descended from settlers who had first come up against the tribes.

Had the British advance into North America been imperial like the Roman, with a frontier consolidated behind the pacifications of soldiers and the barbarians beyond the frontier held in check by forts and garrisons, the result would have been equally disastrous for the natives. But it would probably have been less bloody in the long run, and it certainly would have resulted in far less brutalization of the white population. The endemic bloodshed and eternal danger of every frontier region as the whites advanced into the continent inculcated a lasting strain of violence into American civilization just when such strains were vanishing in Western Europe. The American frontier was armed, turbulent, and lawless, and such social phenomena did not vanish with the disappearance of the frontier.

The British frontier was necessarily wild and brutal because, during the first two centuries of the Anglo-American advance through the continent, neither the British government nor the succeeding government of the United States prevented white settlers from encroaching upon the Amerindians, or offered either race effective protection. People went first into the wilderness, and only slowly and painfully pulled their governments after them.

A great difference between the English and Hispanic frontiers was that a people whose whole lives were devoted to private initiatives also seized military and governmental initiatives. The Anglo-American frontier was never passive, either toward the distant authorities in its rear or the nearby Indians. Frontier people organized their own warfare and rough local governments. Because their measures and their resources were never enough to provide adequate protection, the frontier suffered terribly in many regions— but in the long run the powers of the frontier people, together with the occasional assistance of the population behind the borderlands, were enough to bring destruction to the opposing Amerindians.

The Amerindians almost always won the first round of hostilities. Militias organized or arrived in the frontier settlements normally only in the aftermath of massacre. Distant governments, both of Great Britain and, later, the United States, were unwilling to assume the cost of permanent frontier garrisons; the frontier itself could not afford them. However, in the wooded regions of North America east of the Mississippi, the semiagrarian Amerindians were as vulnerable to frontier counteraction as the isolated white settlements were to raiding. The natives in fact were more so, because their numbers were static; they were undermined by serious losses; and they had neither the concepts nor the resources for sustained warfare as Europeans waged it.

Faced with an uprising, the whites usually took up the war after the Amerindians considered it successfully concluded. They buried their dead and planned destructive campaigns against the marauders. Supported by the swelling population in their rear, the whites could not be deterred by bloody defeats and hideous losses. Anglo-American militias fought summer and winter, carrying out extended campaigns that swept through Amerindian territory, burning fields and lodges. They waged war without ceremony, concluding it only after the dispersal or destruction of the enemy. They usually destroyed the Amerindian confederacies in a single, sustained campaign. Thus the New England lodges were erased, the fields of the Mohawks burned and the tribe left to starve beneath the snows, and the Ohio Valley peoples scattered and driven from their territories. The determined wars of the whites utterly demoralized the Amerindians.

The basic rhythm never changed as civilization pressed deeper and deeper into the continent. A few whites, eager to exploit new lands, filtered into tribal territories. Once the inevitable conflict broke out, the growing white population clamored for the destruction or removal of all Indians. The troubles might be brief, concluded in one season, or, as in Kentucky, they might continue for a decade of bloody raiding. But in every region the final act was the same: the destruction, displacement, or utter subjection of the natives. Where they remained, it was purely on the sufferance of the victorious civilization, and in marginal enclaves not wanted by the victors.

The defeated won small sympathy. There were lingering hatreds; the conquered did not adjust in ways that might have won them acceptance or sympathy. If Amerindian leaders often surrendered with grave, hopeless dignity, the majority of the tribes reacted to their changed conditions in ways that increased their denigration by the white men. Amerindians resisted all sincere imitation of their conquerors. Broken warriors refused to become economic men, to accept the concept of private property or the discipline of incessant labor. They either wandered westward, now strangers in a changed land, or squatted miserably on the fringes of the developing civilization. They clung apathetically but with unbreakable tenacity to whatever they could salvage of their ancient world-view and culture. They absorbed the vices of the white civilization while rejecting its virtues. A common sight in "pacified" regions of the frontier was impoverished bands of Indians, remnants of once proud and independent peoples, who had become purposeless and utterly broken. They wore cast-off clothing and lived in drunkenness and degradation, slinking about the burgeoning settlements. Most nineteenth-century American communities in the new West had their "Indian Joes," dwindling numbers of Amerindians who could not make the full adjustment to the new culture, who were dying out in limbo. Even then they were hated and feared and despised, not because they touched the white conscience, but because they remained a nuisance. Hungry, they stole, and sometimes were gripped by inchoate, murderous rages. In defeat, the Amerindian tragically buttressed the Anglo-American view of the race and culture as dirty, lazy, intractable savages—people who would not help themselves and were therefore irredeemable.

Just as it required too much from human nature for the whites to have eschewed the conquest of the continent, it required too much from the cultural drives of any people to have expected the whites to permit the conquered to redeem themselves under any but the terms of the conquering civilization.

Although the white frontier people descended into brutal savagery themselves in the Indian wars, the wars clearly revealed the great differences in the capabilities of the cultures.

The white conquest in its violent phases was rarely the result of superior numbers or even technology, but of superior organization and superior application of power. The Amerindian could never match the awesome purposefulness of the Anglo-American. While the frontier regions regularly went up in flames, while settlers were besieged in desperate straits, and militias and entire armies from Braddock to St. Clair blundered and were massacred in the forests, the encroaching culture rapidly adapted itself. Just as the early farmers had learned native agronomy from the Amerindians, the frontier whites survived by appropriating the techniques of Amerindian warfare. They discarded pikes and swords and mass formations, taking up the hand ax and the German rifle, far better tools for skirmishes in the densely forested wilderness. They studied the techniques of the enemy to turn his weaknesses against him. Above all, they took advantage of native allies, which the incessant warfare of the tribes always provided, and used these callously. Learning that the random warfare of the Amerindians could rarely sustain a protracted siege, they erected log stockades to serve as community forts in time of danger. By European standards, the rough frontier people were anarchic and undisciplined—but they were far more tenacious, empirical, and flexible than their enemies.

Conversely, the Amerindians seem to have learned virtually nothing from centuries of contact with the conquering civilization. Their very culture barred them from adaptiveness. They took from whites only those things, like guns and iron, that they could fit into their existing cultural patterns. The notion that culture should or could be adapted or adjusted to the pursuit of power or social goals —instinctive to Anglo-Americans—was alien to the Indians. The static Amerindian cultures maintained their strengths and weaknesses to the end.

The long warfare and the total dehumanization of the native race in the American mind eventually had crucial effects in law and policy. Dehumanization obviated any rights the Amerindians might have secured under Anglo-American law, just as a similar dehumanization erased the rights of African slaves. Unlike the Spanish, the British-Americans were not accustomed to accepted hierarchies and legal caste or class distinctions, and this "democracy" actually worked ferociously against "inferior" peoples and cultures. Under Spanish law, an *indio* or Negro could be enslaved while still retaining his essential humanity and certain rights before society. A people who insisted on equal, inalienable rights for all citizens, however, could only subordinate noncitizens by making them into animals. Negro slaves were chattels, like livestock, under Anglo-American law; the Indians became, in effect, trespassing vermin on "American" soil. By the early nineteenth century, such policies had hardened into accepted law.

The American republic granted the Amerindians no ownership rights to lands within the assumed jurisdiction of the United States; they had only treaty rights, which made them tenants at will. Although the fiction continued to be used that the tribes were autonomous "nations," they had become in reality wards of the government. As wards without powers or prescribed rights, they suffered the usual fate of charges of great, impersonal institutions.

Two hundred years of Indian troubles worked cruelly against the handful of tribes that consciously tried to adjust and assimilate to the white world. The Cherokees and certain other southern peoples —the so-called civilized tribes—were making rapid progress toward agrarian civilization early in the nineteenth century. They lived peacefully within their restricted territories; they farmed like whites, built permanent, comfortable houses, and some individuals had even acquired black slaves. The immediate reason behind the expropriation of these Indians' lands and the expulsion of most of them to the newly designated Indian Territory in the 1820s and 1830s was the greed of state governments and individuals who coveted the tribes' remaining territories, and the pressure these forces brought on the federal government. But the American nation permitted the "trail of tears" over which thousands of uprooted agrarian tribesmen were driven toward the western wilderness because the conventional wisdom of most Americans held that there was no place for Indians, as Indians, within the nation. Many people did oppose the ruthless expulsions, but the dominant view was that the two cultures could not meet or merge in harmony, and that therefore the weaker must give way. The tribes stood in the way of the building of a new nation, whose power and security in the 1820s were far from established. The assimilating Cherokees were victims of this great drive to consolidate the nation, but by the close of the century, they had assimilated in any case. The Cherokees were the first Amerindians to gain citizenship, and in fact they disappeared as a distinct people into the white mass.

The gradual destruction of the Amerindians east of the Mississippi had become a series of decreasingly important footnotes in the emergence of the American nation. Yet this advance over dark and bloody ground spawned more than frontier folklore and colorful accounts of Indian wars. While both the American government and people, whatever face is put on it or whatever rationale is made, agreed with Theodore Roosevelt that the continent had to be redeemed from the wilderness in the interests of mankind, rather than left as a game preserve for "squalid savages," the Anglo-Americans carried out the conquest by doing what came naturally. They developed no rationale for empire. Unhappily, the Judeo-Christian ethic, Hellenic rationality, and the premises upon which the republic was based provided no rationale for what happened to the Indians. And just as the bloody frontier turbulence left a cult of violence in America, the ruthless necessity of destroying the original proprietors of the continent left a shadow on the American soul. The wars and mutual atrocities that the passage spawned occurred in modern times, but this was a struggle of a kind that had largely passed from the modern European consciousness.

The Indian wars harkened back to the ethnic conflicts and invasions of earlier ages. The destruction of the Amerindians was another destruction of Canaanites or Carthaginians. Moral considerations were drowned in terrible imperatives, while right and wrong dissolved in mutual atrocity. The closest modern analogy, perhaps, is the war for cultural life or death in Palestine. It was a struggle and experience that Americans survived successfully, but which did damage to American illusions about human nature and conduct, the world, and themselves.

The Indian wars called up forces that could not be intellectually or ethically analyzed within accepted American parameters. The poetic, honorable Amerindian roasted his cultural foes to death over slow fires with apparent enjoyment; many devoutly Christian and well-educated white men coldly shot fleeing Indian women or bashed out infants' brains with gun butts. The wars between civilized whites and barbaric Amerindians were carried out on the same level as the conflicts among the Indians, and many whites never understood this inevitability. On the frontier, it was Them or Us, and They were killed so that We might live. In such wars the defeated vanish in ignominy. The winners hold out neither hope nor generosity.

The wars were therefore high tragedy, between human beings who could not help themselves. The conflict was inevitable. The result was inevitable only in the light of relative strengths and weaknesses. The static cultures failed heroically. The dynamic civilization brutally prevailed, but suffered psychic trauma.

The pattern was set long before Americans came to Texas and so into contact with the powerful Nermernuh on the plains. But in Texas, the racial-cultural conflict was to reach its highest and bloodiest intensity on the continent since the seventeenth century.

Here began the climax of the true American tragedy, the final destruction of the last autonomous North American Indians.

2

PARKER'S FORT

Elder John was killed, scalped, and mutilated.
Granny Parker was disrobed, speared,
and outraged and left for dead.
　　　—Mildred P. Mayhall, *Indian Wars of Texas*

BY THE TIME THE ANGLO-TEXANS FORCED THEIR INDEPENDENCE FROM
Mexico, the Amerindian situation had become confused and turbulent all across the midcontinent. Thousands of eastern Amerindians
were being pushed or had voluntarily migrated toward the fringes
of the Great Plains between 1825 and 1840. The displaced peoples,
regarded as evicted trespassers by the advancing whites, were considered interlopers and invaders by the western tribes. During the
1820s and 1830s, the movements set off terrible conflicts between
impinging and impinged-upon Indians. Despite popular mythology,
the easterners, who were usually better armed and organized than
the western tribes, held their own very well in these bloody clashes,
most of which occurred beyond the American frontier and so never
entered the American consciousness.

From about 1819 onward, large numbers of these "immigrant"
Amerindians passed south of the Red River into northeast Texas.
They settled near the remnants of the Caddoan peoples and the
small Wichita bands along the rivers, taking up great sections of the
rich timberlands that in these years had not yet been penetrated by
Spanish or Anglo-American colonists. These tribes included many
eastern remnants—Delawares, Shawnees, Kickapoos, and smaller
bands—with a very large contingent of Cherokees. All these tribes

were consciously fleeing the borders of the United States, which lay along the Sabine-Red River boundary.

The immigrant Amerindians were primarily agrarian, aware of the futility of further fighting the Americans but also determined to cling to their old life. Mexican Texas was their last refuge, except for the Indian Territory of eastern Oklahoma, which had been set aside for the eastern tribes by the United States government. Moving into Texas, the migrants had run out of territory. Collectively, they wanted only to grow their squash, beans, and corn in peace, and, collectively, their situation was anomalous and tragic. Wherever they went they sparked savage wars with the proprietary tribes. All the agrarian barbarians, like the Cherokees who were refugees from the hills of Tennessee and North Carolina, stood on the last ground they could use in North America. The Cherokees had been ruthlessly dispossessed in the South, while the Algonquian Kickapoos had come originally from far Wisconsin. The Kickapoo tribe was mauled and driven southward into Missouri-Kansas by great wars with the Illinois confederacy in the middle eighteenth century. In the nineteenth century, they came into Texas with the associated Potawatomies, and like the Cherokees, they were through with running. Staking out their fertile fields, they were a nuisance to everyone. The western Amerindians resented them and made war on them; the oncoming whites, desiring their lands, wanted them out of the way of settlement.

Although these migrants were largely peaceful, they willingly returned war on other Indians, and they were not above stealing livestock from the whites or killing isolated settlers they found unprotected. Even the lowly Caddoans occasionally engaged in murderous raids. While few of the displaced agrarians were a real threat to the Anglo-American frontier, they were disliked and distrusted, especially by a white majority who failed to distinguish between different kinds of Indians. Their existence confused matters on the Texas frontier, where the average Anglo-American farmer could not tell a Comanche from a Cherokee.

Few if any of the Anglo-Americans who settled in Texas in the 1820s wanted trouble with the Amerindians. Stephen F. Austin was fully cognizant of the Mexican/Comanche problem and deliberately attempted to avoid being caught up in it. Austin himself was captured by Comanches during a journey into Mexico, but quarrels with strange *americanos* were beyond the purview of Comanche mood or medicine. Convinced that this stranger was neither Spanish nor Mexican, his captors offered him hospitality and let him go in peace, while they rode on to spread terror through northern Mexico. Austin's policies, of course, frustrated Mexican hopes for an Anglo-American buffer; he continually put the authorities off with promises to assist when his colony became "strong enough."

During the Anglo-Texan revolt against Mexico, the rebel government was fearful of an attack by the various Texas Indians. The Texans sent emissaries to all the tribes in the west and north, soliciting peace treaties. The Cherokees and other tribes—who in this period might have wreaked fearful damage on the Texan flank, perhaps even causing a decisive defeat of the Texan cause—agreed to remain neutral. The Comanches, far out on the plains, remained indifferent. The tribes had no understanding that the guns at San Jacinto not only ended the Mexican empire above the Rio Grande but sounded their own death knell.

But by the time the embattled farmers at San Jacinto returned to their fields and homes, Indian trouble could no longer be avoided. Both before and after San Jacinto, new hordes of settlers were pouring over the Sabine. Unlike the essentially capitalistic and relatively affluent slaveholding cotton planters who formed the backbone of the early colony, the later immigrants were largely Trans-Appalachian frontier Americans. They were the descendants of earlier North American pioneers, people without capital or slaves, who were drawn inexorably toward the opportunities inherent in the open western lands. Many were the "leatherstockings" Austin refused admittance into his colony: rifle-toting frontiersmen who went into the wilderness to build lonely cabins and carve out stump-strewn cornfields. At least a quarter were Scots-Irish, descendants of the last European white barbarians, instinctive borderers whose own civilization was a thin veneer. They were a tough, dour, unmilitary yet inherently warlike people, preferring incessant action to self-contemplation. They were not the carriers of the Anglo-American civilization, but rather that civilization's heroic and necessary vanguard.

They moved westward in whole clans, taking wives, children, and old people with them into the unknown wilderness that opened higher on the Brazos and the Colorado. They were fired with visions of endless lands and future fortunes. They staked out farms, hewed timbers, labored prodigiously, and lived poorly in rude cabins. Some were shiftless hunters who never really harvested a crop and who wandered from place to place with defeated, pallid women and hungry, dirty children. But the dominant minority among them attacked the wilderness with ravaging energy, seizing lands and sinking roots, driven by forces they never rationalized to master the earth and bring civilization as they knew it. They cut their way deep into the rolling post-oak belts of central Texas, pushing higher and higher toward the great, rising limestone plateaus of the inner plains. They were a people as much made by their experience on the continent as the Amerindians.

Many of them had come through Kentucky and the Missouri country, and brought vivid folk memories of hideous Indian wars. Yet they tended to ignore the Amerindians, or else to see them as mere obstacles to their progress, like flood, drought, disease, and other natural catastrophes.

They moved not onto the hunting ranges, but into the raiding range of the Nermernuh, beginning the longest lasting and bloodiest confrontation between two races on the North American continent.

THE EVIDENCE IS CLEAR THAT THERE WAS NO IMMEDIATE HOSTILITY between the Texans and Comanches. Until at least 1835, the Texan line of settlement was still hundreds of miles south or east of true *Comanchería*. The Texans on this frontier neither knew nor cared much about the existence of horse Indians. They were wary of them, as most Anglo-Americans had become wary or distrustful of all Amerindians. No settler in his right mind sought trouble deliberately. The Comanches who began to scout the raw new settlements were also uneasy. The whites were too different from People. Thus the first contacts were restrained, and strained, on either side.

It is certain, however, that the Comanches made early, dangerous errors of assessment. Their notion of civilized societies sprang from Spanish-Mexican contacts. Because the Texans followed roughly similar lives and appeared much the same, the People tended to equate them with the Mexicans. They believed that Anglo-Texans had the same social, military, and governmental system as Mexicans, and they approached them much as they would have approached a Mexican community with which they were not at war, such as New Mexico.

Despite their continual unease with outside relations, the bands had grown much more flexible in certain ways. Their history now included truce with Wichitas, alliance with the Kiowas, and a profitable arrangement with the New Mexican Comancheros. The bands were moving toward the pragmatic Great Peace with the Cheyennes and Arapahos. It might have been possible for the Texans and Comanches to have hammered out an ephemeral arrangement like that between the bands and Santa Fe, and it is known that in the first years of contact certain Comanches made trading relationships in which the bands disposed of loot acquired in Mexico. In the early 1830s, farmers and traders in what was then west Texas accepted Mexican goods and horses and asked no questions.

But war was inevitable because of the natures of the two peoples. Though ultimately the white tide would have reached the plains, the conflict came years before that happened, for the Texans went deeper and deeper onto the central plateaus, carving out their isolated farms and settlements within raiding distances. They brought a new, impressive breed of horse from Kentucky and other eastern states, which the Comanches immediately coveted for breeding with their Spanish mustangs. They put heavy horses and unprotected scalps within easy reach of any socially ambitious warrior. Besides the pressure of these almost irresistible temptations dangled in the faces of a race that had come to live by raiding, the Anglo-Celtic Texan frontiersmen were psychologically incapable of acting out the role of Comancheros.

The Texans lacked the subtlety of Mexicans. They regarded the Amerindians as ignorant savages—they could not bring themselves to cater to such folk even when they feared them. Few Texans could gracefully stomach the kind of arrogance the Comanches displayed to the Mexicans. Further, the frontier people were mostly subsistence farmers, whose only wealth was the potential in the lands they cultivated. They possessed no spare livestock or riding horses; they had nothing like the vast, carelessly counted herds of the ranching Mexicans. The demand of the Comanches for presents at every meeting affronted them—and their curt refusal to offer tribute affronted most Comanches. Texans were willing to trade, but they drove hard bargains. They "cheated" the Indians probably less than the New Mexicans, but they traded with far less grace and deference. The notion of buying peace was morally repugnant to their own sense of manhood.

From Comanche accounts, it is clear that all this outraged and provoked the volatile Amerindians. All outside relationships were touch-and-go with Comanche warriors, who were under enormous social pressures to maintain a truculent aggressiveness. While many historians wrote that the Texans were at fault in these early dealings with the Comanches, it is perhaps significant that the anthropologists who have delved most deeply into Comanche culture have said that conflict was unavoidable.

The events at Parker's Fort, and their portents, were as inevitable as a Greek tragedy. Both peoples acted out of their deepest social imperatives.

In the year 1834, the Parkers, a family from Virginia by way of Tennessee and Illinois, migrants in the frontier pattern of the times, explored the country further onto the Brazos bottoms than any white settlers had done before. They discovered a beautiful, open, oak-studded country of rolling plains, well watered and teeming with wild game. The soil was rich for corn, and the stream bottoms thick with deer and turkey. This was nominally Wichita territory; the closest Amerindians were the Wacos on the Brazos; but the land itself was uninhabited. The Parkers chose their fields carefully near the Navasota River, a tributary of the Brazos, in what later became Limestone County, Texas. Here they erected a log stockade, and were joined by several other frontier families, making a small settlement of some thirty pioneers.

Besides the men, women, and children at "Parker's Fort," there were only two other white cabins in the region.

The Parker clan were "Hardshell" Baptists, members of a stern, puritanical Protestant sect who believed in hard work and a rigid morality, and were dubious of any other route to heaven. They were farmers who thought that they had every right to come into this country. They built a "fort" and went armed, because all sensible Americans exercised vigilance on the far frontier. They had no intention of disturbing or fighting Indians, or of fighting anyone. The Parker men took no part in the Texas revolution; the entire clan fled to the Trinity at the approach of the Mexican forces under Santa Anna in the spring of 1836. When they received the news of the Texan victory at San Jacinto, they returned immediately to their fields. Like the thousands of other Texans who did the same, they needed no government or higher authority to give purpose and direction to their lives. Their entire energies were devoted to taming the wilderness and wresting a living from it.

On May 19, 1836, most of the settlement's men went to work as usual in the corn, which was planted just beyond the line of sight of the walled stockade. A few men remained behind with the colony's women and children, busy at various tasks. Thus there was only a handful of males inside the fort when a large party of mounted Amerindians appeared outside the walls. There were at least a hundred warriors, one of whom waved a soiled white flag.

The men inside included Elder John Parker, the patriarchal leader of the clan, his sons Silas and Benjamin, and Samuel Frost and his son. They agreed to parley with the Indians, because the riders continued making friendly signals. The Parkers were uneasy, but did not stand to arms.

Benjamin, who was unmarried, went outside to talk. Silas, who had four young children, held the gate. The Frosts and John Parker remained with the assembled families.

Benjamin Parker conferred briefly with the Indians, who remained on their horses, in pidgin and sign talk. As later verified, the Indians were mostly Comanches from beyond the Red River, together with a few Kiowas, Wichitas, and Caddoans. The nature of this band is obscure. The suspicion remains that this was a war party of convenience, made up of young males looking for adventure. Such bands, in these years, frequently coalesced ephemerally, wild spirits joined together in the borderlands beyond the territory of any tribe. The Plains Amerindians frequently made truces to make war against the interloping easterners; the agrarians formed alliances against the Plains tribes. Such alliances, always brief, were frequently formed against any enemy—a fact that the whites believed justified their distrust of all Indians.

Benjamin walked back to the gate, saying that the Indians asked directions to a water hole and demanded to be given a beef to eat. He stated that he did not think they were entirely friendly. He had refused the beef, but he would go back and try to avoid a fight. Over Silas' protests, he returned to the parley with the now obviously surly Amerindians.

The people in the fort saw the riders suddenly surround him and drive their lances into him. Then, with loud whoops, mounted warriors dashed for the gate. Silas Parker was cut down before he could bar their entry; horsemen poured inside the walls. The two Frosts, father and son, died in front of the women; Elder John Parker, his wife, "Granny," and the others tried to flee. The warriors scattered and rode them down.

There were a few, brief, murderous moments of horror and wild confusion inside the fort. Several warriors seized John Parker and his wife; others rode after the other women and children, in a shrieking, bloody melee.

The early sixteenth- and seventeenth-century European accounts of Amerindian warfare usually recorded events in stark simplicity. This was no longer true by the nineteenth century. Reports became clothed in Victorian delicacy; newspaper accounts and even military records obscured details with awkward euphemisms. Such understatement may have obscured the true nature of events for readers who had never come into personal contact with the frontier, though they deceived no one on the frontier itself. The newspapers of the day printed sanitized versions, often quoted by historians.

But what happened was that John Parker was pinned to the ground; he was scalped and his genitals ripped off. Then he was killed and further mutilated. Granny Parker was stripped and fixed to the earth with a lance driven through her flesh. Several warriors raped her while she screamed. The other women were seized and attacked; two were seriously injured and left with gaping wounds.

Silas Parker's wife Lucy fled through the gate, shepherding her four small children. But the riders overtook her near the river; they threw her and the children over their horses to take them back. Now, however, men were running from the fields with rifles. One David Faulkenberry, a brave soul, rushed to Lucy Parker's rescue. He forced the warriors to drop Lucy and two of the children, but one made off with Cynthia Ann and John Parker, aged nine and six.

Then, as more Parker men arrived, the entire war party leaped for its horses and galloped away from the confining space of the stockade. The horde could have killed all the whites in the vicinity, but the warriors were satisfied with the great triumph they had scored, by their lights, without casualties. They rode north in a cloud of dust toward the Trinity.

They had killed five men, mauled several women and left them for dead. They carried away two young women, Elizabeth Kellogg and Rachel Plummer, and three small children, the two Parkers and Rachel Plummer's fifteen-month-old son, James.

The shaken colony knew nothing about the habits of Comanches. Afraid that the Indians would return, the settlers hid along the river bottoms till sundown. Then, David Faulkenberry and Abram Anglin approached the fort. They found Granny Parker crawling outside the gate, trying to reach water. She had pulled herself free from the Comanche lance; she was a tough old woman, and she survived. But that night two of the other women died.

The men kept the families hidden in the bottoms all night and all the next day, not daring to expose themselves even to bury the fly-buzzing bodies. Finally, the survivors rounded up horses, gathered a few provisions, and fled to the nearest settlement, many miles to the east.

Meanwhile, the warriors who rode away toward the Trinity followed every ancient custom of warfare on the plains. They pushed their ponies furiously till past midnight to put as much distance as possible between themselves and pursuit. The captives were tied to ponies to keep them from falling off; they were battered, bruised, chafed, terrified, and half-conscious when the Comanches halted and made camp. The warriors picketed their horses to graze, then tied all the captives hand and foot with rawhide thongs, and threw them face down upon the ground.

The party now felt safe enough to stage a victory dance. Warriors leaped and pranced about a fire, recounting their individual exploits and brandishing their bloody scalps. This was the sweetest moment of Amerindian warfare. The raid had been a complete success; no one had been lost; and best of all, there were live captives to witness the warriors' triumph and add to it with their own humiliations. In the frenzy of the dance, the warriors kicked the captives and whipped them with bows until blood ran from their backs and legs.

They did not harm the children further. But the two adult women were stripped naked and subjected to more torture. However, this torment was not so much sadistic as part of a rite of total humiliation, which was important to the Amerindians. The two women were not seriously injured, for the warriors had no intention of killing them. They were to be slaves. Captive women who were frightened with torture and threats of torture made less trouble and quickly learned to perform on command. In the final act, both women were raped through the night in full view of the bound children.

Elizabeth Kellogg and Rachel Plummer, both married women, were the first American females known to be taken captive by Comanches. They were treated no differently from women of the Pawnees or Utes. In the reservation years, when Indians were being tried and hanged for "crimes" against the whites, few Comanches, logically, ever admitted to the taking or abuse of captives, and their descendants tended emotionally to deny rapes and tortures for the same reasons that descendants of the Aztecs tried to deny that the Mexica ceremonially ate human flesh. However, to the Plains tribes all females were chattels, and despite a great deal of studied delicacy on the subject, there was never to be a known case of white women captives who were not subjected to abuse and rape. When they could be led to talk, returned captives told the same story, and until the last half of the nineteenth century, Comanche warriors proudly asserted such exploits.

After such initiations, few women ever put up any serious resistance. It was in fact utterly impossible for a captive female to defy a Comanche warrior. The men might kill a troublesome female out of exasperation, but they usually used equally direct but more imaginative means to secure obedience. A captive was always exhausted, bound, and stripped naked in the warrior's presence. The Comanches did not need to use crippling tortures on a captive they wanted to keep. One simple tactic was to make captives run behind a horse, hands bound and attached to the rider by a thong. Bare legs and feet were cruelly lacerated by stones and thorns, and if the captive stumbled or fell from exhaustion, dragging caused exquisite pain. Caucasian captives who were made to walk or ride nude under the southwestern sun suffered agonizing sunburns. Captives quickly learned that complete cooperation was infinitely preferable to the punishments the warriors could devise. There is no record, despite white myths, of women destroying themselves under such circumstances. They clung to life and avoided punishment. Once far out on the plains the captors no longer bothered to keep captives bound, for escape into the wilds meant certain death from thirst or starvation.

Elizabeth Kellogg and Rachel Plummer survived their initial ordeal, the first of many.

At dawn, the Amerindian party broke up. The Comanches and Kiowas went west, taking Mrs. Plummer and the three young children. Elizabeth Kellogg was the property of Caddoans or Wichitas. These warriors took her with them to the Red River. The Kellogg woman was relatively lucky: The Caddoans kept her for six months, but then fell in with a group of Delawares, immigrant eastern Amerindians. They sold her to the Delawares for $150 worth of goods. The Delawares then took her to Nacogdoches in east Texas, where they turned her over to agents of the Republic of Texas for the same price. Here Elizabeth Kellogg vanishes from history.

However, Rachel Plummer and the children were captives of northern or eastern Comanches, probably Nawkohnees, though families came and went between the bands so rapidly in these years that it was impossible to keep track. These Comanches traveled rapidly across the High Plains, finally making camp in eastern Colorado.

The children, even the tiny James Plummer, survived the shock of captivity and were quickly adopted and initiated into Comanche life and culture. Soon, they were dressed like the People, spoke the People's language, and enjoyed tough bison meat. The older Parker children rode like born Comanches within a few months.

The adjustment was entirely different for young Rachel Plummer. Even for a frontier farm wife, her role was now one of degradation. She was a warrior's slave, without status in the camp, assigned the most menial and laborious tasks. She became as filthy and lice-ridden as her captors, insensitive to the humiliations of her lot. She later left a complete statement detailing the cruelties and abuses she suffered.

She bore a child in Colorado, but this infant was killed, according to her account, by being dashed upon the winter ice. One old Comanche female, a relative of her master, treated her to special abuse, beating her constantly and tormenting her with malicious cruelty. One day, she rebelled. She seized a club and knocked the old woman to the ground. Rachel expected to be killed, but she had learned nothing about Comanche culture. Her master was merely amused, and, significantly, the beatings ceased, for she had established herself in the pecking order among the females.

After many months of this life, she was seen by a party of visiting Comancheros. The presence of an Anglo-American woman in the Comanche camp was no concern of the New Mexicans, but it was unusual at this time, and they mentioned it upon return to Santa Fe. The news disturbed an American trader named Donahue. He commissioned the Comancheros to seek her out and attempt a ransom.

The Comancheros located Rachel Plummer in a camp some seventeen days' journey north of Santa Fe, in the foothills of the Rockies. They were able to deal for her, but not for her son James and the Parker children, who had been adopted into Comanche families. The Comancheros carried her back to Santa Fe; she had been in captivity for eighteen months.

Donahue and his wife escorted her over the long trail to Independence, Missouri, where she was met by a relative, who took her back to Texas.

The position of a returned female captive, however, was always anomalous on the nineteenth-century American frontier. The frontier's puritanical views and rigid racial and sexual shibboleths made it impossible for such unfortunate women to be accepted gracefully back into their communities. They were objects of sincere pity, but they were also considered dirty and disgraced, for they had been the playthings of creatures the Americans regarded as animals. They were embarrassments to their families. Some husbands would not receive them or live again with them. Ironically, most returned women suffered more real shame and humiliation among their own people than among the Comanches. If they came back with halfbreed children, their position, and that of the unhappy children, was even more unfortunate. When they could, such women left the frontier and all old associations forever. Rachel Plummer died within less than a year after her ransom and return to civilization.

The Parker raid and the fate of the captives quickly became a cause célèbre across the entire southwestern frontier. The Parker and Plummer families made every effort to find and bring back the children. Americans doing business in New Mexico, which at this time was still Mexican, and United States Army troops in the Indian Territory, who in the 1830s still maintained uneasy but peaceful relations with the northern Comanches, all aided in the search. Although Texas was a separate nation, American and Texan officialdom were united in matters of this kind, and the U.S. Army kept up continual inquiries beyond the borders of Texas.

John Parker and James Plummer were located and ransomed in 1842. The Plummer boy spoke no English, but he was still young enough to make the second transition. John Parker, however, had become too much of a Comanche ever to be reassimilated with his own kind. He was twelve, and he felt close ties only with his sister, whom the bands refused to return, for she had become a Comanche wife. John stayed with his people only until he was big enough to run away, then he moved across the plains, seeking Cynthia Ann. He was in no danger. If he met Comanches, he too could state that he was Nermernuh, of the People, despite his light eyes and fair skin. He never found her, and eventually he took a Mexican girl who was a captive among the Comanches and settled in the desert below the Rio Grande.

Cynthia Ann Parker was now among the Kwerhar-rehnuh, the most remote and fiercest of the bands. Continual rumors of her existence out on the Llano Estacado reached officers in the Indian Territory, and there were occasional sightings. An American colonel saw her briefly at a council when she was seventeen. He said that she refused to speak in English, and burst into tears. He was unable to talk further, because the Comanches became hostile and threatening. All attempts at ransom, which American officers found a frustrating and humiliating experience, failed. Cynthia Ann Parker, now Naduah the Comanche woman, had become the wife of Peta Nawkohnee (Nacona or Nokoni), an important warrior who eventually led his own band. She now had small children and had no desire to return—if she remembered her old life at all.

There was no evidence that she was unhappy on the plains. However, the knowledge that she was a Comanche "squaw" continually fed dark racial and sexual angers across the Texas frontier. A spark of violence and hatred had been lit at Parker's Fort that would burn for forty years. The raid had spawned a tragedy that dogged the Parker blood, and its continuing reverberations would last till the twilight of the Texan-Comanche wars.

Parker's Fort was the beginning of the longest and bloodiest of all the wars between the Anglo-Americans and any single Amerindian people. As if it were a tocsin, in 1836, the western regions of Texas began to flame from Comanche raids. The bands quickly expanded their warfare to include the Texans; they had found the range. The Parker raid was only the first of hundreds like it, which spread killings, tortures, rapes, and tragic captivities all across the borderlands. This was not a frontier of military forts or towns, or of traders and trappers, like so much of the contemporary United States' plains frontier. The Texans were moving thousands of unprotected farming families west. Following their individual stars, the Anglo-Texans pressed on. In the 1830s, what was then west Texas became a bloody ground, filled with pioneer families who had lost fathers and sons, wives and daughters, who had buried their mutilated dead and ransomed young women who returned with demented stares. In a few months blows were struck and insults given that the Texan people could neither forget nor forgive.

One of the deep ironies of history was that the sedentary Amerindians in eastern Texas were to become largely innocent, oblique victims of the opening war on the western frontier. In December 1836, the Texas Congress howled down President Sam Houston's proposal to grant the "semicivilized," immigrant Cherokees full title to their lands, in replacement of mere treaty rights, and thus assure these Amerindians the protection of Anglo-American law. The Congress was in a mood for war: it authorized a mounted battalion for frontier defense and the construction of a string of forts in Indian territory. Shortly afterward, the Congress called for a corps of "600 mounted gun men" for service in the northwest.

Sam Houston, who had lived among the Cherokees in Tennessee, was a genuine friend of the race, which he trusted and admired. He was an anomaly among Americans in high office of his times: he tried to stand between the popular mood and the Amerindians. Despite the fact that Houston refused to implement the congressional measures and spent none of the republic's funds on forts or troops, he could not prevent a war that had already begun. Few Texans knew or worried about variations among different sorts of Indians. They were all "red niggers" to be removed as soon as possible from "Texan" soil. Houston's policy, and his strenuous efforts to make peace with all Amerindians, did not lead to peace with the

Comanches; such efforts merely postponed a full-scale war with the sedentary tribes through the making of promises Houston could not keep.

Meanwhile, the Comanches who now found splendid raiding opportunities down the Brazos and the Colorado were also incapable of understanding the Texan-Americans. They did not perceive that this was a people unlike the other Europeans they had met. Texans appeared to be peasants blundering onto the plains—miserable, grubbing people whose seat in the saddle brought smiles to Comanche warriors' lips; who seemed to fear war and lacked war skills, and who recklessly exposed their women and children.

The People failed to sense the deep-seated belligerence of the Texan-Americans toward anyone who opposed or injured them, or who aroused their passion or contempt. The Texans were not cruel; they lacked the cruelty as well as the subtlety of the Spanish and the French. But they were vastly more brutal and ruthless in sustained determination. That determination was immediately apparent. The shattered Parker clan did not desert the far frontier. It went back to Parker's Fort, tended the fields, and harvested the ripening corn. The men now went armed and vigilant, distrusting and despising all Amerindians. The settlement prospered, and as other hundreds slowly joined them in this country, the family grew prominent in the region.

But Parker's Fort had begun an ethnic-racial war in which there would be no more moral boundaries than territorial ones between the races on the Texas prairies. People who had been raided, who buried their rotting dead and prayed for captured loved ones, only affirmed the old American proverb that the only good Indian was a dead one.

3

ADAPTATIONS:
THE AMERICAN APPROACH TO
THE HORSE AMERINDIANS

The character of the Texan Ranger is now well known
by both friend and foe. As a mounted soldier
he has had no counterpart in any age or country.
Neither Cavalier nor Cossack, Mameluke nor Moss-trooper
are like him; and yet, in some respects, he resembles them all.
Chivalrous, bold and impetuous in action, he is yet wary and calculating,
always impatient of restraint, and sometimes unscrupulous and unmerciful.
He is ununiformed, and undrilled, and performs his active duties thoroughly,
but with little regard to order or system.
He is an excellent rider and a dead shot.
His arms are a rifle, Colt's revolving pistol, and a knife.

—Luther Giddings, *Sketches*

IN 1836, THE REPUBLIC OF TEXAS WAS AN IMPROBABLE NATION. IN
fact, it was an unintentional nation. In the aftermath of the military
victory over the Mexicans, the overwhelming majority of the settlers wanted and expected to join the United States. But annexation
was delayed, despite the obvious strategic importance of the territory to the expanding American Union. Mexico refused to make
peace or accede to the de facto Texan independence, and the government of the United States was constrained by the fear of war
and the 1819 boundary agreement. Even more important, the question of annexation was caught up in the controversy over the extension of slavery. East Texas was slave territory, and its entry into the
Union was vigorously opposed by antislavery interests. The question
was finally resolved by the strategic vision of the Polk Democrats,
but in the meantime, the Americans in Texas remained in a geopolitical limbo for ten years.

So the Texans carried on their lives and purposes in thousands of local initiatives. Americans of this time had less consciousness of or need for a national government than any civilized people on earth. Their social order was individually disciplined, their destinies fused in the destruction of the North American wilderness. Forty thousand Texan colonists, soon joined by new thousands from across the Sabine who had been lured by the republic's open-handed grants of land, held off the power of Mexico and pushed out the Amerindians. In a few more years, they might very well have erected a rival American nation in the West—a consideration that was a real factor in the eventual annexation.

But in the beginning, Anglo-Texas was only a scattering of some twenty-three agrarian counties along the Gulf coast, for all that the republic grandiosely claimed the Rio Grande and drew its purported boundaries into New Mexico and Colorado. Even the oldest Texas settlements were still primitive rural communities. Along the lower Brazos, the slaveholding planters with large acreages produced and exported cotton in exchange for goods, at a still adverse trade balance. The greater planters were approaching prosperity and had begun to raise splendid houses, but the society as a whole was quite poor and undeveloped. The largest towns contained only a few thousands, who walked on mud streets. There were no maintained roads, no school system, no banks, no industry. Everything in the country had to be fashioned individually by hand, or else brought in at great cost from the United States. There was no money, and no money economy. The great mass of the people were subsistence farmers who did a bit of barter on the side. Merchants kept their accounts in kind, and exchanged gunpowder for pigs or corn. There was vast potential wealth in Texas, but in the 1830s it was all held in undeveloped lands.

The newer, western regions up the rivers were even more raw and primitive than the cotton-raising coasts. The immigrants who went here lacked capital of any kind except their "headright"—but this grant of land to which every family head was entitled under Texas law was often in Amerindian country. The pioneers who put up their dog-run cabins and scratched a bare subsistence from the central hills lived far less comfortably than the sedentary Wichitas in this same country. Only a de Tocqueville could have viewed such people as the vanguard of a someday rich and powerful Western civilization.

The panoply of the government of the Republic of Texas, with its presidents and congresses, was patterned after that of the United States. In reality, government usually consisted of locally elected sheriffs and justices of the peace. Texas emerged from the war with Mexico bankrupt and heavily in debt in proportion to its income. The republic's treasury bills were worthless, its promissory notes depreciated. Property taxes were impossible to collect. On the trickle of customs duties that entered the republic's coffers, it could afford neither a government nor an army—yet Texas inherited two border wars at birth.

The never-ending, smoldering hostilities with Mexico absorbed most attention from historians. However, the Amerindian peril was actually far more pressing and dangerous. Between 1836 and 1845, a few thousand mounted Indians killed many more Texans than had all the Mexicans massed below the Rio Grande. The Mexican armies had been badly mauled by the quickly mustered and as quickly disbanded riflemen who gathered at the Alamo and San Jacinto, and the eastern, woodland Amerindians were easily destroyed or expelled by the same forces. Lamar's campaigns in eastern Texas were only continuations of old wars against Creeks, Shawnees, and Cherokees, who were beaten long before they tried to enter Texas as refugees.

But from the environs of Parker's Fort, between the Brazos and the Trinity, and on the frontier of a "west Texas" that still ran east of a line drawn between present Austin and San Antonio, the Texans suddenly came up against conditions, human and geographical, of which they had no knowledge or experience, and against which their tried and true techniques and organization did not serve.

Anglo-Texas was in every way a raw extension of the cotton-planting American southern states, from which 90 percent of the settlers had derived. The coastal communities contained the usual mix of southern American social groups: planter, merchant, lawyer, doctor, soldier, and Negro slave, with the upland fringes of rifle-carrying frontier farmers, small freeholders who dug a hard living from the soil. The dense pine woods of the east and the Texas terrain from the Sabine to the mouth of the Nueces, and from the river deltas up through the post-oak belts into the waxy, black-soiled prairies presented Americans with no geography or enemies they had not encountered and mastered before. Old agrarian techniques and social organization served the immigrants splendidly through half of Texas as it was drawn upon the maps, for this was the conquest of an extension of the geographic southern plain.

Beyond these areas, Americans suddenly confronted the Great Plains, the immense, harshly beautiful, semiarid country that had never left the Pleistocene age. Beginning roughly in the middle of Texas, north to south along the modern Sherman-Dallas-San Antonio line, and curving along the Nueces south of San Antonio to the Gulf, less than thirty inches of rain fell annually. In these vast, chaparraled savannas and brushlands and butte-studded limestone plateaus, and in the breathtaking sea of grass that reached belly-high to a horse as far as the eye could see, the water and wood ran out.

The first vision of the Great Plains stunned most European and Anglo-American travelers. They found it difficult to describe the impact of the blinding sky and distant, vague horizons, the endless expanses of waving grass that ran for miles without break or boundaries. Many compared the plains to the ocean. The light seemed to play across the grasses as on the moving sea, and the scattered clumps of trees and small rises on the prairies stood out starkly, like distant islands. The winds, which blew eternally, cut through the silence with their sullen keening. The impact of this country was devastating on some European minds. None of the early colonists of Texas ever ventured beyond the ninety-eighth meridian.

But if most settlers recoiled from the Great Plains that began in the middle of Texas, and if most farmers' wives were appalled by them, others were fascinated, even exalted, by the prospect of endless vistas and limitless freedom to move across the land. In central Texas, Anglo-Americans stood on the edge of a great scarp that was as mysterious and dangerous to them as the heart of Africa. The plains meant struggle, fear, and loneliness for the families that pushed up against them, but thousands of Anglo-Texans pushed westward just the same. They went into the midcontinent to tame it and carve out their individual destinies.

To approach the plains the Anglo-Americans had to make vast changes and adaptations. Where they could not profitably plow and farm, they had to take up a new agronomy. The border Texans adapted themselves to the arid country by following the Spanish-Mexican practice of ranching—the running of cattle over huge, unfenced regions, a system contrary to all northern European forms of pasturage. They took up the Spanish-Mexican cattle culture almost entirely, together with the vast herds of tough, half-wild Afro-Iberian longhorns that the Spaniards had already seeded across the land: this meant the horse, the *rancho*, the jargon of the northern Mexican range, and the burned cattle brands. In time, they even adopted something of the feudal relationships of the Mexican ranching life, between *hacendado* and *vaquero*, rancher and cowboy. The more permanent American approaches to the plains required newer inventions and adaptations, with the use of the windmill and wire for fencing. Significantly, these came later, in the last quarter of the nineteenth century, and they could not be applied to the plains until the barrier that had halted all the other potential empires in the Southwest had been removed. Even the cattle could not be spread across the great bison range so long as the Comanches roamed there. For the Comanches and Kiowas were more than trespassing vermin; they were men prepared to defend the high country with shield and bow and spear.

The Anglo-Americans had to adapt their warfare to a kind of Amerindian and a type of conflict they had never faced before. More protean than the Spanish-Mexicans or French in their imperialism, they did so quickly.

At the first Comanche raids, the Texans were completely unequipped to cope with horse Amerindians. More and more warriors rode down from the high plateaus under the summer moon, until Comanche raids became a certainty, not a mere threat, all across the northwestern Texas frontier. Tiny parties slipped inside the ranch-farm line, creating more havoc and destruction in a few hours of hit-and-run raiding than Americans had ever faced from small bands of Amerindians. They were incredibly mobile, and incredibly deadly.

Early Texan efforts at coping with Comanches were as ineffective as the Mexican had been. Once again, a thinly scattered, agrarian culture was punished and terrorized by wandering bands of nomads. All other considerations aside, the warlike riders held every advantage in actual combat. The Texans had three great disadvantages in meeting the Comanches on this ground. They were not horsemen; they lacked an effective organization for Comanche warfare; and the weapons they brought out of the woodlands were no good against horse Indians on the open plains.

The old Anglo-American militia system was impossible to implement on a thinly populated frontier. It was cumbersome, and in the absence of rapid communications it reacted with fatal delay. By the time farmers had raised the alarm and assembled with their rifles and muskets, the raiding Comanches had already galloped away with their captives and trophies. They staged their victory celebrations around prairie camp fires in perfect safety, while pursuers on foot either lost the trail or lagged far behind. And on foot, the farmers dared not venture too far out on the trackless, woodless, waterless plains.

For, while the Anglo-Americans brought horses to Texas, they were not horsemen in the Iberian or the Comanche sense. American horses were mostly work plugs; the few fine racing steeds were too delicate to be ridden mile after mile over rough ground like Amerindian mustangs. Evenly mounted, any Comanche warrior could ride rings around the average white man. The Americans worked on foot and fought on foot, and in an open country they were helpless in the face of buzzing hordes of Comanche archers.

Worse still for the Texan-Americans, their vaunted weapons were ill-fitted for either ground or mounted combat. The famed Kentucky rifle, first brought to Pennsylvania by German immigrants and carried to the far frontier, was not a cavalry or even a true military arm. It was long and heavy-barreled, an extremely accurate weapon with a short, awkward stock, designed for shooting from a rest. As long as a man's body, it was cumbersome to reload; it was effective only when used from cover or concealment. In the saddle, the rifle necessarily lost its prime virtue—accuracy. Moreover, in the time it took a frontiersman to get off two shots with his clumsy muzzle-loader, a mounted Comanche could cross three hundred yards and loose a score of shafts. And the hand-ax or tomahawk, an effective weapon for close fighting, was no match for the supple, sixteen-foot Plains lance.

The Texans were thus at a great disadvantage, unless they could fight in timber or from behind rocks or walls. Attacked, Texans were forced to dismount and seek cover, from which their accurate, small-bore rifles, with their long reach, could hold the Comanches at bay. The Indians would not often accept the losses necessary to root them out of such cover. But if the whites did not find natural cover quickly—and such cover was rare on the plains—they were in deadly peril. If they tried to flee across open country, they were usually doomed. Over short distances, no white horsemen could outride the Comanche warriors or outdistance their ponies, and the sight of fleeing enemies spurred every feral killing instinct. Warriors who practiced on running buffalo were deadly in the pursuit.

The worst defeats the Texans suffered, both from Amerindians and Mexicans, came when embattled farmers tried to make stands in open prairie. Swirling, circling archers or Mexican lancers cut them to pieces on the plains. Understandably, the Texans soon became as unwilling to pursue their enemies out on the plains as the former Spanish garrisons had been.

Unable to match their foes in the saddle, with the wrong organization for guerrilla warfare, and armed with weapons unsuited for plains combat, it appeared in the 1830s that the Texans would suffer the same defeat against horse Indians as the Spanish-Mexicans had. The great difference, however, was that the Anglo-American mentality was never trapped in cultural forms; it instinctively obeyed the laws of causality. Faced with any obstacle, whether arid country, Mexicans, or Indians, the Texans adapted to overcome it— for the Anglo-American frontier people, as a people, had all the qualities of conquerors.

In Texas, the frontiersmen had already learned the absolute necessity of becoming horsemen. Distances were so great that even before they took up the cattle culture and stock raising in the Mexican fashion, Texas farm boys had begun to grow up on horseback. A man who could not ride had no business on the Texas frontier; all the while, men who loved the saddle were drawn to the plains. Young Texans quickly came to ride, if not as superbly as Comanches, at least as well as Mexicans. They also quickly understood the inferiority of their horseflesh and bred varieties more suited to the plains. The new stock was developed from Spanish mustangs mixed with Kentucky and Arabian strains: mounts larger and heavier and as long-winded as the Amerindian ponies, though they required grain feed.

The Texan frontier readily and pragmatically developed new Indian-fighting organizations. This took place between 1836 and 1840, so simply and naturally that the nature of the changes were not completely seen. The Republic of Texas could not afford a sizable permanent army, and farmer militias were useless on the western frontier. What evolved was a practical compromise. The government authorized a *mounted* frontier battalion in 1836, and again in 1837, providing legislation for six hundred mounted gunmen for the northwest. But the government did not provide the men, mounts, nor guns. As one Texan of the time wrote, ". . . The government provided for . . . protection as best it could with the means at its disposal, graciously permitting the citizens to protect themselves by organizing . . . ranging companies."

These "ranging companies" of mounted gunmen were unique. The term "ranger" was old and honored in American history; it usually referred to Indian fighters who had operated beyond the frontier. Austin called the companies he organized against the Karankawas rangers, and this title quickly superseded the official "gun men." At first, the ranging companies were only a mounted militia, but they grew into something different—a remarkable body of semipermanent partisans. They were akin to Cossacks, except that they were drawn from the frontier population.

Unlike the Spanish-Mexican governments, the republic permitted armed bands to spring up by authorizing paramilitary forces for frontier defense. The republic supported these forces when it could, but in the main it left recruiting and maintenance to the frontier people. Thus, the people who tended to create their own limited governments in America also created their own army.

The ranging companies were not furnished with uniforms, insignia, or even horses or arms. Members had to provide these themselves. They were rarely paid, but rather were supported by the communities they protected. The early records are filled with settlers' complaints about Comanche raids—and also their complaints about the Rangers' stealing chickens and killing hogs. In the early years, the leaders were not even appointed or commissioned by the government. This was fortunate, because it allowed a competent, indigenous brand of frontier leadership to evolve. The ranging companies emerged not as a true militia, a regular army, or a police force, but as semipermanent, shifting bands of irregulars. They were called into being by the needs of a bleeding frontier, by a society that could not organize or afford another kind of force. The early Texas Rangers were unique in modern Western experience, and therefore also difficult for writers to describe. If analogies must be drawn, they were actually closer to the Amerindian war bands they fought than the advancing civilization they defended.

Although most male Texans on the frontier served in Ranger bands at some time, the hard and effective core of these companies was anything but typical farmers, ranchers, or businessmen. The true Ranger, and especially the Ranger captains who sprang up by consent to command these bands, was a born borderer—extremely young, without wife or property, intoxicated with open spaces, camp fires, and a life of danger. Footloose young frontiersmen passed in and out of the bands; most of the famed captains had completed their careers by the age of thirty. Being a Texas Ranger was not a career; it was a form of adventuring. But because the Rangers were bred on a hard frontier, they were efficient and, for their purposes, deadly. They were volunteers and uniformly courageous, and therefore their accepted and acclaimed leaders tended to be exceptional men—not only men without fear, but canny field generals with a rough and natural germ of combat leadership. The early Ranger captain was produced by the same forces that made the Comanche war chief—except for the visions. The captains had no visions; they were cold, efficient pragmatists, and often superb

Texas Ranger, c. 1840.
Contemporary drawing.

psychologists. They had the hardest of leadership tasks—the command of small groups of men with whom they lived and ate in complete intimacy, whose obedience they gained solely through their personal abilities.

The Rangers were few and almost always outnumbered. They offset this with a violent aggressiveness, and a rapidly building legend of superiority. The Ranger captain who was called to defend the frontier against both Mexicans and Amerindians found his best defense was to attack, kill, strike fear, and dominate. Few Texas Rangers articulated this code; they lived by it. And because the Ranger situation was always perilous, the Ranger bands, unlike the farmer militias, were tightly and efficiently disciplined. There were few of the forms and courtesies of civilized military discipline, but something far more fundamental. Casual orders were obeyed implicitly. No captain asked men to do what he could not or would not do himself. He was the greatest warrior in the band, and his followers knew it.

A great variety of men served in these ephemeral, semibarbarian fighting bands. Most were unlettered farm boys from both Texas and other states; some were gentlemen with classical educations. The Ranger bands, unlike most such fighting men in history, had no taint of cruelty or rapacity. Torture for its own or any other sake was an abomination to the people from which they sprang; and they were men of the frontier, whose conscious mission was to protect the frontier people. But the Ranger bands were inevitably stamped with a deep aggressiveness and brutality toward their enemies. They had to be. The white defenders fought in grim campaigns where there were few protocols and no expectations of honorable surrender on either side. The Texans, with the horse and their own version of the war band, also adopted the fighting styles of their foes. They battled by raid and ambush; they preyed upon the weakness of the enemy; they took few prisoners. They did not make the potentially fatal mistake, in a war of this kind, of perceiving their enemies as men like themselves in red or brown skins. Their outlook and tactics left two enduring legacies: a legend of incredible courage and ruthless boldness, and a smoldering hatred among the descendants of their enemies, whether Amerindian or Mexican.

The Rangers did not comprise a mere reactive force. While they

I. Comanche civil chief.

II. Comanche war chief.

IV.   First contact. Comanches receiving U.S. Dragoons
      under flag of truce, Indian Territory, 1834.

III.   Death on the plains. Comanche lancing Osage warrior.

V. Comanche girls and children.

VI. Comanche buffalo hunt with bow and lance.

were prepared to ride at a moment's notice, they took to the field as a normal practice, aggressively patrolling vast areas. They searched for the tracks of raiders and pursued them. They might very well have ended the horse Indian menace quickly had the Texan republic provided more of them and supported them adequately. As it was, they prevented stalemate and complete destruction of the advancing frontier.

However, the Rangers could not have fulfilled even this mission without one final, decisive factor. The frontier whites were no part of the developing industrial civilization far in their rear, but they could call upon its resources and inventions. No matter how well they rode or how well they organized for guerrilla warfare, the Texans could still not meet the Comanche horse archers on equal terms until they developed a better weapons system than the Amerindians. They found the tool of military superiority in the revolving pistols that Samuel Colt began manufacturing in New Jersey in 1838.

The early years of Colt's enterprise were dogged with failure. There was no civilian need for or interest in such weapons in America during those years. The United States Army did not have a cavalry arm before Americans entered the plains; the government refused to subsidize Colt's invention. But while Colt's enterprise sank into bankruptcy in the East, the Texan borderers immediately grasped the significance of a hand weapon that could be used from horseback and gave one man the fire power of six. Colt named his first working model the "Texas."

The Texans burned the significance and symbolism of the pistol into the American consciousness. The revolver was only another weapon in a long train of evolution, but it replaced the German rifle as the characteristic American arm. For the Rangers quickly embellished the six-shooter with glory and even mythology. It became a symbol of courage and conquest, of American superiority. Colt's invention killed more men in combat, probably, than any side arm since the Roman short sword. Its symbolism, unhappily, outlived its military usefulness.

The Anglo-Texans, quickly seizing new forms and techniques, now approached the last unconquered North American wilderness. This new land meant blood and battle, and its price was high for whites as well as for Amerindians. Frontier ranchers and farmers advanced into Indian country step by step across the rising lime-stone plateaus of central Texas over the bones of their enemies, but also over the graves of their own. On a frontier where Texan settlers numbered a hundred per thousand square miles, each mile of advance west cost seventeen white lives. The Plains bands had raised war and raiding to sheer exaltation; unlike the agrarian Amerindians, they could not be quickly or easily cowed. Most regions of North America were "pacified" in a brief campaign or two. Kentucky was dangerous for white men for a single decade. The Comanches threw up a barrier of bloodshed that denied the Anglo-Americans possession of Comanche hunting grounds for full forty years.

This was the last true American frontier. Here the region that Americans called the West began, and it engaged the consciousness of the American nation as few things had done before or would again. This conquest of an empire was a mere border war, in which only a handful of Americans were ever fully engaged, and which the immigrant hordes who later poured across the sea and into the burgeoning cities never felt or understood. It strewed the plains with the bones of men and animals that soon decayed. It left images and emotions that will live forever in the folk memory of the races that fought and died, before they and the land were caught and carved and swallowed up by the remorseless advance of an all-embracing civilization.

4

BLOOD ON THE MOON

The white man and the red man cannot dwell in harmony together.
Nature forbids it . . . knowing these things,
I experience no difficulty in deciding the proper policy to be pursued . . .
It is to push a rigorous war against them, pursuing them
to their hiding places without mitigation or compassion. . . .
  —Inaugural address of Mirabeau Buonaparte Lamar,
    president of Texas, 1838

THE CONFLICT BETWEEN THE TEXANS AND THE COMANCHES DEVELOPED
explosively after the spring of 1836, because the Anglo-Texan frontier erupted westward under the pressures of renewed immigration
from the United States. The main thrust of this early settlement was
up the south-central rivers, the Brazos, Colorado, and Guadalupe,
and therefore into Pehnahterkuh country. Over President Houston's
veto, the Congress opened all "Indian lands" to white settlement—as
if the Indians did not exist—and surveyors and land hunters were
soon operating far beyond the actual frontier. These parties went
armed into Indian country. Some wreaked havoc on the Wichitas
and similar, settled tribes; some were themselves annihilated by the
Amerindians.

Through the 1830s, the settlement frontier lay east of a line
drawn from San Antonio on the south to not-yet-built Austin,
through the Waco village on the Brazos north of a not-yet-
conceived Dallas at the forks of the Trinity. There was still a wide
buffer zone between the settlements and the Comanche bison range
in the north, but in the south, where the Pehnahterkuh liked to
camp in the central hill country canyons, just above the Balcones
Scarp, the two peoples were beginning to clash. Hundreds of out-

lying farms and a dozen small settlements were being fearlessly carved out by determined pioneers along the fringes of the great escarpment.

Houston did everything he could to prevent a Comanche-Texan war, sending both red and white emissaries to the Pehnahterkuh. He refused to implement the Congress' troop authorizations or to build forts on the frontier. By making promises he could not keep, Houston did preserve an uneasy peace with the eastern, agrarian tribes, broken only by an abortive and quickly crushed Kickapoo rebellion in 1838. But he was unable to make any effective formal agreements with the increasingly restive Pehnahterkuh. As his agent Smithwick reported in 1837, the minimum demand of the Pehnahterkuh chieftains for a peace treaty was the firm guarantee of the existing frontier. This Houston could not grant, and the one treaty he signed with the Comanches was not ratified by the Texan legislature because it attempted to offer such guarantees.

The whites were beginning to disrupt the hunting grounds of the Pehnahterkuh, and they had moved within easy raiding range. Houston's efforts delayed hostilities between the whites and agrarian tribes, but meanwhile, the Texans and the Pehnahterkuh had declared open season on each other.

Despite the enormous number of references to Indian warfare in early Texan accounts, very little of the detail of this opening conflict was ever reported. The nature of the white advance, the nature of the white pioneers, and the virtual absence of formal government did not make for record keeping. The type of white person drawn to the frontier, either as a settler or an Indian fighter, was one whose life was given to ceaseless action, rarely reflection or philosophy. Significantly, not one of the thousand-odd Texans who participated in the momentous battle of San Jacinto saw fit to write down what happened until much later, and much of the true story was lost in differing accounts and political controversies. Similarly, only a handful of the thousands of Texans who battled Indians on the frontier ever bothered to write down their observations. Noah Smithwick, who served as Houston's envoy to the Pehnahterkuh Comanches in 1837, John Holland Jenkins of Bastrop, and John Salmon Ford were rare, literate exceptions. And, except for Ford, these men were called into violent action only by circumstance, never by choice. Thus hundreds of bloody, murderous actions in

Ranger camp.
Nineteenth-century drawing.

Texas received only the briefest, laconic official mention, or were never reported at all. The most effective Indian fighters, such as Hays, would no more have conceived of glorifying the fighting or their own exploits than they would the extermination of dangerous "varmints." Killing Indians did not call for literary effort.

The ranging companies, authorized but not yet supported by the Texan government, were still amorphous, untried organizations. The almost unnoticed but remarkable thing about these forces was how quickly they learned from experience. By the fall of 1836, several such ranging companies were in the field, patrolling between the settlements and the Comanches on the higher, still unexplored plateaus. These riders made cold camps and searched for Amerindian trails or sign. Battle was more often than not a chance encounter, at least during the early months and years.

Noah Smithwick, serving in Tumlinson's ranging company in the fall of 1836, recounted a typical action of that year. Tumlinson patrolled in the general vicinity of the future city of Austin, protecting the settlements lower on the Colorado. One night, as the Rangers made camp beside the river, a young white woman, nude, exhausted, and almost hysterical, stumbled into their midst.

The woman was wounded and bleeding, chilled from running along the shallows of the river. Until the Rangers had clothed and warmed her, and she had calmed down, they were unable to get her horrifying story.

Her name was Hibbons, and her family, consisting of her husband, brother, and her two small children, had been returning to their home on the Guadalupe. The little party had been surprised by a Comanche ambush. The two men were killed. One small child had screamed so hysterically during the attack that a Comanche warrior killed it by smashing its head against a tree trunk. The Hibbons woman and her remaining young son were seized as captives. When the night had turned bitterly cold with the approach of a howling cold front, a Texas "norther," the captors had sought shelter in a cedar brake beside the Colorado instead of riding rapidly back to the plains. The weather was too miserable for sport or dancing, and the warriors were contemptuous of the white woman's ability to escape in the foul weather and rough country. They had not bothered to bind her in the usual excruciating Comanche fashion, and in the dark and under the cover of the roaring wind she had slipped away into the timber. Then, to hide her tracks, she ran a long way under the bank of the river. She would almost certainly have perished had she not stumbled into the Ranger camp by accident.

She had left her son behind in her terror to escape the usual fate of captives. Now she begged Tumlinson and his men to rescue the little boy.

The Rangers mounted and rode back along her path of flight. They found the Comanche camp. The warriors were still snoring in their buffalo robes. Tumlinson attacked. His men reached the Hibbons boy before the startled Comanches could kill him; one warrior was shot down, but the others escaped into the darkness.

As Smithwick later recounted the story, the "boys" awarded him the dead warrior's scalp, since it was believed that his shot had killed the Indian. Smithwick, who had no desire for the bloody trophy, suggested that it go to another Ranger, Conrad Rohrer. Rohrer, however, insisted that "according to the rules of the chase, the man who brought down the game was entitled to the pelt." Rohrer scalped the dead Amerindian, left the corpse to rot, and tied the grisly token to the saddle Mrs. Hibbons was riding, hoping it might afford her some meager satisfaction for her loss. This laconic tale reveals more than a voluminous social study about the kind of warfare that was developing along the Texas frontier.

Yet this was dangerous, chancy "hunting." The small ranging companies could not patrol such a huge frontier, and they themselves were often the hunted, for the Comanches rode boldly through these borderlands in very large war parties. Despite the efforts of men like Smithwick, the western counties suffered continual rape and ruin, and during Houston's administration at least one hundred white captives were carried off by Indians. By the summer of 1838, the situation had become intolerable to the western settlers, and the dissatisfactions found voice in the general presidential election to replace Sam Houston, who under the Texan constitution could not succeed himself.

Texas, like all Trans-Appalachian America in this era, was very much a rough-and-ready male democracy. No bureaucracy stood between the people and even the highest levels of government, and the voters could bring full pressure to bear on their officers. The frontier now formed an enormous, passionate pressure group, demanding that effective measures be taken against Comanche raiding. Most of the ambitious men in politics sensed the power of this group and allied themselves with it, stridently attacking Sam Houston's coddling of the Indians.

The majority of the coastal and eastern Texan cotton growers, whose two great interests were economy in government and annexation by the United States, supported other Houston policies. But few, if any, Texans shared Houston's protective feelings toward the Amerindians, and even the eastern Texans wanted the agrarian, immigrant tribes—who held choice, fertile lands—moved beyond the frontier. And Houston was unable to find any effective leader to carry on his policies. His preferred candidate committed suicide during the campaign, and, in 1838, Mirabeau Buonaparte Lamar, a former Georgian and a hero of San Jacinto, was elected to the presidency almost unanimously.

Lamar began with a policy diametrically opposed to Houston's. He was a fire-eater who believed that Texas should forge its own empire in the West, without worrying about the future interests of the United States. He believed in the removal of all Indians, and in a renewed war with Mexico if that nation did not accede to full

Texan independence. In his inaugural speech he declared war against the red men. He called upon all Texans to put "honor" above niggling considerations of cost, and to take whatever measures full security demanded. He proposed to solve the Indian problem quickly, brutally, and finally, by force of arms. He halted the sending of peace agents among the tribes, and in January 1839, began the mustering of a thousand men into short-term service. His program fitted the mood of the times, and the Congress voted him a million-dollar war appropriation.

In retrospect, historians have been less appalled by Lamar's actions than by his complete, brutal candor in these transactions. He proposed nothing and presided over nothing that was not already fully established in Anglo-American precedent and policy. The people and the courts had decided that true peace between white men and red men was impossible, unless either the Indians gave up their world, or the Americans eschewed the nation they were determined to erect upon this continent. Lamar, however, espoused the cause of naked force without any civilized restraints or expressions of regret at the necessity, and he evinced a lively satisfaction in the destruction of the Amerindians. He did not, per se, advocate a war of extermination. The Indians could have peace if they accepted the conditions of the white conquest and never again lifted a hand to the Texans. Otherwise, they were to be punished so severely that they would either leave the soil of Texas or recognize that they lived entirely on white sufferance, on lands the white men chose for them.

In many ways, this clear, stark policy, without cant or hypocrisy, was more merciful and even understandable to the Indians than the piecemeal death and destruction wrought on both peoples by official fumbling and hesitation. It told the Amerindians the truth about what they could expect from the advancing, conquering civilization. But it haunted many, then and later, that the Indians were not destroyed accidentally, in the French fashion, or by generous white men in a fit of absentmindedness. There can be, however, no denial that the great mass of the population, and virtually all officialdom, supported Lamar at this time. Congress borrowed the funds to support his wars, and during 1839 some two thousand Texans—far more than had ever mustered in the war for independence—volunteered to fight against the Indians.

Lamar was also served by competent officials. Albert Sidney Johnston, the Texas secretary of war, was a skillful soldier. Johnston's strategy was simple but sound: to recruit allies among the Tonkawas and Lipan Apaches, known enemies of the Comanches, for use as scouts or "spies" as they were then called; and then to hunt out and destroy the war power of the independent tribes. There was no problem finding scouts and allies among the Lipan and Tonkawa remnants. Both peoples had been mauled for a century by the horse Indians. They were caught between two powerful forces, and they hated the Comanches far more deeply than they did the white men. Whatever chance of survival these Amerindians possessed lay with the future generosity of the Texans. But even when both peoples understood what kind of gratitude they could expect from whites, they continued to serve the Texans. They both took real joy from the destruction of their ancestral enemies.

There were too few Lipans or Tonkawas to be of decisive use in the fighting. However, their scouting services were invaluable to the very end of the Comanche conflict.

Although dozens of ranging companies were quickly mustered in the west, it soon became obvious that it was no simple matter to root out the extremely mobile Comanches. In 1839 the frontiersmen still did not understand the Comanche mode of war, and they were still unequipped to meet it, in either skills or weapons. Two actions on the frontier quickly proved this ominous fact.

In January 1839, Colonel John H. Moore raised a mounted force from the settlements along the lower Colorado, taking the field with sixty-three Rangers and sixteen Lipan allies, under their chieftain, Castro. Moore rode west, up the Colorado past the confluence of the Llano into the San Saba region, where no Anglo-Texans had yet gone. His Lipan scouts located a large Comanche encampment beside a clear creek, and led Moore's riders to it.

These Comanches were Pehnahterkuh, secure within their ancient range. They now revealed that fatal weakness that was to plague the People to the end, for in their own country the People were lax about security. They could never conceive of white men penetrating into their forbidden fastnesses. Moore's men thus approached without discovery. But Colonel Moore and his Rangers had much to learn about fighting horse Amerindians.

Moore dismounted his command for the assault. The Texans then advanced on foot into the camp, fighting from a line of battle. With complete surprise, they shot down a few startled warriors as they rushed from their tipis. Instead of standing and giving battle, as the Texans expected, the Comanches dissolved in flight, scattering across the stream, rushing for their horses. The Texans had completely ignored the Comanche horse herd—a mistake as dangerous as ignoring enemy armor on a modern desert battlefield. While the Rangers marched about futilely in the deserted village, a few mounted Comanches circled about and stampeded the Texans' own neglected mounts in the rear. Two-thirds of Moore's Rangers were now left afoot.

Moore ordered the recall, without making any attempt to destroy the Comanche lodges or harm the fleeing women and children. His restraint, ineptitude, and retreat infuriated Castro, who deserted with all his Lipan warriors. Although Moore lost only one man, a Ranger fatally injured in the brief action, his victory now nearly turned into a disaster. The Texans only held off the buzzing Comanches with the accuracy of their long rifles; shielded by a thin cavalry patrol, the little army was forced to make a humiliating march back down the Colorado.

Shortly afterward, the Texans suffered another, even more ominous "victory." Captain John Bird rode up the Little River with fifty Rangers recruited in Austin and Fort Bend counties. Striking a band of some twenty Comanches busily hunting buffalo, he immediately attacked. The Comanches ran, and to Bird's dismay, easily outdistanced their pursuers. Bird chased the Comanches for several miles across the open prairie before he noticed that the fleeing Indians were growing much more numerous. Alarmed, he halted the reckless pursuit and turned about in retreat, only to discover, too late, that he had now made the ultimate error in Comanche warfare.

As the Texans turned, the Comanches, now some two hundred strong, immediately wheeled after them in a turnabout pursuit. Screaming, they filled the sky with shafts. Racing for cover, Bird's command survived only because the riders stumbled into a nearby ravine, where the riflemen could dismount and shoot from cover. Now they could stand off the swirling horse archers at long range, firing carefully, always making sure that they kept a few of their muzzle-loaders charged to repel an assault.

The Comanches could easily have wiped out the whole company, but only at a cost in blood that no Comanche chief would accept. After a desultory, angry siege, the Indians soon went back to hunting. The Rangers could thus claim that they had won the field—but it was a Pyrrhic victory. Seven Rangers were dead or dying, including Captain Bird. The bloodied company retreated to the east, and, meanwhile, the aroused Comanches rode on a rampage, carrying fire and death to a wide area of the frontier.

The Texan campaigns were not mounted solely against Comanches. Ranging companies attacked any Amerindians they encountered along the frontier, and in this same month of May 1839, one company scored a great success against a band of wandering, "immigrant" Indians along the San Gabriel River, about twenty-five miles from present Austin. The Rangers captured some one hundred horses, which were carrying a large store of powder and lead. Far more interesting to them, among the dead Amerindians they found the body of a Mexican agent, Manuel Flores, and they took from Flores' body detailed plans for an Indian uprising, planned, supplied, and directed by the Mexican government.

Mexican policy had come full circle: the original plan to plant an Anglo-Saxon buffer between Mexico and the horse Amerindians, which had had such disastrous results, had been supplanted by a hope of erecting a new nation out of the "immigrant" tribes that would drive the Anglos from Texas and create a buffer zone along the Sabine against the power of the United States. To this end, Mexican agents were agitating among the Cherokees and other tribes, and furnishing them arms and advice. Such agents had already fomented one minor outbreak among the Kickapoos in 1838, which was quickly crushed.

Such strategies were not unusual; they had been cornerstones of French and Spanish policies for centuries, and even the British had actively fomented Indian wars in the eighteenth and early nineteenth centuries along the western American frontier. But nothing more aroused the indignation and outrage of the western settlers, and now the Mexican machinations rebounded cruelly against the Cherokees and other sedentary tribes.

Although the Rangers captured papers that indicated the Cherokees had promised the Mexicans assistance in war, these assertions were almost certainly the false claims of a Mexican agent to his superiors. The Cherokees had met with Mexicans, but had resisted every provocation to take up arms in a war that the Cherokee chieftains knew the tribe could not win. Cherokees had lived at peace with the Anglo-Texans now for twenty years, and their lands had already become completely enclosed by the onrushing American settlement. The Cherokees were fast becoming civilized and beginning to organize their lives like white men—the most successful of all Amerindian peoples at this assimilation. Their crime was this: they "squatted" on rich lands desired by the whites, and they were Indians. The discovery of the Mexican conspiracy now gave President Lamar, Secretary Johnston, and Texas Indian Commissioner Bonnell all the excuse needed to destroy or remove them.

Publication of the Mexican correspondence maddened the majority of the Texan population, for the Mexican agents had made it clear that they had promised the Indians complete freedom to massacre all Anglos and to appropriate their property once the war began. Supported by almost all current opinion, Lamar and Johnston massed troops in the Cherokee country, while commissioners met with the Cherokee chief and council to demand their "voluntary" removal. The Texan government agreed to pay for improvements made to the land, but nothing for the land itself, which under the law already belonged to the republic.

The Cherokees behaved with great and tragic dignity. Their chief, Bowles, stated that he knew his people could not win, but when his request that they be allowed to harvest their current crops was refused, he asserted that the Cherokees would fight, even against his counsel. Then the tribe that had tried to live with and like white men tried to fight like white men. They mustered at arms and met the advancing Texan army in open battle, with none of the bloody raiding and indiscriminate slaughter of the normal "Indian war." They were slaughtered themselves by superior force, and the evidence is that Bowles was needlessly murdered. After two days of violent action, the Cherokees were scattered into the pine forests, and their homes and fields were set ablaze.

The Texan commander recommended to his government that he should make a clean sweep of it while the army was assembled: that the entire "rats' nest" in east Texas be cleaned out. The government concurred. By July 25, 1839, the corn fields and villages of all the Cherokees, Delawares, Shawnees, Caddoans, Kickapoos, Creeks, Muscogees, Seminoles, and all the other remnants from the East who had sought refuge in Texas were burned out. Some of the associated tribesmen tried to flee to Mexico; they were pursued and caught up with at the Colorado, the men killed, and the women and property brought back. A few Kickapoos went out on the plains. Most of the dispossessed peoples passed over the Red into the Indian Territory. Only two minor tribes, the Alabamas and the Coshatties, were permitted to remain, and they were moved to new and less fertile territory.

The summer campaigns of 1839 destroyed or removed virtually all the Amerindian population in the eastern half of Texas, opening up thousands of square miles for immediate exploitation. But meanwhile, the conflict in the west—from San Antonio on the south, and northeast to the Little River—remained indecisive. Bands of Rangers and Comanches swarmed along this frontier, but neither Amerindians nor Texans were able to inflict a decisive defeat on the other. Despite Lamar's determination to push his Texan empire westward, the Comanches were a terrible barrier. The frontier could not advance in this region, and the lands lying below the Balcones Scarp were in constant peril from the Pehnahterkuh.

Lamar, whose vision ran beyond the mere extermination of Indians, moved the capital of the republic to this frontier, to the newly laid out site of Austin on the higher Colorado. As the maps of Texas had been drawn, Austin was at its geographic center, but in fact the new capital lay far west of the actual settlement line. Lamar was deliberately attempting to pull Texas' center of gravity westward, for he and other ambitious Texans along the Brazos had begun to dream of a Texan nation that would someday reach the distant Pacific Ocean. It was an American dream, and if the United States refused to carry it out, then the duty—and the glory—would fall to Texas. But while surveyors and engineers laid out Austin's future streets, curious parties of Pehnahterkuh sat on their ponies on the surrounding limestone bluffs above the river, watching.

They did not attack the town, but they rode past it regularly, bringing horror and destruction to the lower counties. The ranging companies often pursued the raiders, and, in some cases, drove them back upon the Edwards Plateau, but there were too few Rangers to patrol this immense, broken frontier; and worse, the white warriors could not meet the Amerindians on anything approaching equal terms in open country. Bird's fate on the Little River made the Ranger captains cautious, although the more intelligent of them had already realized that the Comanche danger could only be ended by determined pursuit and destruction of the Indian camps—in effect, a war of extermination.

The Ranger leaders soon realized that Comanches, for all their warlike qualities and skills at weaponry and horsemanship, were badly custom-bound, forever caught up in worry over magic or medicine. Unlike white men, the Comanches never changed their methods; they surprised only those Europeans who had no understanding of their ways. The Texans saw that, despite their vaunted individualism and warrior freedoms, virtually every Comanche reacted to a given situation in the exact same way. It was possible for observant Rangers to anticipate Comanche actions and reactions, and then, by doing something totally unexpected or seemingly irrational, to startle the enemy and even demoralize him. The Ranger leaders learned Comanche habits in war and raiding, and this made it more difficult for the Pehnahterkuh to ride into Anglo-Texas at will. But for several years there was no way in which mounted Texan riflemen could engage Comanche horse archers in close combat.

The solution arrived on the frontier from the East, out of the budding industrial civilization of which the white Texans were a vanguard. Colt's first commercial repeating pistol, the "Texas," was hardly a true military arm. It was caliber .34, too small, light, complicated, and even ill balanced. Colt designed it with a troublesome disappearing trigger, and it had to be taken down into three component parts for reloading, which effectively made reloading impractical on horseback. But the Texas revolver was no toy. Once loaded, it shot six times, and from the saddle it at last allowed a Texan Ranger to reply missile for missile to Comanche arrows.

The Texas six-shooter was first made famous by a Ranger captain named Jack Hays. John Coffee Hays was a Tennessean, from the same county as Andrew Jackson and Sam Houston; in fact, his grandfather had sold Jackson the Hermitage estate. Hays was a born adventurer, of the type called forth by many frontiers. He went west to Texas as a surveyor, was mustered into a ranging company, and suddenly found his métier. Hays was a natural warrior. He was soon recognized as the captain of his band, and, at the age of twenty-three, he commanded the San Antonio station, the most dangerous and important Ranger post in western Texas.

Jack Hays was the prototype for a certain kind of emerging American hero. He did not look like a fighting man's hero: he was slight and slim-hipped, with a clear, rather high voice; he had lovely manners and was seen as a "perfect gentleman" by the belles of San Antonio. Hays was utterly fearless—but always within the cold, hard bounds of practicality, never foolhardy. He was no talker, and not even a good gunman, but a born leader of partisans who by great good luck had been born in the right time and place. Hays was calm and quiet, almost preternaturally aware of his surroundings and circumstance, utterly in control of himself, and a superb psychologist, in control of all the men around him. His actions appeared incredibly daring to other men who did not have Hays's capacity for coolly weighing odds. It is known that most of the other Ranger leaders, and hundreds of future riders, consciously tried to "be like Jack Hays"—strong, silent, practical, explosive only in action. He put an indelible stamp on the force that was soon to be formalized as the Texas Rangers.

He personally trained the great captains Ben McCulloch and Sam

Jack Hays, c. 1846.
Contemporary portrait.

Walker, and his image and example deeply influenced McNelly, Jones, and Rogers. His example made individual Rangers into one-man armies.

Hays was the first captain in Texas to recognize the potentialities of Colt's newfangled revolvers. Because of this, in early 1840 he fought the first successful mounted action against the Pehnahterkuh Comanches. Riding beside the Pedernales River northwest of San Antonio with only fourteen men, Hays was ambushed by a party of some seventy Comanches. Previously, the standard Texan tactic was to race for cover and hold off the horsemen with their long rifles—heretofore, the only hope for survival. Hays, however, wheeled and led his men in a charge against the howling, onrushing horse Indians; the fourteen rangers rode through a blizzard of shafts and engaged the Comanches knee-to-knee with blazing revolvers. Hays lost several men to arrows—but his repeating pistols struck down a dozen warriors.

Startled, amazed by white men who charged and whose guns seemed inexhaustible, horrified by heavy losses, the Comanche war band broke and fled. The Rangers killed thirty Comanches.

The engagement was quickly celebrated along the frontier: "the best-contested fight that ever took place in Texas," in one observer's view. Hays immediately realized that the revolvers, plus the element of surprise, gave him a great advantage over the raiders. He resolved to patrol boldly and to meet the enemy on horseback at every opportunity.

Only a few days afterward, Hays's company ran into a vastly superior force of Pehnahterkuh in the Nueces Canyon west of San Antonio. Hays allowed the warriors to charge, sweep around, and completely surround him, while his troop dismounted. Then he ordered his men to discharge their rifles, with deadly effect, and as the exultant enemy, sure that the white men were now at the Indians' mercy, swirled in for the kill, he mounted and led a point-blank assault. Each Ranger singled out a Comanche warrior and rode after him. The tactic was so surprising that the Texans were at close quarters before the Comanches reacted.

Hays screamed: "Powder-burn them!" His riders ripped through the Comanche circle, knocking down warriors left and right. Enraged, the Comanches swarmed after the Rangers, believing that they were now fleeing with empty weapons. Hays wheeled about and charged through them again, fire spitting from his men's pistols, shooting down the enemy before they could notch bowstring to arrow. The Comanches, ponies and riders, were thrown into immense confusion. Again the Texans singled out individuals, rode beside them cheek by jowl, and shot them out of the saddle at point-blank range.

Now there occurred that phenomenon that the whites were to see again and again in the coming years, and which the canny Ranger captains were to use to their deadly advantage. In the face of something they could not fully understand—immediate bad medicine—the bravest of warriors' morale cracked. As more of the milling Amerindians were blasted from their horses by guns that never emptied, the Comanches became panic-stricken. They screamed and fled as if pursued by Furies. Great warriors threw away useless shields and spears and rode away howling, bent low over their horses' sides for protection. In their flight the Comanches suffered far greater losses than they would have taken had they pressed the fight. Hays pursued them mercilessly, killing all he could overtake.

Even after the exhausted Rangers broke off the chase, the remnants of the war band fled on to the Devil's River, more than a hundred miles to the west. Fatally wounded warriors fell out and were abandoned all along the trail. Fully half of the Comanches died, and the survivors were gripped with superstitious horror. The war chief, who lived, swore hysterically that he would never face Hays's Rangers again.

Hays gave himself no credit; he credited only the Colt revolvers. This was, of course, too modest, yet the six-shooters did permit white frontiersmen to meet and match Plains Indians at their own mode of mounted warfare. Hays and his band were the new breed of Anglo-American fighting men who had been bred in the West, audacious and coolly competent, ready to seize any advantage and exploit it to the hilt. Hays wrote no books and held no classes, but, by example, he was instructing every Indian fighter near the plains. Incredibly, almost all that is known of his exploits comes from brief, admiring mentions by equally inarticulate contemporaries. These, however, show what he accomplished against the Amerindians.

Hays now took the offensive, riding with confidence into Pehnahterkuh country. He never commanded more than fifty riders, but he had learned almost everything there was to learn about Comanche

Battle scene, Texas Rangers and Comanches, engraved on Colt's martial revolvers, 1840s. Uniforms are actually of Republic of Texas Army.

warfare. He picked up much from his Lipan scouts, but he also taught them a few things. He made cold camps and rode silently by moonlight, like Indians on the war trail, seeking out the Pehnahterkuh in their scattered lodges and secluded but vulnerable encampments. Now he hunted Indians. He had learned how to find them, even when hidden in the most inaccessible canyons, by watching carefully for the swirl of vultures that followed Comanche lodges. The buzzards descended regularly to feed on the bloody Amerindian garbage. Hays's troop rode like Comanches and attacked like Comanches, with one exception: Hays and his men were disciplined, purposeful as well as deadly. They wasted no energy in exultation or victory dances, and no time making ritual sport with captives. They could not be burdened with prisoners, and they took none.

If possible, Hays preferred to surprise the Indians and shoot them down in their sleeping robes, or else surprise a camp and chase its warriors, dismounted, into brush. The Comanche warrior was at a tremendous physical and psychological disadvantage when afoot, and his lances and bows were ineffective in the brushy canyons in which the Pehnahterkuh, the Honey-Eaters, liked to camp. Hays's men mauled the Pehnahterkuh from the Nueces to the Llano, killing Amerindians of every age and both sexes. By their own lights, defending a battered, bleeding, ravished frontier, they were not making war but exterminating dangerous beasts.

Very little mention was made of this, but no one in Texas would have had it any other way. The Lipan chief, Flacco, was in awe of Hays, saying often that he was not afraid to ride into hell all by himself. Lamar's papers, in an age when few systematic records were kept and every Texas political figure was inordinately jealous, indicate that Hays's troop was instrumental in halting Comanche depredations on the southwestern frontier in 1840. Even Sam Houston, who deplored wars against the red men and was disgusted with the brawling Texas borderlands, wrote, "You may depend on the gallant Hays and his companions."

Hays's bloody marauding beyond the frontier was a great factor in the Comanches' decision to seek a truce. Other Ranger companies, formalized by the Texan Congress as border troops, followed his example. The Pehnahterkuh were in no sense exhausted or defeated, but the warfare against the *tejanos* was ceasing to be sport. The Rangers sometimes wiped out camps whose warriors were away raiding deep in Mexico. Also the Comanches quickly overcame their initial superstitious fear of repeating pistols. The People were not given to awe or cringing, and their chiefs quickly understood that these were only guns of a new and better kind. They desired a truce so that they might obtain such firearms from traders.

Ironically, the Pehnahterkuh might have got revolvers from white traders in these years had they permitted white men to enter

Ranger Captain Samuel H. Walker,
co-designer of the "Walker Colt"
caliber .44 revolver.
Contemporary portrait.

their territory. The few rash Texan merchants who attempted to trade with Comanches had been killed, because the Comanches apparently understood the connection between visiting white traders and the smallpox. The traders who were dealing with the People, such as Bent and St. Vrain in the north, did not handle Colt revolvers. The Colt pistol was still far from perfect, but in the meantime, Colt was working to improve it. A Ranger, Sam Walker, visited the Colt factory in Paterson, New Jersey. The Ranger and the inventor combined field experience with mechanical genius, and from this cross-fertilization came the world's deadliest martial handgun: the large-bore, long-barreled, easily loaded, solidly built six-shooter that was to be forever linked with the history of the American West.

The Texan government, even under Mirabeau Lamar, was willing to make peace with the Comanches by 1840. Frontier conditions were chaotic. All the republic's terms, at this time, were that the Comanches recognize Texan sovereignty, stay away from settlements, and allow the whites to appropriate lands up to, but short of, the actual bison plains. It was believed that peace on these terms was possible. But another pressing desire of the government was to recover some two hundred white captives who had been carried off by Comanche raiders since 1836. While this desire made Lamar's government even more willing to hold councils, it also cast ominous shadows over such projected meetings. Texans, officials and settlers alike, considered the capture, rape, and torture of white women and children criminal and bestial, and a deep anger that savage, nonwhite primitives dared to inflict such outrages always bubbled in their consciousness.

When three chiefs of the Pehnahterkuh rode into San Antonio in 1840, asking for a council, Colonel Henry Karnes, who commanded the southern frontier region, met with them and agreed to parley, with one proviso: the bands must return all white captives before serious talks began. The three chiefs agreed to this condition, or at least put up no objection. They promised to return with all the principal chiefs of the Pehnahterkuh Comanches within twenty days.

This casual arrangement was to be one of the most fateful of all Amerindian–Anglo-American councils. Never before had any significant group of Comanches agreed to sit down with Texans, though

Houston had tried to arrange such conferences all through 1837. Both peoples had excellent and pressing reasons to seek a truce, if not a lasting peace. On balance, it was to the Texans' advantage so they might consolidate their frontier communities without Comanche interference. The Comanches, for their part, had only to agree to halt raiding into Texas, accept a fictitious Texan sovereignty (which would have been no more effective than the Spanish was), and give up a few *tejano* captives. There were those on both sides eager to begin trading. For a few years, if not forever, a Comanchero situation like that in New Mexico might have come about, because Texas was at war with Mexico and had no concern whatever about Indian marauding below the border.

But here also, two violent, dominant, and utterly self-assured peoples approached each other, each with no understanding whatever of the other's codes or customs.

Since the Republic of Texas claimed sovereignty over the old Spanish-Mexican province, with its southern and western boundaries at the Rio Grande, by all European custom and precedent, it also claimed sovereignty over all peoples within those purported boundaries. The Texans did not recognize Amerindians as autonomous peoples, but as tenants trespassing at will upon sovereign territories. By the European legal tradition, such Amerindians were fully subject to Texan law, because the European concept of law was territorial. The Texans regarded raiding Indians as punishable under their laws, and beyond the range of normal protocols. They utterly rejected the notion that Comanches might adopt white captives, and thus bring such captives under Comanche law—which could not apply in any case.

The two peoples also had utterly divergent concepts of honor. Comanches believed themselves honorable warriors. The Texans considered them vicious savages. The Comanches, like all Plains Indians, lived by codes and customs that allowed people to wage the most ferocious wars of extermination against each other, but also required them to honor declared truces. Whites had similar codes, but the Texans were not really prepared to sit down and bargain with a folk they saw as either wild beasts or cunning criminals.

The attitude of Texan officers was starkly revealed in the report that Henry Karnes filed with his superior, Albert Sidney Johnston,

Texas secretary of war. Colonel Karnes wrote that he had no faith in these Indians, and the only reason he had not arrested the three Comanche chiefs on the spot was because "they were too few to assure the future"—that is, the bulk of the Comanche murderers were still free, and three chiefs were insufficient hostages to guarantee the tribe's conduct. Karnes, like most Texans, could never see a Comanche, even under the most friendly conditions, without visualizing the barbarities the Indian had done, or might do under different circumstances. The colonel had no taste for bargaining with the savages. He understood government policy, however, and therefore he recommended that commissioners be appointed to deal with the Comanches—but that these officials be empowered to act decisively, without pussyfooting, and further, that troops of the regular Texas army be sent to watch over the council. He urged that if the Comanches did not surrender the prisoners, all the Indians who came to council be seized and held as hostages until the captives were released.

Johnston, a superior soldier but an officer with little sympathy for or understanding of Amerindians, agreed fully. On his recommendations, President Lamar appointed Colonel William G. Cooke, acting secretary of war, Colonel Hugh McLeod, the Texas adjutant general, and Lieutenant Colonel William S. Fisher of the 1st Texas Regiment, as Indian commissioners. Three companies of regular troops under Fisher's command were dispatched to San Antonio. The commission was therefore completely military, and reflected the Lamar-Johnston attitude toward Amerindians. The three officers received detailed instructions: if the Comanches brought in all white captives, this was to be taken as a sign of good faith; the commissioners could then offer them the Texas terms. The Comanches might have peace on three conditions: they must remain west of a line drawn through central Texas; they must never again approach settlements or white communities; and they must not interfere with any white efforts to settle "vacant" lands anywhere in Texas. Further, the custom of giving presents was to be "dispensed with." There would be no ransoming of captives, and if the captives were not freely offered up, Fisher and his soldiers were to seize the chiefs and hold them until the captives had been released.

If these terms were arrogant, actually an ultimatum, the great men of the Pehnahterkuh approached the Anglo-Texans with no less arrogance. They believed that the Texans, like the Mexicans, were eager to buy peace, and that they could wring a great price from the white men for the captives. Mook-war-ruh, the Spirit Talker, a great *par-riah-boh* or civil chief, convinced the band leaders that the captives should be offered up one by one, with hard bargaining. The old, bald headman, like all his rank, was a facile orator, and he was to be group spokesman. The Comanches, who had by then attended many councils with enemies both European and Amerindian, never envisioned violence or treachery. A declared council was sacred. Therefore, the twelve war chiefs who accompanied Mook-war-ruh to San Antonio on March 19, 1840, brought their wives and families. Councils were normally lengthy affairs; sixty-five Comanches arrived to set up their lodges.

Pursuant to their strategy, they brought in only two captives. One was a Mexican boy, who meant nothing to the Texans; the other was a sixteen-year-old girl, Matilda Lockhart, who had been carried away with her three-year-old sister in 1838. The release of the Lockhart girl to the Texan authorities at San Antonio was a terrible blunder; it would have been far better had the chiefs brought in no captives at all. For Matilda Lockhart had been hideously abused in her captivity, and her very appearance was to turn this day, as one of the ladies of the town, Mary Maverick, wrote, into a "day of horrors."

The wife of Samuel Maverick, a prominent merchant, she was one of the women who bathed and dressed Matilda after her release. She described the girl's condition: "Her head, arms, and face were full of bruises, and sores, and her nose was actually burnt off to the bone. Both nostrils were wide open and denuded of flesh." Among the women, the girl broke into tears and said she was "utterly degraded, and could not hold up her head again." She described the horrors she had endured. Beyond her sexual humiliations, she had been tortured terribly by the women, who had held torches to her face to make her scream. Her whole thin body bore scars from fire. To make things worse, she was an extremely intelligent girl; she had learned the Comanche tongue and had actually overheard the Comanches discussing their council strategy. She knew of some fifteen more white captives in the camp she came from. She revealed this, while begging that she be hid away from curious eyes.

When the council was opened in the small, one-story limestone building next to the San Antonio jail on the main plaza—a court-room that ever afterward was called the "Council House"—all was ostensibly calm and peaceful. The twelve war chiefs, led by Mook-war-ruh, arrived in their finest attire, painted for a ceremonial occasion. They squatted on the dirt floor across from the delegation of Texan commissioners and local officials, exchanging greetings through an interpreter. Outside, in the courtyard, the Comanche women, also painted and dressed in their most colorful costumes, squatted patiently; the young boys began to play war games in the dusty street. A large crowd of curious spectators, Anglos and native San Antonio Mexicans, gathered to watch the proceedings. Men tossed coins in the air for the Comanche boys to use as marks for their miniature arrows. The mood of the onlookers was not hostile, but overwhelmingly curious—everyone wanted to see the strange and dreaded Indians.

But inside the Council House, the Texas officials were seething with barely suppressed fury. The treatment of the Lockhart girl was in no way unusual; the Comanches were oblivious of its stunning effect on the Texans. Most of the Texans came from the southern states and had experience with various tribes of Amerindians —but in all the wars and troubles of the nineteenth century, they had not encountered the forms of savagery that were virtually second nature to the Plains Indians. The "semicivilized" tribes of the East, while they had burned men, since the previous century had almost never abducted, raped, or tortured white women. Such practices were unknown among Choctaws and Cherokees and the more advanced Amerindians. And the fury was by no means peculiar to the Texans; it was a common American reaction. The settlers on the Mankato in Minnesota, in 1862, reacted with hysterical cruelty against the Santee Sioux who raped and killed captive women. A similar hysteria pervaded Denver in the summer of 1864, when scalped and mutilated bodies of settlers and their wives and children, victims of the Cheyennes, were put on public display—an event that led to Chivington's expedition.

The chiefs settled themselves comfortably on the packed earth, fondling their favorite weapons, watching the white commissioners impassively. The Texans immediately asked why no more captives had been returned. Mook-war-ruh spoke up eloquently and evasively: there were more captives, but they were in the camps of

Comanches over whom he had no jurisdiction. This was a partial truth, for many of the captives had been taken by other bands than Pehnahterkuh. Then Mook-war-ruh stated that he believed that all the captives could be ransomed. It never occurred to him that the captives were anything but spoils of war, or that the Texans had any inherent right to claim them. He began to indicate the price: a great store of goods, ammunition, blankets, and vermilion. Mook-war-ruh honestly believed his argument was impregnable. He ended his oration calmly with a question: "How do you like that answer?"

Colonel Fisher showed how he liked it by ordering a file of Texan soldiers into the Council House. These men took up positions along the walls, one guarding the door, while the chiefs stirred restively. Then Colonel Cooke, the senior officer, instructed the interpreter to tell Mook-war-ruh that he and the other chiefs were to be made captives, to be detained until every white prisoner of the Comanches was returned. Only after the captives were released would it be proper to discuss presents; the Texans would not be held to ransom.

The interpreter, a former captive of Comanches, turned pale, obviously frightened. He refused to deliver such a message. He said the chiefs would fight to the death before they allowed themselves to be made captive. Cooke was adamant. The man finally translated the Texan statement, then ran from the room before anyone could stop him.

The thirteen prominent Comanches shrieked their war cries, leaping up in outrage. One rushed to the doorway and pushed his knife into the sentinel who barred it. Someone screamed for the troops to fire. The soldiers' rifles filled the room with noise and smoke and ricocheting balls; both white men and Amerindians were struck down. Old Mook-war-ruh stabbed a Ranger captain, Tom Howard, in the side before he was shot to death. Another Ranger, Matthew Caldwell, a mere onlooker at the council and unarmed, was struck in the leg by a wild bullet, but he grabbed a musket from one of the chiefs, blew his head off with it, then beat another Comanche to death with the butt. The Council House reverberated with shots and screams, and reeked of hot blood and powder smoke.

In the melee, several of the chiefs made a valiant effort to fight their way outside. As they emerged, their shouts aroused the Comanches in the courtyard to fury. While the white onlookers, confused and understanding nothing of what was happening, stood dazed, the Comanche women and children seized weapons and turned on them. A child shot a toy arrow into the heart of a visiting circuit judge, killing him instantly. The soldiers who surrounded the area but who had kept in the background then opened fire on all the Indians milling in the courtyard. Indian women and children fell, but the fusillade also killed or wounded several fleeing spectators.

The Comanches, heavily outnumbered, always fearful of fighting in closed spaces, tried to flee. Most ran for the river, while a few tried to seize horses, or take shelter in nearby houses, but by now all the population in the streets, most of whom habitually went armed, were firing on the Comanches. The flight became a bloody slaughter.

The soldiers, idle Rangers, and townspeople instinctively took up the chase, killing without thinking. Several warriors died in the streets, trying to cover the retreat. Others were shot down as they attempted to enter houses. Comanche women and children were shot down with the chiefs and men—but as all observers agreed, the women and children fought viciously, and were as dangerous as the warriors themselves. The whites killed every frightened Comanche who did not surrender.

In the last stages, the fight became a hunt. Two warriors who barricaded themselves in a cookhouse were surrounded by angry whites. When they refused to come out, the little building was set afire with turpentine. As the two were forced out by the flames, one's head was split by an ax, the other shot. No Comanche escaped the soldiers and mob.

Thirty-three chiefs, women, and children died in this massacre. Thirty-two, all women and children, many wounded, were seized and thrown into jail. Seven whites had been killed, including an army officer and the San Antonio sheriff. Ten others were badly wounded, and many whites, officials and onlookers, had suffered minor hurts. In the shocked aftermath of the bloodbath, the single surgeon in San Antonio, an immigrant German, worked through the night to save the injured whites.

Early the following morning, while San Antonio still buzzed with shock and rumor and the great mass of the people stayed behind barred doors, the commissioners took one woman—the wife of one of the greatest dead chiefs—from the jail and put her on a horse. She was given food and instructed to seek the camps of her people, to tell them that the survivors of the "Council House Fight" would be put to death unless the Comanche bands released the white captives described by the Lockhart girl. From where the sun now stood, she had twelve days to give this word to the Comanche nation. The woman listened impassively and was released to ride out of San Antonio. But, though no Texan understood it, from where the sun now stood there would never again be true peace between the *tejanos* and the People of the plains.

The Council House Fight would be seen by all of the People as nothing but the vilest treachery—the breaking of a solemn truce, a crime almost beyond the Amerindians' comprehension.

The chief's widow appeared howling and wailing in the great Comanche encampment set up many miles from San Antonio. She had begun her mourning rites, but she was coherent enough to inform all in the camp of the fate of the delegation. The Comanches were thrown into the most violent confusion. The losses—for the camp counted the prisoners held in San Antonio as lost, too—were horrendous by Comanche standards. All but one of the greatest chiefs of the Pehnahterkuh band were dead—a loss from which, in fact, the southern Comanches never recovered.

The women, wives, daughters, and mothers, practiced the rites of mourning. They wailed and screamed through the night, ripping open faces and breasts, chopping off fingers; some injured themselves fatally. The men rocked and moaned in their robes; they sheared their sacred hair. The profound shock of the massacre at San Antonio upon the Pehnahterkuh was shown in the immolation of the dead chiefs' horse herds, which took two days. Such destructive rites had long gone out of style on the plains, but were now revived in the excess of grief.

The grief soon turned to fury against the Texans, and vengeance was wreaked upon the hapless captives in the camp. One white woman—a Mrs. Webster, who had been taken with her son and infant daughter a year before during a raid in which her husband and several other men were killed—stole a horse and escaped, riding into San Antonio on March 26th. She rescued her baby but had to leave her son, Booker Webster, behind. However, the boy had been formally adopted into a Comanche family, and, of all the captives in the camp, only he and an adopted five-year-old girl named Putnam survived. Booker Webster later revealed what happened to the other whites.

They were tortured to death. One by one, the children and young women were pegged out naked beside the camp fire. They were skinned, sliced, and horribly mutilated, and finally burned alive by vengeful women determined to wring the last shriek and convulsion from their agonized bodies. Matilda Lockhart's six-year-old sister was among these unfortunates who died screaming under the high plains moon.

When the moon set over the charred corpses, there could never again be peace between the People and the Texans, so long as any of the People stood on Texan soil.

These blood rites were left to the women; the warriors of the Pehnahterkuh mounted and rode for San Antonio. The massed warriors of the southern Comanches could have worked a frightful revenge upon that town, and upon the entire frontier, but while they swarmed in the hills northwest of the old Spanish city they were devoid of leadership and medicine. Despite their rage, the Pehnahterkuh fighting men were gripped by confusion and uncertainty. Their great men were dead; their councils were divided; no man had sufficient prestige to bend the others to his will or plan. And the objects of their hatred were behind the limestone walls of San Antonio. Hundreds of angry warriors milled about in sheer frustration.

One warrior rode recklessly into the town with only a single companion. This warrior, painted for battle, actually clattered about the main plaza, screaming insults and defiance. The startled townspeople, both Anglo and Mexican, held their fire, perhaps bemused by his strident challenges to single combat. Finally, some loungers in a saloon shouted out to the two Comanches in Spanish to go to the Mission San José, where the Texas soldiers had withdrawn with the Indian prisoners.

Some three hundred warriors thundered up to the walls of the old mission, hurling challenges to the *tejano* soldiers to come out and fight. Fisher had been taken sick, and the garrison was under the command of one Captain Red. Red had orders to take no action against the Comanches during the twelve days that had been granted for the return of prisoners; he had no knowledge of the massacre of the captives. The truce had three days more to run. Red restrained his troops, who were eager to open fire, and invited the Indians to abide three days, after which he would oblige them with a battle.

The warriors rode about, shouting insults and challenges, but not quite daring to assault riflemen ensconced behind high walls. The troops of the 1st Texas became so unruly and mutinous at being ordered to hold their fire that Captain Red was forced to assemble most of them in the mission chapel. At last the Comanches rode off in frustration, refusing to wait out the period.

They did, however, inflict a certain damage on the soldiers. Red's subordinate, the elegantly mounted and accoutered Captain Lysander Wells—who had pistoled at least one Comanche at point-blank range in the Council House melee—remarked that his commander's strict observance of protocol and orders smacked of cowardice. The proud southern officers exchanged words which in that era could only be satisfied by blood. In the resulting "affair of honor," they shot each other fatally.

Not only a lack of leadership, uncertain medicine, and stone walls frustrated the Comanche horde. They became confused over the thirty-one prisoners held by the soldiers, whom they had considered lost or dead. These were the wives and children of honored chiefs. The soldiers made it clear that they could be exchanged—but the Pehnahterkuh encampment no longer had live captives. These Comanche captives were an embarrassment to both sides. It was impossible for the Texan authorities to kill them in cold blood, despite their bluff; the Comanches did not know how to ransom them.

Until early April there was an impasse. Then, another single warrior, a minor chief known to the Texans as Piava, came into San Antonio accompanied only by a woman. Piava had been selected as the spokesman to attempt a ploy. He was described in Texan accounts as crafty and treacherous; he did facilely distort or avoid the truth during his parleys.

Piava said the Pehnahterkuh had "many captives" whom they would exchange. The Texans agreed to an exchange and gave him and the woman bread and beef and some Mexican brown-sugar candy. Meanwhile, some daring Rangers scouted the Comanche camp, reporting that few, if any, whites were visible. However, the truce held.

On April 4th, Piava returned with a Mexican captive and the little Putnam girl, whose family had been induced to give her up. Before her adoption this child had been abused almost as badly as Matilda Lockhart. Her face was terribly scarred. She knew no English, and cried piteously for her Comanche "mother." Piava refused to say anything concerning the fate of the other captives despite pressing questions, but he finally stated truthfully that he had only one more white boy available for exchange. The Texans gave him two Comanche prisoners, and agreed to accept his choice among the captives in the mission for the return of the boy.

Piava then brought in another Mexican and Booker Webster—who soon told the terrible tale of the fate of the white captives. Shocked by all the bloodshed, the Texas officers grimly held to their bargain. They allowed Piava to choose a woman among the captives and depart. He selected a woman with a broken arm, saying that her family possessed many mules. This woman, however, spurned his selection, and despite his outrage, the Texans honored her wishes. Fuming, Piava then took another female. The Texans added a child and an old, blind warrior, less from kindness than a desire to be rid of them.

These exchanges were not friendly. At many times they were touch-and-go, between men who hated and distrusted each other. The soldiers and Rangers held guns on the Comanches; the warriors sat their ponies with notched bowstrings.

The Putnam child was taken away by relatives and disappeared from history. One of the returned Mexican boys immediately ran off to rejoin the Amerindians. The soldiers, meanwhile, had no more use for the remaining Comanche prisoners. They allowed some to escape through careless guarding; the others were given to residents of San Antonio to be made into servants. This was an old Spanish custom, and the Texans themselves kept Negro slaves. However, Comanche women and children could not be broken to slavery, and within a few weeks all of them had escaped back to the prairies.

The tragic results of the great council at San Antonio in 1840 had darkened relations between the two peoples forever. Worse for the frontier, the Pehnahterkuh were infused with a previously unknown bitterness and energy. For some weeks they buzzed about the frontier. The ranging companies could not contain the widespread raiding. Jack Hays organized a company of "Minute Men" at San Antonio to bolster his hard-pressed troop. This was a posse of townsmen volunteers, who kept horses, arms, and provisions ready for instant service. The Minute Men were mustered by the raising of a flag over the courthouse, and the pealing of the San Fernando church bell. Other similar militias were organized in nearby communities.

These companies saw constant service. They were, however, a reactive force, which rode in the wake of Comanche depredations. They pursued raiders—but not very far into *Comancheria*—and they buried the dead they found on their limited operations. They did not stop the raids.

The regular army was even less effective. The regular Texan infantry, formidable enough against other infantry, invincible when positioned behind stone walls, was as useless as the former Spanish garrisons had been against the Comanche emergency. The wary Comanches refused to battle with massed soldiery; it was impossible for foot troops to pursue, find, or contain a horse Indian enemy.

Only the ranging companies, like Captain Hays's, were able to carry the war to the Comanches. But Hays was thrown on the defensive, and his scouts reported that the Pehnahterkuh had withdrawn their camps from central Texas. By early summer, the southern Comanches appeared to have gone far to the northwest on the higher bison plains.

And by early summer, the raids suddenly slackened. Even the most experienced Comanche fighters hoped that the mercurial enemy had lost taste for further warfare and so had ridden west for hunting. Most frontier people fervently trusted that this was the end of the great fiasco at San Antonio.

They could not know that the Pehnahterkuh Comanches were making medicine for the greatest war in their history.

5

PLUM CREEK

It was a spectacle never to be forgotten,
the wild, fantastic band as they stood in battle array . . .
Both horses and riders were decorated most profusely,
with all the beauty and horror of their wild taste combined.
Red ribbons streamed out from their horses' tails
as they swept around us, riding fast . . .
There was a huge warrior, who wore a stovepipe hat, and another
who wore a fine pigeon-tailed cloth coat, buttoned up behind.
Some wore on their heads immense buck and buffalo horns . . .
They bounded over the space between the hostile lines,
exhibiting feats of horsemanship and daring
none but a Comanche . . . could perform.
     —John Holland Jenkins

THE PEOPLE HAD CLOSE COMMUNICATION, FOR ALL THE LOOSENESS AND
autonomy of their social organization. Pehnahterkuh messengers
rode through all the scattered camps and lodges on the south plains,
crying the perfidy of the *tejanos,* bemoaning the losses and damaged
pride, urging war against the white men. Hundreds of miles northwest of the scattered Texas settlements, council fires burned and
medicine drums resounded through the hot nights. The warriors of
the Pehnahterkuh met in solemn councils with representatives of
the eastern and northern bands, debating strategy, seeking portents.
The mood of the Pehnahterkuh quickly became one of wild exaltation, for the omens seemed good. Signs had come to the great war
chief, Buffalo Hump, that if he made war against the *tejanos,* they
and their seed would be destroyed. Such terror would descend on
the Texans that, like the Apaches and the Mexicans, they would
ever afterward flee in fear at the Nermernuh's approach.

334

While the warriors danced, the women and old men went about the more mundane preparations for war: buffalo meat was dried and stored; weapons were forged or repaired.

But the People, the whole People from Balcones Scarp to the Arkansas, were not moved by the medicine chants, flutes, and drums. They did not come together. The distant Antelope band of the Llano Estacado was too remote, too aloof from tribal affairs. The great northern bands, the Yampahreekuh and Kuhtsoo-ehkuh, were occupied in peacemaking with the Cheyennes and Arapahos at Bent's Fort on the Arkansas, and with horse trading among their newfound friends. Bent, who had done so much to forge the Great Peace, used his influence against a southern war. Dozens of minor bands and families were scattered, hunting, or had ridden off to Mexico. All Comanches sympathized with the Pehnahterkuh, but most believed they had better things to do than to join the southerners in their war. Only a few hot-blooded youths and some Kiowas rode south to Texas.

One great drawback to arousing the other bands was that the Pehnahterkuh no longer had famous war chiefs whose record of successes could bring warriors flocking to them. The galaxy of leaders with proven medicine or prestige had died at San Antonio. There was only one important chief left to the Pehnahterkuh, the war leader who entered history not through his own name, Pohchanah-kwoheep, but its American version, Buffalo Hump.

Like many Amerindian names, Buffalo Hump's was rather scatological. The Comanches took their names without regard to sex and had no patronymics. Names were either acquired, or bestowed, from a variety of sources. Children's pet names were replaced by adult appellations that reflected some medicinal phenomenon, an exploit, or a physical characteristic, the last of which always loomed large in primitive minds. Since Europeans rarely could catch or pronounce Shoshone names, they tended to use names given to the Indians by the Mexicans, or made up English approximations. Nineteenth-century writers, however, faced an embarrassing problem with Comanche and other Amerindian names translating into Bull's Pizzle, Wolf's Behind, or Coyote Dung. Often they refused to translate these, leaving accounts sprinkled oddly with both English and Amerindian terms, or else they bowdlerized names they considered either scandalous or lacking in dignity.

By any name, Buffalo Hump was highly successful. He assembled a vast force on the Edwards Plateau. No one ever counted them—the Comanches kept no muster rolls—but the warriors numbered at least four hundred, and with boys and women, his army probably came close to a thousand. The war party included People of all ages and sexes, because Buffalo Hump envisioned war with the *tejanos* much as the Pehnahterkuh waged it against the Mexicans. He planned an extended campaign, provided with both logistic support and all the comforts of the tipi.

By late July 1840, the Pehnahterkuh war band was ready, fortified with provisions and dancing. On August 1, Buffalo Hump started down the trail from the high escarpment toward the level plains that fell away to the Gulf of Mexico. He carefully avoided San Antonio, with its bristling encampments of Rangers and soldiers, and its dangerous walls and alleyways. The old town was now bad medicine, a place to avoid. But below San Antonio, stretching to the sea, was a great, vulnerable scattering of towns, settlements, farms, and ranches that the Texans had planted between the Colorado and the Guadalupe.

The Amerindian host passed near San Antonio during the night of August 4, moving south of the town, on a route between it and Gonzales. Buffalo Hump rode by the rising moon, and his tactics were flawless. He penetrated the borderlands undetected with a thousand Comanches, and was deep into Anglo-Texas before his trail was discovered.

The sight of this broad, beaten path made by the passage of thousands of unshod ponies raised instant alarm in the town of Gonzales, some sixty miles southeast of San Antonio. The experienced Ranger captain Ben McCulloch read the sign perfectly. Grimly, McCulloch sent riders in all directions to cry the alarm and to call out the militias.

A full understanding of the events of the next few days, which Texans came to call the "great Linnville raid," is possible only by picturing this frontier region. It was hot, dry, and harsh country of gently rolling coastal prairies and fertile river bottoms; its vast open spaces were thinly dotted with farms and small towns and settlements. This region, the great coastal crescent southeast of San Antonio, was still very much a raw frontier, like most of Texas. Its inhabitants were predominantly young, hardy freeholders, men and women who had moved westward with families and often with entire clans to acquire free lands. They were the descendants of old Americans, for the most part; beneath their veneer of civilization lay all the old brutalizations of the North American frontier. Here the people were conscious each day of living in close proximity to an Indian-Mexican frontier. These farmers and small-town men little resembled a European farming population, or the communities of Mexican peasants. The entire male population habitually went armed; a boy got his first gun and learned to shoot it accurately at the age of six or seven. Most settlers were experienced horsemen. For all their small numbers, the tiny companies of Minute Men and Rangers were not made up of soft-handed clerks or humble hoemen; they were heavily salted with frontiersmen who had been accustomed to violence most of their lives. Their leaders were almost never rich, propertied, or professional people but rather that cool, grim, pistol-heavy breed of border riders who had grown up along the frontier, who reacted calmly and purposefully to violent emergencies.

Ranger Captain Ben McCulloch.
Drawing by Lonnie Rees.

Ben McCulloch realized that he had cut Buffalo Hump's trail two days behind the Comanche passage east. He began to assemble armed men on August 6, a few here, a few there from outlying settlements, and to press on grimly behind.

Meanwhile, the Comanches had already ridden around and surrounded the town of Victoria. Whooping warriors appeared out of the blue, taking the settlement by complete surprise, and cut down several luckless inhabitants on the outskirts. They killed a number of black slaves working in the fields. Had they ridden immediately into the town and been prepared to hunt down the whites on foot, there is little question that their hundreds could have slaughtered the entire population. But as always, this was not the Comanche way. Buffalo Hump's warriors circled the town like a bison stand, seizing horses and cattle, running down a small Negro child and carrying her away. And as always, such a medicine circle worked no magic against stout buildings. The walls stood, and the townspeople, alerted, had time to barricade their streets and houses.

The people of Victoria stayed behind cover while the Comanches mutilated the corpses of the dead, speared cattle, and rode around the outskirts in screeching triumph. The warriors kept up this game all day, and kept the town surrounded through the night. Then, on the 7th, when Buffalo Hump persuaded some of his men to ride into the streets, attacking and setting fire to houses, the townsmen opened up with blistering fire from roofs and windows. Quickly losing stomach for a house-to-house search, the warriors retreated, driving off some two thousand mules and horses. One group of Mexican traders in the town lost five hundred head, and the Comanches had killed fifteen people at Victoria.

Leaving the shaken town behind, the host poured across the Guadalupe River and ravaged down Peach Creek. Now, on August 7th, Buffalo Hump spread his warriors in a great advancing semicircle, a crescent sweeping open-ended toward the Gulf. The vast, thin line of warriors cut a swathe of destruction to the sea, surrounding houses, killing surprised settlers, setting homes and barns afire. This was an Indian raid such as no living Texan had ever experienced. It was like Santa Anna's march four years earlier, leaving smoldering desolation in its trail.

McCulloch's and other messengers were riding far and wide, warning the scattered homesteads, crying up the armed men from the towns. Militiamen assembled under Ranger captains at every crossroads settlement. But the veteran Indian fighters read sign; they understood grimly that Buffalo Hump's war party was too big to be engaged by scattered companies. The alerted Minute Men in the path of the host were warned not to try to stand and fight. Meanwhile, McCulloch was moving in cautious pursuit.

On August 6th, when he had cut the trail, McCulloch commanded only two dozen Rangers. He had no choice but to move slowly and carefully in the Comanche wake. He buried the dead and tried to determine the Comanche plan, while each hour he collected additional riders. Other Ranger parties, as yet without communication or coordination, were doing the same along the Comanche flanks. Following close behind the great crescent, Captain Adam Zumwalt's company was also recovering the dead. Zumwalt found the body of one white man whose soles had been sliced off by his torturers; the evidence of his shredded feet showed that he had been made to run behind a horse for miles on the exquisitely tender flesh before he fell exhausted and the Comanches shot and scalped him.

The Comanche army was sweeping rapidly toward Lavaca Bay on the Gulf. On August 8th, Buffalo Hump came upon Linnville, a small settlement on the bay that served as a port for San Antonio and the surrounding region. At Nine Mile Point, his riders seized a woman who was a granddaughter of Daniel Boone, the great Kentucky frontiersman. They killed her baby immediately but threw the woman over a horse for more leisurely diversion.

Linnville was a tiny port whose few buildings provided scant protection. Three whites and two Negroes were killed as the Comanche vanguard reached the settlement. One of these men was the collector of customs, Major Watts. Warriors broke into the customs office and seized Watts's wife, a fair, very handsome woman. They immediately tried to strip her, but they were baffled by the sturdy whalebone corset she wore. Finally, in frustration, they tied her to a pony in her underclothes. This diversion allowed the other residents of Linnville to run to the shore and escape in boats.

One citizen, Judge Hays, was so enraged, however, at the sight of the warriors prancing on the shore that he leaped from his boat and waded back. He waved a shotgun, which was unloaded, and screamed imprecations at the amazed Comanches. They failed to kill him; in fact, they rode around the judge and pretended that they did not even see him, considering him either very courageous or a madman, and in either case armed with powerful medicine. Hays suddenly realized what he was doing, and retreated to safety, rescued by a circling boat.

The Comanches found few victims in Linnville, but they uncovered a different sort of bonanza. John Linn's warehouse was packed with goods awaiting shipment to San Antonio: bolts of red cloth, boxes of fashionable stovepipe hats, umbrellas, and assorted ladies' finery. The warriors, with the women close upon their heels, joyously broke up and despoiled a two-years' store of merchandise. The men put on the tall hats and galloped about trailing bolts of crimson cloth. Others opened umbrellas. Most of these goods were simply destroyed, but the women packed great quantities of things upon the stolen pack mules.

The horde spent the whole day looting Linnville, then set the town afire while its unhappy residents watched from far out on the bay. They were particularly sickened by the Comanche slaughter of the cows and other livestock. Unable to drive these off, the warriors lanced the animals for sport, roaring with savage humor as the beasts died.

Buffalo Hump here began to lose control of his army. The Comanches had ridden out for blood, but the unexpected windfall of loot was destroying the war chief's strategy. The Comanches had taken thousands of horses and mules, and wonderful spoils of every description. In addition to the finery which every warrior and his woman displayed, there were many practical things: pots and pans, ammunition, and a shipment of iron for barrel hoops. This last was loaded on muleback, to be used for forging arrowheads. The Comanches also loaded a bag of law books. The paper leaves were used for fashioning cigarettes.

In theory, all spoils belonged to Buffalo Hump and were at his disposal; in practice, no war chief would have dared order their abandonment. The host had killed many enemies at virtually no cost to itself, and Buffalo Hump reasoned that the score with the *tejanos* was settled. The warriors and their women were eager to return to the plains, and Buffalo Hump, at this hour the most successful war leader in Pehnahterkuh legend, reluctantly gave the order.

The normal practice would have been to turn about and ride hard and fast for many hours, choosing a route through the least populated country, resting only when pursuit was far outdistanced. Normal practice, also, would have been to split the great war party into many small bands, each taking a divergent trail to baffle and confuse pursuers. These options were closed to Buffalo Hump— unless he abandoned his heavy loot, which had to be borne on the slow-footed mules, and also abandoned the immense stolen herd of at least three thousand horses. The pack mules and horse herd were slow and unwieldy; Buffalo Hump decided that they must be guarded by all the warriors. If he had turned south and retreated back to the plains by a route that passed below San Antonio, he would almost certainly have eluded all pursuit, because most of the settlements in this region lay north of the Guadalupe. But Buffalo Hump, perhaps now arrogant in victory, turned north, choosing to march homeward by the most direct route along the Colorado.

The war party was formed in a great column, moving slowly, ponderously northwest, accompanied by towering clouds of dust from the horses' hoofs.

McCulloch and his Rangers arrived at Victoria on August 8th, just as the Comanches were looting and burning Linnville. But here the townspeople swelled his party to more than one hundred, and McCulloch continued riding toward the coast till midnight. Setting out again early on the 9th, he ran into Buffalo Hump's rear scouting parties. One of his Rangers was killed in a brief action, and Mc-Culloch broke off the fight. He and many of his men had been riding for days, and the Texans had only single mounts. Their horses were exhausted. McCulloch stayed well behind, trying to rest his men and animals.

By the 10th, McCulloch realized that the Comanches were also avoiding combat, except for rear and flanking actions. Obviously, they were trying to protect a main column; if they had wanted war, they would have turned upon his small group and destroyed it. Also, they were now moving northwest, toward the high country, and McCulloch did not need a map to visualize their route of march. He knew the country, and knew instinctively the route that Buffalo Hump must follow. The Indians would have to cross Big Prairie, near Plum Creek, which was a small tributary of the San Marcos River.

McCulloch ordered a small group of the most exhausted riders to continue following, and, if possible, harassing the Comanche column. He himself rode for the settlements higher on the Colorado, short-cutting the enemy. Dusty messengers raced across the coastal prairies, alerting men in every bottom, ordering every able-bodied man to muster at Plum Creek. By nightfall on August 10th, every Texan old enough to mount a horse and wield a gun had set out from Gonzales, Victoria, Lavaca, Cuero, and a score of smaller, scattered villages.

One by one the tiny companies came in from the brushy bottoms along Plum Creek on August 11th. They were led by a score of hard-bitten captains: Tumlinson, Matthew Caldwell (who had recovered from his leg wound), John Moore, Edward Burleson, Hardeman, and Big Foot Wallace—all men who had previously faced Comanches along the Colorado frontier. Men and horses arrived in continuous streams and set up a rough bivouac. The Bastrop militia, a large contingent, arrived early on the 12th. The night before, Brigadier General Felix Huston, Texas Army, set up his headquarters, and as the ranking regular officer, took command of all Rangers, militias, and volunteers.

This heterogeneous, buckskin-clad army had assembled none too soon. Behind Buffalo Hump's host, Lieutenant Owens' troop, together with McCulloch's original party from Gonzales, pressed daringly close on the Comanches' heels. Mile after mile, over scores of miles, Owens forced his men forward, staying close to the great column, continually firing at it. The Texans' horses died one by one, ridden out, but the group still maintained so much pressure on the Comanches that some of the laden mules were tiring badly. Owens began to pass mules shot on the trail by angry warriors, and significantly, the trail began to be strewn with abandoned loot, chests of ribbon, bolts of calico.

But the Comanches still clung to the bulk of their loot and the vast horse remuda in the center of their column. They slowly approached Big Prairie, a few miles from the site of the later town of Lockhart, on the morning of the 12th, trailed by a roiling dust cloud.

At the same time, fourteen Tonkawa warriors under their chief, Placido, arrived at Felix Huston's headquarters. Their chests were heaving; they had trotted thirty miles to join the Texans against the hated Comanches. They had no horses, but Huston realized the "Tonks," as the Texans called them, made splendid scouts. He ordered them to tie white rags to their arms to identify themselves as allies, then gave them the most arduous and dangerous task of the day—to scout the Comanche column on foot, and bring him continuous reports.

Thus at Plum Creek a Texan militia army, captained by seasoned Indian fighters, was drawn up to receive a Comanche horde that was peculiarly unprepared for savage combat. The Comanche warriors had dispersed to guard and manage the difficult horses and to drive the tiring mules; warriors were scattered throughout the column with the herd. Only a handful were stationed as outriders along the flanks. In a short four years, the ranging company captains had become expert. They had anticipated the Comanches' moves, and now they almost casually prepared for decisive combat. It would never have occurred to McCulloch, or any other frontiersman, to try to avoid the showdown. Every move had been directed toward forcing a battle.

The captains dismounted their men, many of whom had never actually been in battle, and rested them while the Comanche horde came up. They checked the men and weapons, making the volunteers discard useless impediments. Then, informed about enemy dispositions by accurate reports from the inexhaustible, valiant Tonkawa scouts, the captains stood their troops to horse and led them at the walk out onto Big Prairie. They formed two long parallel lines that enclosed and converged upon the oncoming Comanches.

General Huston was in nominal command; the real command lay with Burleson, Caldwell, and the Ranger officers who rode at the head of their troops.

A Bastrop volunteer, John Holland Jenkins, rode with the Texan line toward the Amerindians. Jenkins was one of those rare literate frontiersmen who found himself a warrior by circumstances. He was by nature a gentle soul, who found himself moving slowly into bloody action with heightened perceptions. He was bemused by the drama of the scene—the grimly converging, silent lines of white horsemen, the now-visible barbaric splendor of their savage enemy. The Comanche outriders wheeled and pranced, engaging in mounted acrobatics, shouting out their prowess and their mighty medicine, performing feats of horsemanship possible only to the people raised on horseback. Jenkins was caught up in admiration, and also struck by the grotesqueness of their appearance and actions. They trailed long red ribbons from their horses' tails; some carried opened umbrellas, contrasting weirdly and ridiculously with their fierce, horned headdresses.

The captains, however, were not bemused. They were calculating the Indian dispositions and actions. Matt Caldwell, who was known as "Old Paint" from his grizzled beard and mottled complexion, saw that the enemy was deliberately putting on a show, hoping to delay the battle until after the mule train and horse herd had passed. The few wheeling skirmishers could never halt a Texan charge. Caldwell, as well as Burleson and McCulloch, knew the time to strike was now, and said so. Huston, however, hesitated.

A tall warrior in a feather headdress rode out of the Comanche press and yelled insults, daring the white men to single combat. He was probably a Kiowa, or from one of the northern bands, who had taken up the practice of the Cheyennes and other northern Amerindians. Caldwell, unimpressed by savage chivalry, told someone to

Battle of Plum Creek.
Engraving by T. J. Owen, from a woodcut by O. Henry.

shoot him. A long rifle cracked and the challenger tumbled into the dust. A throaty moan rose from the passing Comanches; this was evil medicine.

"Now, General!" Caldwell snapped. "Charge 'em!"

Huston gave the order. The Texas horsemen emptied their rifles at the Comanche throng, then, themselves shrieking like Amerindians, they spurred into the flanks of the long column. They struck down the few skirmishers on the flanks and crashed into the main body. The great horse herd was stampeded by their shots and yells.

Horses and heavily laden mules plunged forward out of control. The mule train ran into a spot of marshy ground; tired and over-loaded, they piled up, unable to go farther, and the huge mass of horses crashed into them. Instantly, the whole column became a struggling screaming mass of frightened animals, and the scattered Comanche herders were caught helplessly in the press.

Individual warriors could not maneuver their horses out of the mass. Some went down and were trampled as their mounts fell; others were shot out of the saddle as they struggled to break free. Scores died in this jam, for the Texans rode along the press, firing continuously. A few warriors escaped by leaping across the backs of the bogged-down horses, running for the nearby creek bottom. Even these men were pursued; Burleson and his men chased them, killing them one by one.

This was the battle. The rest was rout. The rear guard, and all the Comanches free of the press, scattered and fled in all directions. Some warriors did put up a desperate fight, but the heart had suddenly gone out of them. Hardeman's horse was shafted, and several Rangers were severely wounded, but, as the fight became a pursuit, all the losses were inflicted by the Texans.

Abandoning the loot that had spelled their doom, the Indians recovered as many dead and wounded warriors as possible, for even in panic the Comanches always tried to preserve their dead and wounded, and fled for their lives. The remainder of the battle was a hunt that eventually covered fifteen miles. Some groups of Indians were chased as far as Austin.

But as the fight dissolved into flight and pursuit, there were many scenes of bloody horror along the trampled trail. The Comanches began killing the prisoners they had tied to horses, both white and Negro. Some of these were tied to trees and filled with arrows, either as an act of defiance or in hope of delaying pursuit. The granddaughter of Daniel Boone died this way. Only one white captive survived, the widow of Major Watts of Linnville. Her captors fastened her to a tree trunk, then shot an arrow into her breast. The same formidable whalebone corset that had protected her chastity blunted the arrow's force and saved her life. She was cut down unharmed, except for a painful sunburn on her exposed limbs.

There was blood lust on both sides. Jenkins was appalled by one act of brutal cruelty he witnessed. A Ranger came across a wounded Comanche woman lying in the trail. This man dismounted, kicked the dying woman, then pinned her to the earth with a discarded Comanche lance. Jenkins later wrote that he was glad that this was not a "Bastrop man." However, there was no general massacre of captive Amerindians. A large number of the women and children in Buffalo Hump's force were ridden down and seized, but they were not killed. An abandoned baby, wailing in the brush, was retrieved and saved.

Afterward, the Texans counted more than eighty dead warriors; they found the body of one Texan, whom some Comanche almost miraculously had found the time to scalp. Buffalo Hump's great war party had lost all its loot, and perhaps one-quarter of its effective men.

The victors casually divided the recovered spoils. Many of the original owners were dead; no effort was made to find them. The militia took sacks of silver and bolts of cloth back to their wives; some men also recovered cases of liquor and kegs of brandy, as well as stores of tobacco, all looted at Linnville, and all of which the Comanches prized. The victors also divided the surviving horses and mules, which were as much a treasure to white men as to Amerindians. Even the Tonkawas got their share, for after the battle every warrior appeared on a fine horse. They must have appreciated these far more than the splendid citation General Huston wrote out to reward them for their services.

No one knew what to do with the Comanche captives. They were finally parceled out to be trained as "servants." One boy was presented to the Comte de Saligny, the French minister to Texas. The diplomat trained the youth to care for one of his horses, but he soon escaped, taking the horse with him. Most of the others escaped in similar ways.

As the battle at Plum Creek ended and the loot was divided, the Texan army simply melted away. No one made much of it, except the gentle Jenkins. The fourteen Tonkawa allies held the only victory celebration. While the moon rose over Big Prairie, they danced about their fire and boasted to each other. They closed the ceremony by roasting and ritually devouring several butchered Comanche arms and legs.

The deadly sequence of cause and effect was not quite over. The news of Plum Creek did not satisfy President Lamar and his secretary of war, who determined that the Comanches needed a bloodier lesson. Lamar called for a punitive expedition to march into *Comanchería* and gave the command to Colonel John H. Moore.

Moore left Fayette County in September 1840, with twelve Lipan Apache scouts and ninety buckskinned riders. He rode west, up the Colorado, actively seeking Indians. The column rode for weeks, seeing nothing but splendid, open country, yet Moore pressed on. He had pack mules and provisions for an extended campaign.

By late October, Moore had penetrated farther west than probably any Anglo-Texan had gone before. He crossed the Concho and the Red Fork of the Colorado; by his own reckoning, he was halfway to Santa Fe. The weather was turning chill on this high, semiarid, grassy plateau when at last the Lipan scouts smelled out a large encampment of Pehnahterkuh Comanches.

The camp lay scattered in the half-moon arc of a small river. Castro, the Lipan chief, counted sixty lodges and estimated a population of perhaps one hundred warriors. Security appeared lax—the Comanche weakness when deep in their supposedly safe domain. Without hesitation, Moore decided to attack the village. His orders were explicit: hunt out and kill Comanches.

Now, not even the Apaches could fault Moore's handling of the mission. He waited until after midnight before approaching close to the encampment. He sent a contingent of riflemen under Lieutenant Owens across the bend of the river to set an ambush across the most likely Comanche escape route. He tethered his pack animals far to the rear, under sufficient guard. At first light, he advanced upon the sleeping village behind a screen of Apache scouts. The Rangers were within two hundred yards of the encampment before they were discovered.

Moore's men attacked on horseback. They stampeded the Indian horse herd, then rode through and around the rows of tipis, shooting down surprised Comanches on every side. As Moore had foreseen, the mass of the Indians tried to escape across the river. The Texans followed them, dismounting at the water's edge to aim more carefully at the running figures. As the screaming, panicked Comanches plunged into the river, Owens' sharpshooters opened up a devastating fire at point-blank range. The action lasted for some minutes; it was a complete and almost casual slaughter of fleeing Amerindians.

Moore spared neither age nor sex and made no attempt to burden himself with prisoners. He operated under clear orders: this was a punitive expedition, in memorial for Linnville and Victoria and a dozen roasted victims. The firing ceased only when the last Comanche was dead or had crawled away.

Moore rode back down the Colorado driving five hundred captured ponies. He made his report to the government in Austin in early November. It stated, succinctly: ". . . The bodies of men, women, and children were to be seen on every hand wounded, dying, and dead." Fifty Comanches had been killed in the camp, more than eighty in the river. One Texan had been fatally wounded.

President Lamar and the secretary of war were satisfied. Whatever later historians would make of the men and their methods, the results were decisive. That year the Pehnahterkuh made no more raids on the Texas frontier.

6

PEACE POLICY

If I built a high wall
between the red men and the white,
the whites would scheme day and night
to find a way around it.
　　　　—Sam Houston, president of Texas

WITH A CLEARER PERSPECTIVE AND WITH GREATER KNOWLEDGE OF what was happening among the Comanches, it is much more obvious to historians than to contemporaries that the power of the southern bands was shattered in the Lamar era. The Pehnahterkuh had been the most numerous of the various Comanches; their misfortune was that they preferred the cedar brakes and sheltered canyons of the central Texas hill country, lands into which a white tide was flowing. Hays and other Rangers had severely mauled several large war parties and, in actions no one bothered to report, had destroyed a number of Pehnahterkuh encampments. The slaughter at the Council House in San Antonio annihilated the Pehnahterkuh leadership and demoralized the band. Buffalo Hump's disaster at Plum Creek, quickly followed by Moore's massacre of Pehnahterkuh high on the Colorado, were staggering blows to the Honey-Eaters' morale and numbers. There were never so many Comanches as generations of Europeans in America believed, and it is probable that a quarter of all the Pehnahterkuh fighting men were destroyed between 1836 and 1840.

These were losses that the fragile Amerindian society required a generation to repair, but time and territory had run out for the Pehnahterkuh, as for so many other tribes and bands. In the fall of

349

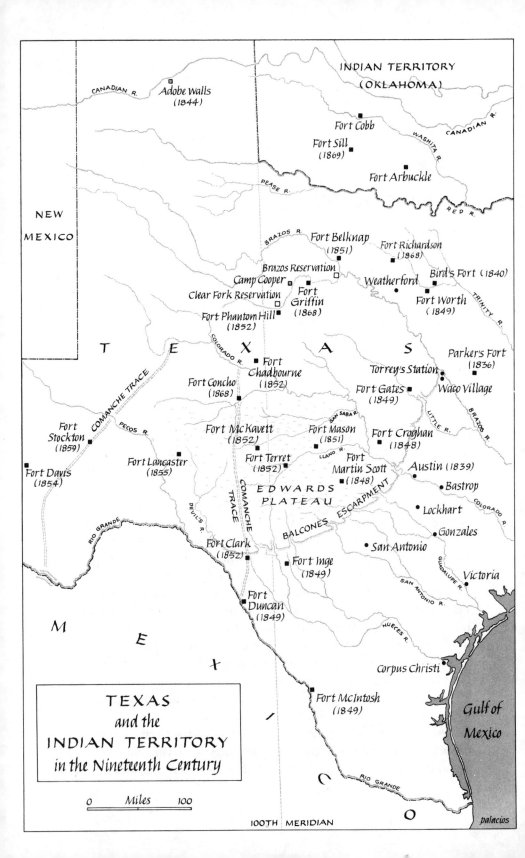

CANADIAN R.

INDIAN TERRITORY
(OKLAHOMA)

Adobe Walls
(1844)

Fort Cobb

WASHITA R.

CANADIAN R.

Fort Sill
(1869)

Fort Arbuckle

PEASE R.

RED R.

NEW
MEXICO

BRAZOS R.

Fort Belknap
(1851)

Fort Richardson
(1868)

Weatherford

Bird's Fort (1840)

Brazos Reservation

Camp Cooper

Clear Fork Reservation

Fort
Griffin
(1868)

Fort Worth
(1849)

TRINITY R.

T   E   X   A   S

Fort Phantom Hill
(1852)

COLORADO R.

Fort
Chadbourne
(1852)

Parker's Fort
(1836)

Fort Concho
(1868)

Torrey's Station

Waco Village

Fort Gates
(1849)

LITTLE R.

BRAZOS R.

COMANCHE TRACE

PECOS R.

Fort McKavett
(1852)

SAN SABA R.

Fort Mason
(1851)

Fort Croghan
(1848)

Fort
Stockton
(1859)

Fort Lancaster
(1855)

Fort Terret
(1852)

LLANO R.

Fort
Martin Scott
(1848)

Austin (1839)

Bastrop

Fort Davis
(1854)

RIO GRANDE

DEVIL'S R.

COMANCHE
TRACE

E D W A R D S
PLATEAU

Lockhart

COLORADO R.

BALCONES ESCARPMENT

Gonzales

Fort Clark
(1852)

Fort Inge
(1849)

San Antonio

GUADALUPE R.

Victoria

M   E   X   I   C   O

Fort
Duncan
(1849)

SAN ANTONIO R.

NUECES R.

Corpus Christi

Gulf of
Mexico

Fort McIntosh
(1849)

RIO GRANDE

TEXAS
and the
INDIAN TERRITORY
in the Nineteenth Century

0   Miles   100

100TH MERIDIAN

palacios

1840, the Pehnahterkuh deserted the hills and canyons they had roamed since the middle of the previous century. The majority of the southern Comanches withdrew north of the Red River.

Thus, Lamar's Comanche campaigns, apparently confused and indecisive in the west, in fact proved decisive. The Pehnahterkuh had been a deadly barrier, keeping a deep zone of settlement below the Balcones Escarpment in constant terror and peril. Significantly, during all the warfare of the republic, Anglo-Saxon settlement never penetrated into actual Comanche territory. Warfare began because the Comanches were long-range raiders. But the defeats, demoralization, and displacement of the southern band immediately opened up thousands of square miles of rich, rolling, and beautiful farm and ranch lands through south-central Texas. Armed parties of surveyors had already marked out these lands, and as the Indian danger eased—as it proved, temporarily—all these southern fringes of the Great Plains were opened for speculators, settlers, and immediate development. Fresh waves of Americans from east of the Sabine poured into them in an inexorable sweep of settlement that would never be dislodged. A vast new tier of settlement was consolidated.

Lamar's aggressive policies toward the Amerindians had resulted in thousands of deaths and had consumed the credit of the republic; even such limited operations drove the Texas government disastrously into deeper debt. But this bookkeeping was balanced by the undeniable opening of an empire in the west. It was hardly accidental that the European powers began to grant Lamar's Texas the recognition they had denied Houston's nation and sent their ministers to the rough capital on the Colorado. The constant and dominant critics of annexation in the United States were also sobered and, in a sense, silenced by the apparent emergence of a rival American empire. The British and French, not yet reconciled to the rise of a predominant American nation in North America, now hoped for the permanent division of the continent between two rival republics, thus forever weakening potential North American power.

Ironically, but perfectly logically in the scheme of things, all this worked to strengthen Sam Houston's hand in politics. Houston never ceased to believe in a single American nation and to pursue his great goal of bringing Texas into the American Union. Lamar's successes worried the United States government and made Americans increasingly determined to achieve annexation, despite the slavery question. Lamar's expensive wars became unpopular in the population centers since the financial burden fell mainly on the planters and businessmen of eastern Texas. The developed regions of Texas had no sympathy for Indians, but the leading men of this still very primitive economy were not willing to spend their substance to push the borders of Texas west. Men of property also had little deep belief in the republic; they overwhelmingly preferred the economic advantages of annexation.

In the east Houston rode a powerful reaction to power in 1841. A conservative, planter-dominated legislature was returned with him. A rhythm of American politics that the Comanches never understood or even imagined worked to stop the enormous pressure that had built up against them. Lamar's campaigns had temporarily opened up more territory than could be absorbed by immigration. The horse Amerindians had apparently ceased their depredations, for at this time, the northern and eastern bands of Comanches had not seriously impinged on the more slowly moving northwestern frontier, which was still separated from the People's hunting grounds by a Wichita buffer. There can be little doubt that if the Pehnahterkuh had continued to tear at the southwest after the bloody events of 1840, the frontier interests would have continued to be more powerful and vocal. The mind of frontier Texas was now fixed: virtually all frontier whites believed that the Lamar-Ranger solution to the Indian problem was the only workable one. If, in retrospect, this attitude seems bloodthirsty, it must be remembered that the Anglo frontier lived all its life amid conditions and with fears that later Americans simply could not envision. The individual frontiersman hardly saw himself as the nemesis of Amerindians. He believed that he was struggling for self-preservation. But by 1841, in the ebb and flow of attitudes and power, the frontier was briefly pacified and satisfied, and the concerns of Texas turned away from Indian wars.

Houston—who showed his true orientation by immediately removing the capital from the west and bringing it back to his namesake city near the Gulf—took up all his former policies. He urged economy in government, peace with the Amerindian tribes, and, though it was never broached in these exact words, the delay of all final solutions until they could be taken up by the greater nation following annexation. Lamar had started up the wars with Mexico; now Houston worked to damp them down again, despite the fact that in reaction to hostile moves the Mexicans twice invaded Texas and occupied San Antonio briefly in 1842. Historically, all but one of Houston's policies were sound. His Indian policy must be considered more an exercise of his own genuine goodwill toward the race, even to the point of wishful thinking, than the practical analysis of which Houston the statesman was usually capable. In the light of history, which illuminates only results, his policies were mistaken, even tragic. They did nothing to preserve the Amerindians in the long run, and, in effect, they permitted a resurgence of bloodshed along the smoldering frontier.

In office, Houston immediately proposed, and the Congress accepted, a changed frontier policy. As in Spanish times, the more distant the seat of power from an Amerindian frontier, the more a government was inclined to see its problems in terms of costs. Houston proposed a simple plan to reduce the cost of frontier defense by three-quarters. The ranging companies were to be disbanded. They would be replaced by trading posts established at strategic points along the frontier, defended only by small companies of no more than twenty-five soldiers. No hostile actions of any kind would be taken against the tribes. The trading posts would satisfy the Indians' economic needs; therefore, they would have no need for further raiding. Meanwhile, as more contacts were made, the Texans would preach friendship and goodwill, and once the tribes became convinced of Texan sincerity they would agree to peace treaties.

This was, of course, a total misunderstanding of the Comanche situation, and of the Comanche society and ethos. Houston, and in fact many Americans of the time, believed that Comanche warfare had at least some economic basis. They understood that the Comanches, like all Amerindian peoples, had depended for centuries on European settlements for their iron, horses, and firearms. But they tended to equate Comanches and other Plains Amerindians with the semicivilized Choctaws and Cherokees, and in fact, to conceive of all Indians in a sort of barbarous European image. Houston tended to admire, and even love, the wild Amerindians without ever understanding them. He and those who shared his views never realized that the Comanche symbiosis with European

settlements was based far less on economic needs than upon san-
guinary social imperatives.

There was another fundamental flaw in Houston's reasoning. He
must have understood—the Pehnahterkuh had made this clear
since the first diplomatic contacts in 1837—that the Comanche
bands would never agree to any settlement that did not give them
guarantees of territory. Here lay an irreconcilable conflict. Every
Texan approach to the tribes had included not only the demand
that they stay away from white men but also that they never interfere with white penetration and settlement. Every Comanche
counterproposal had included the demand that the *tejanos* stop
impinging upon the People's historic ranges. The president of Texas
was forbidden by law to grant the Amerindians any sort of boundary, and by the same law, no officer of government had any powers
to prevent white seizures or encroachment.

Therefore, any genuine bargaining between the Texans and
Comanches was manifestly impossible. The issues between them,
and the natures of the two peoples, made lasting peace or goodwill
improbable; such issues could only be resolved by power.

Houston immediately proceeded to reduce or destroy white
power all along the pacified frontier. The ranging companies were
dissolved by the simple expedient of stopping all official support.
The government provided no more horses, forage, ammunition, or
provisions. The Rangers had rarely received any pay, but now, to
continue in service, they had to take the field supplied from their
own or their captains' pockets. The small frontier communities they
protected lacked the means to support them as a standing force. By
1842, most of the tough young partisans had disappeared into the
frontier society from which they were called by circumstance. Even
the great Captain Hays was released from service. Houston gener-
ously authorized Hays to command a troop of 150 horse, but failed
to provide him with any money for its support. The ranging companies vanished, but not forever, for they had forged an enduring
legend.

Measured by Texan suffering on the far-flung frontier, this disbanding of the Rangers was a ghastly mistake.

The new trading posts were established, beginning in 1842. One,
at Nacogdoches, was to serve the tribes that had been scattered
along the Red River borderlands of eastern Texas. This post was

more an economic venture than part of the new peace policy. Another post, the famous Torreys Trading House, was situated on Tehuacana Creek, a tributary of the Brazos about eight miles below the Waco village. Operated by the Torrey brothers of Connecticut, this post opened up an extensive commerce with the Wacos, Ionis, Anadarkos, and other Caddoan Wichita remnants in the region. Sam Houston himself held a financial interest in this enterprise. Other posts, intended for the Comanches, were eventually opened at Bird's Fort (near the present Arlington-Fort Worth), at the ancient Spanish mission site in the San Saba valley, and west of the Brazos at Comanche Peak. At these posts, white traders licensed by the government were authorized to sell the tribes virtually anything they desired. Most of them did a profitable business in furs and skins.

Meanwhile, Houston's administration pursued an active policy of sending emissaries to the Indians. The great aim was to bring all the tribes to a great council, at which a permanent peace might be forged. There was no problem getting the Wichita-Caddoan peoples and related tribes to such councils; they were caught between the Texan tide and the savage Plains Amerindians, and were now anxious to make peace with the white men. By 1843, Sam Houston's Indian commissioners had assembled representatives of all the minor, semisettled peoples at Bird's Fort, where all agreed to remain northwest of a line drawn along the Texas frontier from San Antonio on the south through Austin to the Brazos and Trinity rivers on the north. But ominously, no Comanches appeared at this council.

The Texan commissioners had great difficulty even locating the Pehnahterkuh. This should have warned the Texan government, but Houston sent his emissaries far up the Brazos to run down rumors of Pehnahterkuh encampments in western Texas, and finally, in 1843, sent them north of the Red, completely beyond the Texas border. Here, after almost two years of searching, three Texan envoys, traveling with guides from friendly tribes under a white flag, at last located one of the main Pehnahterkuh camps on the Canadian, in the Indian Territory.

Despite their flag of truce, the ambassadors narrowly escaped death. When they appeared, asking for a council, the dominant mood of the Pehnahterkuh warriors was to burn them. The southern Comanches were now bitterly hostile toward all Texans and, in the aftermath of the massacre in the Council House at San Antonio, suspicious of all meetings with *tejanos*. While the envoys were kept under guard, the Pehnahterkuh debated a full day in council. At first, only one chief argued against killing them. Fortunately for the Texans, this was the shrewd and highly respected old civil headman, Paha-yuca, who believed in proper procedure and so, gradually, he convinced a bare majority of one to hold out against the breach of custom. When the vote was finally taken, Comanche democracy prevailed, despite the anger of many chiefs, and the Texans were allowed to live.

Their mission, however, was rejected. Paha-yuca showed himself willing to talk with Sam Houston, but even he could not prevail against the deep distrust of *tejano* motives. He put the envoys off by saying that he would bring in some of the Pehnahterkuh by and by, provided there were presents. The Texans tended to exaggerate the authority—and possibly the goodwill—of this *par-riah-boh;* while he was well known and respected throughout several bands for his wisdom, he held no real power over the warlike males. Paha-yuca was a large, fat man, with several wives, who personally did not care for the war trail, but he was in no position to make peace for all the Pehnahterkuh, let alone the northern bands.

Still, he eventually arrived to discuss the matter at the Torreys station on Tehuacana Creek. The whole process was touch and go. Sam Houston himself came to the first proposed council to show good faith, but the Comanches came late and Houston had to depart. Yet even when both he and Paha-yuca sat down together, there was no real progress.

Paha-yuca was no fool, whatever his motives or understanding of the Comanche situation. He probably came to council primarily for the promised presents of trade goods and liquor, but he was also capable of shrewd diplomacy. Like Mook-war-ruh before him, he knew that the key to peace lay in halting the westward movement of the white frontier. By this time, almost all the Comanches as well as other Plains Amerindians understood what was happening to the displaced eastern tribes; in fact, in the Indian Territory and in Kansas and Texas, they were in a wild and bloody confrontation with many of these peoples. Paha-yuca insisted that as a first step Houston mark out a permanent boundary between his people and the

Nermernuh. If the whites wanted the People to remain west of a line on the map, then the Amerindians should have reciprocal guaranties.

Houston, of course, could not even discuss the question. It was difficult to explain to Comanches the European concept of sovereignty that allowed the Texans to claim territory they did not hold and, in fact, over which no Texan had trod. It was even more impossible to explain why the courts of the Americans held Amerindian hunting grounds to be "vacant" lands, and why great white chiefs such as Houston could do nothing about this, even though Houston professed sympathy for the rights of Comanches. Houston was not hypocrite enough to lie to the Pehnahterkuh, while he expressed a certain bitterness toward the land drives of his own kind. Every council was inconclusive, however; nothing occurred but talk.

The Comanches apparently understood the futility better than Houston, since very few warriors ever bothered to attend the councils.

This pointed up the ancient problem of making treaties with the People. Whatever Paha-yuca or another chief agreed to was binding only on his own circle of lodges, and then only if every male accepted the treaty. Any Pehnahterkuh who did not want to accept Paha-yuca's truces could leave his jurisdiction at any time, either by going it alone or by taking up with another group. The evidence is clear that the Comanches continually explained this fact to the Americans as they had to the Spanish a century earlier, and it is just as clear that the Americans were as unwilling to accept such unpleasant reality as the Spanish before them. They insisted upon making treaties that could not possibly be considered binding on any substantial number of Comanches.

The best Houston could do for Paha-yuca was to pledge friendship at their final meeting in 1844, and commit himself to establishing official trading houses and Indian agents to serve the Pehnahterkuh. Paha-yuca agreed to halt raiding, to return any white captives taken by Pehnahterkuh warriors, and to return to annual councils. The Texas government then dispensed its gifts. It is perfectly clear from the statements made that the Comanches did not believe themselves fully bound by these promises because the central issue—the boundary—was never resolved. The vast majority of Comanches, including the majority of the southern Comanches, who never came to Tehuacana Creek, totally ignored the treaties.

The tragedy was that while trading posts were eagerly established by government concessionaires and did a brisk business in pelts, the southwestern Texas frontier was soon exposed to constant peril. Lamar had pounded the borderlands and achieved peace. Houston proclaimed peace and unwittingly encouraged the Pehnahterkuh to filter back to south-central Texas. The result was inevitable.

It was no longer possible for *tejanos* and Pehnahterkuh to live in proximity as independent peoples. Almost every Pehnahterkuh family had its blood feud with the Texans; the white frontier had a collective blood feud with all Indians. The immediate instinct of both peoples was to kill any of the enemy they encountered. Each side considered the other eminently treacherous and murderous. So long as there were autonomous Pehnahterkuh in Texas, there would be trouble.

This was clear even before the abortive councils. The Pehnahterkuh, though driven north of the Red, had still continued to ride a thousand miles to raid northern Mexico. The early 1840s were some of the worst years ever experienced on the north Mexican frontier below Eagle Pass and Laredo. The continuing truce with New Mexico and the new Great Peace with the Arapahos and Cheyennes drove the Comanches toward an intensified raiding war to the south. No chief, or combination of chiefs, could have prevailed against Comanche culture and history. The young men had to ride to war and return with horses and glory. All that Lamar's wars had taught the Pehnahterkuh was that the Texas frontier was dangerous and should be avoided; the survivors still had to make war on *some* frontier.

The last months of Lamar's administration were peaceful, but soon there was a new pecking at the exposed settlements. The problem came from war bands that were passing north and south along the great Comanche Trace that ran west of the Texas frontier and passed into Mexico southwest of San Antonio. On their way to and from Mexico, it was irresistible for small parties of Pehnahterkuh to try hit-and-run raids against the *tejano* enemy.

These raids were refined versions of the old warfare. After their multiple disasters, the warriors never rode boldly or openly into

Anglo-Texas. Tiny war parties, rarely more than a dozen men, slipped down the rivers by night, hid by day, struck usually just at sunset, then raced back several hundred miles deep into the prairies. They made no base camps near settlements, nor did they take along women and children. These war parties had less time to seize loot, and no time to stage victory celebrations or tortures on or near Texas territory. They exercised far greater caution to hide or erase their trails, and on the return, invariably rode a full hundred miles before pausing. In one sense, these sneak attacks were worse: the raiders killed and burned indiscriminately. They often butchered livestock they could not drive away. The Texans called these attacks "murder raids," with reason.

These raids could not destroy the firmly ensconced white settlements. Historically, they were more a nuisance than a vital factor determining the fate of the country. But over a large area, dozens of luckless or unwary frontier people lost their cattle or their lives. By 1842, the Minute Men at San Antonio were assembling regularly to the tolling of the church bell but, as earlier, accomplishing nothing.

This raiding pointed up facts that have often been ignored or overlooked by some historians. It had no economic basis, and it was beyond the control of any Comanche authority. It had some motivation in revenge. But the evidence of the previous century surely showed its real basis in the Comanche ethos. The warfare with north Mexico reached its apogee during the century in which the Spanish-Mexicans ceased to threaten *Comanchería* and tried desperately to placate the bands with tribute. The evidence is overwhelming; had the Texan frontier been stabilized, it must have faced the same sort of problem from the horse Amerindians.

The People could not have halted their warfare, short of a complete reshaping of their world-view and a restructuring of their society. This was to emerge more and more starkly during the advancing decades of the nineteenth century.

Most historians have had a bias toward peacemaking, and most have at least tried to indicate that Houston's efforts had, or should have had, some beneficial results. The entire frontier believed otherwise, and not without considerable reason. While some raiding began again soon after the great battles of 1840, serious forays into the white settlements resumed only after the dissolution of the Ranger defense forces, and once the Pehnahterkuh coming down from the Indian Territory realized that they could again ride through central Texas with impunity.

Word of the peace councils held at Torreys Trading House spread through all the Comanche lodges. This, and the fact that the government-sponsored trading posts proved eager to do business with Comanches in Texas, had one result. By 1844, the Pehnahterkuh were led to believe that they could reenter Texas in safety. They far preferred their old, honeyed ranges to the plains of the Indian Territory, and groups of them began drifting south to the lower fringes of the Edwards Plateau. Another factor aided this migration. In 1844, the great bison herds, always moving on their random, tidal wanderings, tended to flow south below the Red, converging most densely fairly close to the white frontier. Many, though not all, of the Pehnahterkuh followed them.

Thus Houston had planned peace but re-created war conditions.

By late 1844, the frontier seemed to be returning to its old condition. Every week, somewhere in western Texas, whites were killed, cattle speared, and houses went up in flames. The anger of the frontier people followed swiftly.

The peace policy played a central part in the political campaign of 1844. Dr. Anson Jones, Houston's preference for president, pledged to continue Houston's policies, and had the full weight of Houston's support and influence. But although Houston's policies had held down governmental expenses, avoided a major conflict with Mexico, and had brought the United States rapidly toward annexation, his "coddling" of Indians had aroused anger and rebellion in the western counties. In a bitter campaign, Edward Burleson opposed Anson Jones, demanding a return to the Lamar policy of driving Indians out of Texas.

The Texas vote split dramatically between east and west. Jones, by carrying the more populous eastern counties between the Trinity and the Sabine, all far removed from Amerindian danger, won by 7,037 to 5,668. Burleson, however, took all the thinly settled western regions overwhelmingly, proof that the frontier people were convinced there was only one solution to the Indian problem.

Once in office, Jones quickly found the Indians creating new problems for him. The Comanches, understanding nothing of *tejano* politics, were aware only of *tejano* weakness, and became increasingly bold and arrogant. In 1845, a group of migrant Delawares attacked and massacred a Comanche camp in the west. Because the Delawares no longer fought the whites, and often scouted for them, the Comanche bands considered them Texan allies, and on this thin line of reasoning, or from rage that had to fall somewhere, staged a series of bloody raids all along the frontier. Only a handful of the Pehnahterkuh bothered to show up for the annual council in 1845. Conditions had deteriorated rapidly, and it appeared to most Texans that the events of 1840 must be repeated.

However, the Texas frontier was overtaken by greater happenings to the east. In 1845, after a major change in popular and official opinion, the United States government offered Texas a treaty of annexation on very favorable terms. Houston had worked on this sentiment carefully, so that, by 1844, Washington was virtually begging Texas to join the Union. Meanwhile, ten years as a small, isolated, underdeveloped nation had convinced the overwhelming majority of Texans of the wisdom of entering the greater republic. There were ties of blood and history, economic advantages, and other reasons, but the paramount, unifying reason behind the Texans' desire for annexation was that, under the Constitution, the federal government would be required to assume the burdens of frontier defense. After annexation, the United States Army would guard the Rio Grande and, most Texas settlers believed, would quickly pacify or drive the remaining hostile Indians from the state. In this hope and belief, the western counties voted as solidly for annexation in the 1845 referendum as the eastern ones. It carried by 4,000 to 200 votes. Thus, in the end, Houston's great designs prevailed.

Early in 1846, the Lone Star flag was replaced by the Stars and Stripes. The flags changed, and in the joyous ceremony, no one realized that the trail of blood and bones would continue for another thirty years.

V

THE GRAVEYARD PLAINS

THE PEOPLE AND THE AMERICANS

*Our manifest destiny to overspread
and possess the whole continent
which Providence has given us for the . . .
great experiment of liberty.*
    —John L. O'Sullivan, New York *Morning News,* 1845

1

TREATIES

All men from Washington are liars.
      —Spotted Tail, Dakota war chief

In the nineteenth century the forms and practices of United States Indian policy became remarkably like those of the Spanish and other European empires. This was probably inherent in the approach of any European culture to primitive peoples like the North American Indians. The natives were seen as inferior to the claiming civilization in culture, morality, and organization. They were granted no sovereignty over territory or their life styles. The approach was not only imperialistic, but paternalistic and overwhelmingly patronizing.

To Amerindian tribal societies that had no real conception of hierarchs or kings, the American President was described as the Grandfather, or Great Father, who by right ruled both races, and who was alternately pleased or pained by the actions of his children. Like the Spanish, Americans realized that conversion to Christianity would do much to destroy the values and alter the life styles of wild Indians, so missionaries were constantly authorized to penetrate them. However, the separation of church and state in the United States prevented anything like the reducing policy of the Spanish presidio-mission system. Moreover, the proliferation of religious denominations and their mutual jealousy and competition hampered most missionary work among the tribes before jurisdictions were carved out by Congress later in the century. Schools, usually sponsored by religious institutions, had been established early for various Indians. But while the republic unofficially sought to reduce and assimilate the Amerindians, the United States had one great problem that the Spanish had never faced. Missionaries and teachers strove to teach the tribes the English language and Christian culture, but the American republic had no place for assimilated Indians.

Anglo-American society lacked the class-caste structures of the Hispanic American world. North American Indians could not be made into slaves, like Africans, even before slavery disappeared in the middle of the century. While the Spanish utilized a form of serfdom in Mexico and Peru, English society had nothing similar to offer. The fact that the United States was faced with assimilating Amerindians as full citizens—which was difficult under any circumstances and which most white citizens were not prepared to accept—tended to hamper all assimilation. The United States had no real means of bringing even educated Indians into its society as a lower or subordinate class. The loose, rough and tumble, flexible society that emerged, generally without government control or supervision, in effect made it more difficult for Amerindians to find a niche.

Ely Samuel Parker, a Seneca who secured an elite education in the nineteenth century, is a case in point. Parker, as assimilated as any Indian could be, wanted to practice law but was refused admission to the bar, a decision upheld by the Supreme Court, on the grounds that Indians were not citizens. He did become an engineer, and during the Civil War served as Grant's military secretary and a lieutenant colonel. He was present at Appomattox, where General Lee shook his hand and said: "I am glad to see one real American here."

Parker replied, "Sir, we are all Americans."

But Parker's belief had no currency in American society. The result was to make the vast majority of surviving tribesmen eventually dependent upon the federal government and to maintain them indefinitely as wards of the government. Whatever the Indian's failures to come to grips with his reality, the American society's policy of assimilating them was a total fiasco.

Like the European colonial powers before it, the United States government sent political officers among the tribes. These were called Indian agents; the system was adopted in the 1780s. It proliferated into a bureaucracy: the Office of Indian Affairs. The agents had authority to look after the wards of government and to deal with them in the name of government. Their duties with the still wild tribes lay mainly in peace keeping; with the pacified peoples, their task was to supervise the subsidies, called annuities, usually paid in foodstuffs and goods, which allowed the conquered tribes to exist. The control over annuities voted by Congress gave the agents enormous powers over their charges, and equally enormous opportunities for corruption. Annuities were sometimes proposed, and voted by Congress, with the expectation that white agents and contractors would profit more from them than would the Amerindians. Annuities were paid in goods or rations; much of the money was diverted and never spent at all; and the shoddiness and even uselessness of delivered goods or food was documented again and again. The federal apparatus, especially in the era before the civil service law, was never able to discipline the Indian office into an effective bureaucracy. The jobs were filled with political appointees, few of whom were ever qualified, and many of whom sought appointment mainly for the opportunity to rob the Indians. The Amerindian wards were peculiarly helpless to protest or complain. Unlike the citizenry, they had no recourse to law. No United States official agency had a worse record, or deserved a fouler reputation, than the Office of Indian Affairs.

In its dealings with the still autonomous tribes, the Indian agency repeated all the old travesties of the Spanish. Chieftains were bedecked with medals and diplomas and empty titles and honors were lavished upon cooperative tribal leaders. George Washington presented the first American peace medal in 1792, and by the time the Americans reached the plains, such practices had become customary. The whole process had an air of unreality, because the Indian commissioners, like the Spanish before them, were frustrated by the lack of hierarchy in the Plains war societies. White agents insisted that the Indians produce leaders with whom they could negotiate, despite the Amerindian explanation of the Plains form of warrior-male democracy. United States commissioners took to appointing such spokesmen arbitrarily when the tribes were unable to agree upon a paramount chief. Federal officials were impatient with the diffused democracy of the Indians and demanded a responsible leadership. Sadly, however, they were unable to impute any real powers to the white-designated chiefs. These were inevitably patronized by the whites and spurned contemptuously by their peers. Some such chiefs were consciously tragic figures; others were merely bewildered until they were killed by either the whites or their own kind. The appointees got medals, batons, uniforms, and were often paraded to Washington for audiences with the Great Father. One Sioux was "made" a brigadier general with sword and epaulets, and was received with field music; he died as tragically as did most of his kind.

The United States soon resorted to the old Spanish practice of enticing warriors to councils with gifts. Presents provided a chance to buy peace at small cost. This practice was even more patronizing than the rendering of tribute, for most of the goods offered were grotesque gewgaws or worthless commodities. The Indians liked such goods, and accepted them with pleasure, which demeaned them further in white eyes. American officials never followed the Indian practice of giving presents out of sheer hospitality.

The greatest of all travesties, however, was the incessant seeking and signing of peace pacts or treaties with the different peoples. A legalistic approach was inevitable for a civilization that professed the rule of law and in practice tended to be governed by a corps of lawyers. Anglo-Americans instinctively approached Indians with treaties and compacts. The British had used the same approach, but the American republic carried the practice to ridiculous extremes.

Throughout the nineteenth century, the U.S. federal apparatus was extremely loose and weak in European terms; no government anywhere had quite so little authority and control over its citizens. While no nation or people was more eager to solve problems by negotiation, no government on earth had a poorer record of keeping its ratified agreements. The problem was inherent in the Anglo-American form of democracy. Representatives were empowered to make laws or treaties, but the government had little power to force them upon the citizenry. Unpopular treaties could not be enforced without political repercussions. Government at all levels was extremely sensitive and vulnerable to shifting public opinion and especially to powerful pressure groups. Any agreement that provided the tribes with rights, privileges, or territory was inevitably challenged—sooner or later—by some part of white society, and government was more susceptible to citizens than to alien wards.

This was not so much an inherent ethnic problem as a political one. The British in Canada managed differently. They made pragmatic arrangements with the tribes, gave them certain rights, then rigidly enforced the rights they granted. Although the end result was the same—the Amerindians were engulfed—the Canadian conquest was carried out with a maximum of justice, good faith, and rationality, and almost without bloodshed or lingering psychic trauma.

The inability of the American government, usually distant and only weakly felt on the North American frontier, to enforce treaty provisions on white citizens was historic. It began in British times. In 1768, in the worried aftermath of Pontiac's great uprising, the British commissioners for North America negotiated treaties with the Trans-Appalachian tribes, with the avowed purpose of guaranteeing these Indians their ancient hunting grounds.

The British designated the Appalachian-Allegheny chain as a line of demarcation. Surveys were made, boundaries set. But the ink was hardly dry on the documents sent to Whitehall or the peace pipes cold before white settlers had blazed new trails through the Cumberlands, and thousands of frontier people were pouring into the Ohio Valley wilderness. The authorities were unable or unwilling to prevent this, or to meet the expense of providing adequate protection for both red and white subjects of the Crown. Government indifference allowed whites and Indians to fight it out. The United States, after its creation, continued this great failure, not only across the Appalachians but eventually to the far Pacific.

There had been a fundamental misconception behind the treaty making of 1768. Authorities utterly underestimated the explosive growth of the Anglo-American population and its restless, pioneering drives. U.S. governments continued to make this error for another century, setting aside reservation after reservation for the Amerindians, then refusing to force their voters to respect these territorial pacts.

And there can be no question that a powerful element of sheer hypocrisy reinforced these constant "errors." In 1768, Lord Shelburne believed and desired that Anglo-American settlement would quickly reach the Mississippi, in the interests of British trade. He approved the peace pacts simply because he hoped they might buy time from the warlike Amerindians. This was not the last treaty that was offered in bad faith. Peace treaties were often seen as placebos for the Indians, to delay the expensive and inconvenient warfare that a blunt statement of white thinking must immediately have provoked.

White negotiators justified such false treaties on the grounds that even a brief peace based on deception was preferable to an honest war. Peace inevitably favored the whites; each year they grew stronger on the frontier, while the Indian was destroyed in myriad peaceful ways. As Ben Franklin remarked, Providence had apparently chosen whiskey as its principal instrument for preparing the continent for agriculture and civilization. There were other effective instruments, for the Indian continued as physically vulnerable to European diseases as his metabolism was to alcohol.

The tribes, true to their cast of mind, demanded pacts that would run so long as the hills stood or the grass grew green on the meadows. Indian agents acquiesced to such language, sometimes even remarking on its quaint symbolism. Any agent with an ounce of historical perspective must have known that no American government could sign such a treaty in good faith—yet such pacts were ratified into the last half of the nineteenth century.

The entire process of peace-keeping with autonomous tribes had become shot through with ambiguities and hypocrisies by the time the United States impinged upon the Great Plains area. Under American law, the plains region north of the Red River had become U.S. territory through the Louisiana Purchase. The tribes inhabiting it therefore could not be sovereign, and the government did not accept them as sovereign; yet they were in fact autonomous and were dealt with as separate "nations." Indian treaties were ratified by the Senate just like agreements with foreign countries. This fiction was carefully preserved, to the considerable bewilderment of many intelligent Amerindians, who were invited to councils ostensibly as equals, the representatives of free peoples, only to be presented with actual ultimatums.

The process permitted unlimited debate, yet it really meant wearing down the Amerindians. Few, if any, of the signatories could read the texts of treaties, or even sign them—they gave assent by touching the pen with which the whites signed—and they assented to loose translations. Often, neither party understood the exact territorial definitions or proposed boundaries; American commissioners frequently set boundaries that were never surveyed. Almost all the Plains tribes had the same social and political organization as the Comanches; this meant that every adult warrior must touch the pen before a treaty became binding upon an entire band or tribe. No treaty ever signed with any tribe upon the plains was ever completely valid, from this fact alone—which every American commissioner refused to recognize. This rendered effective diplomacy with the warrior tribes almost impossible, if not ridiculous. American agents described Cheyenne, Dakota, and Comanche "nations" as determinedly as did the Spanish scribes.

The American Indian bureaucracy tended to accept treaty-making as an end in itself, and measured its progress by pacts signed, without regard to their eventual ramifications. Expert white advisers often pointed out that certain clauses were impossible to implement, especially those that required the Plains tribes to cease their warfare against each other. The whites violated the concept of the brotherhood of man; the Plains Amerindians did not even possess it. The first or second clause of all the early Plains treaties was a pledge by the tribes that they would not raid each other in the future—always inserted on white insistence.

Moreover, the whites often failed to deliver the presents they had promised the tribes in order to lure them to council. To the Amerindian mind, this was bad faith, and rendered all the other agreements invalid. Amerindians neither understood nor accepted white excuses such as a failure of appropriations or problems with delivery. As when the French failed to deliver promised arms in the eighteenth century, a failure to deliver promised goods or annuities not only abrogated treaties, it occasionally caused hostilities.

And sometimes, a treaty secured with vast effort failed to be ratified by the Senate for purely procedural reasons, or appropriations were stopped by administrative problems having nothing to do with the Indian question. The tribes had no patience with such bureaucratic nonsense, and such things left a bad taste among the Indians. Many councils did more damage to relations than a brutal confrontation would have done.

There were countless facets of white diplomacy that bewildered or deeply worried council-attending Indians. Every Comanche description or legend of a council with whites revealed a feeling of unease or ambivalence. These folk memories lingered far into the twentieth century. The chiefs were invited to speak their minds, and did so. The whites then made demands as if they had never spoken. The Comanches never liked to attend a council; they avoided at least one major council on the plains on the grounds that their enemies had been invited. The Americans rarely understood why it was unthinkable for People and Apaches to sit together.

The bureaus of the Office of Indian Affairs became stuffed with hundreds of separate Indian treaties, many of which were invalid from the start since the Amerindians touched the pen with stated reservations. The office, and the government, set great store by such cheap peace-keeping. Pacts were triumphantly carted off to Washington and successful treaty writers were promoted. But peace was rarely cheaply purchased; whatever treaties were signed, the final peace was paid for in bloodshed across the entire frontier.

This travesty was an ineradicable blot upon the honor of the United States and its officers and citizens. In historical perspective, American diplomacy with the Amerindians was more reprehensible than the brutalities inflicted upon them. Massacre matched massacre; tortures were repaid in displacements and exterminations. The same forces that impelled the modern European nations to world power made the conquest of the American continent inevitable. From the late eighteenth century, most intelligent Europeans understood that the white entry into the Americas spelled at least a cultural death warrant for the natives. The question facing the United States throughout its advance across the land was never whether the aborigines should be removed as a barrier to its civilization, but only the best means and timetable of the removal. The question was bound up in politics, ethics, morality, and even sentimentality—but it was handled almost throughout with pervasive hypocrisy.

The Plains Amerindians, ironically, would have better understood a direct approach; this would have fitted into their worldview and ethos. The Mexica admitted to Cortés that they had come into the Valley of Mexico without lands, but that they had seized the lands of others with shield and arrow. They understood when Cortés told them that he had come with shield and spear to take their lands and give them others. Had every American told the Plains Indians what many already knew, that because the white men had come the tribes' days were numbered, and that as conquerors they demanded the Indians' lands, the warrior societies could have understood this perfectly. Their tragedy would not have been deeper, nor their sorrow any greater. Amerindians would have fought and died, killing no more and no less. In the end, however, victors and vanquished might have found an only slightly haunted peace which, as between Union and Confederate soldiers, emerged from warfare declared and accepted by both sides.

The Plains peoples never approached the whites begging for peace and mercy. It was the whites who came with professions of humanity and protection, insisting upon promises they could not keep. The whites sought out the tribes and encouraged the chiefs to speak in their splendid, vivid, soaring, useless Amerindian oratory. White representatives sat stunned, and the best of them shamed, at the Indian recitals, knowing that not one word of all the great orations would affect one jot of an American agenda, or alter a single goal of American policy. Nor would the Amerindians be told the truth when it was not to the American advantage.

Harney the soldier, who hated Indians and made no bones about it, was the most respected white chief on the plains before the Civil War. Harney spoke the truth: when he said there would be war, there was war; he said the whites would take Indian lands, and the whites did seize the Indians' territories. Harney was remembered as a great chief whose straight speaking entered Dakota, Cheyenne, and Comanche legend. In the West, only a few Americans dealt honestly with the natives who stood between the Americans and their imperial dreams. It was significant that while many whites despised Harney, as they professed to despise Lamar, the warrior peoples understood and respected him.

The American experiment in liberty, as the Founding Fathers called it, could not be extended to the Amerindians for a multitude of cultural reasons. Yet the savages deserved better than hypocrisy and treachery and the false humanitarianism that was continually professed but could not be implemented. Hypocrisy was perhaps inevitable in a people who convinced themselves that they were creating something new in the New World, while actually carrying out the most primordial form of conquest.

AMERICANS OTHER THAN THOSE IN TEXAS FIRST MADE CONTACTS WITH the Nermernuh in the Indian Territory, in what is now western Oklahoma, in the 1830s. As usual, the first contacts were diplomatic missions. Envoys escorted by dragoons went through the plains territory, attempting by treaty to make arrangements for the east-ern tribes that were being expelled from the United States. The Comanches and their Kiowa allies received the American agents and soldiers with characteristic hospitality. American traders such as William Bent had already penetrated the Santa Fe Trail; the early relationships were amicable.

The American dragoons, with their heavy, colorful, almost comic-opera early-nineteenth-century uniforms, impressed the Indians favorably. The Arbuckle and other expeditions spent weeks in or beside Comanche-Kiowa encampments. Captain Randolph Marcy of Virginia and Colonel Richard Irving Dodge and the artist Catlin recorded their first impressions of the Comanches as generally un-prepossessing compared to the northern Plains Indians. There were no hostilities or confrontations. The troops were only visiting; they made no attempts to place permanent garrisons so far west; and the tribes saw the white men as passing novelties. The diplomacy that was supposed to carve out a place for the expelled tribes was mostly futile. The tribes sat in council, accepted presents, and returned to their time-honored raiding as soon as the white men departed.

At this time, Texas was still a Mexican province, and the U.S. envoys made it clear to the Kiowa-Comanches that the Americans and the peoples of Texas belonged to entirely separate nations. The bands absorbed this fact quickly. The vicious Texan-Comanche hostility that developed during the late 1830s played no part in Comanche-United States relations.

The Americans called the People "Nerm" or "Nimma," from their language, but the Spanish "Comanche" soon drove out the other terms. Conversely, while the Comanches also used the Spanish description, *americano*, their general term for an American was *tahbay-boh*, or white man. Americans recorded this name as "tabby-boo" or "tavahoe," while noting that the Comanches invariably called the Americans in Texas *tejanos*. From the very first, the Comanches of all bands learned to distinguish *tahbay-boh* and *tejanos*. The two appeared quite different to them: white men al-ways wore gaudy blue uniforms, while the Texans rarely had uni-forms or any regular dress, and their official tunics were plain gray. Above all, the two kinds of whites, above and below the Red River, approached the People in entirely different ways. Americans were friends; *tejanos*, vicious enemies. This early impression was so marked that it was never quite extinguished in the Comanche mind.

The U.S. Army, on its infrequent sojourns along the Santa Fe Trail, maintained excellent relations with the scattered Comanche bands throughout the 1840s. American officers, following an emerging Indian policy, tried to ameliorate conflicts between tribes, especially Osages and Kiowas, and, generally, between displaced eastern tribes and the warlike horse Indians. They scrupulously did not interfere in Comanche internal affairs. On many occasions soldiers saw white Texan captives with the bands, including the celebrated Cynthia Ann Parker. They made no attempt at rescue, and ransom efforts, while always attempted, were muted and not pressed in the face of Comanche surliness. Many American officers chafed at such orders. Texas might be a separate nation, but blood called to blood, and the sight of Anglo-American women in Comanche hands aroused deep antipathies. But peace on the plains was considered more important than the fate of a few bedraggled captives.

Those efforts at ransom, however, which were often successful, had one unfortunate historic effect. They encouraged the northern bands to take more captives in Texas, because they could always obtain a good price for them above the Red boundary. Comanches were not encouraged to keep such captives in good shape, since they also discovered that the more abused a white captive was, the more eager the white men were to buy the woman or child.

These somewhat uneasy but basically peaceful relations were founded on an emerging United States Indian policy that was now being applied uniformly and with reasonable consistency to the West. Within the organized American states, all the powerful or warlike Amerindian peoples had been pacified, expelled, or else relegated to remote enclaves. There were few dangerous Amerindians along the American frontiers, for the white line of settlement was still far to the east of the true Great Plains. Anglo-Americans were fully absorbed in developing the vast, newly opened territories of the midwestern prairies. Indian troubles were minor, and easily handled by militias in a single campaign. The largely Siouan peoples who had farmed the bottoms of this region for a thousand years were easily destroyed or displaced, without general wars and, as a rule, without national attention.

The beginning of the true plains, still imperfectly explored, seemed to mark a possible line of demarcation between the American civilization and the remaining North American Indians. This great interior region, and most of the American West, was denoted on the maps as the "Great American Desert." It was largely unfit for the agriculture practiced in America in the first half of the nineteenth century; the Spanish-Mexican cattle culture had not yet been transmitted northward out of Texas. Except for trappers and traders, few Americans saw any profit in the entire plains region, and small future for development. Therefore, the early Anglo-American approach to the plains was much like that of the earlier French. The object was to establish a loose sovereignty, primarily to impress potential European rivals, and to maintain good relations with autonomous tribes so that the area might provide a profitable fur trade.

Here the Americans made an error comparable to the British mistake of the 1760s, when the British believed that Anglo-American expansion would halt, perhaps for centuries, along the Appalachian-Allegheny chain. The United States government did not yet fully appreciate the explosive growth rates of the population— in the 1830s, the highest in the world—or the dynamism inherent in the burgeoning Industrial Revolution. Thus, official Washington, and easterners generally, made the classic error of again believing that a new balance might be created between the races, and that much of the West could be reserved as a sort of expanded Indian Territory for the remaining wild tribes.

The United States was peculiarly unmilitary and maintained extremely small regular forces; the army numbered only eight thousand men in 1846. There was only minimal interest in Washington and in the power and population centers of the East for military operations in the western Indian country. Such operations consisted mainly of exploring and mapping. There was no interest at all in campaigns to reduce the savages. This would be expensive for the government and appeared to offer no recompense. Once reduced, the tribes would have to be maintained and would become a source of new embarrassment. Therefore, the concept of using the West for an Indian preserve made good sense.

A certain sentimentality was mixed in with this practicality. The tragic removals of the southern tribes had aroused a vocal, if ineffective, opposition, and in the aftermath a widespread, though relatively shallow, sympathy for the "vanishing red men" developed. This tended to be primarily intellectual; it was widely reflected in American literature. Still, many Americans, appalled at the rapid destruction of the race, felt an almost nostalgic need to preserve the "natives." Sympathy was strongest on the eastern seaboard, where the Indian wars were two centuries past, and where Americans had little personal interest in the West and, for the most part, had never seen an Amerindian. Americans who had no concept of the true life styles of the Plains warrior societies tended to idealize them as noble savages. Such sentiments among a large part of the American elite did color official thinking and affect official policy.

Of course, this view of the red men was not shared by people close to the actual frontiers. The great mass of frontiersmen and western immigrants never looked on Indians as anything but obstacles in the way of rightful progress, and where there was actual conflict, as in Texas, there was a deep hatred of the entire race. The westerners who knew Amerindians best, such as the mountain men who had lived among them, almost never idealized them, though these Americans understood the native viewpoint and sometimes wanted the tribes to be dealt with fairly. Thus by the 1830s, there had developed a certain dichotomy between the western and the eastern views toward Indians which had very serious implications. It was to paralyze American Indian policy in the coming years, with tragic results—particularly in Texas.

By 1845, when Texas was annexed, the western Indian policy had become fairly uniform from the Red River to the Canadian line. The army had principal jurisdiction over the Indian Territory and the wild tribes. It scattered forts along the frontier but did not seriously impinge on the Amerindians. Both the army and the government were disturbed by the wild wars set off by the forced entry of the immigrant tribes onto the plains' fringes, but the policy was to enforce peace through diplomacy. The army did not offer the displaced peoples much protection, either from the Plains tribes or from advancing whites. It was policy to prevent the indiscriminate slaughter of game along the frontier, so that the Indians would not lack food, but this was only spottily enforced.

The annexation of Texas—where very different frontier conditions existed—threw an immediate strain on the whole system. In

1845, the Texans had confidently expected the federal government, through its army, to rid the new state quickly of its dangerous Indians. There was no understanding in Texas of the newer, post-Jacksonian Washington policy which reserved the plains for the Indians. Conversely, there was no understanding in the government of the Texas situation, or of the nature of the southwestern horse Indians, whose long-range mobility and aggressiveness transcended those of any savages so far encountered by Americans.

Washington dispatched Indian commissioners to Texas even before the date of official annexation, with instructions to seek out the Texas tribes and make peace treaties with them. Commissioners Pierce Butler and M. G. Lewis, a younger brother of the explorer Meriwether Lewis, began work in January 1846. By April, with the help of the former Republic of Texas Indian Agent Major Robert S. Neighbors, they had gathered sixty-three prominent chiefs in a council at Comanche Peak, near Granbury in the present Hood County. The parleys with the Wichitas, Caddoans, Kichais, Tonkawas, and other remnants were a continuation of earlier dealings these same tribes had had with Texas. These peoples had no choice but to take the American presents and accept the American ultimatums. However, a large number of the Pehnahterkuh Comanches came to Comanche Peak, more than had ever attended a council, to hear the words of the new Great Father of the white men.

The treaty offered by Butler and Lewis incorporated current Indian policy. The Comanches were asked to remain west of the white settlement line, to acknowledge the sovereignty of the United States, to surrender any wanted men on demand to American authorities, to return white captives and any and all horses that might be stolen in the future, and to help the Americans suppress the illicit arms and liquor traffic by doing business only with licensed traders. Comanche representatives indicated that these would be difficult to enforce on the People's warriors—the American representatives could not know how difficult—but that they would accept the terms provided the white men gave the Pehnahterkuh what the *tejanos* refused them: a permanent boundary over which no white man or Texan would be allowed to cross without the permission of the tribe.

Here the Pehnahterkuh put Butler and Lewis in a most awkward position. This was the heart of the matter, the basis upon which any lasting peace must rest. But the U.S. commissioners lacked any authority to grant the Indians a line of demarcation anywhere within the borders of Texas.

Uniquely, in the years since 1789, Texas had entered the American federation from sovereign status. No part of its territory had previously been claimed by the United States. Every other state beyond the original thirteen had petitioned to join the Union from territorial status, and in these formerly federal territories, the title to unpreempted lands automatically rested with the government. But because the treaty of annexation reserved title to all vacant lands to the state government, there was not an acre of public lands within the state. Under both state and federal law, the Comanches were trespassers on state lands.

Another facet of the Texas situation was unique. Formerly, Indian pacification or removal had been almost a condition for statehood. But Texas, out of a peculiar set of historic and geopolitical conditions, came into the Union with a full half of its recognized territory still unsettled and roamed by powerful, warlike bands. The rights of Amerindians, of course, were no more considered in the Texas-United States deal than in any other white territorial treaties in the Americas, yet certain aspects of this situation should have been thought through during the transaction.

It immediately called into question the whole Indian policy of the United States in the West. Under the law, Amerindians were wards of the federal government; the state had no responsibility for them. The federal government was also responsible for frontier defense under the Constitution. The Texas government made it perfectly clear that it would not, then or later, agree to set aside half its territory for an Indian reservation. In fact, the state was already busily granting and selling Indian lands to encourage immigration and development. Meanwhile, both the state government and the white frontier, and a horde of land speculators, demanded that federal authorities do their duty under the law and remove the squatting Indians.

The federal government opposed this demand as unreasonable. For whatever reason, Washington was totally opposed to large-scale military operations. Almost from the day of annexation, these opposing interests and views complicated and even embittered state-federal relations.

The majority of Texans were convinced that there could be no peace until the Indians were removed. Washington did not, then and for many years to come, intend to implement such measures. The disagreement became emotional. The Texans, to enhance their legal arguments, emphasized the bestial nature of the Comanches. In a counterreaction, their opponents tried to deny such savagery; they deprecated continual reports of raids, rapes, and burnings, blaming all violence upon the white frontiersmen. Most of the arguments on each side, whether self-serving or humanitarian, failed to deal with the basic questions.

There could be no real hope of permanent peace with the Comanche bands unless they were granted inviolate territories. This the federal government could not do. Therefore, there would be no end of raiding and killing along the Texas frontier until the government afforded adequate protection. This the government was unwilling to do. The result was a repetition of so much of American frontier history since British times: the government failed both the citizens of its frontier and the Amerindian wards. It ensured the continuation of a terrible brutalization of the white frontier, and the eventual destruction of the remaining Indians.

The Butler-Lewis commission tried to get around the principal problem without facing the requirements of a workable policy. There can be no doubt that Butler would have promised the Comanches their west Texas ranges had he been able. In this era of wholesale treaty-making with the Plains tribes, far more incredible promises were ratified by the United States government. The great northern council at Laramie, in 1851, ceded whole future states to a handful of horse Indians. All western Kansas and most of Colorado were assigned to the Cheyennes and allied Arapahos in perpetuity. The Black Hills region, that ancient Amerindian battle ground, was granted to the Plains Dakotas. These promises were signed when the concept of "manifest destiny" had become common currency, and the West was already exploding with streams of settlers and miners. Butler refrained from ceding the Pehnahterkuh the Texas bison range, but the American commission indulged in another sorry business. It solemnly promised to halt white encroachment on the Pehnahterkuh territories by requiring every white man to obtain a pass signed by the President before crossing the frontier.

This pledge was not entirely cynical; the white treaty makers probably thought that they could write new law. If such a provision were included in a ratified treaty with a "foreign" power, it perforce would become federal law. But any such view ignored reality. A pass system was not practical. No agency, certainly not the army, could hope to enforce it. History gave small promise that any elected American official or Congress would even consider employing force against citizens in defense of noncitizen Indians—the pressure was entirely in the other direction. And the legal grounds were dubious. No American court was apt to uphold the constitutionality of an edict that required a citizen to secure a presidential pass to visit property to which he had obtained legal title.

The Pehnahterkuh had begun to recognize evasions, and the chiefs were not satisfied. To secure a pact, the commissioners further promised to supply special trading posts, and to provide the Comanches with blacksmiths and gun repairmen to solve their continual problem of keeping firearms in good order. They also promised ten thousand dollars' worth of presents to be distributed to the chiefs. Finally, the Pehnahterkuh chiefs touched the pen, with reservations. No other Comanche band was represented. In this manner, the Butler-Lewis commission believed it had arrived at peace, and bore its treaty and a gaggle of chiefs on the ritual passage to Washington to parade before both the Senate and the President.

The Senate ratified the Butler-Lewis Treaty, and the President signed it personally, early in 1847.

By this time, it was already violated. The army never marched to the Texas frontier to police a pass system; it went to the Rio Grande, where General Zachary Taylor, under presidential orders, quickly involved the United States in war with Mexico. Meanwhile, no effort was made to keep Americans out of the treaty territory; in fact, once the war with Mexico began, the army itself poured across the Santa Fe Trail toward the Mexican provinces of the Southwest. At the same time, the annexation of Texas had brought new hordes of American land seekers across the Sabine. These immigrants filled up the frontier and continually pushed it westward. For the first time, the northwestern frontier along the Brazos and Trinity began to impinge upon the plains. The central hill country north-northwest of San Antonio was settled by German immigrants, who did try to make special treaties with the southern Comanches. Instead of halting this settlement along the current line of demarcation between Anglo-Texas and Indian country, the State of Texas did everything possible to encourage more settlement by granting headrights and homesteads liberally throughout the western regions. From the very first in Texas, the state and the Office of Indian Affairs worked completely at cross purposes.

It cannot be stated that the Pehnahterkuh carried out their part of the bargain either. The 1846 treaty—as all subsequent treaties —made impossible demands on Comanche society. It was only realized much later that asking the Comanches to halt raiding and to return all horses and captives in effect demanded that the Nermernuh cease to be Comanches. There is evidence that the chiefs and warriors who actually signed the treaty were reasonably sincere, but, again, they could speak for no one except themselves. Any American who understood the society of the Nermernuh must have realized that no solutions to the southwestern Indian problem could be derived from treaty negotiations, whether the United States observed the pacts or not. A separate peace could not be made with every young warrior on the Texas plains, and short of this, no peace was valid.

Surprisingly, a sort of peace did hold for a time. The southern Comanches did not carry out extensive raiding from 1846 through 1848, although the situation remained volatile. There were two reasons for this fragile peace, neither of which depended on the document signed at Comanche Peak.

One was that the Texan frontier was well patrolled, and the Comanches knew it. Texas had raised a regiment of Rangers in 1846, with Jack Hays in command. This, and another regiment, were diverted to service with the army in Mexico after the outbreak of war. But the federal government authorized Texas to defend its frontiers at federal expense, and, subsequently, nine Ranger companies were stationed along the frontier. The Pehnahterkuh feared and respected the Texas Rangers, and their presence was an effective deterrent, for the southern Comanches had no illusions about the Ranger mode of warfare.

The other reason was Major Robert S. Neighbors, the former Texas Indian agent who was worth another regiment to the white frontier. Neighbors was appointed United States Indian Agent for Texas early in 1847, one of the most sensible appointments the Indian office ever made. Neighbors understood Comanches, due to his long service to the Republic of Texas, and beyond this, he possessed remarkable personal qualities. He was without greed, personal ambition, or arrogance, neither a true political appointee nor part of the federal bureaucracy, and possessed of infinite patience, tact, and wisdom. Neighbors had no illusions about the Indians, but he met and sat with them as equals, and spoke without hypocrisy. The Pehnahterkuh came to respect and even like him as they did few white men. For some two years, Major Neighbors kept a sort of peace single-handedly, through the force of his personality, and through some extremely effective personal relationships with the Pehnahterkuh civil chiefs.

The Comanches had always had many wise and capable camp headmen, such as the shrewd Mook-war-ruh and Paha-yuca. These men were still only minor civil magistrates, whose authority rested more upon personality and use and custom than any official sanction. They could offer advice only when sought, and about their only arbitrary power was the right to move the encampments. However, in this period the destruction of virtually all the great war leaders of the band had tended to enhance the position of the civil chiefs. The natural imperatives of the camp headmen, which ran counter to the arrogance and ambitions of the prestige-hungry younger warriors, had greater play. Wiser than the average warrior, instinctively jealous of potential war chiefs, these men were drawn into a natural alliance of interests with the Texas Indian agent.

Paha-yuca and the others almost always spoke against a renewed war with the *tejanos,* and advised the People to trust the white man Neighbors. They could not prevent the young warriors from making medicine and taking the blood trail, but they discovered one almost Machiavellian ploy. When hunting slowed, or the warriors appeared too restless, Paha-yuca and the others took to moving the camps as far as possible from the white frontier, ostensibly in search of more buffalo. They also informed the northern bands that raids conducted through Pehnahterkuh territory were unwelcome to the southern Comanches, unless they were directed at Mexico, in which case the restless Pehnahterkuh often joined them. Thus in a sense, because the normal drives of Nermernuh society could not be entirely bottled up, Neighbors saved the Texas frontier by diverting Comanche energies toward long-suffering Mexico.

But it was not possible for this tenuous peace to hold; too many factors worked against it. The twenty thousand Nermernuh on the plains—Neighbors' 1849 estimate—were the real if not the titular masters of all the territory between central Texas and New Mexico from the Arkansas River to the Rio Grande. Peace depended on three things: respect for Amerindian territoriality by the whites; the horse warriors' restraint along the exposed Texan frontier; and a continued outlet for Comanche aggressions to the south, in Mexico. But even a stabilization along these lines, had it been possible, would probably not have long preserved either peace or the People.

Time still seemed frozen on the prairies of North America. The land had not changed for ten thousand years; the buffalo still roamed in their uncounted millions. The Plains peoples had hardly changed for a thousand generations. For them, this was not the hopeful middle of a progressive century; they were living in the fortieth millennium of a static existence. This fact alone made the middle of the nineteenth Christian century not the zenith but the fast-approaching twilight of that existence.

Because of the injuries knowingly inflicted on the primitive peoples of the plains, Americans have tended to take too parochial a view of the tragedy that befell that native population. The sweep of American civilization across the continent was part of a worldwide phenomenon, only one expression of an explosion of European power, population, and technology across the earth. Whatever the means used against them, soldiers or merchants or missionaries, the primitive folk everywhere on earth, from the plateaus of central Asia to the North African Sahara, from the savannas of the Argentine to the deep forests of the Congo, faced imminent disaster in the nineteenth century. In the same decades in which Americans penetrated the Great Plains and Rocky Mountains, Russian and Chinese armies crushed the independent existence of the Asian steppe barbarians who had menaced Eurasian civilizations for millennia. Modern arms, techniques, and organization were opening all the "dark" places of the world. The Argentinians exterminated the pampas *indios* by military operations; Europeans destroyed native hordes below the Zambesi; Mexican artillery, transported by rail, blew apart the last strongholds of the Yaqui tribesmen who had defied the Spaniards. Gentler, but even more destructive, means were employed against the aborigines of the Pacific islands. The nineteenth century was a time of tragedy and horror for primitive cultures everywhere.

2

THE GREAT DISASTER

*The Comanches were terribly wasted
in the [nineteenth] century.*
   —Frederick W. Hodge

THE GREATEST SINGLE DISASTER THAT BEFELL THE NERMERNUH IN THE nineteenth century was not the final destruction of the buffalo, their staff of life, nor the pursuit that drove their last remnants starving and freezing across the barren plains, until their infants died of hunger and exposure and the last pride of the survivors broke. These were only the final acts of the tragedy.

The critical period in the life of the Comanches began when the Anglo-Americans appeared on the Great Plains. Unlike the Spanish, the Americans represented a culture that had not exhausted its energies; unlike the French, they would not disappear because of some distant cataclysm. The Anglo-Americans were already numerous and powerful, a fact that, even in 1846, the wisest of the Nerm chiefs at least dimly understood. When they first met in the Indian Territory north of the Red River, the two peoples had no quarrel. First penetrated by judicious traders such as William Bent, the Nermernuh sat uneasily but peaceably with the soldiers who began to arrive along the Santa Fe Trail in the 1830s. The Comanche warriors neither liked nor trusted the representatives of the United States, the *tahbay-boh* or "white men," but they did distinguish between their tribe and that of the Texans, with whom they soon had blood feuds. While the white men drove thousands of eastern Amerindians into Comanche country, the People held this fact against the trespassers rather than the white traders and soldiers.

385

In this critical period, it was of paramount importance that power relationships be quickly established and understood. Here the fault was entirely that of the United States. The Texan wars had shown that the Comanches, though they could be vindictively hostile, were not inherently suicidal. Mauled savagely by the Texans, the Pehnahterkuh had abandoned the field. In the deep winter of 1840, no Comanche chief or medicine man saw signs or heard oracles encouraging him to ride against the *tejanos*. The survivors of war bands decimated by Jack Hays and other Rangers hated *tejanos* with a consummate ferocity and ever afterward were prepared to kill any Texan who fell into their hands. But the bravest of warriors did not ride back to seek vainglorious death from the muzzles of Texan guns. The Pehnahterkuh abandoned Texas, until they were lured back by a series of white errors, committed by both the then-independent Texans and the Americans.

The United States, in the initial confrontation, believed that the People could be controlled by treaties, and their independence taken away from them merely by reading them the white men's law. A great show of force would have been more to the point.

This was still not the greatest disaster for the Comanches, although confused policies led to warfare. Even after bitter fighting with the United States, they might still have been conquered and cowed, but have survived more or less intact as a people. The fate of the Navajos might have befallen them. The Navajos, warlike Athapaskans, were driven into their last refuges and smashed forever as a war-making tribe by the frontiersman Carson in 1864. After defeat, they were stripped of their weapons and removed from their historic canyons. But when they showed themselves pacified, they were kept from starvation by a United States commander who put his own men on half-rations through the winter in order to feed them. Later, they were allowed to return to their own lands. Only some seven thousand Navajos remained. They did not survive in glory, but they survived as a coherent tribe. There had never been half as many Navajos as Nermernuh. But by the twentieth century, the Navajos had become the largest of all Amerindian tribes, while the Nermernuh had almost vanished.

The Navajos were conquered, but not entirely demoralized. Their greatest disaster was a transition from a proud independent existence to a meager future that still had hope.

The disaster that befell the Comanches was not soldiers, settlers, nor *tejanos*. It was an almost unseen calamity that destroyed the coherence of all but the smallest band, the remote Antelopes of the Llano Estacado. It was the great epidemic that swept the southern plains in the summer of 1849, killing half of the remaining Pehnah-terkuh and decimating the other bands. This was the deadliest blow given the People by the white men, one from which they never recovered, and one which was not fully understood by the whites, although they saw and understood the vanishing of the red men.

The fundamental absurdity of the developing western Indian policies should have been apparent by the spring of 1849. The policy was to avoid western Indian wars, and to preserve the remaining peoples on their vast but "useless" prairies. This policy, formally adopted and confirmed by innumerable treaties with the tribes, flew in the face of developing realities.

The mood of the American nation—not just its pioneer frontier—was clearly expansionist. Out of the Mexican War, the United States not only secured its strategic position on the continent, but seized a huge tier of southwestern territories: the future states of Colorado, New Mexico, Arizona, Utah, Nevada, and California. In the same year, 1848, the Oregon Territory was secured, completing the American domination of the continent. Thus, the republic acquired a western empire that lay across and beyond the tribal treaty territories, and through which it had to have land communications. The process was accelerated when gold was found in California, starting one of the greatest mass movements in all history. Thousands upon thousands of Americans, gold seekers and land-hungry developers, rushed through the Great American Desert toward this glittering Pacific empire. The U.S. government could not have halted this, nor did it want to. The great thrust of the United States now became one of filling and consolidating the new western domain. This was the age of manifest destiny.

The events of 1846–49 destroyed all hope of genuine stability along the plains frontier. Every territorial treaty west of the Missouri was immediately violated. Hordes of Forty-Niners, none of whom acquired presidential permission, poured down the Santa Fe

Trail. Thousands more cut new trails west from San Antonio to the remote outpost of El Paso, and on to the Pacific. Wagon trains and riders pushed through the plains in such strong parties that the tribes could only watch them in amazement—in this period, contrary to popular cinema and mythology, the trains were rarely attacked by hostile Amerindians, though there were occasional brushes and clashes. Europeans had never dared pass through these lands before, except in large, armed parties. Now, the Americans went armed, and passed by the thousands. In 1849, three thousand immigrants cut a new route along the Canadian River toward New Mexico and California, pushing through the very heart of the Comanche bison range. They sowed disaster.

The lure of gold, especially, had brought a newer sort of immigrant. Men and women came from every city in the world, poverty-stricken slum dwellers as well as fortune hunters from the farming frontier. They traveled for protection in tightly packed caravans, with only a rudimentary knowledge of sanitation. They brought all the diseases of the Old World with them. They sickened on the prairies, leaving behind a trail of polluted water holes, discarded garments, and fresh graves—which Amerindians sometimes violated. They spread a virulent plague of Asian cholera across the whole expanse of the southern plains.

Attack on wagon train by Plains Indians.
Nineteenth-century lithograph.

Cholera, and smallpox as well, was loose in the Comanche lodges by midsummer.

The People had never faced a truly disastrous epidemic. There had been outbreaks of smallpox in 1816, and again in 1839, brought back, along with syphilis, from Mexican raiding. But the great aloofness of the bands kept them free from European diseases; the horse warriors had avoided congregating around trading posts or permanent settlements. They made the Comancheros and others come to them, and even then the Nermernuh rarely allowed a foreigner to enter their lodges.

The strongest Comanche warrior tended to be more susceptible to infectious disease than the weakest slum-born child of a crowded civilization. While the People's treatment of externally caused ailments was often empirical and quite effective, they possessed no understanding of or means of combating invisible killers. Measles, cholera, and the like were treated with prayers and incantations, magical markings upon the body, and purification rites that in themselves almost killed the patient. The most favored cure for smallpox was the sweat lodge, followed by an immediate plunge in a cold stream or river. All such remedies, of course, had no effect on the plague, and worse, weakened its victims. There was always a tendency among the Plains tribes, who regarded illness as the work of evil spirits, to view the very sick with superstitious horror, and they had learned that such "bad luck" was contagious.

The People were technically, socially, and psychically unprepared for such a crisis. As cholera infected whole encampments, the dying could not be adequately cared for, nor the dead properly mourned or buried. Among a folk with no understanding of the forces at work, and with a vast, frequently hysterical dread of all such things, the epidemic soon sent families fleeing across the plains in blind terror.

In the ultimate horror, the stricken were abandoned to die alone on the windswept prairie. Bands and families dissolved. But the People were gregarious. They fled one stricken camp only to seek security and comfort in another, thus spreading the epidemics like grass fire across the thinly populated wastes of *Comancheria*. As more unfortunates came down with raging fever or erupted in hideous, blinding pustules, the still healthy again fled into the wildernesses. This abandonment of the dead and dying, inspired by terror and superstition, probably did save the bands from virtual extinction. No Comanche ever again returned to a site of death, and thus a source of infection, and eventually the epidemic ran its course.

How many thousands of the Nermernuh died in this disaster cannot be known. Anthropologists who later sifted the old legends believe that half the Pehnahterkuh were destroyed, and other bands, except the Kwerhar-rehnuh, suffered only slightly less. The raging pestilence of a single season wiped out at least the increase of a century on the meat-rich plains. Even worse, the death that struck blindly through the camps left in its wake not only a psychic horror but a definite social dissolution. Every member of the Comanche family, every warrior, child, and aunt or uncle, was essential to the fabric of the culture. Great wounds were inflicted on this primitive, but very definite, society that were never healed. It is known that every important camp headman or civil chief died in 1849, destroying the last vestiges of social leadership along with the wisest members of the race. The southern Comanches dissolved as a coherent band, and from this time forward the surviving eastern and northern bands were split into confused and traumatized fragments, which began to show signs of social and psychic disintegration.

The destruction was not confined to the Comanches. The Cheyennes and other southern Plains peoples were also decimated by white penetrations of their territories. The numbers of many tribes of Plains Indians were vastly reduced before the American nation came into close contact and confrontation with them. Nineteenth-century Americans perceived these events on the Great Plains imperfectly—even the Indian agents continued to use Neighbors' older, inflated numbers in their reports—and were ignorant of the true extent of the "vanishing red man's" disappearance. For more Amerindians fell to the invisible terror loosed on them by white disease than to all the American bullets later fired at them by settlers and army. The numbers of the Comanches had usually been overestimated because of that people's mobility. From this time forward, the Plains tribes became even more mobile—and more hostile.

The Comanches, like the Cheyennes, did not sink into that final apathy characteristic of so many of the semiagrarian tribes when disaster struck. While the evidence that the tribes correlated the epidemic with the incursions of the whites is tenuous, it is certain that they must have made some connection. The Comanches in Texas had definitely understood that disease followed contacts with the whites; they had seen the Tonkawas destroyed by the proximity of the Spanish, and they had been wary of *tejano* trading posts. Some Great Plains tribes saw the disaster as an attack by the guardian spirits of the white men, which overcame their own invisible guardians. At any rate, the deadly epidemic seems to have sent many Comanches plunging downward in that manic cycle to which they were so prone, and to have pushed them viciously, even despairingly, onto the war trail. From 1849 onward, the northern bands in the Indian Territory developed something like a compulsion to strike continually at the Texan frontier. The Pehnahterkuh had been terribly weakened, and half of the southern Comanche families were no longer able to carry on warfare—it took their full efforts merely to hunt and stay alive. But their place was taken by long-ranging parties from above the Red. The Texans did not notice the change for many years.

The fragile peace broke, and the bands ran wild in 1849. Admittedly incomplete reports show that in this year, 149 white men, women, and children were killed on the northwest quadrant alone of the Texas frontier. While the southwestern regions were punished as never before, even in the late 1830s, Comanche terror descended particularly upon the reaches of the upper Brazos and Trinity. From this time forward, rarely were fewer than a hundred whites killed every year on the frontier.

If the Comanches and other Amerindians of this era only dimly perceived the shape of events, the American government and the Office of Indian Affairs do not seem to have seen them at all. The significance of the new outbreak in northwest Texas was missed, or ignored, because it upset committed policy. The Indian office did not consider that the whole Plains structure—the establishment of demarcation zones and the creation of Indian territories or reservations on a vast scale—had collapsed when the Forty-Niners and others breached the midcontinent. Texas was still the only region where permanent civilian settlement was within the raiding reach of a horse tribe, and the Texas situation was considered to be peculiar and unique—and, moreover, the fault of the Texans, because they would not stay out of Indian range and territory. The treaty-territory policy was not changed; rather, it was consolidated in a triumph of ideology over evidence.

In 1849, the Home Department (later the Department of the Interior) took over jurisdiction of the Office (later, Bureau) of Indian Affairs from the army. There was, of course, a certain logic here; the army was hardly trained or fit to manage the autonomous tribes or to negotiate treaties with them for Washington. But there was also illogic, for the tribes were far from conquered or pacified, and the mere claim of United States sovereignty over Amerindian country by agents did not make it fact. A great many Americans seem to have thought that the tribes would respond to a simple laying down of the white man's law, if the declarations were accompanied by promises and presents. A further illogic was present in American thinking. All past experience indicated that the true, if unadmitted, American policy could not be carried out without a decisive confrontation at arms. But both the Office of Indian Affairs and the government, now and for many years, were determined to avoid serious Indian wars in the West. Further, an unmilitary and even antimilitary attitude characterized most American thought and politics. The military was unpopular and had almost no political constituency; it had far less influence in Congress and in the executive branch than the minor civilian agencies and interests. By the 1840s, the army had come under serious criticism for its handling of Indian problems in the West.

As Americans poured into and across the West, the army had found itself in many local confrontations with the tribes. Sterling Price reduced some pueblos in New Mexico; there was bloody trouble in the high Northwest. Whenever large numbers of whites entered a territory, they made a shambles of treaties and the peace policy, and the army had to pick up the pieces, invariably by moving against and crushing the local natives. War was the army's business, and few commanders were loath to engage in it. However, in this era the army got much of the blame for causing the wars.

There were, then and later, glory seekers, war lovers, and sheer incompetents commanding western garrisons who did provoke trouble, or allowed it to come to a head. But the evidence presented by almost all historians shows that the army was unjustly maligned in this. The vast majority of officers in this period were professionals, career men who neither loved nor hated Indians, and who often despised the drives and attitudes of the white frontier they were duty-bound to protect. They were prepared to implement any rational policy; but policy was irrational, and army officers often infuriated the Indian office by saying publicly that the treaty promises made to the tribes were absurd because the government had no discernible intention of enforcing them. To consolidate the seizure of the Southwest and the Pacific coast, to protect the long lines of communication passing through Indian country, and to guard the hordes who insisted upon rushing through or into the treaty territories, the army was frequently forced to fight or destroy Indians. If it carried out operations efficiently, it was accused of bloodthirstiness and a considered policy of extermination.

Civilian Washington believed that the tribes could be managed peacefully, while the military and the frontier, with direct experience in the field, did not. In 1849, and generally for more than twenty years afterward, the civilian viewpoint won out in government, and created a disastrous situation on the plains.

With the Office of Indian Affairs in the Home Department, the army, still with the responsibility of policing and peace keeping in the West, was forced to operate under civilian viewpoint policies. The military, however, was not brought under the direct control of the Indian agents; this would have been impossible to implement. What emerged was a situation in which the Indian office dictated policy, but without direct control over the policy arm, while the army, charged with enforcing policy, had no voice in its creation.

This divided authority and responsibility between two inherently jealous and hostile federal agencies came just at a time when the government was facing wholesale problems with Amerindians on the plains. The whole history of the American West was to be stained by disputes and bureaucratic bickering between the army and the Indian bureau. The army branded Indian policy as ridiculous and impossible to implement and accused the agencies of malfeasance; the agents accused the army of preferring war to peace and of failure to protect the Indians.

The Indian office, unfortunately, was as poorly fitted as the army to manage Amerindian affairs. Those at the policy-making level—and, incredibly, even those sent to the West—were mostly easterners with little knowledge or understanding of the Plains peoples. The dominant view of the Plains warrior societies held throughout the period by the Indian office was one of childlike primitives who would respond to the moral authority of white men.

The corruption of the office, admittedly heightened in the American consciousness by the telling arguments of soldiers in the West, became proverbial. Many of the same agents who cried loudest about military operations against Indians saw no shame in robbing them. Honest Indian agents were unpopular in the service. Neighbors was vastly respected but liked by only a few of his white colleagues, and, in fact, he was dismissed in the politics of the reorganization of the office in 1849.

The dishonesty of Indian agents probably instigated more bloodshed than the Indian office's policies prevented. The Amerindians did not brook bad faith easily. Again and again, the failure of promised annuities to arrive abrogated a treaty or sparked an uprising. A large factor in the Santee war in Minnesota, in 1862, was the hunger of the treaty Indians, who had been told by their agent to try eating grass. After the uprising, which cost thousands of lives, both white and Indian, the corpse of this agent was found with his mouth stuffed with weeds.

Whatever the reasons, the Indian office failed monumentally to preserve either peace or the Indians. Less apparently, its overall policies cost many thousands of lives that might have been spared had the makers and administrators of policy not confused the issues.

By 1849, as always, the issue confronting the American nation was how to remove the remaining tribes that barred white passage and development of the continent. By determinedly holding to rapidly outmoded practices and policies, the authorities allowed a long period of slow attrition, a piecemeal destruction and demoralization of the free Indians. And as always in the trail across the continent, the greatest damage done was not the countless graves, but the effects on the survivors. The terrible brutalization of the American frontier continued until the last quarter of the nineteenth century. Both whites and Amerindians were left with unbearable memories. The savage process heightened the stubborn resistance of the natives, while it made inevitable the final humiliation and degradation of the conquered tribes.

The failure to solve the Amerindian problem relatively rapidly and cleanly did not just provoke Indian hatred of Americans. It also spurred the frontier hatred of all Indians. If many easterners believed that Amerindians were victims of the progress of a rapacious civilization, the whites in Texas saw themselves as aggrieved victims of a horror that went on endlessly.

The dangers, harshness, and brutality of the Texas frontier in the middle nineteenth century probably cannot be fully understood by later generations. Conditions were similar to the horrors of the Appalachian frontier in the previous century, but the brutalities continued over many more years. The whites had come into a country that was innately harsh and strange to them; as the wood and water ran out, it was harder to grow their crops, build their houses, and erect their enclosing fences. The families in the Texas west lived in much greater isolation than the embattled Kentucky pioneers closely clustered in their hollows. Often, a single family held sway within a hundred square miles. Moreover, the horse Indians were far more formidable raiders than the forest Shawnees.

Even without the growing Indian peril, life was almost impossibly difficult on this frontier. The land seekers who went west had little or no money; they made everything they owned or used, except for firearms and iron tools. They erected their cabins and sod shanties with their hands, without the precious nails they could not afford—transportation alone cost more than the price of manufactured goods. Thousands died, thousands more retreated, beaten, back to jobs or tenantry. But some always stayed, won out, and slowly prospered. Like the incredible Parker clan, they took their losses and held on, acquiring more land. Their fields took form. As more families joined them, they sold off excess lands and found markets for their grain and beef. They built permanent, solid houses, and made towns rise incongruously on the prairies.

No one asked them to come into Indian country; they came naturally, pulled and driven by their deepest instincts as a people. They understood the risks, but unlike Mexicans, they did not accept them. Every outlying, dog-run cabin or sod hut was a potential fort. Living quarters were built with window bars and gun ports and noncombustible roofs. Every sundown before a rising moon held dangers over thousands of miles of forlorn frontier, even a hundred miles within the farthest settlement line. No man left his fortress for his fields or pastures without fear for his family; no woman was left alone without the same emotion. Every bird call or animal chatter-

ing was ominous. The weak died or departed; the careless or unlucky perished. Those who stayed feared Indians, fought Indians,
and all had family or neighbors plundered, burned out, or killed
and mutilated by Indians.

The disgust of this white frontier with any Indian policy other
than immediate removal was enormous. This view was not peculiarly Texan or parochial. It was the dominant view of all Anglo-
Americans and Europeans exposed to warlike Amerindians. It was
most vividly recorded in Texas because the Indian frontier there,
uniquely, spanned two generations, and survived into recent history. The American and European settlers on the Mankato in Minnesota showed the same passions in the 1860s; the hatred for Plains
Indians in Denver of 1864 was far more hysterical than any produced in Texas.

As Walter Prescott Webb wrote a century afterward: "The Texans had very definite ideas as to how the Indians should be treated
. . . out of the maelstrom of their past and its many bitter experiences
they had come with hard and relentless methods. Their independent existence for ten years had fostered self-reliance and created
new institutions suited to the circumstances. They convinced themselves that the Texas Rangers knew best how . . . to exterminate
Indians, and their impatience with the clumsy methods and humanitarian policy of the United States . . . was colossal."

In September 1849, the *Texas State Gazette* editorialized:

I see that the Comanches are still continuing their forays upon the
Texas border, murdering and carrying off defenceless frontier settlers
who had been granted protection. . . . They must be pursued, hunted,
run down, and killed—killed until they find out we are in earnest. . . . If
Harney can have his own way, I cannot but believe he will call in Hays,
McCulloch, and all the frontier men, and pursue the Comanches to the
heads of the Brazos, the Colorado, and even up under the spurs of the
Rocky Mountains—they must be beaten in all their covers and harassed
until they are brought to knowledge of . . . the strength and resources of
the United States.

The frontier view, fully articulated by 1849, was that there could
never be peace with the horse Indians so long as the tribes roamed
free and were granted a privileged territory. The Texas West had
discovered the only effective countermeasure to the classic guerrilla

tactics of the Comanches: the brutal punitive campaign that pursued and destroyed them in all their sanctuaries. And these were the very tactics that the United States Army was to use in later years, from Texas to the Canadian border—but not this year, or for many years to come. Harney, the army commander, was not to have his way, and neither the Office of Indian Affairs nor the army sought the advice or experience of the hard-bitten, relentless Rangers.

Once again, as in Spanish times, mistaken policies dug thousands of graves, cloaked whole families in mourning, and made a bloody shambles of a wide frontier, while uninvolved, distant men argued priorities and procedures. The "humanitarian" policy toward the Amerindians was not merciful, for either white or red men.

It was to be, in fact, almost as great a disaster for the Plains tribes as the epidemics the white trespassers loosed among them.

3

FORTS ON THE FRONTIER

O pray for the soldier you kind-hearted stranger;
He has roamed the prairie for many a year.
He has kept the Comanche away from your ranches,
And followed them far over the Texas frontier.

> —Epitaph on a nineteenth-century grave,
> Fort Clark, Texas

FEDERAL AUTHORITIES ALWAYS INTENDED TO FULFILL THE GOVERN-
ment's responsibility for frontier defense in Texas. The problem
was that men on the policy level rarely understood the nature of
the problem and its true scope; it was remote, and out of sight was
out of mind. The cost was deeply resented: dominant interests in
American society throughout the century always resented military
expense. And in the first years even the little that was done tended
to be disastrous, because the armed forces were ill equipped and
inexperienced to handle the challenges of the Comanche confrontation.

Immediately upon the conclusion of the Mexican War, the federal subsidy of the Texas Rangers was discontinued, and the state
disbanded its frontier force. This was a mistake by both parties. The
infantry and few dragoons who arrived in Texas during 1848, to
establish a defensive cordon between the settlers and the Amerindians, soon inspired as much contempt among Texans as the policies
they followed, and they totally failed, despite easterners' confident
expectations, to overawe the primitives.

The United States Army had been operating along the fringes of
the plains country for years, but the top echelons of the War De-

398

partment did not yet grasp the differences between the West with
its Plains Indians and the terrain and tribes with which they were
familiar. There were plenty of Indian fighters in the army, but none
who had marched against the horse tribes. The policymakers did
not understand the enormous distances in the West, the nature of
the thinly settled, far-flung frontiers, or the normal tactics of the
horse barbarians. For ten years the military policy forced on the
army was purely defensive and passive. It was ordered to build
barrier fortresses, but not to fight Indians unless attacked. Indians
were not to be molested unless actually caught in some criminal act
on the frontier; in fact, the army was to protect them from the
white settlers.

The army was not prepared to take stronger measures, in any
case. The United States, incredibly, still possessed no cavalry arm.
Cavalry had not been needed east of the plains, and afterward,
while it was apparent that foot soldiers were ineffective against
mobile tribesmen, the government hesitated to use mounted forces
because of the greater expense. A regiment of infantry cost
$300,000 per year to maintain in camp, while the forage, remount-
ing, and transportation expense for horse troops was double this;
and when a horse regiment took the field, the cost—$1,500,000

*Meeting of U.S. 1st Regiment of Dragoons and Comanches under
flag of truce, Indian Territory, 1836.*
Drawing by George Catlin.

annually—was considered astronomical. Therefore the majority of troops sent to Texas were foot soldiers, sometimes mounted on mules.

The elite of the army were the dragoons, created in 1833, and elements of the two dragoon regiments were dispatched to Texas. The dragoons, however, were not a true cavalry trained or equipped to counter the lightning thrusts of the Amerindian "light cavalry." They were essentially mounted infantry, patterned after European models, who were trained to fight on horseback. Dragoons fought as heavy cavalry, and would have been quite effective against a proper army of the times. Against horse Indians, however, the dragoons, self-consciously gallant in their French-inspired blue jackets, orange forage caps, white pantaloons, and sweeping moustaches, were more impressive than useful.

Dragoons considered a day's march of thirty miles an extraordinary effort. Each trooper had one mount; there was a very limited number of remounts. On the march, dragoons had to walk as much as ride, in order not to exhaust their horses. The evidence that a Comanche war party could cover fifty miles in seven hours, and ride a hundred miles without once halting, confounded American military experts, who refused to credit this. The Comanches rode light, without accouterments or heavy saddles, and changed ponies rapidly. Dragoons had no chance of catching a war party.

Nor could they have done much damage had they caught them. Dragoons were armed with single-shot pistols, sabers, and the Springfield Arsenal Musketoon, Model 1842, which, as Philip St. George Cooke, the army's contemporary cavalry expert, wrote, was "utterly unreliable at any range." The Plains Amerindians quickly learned the range of the musketoon and rode beyond it. The cherished saber, which military tradition clung to stubbornly in most nineteenth-century armies, was never of much military use against Plains Indians. Significantly, in this same period the British dragoons in India unofficially but pragmatically took to using pigsticks. The Comanches, if pressed into a fight, could not only hurl a greater weight of missiles, but their supple lances were deadlier than sabers in a close melee. As Colonel Richard Irving Dodge wrote unhappily in the 1850s, American troops were inferior in every respect to Plains warriors except one: their disciplined constancy. A Texas Ranger expressed it more cruelly: the Indians were in no danger from dragoons, unless their gaudy appearance and clumsy horsemanship caused them to laugh themselves to death.

The initial appearance of the American military on the plains thus excited contempt from both Amerindians and civilians. This early impression was lasting, and colored later songs and stories. Bitter lessons had to be learned, but in fact, Bonneville, Frémont, Dodge, and Kearney were as observant as any hard-bitten Ranger, and dozens of intelligent subalterns served on the prairies. Unlike the Rangers, army officers had to carry their notions for reform against an established tradition and ensconced bureaucracy. They could not throw away their sabers and purchase the best firearms available on the open market any more than they could discard the books on tactics. What was significant, in world military terms, was that the army changed within a decade. It learned its lessons rapidly; they were all well absorbed before the outbreak of the Civil War. The army was placed in a bewildering political, strategic, and tactical situation in the West. As British observers wrote admiringly, they were less impressed by the constant errors than by what the army finally accomplished.

To CARRY OUT THE INITIAL SCHEME OF OPERATIONS, THE ARMY planned and established a string of garrisons through central Texas, running generally along a southwestern slant that intersected the present cities of Fort Worth, Waco, and San Antonio, and continued to the Rio Grande. These forts, actually cantonments, were crudely thrown together in 1848–9. They were no sooner built than they were obsolete, because events ran ahead of planning.

They were too close to the actual line of white settlement; in fact, as they were built, they attracted settlers and were soon enclosed by the settlement line. None of these early posts—Duncan, Inge, Croghan, Gates, or Worth—served a military purpose, though they did hasten the process of settlement and town building.

However, explorations were being carried out across all western Texas. Robert Neighbors and Ranger Captain John S. Ford scouted routes and crossings for the army; Captain Randolph B. Marcy, 5th Infantry, made an extensive survey during 1849. Marcy wrote a widely heralded account of his adventures and observations, and

one of his recommendations, that the outpost line be moved approximately a hundred miles westward to strategic sites at river crossings, was almost immediately implemented. The outbreak of Comanche raids in 1849 hastened this decision. Another factor was a
clause in the Treaty of Guadalupe Hidalgo that ended the Mexican
War and ceded the Southwest to the United States. Both Mexico
and the United States pledged themselves to halt Indian raiding
across the new border, and the United States, at least, attempted to
carry out this provision.

Considering logistics, distances, and communications, the new
line was rapidly constructed and was virtually complete by 1852.

The cordon now ran from Fort Belknap, high on the Salt Fork of
the Brazos, to Phantom Hill, on the Clear Fork of the same stream,
near the present Abilene; then to Fort Chadbourne, on a tributary
of the Colorado; thence south to McKavett, fifty miles south on the
San Saba; and to Fort Terrett at the headwaters of the Llano. Continuing to the south and east, Fort Mason was sited to guard the
expanding Austin–San Antonio region, and the bottom anchor of
the line, Fort Clark, was set athwart the eastern Comanche Trace—
the raiding path that entered Coahuila a few miles south of the
present Brackettville.

Later in the 1850s, newer forts were built to protect the increasingly important San Antonio–El Paso route to the Pacific coast:
Fort Lancaster, at present Ozona; Fort Davis, at the juncture of the
stage route and the western Comanche Trace that entered Chihuahua through the Santa Elena Canyon; and finally, Stockton, at
the then strongly flowing Comanche Springs, an oasis where the
Comanches passing into Mexico camped regularly.

The new fortress line lay generally along the 100th meridian, and
thus far west of the nineteenth-century dry-farming frontier. The
posts were inside the bison plains, beyond the edge of what was
then the wilderness. The sites were well chosen strategically, but
they created a logistic nightmare. Americans were used to building
with wood, not stone like the Spaniards, and the timbers for some of
these outposts had to be hewed far to the east and hauled as much
as a hundred miles. The army had no support services in the West,
and the labor, freighting, and actual construction of the forts had to
be done by the troops who were sent to man them. The posts rose in
the crudest fashion from raw timbers: they were primitive stock-

ades, inferior to those that had once guarded the Allegheny frontier. The quarters, bakeries, and hospitals within the log walls were, as one inspection report read, "unfit for human habitation," miserable under the summer sun and freezing in deep winter.

The local water was often undrinkable, and supplies had to be transported over many miles.

These were the western army "forts" that would be immortalized in American history and legend, and, in the next century, glamorized on the screen. Each played its role. But the men who went to them saw them only as hell holes, dangerous, dirty, monotonous sinks where men wasted away their lives. It was after a tour at Fort Clark, the later location of countless Western movies, that the future General Sheridan made his famous remark that if he owned both hell and Texas, he would rent out Texas and live in Hades.

Unfortunately, the forts could not at first fulfill their mission. They were far apart, held only small contingents, too small for either combat or patrol, and were manned by footsore infantry. Thus in the early years they were passive symbols of a useless military presence, which provided the frontier no sanctuary. Like the former Spanish presidios, they were more impressive on maps in the capital than on the ground.

THE HUMAN ELEMENT OF THESE FORTS ALSO ENTERED AMERICAN HISTORY, but not always accurately.

The nineteenth-century regular military service was in no sense a national army. In composition it was closer to the Foreign Legion that manned French outposts of empire. It was a mercenary force, commanded by native professional officers. Only a tiny percentage of the men in it were native-born Americans. The majority, prior to 1860, were Irish and German immigrants.

In this era, only men fleeing society, a woman, the hangman, or themselves volunteered for military service. A criminal element was prominent. As in the contemporary British army, on which that of the United States was modeled, the service was the last refuge of the hungry or the hopeless. The ranks were viewed, and described, both by society and by their own officers as a "low lot," "scum," or "outcasts." Thus the gulf between society, and officers and men, was far deeper than in a citizen army raised by conscription. And in the United States Army the gulf was ethnic as well as cultural and social. Soldiering in the ranks was not in the English-speaking tradition; the term "soldiering" itself meant loafing or malingering in the American vernacular. The alienation even applied to the American officers, because, except in the South, there was no aristocratic ideal of service.

Consequently, this army, like the British forces and the French Foreign Legion, was handled roughly and contemptuously by the government and people it served. Officers treated enlistees with an expressed contempt unthinkable in a citizen army. They broke down work parties and fatigue details according to supposed intelligence or national origin, giving axes to native-born Americans, picks and shovels to the Irish ("That's all they are good for, Sergeant"), and setting Germans to pulling weeds. Men were not permitted to think, or at least not permitted to express opinions; they were trained to follow orders mindlessly. They enlisted for five, later ten, years and as much humanity as possible was quickly ground out of them.

The codes and conditions of the army were generally no worse than those of similar contemporary forces, which meant that by present standards soldiering was similar to penal servitude.

These outcasts of all ranks were poorly paid and miserably maintained. Privates received $5 per month, which was subject to stoppages. Sergeants drew $13, lieutenants, $25; a colonel commanding a regiment was paid $800 annually. In an army of only a few thousand, ruled rigidly by seniority, promotion was painfully slow. Irish recruits, starting with the advantage of speaking English, took several enlistments to make sergeant. The turnover in officer ranks was slower. There were lieutenants on the frontier in their forties, and captains on the active list past sixty.

Only the barest minimum of necessities was provided. The troops built their own quarters—crude, dirty, uncomfortable barracks— and were issued uniforms and blankets. They ate salt pork or beef, often spoiled at issue, rice, hard peas, beans, with bread or biscuit and coffee. There was once a daily gill of rum, but this was stopped both because of the cost (over $22,000 per year) and to enhance "morality." Food, quarters, and comforts in an army post were worse than in any later American prison.

The army was neither young nor healthy. Physical standards were low; they had to be, to maintain numbers. The exposures of the life crippled many long-service men with rheumatism. The lack of sanitation and medicine produced horrendous sick lists and death rates at every station. At one western post, six officers and 293 men died of natural causes in a two-year period.

Officers were permitted to marry and could maintain wives and daughters at cantonments; they could also keep spirits. No such provisions were made for enlisted men. The only females officially recognized by the army other than officer wives or family were "laundresses." These were allowed quarters and received pay for their work—out of the enlisted men's pockets—and were almost always the wives or daughters of corporals and sergeants. There was no other provision for married women, though they were sometimes permitted at posts as camp followers. The wife of a private who followed him was not necessarily "following the drum" or whoring, but she had to share the common barrackroom and be listed as a camp follower. Understandably, there were few wives with the army.

However, the troops were not without spirits or women. These were regularly smuggled in, or were available at the more or less clandestine "blind pigs" or "hog ranches" that sprang up near posts to purvey sex and rotgut whiskey. Collectively, an army payroll was big business in the cash-poor West, and there was an even more miserable class of society that lived off the lowly soldiers.

Many rankers formed formal or informal liaisons with Amerindian women, especially the girls of the "high barbarian" tribes forced into the Indian Territory. The Cherokees were prized for their beauty. The Indian women could endure the hardships of such a life better than white women, and a soldier, as a warrior, might also find respect with them. The army was the principal instrument of a widespread assimilation of the "civilized tribes" in the Indian Territory.

The troops were further demoralized by incessant labor. Besides building posts and quarters, hewing wood and hauling water, there were more fatigue duties and drills than patrols—which came as welcome diversions. Contrary to opinion, soldiering was life at hard labor on the frontier; in fact, some units devoted so much time to maintenance chores that they neglected military functions. Monotony added to the prison atmosphere, and caused many disciplinary problems.

As in contemporary mercenary armies, these were handled with severity. American discipline followed the British practice, and therefore was rigid and bloody. The rulers of the army believed that the kind of human beings that composed the troops could only be treated roughly and would understand no other kind of treatment. Drunkenness, insubordination, malfeasance in a hundred trivial ways were punished by loss of pay, bread and water, or forced marching, but military courts could also impose the wearing of a ball and chain, an iron collar, and flogging, and these were favorite sentences for hardened cases. Flight in the face of the enemy, cowardice, or striking an officer could mean death. Desertion also was legally punishable by death, but this sentence does not seem to have been imposed. Deserters, when apprehended, were given fifty lashes—the legal maximum in the more enlightened era of the middle of the century—and branded. The army considered imprisonment a waste of time; officers believed that men responded better to pain inflicted on their bodies than on their probably nonexistent minds.

Officers could and did impose arbitrary punishment—flogging, hanging by the wrists, "railing," or sweat boxing—without formal charges or trial. The records for the whole period indicate that about 10 percent of the ranks were undergoing punishment at any given time, and that about one-third deserted or tried to desert from some posts in some years. Recruits normally arrived at stations under guard.

The officers did not have it much better on this service. They were more comparable to prison warders than gentlemen. They lived in the same forlorn surroundings, faced the same dangers from disease, and endured the same monotony. There were never more than a few officers at the small posts. Sharing nothing, as they believed, socially or intellectually with the ranks, they were utterly isolated. Loneliness and boredom led many to alcoholism.

A less known but equally troublesome problem was sex. Most officers were separated from their wives during western tours; many never married. The few women who arrived at the outposts often caused serious trouble along Officers Row. The severe hardships and the monotony of women's lives in these restricted places put great strains on marriages. Divorce was not respectable among army officers. Adultery became a fearsome problem at many posts; it was sometimes carried on openly among multiple partners. Scandals were very frequent. Together, alcoholism and adultery ruined more military careers than Indian arrows did.

And yet, this pitifully tiny force was to become a veteran, reliable, and even efficient army on the frontier, more understood and admired, however, by foreign observers than the society it served. The army proved more than adequate for its mission, despite vast distances and logistical nightmares, despite the fact it never had nearly enough men, and despite countless errors in directives and policies. There were two basic reasons.

The first was that the ranks, whether from training, rigid discipline, or some innate human quality, had constancy, which in nine out of ten military situations was more valuable than high courage or élan. The soldiers endured everything: incredible hardship and suffering, stupidity, disease, and danger. When they were defeated, it was almost always because of the mistakes of the men who commanded them, like Custer's at the Little Big Horn.

The second reason was the professionalism that prevailed in the officer corps, which was remarkable for its time and place. Half of the officers emerged from the United States Military Academy at West Point. The institution and its training were unique, imbuing officers with a professional mystique found then in few standing armies. This mystique transcended background and region; the majority of West Pointers from the South remained in the United States Army during the Civil War. The exceptions were most often the Southern gentlemen who, despite their splendid qualities as soldiers, were not the American military norm.

Most army officers came from the small-town or rural Anglo-American middle class. They emphasized their British background and, like others of this class, clung consciously to British forms and traditions throughout the century; their outlook and ethos were that of the English lower-middle classes that had settled North America. Army officers came from the same people who produced the small-town bankers, merchants, and professional men of the United States, and they brought to the service the same inherent industry, practicality, and efficiency their civilian counterparts infused into American business, law, and medicine. They tended to be hard-working, present-minded, job-oriented, and empirical. If they had all the prejudices of middle-class America, they carried all its strengths.

Despite their "Anglo-Saxon" consciousness, they were far closer in social background, spirit, and education to the men then building the Prussian military and industrial machine than to the gentlemen who purchased commissions in the British service, and who had to have outside incomes almost of necessity. The American officer was poor, and therefore attached to his career. Alienated, he fell back on his professionalism.

Though the average officer had both a racial and a cultural contempt for his men and the Amerindian enemy he faced, this was tempered by his professionalism. The western officer remained remarkably good-tempered and even good-humored toward the "savages." He did not overly despise them, for they taught him too much, which he was professional enough to grasp. It became his duty to control Indians, killing them when necessary, but not to hate Indians. This was a luxury professionals could not afford. Officers avoided the blind passions of the white frontier, and also the rapacious hypocrisy of political officialdom. The army had its share of romantics, glory seekers, and incompetents, but these were usually soon found out. The career men distrusted those who were less than truly professional. As Sherman pointed out, the army had little to gain and much to lose by fighting aborigines, and few officers forgot it.

Military historians have noted that, in all wars, the higher the proportion of civilian or popular participation, the more terrible the passions, brutalities, and lasting hatreds engendered. This held true in the American West. Soldiers were defeated, slaughtered, tricked, scalped, and tortured by Indians, but this merely became the normal hazards of the job. Noticeably, almost all the historic massacres of Indians were perpetrated by volunteers or militias recruited from the white frontier, rarely by regulars.

Despite all this, the army was to be used too little and too late.

4

THE CAVALRY

The Indian character is such that
he will not stand continual following, pounding, and attacking . . .
none of our campaigns have been successful
that have not been prepared to follow the Indians
day and night, attacking them at every opportunity
until they are worn out, disbanded, or forced to surrender,
which is the sure result of such a campaign.
　　　—Colonel Richard Irving Dodge,
　　　　in an instruction to the troops

A FULL UNDERSTANDING OF EVENTS IN THE WEST PRIOR TO THE CIVIL
War never really entered the American consciousness. The period
has been generally ignored by historians; during the 1850s too much
attention was focused elsewhere, especially on the growing storm
over slavery and secession. Most Americans began to focus on the
Amerindian question in the deep West only after Appomattox, but
by that time the problems had all been encountered, and the countermeasures largely learned and set. The "brutal operations" against
the Plains Indians that some historians later discovered actually
began in the 1850s, almost without national attention. And many
historians, with only a faint understanding of the southwestern
Texas frontier, did not understand the origin of these operations.
Two Plains peoples, the Comanches and the Kiowas, precipitated
them, by incessantly transgressing the frontier military cordon to
raid white settlements beyond the farm line. The trouble was not
confined to Texas; by the late 1850s the Kiowas had begun to rav-
age the Kansas frontier, where white settlements had also come
within their range.

The situation was intolerable to those Americans who faced it. Unfortunately, it carried tragedy not only for the predators who assured their own destruction, but also for thousands of western Amerindians who stood only on their ancient territories and never raided beyond them. Twice, in the 1850s and again in the 1870s, the rampages of the southern Plains tribes were to bring *revanche*, and all the autonomous Plains peoples were to be swept up in the conflict.

Again, the final destruction, at least of the Amerindian independence and way of life, was assured in any case. A hundred thousand western Indians must have died of war, disease, or dispossession beyond the Mississippi just as a hundred thousand had died earlier in the Jacksonian era of mass removal. The western Amerindians were enclosed within an American empire; the only question remaining was the date and means by which their cultural death warrant would be executed. The tragedy within the tragedy was that the intransigence of the southern predators brought revenge down upon the Sioux and Nez Percé, and, in fact, all remaining American Indians.

The period between 1846 and 1853 was peculiar in one sense: Anglo-American expansion westward proceeded largely undirected and uncontrolled. The United States, about to be torn apart by internal quarrels, was not prepared to cope with the realities of the new empire in the West, either militarily or politically. Important questions were ignored or not thought through. The seizure of the Pacific coast, a long-term American dream, and the gold rush of '49 had made a shambles of the peace policy on the Great Plains; it was impossible for the United States to permit the Amerindians to hold huge barrier enclaves in the middle of the continent. Final tests of strength must have come eventually over this question alone, for the Indians must and did contest untrammeled passage across their territories. But the patterns of the wars were precipitated by the inability of the southwestern tribes to eschew their ancient war customs.

The passive peace policy of the United States lasted less than a decade after the annexation of Texas and the vast Southwest. In effect, while rarely articulating the philosophy, Americans generally adopted the Anglo-Texan approach to the plains and Plains Indians. What marked the 1850s was the rapidity with which the

American nation began to react. The entire Amerindian question would have been settled within another decade, except for the intervention of the Civil War, which relaxed the pressure on the Amerindians and, in the exhaustion that followed Appomattox, ensured ten more years of brutality and horror across the plains.

The army in the Southwest had perceived almost immediately that the passive American defense policy was not working, and that the army itself was not organized to police the Amerindians. After 1849, the line of forts along the hundredth meridian could not and did not protect either the Texas or the Mexican frontier. The military, under orders not to fight Indians unless it found them actually raiding, tried to establish the same relations with the Texas tribes that existed in the Indian Territory north of Texas. It could not, because of the viciousness of the Pehnahterkuh and other Comanches toward the Texans, and because of their long-established raiding patterns. The Comanches and Kiowas did not fight the army —posts and troops were not attacked in Texas as the garrison line was fixed—and for some years the raiders even maintained fairly amicable, if uneasy, relations with the *tahbay-boh* soldiers. Parties camped near forts, held councils and horse-trading sessions, and soldiers and warriors even engaged in games and horse racing. The Comanches, inveterate gamblers, enjoyed such contests, and shrewdly won many wagers from the ignorant white men, who learned to their cost that the Indian ponies, progenitors of the southwestern quarter horse, could outdistance the finest-blooded Kentucky stock over short courses. But in the meantime, the bands bypassed the forts to burn, kill, and plunder both *tejanos* and the Mexicans, and this became intolerable to the army commanders.

Relations soon deteriorated. A war party, more in sport than anger, stole the horseflesh at one garrison. At another post an officer, believing that a passing group of Comanches had been raiding on the frontier, tried to arrest them. Blood was shed on both sides. Trust ended, and the Indians avoided soldiers. Conversely, knowing the depredations that continued to their rear, the soldiers came to look upon all Amerindians on the Texas plains as potentially hostile.

If many white customs were bewildering to the Comanches, Americans also found it impossible to understand the Comanche delineation of truce and war. Army officers generally felt that the Comanches were making fools of both the Washington policy-makers and themselves. When confronted, the Comanches rarely dissembled; they learned to do this only after they had come to fear the power of the white soldiers. They made it clear that while they had no quarrel—yet—with the white men in blue coats, they had an ancient war with Texas and Mexico that they had no intention of giving up. It was no concern of the Comanches if the United States had annexed Texas and made a treaty with Mexico—the bands had not been parties to the agreements. But Mexico protested, the Texan frontier hurled its contempt on the useless protectors, and most officers grew sick of what they considered to be aboriginal arrogance. Yet under the strictures of policy, which did not allow the army to initiate hostile actions against the tribes beyond the frontier, nothing could be done.

Meanwhile, the weird legal problem of jurisdiction continued. The military and the Indian office shared responsibility for controlling the tribes, but each lacked authority over the other. Co-operation depended upon personalities and local arrangements. Furthermore, federal officers, military or civilian, had no jurisdiction over white civilians within the boundaries of a sovereign state. State officials rarely cooperated with the federals. The State of Texas demanded removal of Indians; the Indian office demanded peace with Indians; the army was caught between two fires.

The codes and regulations that governed operations in Indian territory did not apply within a duly constituted state. Both the army and the Indian agents in Texas had to work within the confines of state law. One case in point showed the complexity of this problem. An American, George Barnard, opened a trading post high on the Brazos, from which he began to dispense both firearms and alcohol to all the tribes. He caused enormous trouble, both among the tribes and for the frontier. The army wanted to remove Barnard; the Indian agents wanted to stop him; but both lacked any jurisdiction over such activities in Texas. The new state had failed to enact laws against the sale of whiskey or firearms to Indians. The Texas governor did not approve of gun running, but was unable to get the requisite legislation through his legislature. For some years Barnard operated profitably in this state-federal limbo.

The same lack of jurisdiction had caused the situation of the so-called tame Indians in Texas to become desperate. All the Wichita-Caddoan-Tonkawa remnants, and the migrant eastern Amerindians, were official wards of the federal government, but all of them were trespassers on either state or private property. The Indian agents had no authority to allow these peoples any sanctuary in Texas. The agents regularly rounded up the tribes that migrated down from the Indian Territory and sent them back, but there was nothing they could do about the native remnants. By the early 1850s, the farm line had about reached its natural geographic limits along the ninety-eighth parallel. This meant that the Wichita-Caddoan survivors no longer had any secure territory. They were dispossessed from the lands on which they had "squatted" for generations, and retreated just beyond the white frontier. But in these borderlands, so close to the white frontier, there was insufficient game to maintain them. The pacified Amerindians now could neither grow corn in the arid west, nor find sufficient flesh. They were starving, and understandably, many, even the unwarlike Caddoans, began to commit depredations against white farms and ranches.

The state argued that the federal government should remove them to the Indian Territory—but the Oklahoma strip was also overcrowded, so much so that thousands of Seminoles, Shawnees, Delawares, Kickapoos, and others continually strayed into either Texas or Kansas, looking for fresh game. And the movement of these tribes, as well as the pushing of the Wichita-Caddoan remnants westward, set off the last, vast internecine tribal wars among the continental Indians. The Plains peoples—the Comanches, Kiowas, Cheyennes, Arapahos, and others—hated these interlopers more than they did whites, because such trespassing on their hunting grounds aroused outrage. Ironically, some of the greatest alliances forged between the tribes were now combinations of eastern and western Amerindians against each other; even Kiowas and Osages would bury their ancient hatreds to ride against the easterners; Comanches and Utes would interrupt their own warfare to eject the Kickapoos. The easterners and Plains peoples destroyed each other by the thousands in this era.

The easterners were not entirely helpless before the fiercer horse Amerindians. They were now mounted, and generally they had become well-equipped with firearms acquired at trading posts. They also had their own war skills. In 1849, American travelers discovered a large party of friendly Kickapoos camped in southern Colorado, who boasted that they had come to stay the winter. Other easterners wandered all through the fringes of the plains. In 1853, one hundred Sauk and Fox Amerindians held off a great alliance of some fifteen hundred Comanche, Kiowa, Cheyenne, Arapaho, and Osage warriors by rifle fire in a battle along the Kansas River. But significantly, even the powerful Kickapoos were never able to make a successful transition to the Plains culture or carve out a secure niche on the bison grounds. The easterners remained lonely wanderers from place to place, whose condition gradually became pitiable through attrition. They kept the plains from Texas to Kansas in turmoil throughout the 1850s, until finally what was left of them either retreated into the narrow Indian strip, or a few remnants sought refuge south of the Rio Grande in Mexico.

John H. Rollins, the Indian agent who replaced Neighbors in 1849, fought a losing battle with chaos and starvation. He was unable to do much about the autonomous Comanches and knew it. Although he got a number of Pehnahterkuh to a council in 1850, getting them to agree not to ride south of the Llano River, this treaty actually made matters worse; the Pehnahterkuh and the northern Comanches who did not sign became very angry, and for the first time, so far as is known, the northern bands actually carried out some raids against the southern Comanches. The few Nermernuh who despaired of further war and wanted to accept peace with the *tejanos* now faced a new danger—the hatred and frustrations of their own People. In 1851, Rollins secured a large annuity for the Pehnahterkuh, but this could not bring peace or halt the incessant raiding from beyond the Red River. And as those older Pehnahterkuh warriors who were willing to stop raiding told Rollins, they had no control over individual warriors even in their own camps. As new men came of age, they dreamed of prestige and plunder and were driven to take the blood trail. Rollins understood this, but could not impress it upon his distant superiors. About all he could do was to try to save the hungry peaceful Amerindians; he filled his reports with descriptions of starving women and children and proud warriors forced to eat their dogs and horses.

Official Washington then, as it would again in the 1860s, tended to believe that the entire Indian problem was vastly exaggerated. Many easterners thought the whole trouble was caused by the entry of whites into Amerindian lands and were not sympathetic to frontier problems—though officially or otherwise, nothing was done to prevent white encroachment upon Indian territories. The notion that Comanches or Kiowas would raid the Texas frontier without current provocation was rejected by many officials who knew nothing but their own conception of Amerindians. The reports of white deaths and captures on the frontier were also considered highly exaggerated. A typical contradiction within American ideology was that while most Americans instinctively believed in "manifest destiny" many Americans detested "land speculators" who were continually bringing pressures on Indian lands. Washington and Jackson, neither of whom had any tenderness for the American Indian, shared this dislike—at least outwardly, for Washington himself was a speculator beyond the Appalachians. The net effect of a refusal to protect the Indian territories coupled with a dislike or disdain for the land-hungry frontier was to create the worst of all possible worlds in the West. Viewpoints were further complicated by the fact that the Indian office put the best possible face on things, while blaming the military for wanting trouble, and the military naturally pointed up the worst, calling the peacemakers idiots or worse. It is certain, however, that aside from some spectacular massacres, officialdom rarely understood the nature or the extent of the annual bloodshed.

Officialdom did see, however, that lines of communication had to be maintained across *Comanchería* to the Pacific. The Kiowas and Comanches after the summer of 1849 had become very troublesome along the Santa Fe Trail. Washington again decided to resolve this problem by diplomacy, although there was some pressure for a military campaign to teach the savages that they must not molest travelers crossing out of Missouri.

Commissioner Thomas Fitzpatrick convened a council in the Indian Territory with representatives of the northern Comanches, Kiowas, and Kiowa Apaches in the summer of 1853. Here he rammed through a treaty that gave the government rights to build roads and forts in Comanche country, forbade the tribes to raid in the future, and also pledged them to return all captives. In return for this agreement, Fitzpatrick offered $18,000 in annuities for five years, or longer, if the President directed.

The 1853 treaty was another fraud. The annuity goods were not delivered as promised, though someone made a fortune from this appropriation; the tribes gave up no captives; raiding was not stopped. There was clear evidence that the chiefs came to the council primarily to see what presents the white men would offer and were affronted by the shoddy goods they received. What Fitzpatrick gained, if anything, was the moral advantage of making the Indians treaty-breakers if they continued to make war, and this, as always, was important to the Anglo-American mind. The treaty thus did lay a moral, and perhaps a quasi-legal, basis for the actions of the secretary of war.

Jefferson Davis, who became war secretary in Pierce's cabinet in 1853, seems to have been the first American in high national office who understood the radically different military and geographic conditions that faced the United States in the trans-Mississippi West. Davis, a southerner, was prepared to make radical changes in both policy and organization to extend the southwestern frontier to the Pacific as quickly as possible.

Davis was imperialist in the true nineteenth-century sense: he had no doubt of the rightness of the civilized nations' exerting their sway over the primitive regions of the world; he believed instinctively in the explosion of the American empire, and he believed that it was the duty of government to assist it. He saw the aboriginal inhabitants of the American West almost exactly as his British counterparts looked on the tribesmen of Northwest India, or the French in North Africa regarded the Saharan nomads: as barriers to the rightful progress of a beneficial civilization. He had no particular interest in exterminating primitives; he felt a definite concern that they should not be allowed to deter the national interest, which demanded the seizure and exploitation of new territory.

Davis' career as secretary of war between 1853 and 1857 was decisive for the West in a way that few Americans noticed. Davis placed great emphasis on winning the West; he strengthened and reorganized the United States Army; he changed military policy; and he trained a whole generation of soldiers for horse operations on the Great Plains. It was his army and his policies, renewed in the 1870s after they were aborted in the Civil War, that carried out the final conquests of the western Amerindians.

The domestic controversies of the 1850s tended to obscure Davis' accomplishments in the West, and his later services to the Confederacy obscured his services as a cabinet officer. Davis was accused, then and later, of seeking only to advance the southern cause, both by concentrating the army in Texas and by training southern officers. His contemporary papers refute this: as secretary of war Davis did not yet contemplate two American nations, and as a West Point graduate and former army officer, he believed he was serving a great national purpose in consolidating the conquest of the West. He did want to expand Texas, and extend a tier of southern-attached and -oriented states to the Pacific to match the extension of the political and economic influence of the Northeast across the prairie states behind the railroads. He thought in terms of the relative power and influence of the southern region within the American confederation, hardly a traitorous notion at any time. Davis had ability, energy, and a powerful political position within the cabinet and with Congress; therefore he was able to begin incisive changes of western policies without actually articulating a formal transformation.

By 1853 Jefferson Davis was convinced that the western Indians could not be handled by the time-honored American custom of taking down the family musket and assembling the militia on the green. It had been obvious for years that infantry could not operate effectively across the terrain and enormous distances in the West, and also that the tiny, passive garrisons of foot soldiers scattered along the frontier excited more contempt than respect. Davis understood the Anglo-Texan experience, and he believed that the Texas Rangers had devised the best procedures for countering horse Indians. He decided that the garrisons must be large enough to provide powerful concentrations of troops capable of meeting any Amerindian threat, and further, that the Texas situation demanded aggressive patrolling of the frontier by cavalry, which might "pursue and punish the offenders." On an extended, arid frontier where the potential enemy were mounted nomads, defensive forces must be both mobile and aggressive. Davis drew on French experience in North Africa as well as the lessons of the Texas Rangers. The Algerian analogy was good, though Davis erred in importing camels for the army. Camels did well in arid country, but they did not thrive on corn; and the stony terrain of the "American deserts," unlike the soft sands of the Sahara, hurt the camels' tender pads.

Davis countered the great objection to cavalry—its expense—by arguing cost effectiveness. If cavalry cost three times as much as infantry, it was ten times as effective. This argument eventually carried with the Congress, which authorized a horse regiment in 1855.

In the meantime, Davis sent more soldiers to Texas, increasing the garrison there to more than three thousand in 1853. He also tacitly gave commanders greater license to act against the raiders. While infantry and even the dragoons were still unable to perform the mission competently, the troops were greatly strengthened by the adoption of muskets firing the new .69 caliber Minié ball, which gave military firearms an effective range of six hundred yards. All this had its effect, as Comanche raiding slackened considerably during 1853.

Davis was familiar with John Rollins' reports of the pitiable condition of the tame tribes and believed that the only answer to this situation was the provision of fixed domains for these peoples. The reservation system had existed since the 1820s; there was plenty of vacant land in Texas; only the state-federal imbroglio over land ownership had prevented the formation of federal Indian reservations. Davis wrote to the Texas governor, stating that the federal authorities could do little to solve the problem of wandering tribesmen unless the state provided the Indians with a defined territory. He promised to use the army to put the Indians on reservations and keep them on them. Through his offices and influence, the Texas legislature voted a grant of twelve square leagues (about seventy thousand acres) of unpreempted lands to be used by the Office of Indian Affairs for reservations.

Captain Randolph Marcy and Robert S. Neighbors, who was now brought back into service, surveyed likely sites on the upper Brazos. They found an excellent location near Fort Belknap, in attractive, wooded, and well-watered rolling country along the river, an oasis suitable for farming Indians. They designated this the Brazos Reservation and planned to locate the Wacos, Ionis, Anadarkos, Tawakonis, and other Wichita-Caddoan remnants here, on eight square leagues of land. Then, as Neighbors believed he could bring in the Pehnahterkuh Comanches, another site was designated some twenty miles to the south on the Clear Fork of the Brazos, enclosing twenty thousand acres.

Neighbors had the thankless task of assembling the Amerindians, few of whom wanted to go to the white man's reservation. The problems were enormous: the scattered bands had to be located, persuaded, guided, and provided for in transit and after they arrived. Neighbors' assistants were incompetent; some undid his work as fast as he accomplished it. And as he rode the frontier fearlessly, contacting and gathering tribes, the white frontier people, state officials, and the army itself made his job almost impossible.

Whites fired on one group of Tonkawas he gathered, scattering them again. Soldiers attacked another encampment of peaceful Indians. Rations and supplies were not delivered on time. There were problems with the Indians themselves, as the Tonkawas were mortal enemies of all the other tribes. But somehow, aided by an unusually harsh winter in 1854–55, Neighbors got the various remnants to the reservation, and in doing so, he earned the grudging admiration of every federal and state officer in Texas—though not that of the civilian frontier, which distrusted the whole reservation plan. The Texas frontier people preferred that the Indians be removed entirely from the state.

Because many of the Pehnahterkuh were now hungry and fearful of Neighbors' warnings that if they did not come to the Clear Fork Reservation the soldiers would pursue them, he was able to bring in 431 of the southern Comanches. He split the band, for about five hundred retreated north across the Red. Neighbors found the Pehnahterkuh badly wasted, their families dissolved, but not so shrunken as the agrarian peoples. There had probably been some thirty thousand Amerindians in Texas at the beginning of the century. Now, Neighbors found only approximately one thousand native Pehnahterkuh, and only one thousand other Indians. A few small bands of various Indians refused to come in, and the Lipan Apaches still hid out along the Rio Grande.

The Wichita-Caddoan elements fitted rather easily into reservation life. They were soon busily erecting thatch-roofed houses and putting in corn crops. The Brazos Reserve was large enough for a thousand peaceable tribesmen. But the fewer than five hundred Pehnahterkuh on the Clear Fork presented problems. No Comanche had ever planted a seed, and while these Comanches had made peace, they had no intention of changing their manner of living. The men refused to do any work except hunting, and the small Clear Fork preserve could not support so many human predators. Neighbors was forced to supply his charges with cattle, while he hoped to bring them around by example.

The die-hard Pehnahterkuh who went north to join the remaining free bands created another sort of problem. Once again, these Comanches had been expelled from their ancient hunting grounds; they retreated with a burning sense of grievance. They refused to make peace with the *tejano* frontier. A peculiar pattern now emerged in Comanche-American relations: The Indian agents north of the Red River line welcomed the Pehnahterkuh and did not interfere with them in any way, and north of the river peace continued, at least officially. But there was no force to prevent the Pehnahterkuh from slipping back to the Brazos to raid the white settlements, and Pehnahterkuh raids encouraged the other bands and the Kiowas to intensify their own raiding. By continuing to act as if there was peace between Comanches and Americans in the Indian Territory, federal agents actually encouraged this activity, and perhaps convinced the bands that the whites were indeed two nations.

The old patterns were only slightly changed. The war parties tended to be smaller than ever, sometimes only five or six warriors, and now women or families were rarely taken along, even to base camps in Texas. The Comanche and Kiowa lodges remained secure along the Arkansas while the adventurous young men slipped away, rode fast and far, and again created chaos from the Trinity to the environs of the sea-coast settlement of Corpus Christi.

The raiding in the 1850s was charged with a newer ferocity, for the Comanches were beginning to display something akin to the sustained hostility of the Apaches. The northern bands were now quite hostile to the reservation Comanches on Clear Fork. One sign of this was that raiding parties from beyond the Red sometimes left broad, clear trails from the scenes of their depredations ostensibly leading directly to the reservation.

The great hopes that had attended the opening of the two Texas reservations were immediately shattered. The "tame" Indians—who had been blamed for more depredations than they actually committed—did not leave the enclaves, but they continued to be blamed. Neighbors and several experienced Texas Rangers understood that the reservation Indians were guiltless, but the white frontier quickly came to believe what it wanted to believe: that Neighbors' "pets" were using the reserves as sanctuaries for murder raids.

Unfortunately, demands in other regions had required a large part of the reinforced garrison to be removed by 1854. At the beginning of 1855, conditions across the entire Texas border grew much worse again. War parties from beyond the Red now penetrated through the frontier regions, where the settlers were armed and wary, and sometimes struck a hundred miles into supposedly secure country. In the 1850s the area around San Antonio was harassed again. An entire German settlement was destroyed northwest of San Antonio, and raiders rode down Buffalo Hump's old trail to the Gulf.

The continuing disasters caused a political clamor in Texas, with demands that the state again raise Rangers. This cost Sam Houston his seat in the United States Senate, because Houston tried to oppose harsh measures against Indians. But, because Jefferson Davis was determined to do something about the raiding, the cycle swung again in 1856.

The first United States cavalry regiment, by some obscure military logic officially designated the 2nd Cavalry, was authorized in March 1855. It was organized at Louisville, Kentucky, in the heart of the American horse-raising country. The regiment—"Jeff Davis' Own"—was planned especially for operations in Texas, with great attention by the secretary himself to detail. Davis personally selected every officer for the regiment, setting aside the crippling strictures of seniority in the service; he even went outside the regular service, offering commissions to certain experienced Texas Rangers. The regiment's commander, Colonel Albert Sidney Johnston, was the former Texas secretary of war. The senior officers of the regiment were permitted to choose their NCOs from the army at large. The ranks were largely recruited, like the horses, from the Kentucky, Ohio, and Indiana countryside.

No expense was spared in equipping the 2nd Cavalry. Only the finest blooded horses were purchased by special teams. Each of the ten companies was to ride mounts of a single color: grays for A; sorrels for B and E; bays for C, D, F, and I; while G and H had browns, and Company K was roan. The troopers were furnished brass-mounted saddles and gutta-percha cartridge boxes. More important, their arms were the latest model: new breech-loading Springfield carbines and .36-caliber Colt's Navy Model revolvers. NCOs were also issued heavy dragoon sabers, though more for show than military use. Jefferson Davis authorized officers to wear ostrich feathers in their hats. All this made the regiment a brave sight on parade, but far more to the point, it carried twelve-pounder mountain howitzers which could be disassembled for transport and it was half again as large as later cavalry units: 750 officers and men, eight hundred horses. It was unique in every respect, from its weapons to the heavy salting of southern gentlemen posted to it by the war secretary. Inevitably it was the elite outfit of the army, and even its junior subaltern was considered a lucky man and one to watch.

The forty-odd officers who served in the 2nd Cavalry during its brief five years of existence more than justified Davis' expectations. No single regiment in American history produced so many general officers. Albert Sidney Johnston, his second in command, Robert E. Lee, Captain Edmund Kirby-Smith, and Lieutenant John Bell Hood were to become full generals in the Confederate States Army. Major William Hardee gained three stars, and Earl Van Dorn, Charles W. Field, and Fitzhugh Lee became major generals in the same service. Three more southern officers were later brigadiers. Nor was the 2nd Cavalry exclusively a southern regiment, for George H. Thomas, Kenner Gerard, George Stoneman, Jr., and Richard W. Johnson all became Union major generals. Almost all others who survived were promoted to full colonel in either service.

The southern image, however, caused the regiment's dissolution and dimmed its luster in United States military annals, and in fact, it was an anomaly in the professional ranks. Elegant officers with black servants and ostrich-feather hats, notwithstanding their great abilities, were not in the American vein, although the 2nd Cavalry established a tradition of a kind that did not die in the Civil War. Its organization, in any event, formed the tradition for a new kind of mounted service on the frontier, and the lessons learned in twenty-five campaigns laid the groundwork for all later cavalry operations in the West. The 2nd Cavalry became the army's school for western Indian warfare.

The regiment marched from Jefferson Barracks, Missouri, to the Texas border in the fall of 1855. It crossed the Red during a howling norther, in which several horses died of cold and a crazed mountain lion attacked the picket line at night. The long march partially seasoned the troopers for what was to come. Even in an elite regiment there were disciplinary problems, as Eliza Johnston's journal testified. After viewing a punishment parade, with its floggings, ripping off of buttons, and drumming out of the service, the Colonel's lady wrote down her wish that the army could find some less "degrading" way of treating men.

Crossing the Red River into Texas, the regiment split up into segments to garrison the frontier. Headquarters and six companies were assigned to Fort Mason; the remainder journeyed on under the senior major to establish a new outpost on the Clear Fork of the Brazos, west of old Fort Belknap. At both sites the regiment had to pitch canvas, for Fort Mason, earlier abandoned, had fallen into ruin. But by January 1856, all companies were on station, and long before quarters were finished, the regiment was in action.

Since the other Texas garrisons were infantry, almost the entire burden of the active defense fell on the cavalry. Colonel Johnston welcomed this, and relished the orders received from the war secretary—to patrol, pursue, and punish any wild Indians found in Texas—because the regiment was out to prove both itself and the effectiveness of horse soldiers. The 2nd Cavalry had been freed from the galling problem of determining which Indians were "friendly" and which were "hostile." Any encountered between the Red River and the Rio Grande, outside the reservations, were to be fair game.

The mix of ex-Rangers, civilians, and West Pointers in the officers' ranks produced some of the finest tacticians ever to appear in the army. Although the ex-Ranger Captain Charles Edward Travis, son of the hero of the Alamo, was accused of slander, convicted by courts-martial, and dismissed from the service for "conduct unbecoming a gentleman"—a sentence many thought too harsh, but which President Pierce upheld—and Lieutenant Charles Field scandalized Mrs. Johnston and other officers' wives by living in sin with a married woman who followed him from St. Louis—a fact that was officially overlooked and did not interfere with his brilliant career—the officers as a whole pursued their tasks as expected. Skilled engineers—Robert E. Lee was one—quickly mapped the theater of operations. Delaware scouts had been secured in the Indian Territory. Plans for extensive patrolling, which provided for interlocking patterns from each base, rapid communications, and frequent contacts and reliefs, and for strong reserves for possible pursuits were painstakingly drawn. The concept was to cover the entire frontier region by a continuous scouring of each river crossing, bank, and bottom. The patrols were even carefully scheduled so that they would appear random and without pattern to the enemy. The patrols were to be aggressive; they were to go beyond the frontier and search for Indian sign. Whenever a patrol cut the trail of unshod ponies, it was immediately to take up pursuit and bring the Indians to battle.

Johnston was determined to keep as many patrols in the field as horseflesh and human endurance could support.

First blood was drawn quickly. At this time small parties of Lipan Apaches, and a few Wacos and Kickapoos who had avoided the reservations, were committing depredations in the borderlands. These warriors dared not venture too far out onto Comanche country, and their trails were turned up immediately. In late February, a detachment of G Company tracked a group of Wacos for six days, overtaking and scattering the war party after killing several. Two troopers were wounded in this action. A few days later, the bay-mounted C Company successfully ambushed some Lipans returning from a raid south of San Antonio. The Apaches lost several warriors and all their horses and supplies. Then, in April, Captain Oakes of C Company pursued a Comanche war band for three hundred miles, catching up with it on May 1 and killing more Indians without loss to himself. On this operation C Company covered six hundred miles in twenty-two days. It was discovered that the heavier, grain-fed cavalry horses could overtake the Indian ponies on grueling pursuits, especially if one patrol relieved another.

In June, Lieutenant Colonel Lee directed an extensive campaign that took two hundred cavalrymen into the field for seven weeks, but that failed to find any Amerindians.

These patrols were punishing to man and beast, and they used up corn and horses—but they were even more punishing to the Indians. They disrupted Comanche raiding patterns by striking trails beyond the frontier, and served a purpose by causing war parties to turn back even when no blood was drawn. Above all, this patrolling made life untenable for the hold-out bands of native Texas Amerindians, caught between the Comanches and the cavalry.

Few if any of the actions could be termed battles, and the operation itself hardly seemed to justify the name of campaign. But this type of military response was extremely effective in inhibiting the Indian guerrilla warfare. As time passed, the patrols became more aggressive, "searching and seizing" farther into Amerindian territory. By the close of 1856, the normal patrol traversed six hundred miles and remained in the field for thirty days. Base camps and field headquarters were constantly shifted about; at times only the regimental band remained in garrison at Fort Mason.

In November, Lieutenant Jennifer of B Company surprised a small party of Comanches on the Llano River. He attacked, scattering the warriors into the brush, capturing all their horses and equipment. Captain Bradfute struck a more powerful band on the Concho that same month. He killed four Comanches, wounded several others, and seized one warrior and more horses. Continuing on patrol, Bradfute covered five hundred miles before returning to quarters in December.

The cavalry learned rapidly, from both success and failure. The young officers were too fond of sounding the trumpet and charging with the saber, as Jennifer did on the Llano. Many hostiles escaped these tactics, but the continuous summer and winter war waged by the bluecoat soldiers soon demoralized the raiders. Patrols were sent out in the foulest weather, and gave up pursuit, once a trail was cut, only under the most pressing conditions. Significantly, by the beginning of 1857 the cavalry was finding few traces of Indians.

In February the regiment's junior officer, Lieutenant Wood, followed a fresh trail with his Delaware scout and fifteen troopers. He continued pursuit relentlessly for days, finally overtaking five Comanche warriors near the North Concho. He killed three by gunfire, and seized the others, though he himself was wounded in leading a mounted charge upon the startled Indians.

Then, in July, Lieutenant John Hood fought the bloodiest action the 2nd was to win in Texas. Hood, an energetic Kentuckian, pressed out of Mason on a Comanche hunt with his scout ranging far ahead to smell out sign and prevent an ambush. Hood pushed his twenty-four soldiers for twelve brutal days of riding,. before his Delaware scout cut a three-day-old pony trail. The trail led toward the Rio Grande border, over extremely rough and desolate country in which water holes ranged up to fifty miles apart, and in some of these holes the scummy water smelled so foul that men could hardly drink it. Without hesitation, Hood took up pursuit, hoping to catch the estimated twenty Comanches before they slipped into Mexico.

For four days the lieutenant pushed his gamy, bearded, and dust-covered troop south, until several of the horses were staggering with exhaustion. On July 20th, he came across a fresh camp site with still smoking embers. He was closing, but his scout reported gravely that more Comanches had come together, and that the troopers were now pursuing some fifty warriors. Here, near the headwaters of the Devil's River, Hood took stock of his situation. He was now outnumbered, with exhausted men and jaded horses. But he could see the blue-shadowed eastern Sierra Madre just to the south, and he determined to ride at least to the Rio Grande.

Finally, the soldiers spotted Indians on a bluff overlooking the clear Devil's River. The warriors appeared boldly, waving what appeared to be a large white sheet—a sign of truce. Hood suspected ambush, but led his troop forward into an expanse of spine-tipped yucca to meet the Indians. He was far in advance of his own line, which rode forward with cocked carbines at the ready, when the waiting Amerindians threw down their "flag" and charged at him on foot. At the same time, the thicket was set ablaze ahead of the cavalry, and some thirty mounted, painted warriors raced out toward Hood's flanks, while others fired from the spiny thickets. A thirty-foot-high wall of flame blazed up, throwing the cavalry horses into confusion as they wheeled to meet the charge.

Two warriors rushed at Hood, hoping to drag him alive from his horse. But the lieutenant had learned one trick of Comanche warfare: he carried a short, double-barreled shotgun across his pommel, similar to the eight-gauge weapons the horse Indians favored. He literally blew both attackers apart at point-blank range, then wheeled and rejoined his small band of surrounded troopers.

Fifty Comanches with lances and buffalo-hide shields were already among his dissolving line, attacking both on foot and horseback. But in this melee the iron discipline of the 2nd Cavalry held, and the Colt revolvers did fearful execution. Men and horses went down, buffeted by the iron-hard shields, while Hood and his sergeant wielded their sabers. The sergeant clove one warrior to the chin with a powerful stroke. By then, Hood's soldiers had emptied their revolvers. They could not reload on horseback. Somehow, the whole command fought its way back out of the thicket and dismounted in a tiny press to reload. The soldiers were under continuous fire, for a number of Comanche women apparently were reloading the Indian muskets and passing fresh ones to the sniping warriors.

Hood's left hand was pinned to his bridle by an arrow. Cursing, he broke the shaft and withdrew it, wrapping his torn hand in a kerchief. At this moment, with several men and horses down and only a half dozen troopers with loaded weapons, Hood's command could have been utterly destroyed by any determined charge. He was saved, incongruously, by the Comanche women, who as the smoke cleared saw the Indian casualties and commenced a fearsome howling. Hood later officially estimated that his men had killed eight or nine warriors, and wounded perhaps twice that number. He was too conservative, though he had had no time to count the fallen, for Comanche survivors of this engagement later verified on the reservation that there had been nearly a hundred Amerindians, and that the soldiers had killed nineteen and wounded many more. Disheartened, the Comanches failed to destroy Hood's battered troop. They retrieved their dead and wounded and slipped away through the scrub.

Hood let them go. Two of his men were dead; he and four others seriously wounded. His horses were in poor shape, and he was without food or water. He retreated to the river and sent a rider to Val Verde County for medical assistance. The next day a relief column from the 8th Infantry out of Camp Hudson arrived to help bury the dead and resupply Hood for a march to Fort Clark.

After five weeks in the field, Hood brought his survivors back on August 8th to Fort Mason. He and his men were commended for gallantry by Winfield Scott, commander-in-chief of the U.S. Army.

Dozens of similar, if less dramatic and bloody, patrols cleared the Texas frontier of hostile Indians during 1857. The Comanches were never suicidal; they began to give the Texas borderlands a wider berth. At the same time, it became almost impossible for the northern raiders to pass freely to and from Mexico. A string of forts and constant cavalry patrols crossed the ancient Comanche traces; Hood's action had been against raiders bound for northern Mexico. Now, a century of Comanche terror in the Mexican borderlands suddenly ceased. The peasantry gave thanks to God, but probably never understood the role of the American cavalry.

These months and years also destroyed the last of the other Amerindian remnants struggling to survive in Texas outside the reservations. By 1857 the Lipan Apaches in southwest Texas were virtually exterminated. The Apaches deserted their old ranges above the Rio Grande and sought refuge in Coahuila, where remnants of the Kickapoos and others began to join and amalgamate with them. The few Lipans and Kickapoos still caused trouble from south of the border; they raided into Texas and stole stock until the 1870s, when Mackenzie's punitive expedition finally rooted them out and scattered them through the Mexican sierra. In 1903, nineteen Lipans, all those remaining, were permitted to recross the border and enter the Mescalero reservation in New Mexico. There were then only three other surviving members of this tribe: two who had joined the Tonkawas, and one with the Kiowa Apaches in the Indian Territory. Thus the eastern Apaches, the former terror of the Spanish borderlands, were destroyed, victims of both red and white men.

THE CAVALRY PATROLLED ONLY THE TEXAS FRONTIER COUNTRY. IT DID not pursue Indians north of the Red River, nor did it strike into the high, distant, and still mysterious Llano Estacado. Its stance, for all its aggressiveness, was entirely local. Therefore the 2nd Cavalry was only half effective. It inhibited raiding, but it did not destroy the sources of the Amerindian terror on the Brazos frontier.

This was, or should have been, demonstrated to the federal authorities when Davis left the War office in 1857, and his successor, Floyd, believing the Texas trouble controlled, ordered the greater part of the 2nd Cavalry off to the Utah territory. The Comanches were always ignorant of white politics, but they were extremely sensitive to actual events on the frontier. The bands in the Indian Territory knew within weeks that the horse soldiers were gone, and war parties again probed the Texan frontier.

Within a few months after the patrolling ceased, a hundred Texas farm houses had gone up in flames and more than a hundred sun-bloated corpses were buried in the bitter frontier soil. The return of the terror, after many months of relief, was now intolerable. It caused a great political furor in Texas, in which contempt for federal policy was mixed with clamor for local action. As editorial after editorial demanded, if the distant federal government and the Indian-petting agents refused to take action, then the state should defend itself with the most direct means at hand, the Texas Rangers.

Hardin R. Runnels, a blunt, direct politician who was already tending toward secession, came into office in January 1858, riding on this widespread discontent. Runnels believed that he must take decisive action quickly to protect the deteriorating frontier. He got the legislature to appropriate funds for frontier defense, and he appointed John S. Ford—known as "Old Rip" from his habit of writing the letters R.I.P. at the close of his casualty reports—then the most experienced Ranger officer in service, as senior captain and supreme commander of all state forces.

The title was more imposing than Ford's projected army: he was authorized to enlist one hundred mounted Rangers and establish them at a base camp on the Indian frontier. The Texas Rangers were still not a permanent, standing constabulary, though their fame was thoroughly established. The state appointed Ranger captains from time to time for specific purposes, then allowed these captains to raise their own troops for a specified time. Ford's authorization in 1858 was unique, for he was allowed to dismiss any captains then in service and replace them with his own officers.

Runnels gave Rip Ford both clearly written and additional clearly understood unwritten orders. He was to "follow any and all trails of hostile or suspected hostile Indians" and to "inflict the most summary punishment" on them when he found them. He was to cooperate with federal officers and Indian agents, "but to brook no interference with his plan of operation from any source." In effect, the orders and plan were nothing new; this was to be a punitive expedition such as Hays and John S. Moore had led years earlier. Ford was given a completely free hand, and urged to take immediate, drastic action, because his funds were severely limited.

The task called for an experienced Indian fighter, but also for an officer with keen tact and judgment: Ford's orders called for nothing less than a war against the Indians in defiance of federal policy. The governor made it clear, and Ford understood, that both men's reputations would ride on successful action. Runnels was not to be disappointed, for Ford was the best possible man to handle both the fighting and the delicacy.

Here began the bloodiest two years in Texas since the war years of 1835–36.

Ford raised his small army of tough frontier riders, most of them experienced veterans of the frontier style of warfare. He moved to the northwest, setting up his base camp, which he called Camp Runnels, near the Brazos Reservation. Nothing showed Ford's wisdom more than his plan to enlist an equal force of reservation Indians. The Tonkawas and other ancient enemies of the Comanches as always were eager to serve the Texans, and in this Ford gained the full support of the son of the Indian agent, L. S. Ross. Ross, who had no official status, raised a force of 113 warriors from various tribes on the reservation, then accepted an appointment to lead these Indians under Ford's command.

With the help of the reservation Indians, Ford quickly obtained excellent intelligence. Scouts rode out and reported back that while no Comanches appeared to be camped in Texas, there were large encampments north of the border in the Indian Territory. The country north of the Red River, of course, was completely beyond Ford's jurisdiction as a state officer, but as he said, his orders were to find Indians, not learn geography.

Ford's column—102 Rangers with pack trains and at least a hundred Indian allies—left Camp Runnels on April 22, 1858. He rode directly for the Red behind a wide screen of Amerindian scouts, and crossed the river on April 29th. By May 10th, he was finding Indian sign everywhere on the Oklahoma plains: the trail marks of meat-laden Comanche travois, and a bison carcass that held two distinctive Comanche arrows. On May 11th, his careful scouts had discovered a large Comanche camp, and Ford prepared to attack.

The Rangers had not been discovered by the Amerindians. They moved differently from the army, quietly, grimly, making cold camps and without all the military jangle and furor and constant bugle signals of the cavalry. Like most old Rangers, Rip Ford fought Indian-fashion: surprise the enemy and, if possible, kill them in their lodges. His plan, however, was almost ruined by some Tonkawa allies, who, overeager, attacked and demolished a small outlying encampment of five lodges, which lay about three miles beyond the main Comanche concentration. Two Comanches escaped on horseback, crying the alarm.

Ford did not hesitate in this situation. He rode hard toward the main encampment, which spread along the shallow Canadian.

The Comanches, forewarned, failed to scatter. There were some three hundred warriors along the Canadian, and this was deep in their own country. The chiefs determined to give battle, to teach the *tejanos* and their despised allies a bloody lesson. Hastily painted, black for war and death, the warriors rode out in magnificent array, their great bison-horn headdresses and iron lance points glinting in the bright May sun. As Ford approached across the rolling plain, they shrieked and capered, whirling and thundering in front of the slowing Texan advance. Hundreds flowed around the Texan flanks, shouting insults, invoking powerful medicine.

Here was a scene that was to be repeated many times in the tragic Amerindian twilight on the plains: a savage horde, resplendent in their valor and barbaric finery, swirling to meet a small, sweat-stained band of bearded white riders who watched them grimly, now and then spitting tobacco juice. The Rangers, calm among their own screaming, gesticulating red allies, invoked their own rites. They cocked their rifles, and checked the seating of the red copper percussion caps on the nipples of their Colts. They wore no uniforms, but they had the discipline of combat veterans. They watched Ford, who sat staring shrewdly at the enemy, calculating the best way to break the Indians' medicine.

And as so often, the splendid horde played into his hands. A great chief of the northern Comanches, whom the whites knew as Iron Jacket, rode in front of the Amerindian van, brandishing his long Plains lance and daring the white men to personal combat. Iron Jacket wore a burnished cuirass, left with his bones by some forgotten Spanish soldier on these plains. The overlapping iron plates had gained the chief a fearsome reputation of invulnerability in war against other Amerindians. But no Spanish armor could turn a Sharps' rifle ball. Several Texans took aim; their guns roared, and Iron Jacket and his horse collapsed into the dust.

As Iron Jacket fell between the two hosts, Captain Ford immediately ordered the charge. Revolvers blazing, the Rangers crashed into the milling Comanche masses—riding into three times their number of horsemen. But the Texans were grimly fighting for their lives, and to wreak execution; the Indians were already half demoralized.

What should have been a desperate battle dissolved into a bloody slaughter that swirled over six miles. In this kind of melee the Comanche spears and arrows were no match for long-barreled revolvers in the hands of skilled gunmen. Again and again charging warriors were knocked from their horses by the repeating pistols. Ford kept his men pressing into the Indians, stirrup to stirrup, giving them no chance to form their deadly circle. Soon, the Comanches lost all order or cohesion, and the Rangers pursued them for seven hours, until the Texan horses were staggering. By the end of the afternoon, Ford's Rangers had killed seventy-six warriors, seized three hundred horses, and captured eighteen women and children abandoned by the fleeing band. Ford lost two men dead.

Ford arrived back on the Brazos on May 21st. Here he wrote a report to Runnels, stressing the fact that he had proved so bloodily: that the Comanches could be pursued, found, and defeated by a properly organized expedition anywhere in the western territory. Ford and a hundred Rangers had smashed a force of three hundred Comanches, whom at this time the army considered the most fearsome opponents on the plains. His company had penetrated a region the Spanish had not dared to enter for a century, and in which American military forces were reluctant to undertake extended operations. Ford requested permission to continue his campaign through the summer and winter, in an effort to destroy the Comanche threat forever.

His victory was hailed, but his request was denied. Ford had spent all of the funds authorized in this month-long campaign, and the governor now disbanded his little army.

However, his successful penetration of the Indian Territory had an effect far beyond his single victory over the Comanches. The Ranger operation aroused the U.S. Army, which regarded the Texans' triumph as something of a humiliation. Although the cumulative efforts of the cavalry had proven enormously effective, the thousands of regulars stationed in Texas had never achieved such a signal victory. The army's pride was stung, and Brigadier General David Twiggs, commanding the Texas Military District, now began to protest vigorously against the restrictions placed upon the army. No outcry was made against the Texans' invasion of federal territory; instead, the army now demanded permission to pursue Indians beyond the borders of Texas, to hit the hostiles and destroy them wherever they might be found.

Twiggs wrote through channels to his superiors that the Indian problem on the Texas frontier would never be solved without a drastic revision in military policy. He denounced the notion that a true peace would ever be possible so long as the Plains tribes retained autonomy and freedom of action. He urged that a full regiment of cavalry be sent into Comanche country, to take the offensive and harass the Indians on their hunting grounds throughout the entire year, giving them no breathing spell to raid the white frontier. "As long as there are wild Indians on the prairie," he wrote, "Texas cannot be free from depredations." He also wrote to Runnels, expressing full support and sympathy.

Twiggs based his argument not only on the nature of the southern Plains tribes, but also on the fact that the army did not have, and probably never would have, sufficient numbers to prevent raiding by a mere policing of the frontier. In this he was entirely correct. The army was painfully discovering the only effective countermeasures to the form of warfare practiced by the horse tribes. Guerrilla warfare could not be halted by barrier fortresses, even with aggressive local patrolling. The guerrillas could only be controlled by destroying them in their distant sanctuaries on the High Plains.

Twiggs' reports, extreme political pressure from the Texas government, and Indian Agent Neighbors' private assertions that if the federal authorities did not end the Indian trouble, the state apparently was prepared to wage its own war north of the Red River, shook the faltering Buchanan administration—not into decisive action, because President and Congress were almost immobilized by the stresses of the slavery controversy, but into letting the military seek its own solutions in the West. The total problem now extended beyond Texas. There were Amerindian rebellions in many areas as whites flowed through the Rockies, and in Kansas the prairie frontier had at last come within the range of the marauding Kiowas and Cheyennes. Americans were at war with these tribes in Kansas, whatever name was put on it.

War Secretary Floyd tacitly agreed that Indian aggressions against whites should be destroyed at the source, and that the army should take whatever steps were necessary to ensure its power and control over the entire western territory.

The 2nd Cavalry Regiment came back to Texas with these orders, and also with a burning determination to demonstrate that the regulars could do anything the Rangers could do, given the opportunity. Major Earl Van Dorn received instructions to march into the Indian Territory with four companies of the 2nd and one of infantry, to set up a base camp in the Wichita Mountains, and to scour the entire region between the Red and Canadian rivers for hostile or potentially hostile Indians.

Van Dorn engaged the services of Lawrence Ross and his scouts at the Brazos Reservation and moved north of the Red in September 1858. Far-ranging Amerindian scouts again located a Comanche encampment. Leaving his infantry behind, Van Dorn marched ninety miles in thirty-seven hours, and on October 1st moved into position to attack the lodges of approximately five hundred Indians.

This time there was no warning, no dramatic confrontation. The cavalry struck the sleeping encampment at dawn. This was again more of a massacre than a battle, but even with these advantages the heavy cavalry was not as effective in this kind of melee as the Rangers. The soldiers killed fifty-six Comanches of both sexes and all ages, took some three hundred horses, and burned the lodges, destroying tons of Indian rations. But the great majority of the Comanches escaped, and in the confusion they inflicted many casualties on the horse soldiers.

Two officers and a number of men were killed by arrows. Ross and Van Dorn were wounded, the latter so seriously it was thought he would never return to duty. Despite this, General Twiggs reported the "victory was more decisive and complete than any recorded in the history of our Indian warfare." This exaggeration, and the methods by which the "victory" was achieved, showed how profoundly the army had been influenced by Ford's exploits.

MEANWHILE, A DIFFERENT FORM OF DESTRUCTION FACED THE RESERVAtion Amerindians, Comanches and others, on the Brazos preserves. The scouts who rode with Ford and Van Dorn were now to receive an all-too-common reward from white men.

Two factors had doomed the Texas reservations from the start. One was that their very presence, and the good lands lying around them in the river bottoms, attracted heavy white settlement to these areas between 1855 and 1857. Both reserves were completely enclosed by white farms and ranches by 1858. The other problem was that when the northern Comanche bands returned to raiding late in 1857 after the removal of the 2nd Cavalry, the Brazos frontier blamed these depredations on the reservation Indians.

Neighbors, who believed deeply in the reservation policy, understood that the reservations could not succeed so long as wild tribes still remained free beyond them. His own Indians would never be accepted as peaceful until all raiding was stopped. He wrote out a lucid explanation of this situation, and urged the federals to move quickly to enclose all the western tribes on defined territories, stressing the innocence of his own charges and their services to the state and army. The army was moving in this direction, but it lacked the capability to enclose the Comanches beyond the Red quickly enough to solve the problem. As raiding continued, Neighbors and his pacified tribesmen faced mounting hysteria on all sides.

One man in particular did much to stir up trouble. John R. Baylor, a former Indian agent who had been dismissed by Neighbors in disgrace, was blind with rage and prejudice against both Neighbors and his "pets." Baylor traded on his reputation for "knowing Indians" among the local settlers. He accused the reservation people of every crime committed in Texas, and charged that Neighbors was knowingly protecting them. Baylor played cruelly on the emotions

John R. Baylor in Confederate uniform c. 1862.

of Texans who had lost loved ones in Indian raids, until the whites in the vicinity threatened to attack the reservations and massacre every Indian.

Ford was stationed at Camp Runnels with a handful of Rangers. He investigated the charges, found them false, and demanded that Baylor put them in writing for official action. Ford also angrily rejected a suggestion that he assist the settlers in "getting rid of the reservations" by manufacturing evidence against them. Ford knew perfectly well that the raiders came from far away, and that the reservation bands were guiltless. And though he had no love for Indians, he respected Neighbors' courage and integrity.

However, Baylor continued his slanders at stump meetings, fostering a mob atmosphere along the Brazos. Neighbors himself was a poor man to offset this hysteria, because although infinitely religious and infinitely patient with his wards, he was totally impatient with white prejudices and rhetorical piety. Defending his charges, Neighbors quarreled with all the local people. But Neighbors was utterly rational, and by the fall of 1858 he realized that his Indians would be in physical danger if they remained in Texas. He traveled to Washington and urged the Office of Indian Affairs to remove his people to the Indian Territory, for their own protection.

His fears were justified. Two days after Christmas 1858, seven Indians were found shot to death in their blankets beside the Brazos. Four were men, three women, all Anadarcos and Caddoans. As the subagent reported, these seven had never caused anyone trouble. Evidence quickly pointed to six white men as the probable murderers. Accused by Rip Ford, one of these men, Dr. W. W. McNeill, wrote an account stating the six had been following some Indian horse thieves, had overtaken them, and killed them after a desperate battle. When it was shown that the dead people had been killed in their sleep, the judge of the Texas 19th Judicial District requested Ford to arrest the six white men.

Now Ford was caught in the painful dilemma that confronted even honest officials in such racial-ethnic controversies. Ford was fearless, but without Neighbors' rigid ethics. He knew first that the arrests would cause widespread disorder, and that more people would probably be killed; he knew also that no jury in frontier Texas would ever convict white men for killing Indians. Believing the arrest of McNeill and the others to be a dangerous, futile exercise, he refused the judge's orders, on the rather specious grounds that he was principally a state military officer, with no jurisdiction over civil criminals. Neighbors charged scathingly that Ford was pandering to the prejudices of the frontier against the interests of the very scouts who had led him to victory. And Ford candidly admitted that, right or wrong, as a Texan he found it difficult to take the side of Indians against his own people. Nothing Ford could have done would have turned out well. By doing nothing, he won the approval of his own Rangers and the whole frontier.

By spring, armed whites were prowling all around the reservation, hunting Indians like wild animals. Only the company of United States Rifles stationed on the Brazos prevented bloodshed, and John R. Baylor told the commanding officer that he would kill any federal soldier who stood in his way. Then, on May 29, 1859, whites entered reservation grounds and fired on Amerindians. In this atmosphere of madness, all work stopped, and the thousand tribesmen huddled around Neighbors' headquarters for protection.

Finally, Neighbors received word, on June 11th, that Washington and Texas had agreed to the conditions of the reservations' removal. Ranger Captain John Henry Brown arrived to help the Rifles escort the Indians to the border. However, Brown refused to allow the Indians to scatter to round up their livestock, which grazed all over the large reservation, on the grounds that some might "escape." After a bitter quarrel with Brown, Neighbors was forced to inform his people that they must leave their horses, cows, and pigs behind.

The reservation Indians left their houses and greening fields and were herded north toward the Red. It was a long, arduous journey on foot, punishing both to troops and to Indians. On September 1, 1859, Neighbors led his charges into the strange land of Oklahoma and turned them over to the Indian agent in that jurisdiction. There is no record of his final words to the Comanches, Wichitas, and other remnant Indians who had trusted him. But that night he wrote his wife in Texas:

I have this day crossed all the Indians out of the heathen land of Texas and am now out of the land of the Philistines.

If you want a full description of our Exodus . . . read the "Bible" where the children of Israel crossed the Red Sea. We have had about the same show, only our enemies did not follow us. . . .

The next day Neighbors returned to Texas, to post his final report to the Indian office from Fort Belknap. There, for reasons never explained, a man named Cornett walked up to him and shot him in the back.

The codes of the frontier permitted the murder of Indians, but they did not admit of even an Indian-loving white man's being shot in the back. After some discussion, a party of Minute Men hunted down the man Cornett the following spring and disposed of him without benefit of judge or jury.

NEITHER THE RANGER-ARMY OPERATIONS IN THE INDIAN TERRITORY, nor the removal of the reservations, halted Comanche-Kiowa depredations in 1859. The first in fact brought retaliations: a few small parties of Comanches rode to Texas for the express purpose of killing white men in revenge. The Comanche codes required vengeance by men whose sons, fathers, or uncles had been killed. Such war parties rarely committed extended depredations. They rode until they encountered some unfortunate traveler or isolated farm family, slaughtered them, and took scalps back home for consolation. Understandably, even a few such raids kept the entire white frontier in fear and uproar.

However, while to many Texans it appeared nothing was being solved, the pressures on the distant Amerindians were mounting terribly in these years. The government had halted annuities to the Kiowas and had given the military full license to pacify, cow, or destroy as necessary the remaining natives on the prairies. And under an otherwise futile administration, the military was succeeding rapidly. Formerly remote strongholds of the Plains tribes were being penetrated and mapped. Under the succeeding commanders, Robert E. Lee and George H. Thomas, the 2nd Cavalry continued its violent patrols. The cavalry and its leaders learned the hard and brutal facts of horse Indian war. Colonel Thomas, like Earl Van Dorn, took his wounds, and Fitzhugh Lee nearly died from the arrows he received.

The losses meant little to the cavalry, though every trooper was ceremoniously buried and mourned. The streets and slums of the distant cities promised more recruits. But the operations were crippling and demoralizing the warriors of the southern plains, who now numbered barely in the thousands.

In Texas, federal and state policy now pursued the same goal, with greater cooperation between officials. Sam Houston was elected governor of Texas in 1859, ironically, considering his historic stands, as an old Indian-fighter who pledged to defend the state's frontiers. Houston had vaster, if inchoate plans; there is evidence that he thought he could save the dividing Union by involving Americans in a war with Mexico. Houston immediately began to raise state troops, five hundred standing Rangers during 1859. He put Minute Men under arms in every county, organizing twenty-three companies by 1860. The army maintained 2,500 troops in Texas, two-thirds of its actual fighting forces. All together, more than three thousand combined troops operated against the Indians along the western frontier. Comanche raiding now brought swifter and more merciless retribution than ever before.

In the fall of 1860, the war chief Nawkohnee (usually called Peta Nacona in Texan accounts) led his small band of eastern Comanches deep into Parker County, passing close to the site of the old Parker fort. But this was now a long-settled, armed, and highly organized frontier. Nawkohnee soon withdrew and raced westward toward the High Plains, for he had stirred up a hornets' nest of vengeful Texans.

Ranger captain Sul Ross, an experienced leader, took up the chase with sixty riders, some Tonkawa scouts, and seventy settler volunteers. A patrol from the 2nd Cavalry, a sergeant and twenty troopers, joined him, placing themselves under the state officer's command. Ross rode further and further, determined to catch the marauders and teach them a Texas lesson they would not forget. He drove his command high onto the plains in the teeth of winter. Finally, his scouts reported the Comanche lodges on the Pease River, near what was to become the tiny town of Quanah.

On December 17, 1860, Ross came down on the Comanche camp behind the noise and dust of a howling west Texas norther. This was the camp of Nawkohnee, but it held only women and children and a Mexican male slave. The chief, his sons, and warriors had gone hunting, never dreaming that white men would pursue him to the heart of the bison plains.

The Rangers, volunteers, and soldiers crashed through the camp.

There were the screams and shots, ripped away by the wind, the usual killing. Accounts vary as to what happened. Captain Ross, who was acclaimed a hero for the deed, claimed and probably honestly believed that he had caught and killed Peta Nacona. But in the melee he pursued and shot Nawkohnee's Mexican slave, who was trying to save the fleeing Comanche women.

The plunging horsemen fired at every running figure, killing, as Ross reported, "several" females. But then, as Ranger Charles Goodnight took aim at a small running form, the wind caught and turned back a blanket, exposing dirty, dung-greased, but unmistakably blond hair. Goodnight screamed: "Don't shoot her! She's white!"

This woman was spared and seized. Ross examined her. She seemed to know no English, but her eyes were blue, and although wrinkled and browned by the elements, her exposed skin and features were distinctly Caucasian. She carried a little girl, a small, dark, eighteen-month-old baby. When the Rangers and soldiers left the burned camp with its scattered, tumbled corpses, they carried the woman and girl back with them.

The woman created a great sensation, for she was positively identified as Cynthia Ann Parker. She was the right age, the right coloring, and had Parker features. And when her name was spoken, she broke into tears, although she had forgotten every other word of English.

The Parker clan had become prominent in this part of Texas. They received Cynthia Ann back with rejoicing and tried to give her love; Parker blood had helped win Texas, and the family cared nothing for popular opinion. But opinion now was highly sentimental. The state legislature granted Cynthia Ann Parker a league of land and an annual pension of $100 for life to ease her return to civilization. Her family and her people now did everything they could for Cynthia Ann, as they believed, and so destroyed her.

For this blue-eyed, yellow-haired survivor of an almost-forgotten massacre was no longer a Parker, or a Texan. She was Naduah, Nerm, a woman of the People, who had belonged to them now, for twenty-five years. Her husband was Nawkohnee, the respected chief; her sons were still out on the prairie. Every account or memory of the People has agreed that this family was a singularly happy one, and that Nawkohnee the chief, when he returned to his ruined and death-filled camp, never took another woman. The Parkers would not grant the woman Naduah the one thing she begged of them—to return her to her man and two sons on the High Plains.

When she tried to escape, sadly but adamantly the Parkers put her under guard.

There was no hope of adjustment. This, probably, did much to kill the little girl, Topsannah or Flower, who died from a "civilized" disease. Naduah then, to the horror of her blood kin, mourned her dead child like a woman of the People. She mutilated herself, cried and howled. She had nothing more to live for; she sank into deep apathy and starved herself to death.

But the Parker saga was not ended, nor would tragedy cease to haunt the Parker blood. Far to the west, the grieving Nawkohnee died from an infected wound. His younger son Pecos, or Peanut, fell prey to some disease. Such losses were not unusual for a Comanche family in these years. But the elder son, born about 1847, who was called Kwahnah (Quanah) or Sweet Odor, was growing tall and strong. Already as a boy, he showed intelligence and spirit and great character. In his twenties, he was to be acclaimed a war chief and, in his way, to become the greatest Comanche chief of all time. The Texans would hear of him, fear him, hate him, and eventually come to honor him, writing—half in boasting, half in bitterness— that blood would always tell.

IN THE DESPERATE, HAUNTED YEARS JUST BEFORE THE CIVIL WAR, THE American nation paid attention to only one kind of bloodshed in "bleeding Kansas." The remarkable military accomplishments of a tiny regular army in the Great American Desert were virtually ignored. In a few short years, facing unprecedented distances, logistical problems, and unknown terrain, the tiny, alienated, professional frontier army had extended American power and control over almost every remote region between the Canadian border and the Rio Grande.

There was little glory in this campaign: the primary problems for the army had always been geography and civilian policy, not the enemy. But the enemy was formidable enough. If Americans took the conquest for granted, and millions in fact felt at least some sympathy for the Amerindians, the true grandeur of the achievement was revealed by comparison with the failures of France, Spain, and Mexico. Failed empires somehow become romantic; successful ones seem, in retrospect, to have been juggernauts.

Despite the countless clear reports that piled up on military and civilian desks, mythology entered in the picture. But neither the "cowboys" nor the farming pioneers won the West—for in every region where there were horse Amerindians, there had to be soldiers long before there were cowmen or agrarians. Neither cowboys nor settlers pushed forward the Texas frontier. The great majority of the thousands of whites who died on the plains frontier from Kansas to Texas were not, in fact, killed in "Indian country." They were killed by Comanche and Kiowa raiders within, and sometimes far behind, the agrarian frontiers.

The Amerindians were killed in Indian country. They were killed most of all by disease, but those who died violently were killed by military operations. They were killed by soldiers, and by ranging companies and posses that were cavalry in everything but name. As the Texans discovered quickly, white farmers could not live in close proximity to a horse-Indian frontier without protection, and the only effective protection against Plains Indians was a form of Indian warfare: the counterraid, which civilized men called the punitive expedition. This was a lesson learned bitterly, one that had to be relearned again and again from the seventeenth century onward. The various Europeans who entered the western plains found no way of controlling the Plains Amerindians short of slaughtering them.

Every military force that operated in the Southwest came to this conclusion, and every soldier from Spanish times forward in some way had to face opposition or reluctance from civilian or religious authorities. There was less controversy and a clearer policy overall in Anglo-Texas for one reason: in a real sense all the Texans comprised a frontier population.

In the years just before the Civil War the United States Army was becoming allied psychologically with the frontier people and increasingly estranged from its civilian policy-makers, who, like the Spanish, were never willing to support large-scale warfare against Amerindians. There was little love lost between the military and the frontier civilians who professed to despise it. However, the army buried civilian dead and daily saw the result of raiding atrocities; and on the southwestern frontier, at least, the army rejected the eastern *idée fixe* that white men were normally the aggressors. In any case, both the Constitution and duty required the army to protect citizens against aborigines on any soil beneath the flag. The military faced an extremely frustrating problem in that it was always too small to police adequately; it could not prevent whites from moving into Indian raiding range, nor throw up any really effective cordon to protect them. The army therefore, to be effective, could not act as a police force—as had been envisioned. It had to carry out antiguerrilla measures, which meant that the raiders must be pursued to the ends of the country if necessary, and cowed or destroyed in their remote sanctuaries.

Few professional soldiers shared the frontier hatred of the entire red race; for one thing, the soldiers rarely exposed their families, if they had any, to Amerindian warfare. But there is no question that, whatever they felt, the soldiers took up the punitive practices of the Texas Rangers by the 1850s.

The United States never formally adopted the policy of massacre authorized by both the Republic and the State of Texas. Many commanders, however, came perilously close to authorizing it in field orders. In the great sweeps of the later 1850s, it had become permissible to kill all males twelve years and older; many attacks on Indians—Harney's operations in 1855, Van Dorn's in the Wichitas in 1858, Custer's later activities on the Washita—were indistinguishable from massacre.

The problem was that the loose ordering of Plains Amerindian society and the random nature of Amerindian warfare made the army's instructions to distinguish between "hostile" and "friendly" Indians virtually impossible to implement. With regard to Comanches, Kiowas, and similar peoples, it was impossible to define "peaceful" or "hostile." The Comanche "tribe" or "nation" never went to war with Americans north of the Red River. Lodges were set up peacefully along the Arkansas, and these peoples accepted annuities from federal agents at the same time that dozens of war parties were raiding into Texas. *Every* Comanche camp held warriors who took the war trail when the spirit moved them. Many of the bands who were massacred by frontier whites or soldiers were indeed peaceful at the time—but like Black Kettle's Cheyennes, slaughtered in 1864, they most certainly had been at war shortly beforehand, and the whites believed with reason that they would be "hostile" again in the near future. This was why the army wanted to establish clearly defined reservations. Harney also suggested in the 1850s that the Amerindians be allowed to police themselves, through the appointment of native Indian agents and officers, and that the military should supervise payment of annuities to prevent corruption; but his ideas met powerful political opposition. The question of exactly what was a "hostile" Indian was not clarified until the 1870s, with the full implementation of the reservation policy.

Throughout the entire history of the confrontation, it was apparent that Amerindian warfare quickly brutalized most white men, soldiers or eivilians.

The warfare proved or at least strongly indicated that the principal difference between primitive warriors and the soldiers of a civilized power was in amassed knowledge and assumed habits. The nature of the country and the fighting made the whites as savage as their enemies, as they found they had to slough off former restraints and habits to accomplish their aims. Recruits who vomited at the first sight of an Indian "atrocity" with its tortured, blackened corpses, hideously mutilated, soon grew inured. Many veteran soldiers, like experienced frontiersmen, took scalps. Like the savages, whites made war on women and children. There was some excuse for this. When an Amerindian camp was attacked, women and boys were hardly noncombatants. All white accounts attested to the fact that they were almost as deadly as adult warriors when pressed. In the wild melees, the sexes were not easily distinguishable. Rangers and soldiers soon ceased trying to distinguish them, for hesitation often proved fatal. And the awareness of the women's role in torturing captives destroyed most white sympathy and restraint. However, many Rangers and soldiers did refuse to make war on women. Every punitive raid threw up examples of whites who failed to shoot, or else protested the killing. One of Moore's Rangers narrowly escaped death because he held back from shooting an attacking woman; in fact, he was only spared because his comrades killed her. The majority of whites, descending on an Indian encampment, closed their minds to the question, took no chances, and afterward seldom discussed the issue.

By 1860, such measures had clearly defeated and demoralized the Comanches, who were on the defensive not only in Texas but throughout the Indian Territory. The historic raiding into Mexico had virtually ceased, and the wiser chiefs had developed second thoughts about provoking the *tejanos'* wrath by harassing the Brazos frontier. Meanwhile, U.S. cavalry had the bands on the run in the very heart of *Comanchería*.

Most American historians of the Indian wars believe that the pacification of the southwestern horse tribes was far advanced by the eve of the Civil War. Thousands of armed men in Texas were poised and preparing to destroy the war bands. The Comanches north of the Red River could not have withstood much more of the pounding they had received from Ford and Van Dorn. The Pehnah-terkuh were finished; the other bands were showing signs of physical and psychic exhaustion. The end of the autonomous Plains cultures seemed to be approaching swiftly. But now, as the Anglo-American civilization turned from wresting the continent from the aborigines toward a bloody, intestine struggle, the tribes were to receive a brief, though hardly merciful, stay of execution.

5

TRAGIC REPRIEVE:
THE CIVIL WAR
AND THE AMERINDIANS

During the Civil War, the Indians, unrestrained
by the United States Army, held carnival across the plains—
north to south and east to west—looting, pillaging, and marauding
over a wide area, especially to the west and south
of the federal troops at Fort Leavenworth,
burning out the stage stations and
disrupting travel across the plains.
  —Mildred P. Mayhall, *Indian Wars of Texas*

THE SITUATION THAT DEVELOPED ON THE GREAT PLAINS DURING 1861–65 was a classic example of the nature of the ebb and flow of relative power along a civilized/barbarian frontier. At the beginning of the American Civil War the tribes were everywhere on the defensive. Epidemics had ravaged them. The cavalry was penetrating their remote sanctuaries and terrorizing them on their home grounds. Most of the Plains peoples already understood that their autonomy was ending; all that remained were the final, decisive blows to end all resistance. But when the Civil War halted the offensive against the Plains Amerindians, this did not bring peace. What happened was that the warlike tribes were given a respite; the Comanches, Cheyennes, and Kiowas threw off much of their earlier demoralization. They soon discovered that the white soldiers had departed from the frontier, and if the reasons were unfathomable to the Plains warriors, they reacted to the situation according to their culture. The power balance did not and could not, in this situation, remain stable. The flow of aggression was reversed, and terror again descended on the white frontier.

446

Now, however, the range of Amerindian warfare extended far beyond the Texas plains. During the 1850s large white communities had been created in Minnesota, Kansas, and along the fringes of the Great Plains. Mining camps and other small settlements had been established in the Rockies; a network of communications, roads and stage stations, had spread across the prairie. Thus a greater area was vulnerable to Indian warfare than ever before.

By 1864, this entire frontier region had become a bloody shambles. Communications were disrupted; many communities were under virtual siege; and in Texas the white frontier actually retracted. Almost unnoticed during the slaughters in the East, the West formed a secondary front, where Americans and Amerindians carried on a vast and terrible guerrilla warfare. And in its way, this secondary western front was as tragic as the secession holocaust. White-Amerindian conflict took on deeper and bloodier dimensions; a new generation was brutalized; and both whites and Amerindians suffered terribly from a long attrition.

It is understandable that while the greater question of the form of the American republic and the shape of its society was hammered out between North and South on the battlefield, both the Confederacy and the United States were forced to leave the West largely to its own resources. There were few regular forces west of the Mississippi, and even these were of dubious quality. It was fully understood at the time that many of the men who chose to serve in the various state or territorial militias did so deliberately because they were not willing to fight to preserve or destroy the Union, but also that many of the western volunteers hoped to avoid the greater dangers of the eastern battlefields. Though they wore the same uniforms and have often been confused with the pre-1861 regulars, the various Minnesota, New Mexico, Colorado, and other territorial forces comprised a less trained and much less disciplined army. The Confederate or Texas state militias left to defend the Brazos frontier were of even poorer quality. The best regular officers and troops departed to serve under Grant and Thomas, Hood, Johnston, and Lee, in the Mississippi Valley and in Virginia. This, and the fact that there were never sufficient territorials in any case, lent the western operations their remarkable savagery.

Along the white frontiers from Colorado to Texas, conditions reverted to something like the Appalachian frontier in the mid-eighteenth century. Frontier feelings and prejudices prevailed. Toward the end of the Civil War period, the white-red struggle devolved into a series of slaughters and countermassacres, in an all-out ethnic warfare.

The pattern of events should have laid to rest forever all future mythologies of "cowboys and Indians." Left to their own resources, the various western pioneers held out very poorly against horse Indians. Although armed and brutalized, the mid-nineteenth-century frontier people could not handle the Indian problem. By 1864, from Pikes Peak to the Brazos bottoms the ranchers, miners, wagon masters, and farmers of the West were in states of panic and near-demoralization. Texas ranchers had "forted up" like their fore-bears in Daniel Boone's Kentucky. Wagons no longer crossed the Kansas plains, and flour reached the astronomical price of $45 a sack in the Denver settlement. The frontier was paralyzed, and worse, approaching a sort of hysteria.

This was not a warfare that the Plains tribes had any long-term hope of winning. But the few, valiant, and now utterly hostile peoples of the southwestern plains did not understand the true nature of the ebb of white power. Initial victories restored their hope, and even much of the old Comanche arrogance. In the march of the American nation, the stay of execution was brief, and the warfare in retrospect appeared minor. But it wiped out twenty years of white "progress," sowed new hatreds, and in the end, caused immense havoc for the future.

NINETY PERCENT OF THE TEXAS SETTLERS HAD COME FROM THE southern states and culture; therefore, it was inevitable that once secession began, Texas should enter the Confederacy. On Secession Day, March 16, 1861, 2,700 federal troops were deployed along the Texas frontiers. These regiments immediately dissolved. Some federal soldiers were able to leave the state; some were made prisoners; and large numbers, particularly officers of southern origin, resigned to accept commissions with the Confederate States Army. This dissolution destroyed forever the 2nd Cavalry. The frontier forts were all abandoned, and some were burned upon evacuation.

Confederate forces out of Texas invaded the Indian Territory and

seized three military posts, forcing the United States Army to retreat above the Kansas line.

The Indian policies of the Union and the Confederacy were essentially the same: both tried to recruit the settled or "civilized"
tribes while attempting to make peace treaties with the still autonomous and warlike Plains peoples. Initially, Confederate Indian
Commissioner Albert Pike enjoyed great success with both groups
of Amerindians.

The white men's war caused enormous bloodshed, havoc, and
confusion among the long-settled eastern tribes in the Indian Territory, although in the long run this had no real effect on the course
of the war itself. The more advanced tribes, all coming from the
southern states, were slaveholders. Over the years, they had captured hundreds of runaway Negroes and held them in servitude,
and for this reason the Cherokee, Choctaw, Chickasaw, and Seminole tribal councils "seceded" from the United States and declared
for the Confederacy. Some tribes split; the Cherokees were not
completely united on the issue. The Creeks, Shawnees, Delawares,
and others tended to side with the Union. The Indian Territory
tribes began to fight their own "Civil War," but then and later the
conflict had much deeper roots in tribal hatreds and antipathies
than in slavery or extraneous white ideological issues. In 1861, the
other tribes inflicted a terrible massacre on the Creeks, killing seven
hundred and driving the survivors into Kansas to seek the protection of the Union forces.

Commissioner Pike was anxious to make peace treaties with the
Comanches, Kiowas, and other wild tribes. He was able to secure
the help of the "Confederate" Amerindians, and was assisted by the
fact that for two years the bluecoats had been at war with the
Kiowas and Comanches. In August 1861, Pike held a convocation of
both wild and agency Indians at the former federal Wichita agency
in the Indian Territory, which the Confederates now administered.
Significantly, the remnants of the Pehnahterkuh were considered
and listed as "agency Indians," for most of this band had now settled at the agency to which Robert Neighbors had delivered them.
However, Pike assembled at least a dozen chiefs from all the important bands but one: representatives of the Nawkohnee, now called
Dertsahnaw-yehkuh, Those Who Move Often, the Kuhtsoo-ehkuh
or Meat Eaters, the Yampahreekuh, and even a remnant of the

Tahneemuh, the Liver Eaters. The only Comanches not represented were the Kwerhar-rehnuh, the Antelopes of the Llano Estacado, who still would have nothing at all to do with white men.

Pike, who called his treaty "A Treaty with the Comanches of the Prairies and Staked Plains," largely wrote it from old scripts. Both sides were to return any captives, the Comanches to be paid for theirs; the Confederate government was to supply the bands with food and goods "until they could become self-sustaining," as well as cattle to start herds. In return, the treaty read, "the Confederate states ask nothing of the Nerm except that they prepare to support themselves, and live in peace and quietness." As Wallace and Hoebel observed in their study of the People, nothing was asked except that the People should cease to be Comanches forthwith, by giving up war and settling down as ranchers.

The Confederate government provided more than $60,000 in supplies to implement the treaty. Other than the Pehnahterkuh, the bands never came to the agency except to demand presents, but when they did Agent Mathew Leeper was able to supply them for about a year. During this year, there were almost no raids on the Texas frontier. The treaty was one reason. The other was that the battered bands out on the prairie did not yet sense the growing weakness of the white frontier.

The situation in the Indian Territory, however, remained highly unstable. There was a series of massacres and retaliations between the reservation or agency Indians. The Tonkawa remnants that had been removed to Oklahoma by Neighbors were almost exterminated, ostensibly because of their "cannibalism," but more likely because the tribe's services as scouts for the Texans had made them hated by the other Amerindians. Federal agents also filtered back into the Indian Territory by 1862. Some tribes changed sides: the Cherokees defected and rejoined the Union. And in October 1862, "Union" Delawares and Shawnees raided and destroyed the Confederate Wichita agency. The Pehnahterkuh Comanches were dispersed into the Wichita mountains, and the link between the Plains bands and the Confederates was broken.

The federal agents now tried to restore relations with the Kiowas and Comanches, who posed dangers to Union communications along the Santa Fe Trail. The band councils, approached for an armistice, apparently saw no reason why they should not accept presents from each faction of warring white men. Comanche treaty-making had evolved: it was becoming as cynical as the Anglo-American. A party of Comanche and Kiowa chiefs was taken to Washington, where, in April 1863, they reaffirmed the old treaty of 1853. The tribes promised not to harass the Santa Fe Trail and to hand back white captives, in return for which the United States was to resume a $25,000 annuity. This treaty turned out to be one of the true disasters for whites in the Southwest.

The Senate failed to ratify it. But meanwhile, thousands of Comanches, Kiowas, and Kiowa Apaches had drifted toward the Arkansas River, expecting handsome disbursements, for word of the terms had spread rapidly. By the fall of 1863, when no goods arrived, many of the tribesmen had become angry over the apparent perfidy. There is evidence that disgruntled Comanches and Kiowas held councils with the Cheyennes and Arapahos and Dakotas, discussing war. These events led directly to the mass "outbreaks" across the southern plains in 1864.

Trouble had already reappeared in Texas. Soon after the destruction of the Confederate agency in the Indian Territory, war bands probed the Brazos frontier. These discovered that the horse soldiers and Rangers had vanished, and that the frontier lay open and inviting.

The Confederates in Texas had never intended to neglect the Indian frontier. In addition to the diplomatic efforts in the Indian Territory, a mounted regiment, commanded by Neighbors' old nemesis, John R. Baylor, was assigned to garrison the abandoned federal forts along the one hundredth meridian. But Baylor was now caught up in far more grandiose schemes than guarding against Indians. He launched an invasion of the New Mexico and Arizona territories, reaching Tucson and establishing a provisional Confederate government, manned by Texans. This pulled other Texas forces west, and General H. H. Sibley, with three regiments, seized Santa Fe in February 1862. However, the federal forces were strongly reinforced out of California, and the Colorado Territorials under Chivington decisively defeated the Texan column. Badly mauled, the Sibley-Baylor expedition was driven back across the El Paso–San Antonio trail; the three Texas regiments were almost completely destroyed.

This campaign had terrible consequences for the western counties of Texas. The wasted regiment could not be replaced by the Confederacy or the state. By the end of 1862 Texas had sent more than 62,000 young men to the southern armies; there were only 27,000 males between the ages of sixteen and sixty within the entire state. The good men and good horses that might have protected the frontier were leaving their bones scattered across a dozen states from the Mississippi to Virginia. The manpower that remained for use on the frontier was unwarlike, ill-equipped, undisciplined, and untrained. The posses and local militias (some called by imposing military names) were as useless for anti-Indian warfare as they had always been on the plains frontier, and, even worse, they were now of lesser quality.

The old terror inevitably returned, as the Comanches and Kiowas found they could ride to the Brazos with impunity. By 1863 many northwestern counties were under virtual siege: Clay, Cooke, Denton, Jack, Montague, Palo Pinto, Parker, Young, and Wise all suffered from "murder" raids, and now a new phenomenon, the cattle raid. The raiders had discovered that they could trade livestock to the federal army contractors in New Mexico and the Indian Territory. Union agents thus loosed a new form of warfare on the far-western Confederate frontier. Ten thousand head of cattle were driven off during 1863–64.

By 1864 the entire frontier was crumbling. Thousands of terrified women, children, and old men packed their belongings and abandoned their fields and homes. Within two years great stretches of the lands settled in the 1850s again became depopulated. The true frontier retracted eastward between one and two hundred miles, back to where the settlement line had rested in the mid-1840s. Comanches again swarmed near Fredericksburg and the vicinity of Austin.

The few families who stubbornly remained in the new territories were closely congregated for mutual protection. They erected log stockades, square in shape with picket bastions, as places of refuge in times of danger. A few forts, such as old Fort Belknap on the Brazos, were manned by wartime "Rangers." Most such forts were garrisoned like those of an earlier century, by embattled settlers. The people of Young County, which had been organized along Elm Creek soon after the removal of the nearby Brazos and Clear Fork reservations, built Fort Murrah. There were also Blair's Fort in

Eastland County, and Fort Hubbard and Fort Owl Head nearby. The whites huddling around these stockades suffered constant alarms, cattle raids, and casualties.

During 1864 there were fewer raids, but the Comanche war parties increased in size, a sure sign of growing Amerindian boldness.

The Brazos frontier was not the only region affected. To the north, the Cheyennes and their allies and the Kiowas and Comanches had taken the warpath against the Colorado-Kansas settlements. The Santa Fe Trail was paralyzed; stage stations were attacked and burnt out and wagon trains massacred. This did great damage to Union military communications in the West. It also halted immigration, which never entirely ceased during the Civil War, as hundreds of whites were slain on the Kansas-Colorado plains and the survivors flocked to the nearest military outposts.

This situation, the great "outbreak" of 1864 on the southwestern plains, became intolerable. The various territorial and army forces in this country began organized campaigns against all Indians. When these started, they had the effect of pushing many Comanches and Kiowas south into Texas. In the early fall of 1864, some thousands of Comanches and Kiowas camped along the Canadian River in the Llano Estacado, and along the Red River south of the Wichitas. Spoiling for war, they came under the influence of an ambitious leader known as Little Buffalo.

Little Buffalo had carefully scouted the Brazos country on earlier raids. He moved from camp to camp, holding council, telling the Kiowas and Kiowa Apaches that the horse soldiers were gone, and that the *tejano* Rangers were too few to matter. He held out the vision of great victories, with immense spoil and prestige accruing to all warriors who rode with him. By October 1864, he had gathered at least seven hundred warriors; he crossed the Red into Texas with a great band of approximately a thousand allied and associated Amerindians. Large numbers joined from all the northern bands of Comanches, and the famous war chief Aw-soant-sai-mah (Aperian Crow) led a powerful contingent of the Kiowas. Many horses were assembled, for Little Buffalo had learned Buffalo Hump's hard lesson: this was to be a heavy but a lightning blow, with a quick return from the Brazos.

On October 13th Little Buffalo's horde crossed the Brazos about ten miles above Fort Belknap, where Elm Creek poured into the river. The Comanches and Kiowas swarmed up the creek bottoms, which were inhabited by between fifty and sixty stubborn white frontier people. The raiders, bold in their numbers, split and rode along both banks at noon on a bright, crisp, beautiful day. The burning and killing began.

The Comanches came upon a settler and his son, who were looking in the brush for strayed livestock. They killed, stripped, and mutilated the man and boy. They then moved along the creek to the Fitzpatrick ranch. Here there were three women and a number of children. The men were away, gathering supplies at the Weatherford trading post. As the Indians rode up, young Susan Durgan seized a gun and rushed outside. She fired on the warriors, but they cut her down and stripped her naked, mutilated her corpse and left it lying in the yard. They captured the other women and children: Elizabeth Fitzpatrick, Mary Johnson—the wife of Nigger Britt Johnson, a black man who was legally a slave but treated as a free man on this frontier by an owner who had inherited him—and three black and three white youngsters. Two warriors quarreled over who had seized the oldest black child, and settled the matter by killing the boy. The women, the two surviving Negro children, young Joe Carter, aged twelve, and Lottie and Millie Durgan, aged three and eighteen months, were carried off.

But now smoke was rising in the clear air, and the shots had been heard. The Hamby men, one of whom was a wounded Confederate veteran on recuperation leave, rushed their women and children into hiding in a cave and mounted their horses to spread the alarm through the valley. The Hambys raced along the stream, firing at pursuing Comanches as they rushed from homestead to homestead. The Williams family hid in the thick brush, guarded by a fifteen-year-old boy with a rifle. While Judge Williams' house was looted, the women and children were not discovered.

The two Hamby men, with Tom (Doc) Wilson, rushed for the George Bragg ranch house, which was a small but picketed and sodded cabin, built to serve as a fort. As the three men abandoned their horses in the ranch yard, Doc Wilson was struck in the heart by an arrow. He staggered into the house, jerked the missile free, and died in a gush of blood. George Bragg, five white women, a Negro girl, and a large brood of children were in the house. The ranch was immediately surrounded by a horde of howling warriors.

As Thornton Hamby, the Confederate soldier, later said half-humorously, he might have hid under the bed—except that three families of refugees already had preempted that dubious spot of safety. With young Hamby coolly directing the defense, the whites prepared to stand off a siege.

The women were directed to reload all the rifles and pistols. One woman stood at Thornton Hamby's elbow and gave him great assistance. As the Comanches rushed the cabin, trying to dig out the pickets, he opened fire from the tiny gun ports that were a feature of all west Texas ranch houses. The elder Hamby killed one Indian, but he had suffered four wounds, and old George Bragg was not much help. Young Hamby saved the whites as he emptied pistol after pistol pressed into his hands by the desperate women who reloaded them at a table. All afternoon, while some unseen warrior blew mournfully on a captured army bugle, Hamby held the fort. He was wounded again; then he killed Little Buffalo himself, who was directing the attack, with a lucky shot. The Comanches withdrew, after a few parting shots and a bugle blast.

Meanwhile, the Pevelers, Harmonsons, and other local clans had assembled within the walls of Fort Murrah. The warriors who now swarmed everywhere along Elm Creek were frustrated by this small stockade. They stayed beyond rifle range, rampaging up and down the creek. France Peveler, who had a spy glass, saw warriors gathered in the mesquite around two white men. He told his companions that the Comanches were killing "old man McCoy and his son right now." One of them told him to keep quiet. The McCoy women had made it to the fort, and would be "mightily distressed" if they knew that the Indians had their menfolk.

On this same afternoon, realizing that there was trouble, Lieutenant N. Carson of Bourland's Border Regiment of militia rode toward Elm Creek from Fort Belknap with fourteen men. He struck some three hundred warriors. Five militiamen were killed at once, several others wounded; the rest fled for their lives. A stand would have been futile in any case. The militia did save several women on their mad dash to safety at Fort Murrah. They came in riding double; some horses were pin-cushioned with Comanche-Kiowa shafts.

That night, while the courageous Thornton Hamby left the Bragg ranch under the cover of darkness and slipped through a screen of warriors to reach the Fitzpatrick place and bury the corpses there, the survivors in Fort Murrah prepared for what they believed would be a dawn attack. They could see Indians moving constantly on the ridges, and a great fire blazed up in the north as somewhere a house went up. The settlers agreed that someone had to ride for help. The state troopers (Carson's report maintained that they "acted with unexampled bravery") absolutely refused to leave the fort, so two settlers, France Peveler and a man named Fields, volunteered to go. They slipped past the nervous outside picket, a boy of seventeen who had taken this dangerous duty beyond the walls, and rode along the low ground, so that the Indians would not "sky-light" them against the ridges. They passed a nude white body in the dark, and a pitiable horse pinned to the ground by a lance, still trembling in its agony. They dared not stop; when they were clear, they galloped the full six miles to Belknap.

All the militia was gone—out hunting Indians, someone said. But among the people forted up at Belknap, a young boy, Chester Tackett, volunteered to ride seventy-five miles to Veal's Station. Tackett slipped away at one in the morning, and changing horses at every white cabin he passed, arrived at Veal's Station, the closest white settlement, at nine. But again there was no militia to be found. Another volunteer raced on to Decatur, another thirty miles. Here, at sundown, Major Quayle, commanding the local militia, heard the news. Quayle pushed his men for sixty miles without halting, until, when he was still some twenty miles from Elm Creek, he met a rider who told him that the Indians had withdrawn. He rode after the Comanches for about a hundred miles, because the raiders had taken white women and children, but at last broke off pursuit.

This was a classic frontier Texas Comanche raid, different only in the greater scope such raids were once again assuming. Eleven settlers had been killed, eleven homes destroyed, seven women and children carried off. The frontier people survived as they could, both by heroism and flight. The militia, as always, arrived too late. The Comanches and Kiowas had taken almost everything, and what they could not carry or had no use for, they had destroyed. Flour sacks were emptied, or mixed with sand, livestock was killed. That winter was a hard one on Elm Creek.

The Elm Creek raid had its aftermath, as did every Comanche descent. Britt Johnson returned to the Fitzpatrick ranch to find his son buried, his wife and two small children gone. Johnson was determined to rescue his family. With the help of the Hambys and others, he got together a pack horse, provisions, a rifle and two six-shooters, and struck out north-northwest, into the vast wilderness that lay beyond the Brazos settlements.

After covering sixty miles, the courageous black frontiersman reached the Wichita River. Here he came across a lone Comanche guarding a horse herd. Johnson could "talk Mexican," which most Comanches and Kiowas understood, and he made the peace sign and advanced boldly. The warrior, and a party of Comanches who rode up, were more curious than hostile, and they accepted truce with the black man. Some of the Comanches were Pehnahterkuh who had been at the Clear Fork Reservation, and they remembered Johnson. Johnson, meanwhile, ignored the fact that he recognized the Peveler and Johnson brands on some of the Comanche horses. He had found some of the raiders.

The friendly Pehnahterkuh told Johnson that there was a single white woman in their camp, but that the Kiowas had taken all the *negros*. They agreed to let him ride with them to the encampment. This meeting, and the casual truce Johnson forged, was an immense stroke of luck. From now forward he enjoyed hospitality, and even a certain interest among the Comanches in his project.

He found Elizabeth Fitzpatrick in the camp, which lay somewhere on the high Canadian. From her he learned that Little Buffalo and twenty warriors had been killed at Elm Creek, which had caused the great war party to break off and retreat. On the return, the Comanches had killed little Joe Carter, Mrs. Fitzpatrick's son by a former marriage, because the boy took sick. The two Durgan children and Johnson's family had been taken by Kiowas. Elizabeth Fitzpatrick begged Britt Johnson to try to ransom all of them; she was a relatively rich woman in Texas and would pay any price.

Johnson now made four incredible journeys into the heart of *Comanchería*, searching for the captives. He could not have succeeded without the good offices of the friendly Pehnahterkuh, who not only instructed him in dealings with the "tricky Kiowas" but gave him two warriors for escort. He made a deal for Elizabeth Fitzpatrick and brought her out. He located his wife and bought her back for the equivalent of two dollars and a half. He also ransomed his children and little Lottie Durgan, Mrs. Fitzpatrick's granddaughter. He failed to bring out Millie Durgan; she had been adopted into the family of the Koh-eet-senko Aperian Crow and was not for sale.

Elizabeth Fitzpatrick, who owned much land and many cattle, fared better on return than most captives; she was able to marry again. Johnson's indomitable efforts bespoke his own feelings for his wife, and her return was a happy one. There was grief over the Durgan child, who was never seen again. However, the grief was perhaps misplaced. Sixty-six years afterward, the old Kiowa woman Saintohoodi Goombi was identified at Lawton, Oklahoma, as the Durgan girl. Her life had not been an unhappy one. In the clannish Kiowa circles she had been raised as the daughter of a great chief; she had married and reared a family. She had no memory of her origins or white blood, and when she died in 1934, she had made it clear that she desired nothing whatever from her former people.

Nigger Britt, meanwhile, had won the respect of the entire white frontier. After the war, in a Texas harvesting the bitter fruits of Reconstruction, he opened a successful freighting business in partnership with three other former slaves, carting supplies between Weatherford and the army forts that were eventually rebuilt in the west. This was extremely dangerous business on this Comanche-infested frontier, but then, as the Brazos country agreed, Britt Johnson was an extremely courageous man.

ALMOST UNSEEN AT THE TIME, THE AMERICAN CIVIL WAR BORE EVIL fruits not only in Texas but throughout the West. The Plains tribes had been sullen and desperate at its beginning. Toward its close, the tribes were still angry, fragmented, and desperate—but they had also become self-confident. What the entire Western frontier got, by 1864, was a horrendous warfare, in which both sides sowed vast evils.

The Santee Sioux uprising in Minnesota in 1862 presaged the form and texture of this struggle. Few of the thousands of white settlers who had arrived on the Mankato in the 1850s were true frontiersmen. Many were farmers coming directly from the East, and many were new European immigrants. Few had ever had contacts with any Amerindian. They were guilty of no crimes against

Amerindians—except that of being part and parcel of a destroying civilization. The bloody, almost mindless rebellion of the Santee, in which hundreds of whites were slaughtered and up to 40,000 made refugees, fleeing from the country, produced first shock and horror, then a call for retaliation. The Siouan uprising revealed something as yet strange to the northern pioneer consciousness: the calculated, not casual, rape of white female captives. One band of Santee, surrounded and facing destruction themselves, indulged in an orgy of torture and degradation of their female captives.

The reaction of the northern territories from Minnesota to Colorado was more hysterical than that of the Texan, pioneer-descended frontier. The Texans arrived in the West with the dehumanization of Indians deeply imbedded in their consciousness, expecting nothing but trouble, believing that the Indians had to be destroyed in the name of peace and progress. The question of whether the calm brutality of the Texans in the face of injuries or the violent, semi-hysterical reaction of the eastern and European immigrants was more horrifying is a matter of individual judgment. The Texans believed in turning loose the Rangers or the cavalry. In Minnesota, once the blue-coated volunteer regiments had crushed Santee resistance in the forests, mobs clamored for the execution of hundreds of Indian prisoners.

Hundreds would have been hanged, except for the intervention of President Lincoln, who required the army commander to act with great restraint. Lincoln refused to permit the execution of prisoners except where "guilt" was proven. In the end, thirty-eight were hanged, and most historians believed that many of these were innocents who had taken no part in the uprising. The warlike tribesmen had run off to the Dakota plains, but they were hardly safe there, since the troops pursued them. The Union general Sibley, without supplying details, reported that he had killed "500 Indians" on a single punitive expedition. Sibley commanded volunteers, raised in the local communities, who came from the same mobs that had screamed at the wretched captives in their cages, and had even broken through on one occasion and castrated several warriors.

As the Kansas, Colorado, and New Mexico regions were subjected to the same horrors as the Texan frontier, the white newcomers in these territories were gripped by similar hysteria. Between

1863 and 1865 thousands of "Union" soldiers were raised for the various territorial regiments, but none of these were used against the Confederates. After 1862, there was no Confederate threat in the West; the Indian problem was primary.

For many of the territorial volunteers the Indian wars had become personal. The old hands, such as Jim Bridger, who advised and scouted for the army, and Kit Carson, who commanded the New Mexico militia, had lived among the tribes and kept a certain equanimity. They understood the humanity of the Amerindians beneath their barbarity. But these men were in a minority. Carson's grim subordinate Captain, later Colonel, Pfeiffer, of the New Mexico territorials, had buried the mutilated bodies of his wife and her maid, seized by Indians while on a picnic outing. Pfeiffer became a legend in his own time, not only among shocked whites, but among the Amerindians, who said that whenever he rode out, the wolves came down from the mountains and hovered behind his column, certain of Indian carrion. It was Pfeiffer, as Carson's good right hand, who trapped the Navajos in the Canyon de Chelly in 1864 and destroyed them so completely that they never made war on white men again. Despite requests of the regular military establishment for magnanimity and rehabilitation of the stock-raising Navajos, the survivors were herded into arid country and left to starve by the territorial forces. It was these Navajos that Carleton, the Union commander in New Mexico, saved by putting his own soldiers on half rations and feeding the Indians through the winter.

The Indian-fighting regiment recruited in Denver in the summer of 1864 was mustered in an atmosphere of hatred and hysteria. This was the summer that the Cheyennes and Comanches and their allies ran amok, destroying communications and trapping hundreds of hapless travelers. Cut off, the Colorado mining camps were almost starving. J. M. Chivington, the former Methodist minister who was now a brigadier general in the Army of the United States, the officer who had saved New Mexico for the Union, enlisted his territorial volunteers for one purpose: to destroy Indians. To spur recruiting, the mutilated corpses of a white immigrant, his wife, and two children were displayed in the center of Denver beside the drum and enlistment table. Chivington did not dissemble. He instructed his regiment: "Kill and scalp all, big and little; nits make lice."

The Colorado territorials attacked a large encampment of Cheyennes on Sand Creek. This was the village of Black Kettle, who had been at war but had recently made truce and, according to some accounts, flew the American flag above his tipi. The volunteers came down on the camp. They bombarded the tipis with howitzer shells, then raced among the tents, stabbing and shooting. When the screaming and bloodlust was over, there were three hundred Cheyenne bodies scattered along Sand Creek. Twenty-six of these were warriors; the rest were women and children. Throughout the entire territory, Chivington's coup was hailed as a great victory.

The great difference between the Chivington massacre and at least a dozen similar actions was simply that Chivington, who by his own lights was a hero, received more publicity. Many of his volunteers shot squaws and bayoneted Cheyenne children with relish, but the heterogeneous Colorado column also contained many men whose stomachs revolted. As detailed descriptions, which were rare in the West, emerged and were published in newspapers, a wave of horror swept the distant East. But significantly, a fact not always noted by historians, the outcry was confined to the East and to the regular army, which disavowed Chivington as a volunteer officer and forced him to resign to avoid court-martial. No action was or could be brought against the regiment, as it had passed out of service.

The army had its own reasons for this condemnation, including both jealousy and the desire to free itself of blame for similar actions. For all commanders in the West were now operating under "pursue and punish" orders. Shortly after the Chivington massacre, General P. E. Connor at Fort Laramie in the Wyoming Territory issued written instructions to "kill all Indian males over 12." Sibley had killed more Sioux, in the same fashion, in the Dakota territory. The outcry that was made over killing women was not joined in by the West. The condemnation of using howitzers against the village was not even understood, for the mountain howitzer had become one of the military's most effective tools in all Indian operations. The army's great distaste stemmed from the fact that Chivington's men displayed the undisciplined savagery of raw recruits; they ran amok, scalping and mutilating, matching Cheyenne and Comanche ferocity in every respect.

William Bent, Kit Carson, and several other old hands were outraged, but not by the details of the massacre—these men had, after all, witnessed many massacres perpetrated by Indians. What angered them was that Chivington had broken the code by allowing his men to attack a village under truce.

The making of Chivington and his Coloradoans into scapegoats obscured rather than revealed what was really happening in the West. For as General Sherman wrote in a defense of army operations, this was "inglorious war" at best. Any campaign against the savages was unpleasant duty. It required hunting down and killing, without banners or bugles or all the panoply of the military mythos. The line between battle and massacre was a thin one in this guerrilla warfare. Sherman further advised his officers, in a special instruction, that if the war with the white man "results in annihilation, the Indians have been warned." They were not to be allowed to kill white people, or to impede the progress of the nation. He reassured his officers that he would "not allow charges of cruelty to tie the hands of soldiers on the spot." The soldiers were to "use all powers so that, these Indians, the enemies of our race and of our civilization, shall not again be able to begin and carry on their barbarian warfare. . . ."

Sherman wrote with the eastern newspapers, which had condemned Chivington, and history in mind. But his orders to the army were only a more literate and measured version of what the preacher Chivington had succinctly told his volunteers.

6

MEDICINE LODGE

It is too late . . . We wish only to wander
on the prairie until we die . . .
> —Par-roowah Sermehno (Ten Bears)
> at Medicine Lodge, Kansas, 1867

THE RESPITE GIVEN THE PLAINS TRIBES BY THE CIVIL WAR WAS NOT enough to allow them to rebuild their numbers. In the closing months of that conflict, the United States military commands in the West were moving swiftly to regain the initiative and effect a bloody retribution. While the Colorado militia was mopping up Amerindian villages without regard to guilt or innocence in the wars, Colonel Kit Carson of the New Mexico Territorials had crushed the Navajos. By the fall of 1864, Carson's superior, the district commander General James H. Carleton, was ready to turn the army's attention to the Comanches and Kiowas, who all year had raised havoc along the Santa Fe Trail.

Angry bands of southern warriors threatened to cut completely this route of communications with Missouri and the East. During 1864, virtually every wagon train proceeding down the Canadian River to New Mexico was attacked. Even large and powerful parties lost horses and oxen to raiding Amerindians. Small groups, whether military or civilian, had been massacred. In October, therefore, Carleton received orders to restore full communications and to "punish the savages" responsible for the depredations. He authorized Colonel Carson to sweep through the valley of the Canadian with a strong force of New Mexico and California territorials.

463

It was known that large numbers of Comanches and Kiowas were wintering on the rich bison plains of the Texas Panhandle, and it was believed that these Indians would not be prepared to fight a winter campaign.

Carson marched out of Cimarron, New Mexico, in early November with more than three hundred mounted troops and seventy-two Ute and Jicarilla Apache scouts and auxiliaries. The Utes were promised scalps and plunder, and some warriors brought along their women. Carson was well supplied: he had a well-stocked train of twenty-seven wagons and six thousand rounds of ammunition. He was also furnished with two excellent little twelve-pounder mountain howitzers, fitted on special traveling carriages.

The column followed Ute Creek to where it pours into the Canadian, then rode east into the high Texas plains along the broad, flat river bottoms. The scouts went far ahead. At night, Carson camped among tall cottonwoods in the gulches or *cañadas*. The weather was already bitter, with snow flakes appearing. For days he saw no Indians. Then, at sundown on November 24th, the scouts reported an encampment about a day's march to the east, near the old, abandoned Bent and St. Vrain trading post on a small tributary of the Canadian. This place was known as Adobe Walls, from its still standing sun-dried brick structures. Carson at once marched toward the Indians, pushing his column through the frosty night for fifteen miles, allowing no fires or smoking during rest breaks.

He was in sight of the Indian camp at daybreak. Lieutenant George Pettis of the California volunteers, the officer in charge of the two-gun battery, thought he saw gray-white Sibley tents in the distance. Carson informed him that these were the sun-bleached tipis of Plains Indians. The Utes reported a camp or village of 176 lodges. Without scouting farther down the river valley, Carson detached his baggage train with a guard of seventy-five men, and with a squadron of some 250 cavalry attacked across the two-mile-wide valley toward the village. This was open country, surrounded by low hills or ridges, and covered with dry grasses that rose horse-high in many places.

The Ute and Jicarilla auxiliaries left the column and tried to steal the enemies' horse herd. The camp, which was Kiowa Apache, was alerted before the cavalry reached it. The warriors formed a skirmish line to cover the flight of their women and children, who abandoned the tipis and ran for the ridges behind the river. The Plains-culture Athapaskans, who were "Apache" only in dialect, often created a confusion in accounts, which sometimes called them Kiowas, sometimes merely Apaches. This led some whites to believe that there were still Apaches on the Texas plains, and that they sometimes fought alongside Nermernuh—the last unthinkable. The Kiowa Apaches formed an integral part of the Kiowa tribal circle, and on this day one of the great war chiefs of the Kiowas, Dohasan (To'hau-sen, Little Mountain, also often called Sierrito), was in their lodges. Dohasan organized the defense, while also sending for help from Comanche and Kiowa lodges downstream. He rallied the warriors, and his swirling, shooting horsemen slowed the white attack and assured the escape of the women. Carson's cavalry killed one warrior who wore a coat of mail, but when they reached the tipis they were deserted.

Dohasan exhibited great bravery. His horse was shot from under him, but he was rescued and rallied his warriors. The cavalry pushed on against the retreating Kiowa Apaches for about four miles, finally reaching the crumbling Adobe Walls buildings. Here, more and more Indians seemed to be appearing. The whites dismounted, and sheltering their horses behind the trading post, began skirmishing on foot. Carson came up to Adobe Walls with the battery, and now both the old mountain man and the inexperienced Pettis saw another camp of some five hundred lodges rising less than a mile away, along the river.

This was a Comanche encampment, and hundreds of warriors were streaming from it across the prairie. Pettis counted "twelve or fourteen hundred." The Indians formed a long line across the ridges, painting their faces while their chiefs harangued them. The Kiowas, who were also arriving in large numbers, roared the battle songs of their warrior societies. Pettis feared that the horde would charge the white squadron at any moment.

Carson ordered him to throw a few shells at the crowd of Indians. The howitzers were unlimbered, wheeled around, and fired in rapid succession. The shells, screaming over the warriors' heads and bursting just beyond them, seemed to startle the Indians badly. Yelling, the host moved precipitously out of range.

Carson told his troops that the battle was over. He ordered the horses watered in Bent's Creek. The surgeon looked after several wounded men while the others ate cold rations. However, the tall grass was swarming with distant Comanches and Kiowas. Within the hour, a thousand warriors surrounded the trading post, circling and firing from under their horses' bellies. Surprisingly, most of the warriors appeared to be equipped with good firearms. However, the twin cannon broke up their attacks, and the exploding shells knocked down both men and horses at a great distance. The enemy swirled about for several hours, not daring to press too close, while the howitzers killed many on the ridges. But Carson was becoming apprehensive. He had never seen so many Indians. Pettis was sure that there were at least three thousand, and small parties could be seen still arriving. The expedition had marched unwittingly into a vast winter concentration of the tribes on the southern bison range. Carson, with a split command, was worried about his trains. His rear detachment, without cannon, would almost certainly be overwhelmed if the enemy discovered it. He now made a cautious but quite sensible decision: to break out of Adobe Walls and regroup with his supply column, which had his food and ammunition.

The cavalry mounted and retreated behind the fires of the battery, which stayed constantly in action. The Indians fired the grass, but this helped, because the smoke concealed Carson's retiring column. About sundown, the whites arrived back in the deserted Kiowa Apache camp, where Pettis noted that the Ute women had mutilated the corpses of several dead Indians. Carson ordered the lodges fired; then, under the cover of darkness, he moved out rapidly to the west. The enemy did not attack. Three hours later, he rejoined his wagons.

The next dawn, the Indians still held back. Some of the territorial officers insisted that the expedition take up the attack, but Carson ordered a withdrawal. The odds were much too great; Carson, who later wrote that he had never seen Indians who fought with such dash and courage until they were shaken by his artillery, did not make the error of despising horse Indians. He had so far lost only a few dead, and a handful of wounded, while his guns had inflicted serious losses, killing and wounding perhaps two hundred Indians. He could claim a victory, and did this when the column arrived back in New Mexico. Carson's official report stated that he had "taught these Indians a severe lesson," to be "more cautious about how they engage a force of civilized troops."

Privately, he thought himself lucky to have extricated his command. In fact, the howitzers and his own caution had probably saved him from Custer's fate on the Little Big Horn. The Kiowas and Comanches told some Comancheros who were in the Indian camps at the time that except for the "guns that shot twice," the twin battery, they would have killed every white man in the valley of the Canadian. Carson himself said as much to Lieutenant Pettis.

Carson was angered by the presence of Comancheros with the Kiowas and Comanches, which explained the source of the Indians' guns and ammunition. He "had no doubt," he stated, "that the very balls with which my men were killed and wounded were sold by these Mexicans not ten days before." He wanted the New Mexicans barred from trading with the wild tribes while the army was at war with them. This was the beginning of what was to become a historic hatred between the soldiers and the Comancheros.

Overall, the expedition had been less than completely successful, and the white withdrawal left the Indians in full control of the territory. Carson urged that the campaign be renewed, but with at least a thousand troops, who, he thought, would destroy the Indian concentrations in winter. The military authorities were planning extensive, determined operations from Kansas to New Mexico when the sudden collapse of the Confederacy changed everything again. The Comanches and other Plains peoples were now to be granted their second stay within the decade.

A NUMBER OF REASONS BROUGHT EXTENSIVE OPERATIONS AGAINST THE hostile western tribes to a halt following Appomattox. One was that the old regular army had in effect disappeared during the war. The government had chosen not to expand the regular service but to fight the war with regiments of volunteers, later expanded with conscriptees. The professionals were taken to command these state and territorial forces. Most regular officers reached dizzingly high ranks, many going from lieutenancies to general's stars, but in the process the old regular army, as such, dissolved. At the end of the conflict, the regular establishment commanded hordes of civilian soldiers who now had to be disbanded quickly. In the West, the various territorial and militia units had been raised under the national emergency powers. These volunteers were due for release; few were available for permanent duty. In the aftermath of victory, the United States Army became an imposing façade of experienced generals and officers, without rankers. The army thus could not fight the Indians without an extensive and time-consuming reorganization.

But as this reorganization was carried out, establishing an army of 75,000 by 1866, other factors also prevented a resumption of white hostilities against the red men. One was a change in government that caused a pervasive change in western policies. Following the assassination of Lincoln, Congress emerged as the most powerful branch of government and dominated the federal apparatus during the administration of the futile accidental President, Andrew Johnson. This had repercussions that affected the West as well as the South, where Congress was soon carrying out Reconstruction through military occupation.

Whatever name was put on it, the American acquisition of the western territories was always at bottom an imperial venture; as such it was fostered and directed by the executive branch rather than by the legislature. For Congress inevitably reflected the views and imperatives of its major constituencies, which were the older, long-settled, and more populous eastern regions. Although thousands of Americans went West, the great majority of the population were not aroused by the "winning of the West" until the romance was popularized long after the Civil War. The western acquisitions were initiated and pressed by presidents, from Washington to Jefferson to Polk, who normally exceeded the accepted limits of their powers by such moves and measures. Western military operations against Amerindians—which were hard to dignify as "wars"—had come to be decided upon, "declared," and carried out, not by Congress, but by the President and his cabinet. The legislature had paid little attention to Jefferson Davis' cavalry, beyond reluctantly authorizing it.

Between 1865 and 1869 the new President was unable to command the federal bureaucracy or the army against the dominant power of Congress. Congress was understandably far more concerned with bringing the rebellious southern states back into the Union, under the terms of the dominant Republican majority, than with pacifying a handful of recalcitrant savages who posed no danger to the nation. The few whites in the western territories did not comprise a powerful constituency. The Texans, who suffered most, were not even part of the congressional constituency. Texas, despite the rationale that a state could not legally secede and there-fore, even in rebellion, had never left the Union, was treated as an occupied province. Thousands of federal troops arrived in Texas in 1865, but all were stationed in the eastern centers of population to police the former rebels, or sent to the Rio Grande to confront the French intervention in Mexico. None of the old frontier forts was manned.

The nation was understandably sick of warfare and weary of military operations. Congress faced an enormous war debt and was extremely reluctant to spend more millions on the Indian frontiers. The widespread publicity concerning the Chivington affair, and the horror that single massacre aroused in the East, made further puni-tive measures against the tribes unpopular. The authorities were anxious to find peaceful solutions, and this allowed the Office of Indian Affairs, submerged in the 1850s, to reemerge powerfully in the political arena on Capitol Hill. Early in 1865, J. H. Leavenworth, the agent for the Kiowas and Comanches, convinced Washington that he could accomplish more by kindness and understanding toward these Indians than by further killing, and military measures were halted while Leavenworth tried to forge a new peace treaty.

All these factors together brought about a return to the old "peace policy."

The new-old policy appeared practical and humanitarian to men in government distracted by other affairs and with no real under-standing of conditions in the West. But it was nothing of the kind, because it did not take history or circumstances into account. It had several flaws, all of which contributed to disaster.

The only kindness Americans could have done the southern Plains tribes, short of leaving the continent, was to grant them fi-nally a fixed, inviolate territory, halting all encroachments upon it or communications through it. This was impossible. Not even the genuine humanitarians who were appalled by the destruction of the tribes considered abandoning the Santa Fe Trail or halting the con-struction of railroads across the Great Plains. The tribes would simply have to learn to live with these invasions. Further, it was still legally impossible to grant the Comanches any part of the soil of Texas, for the legal fiction that was maintained—that the rebellious states had never been out of the Union—made the 1845 annexation treaty still valid. The Staked Plains and broad Panhandle region, the richest portion of the shrinking bison plains, remained public lands belonging to the state, and no Texan government, however constituted, would ever give them to Indians.

The fact that the federal government neither would nor could halt white passage through *Comanchería* or grant the Indians an adequate hunting range made peace through diplomacy impossible, unless the tribes were first overawed or overwhelmed by force. The Comanches and Kiowas, now thoroughly hostile and even on the offensive, would never submit meekly to dictates that took away their ancient territories and threatened their whole scheme of things.

And the nature of Comanche society, its inherent war ethos and its organizational fragmentation, still made meaningful diplomacy impossible. Even if white men stopped injuring the southern Plains peoples, the culture simply could not coexist with another civilization within their raiding range, unless the civilized frontier was made invulnerable. Peace was possible only if the white frontier presented overwhelming force to the restive warriors. This was perhaps the hardest thing for many Americans to understand. It was an article of faith among many Americans of peaceful persuasion that the Amerindians were driven to war by white injuries, or by poverty, and therefore that Indian wars were the fault of white men. Except for some Texans and a few experienced military men, not one American in a million knew the history or the nature of the Comanche-Kiowa descent upon northern Mexico.

The mere mechanics of European diplomacy were also, as always, virtually impossible to implement. After the 1840s, there were never any paramount chiefs who could influence more than a few warriors. To secure a comprehensive treaty, the whites would have had to bring every single Comanche warrior to council and get his pledged agreement. Finally, the Comanches themselves had become understandably cynical toward councils and treaty-making. Treaties never changed anything. Most warriors did not feel bound by the white-dictated "agreements."

The post-Civil War peace policy, therefore, was another substitution of theory and expediency for knowledge learned in bitter lessons. It paved the way for Americans and Comanches to relive all the old, tragic experiences. It was to result directly in the deaths of some thousands of whites across the western frontiers, deaths that could have been prevented by forceful government policies. It made inevitable the piecemeal destruction of the Indians.

AFTER EXPLORATORY MEETINGS, AGENT LEAVENWORTH AND THE U.S. commissioners met with representatives of the Comanches, Kiowas, and Kiowa Apaches in October 1865, on the Little Arkansas River, near present Wichita, Kansas. Only "six of the nine bands which compose the Comanche tribe" attended. The Kuhtsoo-ehkuh were too busy hunting meat; the remote Kwerhar-rehnuh were still unapproachable on the Llano Estacado. This did not prevent the commissioners from securing a new treaty.

The terms required the tribes to stop raiding, give back all captives, and now to remain within a more limited range than formerly specified. The new "reservation" generally included the western Indian Territory and most of far-west Texas, near New Mexico. This last the commissioners had no authority to award.

None of the parties lived up to the agreement. An investigative commission, sent out in 1866 to determine why there was no peace, reported that all the tribes were flagrantly evading the treaty terms. They rode where they willed, they raided, they took more captives. The investigators also wrote that the annuity goods delivered by the government were so shoddy that the blankets were hardly fit to be used under Comanche saddles, and many Indians were not bothering to show up to get them. The army officers stationed in the Indian Territory were "utterly ignorant of the Indian character and of the proper method of dealing with Indians." The investigators predicted a much-widened warfare the next spring unless something was done.

The report resulted in the appointment of a new Indian Peace Commission by Congress in the summer of 1867. The commission was instructed to correct deficiencies and secure a lasting peace with all the southern Plains tribes. This meant a new council and a newer treaty, and led to the last, sad charade performed in the West between Americans and the southern Plains Amerindians.

A great council was convoked at Medicine Lodge Creek, in the present Barbour County, Kansas, in October 1867. Comanches, Kiowas, Kiowa Apaches, Cheyennes, and Arapahos attended, but again the Kwerhar-rehnuh and part of the Kuhtsoo-ehkuh refused to come. Some warriors stayed away because of indifference, some from fear, and some simply because they believed that they did not know how to deal with white men. Still, Medicine Lodge was the most representative gathering on the plains.

This last great council followed the pattern that was now almost a ritual. Both sides deliberately made a great effort to impress the other. The American commission arrived with a large escort of soldiers, drawn up in dress uniforms. The chiefs appeared fully armed, backed by warriors gaudy in council paint that had taken hours to prepare. The army set up field kitchens to dispense food and coffee so that there would be no interruption of important business. Presents were exchanged—some Comanches came early, hoping to get choicer gifts. Finally, the chiefs, commissioners, and officers sat together in a circle, with followers and interpreters in the background. The peace pipe was passed in unbroken silence. The Plains warriors were naturally grave and dignified at such ceremonies; the whites tried to match their demeanor. When each participant had taken a puff from the brass pipe, the commissioners opened the proceedings.

The whites stated the purpose of the council, according to the wishes of the Great Father. The tribes were to be given lands away from the white settlements and travel routes, so that there would not be war between the peoples. The tribes would also be given food, seeds, and instruction in farming. They would receive tools, and a carpenter would be furnished to show them how to build houses. The Great Father was also prepared to build them schools and furnish a doctor for their children. Annuity goods—$25,000 worth of clothing and other things as might "seem proper" to their "condition"—would be furnished them for thirty years. In return, the tribes must cease all wars against the white men, and not interfere with the roads, rails, and forts that would be constructed in their country.

The commissioners expressed their love for their red brothers and reminded them of the vast power of the Great Father. They told the assembled chiefs that the Indians had behaved badly. The warriors

The Koh-eet-senko Set-tainte or White Bear, c. 1870.
Photograph by William S. Soule.

were still raiding in Texas and Kansas. Now the whites were willing to hear the Indians' side of it: if they had been wronged by white men, they were to say it, but if they had wronged the whites, they should admit it.

The aged Kiowa Koh-eet-senko Set-tainte or White Bear, whom the whites called Satanta, spoke first for the Amerindians. His oration was defiant, even belligerent. He said bluntly that the Kiowas did not want schools or "medicine houses," and that the Kiowa warriors would never submit to performing labor. To Set-tainte, this ended the argument.

Par-roowah Sermehno, or Ten Bears, a chief of the Yampah-reekuh, spoke for the Comanches. Ten Bears was as rehearsed in his speechmaking as Demosthenes, and he stunned the white commissioners with his powers. His words were set down and published in the record of the proceedings, and they still stand as one of the finest examples of Amerindian oratory. His speech was a splendid expression of the People's views: simple but intelligent, both logical and illogical, honest and self-serving, with a true but limited perspective, highly personalized, and at last, despairing:

My heart is filled with joy when I see you here, as the brooks fill with water when the snows melt in the spring; and I feel glad as the ponies do when the fresh grass starts in the beginning of the year. . . .

My people have never first drawn a bow or fired a gun against the whites. There has been trouble between us . . . my young men have danced the war dance. But it was not begun by us. It was you who sent out the first soldier. . . .

Two years ago, I came upon this road, following the buffalo, that my wives and children might have their cheeks plump and their bodies warm. But the soldiers fired on us . . . so it was upon the Canadian. Nor have we been made to cry once alone. The blue-dressed soldiers and the Utes came out from the night . . . and for campfires they lit our lodges. Instead of hunting game they killed my braves, and the warriors of the tribe cut short their hair for the dead.

So it was in Texas. They made sorrow in our camps, and we went out like the buffalo bulls when the cows are attacked. When we found them we killed them, and their scalps hang in our lodges. The Comanches are not weak and blind, like . . . pups . . . when seven sleeps old. They are strong and far-sighted, like grown horses. We took their road and we went on it. The white women cried and our women laughed.

Par-roowah Sermehno or Ten Bears, civil chief of the Yampahreekuh, wearing peace medal.

But there are things which you have said to me which I do not like. They were not sweet like sugar, but bitter like gourds. You have said that you want to put us on a reservation, to build us houses and make us medicine lodges. I do not want them. I was born under the prairie, where the wind blew free and there was nothing to break the light of the sun. I was born where there were no enclosures and everything drew a free breath. I want to die there and not within walls. I know every stream and every wood between the Rio Grande and the Arkansas. I have hunted and lived over that country. I live like my fathers before me and like them I lived happily.

When I was in Washington the Great Father told me that all the Comanche land was ours, and that no one should hinder us in living on it. So, why do you ask us to leave the rivers, and the sun, and the wind, and live in houses? Do not ask us to give up the buffalo for the sheep. The young men have heard talk of this and it has made them sad and angry. Do not speak of it more. I love to carry out the talk I get from the Great Father. When I get goods and presents, I and my people feel glad, since it shows that he keeps us in his eye.

If the Texans had kept out of my country, there might have been peace. But that which you now say we must live in, is too small. The Texans have taken away the places where the grass grew the thickest and the timber was best. Had we kept that, we might have done the things you ask. But it is too late. The whites have the country which we loved, and we wish only to wander on the prairie until we die . . .

Other speakers said essentially the same thing. Like Ten Bears, they represented themselves as men of peace, unwilling to fight the white men. But they were unwilling to agree to any further encroachments upon their historic ranges, either by whites or other red men. Without the Texas ranges, *Comanchería* was too small. They did not want the soldiers to put buildings in their country. There was no need for the peoples to farm so long as there were buffalo, and there would be plenty of buffalo if the whites would stop hunting them. They had no trust in the Indian agents' promises to take care of them. They had all seen the "white" Indians, those who had submitted and lived at agencies. Those peoples had once been proud and strong; now they were weak and poor, and could no longer manage their affairs without running to the white men. The free peoples despised them; they would never willingly give up the ways of their fathers and become like the reservation Indians.

The commissioners and soldiers listened to all this patiently; it changed nothing, because the Peace Commission had decided all the issues before the council opened. While the whites wanted peace, there could be no real bargaining. The terms were an ultimatum: if the chiefs agreed, they would get presents and annuities; if they did not, there was in the background a strong threat of a renewed war that would destroy the tribes.

General William T. Sherman, representing the army, expressed this bluntly and honestly. He told the chiefs that no matter what they wanted, they had to give up the old ways and follow the ways of the white men. They could not stop the roads and rails coming into their hunting ranges. They would have to learn to live like white settlers, from farming and ranching. The "former agreements" made by the Great Father had "not made allowance for the rapid growth of the white race." Sherman told the Indians that "you can no more stop this than you can stop the sun or moon; you must submit and do the best you can."

Sherman, and many of the American officers and officials, did not like the ethics of the situation, and said so. But to them ethics really played no part in what was happening. The rights of savagery must yield to the rights of civilization. Ten Bears, who had been to Washington, understood this; he understood the great power of the whites, and he also knew that just as the old Comanche headmen could not control the young warriors, the Great Father of the whites could not, apparently, control the actions of his own tribe. But Ten Bears and the others still pleaded that the whites make the sun stand still in the heavens.

In the end, ten chiefs made their mark on the document presented to them. They did not "agree"; they signed out of resignation and the hope of getting the promised gifts. As a contract, the treaty would not have passed the acid test of examination in an Anglo-American court of law. The Kwerhar-rehnuh, whose names were made a party to the treaty, were not at Medicine Lodge, nor many of the Kuhtsoo-ehkuh—perhaps one third of the People were not represented at the council, yet the treaty was to be binding on the whole tribe. The contract was not with citizens, however, and it would not be reviewed. The government had a purpose beyond its hopes of procuring peace in getting this treaty "signed." By the terms of Medicine Lodge, the Plains tribes "ceded" back to the government most of the territories awarded them by earlier treaties, the terms of which were now an embarrassment,

The new treaty, ratified in August 1868, restricted the Kiowas,

Comanches, and Kiowa Apaches to a much smaller territory, much less than the land they then actually held by force of arms. This new reservation lay in the Indian Territory west of the ninety-eighth meridian, bounded on the north by the Washita River, on the west by the north fork of the Red, and on the south by the Red River. (The new reservation given the Comanches and their allies had earlier been awarded by the government to the Choctaw and Chickasaw tribes, but had been taken back in 1866.) This was good, rich country, 5,546 square miles of rolling plains, hills, and valleys, 2,968,893 acres in all, stretching from the hazy granite slopes of the Wichita Mountains to the brush-lined bottoms of the Texas boundary. It was warm, with killing frosts only between November and April, and with ample rainfall, averaging thirty-one inches annually. It was part of the historic *Comancheria*. But it excluded the richest hunting grounds, the Texas bison plains. The Comanches still considered all the lands between the Arkansas River and the Rio Grande to be their ancestral territory. The Peace Commission tried to assuage their fears by agreeing to stop all buffalo hunting by Americans south of the Arkansas.

The remaining clauses were entirely paternalistic, and the commissioners believed them humanitarian. In the restricted territory the tribes would be secure from further white aggression and aggrandizement, and as they became farmers they would be freed from the necessity of hunting and the tyranny of their primitive circumstances. The Comanche arguments that they were being subjected to a different kind of tyranny were brushed aside.

7

QUAKERS AND INDIANS

*I have never seen an Indian so demoralized
that he was not a shining example
of honor and nobility compared with
the wretches who plundered him
of the little our government
appropriated for him.*
          —General George Crook,
             on Indian agents

THE BEGINNINGS OF THE COMANCHE-KIOWA RESERVATION-AGENCY
were not auspicious. The entire process brought sullen anger and
bewilderment to an already confused and surly People. The agency
was first established in the north, on the Arkansas River, and during
early 1868 considerable numbers of Comanches and Kiowas congregated around it, expecting a momentary disbursal of food and goods.
But the Senate did not ratify the treaty for many months, and there
was no issue until December. In the meantime, the waiting Comanches and Kiowas grew increasingly impatient and angry.

There were many peaceable reservation Indians in the vicinity,
and the warlike bands began to raid them, stealing horses, cattle,
and mules. In order to convince the Plains tribes that the government wanted peace, the Indian office had forbidden the stationing
of troops at the agency. The settled Amerindians were terrorized;
the local agent could do nothing, and finally deserted his post entirely, out of disgust or fear. After this, large numbers of the congregated tribesmen began drifting away. Most of them wandered
back to the Texas bison ranges.

479

Meanwhile, there was an outbreak among the Cheyennes north of the Arkansas. A war party killed four whites and raped three women at Spanish Fork. The army moved to apprehend the hostiles; soon, a full-scale war flared across western Kansas. By the time the Indian office was prepared to make its first issue to the Comanches, late in 1868, the situation was so volatile that the government believed the Comanche-Kiowa agency should be moved south, to separate these potential allies from the Cheyennes. Soldiers therefore escorted the tribesmen still gathered on the Arkansas deeper into the territory, near the Medicine Bluff that was an ancient sacred site on which warriors had long sought medicine. A new fort was laid out three miles from the agency, because the interim agent, Hazen, realized that those tribesmen who were willing to remain about the agency had to have protection against the wild bands. This post, Fort Sill, was built beginning in February 1869.

Hazen did his best to start as many Comanches and Kiowas as possible on an agrarian program, but he immediately met insurmountable problems. The men had no interest in learning to farm; they were hostile to the idea of taking up any kind of labor except hunting. Meanwhile, hundreds of Amerindians remained around the agency headquarters, expecting to be fed, especially during the winter months. Hazen had to hire a white farmer to plow the fields and plant crops. Then curious tribesmen plundered the fields before the crops ripened: some Comanches ate green watermelons, became violently sick, and branded all farming as "bad medicine."

The People were also disillusioned by the annuity program. Much of what was delivered was useless to the aborigines. The clothing issues were grotesque. The government specified that each male tribesman was to get a suit, a shirt, a hat, and a pair of socks, and each woman a skirt and twenty-four yards of material to fashion clothing, so that they could adopt "civilized" dress. Both the ready-made clothes and the materials were incredibly shoddy. The men got black suits, red flannel shirts, and a curious hat that strongly resembled those worn by the Pilgrims in the early seventeenth century. The suit trousers were all of one size, which would only have fit a man who weighed approximately two hundred pounds. Obviously profits were made out of these contracts; the money would have been wasted in any case, because the Comanches refused to dress like pioneers going to a camp meeting. The men discarded the hats, ripped the sleeves from the suit coats (using them for leggings for children), and cut the seats out of the issue trousers, so they would be comfortable on horseback. The women used the cheap calico as blankets.

The food issues were almost equally disastrous. The Plains peoples subsisted largely on fresh meat, but they were issued much salt pork and corn meal. They fed the corn meal to horses. They did like the coffee and sugar rations, but they threw away the pound of soap included in the issues after tasting it. The government had planned to furnish seeds and tools for three years, and the rations had been intended as supplementary to the diet the Indians were supposed to produce themselves. However, the agent found he had to spend all his money allowances for beef rations. Nothing was left over for capital improvements, and none were made.

Neither the goods nor the projected life at the agency was attractive to the tribal people, and they immediately began to drift away. By summer, two-thirds of the supposed reservation Indians had gone back to hunting on the bison plains, paying no attention to their imposed boundaries.

THE PEACE-AND-RESERVATION POLICY WAS FAILING WITHIN A YEAR. The failure of the peace portion of the policy was preordained because there was no comprehensive effort to force the tribes onto the reservations or to keep them there. This could have been accomplished only by military force, but this ran contrary to policy. At least one-third of the Comanches never showed up at the agency. These bands continued hunting and making war as they had always done. They fought the Utes; they did business with the Comancheros, trading hides for guns and ammunition; and they raided the Texas frontier, now almost as a religious mission. The presence of these small but warlike and dangerous bands all across the plains made white passage unsafe, and the environs of Indian country terribly insecure. But they also prevented any true acceptance of changed conditions by the agency Indians, with whom they kept close contacts.

The warriors who remained free on the prairies were a constant reproach to those who had made peace. Restive young men constantly joined them for wars against the Utes and other enemies. With summer, the urge to join the free bands was irresistible for most agency Indians. A pattern had developed by the summer of 1869: thousands of tribesmen were willing to take rations from the agents during the hard winter months, but with the new grass they rode away to follow the buffalo. There was relative peace in winter; come summer, there was sporadic raiding and warfare from the Arkansas River to the Rio Grande. In Kansas and Colorado, where white passage was heaviest following the Civil War, there was constant bloodshed.

The army immediately found itself engaged in dubious but savage warfare. The army had again been reconstituted by 1869. It was now reduced to 25,000 officers and men, but this force included ten cavalry regiments for use in the West. The new horse regiments comprised five hundred men, broken down into ten companies of fifty soldiers. Each company was commanded by a captain, with a first and second lieutenant. The regimental staff consisted of the commanding colonel, a lieutenant colonel, two majors, an adjutant, and one second lieutenant quartermaster. About half of the officers were West Pointers; almost all, except the newest lieutenants, were veterans of the Civil War. Far more important, veterans of the old Indian wars were scattered through the regiments, which were themselves fragmented into distant small garrisons throughout the western territories.

The ranks were recruited from the same sources within society, but they were now more heterogeneous. There were fewer Irish and Germans, more Southerners, Slavs, Italians, and even Armenians. Many Negro freedmen were also enlisted in black regiments. The 4th and 10th Cavalry were black, commanded by white officers. Native-born white Americans were still a tiny minority of the service. Some authorities have held that the quality of troops was poorer than before the war. The desertion rate, in any case, was tremendous. Consistently, half of the new recruits sent West, when they learned their destination, tried to desert in transit. The conditions of service had in no way improved, and discipline was still ferociously enforced.

The new army, however, was more relaxed and raffish than the tradition-bound, consciously British-patterned older service. Officers who were western veterans were less interested in dress and parades. Heterogeneous uniforms replaced the elegance of the old 2nd Cavalry. This was an army in "dirty-shirt blue," which began to discard ceremony and dress sabers and to move onto the prairies without making campfires or using bugle calls. The new cavalry was less impressive to European observers—except for certain British officers who had fought primitive tribesmen in India—but, as it became trained, far more dangerous to the Amerindians.

However trained and ready, the cavalry faced the old, insurmountable problem. Ten regiments were not adequate to *police* the immense distances of the Amerindian frontiers; they were sufficient to search out and destroy the tribes if they were unleashed upon them. Many Americans, then and later, never understood the fundamental tragedy induced by military economies. The only really effective warfare the cavalry could wage against horse Indians was pursue and punish actions, which turned into a war of extermination.

For several years after 1865 the policy-makers forbade such missions. This did not mean that the army never undertook them. Hundreds of whites were being killed in the post-Civil War years north of the Arkansas River; a number of the small military commands, such as Fetterman's outpost on the Bozeman trail, and Elliott's squadron on the Washita in 1868, were cut off and slaughtered. In retaliation, Amerindian villages were razed in fire and massacre. Custer carried out limited operations on the Washita in 1869 that were fully as savage as Chivington's five years earlier. Troops out of New Mexico struck Comanche camps in the dead of winter, scattering them. But there was no comprehensive, concerted effort to crush the tribes so thoroughly they could no longer continue roaming, hunting, and raiding.

Both the army and the Indian service found the situation exasperating. Each blamed the other for its problems. Neither had any control over the other; therefore, there was no real policy. Inevitably, the two bureaucracies were in constant confrontation, and the rhetoric of their arguments grew violent. General Sherman, the military commander-in-chief, frustrated by the rhythm of summer failures and enforced winter passivity, instructed the cavalry to destroy as many tribesmen as possible during authorized operations: "The more Indians we can kill this year, the less will have to be killed the next . . ." The Indian office branded this as genocide. Hostility between the two governmental agencies approached the intensity of verbal warfare between the earlier Spanish missionary priests and soldiers.

The generals said that the Indian office was filled with "rose-water dreamers" whose only interest was in living off the reservation Indians by robbing them, and that this plundering was the true cause of the incessant warfare. The military resisted the counter-propaganda of the office, whose "*idée fixe,*" as one officer, Colonel Tappan, wrote, was "that whites were always the aggressors, forcing Indians to war."

The Office of Indian Affairs branded soldiers in the West as "butchers, sots determined to exterminate the noble redmen, and foment wars so that they had employment." The Indian Commissioner, N. P. Taylor, a moralistic Methodist, who stated that he intended to "improve the social status of the American aborigine," became a humanitarian symbol, but only east of the Mississippi. In the West, he was called a "simpering incompetent, whose Methodical sanctity clung to him like a tailored coat." The military and the white settlers detailed countless reports of "Indian atrocities." The Indian office replied that all such reports were grossly exaggerated: the Comanches and other primitive tribes never killed whites unless they were provoked, and they would live in peace if treated with simple kindness.

The army and Western whites retaliated with descriptions of the residue of Plains raids. For example, the surgeon's report after examination of the unburied remains of Elliott's squadron began: "Major Joel Elliott, one bullet hole in left cheek, two bullets in head, throat cut, right foot cut off, left foot almost cut off, calves of legs very much cut, groin ripped open, and otherwise mutilated." All of Elliott's troopers were "otherwise mutilated," the description of which went beyond the bounds of Victorian decency. The Amerindian methods of warfare did not really bear on the morality of the Amerindian question, but atrocities had such an effect on American opinion that the Indian office took to denying them, convincing many well-intentioned Americans that the constant reporting of rapes and tortures and mutilations were propaganda put out by the army and "border people."

While the professional exterminators and professional humanitarians had at it, all real perspective of the Indian problem on the Plains was lost. Civilization was continuing to penetrate Comanche-Kiowa-Cheyenne ranges; rails and settlements were disrupting the bison herds; the warlike tribes had in no sense been pacified; and they were not being taken care of adequately on the reservations to which they had been arbitrarily assigned. The Amerindians were being made more hostile; hundreds of whites were being killed each year; and the army was continuing to destroy the tribes piecemeal. The "peace policy" was neither peaceful nor humanitarian. It continued because the Congress and public it represented were dominated by lack of interest and a determination to avoid any costly solution, whether it involved military pacification or adequate provision for Amerindian welfare.

If the hatred of Indians that existed in the white West continued unabated, if the military were callously brutal in carrying out their responsibilities to protect the frontier, the policies of the Office of Indian Affairs in retrospect appear insane. Agents continued to believe that Comanches and Kiowas would take up agriculture, wear white clothing, and live in houses if the government provided them with funds and a little more time for adjustment. The crushing paternalism of this policy was never questioned, least of all by the most avowed humanitarians. Soldiers or settlers were blamed for every trouble, while nothing was done to halt the ceaseless grafting of Indian appropriations. Agents consistently made promises they could not keep—some of which, made by special peace commissions, were so impossible that they were repudiated by the office itself. Some commissioners appear to have thought that lying to the tribes was infinitely preferable to the truth, if the truth seemed likely to bring on more hostilities. There was a wholesale avoidance of basic problems by a passing horde of political appointees.

A number of Plains chiefs made fools of peace commissioners. Listening to constant Indian complaints about the "lack of guns," some whites became convinced that the Plains tribes needed more firearms in order to feed themselves by hunting. The Department of the Interior actually delivered several tons of arms and ammunition to various groups of Plains Amerindians, although it was illegal under federal statutes to sell guns to Indians. Many of the weapons furnished were new-model repeating Spencer or Henry rifles and carbines. The army was still equipped with single-shot rifles; many

Plains warriors were better armed, courtesy of the government, than its own soldiers.

The incompetence of the Office of Indian Affairs finally destroyed it, though its arguments and policies lingered on. By 1869 the corruption of this agency was so clearly known that the Congress, even in an era of rampant graft, abolished it. The President was authorized to form a new Indian commission, the Indian Bureau, which would have joint jurisdiction with the Interior Department over Indian affairs and appropriations. President Grant, a former soldier, wanted to turn the operation of the Indian agencies over to the army, as the army had long requested. However, Congress would not stand for this, and a compromise was reached by offering the agency posts to the nominees of various religious denominations, who, it was hoped, would be more honest than the former appointees, and would also pacify the tribes by converting them to Christianity. Probably neither Congress, the President, nor the various groups who immediately accepted the challenge—furnishing agents, teachers, and other employees—knew anything about the Hispanic experience in the Southwest. Thus the Plains Dakotas were to become Episcopalians, and Ulysses S. Grant, either with the utmost sincerity or with a sardonic sense of humor, gave over the stewardship of the Comanche people to the Quakers.

The policy was still peace, and many people in government believed that the Friendly Persuasion might bring about a reformation of the plains' most unregenerate warriors.

THE NEW QUAKER AGENT FOR THE COMANCHES, KIOWAS, AND KIOWA Apaches arrived at the Fort Sill agency in July 1869. Lawrie (spelled Laurie in some accounts) Tatum wrote that although he knew nothing about this work, God had called him to it, and God would provide him information as needed. He believed deeply that the Friends could solve whatever problems still remained with these Indians, through gentleness and honesty. As he reported to the Indian Commissioner after his arrival, he intended to defend the Comanches and Kiowas in their legal rights and assist them quickly toward civilization. He totally disapproved of the use of any sort of force against the tribes, and he would never allow troops to molest them on the reservation. The Comanches called him Bald Head, and if he knew nothing about Comanches, it is certain that they never understood him.

Agent Tatum was honest, unimaginative, and fearless—a timid man would never have taken the job. He was annoyed to find soldiers guarding the agency headquarters, ordered them to remain at Fort Sill, and went single-handed among the Indians. Tatum was sincere, and it would be a needless cruelty to his memory to detail every aspect of his progressive disillusionment. His problems were immediate and interminable.

Only a few Comanches were staying at the agency. No matter how many discussions Tatum had, or how many messengers he sent out, the bands refused to come in. As Mow-way (Shaking Hand) of the Kuhtsoo-ehkuh told him, he saw no reason to come back to the reservation until the People there lived better than those who still roamed the prairies. And those families who set up residence near the agency would not perform useful labor. Not only would they not grow vegetables and grains; they were not interested in eating them, except experimentally.

The first issue day proved shocking. The Comanches knew only one way to draw their beeves: they wanted the animals released

Lawrie Tatum with young Kiowas, c. 1872.
Photograph by William S. Soule, c. 1867–74.

one by one; then the warriors to whom they were assigned rode after them, shouting and filling the poor beasts with arrows. When they collapsed, the women and children ran shrieking upon the carcasses for blood and butchery. The Comanches had never needed hunt police out on the plains, but now it was clear that ancient customs and disciplines were cracking on the reservation. There was rarely enough meat at issue; there was bickering and quarreling over the carcasses. Also, wild groups showed up on issue days, ready to maraud and rob the agency Indians. Tatum immediately found that he could not keep order; frightened, he called for soldiers. With troops from Fort Sill overseeing the Comanche butchery, there was at least a fair distribution, and the weak were not robbed of their share of meat.

The bands continued to visit and depart as they pleased. Reports of their raiding in Texas and Kansas constantly reached the agency. The garrison at Fort Sill, a regiment of cavalry, could do nothing to halt this. Through 1869, the soldiers were engaged in erecting their walls, and furthermore, they had no authority to do anything except protect the agency under Tatum's instructions. Under federal policy, Indians on a reservation could not be attacked or even arrested by soldiers or other federal officers without the agent's express permission. Troops pursuing raiding parties were legally forced to halt at the reservation boundary. Lawrie Tatum, like most agents nominated by the religious denominations, arrived in the West believing that his principal duty was to protect Indians from the army; like most agents in this period, he steadfastly refused to permit the soldiers to carry out reprisals. It was soon apparent, however, that the mere presence of troops at Fort Sill in the Indian Territory did not overawe the warlike peoples.

The depredations continued, and in 1869 Tatum's monetary allowance was cut, the money going to pay indemnities for the raiding. This hardly pacified the Comanches and Kiowas; it made them even more dissatisfied with the 1867 treaty. Several chiefs approached Tatum, telling him that the present treaty was no good, and wondering out loud if the tribes might not get a better one if they renewed their all-out warfare against the white men. The band councils seriously discussed the feasibility of taking the warpath en masse, in the hope that this would force the Great Father to call a new council. Councils and treaties were now indelibly connected in

Mow-way or Shaking Hand, chief of the Kuhtsoo-ehkuh, Sill Agency.
Photograph by William S. Soule, c. 1867–74.

the Comanche consciousness with lavish gifts and disbursements; it was not lost on them that the peace commissions in effect tried to buy peace with tribute, whatever different name they gave it. And the Comanches, as they remarked to Tatum, saw something that few whites did: that only the Amerindians who made big trouble for the white men were invited to councils, given presents, and taken on the grand tour to Washington. The tribes that submitted meekly to the whites and never broke treaties were allowed to starve in obscurity, forgotten on their reservations.

The situation grew increasingly tense through 1870. In June the Comanches held council with all the circles of the Kiowas on the occasion of the Kiowa sun dance and debated whether both peoples should join in a general war. Peace won out, barely. However, some chiefs refused to accept the verdict and went off to make war on their own. The passivity of the soldiers at Sill puzzled the tribes; they could only interpret this according to the values of their own culture and assume that the white soldiers were afraid. Tatum and his Friends meanwhile insisted upon interpreting Comanches according to their own view of human nature, while the warrior peoples turned increasingly restive.

That summer the war chief Tahbaynaneekah (Hears the Sunrise) sent word in to Tatum to tell the soldiers to come out onto the prairie: he wanted a fight. Colonel B. H. Grierson, the commandant at Sill, could not oblige, whatever his real feelings. Grierson, who had led one of the boldest cavalry operations of the Civil War, raiding deep through Confederate territory, had to endure countless humiliations in these months. He was not permitted to attack Indians in any way, but he was required to ransom white captives. The government paid a "reward" of $100 in goods for the return of each captive. Anxious groups of seekers, families and relatives of women and children carried away from the frontier, continually plagued the military, which sympathized but could do little to help them. The standing "reward" was a mistake; it encouraged the raiders to search out captives for the bounty. In fact, the taking and ransoming of captives was becoming a great game on the Indian Territory reservation, and the government had lost all control over it. The warriors took captives as they chose, and returned them when they wanted to.

The warriors were bold and insolent as they returned whites in various states of repair: battered children, filthy, bedraggled, lice-ridden women who could hardly look the soldiers in the face. On one occasion, Grierson had fresh, bloody blond scalps waved in front of him. He was told that, unfortunately, it had not been possible to deliver these *tejanos* alive, but perhaps the scalps were worth something to the white men. One white girl, who was more honest and lucid than most returnees, stated frankly what everyone knew but seldom mentioned. She had been kept for a winter, passed from hand to hand and raped continually before her owner decided to redeem her for the standing price. In the process, she had learned some Comanche speech, and had heard the Comanche women boasting about the "fine things those damned fools, the *americanos*, would give their men for a few *tejano* rats" such as she.

None of this was new; it had always existed on the Comanche frontier; but now it seemed to soldiers like Grierson that the United States was actively abetting raiding and ransoming through its "peace policy."

Many of the Comanches were busy seizing captives and cattle along the Texas frontier, but the Kiowas created more problems around the agency. During the summer of 1870 they continually rampaged, shooting livestock, tearing up the few fields Tatum was able to put under cultivation, and stealing seventy-three mules from the Fort Sill garrison. Grierson could do little but keep his men inside the fort. The actual culprits could not be identified. The only alternative would have been to take indiscriminate punitive actions against the tribe. Grierson was a professional; unlike Custer, he followed orders scrupulously. And only because most officers were more like Grierson than Custer was the peace policy so long preserved by the army.

At Tatum's request, Grierson did supply the agent with a guard for the agency, for by now Tatum could not assure the security of the issue beeves or his storehouses without a constant garrison of soldiers. Tatum took this step with enormous reluctance, for he was a sincere Quaker, who despised even a show of armed force. He did it to protect the supplies of the peaceable tribespeople who stayed at the agency and made no trouble, a small minority.

In the fall of 1870, the Kiowas sent word to Grierson through Tatum that they were coming in for the winter, and that the soldiers might now have peace. Grierson was informed grandly: "The white people need not sit trembling in their tents, peeping out to see if our warriors are coming. You can now send your horses out to graze, and your men out to chop wood."

This was consistent with the pattern developing among all the warlike Plains peoples; they preferred peace at the agencies during the snows; their restlessness increased with the warm spring rains.

Meanwhile, a group of touring Friends visited Tatum's agency. They were horrified that he permitted soldiers to guard his buildings, insisting that he get rid of them. Tatum obeyed, for under the new system every agent had two masters. He served the government, but he was also responsible to the sect that controlled his appointment. This placed Tatum under impossible strains, both of conscience and politics. He was slowly coming to the belief that the Plains warriors despised meekness and respected only strength, even violence. He realized his job could never be carried out unless the recalcitrant bands were rounded up and kept on the reservation, and by 1870 he saw no way to accomplish this except through the military. But when he broached this idea to his Quaker superiors, it was dismissed coldly.

Tatum tried to discipline his charges in the only way open to him, by withholding their rations. This did not work; the Indians who were engaged in raiding simply stayed away from the agency. There were still millions of buffalo on the high Texas plains, and thousands of cattle roamed the west Texas frontier. The Comanches and the Kiowas were getting all the weapons they required out of New Mexico. They stole cattle in Texas, then traded the herds to the Comancheros for rifles. They killed buffalo and raided the surrounding territory, as they always had done.

Nothing had changed, and with the coming of the new grass and the soft summer moons, the stolid, patient, but now disillusioned Lawrie Tatum was close to despair.

8

THE GRAVEYARD PLAINS

White hunters assist the advance of civilization
by destroying the Indians' commissary;
and it is a well-known fact that an army
losing its base of supplies is placed
at a great disadvantage.
Send them powder and lead, if you will,
but for the sake of a lasting peace,
let them kill, skin, and sell
until the buffaloes are exterminated.
Then your prairies can be covered with speckled cattle,
and the festive cowboy, who follows the hunter
as a second forerunner of advanced civilization.
                    —General Philip Sheridan,
                      to the Texas legislature

IN THE 1860s THE STRUGGLES OF THE NORTHERN CHEYENNES AND
Dakotas against incursions across their hunting grounds occupied
the energies of the army and the government and stole national
attention from the real running sore in the West, the Texas frontier.
The peace policy ushered in an era of disaster for the whites who
lived along the southern fringes of the great grass ocean.

The federal authorities who placed Texas under military occupation in the summer of 1865 disarmed and disbanded all the paramilitary forces that had protected the Amerindian frontier. In any
case, these forces had never been effective. In the last months of the
Civil War, the militias had attacked a party of Kickapoos moving
south from the Indian Territory seeking refuge in Mexico. The
Kickapoos drove the Texans off with heavy losses. The Minute Men

493

were never of much use against Comanche raiders. Nonetheless, after their disbanding, the entire frontier was left without any sort of organized defense. The federal authorities, concerned about a possible Confederate resurgence and the French operations in Mexico, paid no attention to the Indian question. The treaties signed in Kansas with the Comanches were supposed to settle this problem. Instead, the weakness of the Texas frontier encouraged raiding by aggrieved tribes, the Comanches out of the Indian Territory reservation, and the Kickapoos, now amalgamated and allied with Lipan and Mescalero remnants, from south of the border.

As the Texas historian Rupert N. Richardson wrote: "Indian raids, severe during the war, continued with increased fury. . . . The frontier was scourged as never before in its history. In some places the line of settlements was driven back a hundred miles. The country west of a line drawn from Gainesville to Fredericksburg was abandoned except for a few courageous people who moved into stockades. The worst raids were made on moonlit nights, and the soft summer moon became a harbinger of death. Charred rock chimneys stood guard like weird sentries, symbolizing the blasted hopes of pioneers and often marking their graves. Incomplete reports from county judges covering the period from the close of the Civil War to August, 1867 showed that 163 persons had been killed by Indians, 43 carried away into captivity, and 24 wounded."

The situation was similar to if not worse than the chaos of the early years of the Republic of Texas. If there were only a tenth of the Comanches on the Texas plains that there had been thirty years before, that remnant was ten times as vindictive and murderous. All Comanches blamed the *tejanos* for their misfortunes; whatever the treaties they signed with *americanos,* most Comanches refused to make peace with Texas. The small but very warlike Kuhtsoo-ehkuh and the remote Kwerhar-rehnuh of the Llano Estacado had never signed any agreements with anyone. These bands, joined by warriors who regularly slipped away from the Indian Territory reservation, terrorized the western and central counties.

As in Lamar's time, the Texans had an answer. In 1866 the reconstituted Texas legislature authorized the governor to call a thousand Texas Rangers for Indian border service. But the state was still subject to federal military control, and General Sheridan overrode the legislature and governor. Washington was committed to the peace policy, and the army was still suspicious of armed ex-Confederates. Because of the governor's earnest pleas, however, Sheridan at last ordered some federal soldiers into the central and western counties.

Troops arrived at Fredericksburg in September 1866. Sheridan authorized two cavalry regiments for frontier service. However, the regarrisoning of the old frontier line was carried out with painful slowness. In these years the army was being constantly reduced and reorganized, and the ranks were filled mostly with raw and inexperienced immigrants, who needed time to be hammered into horse soldiers. The new Negro regiments, one of which went to the Texas frontier, had to be completely trained. Old errors were still made; the Rio Grande posts were manned by infantry. Therefore, even as the old stations along the hundredth meridian were gradually reestablished, with certain modifications, the army's stance was defensive and even passive, with no aggressive patrolling.

The primary restrictions on the army stemmed from policy set by the terms of the Medicine Lodge Treaty of 1867. No operations were carried out against the Kwerhar-rehnuh of the Texas Panhandle, even though this band did not go to the reservation. By 1869, therefore, the Texas frontier lay generally where it had in 1849 and was suffering far more severe punishment. The Comanche and Kickapoo raiders avoided the military outposts and drew blood in the unprotected rear.

To the majority of Texans, the policies appeared mad. They created a bitter, long-lasting legacy of animosity toward the federal government and easterners in general. Many Texans thought that the dominant powers were letting them suffer deliberately, either out of anti-Texan prejudice or hatred for former Confederates. This was not the case; rather, first the Indian office, and later the Quaker-dominated Indian commission, mistakenly thought that the policies were working, and that the Texan complaints were grossly exaggerated. The Texan hatred for Indians was well known, and many officials saw no reason why they should destroy Indians simply so that the Texans might seize Indian lands. Ironically, by blaming the Texans, the easterners showed that they understood them; by blaming them exclusively, they showed that they did not understand the southern Plains tribes.

The Indians had supposedly been driven from Texas, and it was expected that the agents in the Indian Territory would soon turn the former warriors into peaceful agrarians. Actually, the entire frontier remained in bloody turmoil from long-range raiding, and the white advance westward was completely halted.

The farm line had stopped generally along the ninety-eighth meridian running through central Texas, because west of this line rainfall was too scant for agriculture without extensive irrigation. Beyond this line, the Texans had created the so-called cattleman's frontier, which extended outward from thirty to one hundred fifty miles. This frontier lay between the farm line and the military cordon. It was a broad steppe that contained about one white person per square mile toward the east, but only one white per thousand square miles near the western limits.

This was the era of the first great western cattle boom, and ranching had become highly profitable. The burgeoning northern and eastern urban markets had become ravenous for Texas beef. Hundreds of thousands of Texas range cattle were being driven north toward the Kansas railheads. But despite enormous pressures for new lands and grass to expand this industry, the cattle frontier could not push westward beyond the hundredth meridian. The reason was not ecological: beyond the lonely forts, across the ancient Comanche traces, past the Comanche springs and all across the high Llano to the mountains of New Mexico, rich prairies rose endlessly, filled with tall grasses. But they fed only millions of wild buffalo, because the cattle frontier met an invisible block.

The Comanche barrier had stopped European penetration of these plains for almost two centuries. It did not show on maps; it had no shape or form. The Comanche barrier was a wisp of smoke on the horizon, riders appearing suddenly on the ridges, shots and screams at sunset, horror under the summer moons. It was the death that threatened all whites who moved into this vast country. Medicine Lodge had "restricted" the Comanches and Kiowas above the Red River, but as the policy evolved it left a few small, wandering hostile bands in complete control of one half of the entire expanse of Texas. They crossed the Red at will, destroying any encroachments on this, their ancient country. Fewer than three thousand Amerindians still halted the pressure of white millions.

Significantly, the Texans had already vastly expanded the cattle culture they had adopted from the Mexicans and had turned into a vast enterprise far beyond Comanche territory. In the 1850s ranchers entered New Mexico from the south, bypassing *Comanchería.* They were moving herds north, to stock distant ranges. But they could not advance into Comanche-disputed territory. Only the bravest, hardiest, and most belligerent, and also the luckiest, could even exist on the fringes of the Comanche-patrolled plains.

Despite its warlike image and mythos, the southwestern cattle culture was basically a business. Cowmen and cattle companies made no profits from fighting or killing Indians. They were prepared to challenge Indians like other predators, but only fools took needless chances. Behind the military cordon, which offered only the scantest protection, the cowmen lived in fortress houses and went heavily armed in bands. On the free range they lost great quantities of cattle and horses, but because they were armed and were duly cautious, rarely leaving their homes or families unprotected, they suffered fewer dead and made captive than the more vulnerable farmers in their rear. But the cowmen did not destroy the Indians, or push back the Comanche frontier, except in American myth. *Homo economicus,* whether his business was raising beef or grain, was no match for horse barbarians whose way of life was guerrilla warfare. Throughout history, civilized men conquered savages and barbarians only through superior organization, and this atomistic frontier of individualists possessed no organization. It endured, as the Mexican peasantry endured, and some people prospered. But the skeletal chimneys that rose starkly over many blackened ruins across the Texas prairies stood watch over the bodies and broken dreams of countless others.

A few thousand untamed plainsmen kept an exploding civilization at bay through sheer ferocity. In retrospect, because of the tremendous disparity of the two forces and the final outcome, this fact is often overlooked or forgotten.

It could not be overlooked or even tolerated by a frontier folk who in the half-decade following the Civil War suffered the worst Amerindian depredations in Anglo-American history. In the late 1860s the Kickapoo-Lipan-Mescalero remnants began to strike deeply across the unprotected Rio Grande into southwest Texas. These aggrieved, dispossessed, and dying peoples had discovered their own version of enterprise. They looted Texas ranches of $48 million worth of property in five years, if contemporary claims are to be credited. They had found a ready market for all stolen stock and goods in nearby Mexican communities, which shared a common hatred for *tejanos*. The United States Negro infantry that guarded the border was as ineffective as were the continual diplomatic protests dispatched through the State Department. The Mexican regimes of Benito Juárez and Lerdo de Tejada did not sanction the raiding; they had little control over the wild Mexican north and were powerless to halt it. The problem was compounded because these governments were extremely jealous of Mexican sovereignty. Not until the regime of Porfirio Díaz was any Mexican government strong enough to move against the northern *indios*, or willing to cooperate with United States military forces.

The situation on the border between Eagle Pass and Laredo was so bad that the army garrisoned the old border forts before it moved back to the edge of Comanche territory. The potential international problem also drew Washington's attention from the more deadly Comanche menace to the northwest.

Meanwhile, during the Civil War, when they had been able to sell Texas beef to federal military meat contractors, the Comanche bands had found a new form of business. That outlet was now closed, but New Mexican and Arizonan ranchers eagerly sought thousands of Texas cattle. They would buy them, no questions asked, from enterprising Comancheros. Whether the New Mexican traders instigated the raiding or not, they supplied the bands with a great incentive. Comancheros went out on the Comanche plains with wagonloads of new repeating rifles, which they exchanged for herds that small parties of warriors drove away from the Texas frontier.

These arms made a difference: they at last overcame the Anglo-American superiority acquired through the revolving pistol. The United States Army did not adopt the new Henry and Winchester repeaters, for they were not suited for universal military needs. They were highly inaccurate beyond a hundred yards, with a fifth of the effective range of the military breechloaders. But they were splendidly suited for close-in mounted actions; they threw up a far greater volume of fire. The Comanches quickly saw the advantages of ten-shot, lever-action rifles over their traditional bows and arrows. Now again they changed their weapons system; and every warrior who raided in Texas soon possessed a modern repeater.

With it, he was better armed than the average Texas farmer or United States cavalryman.

Spare parts, the difficulties of keeping the complicated weapons in repair, and the need for ammunition—which was produced and sold in a great miscellany of calibers in these years—however, remained serious Comanche problems. Ammunition was expensive at ten cents a round on the frontier. It took many stolen herds to satisfy the Comanche needs, because the friendly Comancheros had a seller's market and made enormous profits. Some estimates of the Texan cattle losses in these years run as high as three hundred thousand range beeves.

The loss in blood was far less tolerable. By 1870, the complaints recorded in the Texas newspapers read like a litany, with prayers, entreaties, and finally, fury, offered up to distant authority. In August 1870, the following reports were typical of hundreds being written and published in every dusty town, each of which in those days had its little press. The *Daily State Journal* of Austin stated that "The counties of Llano, Mason, and Gillespie swarm with savages. The farmers are shot down in their fields, and their stock is stolen before their eyes. . . . Not for twenty years back have the Indians been so bold, well armed and numerous as now. At Llano, the frontier is breaking up. . . ."

From Lampasas, where within a few years the People's or Populist Party would be formed by angry farmers, came the report: "During the last moon our entire county, and so far as reports can be credited, other surrounding counties, have been infested by large bodies of hostile Indians. The truth is, if something is not done soon for the relief of the frontier, it will have to be abandoned."

At San Saba the settlers reported that the situation was relatively peaceful: "The Indians are not worse than usual. Only one man killed, two children captured, and about seventy-five head of horses driven away during the past 'light moon' in this vicinity." The comment was not intended to be satirical.

All this took place in farmer country; there were no newspapers and few reports from the cattlemen's frontier.

Editorial comment was bitter. One of the mildest broadsides issued in the Texas of 1870 was the following from Austin: "The idea of making 'treaties' with the Comanches is supremely absurd; just as well make treaties with rattlesnakes and Mexican tigers. Property will be stolen, men murdered, women ravished, and children carried into captivity on our frontier until the Indians are all killed off, or until they are all caught and caged."

This view was essentially correct, if unpalatable to the peacemakers. History simply could not be set aside. Either the whites would have to surrender the country, or the Amerindians would have to be so crushed that they would never make war again. Long-settled regions were regressing toward depopulation. Only hundreds of settlers were being killed, but meanwhile thousands were deserting the frontier. The panic was very real. It was quickly forgotten in retrospect, because only handfuls of mounted Comanches were responsible for all the chaos, and the helplessness of the frontier folk did not fit easily into the Anglo-American self-image. Deprived not of the right to bear weapons, but of the ability to organize and bring concerted, disciplined power to bear, the American frontier was as defenseless as the Mexican.

The reports out of Texas, Kansas, and other points west continually piled up on the desk of Secretary of the Interior Delano. The entire role of the civilian authorities in the Interior Department and on the Indian commissions appears ambivalent. Easterners did believe the problems to be exaggerated—but there is evidence that the secretary deliberately changed or falsified the reports of losses for the federal record. Many Indian agents were reporting that the peace policy was not working, and that the reservation tribes were out of control. The Interior Department and the Quaker commissioners resisted this, apparently for two reasons. The widespread belief was that western whites were out to destroy the tribesmen, and that the aborigines must be preserved. A more compelling reason, probably, was that the Department of the Interior and the Bureau of Indian Affairs were fearful that the military would again gain full jurisdiction over Indian affairs if there was an admitted war. When army officers in the West confirmed current atrocities, there was talk within the bureau of a "conspiracy" by the army to join the "border people" in a war of extermination against the American Indian.

The Quaker sentiment, tragically, was building toward such a war of extermination by not realizing that some military measures had to be used against tribes like the Comanches, if only to "cage" them on their reservation.

The Washington policies had passed from provoking concern to provoking outrage on the border. The Speaker of the Texas House prepared a joint resolution to present to Congress in 1870, stating "that while Great Britain, the greatest civilized power, went to war with Abyssinia because of the detention of a half-dozen of her subjects, the United States has not even raised her voice in protest . . . for the murder of one hundred of her citizens."

There would probably have been no relief out of Washington for many years if the "vexed Indian question," as Sheridan called it, had continued to be debated as a moral or a bureaucratic problem rather than admitted to be what it had become, a military one. The Comanche barrier, and the Comanche terror, were removed only by generals in Union blue who had earlier destroyed the rebellion, and who now began to force a solution to the Indian problem very largely, if not entirely, against the wishes and policies of the civilian government.

When Grant became President in 1869, his old comrades in arms who commanded in the West, Philip Sheridan in the Southwest, William T. Sherman of the Army of the Missouri, believed that they might enjoy greater influence. They did have Grant's ear; but Grant was not a forceful President. His great—and only—talent was generalcy, not politics, and he was never able to discipline his rampant, corrupt Congress or cabinet. Grant sympathized with his army commanders, who argued that their constitutional duty was to protect American citizens, not noncitizen Amerindians, and that they could not do it because they were hamstrung by official policies. But U. S. Grant was not the kind of civilian leader to blaze new policies. He was to exert a tremendous influence on western events, but only indirectly. Usually balked when he tried to ram something through Congress, he adopted a passive role. What made his influence on the Indian question profound was that he tended to let the commanders in the West have their heads. Sherman and Sheridan dared to take actions that violated policy or even the law, because they clearly understood that they had Grant's protection, if not his avowed approval. The generals almost always first cleared their proposed actions with the President.

In 1869, Phil Sheridan convinced Grant that treaty-making with the tribes was a travesty. If the Indians were wards of the federal government, they could not be autonomous nations. Grant agreed, and thus the hopes of the Comanches for new councils were shattered; there would be no more presents for making peace. Similarly, certain promises made by the various peace commissions were repudiated. Only the clearest-minded saw this as progress. Sheridan's and Sherman's position was that whatever the United States did with Indians, it was dishonored by making promises it could not keep.

The turning point, however, did not come until 1871.

In frontier terminology, this promised to be a "bad Indian year." The warriors at Tatum's Sill agency were out of control. They had raided for several seasons into Texas, and while soldiers there chased them if they saw them, none ever pursued them onto the reservation. The lack of punishment, even after Tatum became aware of these activities, made most of the warriors extremely arrogant. Two old chiefs, Set-tainte and Set-tank (Sitting Bear), and an ambitious younger Kiowa, A'do-eete (Big Tree), were very active and boastful of their accomplishments.

On January 24th a party of Indians crossed over the Red River and came down Salt Creek, in Young County. Here they laid an ambush along the old Butterfield Trail, which ran between Weatherford and Fort Griffin, a new post on the Clear Fork of the Brazos that had assumed the function of old Fort Belknap. They jumped a wagon train that came by, manned by four black teamsters.

The freighters put up a brief, desperate fight from behind a barricade of dead mules before they were overwhelmed, killed, and scalped. The war party rode off in triumph with the teams and trophies. The Indians soon became disgusted with the short, woolly Negro hair, however, and threw the scalps away. Other travelers discovered the stark, stiff, mutilated bodies on the trail; cavalry from Fort Richardson, at Jacksboro, came out and buried them. This was the death of Nigger Britt Johnson, that true hero of the Texas frontier, and his three business partners.

War parties continued to haunt this vicinity. On April 19th a white traveler was taken and scalped alive; during the next several days men were attacked almost in the shadow of Fort Richardson. Fourteen persons were known to have been killed by Indians in Young County through April.

The protests out of west Texas were now a clamor. Official and private letters went to the governor, the legislature, the Congress,

The Kiowa warrior A'do-eete or Big Tree, c. 1870.
Photograph by William S. Soule.

the Indian commissioner, and the army. The constant complaints caused General of the Army William Tecumseh Sherman to decide on a personal inspection of the Texas frontier. In early May 1871, he left San Antonio for the northwest, traveling with a small staff that included Major General Randolph Marcy, an ambulance, and an escort of fifteen cavalrymen.

At the Sill agency, meanwhile, the tribes were becoming intoxicated with these small victories. The Kiowa Maman'te (Sky Walker), who was also known as Do-ha-te (Owl Prophet, or Medicine Man), proposed a major foray into Texas. The drums sounded through the nights along the North Fork of the Red River, and some 150 Kiowas and Comanches, including boys and women, were recruited for Owl Prophet's war trail.

Agent Tatum was not ignorant of these events. In fact, many of the war chiefs were boasting openly of their exploits. Now, old Settainte, who with Sitting Bear and Big Tree was included in Owl Prophet's expedition, informed Tatum that the warriors were going to Texas to make war on the Tonkawas. The last surviving Tonkawas, after their near-extermination by the other tribes in the Indian Territory, had been permitted to stay near Fort Griffin, where they scouted for the soldiers. Tatum knew that whites were being killed and property plundered on these raids by his charges. But his Quaker code held him back: he refused to call out Grierson's soldiers, because this would mean violence; therefore, he in effect countenanced the violence loosed on the Texan frontier.

The great war party crossed the Red, making a base camp near the present Vernon, Texas, and leaving women and boys guarding its supplies and extra horses. Two women insisted on riding with the warriors, and they were with them when they assembled on a small hill that overlooked the trail across Salt Creek Prairie on the night of May 17th. Final medicine was sought under the high moon, and war shields were purified. Owl Prophet received a vision in nocturnal owl hooting, and instructed the warriors that two groups of white men would pass this way. The first party must not be molested, but the second would be massacred. Encouraged by this medicine, more than a hundred warriors set up their ambush.

So it came about that when General Sherman and his little escort passed under the hill on May 18th, the soldiers rode past unaware that they were escaping certain death by sheer good fortune. Some of the Comanches wanted to attack, but Owl Prophet swore that this would destroy the medicine. Sherman and Marcy rode innocently into Jacksboro and Fort Richardson, which they reached at sundown.

Marcy, who remembered this country from his earlier service in Texas, had been depressed by its changed aspect. On May 17th he wrote in his private journal: "This rich and beautiful section does not contain as many white people as it did when I visited it eighteen years ago, and if the Indian marauders are not punished, the whole country seems to be in a fair way to become totally depopulated." But Sherman so far had not shown himself convinced that the reports of Indian damage were not exaggerated. At his various stops along the way he had been confronted by groups of complaining citizens; he was noncommittal and gave the deputations little encouragement. That night at Jacksboro he met with a local delegation, listened to strident complaints that reservation Indians were rampaging in Texas, but only said mildly that he would make an investigation.

Back on the trail, the waiting war party had descended on the second group of white men who passed near Cox Mountain. This was a train of ten wagons carting supplies to Fort Griffin. More than a hundred warriors, all armed with Spencer repeaters and revolvers, charged out on the train, shrieking and shooting, eager to make coup, while the two women yelled encouragement. The teamsters tried to turn their wagons into a circle, but the attackers were immediately upon them. Their fire killed one Comanche and wounded a Kiowa, but the wagon master and several teamsters fell dead or wounded. The remainder panicked and tried to run for nearby timber. Two more men were shot down; five reached the brush, though all were wounded.

Instead of pursuing, the warriors ran to ransack the wagons. One young Kiowa, too eager, was shot in the face and badly wounded by an injured white man who had crawled into a wagon. Enraged, the warriors shot holes in all the wagons; they dragged out the wounded teamster and tied him head down to a wagon wheel. After ripping out his tongue, they built a fire under his face. They found axes in the wagons, and chopped and smashed the corpses of the six dead white men. The bodies were cut apart, and arrows were shot into some of the pieces. Then, when the tortured teamster was dead, his head burned black, they loaded the loot from the wagons on the mules and departed quickly. A great storm was brewing. The war party buried the single dead Comanche on the hill and carried the wounded, tied to horses, back across the Red onto the reservation. Here the inexperienced young Kiowa warrior, whose wound became fly-blown, died horribly as the dreaded Texas screw worms ate into his brain.

This was the "Wagon Train Massacre"; it was no different from, and no worse than, many others in these months. But it was to have far-reaching results, because one of the escaping teamsters, though shot through the foot, dragged himself to Fort Richardson. Sherman was still here, and he questioned the wounded man, Thomas Brazeal, carefully in the hospital. The full realization of the pattern of events appeared to shake him. He immediately ordered Colonel Ranald S. Mackenzie to investigate and pursue with four companies of the 4th Cavalry. Mackenzie was ordered to meet with Sherman's party at the Fort Sill agency, although Sherman had no authority to order the cavalry onto the reservation. And that night, May 19th, General Sherman quietly told a citizens' delegation from Jack and Parker counties that he would do everything within his powers to change national policy and halt the Indian menace. Here, the army unofficially joined the "border people" in common cause against the Interior Department and the Indians.

Mackenzie took the field in a blinding rainstorm. His men buried the mutilated bodies of the freighters at Cox Mountain, where their graves still remain beside the trail. One of his columns brushed with part of the retreating raiders, who had stopped to hunt a clump of buffalo. The troopers killed and scalped one Indian, but the others got away, and the rain washed out their tracks. Mackenzie then crossed the Red River, to rendezvous with Sherman at the Sill agency.

Sherman arrived at Sill on May 23rd in a grim and inquiring mood. He demanded of Agent Tatum if any of his Indians were off the reservation. Tatum answered truthfully that Set-tainte and some others he knew of were gone, but that as an issue day was coming up, he expected them back shortly. Tatum now confessed to Sherman that he had believed for some time that force would have to be used against the warmakers, but he could not convince his superiors. He indignantly denied that he had sold any firearms. Later, it became known that the tribes were getting guns through one Caddo George, an employe, at Anadarko. Tatum promised that he would question the Kiowas and Comanches when they arrived for issue.

Set-tainte, who was about fifty, not only admitted the raid, but tried to claim all the credit from Owl Prophet. He said, according to Tatum: "Yes, I led that raid. I have repeatedly asked for arms and ammunition, which have not been furnished. I have made many other requests which have not been granted. You do not listen to my talk. The white people are preparing to build a railroad through our country, which will not be permitted. Some years ago they took us by the hair and pulled us here. . . . But that is played out now. There are never to be any more Kiowas arrested. I want you to remember that." As Tatum reported, he then named other chiefs who had led the raid, including Big Tree and Set-tank, admitted that they had killed seven whites and lost three, and that there was no need to say any more about it. Set-tainte was neither mad nor senile; like most of the reservation Amerindians, he now completely misunderstood the Quaker peace policy. He told Tatum that the warriors had no intention of raiding "around here"; the *americanos* were safe. But they would make war on the Texans whenever they felt like it. With this, Tatum's scruples broke, and he sent for Colonel Grierson.

The several chiefs were confronted by Grierson, Sherman, and Tatum in Grierson's bungalow. The whites seized on Set-tainte, Set-tank, and Big Tree as the principal culprits, and Grierson, with Tatum's consent, placed them under arrest with a file of soldiers. This was the first time any Indian agent had permitted agency Indians to be arrested by soldiers, and it produced consternation among the tribesmen. There was a melee; Sherman was almost killed; one warrior died and another was wounded fighting the soldiers. All of the agency residents fled amid scenes of panic and disorder.

When Mackenzie arrived at Sill with his column, Sherman ordered him to take the three chiefs back to Texas, to be turned over to the civil authorities for trial. The three chiefs, in irons, were forcibly dragged to wagons and sent back guarded by a file of cavalrymen. The old chief, Set-tank, complained that he was a Koh-eet-senko, one of the ten greatest warriors, and should not be humiliated in this way. He made up his mind to die.

A few miles from Sill, Set-tank began to wail his death song:

> Aheya aheya ya-heyo
> Ya eye heyo aheyo—
> O Sun, you live forever
> But we Koh-eet-senko must die—
> O Earth, you remain forever
> But we Koh-eet-senko must die . . .

The other two chiefs sat frozen; Caddo George, who was interpreting, tried to warn the uncomprehending soldiers, who were commanded by a green young corporal, John Charlton; an Indian woman with the wagons began to ululate in honor of Set-tank's bravery. Beneath a concealing blanket, the old Kiowa gnawed the flesh of his wrists until he could slip off his hand irons. He leaped suddenly upon his guards, almost killing one before another shot him through the lungs. He died gasping in the dust, but with his honor as a Koh-eet-senko intact.

The other prisoners arrived at Jacksboro, Texas, amid wild hatred and jubilation. Hundreds of frontier people crowded around the tiny courthouse, where a great travesty began. The murder trial of the two Indians was not just a local sensation; it received national attention. The Salt Creek Wagon Train "massacre" was revealed in all its lurid details. Here the state's prosecutor, W. W. T. Lanham, began a career that took him to the governor's mansion. The white lawyers who defended the Indians did so at the risk of their reputations and even lives. The two Kiowas denied nothing, expected to be killed by their enemies, and asked for no mercy. Set-tainte predicted that his people would avenge him according to their ways. The jury found them guilty of murder; the judge sentenced them to be hanged. The travesty was not in this, but in the fact that the Kiowas had no understanding of the process or the legal nature of the crimes for which they were condemned. They had been made captive; they expected to be humiliated and slain.

But they did not die, because of events the Indians must have found even more bewildering. There was much popular sentiment in the East against hanging the aborigines; more important, the

The Koh-eet-senko Set-tank (Setangya) or Sitting Bear, killed May 1871.

Indian Bureau and the Department of the Interior strongly resented the army's interference in Indian affairs. The Indian commissioners, with an imperfect understanding of the Plains societies, feared that the hangings might provoke all the Plains tribes to war. Enoch Hoag, superintendent of the Indian agencies, begged the President to set aside the sentences. This was not legally possible, for Grant had no jurisdiction over nonfederal crimes, but under considerable pressure, he wired Governor Edmund J. Davis of Texas, requesting a commutation to life imprisonment. Davis, whose Republican administration in effect rested upon federal bayonets in this southern state, complied. The two were sent to the state prison at Huntsville.

The two prisoners had become pawns in a vast bureaucratic struggle between General Sherman and the army, and the Indian commissioners. Both sides acted rashly. The Indian Bureau tried to blame the admitted unrest among the Plains peoples upon the trial and presented the two Kiowas as martyrs. Most of the agents in the West were reporting Indian agitation—Tatum admitted that the spirit of the Kiowas was very bad—and the Indian commissioner called a great conference (Grant would no longer authorize councils with treaty-making powers) at St. Louis, Missouri. Representatives from all Plains tribes were brought to this, and at the Interior Secretary's strong request, Governor Davis allowed Set-tainte and Big Tree to attend, under guard. There is no evidence—quite the contrary—that the different tribes had heard of the two Kiowas, and even the Comanches in the Indian Territory were hardly angry at their fate. A certain portion of the Kiowas, a burgeoning "peace party," even blamed them for making trouble for the agency Indians. But the agents at St. Louis announced that only a return of the Kiowas would guarantee peace on the plains, and they promised this at the conference. This was of course totally beyond their legal power to bring about.

The Texans, already angry over the commutations, reacted with enormous indignation. The state legislature—Davis' legislature—overwhelmingly passed a resolution to the effect that the two Indians should never be released. Sherman wrote the Secretary of the Interior, advising that this act would be a mistake, that if the chiefs were freed, they would almost certainly raid again—it was their nature; they couldn't help themselves, as Sherman put it in contemporary language. But the Secretary put every pressure, official and political, on Governor Davis to pardon the two.

Davis' peculiar political position as a Reconstruction governor in Texas made him vulnerable to federal pressures. He did not quite dare pardon the Indians, but finally he paroled them back to the Indian Territory. He lost little support in Texas because of this, because he had very little to begin with among a population that was ninety percent ex-Confederate, but significantly, he infuriated the United States Army. Sherman wrote him a vitriolic letter that was remarkable for its bluntness, stating that the freed chiefs would "take scalps" again, and adding that the governor deserved to lose his first.

This furor over two Kiowas showed that the peace policy was not easily changed in official circles, whatever the President's generals thought. However, Lawrie Tatum gave Sherman an opportunity to move in Texas, by requesting the army's assistance in getting the Kwerhar-rehnuh and Kuhtsoo-ehkuh bands to enter the Indian Territory reservation. Tatum had already earned the disapproval of his Quaker superiors by permitting the arrests on the reservation, with the attendant violence and the "frightening" of the agency Indians. This direct cooperation with the military proved to be the last straw. It led to the Quakers' withdrawal of their nomination of Tatum, and his dismissal and replacement in early 1873 by a more committed Friend.

Despite Tatum's request for assistance, the army made only abortive attempts to force the Kwerhar-rehnuh and Kuhtsoo-ehkuh bands onto the Indian Territory during 1871. Mackenzie mounted an expedition with the 4th Cavalry into northwest Texas in October, moving through the Blanco Canyon. This was very much a move into *terra incognita;* none of the white officers and not even the Tonkawa scouts had ever penetrated very far toward the remote and dangerous Llano Estacado. Mackenzie and his troopers had to learn the country, and also how to deal with Comanche warriors on their own ground.

The Blanco Canyon expedition brushed many times with Kwerhar-rehnuh warriors under the young chief Kwahnah, who was beginning to earn a great reputation. In Texas, he was referred to as Quanah Parker, and the Texans, aware now of his ancestry, even took a certain pride in him. Quanah and his Antelope band

Quanah Parker.
Posed reservation photograph, late nineteenth century.

held the cavalry at bay superbly. He made Mackenzie relearn old lessons, and some new ones. Out in the high grass prairies, the cavalry were as much the hunted as the pursuers. Quanah never gave battle, but he hovered around the cavalry column, threatening camps and picket lines, now and again attacking suddenly, killing sentries and stampeding horses, vanishing back into the tall grass before the soldiers could react. On one occasion, the Comanches even put an arrow into Mackenzie.

The Comanche tactics intrigued and baffled the American veterans of the Civil War, who thought that they understood cavalry combat. The warriors would swirl off the ridges in a wide, inverted V-formation, sweeping around them. The cavalry was not trained to meet them horse to horse, like Texas Rangers, but to fight as units. As always, mass tactics were useless against Comanches; they swerved away from charges. Even musketry or massed fires were ineffective, because Quanah's warriors never presented a bunched target. Volleys were dissipated as uselessly as the saber attack. Mackenzie learned to keep his horses under close watch, and to put sharpshooters, men who could fire at will and hit bobbing, weaving, racing targets, on his perimeters. Individual marksmen were at a premium, and received recognition and extra pay. In this way Mackenzie could keep the Comanche riders at a distance, but the result was more a standoff than a victory. The cavalry learned to cope with Comanche tactics, but never quite to defeat them.

Pressed, the Comanches simply dissolved and vanished into the plains. Their ponies could invariably outrun the heavier cavalry mounts over short distances. In the 1871 campaign Mackenzie failed to "catch" or punish Quanah Parker, for the Kwerhar-rehnuh retreated higher and higher into the Llano Estacado until cold weather halted the cavalry operations. Mackenzie could not even estimate how much damage he had done in the brushes, because the Comanches always retrieved their dead and wounded before breaking off. But the colonel and his black troopers were learning bitter and extremely useful lessons for future operations.

There was little change in the situation as 1872 began. The Kiowas had got over their fright and were again on the offensive. The Kwerhar-rehnuh were free and untamed, and more and more Comanches were becoming disillusioned with the reservation. Mowway, the Kuhtsoo-ehkuh band leader, brought his people in during the winter for rations, but with the greening of the grass, all the Comanches were restless. They were angry over an increasing penetration of grounds they still considered their own by buffalo hunters operating out of Kansas; many families wanted to seek revenge for members killed in Texas the previous year; and above all, the younger warriors were still eager for fame and prestige. It was very difficult for a chief to maintain his position on the reservation. Accepting rations from Tatum inevitably damaged a chief's prestige, and the younger warriors complained that the older men who advised peace with the white men were becoming intolerably "arrogant." They preferred to gather around Comanches who made medicine and spoke of new glories on the war trail. Mow-way, who personally was prepared to give up war, took his band back onto the Texas plains.

Special Commissioner Henry Alvord tried to tell the Amerindians that they must change their ways, for the buffalo would soon be gone. None of the Comanches accepted this; they could not envision such a thing. And the discussion of it made them desperately angry. Tahbaynaneekah, Hears the Sunrise, shouted at Alvord in a voice that could be heard a quarter mile that before he would be caged on a reservation he and his people would "learn to eat shit on the prairie."

The Quakers tried to use other Amerindians to influence the Comanches in 1872. Members of the Cherokees, Choctaws, and other "civilized" tribes met with the Plains peoples at Fort Cobb. These Amerindians had seen the game vanish in their own lands, and advised the Comanches that this would soon happen to them, and that they must learn to farm or starve. But the few Comanche representatives who met with them fixedly rejected the notion; there might be a bad year or two, but the buffalo always returned. Meanwhile, they asserted that they could always live off Texas cattle. The civilized tribes told the Quakers that there was no reasoning with the Plains warriors and returned to their own reservations.

Meanwhile, 1872 was a bad year "for Injuns." By early spring raids were in progress all across the bloody northwest Texas frontier. Dozens of frontier families were killed or burnt out. There was a repetition of the Salt Creek wagon train massacre in Crockett County in April. This time sixteen white freighters were killed, and the attackers held off two full companies of cavalry before they escaped back into the sanctuary of the Indian Territory. Agent Tatum's own reports were filled with accounts he had heard secondhand of rapes and slaughters. His supposed charges also bargained regularly with him for the return of captives. "[They] have taken one young woman and two children captives and murdered in Texas twenty-one persons that I have heard of. . . . They brought in two of the captives, Susanna and Milly F. Lee. . . . They promised to bring in [the girls'] brother in two weeks." Tatum's principles were now strained beyond endurance. He reported that he would never issue rations to these marauding Indians again, unless he was expressly so ordered. He also reported that the Indians at Sill had stolen 16,500 horses and mules out of Texas to his personal knowledge. And in June, a small party of Kuhtsoo-ehkuh raided the corral at Fort Sill and got away with fifty-four government horses and mules.

The United States Indian Commissioner admitted in his official report for 1872 that "100 persons had been murdered and 1,000 horses stolen by reservation Indians" across the West. This report was certainly deliberately falsified by the bureau. It did not correlate with the reports of its own agencies, which revealed far greater depredations.

In this era the views and feelings of the white frontier were summed up vividly in a letter dispatched to the President by Charles Howard, judge of the 13th Judicial District in Texas:

For a long time have this people endured an almost uninterrupted war-fare bloody and savage at the hands . . . of Indians. But sir those depredations have been growing from bad to worse until they are perfectly alarming to our people. I might give your Excellency scores of instances of recent date of murder, rape, and robbery which they have committed alone in the counties composing my Judicial District. It has been but a few days since the whole Lee family, three of them being females were ravished, murdered and most terribly mutilated. Then Mr. Dobs, Justice of the Peace of Palo Pinto County was but last week murdered and scalped, his ears and nose were cut off. Mr. Peoples and Mr. Crawford of said county met the same fate. Wm. McCluskey was but yesterday shot down by those same bloody Quaker Pets upon his own threshold. I write to your Excellency, as to one who from your Exalted Position in our nation *can* if you *will* protect us from this inhuman butchery. . . . Your humble correspondent believes your Excellency to be en-

dowed with at least a moderate amount of human feeling and a mind that
cannot be trammeled by this one dred insane Pseudo humanitarian Policy: called the "Quaker Indian Peace Policy." Am I mistaken?

Judge Howard was not mistaken. Grant's mind was untrammeled,
and if his hands were tied by eastern opinion and his own bureaucracy, he possessed multiple agencies. The military operated under
executive control for operations too small to be dignified as "wars,"
even in the nineteenth century. Grant now agreed with Sheridan
and Sherman, the generals in the West, that the army must take the
initiative with the Indian problem. The generals were quietly authorized to clean up the mess in Texas.

The army had an excellent instrument in the commander of the
4th Cavalry, Ranald Slidell Mackenzie. Like Sheridan, Mackenzie
was from New York State, the son of a distinguished naval officer.
He had graduated from West Point with the class of 1862, and in
three brief years of war he had been severely wounded four times,
losing part of one hand and receiving one injury that never properly
healed. More important, he had been promoted seven times, to lieutenant general. Sheridan and Grant knew him personally and
greatly respected him as a soldier. He had been assigned to the
Texas frontier because it was thought his talents could be best employed there.

Mackenzie had been retained as a full colonel at the end of the
war, although he was only twenty-five. The army still maintained
the confusing system of brevet ranks, borrowed from the British;
thus most of the veteran officers held honorary grades far above
those in which they actually served. Mackenzie was a lieutenant
general, Grierson and Custer major generals, allowed to employ the
titles and wear the insignia of these superior ranks. Brevet rank
perhaps assuaged the frustrations of an incredibly slow promotion
system, for some brevet colonels never went above first lieutenant in
the reduced army of 1869. Most officers sensibly demanded the
honors of the grade in which they were paid, like Mackenzie;
though Custer, a lieutenant colonel on the regular list, insisted upon
his stars and titles.

Ranald Mackenzie became and remained the best Indian fighter
in the West. He combined great military talents: the initiative to
operate under mission-type orders, needing nothing spelled out for

him; the ability to pay minute attention to detail, while never losing an almost incredible aggressiveness. It went without saying that he was fearless, both of others' opinions and the enemy. Mackenzie made the Negro cavalry a splendid military instrument; he refined the plains tactics of the army in countless ways, from using infantry in wagons as mobile weapons platforms to the use of multiple columns in the techniques of pursuit. Above all, he brought the cavalry back to the practice of the relentless hunt, the most effective of all measures against guerrilla tactics. He organized and carried out the destruction of Comanche resistance on the plains; he then destroyed the Cheyennes to the north; and his techniques were consciously adopted by all later commanders for all Indian operations, from the Dakotas to Arizona. But Mackenzie was to be one of the most tragic American military figures, who after decisive accomplishments left the army in bitterness at the age of forty-two. Despite the fact that Grant described him as the most promising young officer in the army, he was to die forgotten, and to remain forgotten by his countrymen. Mackenzie could not fit the image of the standard American hero.

He was cold, remote, taciturn, utterly professional, a "monk in boots" who had no interests except in carrying out combat missions. He was not arrogant, capricious, unfair, or vain—his staff constantly attested to the high respect in which they held him. But Mackenzie was merciless where the performance of duty was concerned. He was hard on officers, hard on men, hard on horses, and hardest of all upon himself. He did not build "smart regiments" but unkempt, long-haired, dirty-uniformed Indian killers. He took his illiterate mercenaries, black and white, and made them almost as efficient as himself. Mackenzie was no book soldier, whether in discarding bugles and sabers, or in spread-eagling every enlisted slacker against a wagon wheel. He would never be a popular hero, because his methods would not stand popular inspection. He and his black heroes, probably, had to be expunged from the popular history books, because he and his colored cavalry did not quite blend with the rising America's image of itself.

His contrast with Custer could not be more extreme. Mackenzie never permitted correspondents to ride with him; his reports never spared himself or went into detail. He knew the top echelon could read between the lines; he was uninterested in the public's opinion or approval. He went out of his way, as a professional, to win his war without colorful but costly battles. This caused his men's feats to "go unheralded," as one unhappily recalled in his memoirs, while other commanders stole the stage. It was no accident that Custer was killed by Amerindians, but that Miles, Terry, and Crook followed Mackenzie's procedures of survival training, scouts, converging columns, and relentless pursuit down to the close of the Indian wars.

Operating out of Forts Richardson, Griffin, and Concho—a new post that replaced the old Chadbourne at the headwaters of the Concho River—Mackenzie instituted vigorous patrolling. He put men in the field and kept them in the field, resupplying them from month to month. He believed that the Comanches would be most vulnerable during the fall hunting season; he wanted to give them no chance to store their winter meat. He personally led a column of twenty Tonkawa scouts and 222 soldiers across west Texas, drawing new supplies in New Mexico. The patrolling paid off in late September 1872. The Tonkawas located Mow-way's encampment on McClellan Creek, a branch running into the Red River, high in the Texas Panhandle.

As the delighted Texans said, Mackenzie dosed the Kuhtsoo-ehkuh with their own medicine. He came down on the village and destroyed it. At least fifty Comanches were killed and 130 captives taken. Significantly, perhaps, there were no adult males among the prisoners. The Buffalo Soldiers, as the Plains Amerindians called the black troopers to distinguish them from white men, burned everything—lodges, poles, hides, blankets, and all the drying winter meat. They also seized a huge herd of horses.

The great remuda was difficult to guard, and the following night several desperate warriors attacked, stampeding it. They also drove off some cavalry horses. After this Mackenzie gave standing orders that all captured Indian ponies must be shot at once.

In these operations the 4th Cavalry lost some twenty troopers killed or wounded, and the Comanches did recover all their horses. But the Kuhtsoo-ehkuh band was virtually destroyed, and the survivors were demoralized. Some warriors escaped, but their women and children were held by Mackenzie at Fort Concho. Representatives came in under flag of truce, asking for their return. The prisoners were not harmed; in fact, some of the ladies at Fort Concho tried to make friends with them. Mackenzie's terms were simple: the Comanches must go to the reservation and return all white captives. The Kuhtsoo-ehkuh were humbled; they gave Mackenzie assurances of friendship, and there was an exchange of prisoners at the Sill agency.

That winter there was no raiding. The Kwerhar-rehnuh left their hunting grounds and camped on the reservation near the present Lawton, Oklahoma. Through the spring of 1873 few Comanches were reported anywhere along the Texas frontier.

Tatum strongly supported Mackenzie's operations, and stated that the Comanches had become more passive after Mackenzie's punishment. This apparently was the last straw for his coreligionists, as one observer wrote. He was replaced on April Fool's Day, 1873, by another Quaker, J. M. Haworth, who asserted his unshakable belief in nonviolent principles. Haworth immediately dismissed the military guard that Tatum had again established around the agency and appointed one aged and peaceful Kiowa to oversee the rations issues. One month and one issue day later, Haworth wrote to Lieutenant Colonel Davidson at Fort Sill, requesting a restoration of night guards. With some satisfaction and perhaps a little needless cruelty, the soldiers now refused to do anything for the Quakers unless they begged in writing, for the record.

Mackenzie could now turn his attention to the other problem, the bleeding Mexican border. In May 1873, he carried out one of the strangest, least celebrated, and most effective cavalry operations in history. Continual protests to the Mexican government about the cross-river raiding of the Kickapoos, Lipans, and Mescaleros had brought no relief. In March, Sheridan sent Mackenzie written orders to proceed with the 4th Cavalry to Fort Clark, some twenty miles from the Rio Grande, and to "take whatever action your own judgment deems fitting" to halt the raiding. The true orders could not be put in writing, but Mackenzie understood them, and Sheridan understood that he had the backing of the President. Mackenzie was to cross the border.

Seminole scouts crossed the Rio Grande and pinpointed the bases of the raiding Amerindians at Santa Rosa, in the arid Bolsón de Mapimi region of northern Coahuila. The villages lay eighty miles inside Mexico, across extremely rough and waterless country. Mackenzie made his preparations with utmost thoroughness. For days he kept the troopers on the target ranges for carbine practice. He ordered sabers honed, contrary to regulations, for he fully expected to have to fight Mexican cavalry if he was discovered. Then, before dawn on May 17th, he led four hundred cavalrymen to the Rio Grande and clattered across. Such was his command and control of the regiment that the startled officers, to whom he had told nothing, made no protest.

Changing gaits to rest the horses but never stopping, Mackenzie drove his column across the alkali desert toward the Indian villages. At nightfall, still with far to go, he cut loose the pack animals, after loading his troopers with ammunition and biscuit. The next dawn the grimed, weary horsemen came up to the scouts, who pointed out three Kickapoo–Apache settlements in a valley. Mackenzie had already outlined his plan, and the regiment, in two waves, galloped immediately to the attack.

The cavalry smashed into the villages in a maelstrom of gunfire and flashing sabers. There was no battle. Mackenzie's report of the action was deliberately brief and vague: ". . . Nineteen dead warriors fell into our hands." One chief was captured and forty women and children were seized, together with many horses. How many Indians were killed but not counted will never be known. The villages were lifeless when Mackenzie burned them and immediately turned back toward the Rio Grande.

It was a terrible march for men and horses without rest or sleep, although the expected contact with Mexican forces never materialized. The captives were tied to their horses, Indian fashion. Finally, after sixty hours of constant riding and one brief action, the column splashed across the border river. When the halt was called, the troopers fell from the saddle like dead men. Mackenzie then informed his officers that he had made the raid on his own authority, undoubtedly for the record. When one, shaken, demanded to know what the colonel would have done if he had refused to cross, Mackenzie answered: "I would have had you shot."

During the inevitable international and political furor that followed, Sheridan and Sherman stood steadfastly behind Mackenzie's actions. He was sheltered but not entirely absolved, and here he may have destroyed his chances of again reaching a generalcy. But Mackenzie was a hero on the frontier, where he was now regarded with a certain awe. There was no more raiding across the border by Amerindians, because Mackenzie had destroyed the tribes that had

used Mexico as a sanctuary. Years later, the surviving handful of
Kickapoos and Lipans were permitted to come back to reservations
in the United States.

The coming of Mackenzie brought brutal times for the Comanches still trying to hold their hunting range in Texas. All through
1873 the 4th Cavalry kept up a constant patrolling. There were few
fights; the Kwerhar-rehnuh avoided them and Mackenzie did not
try to press them into battle. He was not interested in exterminating
the Comanches, but in giving them no peace so that they would be
forced onto the reservation. Unlike the Kuhtsoo-ehkuh, Quanah
Parker's Kwerhar-rehnuh were still uncowed, but Quanah could
camp safely nowhere in his ancient Llano Estacado territory. Comanche smoke constantly reported the approach of bluecoat columns scouring the plains; the Comanches were constantly on the run.

But Quanah was a wily antagonist, an expert at this kind of warfare, and Mackenzie's more ponderous columns could not catch
him. Again and again, after light brushes, the Kwerhar-rehnuh
Comanches lost themselves in the trackless Texas Panhandle. The
record must show that Mackenzie never defeated Quanah and his
Comanches in battle. The reduction of these few stubborn warriors
might have taken years if the army had not now gained a valuable
ally in the buffalo hunters operating from the Kansas railheads. The
final fate of the southern Plains peoples was to be destroyed, not in
battle with white men, but through the whites' destruction of their
environment.

The bison had been disappearing from North America for many
years. In the 1830s they vanished from the fringes of the Great
Plains and the prairie states; a characteristic of the buffalo was its
departure from territory where there was permanent settlement.
The advancing whites drove the bison west. By 1841 the Osages
were short of game; by the 1850s all tribes who could not maintain
themselves as true Plains Amerindians were starving. The railroads
disrupted the hunting grounds of the Arapaho, and split the great
plains herd into northern and southern segments. But as late as
1869 the southern herd, which roamed south and west of the Arkansas River, was still immense. The buffalo hunter Robert Wright
rode through this territory for days, passing millions of animals
along the Arkansas and Cimarron. There may yet have been as
many as sixty million surviving bison.

Up to this time neither Amerindians nor Americans believed the bison could or would be destroyed. Government policy, begun in the 1850s, was to preserve the animals for the subsistence of the reservation Indians. The treaty of Medicine Lodge guaranteed the tribes the sanctity of the southern herd, by forbidding white hunting below the Arkansas. Up to this time, Americans had had no great reason to slaughter buffalo. Both peoples used the beasts for meat and hides, but there were not that many whites in the West. Buffalo coats and robes were fashionable, but this use never developed into a big business; about 100,000 hides were sold per year. The rail crews, like the army, used the bison for fresh meat, but this butchery was minimal, and dented the herds only in small localities. William Cody, hired to supply meat to one railroad, killed 4,280 bison over seven months, earning the nickname Buffalo Bill—but even this kind of killing could not exterminate the immense, prolific stands.

The slaughter of the bison has often been described as senseless, and certainly, there was much wanton destruction. Whites crossing the plains on rails often shot the beasts for sport from their coaches; "sportsmen" even came from Europe to sate their appetite for easy shooting. Significantly, however, the real slaughter of the hapless buffalo only began in 1870, when the American leather industry developed processes that made hides valuable. Raw hides by 1872 brought $3.75 apiece in the industrial market, and this gave rise to a vast new enterprise.

W. T. Hornaday of the Smithsonian Institution later wrote bitterly that "perhaps the most gigantic task ever undertaken on this continent in the line of game slaughter was the extermination of the bison in the great pasturage region by the hide-hunters. Probably the brilliant rapidity and success with which this lofty undertaking was accomplished was a matter of surprise even to those who participated in it." Hornaday's anger was not misplaced, but his understanding of the phenomenon was imperfect. The Anglo-American business ethic destroyed the buffalo. Once a commercial use was found for hides, the bison gave thousands of men employment and income. The millions of robes sold, and the seven million pounds of bison tongues shipped from Dodge City, Kansas, within two years as table delicacies, were merely by-products of a burgeoning industry. The extermination was a consequence that at the time only a few non-Indian people thought unfortunate.

Technical advances in weaponry made the slaughter bloodily

efficient. The .50 caliber Sharps rifle, firing a 600-grain bullet driven by 125 grains of black powder, could knock down a full-grown bison at extreme range. The nature of the beast, which would not stampede or flee so long as it could not see the source of danger, made it possible for concealed marksmen to kill entire stands in one spot. One hunter, Wylie Poe, who operated out of Fort McKavett, Texas, once killed ninety animals in a single stand without moving. Another famous hunter, Brick Bond, normally killed 250 beasts per day, keeping fifteen skinners busy in his wake. The average hunter killed twenty-five to forty.

The hunters (more accurately "shooters," since no real hunting was involved) were the aristocrats of the new enterprise. Each hunter was supported by about twelve hide skinners. The crews moved out upon the plains with lines of wagons and tons of ammunition. The shooters slaughtered stand after stand; the lowly, sweating, stinking skinners stripped off the hides, leaving the carcasses to rot. Wagons filled with bloody hides rumbled into Fort Griffin, Fort Worth, and went on to Dodge City, for shipment over rails. Behind them, for miles and miles the high plateaus swarmed with circling vultures, which left acres of whitening bones. This was neither senseless nor a sport; it was butchery for profit. Buffalo hunters made good money. There were men who sickened in a single season and quit the business, but there were more than enough eager to take their places.

The hide hunters were naturally a rough, dirty, violent breed. They worked hard, at a job that was frequently dangerous, because the Plains tribes would attack any party they surprised on the range. They also played hard, and like the miners, soldiers, and frontier cattlemen, they brought their forms of civilization to the plains. Wherever they congregated, western hell-towns rose. The Flat, outside the walls of Fort Griffin, was a typical example. Here unpainted frame buildings were slapped together out of lumber hauled in over hundreds of miles, creating dance halls, hotels, and saloons. Hundreds of "hookers" (named for "Fighting Joe" Hooker, the Union general of the Civil War with a penchant for prostitutes) and "whirlago" girls poured in, with cardsharps and gunmen. Here Lottie Deno, the legendary red-haired Texas poker queen, reigned supreme. She ran her game, and her hired gunmen shot any man who questioned it. The army had no jurisdiction and never interfered. There was no civil law for years, and when it came, it arrived in the form of gunmen wearing shields, hired by the mercantile interests. Like Lottie Deno and her colleagues, these peace officers rarely fitted any later legends of rough gallantry. They drew their deadlines, enforced their curfews with sawed-off shotguns and a dozen desperate deputies. Whether Wyatt Earp or Wild Bill Hickok, they were uniformly killers. The boom towns roared, and rocked the West with new prosperity.

Hide hunting was big business. Forty thousand hides left Dodge by rail in a single day. Robert Wright shipped two hundred thousand over the Atchinson, Topeka, and Santa Fe in a single winter. During 1872–74, 1.5 million hides went out of Dodge alone. After this, the trade slackened, for the very efficiency of the hunters rapidly put them out of business along the Arkansas. In the December–January hunting season of 1877–78, only one hundred thousand bison could be found and killed. Some querulous hunters turned to bone picking, and the records show that between 1868 and 1881 the bones of thirty-one million animals were sold for fertilizer in the state of Kansas. After 1881 there are no records, for there were neither bones nor buffalo.

Scalped buffalo hunter, Ralph Morrison, near Fort Dodge, 1868.
Photograph by William S. Soule.

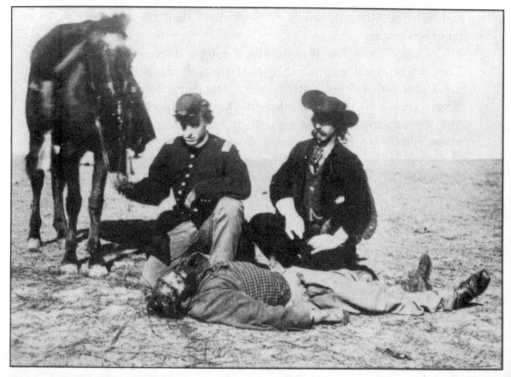

By 1873 the main action centered on the Texas plains, with the principal hunters outfitting at Fort Worth, and operating out of the Flat at Griffin and other raucous boom towns that sprang up around the frontier army forts. This killing violated the 1867 treaty with the Comanches and Kiowas. But the treaty itself stood in violation of the rights of American citizens making a living on Texas soil. There was no legal means of halting the hunters who now began to penetrate the high bison plains of the Panhandle in large, armed, and truculent parties. The truth is that the army had no desire to halt them, because most of the officers in the West now saw the hide hunters as allies. As General Sheridan, commanding the Southwestern Military District, put it, they were destroying the Indians' "commissary."

The army, in fact, was instrumental in preventing any halt to the slaughter. Many Texans had become appalled at what was called an insane butchery of God's creatures, and a bill was introduced in the state legislature to halt all such hunting. This bill was strongly opposed by leather lobbies and ranching interests—for the western cowmen saw the bison as useless and an obstacle—but it would probably have been enacted, had not Sheridan, with Sherman's approval, made a special trip to Austin to address the legislature. Sheridan argued vehemently that to oppose the killing of buffalo was to oppose the advance of civilization. The alliance of ranchers, eastern leather-makers, soldiers, and Indian-haters won over the politicians. The bill was killed and never resurrected.

The high plains of Texas, like those of Colorado-Kansas, became a bison boneyard. With winter, the Indian Territory buffalo moved south, onto the Texas plains, and with winter, the hide hunters went out with their guns and wagons and exterminated them.

The tribes did not quickly comprehend this phenomenon. Raiding and dodging soldiers all summer, keeping to their tipis in the Indian Territory reservation by winter to avoid Mackenzie's cavalry, they came to understand its meaning only when the slaughter was far advanced. In the spring of 1874, startled scouts, ranging out to locate the herds for hunting, rode past miles of rotting carcasses and whitening bones.

Thus was precipitated the last great crisis on the southern plains.

9

THE DESTRUCTION OF THE COMANCHES

Briefly, the obliteration of Texas Indians
was but a small part, a footnote really,
to the nineteenth-century development and emergence
of a new, and in technological terms,
a tremendously powerful nation-state.
      —W. W. Newcomb, Jr.,
        University of Texas anthropologist

THE PEACE ON THE TEXAS FRONTIER FOLLOWING MACKENZIE'S RAIDING was ephemeral. In June 1873, Agent Haworth insisted upon releasing the imprisoned captives Mackenzie had taken. As soon as these had rejoined the bands, many of them again began raiding. There were, however, a few signs of change. More Comanches had given up marauding, and some headmen returned stolen horses to the agency. Quanah and several other war party leaders, meanwhile, instructed their warriors to stop taking white women and children captive, for they understood, imperfectly, that this seemed to provoke the white men to murderous fury. When the soldiers found a white woman captive in a camp, they did not always bother taking prisoners.

When 1874 came, the hide hunters were not solely responsible for the cracking peace. Other promises made to the Comanches and Kiowas were being broken. The annuities had always been intended as a supplement, and the beef rations were never enough to feed peoples who lived almost entirely off meat. There were also inefficiency and major graft involved in the disbursements. The piety and humanitarianism professed by the Indian commissioners of the

Grant administration often got strangled in bureaucracy, and there were religious men who railed against the killing of Indians while they lived by cheating them. The People did not live well on the Fort Sill reservation.

Early in 1874, heavy rains delayed the shipments. Agent Haworth cut the agency Indians to half-rations, forcing them to kill their horses for food. As he reported, the bands became unruly and he understood that they were holding councils with the still untamed Comanches who never appeared at the agency. If Haworth had been more aware, or understood the signs of human beings in crisis, he would have seen and reported ominous portents.

For the People collectively were sinking into a terrible social and psychic crisis. For a generation now families and band structures had been undergoing steady dissolution by disease and by bullets. Gathered together on the reservation, the shrinking bands were painfully aware of the thinness of their numbers. The band camps were little clumps of tipis, holding a few hundreds, where once encampments had stretched for miles along the Cimarron and Canadian. Worse than this, the survivors were faced with a future that spelled out psychic horror to them.

When there was no more war, no more hunting, there was no longer any purpose to Nerm existence. The males, in their own minds, were being made slaves. They waited for beef that did not come, while the women and children complained. What was a warrior for? What could a man teach his grandchildren or his nephews, except to make them restless with tales of the thrills of hunting and old war parties? The youths coming into manhood were already sick to death of old men's reminiscing, of chiefs who advised against new wars but demanded the prestige and privileges they had won in old ones. How could a young man gain honor in this changing world, to make the women praise him?

The failure to provide the peoples on the reservation with sufficient food was one shame for the American government. The other great failure was unintentional, and sprang from ignorance, but it was probably more cruel than the actual starvation of the Amerindians. The rigidly moralistic Americans who believed that they were "raising the social status of the aborigines" were actually destroying the Amerindians' entire system of values, but without opening avenues to genuine status or prestige in the new universe of the whites. This dismal failure, which persisted after the end of bloodshed and resistance, was less the result of racial discrimination than an utter incomprehension of the Plains cultures. Historically, the subjugation of the Plains tribes was inevitable, and once the conflict began, necessary. However unpalatable in memory, the white frontier's own descent toward barbarism is understandable. But the reservation policies of the government, in conscious conflict with that barbarism, were barbaric in a different way. They were the more offensive because they violated the victors' own codes of decency. Once the Plains tribes no longer barred the advance of civilization and had begun to surrender to superior force, they deserved to be treated according to the codes of the victors, rather than by the practices that were inevitable between races and cultures still in violent conflict.

The Comanches, like other warlike tribes, did not of course make the task easier for the Americans. They never grasped the motives or drives of the whites, never understood the Anglo-American nature. They grasped only a knowledge of its hypocrisies. The land was no longer theirs, and they could no longer enjoy their old freedoms; the freedoms the Comanches still longed for on the reservation were impossible within the framework of all civilized societies. They were liberties that civilized men no longer even remembered. These things were certain: The Comanches could no longer live by raiding and hunting once the Anglo-Americans had enclosed their lands, nor could they live a life of the spirit or rekindle ancient magic. The desire of course lingered stubbornly among the survivors, but there could never be a resurgence of red power on the continent except one that conformed to and used American political and social processes. The warrior peoples would have to learn the tyranny of cause and effect, and they could never live effectively within a capitalist social system without adjusting to the rationales and forms of private property, social hierarchy, and labor for economic gain.

The Quaker keepers of the Comanches had reason to understand all this, but just as persistently as the Comanches failed to understand the nature of the white world, the Quakers refused to credit the basic nature of the Comanche ethos and society. What the People were, the Quakers could not accept as anything but a terrible aberration. Comanche mores flew in the face of the religious denomination's concept of human nature and human society. Thus the Tatums and Haworths failed to face the true problem of assimilation, and in the coming generations their successors persisted in that failure. They did not know how to win respect, or how to redirect Comanche pride and aggressions toward new goals, because they had no understanding of the Nermernuh as men. They prolonged the agony of the subjugation for a decade, because their own culturally acquired hatred of war and violence was so ferociously held that they could not admit the true situation: that the Comanches required a display of complete and overwhelming force before they would even consider an adjustment. They went out to protect the aborigines from white aggressions; they failed because they could not cope with red ferocity. But their greatest failure was that after the red men were at last subdued, they became not their red brothers' keepers, but keepers of Amerindian jails or zoos.

They ended by instigating one of the most fearsome tyrannies in human history. They allowed the conquered no graceful, dignified approach to adjustment or assimilation. They treated Comanche customs as those of erring children. They interfered with the Amerindian religion, marriage customs, medicine. They took children away from parents to white schools, and as when they withheld rations, they saw this as disciplining and uplifting, never as a fearful humiliation. Believing their own parochial set of ways to be "natural," the keepers expected the Amerindians to adopt them. In the end they used force and delayed assimilation interminably. The Indian bureau was to become the only Anglo-American institution the western tribes ever saw or had contact with, and what people could assimilate with or admire their jailers?

By the early 1870s most of the soldiers who were penning the Plains warriors in their new cages had become outraged by the government's handling of reservation Indians. Crook and Miles, especially, admired the warriors as warriors, as valiant if cruel and ferocious savages. The generals who defeated the tribes respected their dignity as men, although they never confused this sympathy with a belief that the tribes had any hope, or even right, to halt superior power. Crook argued that Amerindians should be enrolled as American citizens by birthright, a generation before citizenship was granted the Cherokees, in 1906. The grim Mackenzie, like Miles, had no interest in exterminating the United States' Indians.

Extermination was not the issue. The issue was this: how quickly, and how cleanly, could the conflict be ended, and the inevitable process of readjustment and assimilation begun? Thus Miles and Mackenzie both promised the tribes "no mercy" while they resisted, but promised fair treatment after final surrender—promises the government never kept.

The reservation theory was good, like the Spanish concept of tutelage of Indians until they could be brought as equals into the new world. The practice was as patronizing and as self-serving, in the long run, as that of the friars, but worst of all, the institutionalization of reservations made the Amerindians helpless and vulnerable within the nation. Once they had ceased fighting, the tribes passed from national attention. The western whites were naturally vindictive, the easterners basically indifferent. American democracy, in the continual absence of high ethic, responded only to pres-

Comanches on the reservation.
Photograph by William S. Soule, c. 1867–74.

sures and pressure groups, and all the pressures exerted were invariably against the Indians. The reservation peoples exerted as much influence on the body politic as imprisoned felons. Thus cruelties continued long after Amerindians had ceased to trouble the nation. The original western preserves were adequate for the depleted numbers that finally entered them, but afterward none were preserved intact against further aggrandizement. Cuttings-up, reductions, openings, violations of treaty rights, and outright starvations, like the cultural humiliations, went on inexorably.

Most high government officers expressed ignorance of the operations of government reservations. That was the province of a specialized bureau. The transfer of responsibility to the religious denominations in the Grant administration in the long run had little good effect. Few high-minded persons would take a job living with and keeping Indians, and those who would were usually unfitted for the task for many reasons, and they were very hard to direct or discipline. Many appointees had influence, and the organizations backing them were prepared to make a clamor if new reforms were threatened. The bureau, like any normal bureaucracy, devoted itself to its self-preservation and perpetuation, and faced little difficulty in doing so. Once the western Indian wars were closed, the public showed as little interest in what went on in government reservations as they did in military prisons.

Before their last war powers were destroyed the tribes learned the shape of their intended future, and saw promises broken. What they saw made the last desperate stands inevitable from Texas to Montana. Toward the end, they resisted savagely, whether Comanche or Dakota, and ironically, this resistance only solidified a future in which all promises might be broken with impunity.

THE PEOPLE WERE IGNORANT, BUT NOT STUPID. WHEN THEY PASSED the piles of moldering bones on the plains and waited for beef that did not come, even primitives ignorant of the great forces moving the world could see the outline of the future. Their world was filling with deep shadow.

The bands were unsure of everything, except their fear of the reservation life and their hatred of *tejanos*. This very hatred had perhaps kept them sane for several years, because year after year they had slipped off the reservation to dissipate their aggressions and wreak blood vengeance. But in this late autumn of their tribal existence, the Nermernuh were socially and psychically insecure, and the insecurity showed in many ways. Once the People had been exceptionally parochial, rejecting all other folkways. They had watched the rites and folk magic of their neighbors with indifference. Now, they had become vulnerable to countless foreign influences. War chiefs took up the streaming feather bonnets of the Cheyennes; some bands adopted the burial customs, with scaffold biers, of the northern tribes. The People were desperate, searching. Many warriors had a paralyzing suspicion—which could not yet be broached openly—that the medicine of the white men and *tejanos* was more powerful than that of the Amerindians. Within their world-view, they could explain the disasters that had befallen them in no other way. The warriors were still fearful of their guardian spirits, still frightened by the accidental violation of taboo, but very few really believed any longer that their medicine could turn a *tejano* pistol ball. They had adopted the guns of the whites, and some customs of the Kiowas

Comanche feathered war bonnet, copied from Cheyennes. Late nineteenth century.

and Cheyennes, and might even have been willing to try the medicine of the white men—but they could not understand how it was derived.

They had two things left in the hungry spring of 1874: a deepened psychic savagery toward the outer world, much like that of the Apache, and a desperate longing for an atavistic reaffirmation of their ways. They had no real concept of a succoring Great Spirit or God, but they were ripe for a messiah. Inevitably, one was called forth among them.

Eeshatai (Coyote Droppings) the medicine man was a phenomenon that had appeared, or would soon appear, among many disintegrating Amerindian peoples from the Southwest to the Pacific Northwest. He was less a symbol of hope than of extreme social decay and despair. He was a common reaction thrown up by despairing societies. He was a Nerm, and therefore he moved and spoke within the traditions and consciousness of the People. He reaffirmed the primacy of the spirit world, and he rallied the spirit world behind the People for war.

Eeshatai had not proved himself in war, but he was a young man who claimed powerful *puha*, medicine. He was immune to bullets, and he had performed certain miracles, such as bringing back the dead and belching forth a wagonload of cartridges. The Comanches were familiar with such magic; but they took the power of Eeshatai seriously when he predicted that a comet that blazed across the heavens would last five days, then be followed by a drought. This happened (Coggia's comet) and the People began to believe in the magic of Eeshatai. They needed desperately to believe. When he spoke of having "ascended above the clouds" and communed with a Great Spirit, even great warriors were impressed.

This prophet moved through the bands during the spring of 1874, telling them that if they purified themselves, the time of deliverance was near. He professed a power that could save them from their enemies. By May he had gathered the restless remnants of the Comanches together north of the Red River as no past war chief had ever done. For the first time in the People's history, a leader brought together almost all the lodges of the tribe in one encampment.

He told the People that this year they must perform the sacred sun dance, as the Kiowas and Cheyennes and Dakotas did. It apparently occurred to no skeptics that the Plains sun dance was not saving the other tribes; this was a magic whose framework was familiar to them. The Comanches had neither the cultural nor the social equipment to perform the true sun dance. The Nermernuh lacked *taime* dolls and priesthoods, even the "sacred bundles" of the Cheyennes. They did not understand the ancient symbolism of the rite. But Eeshatai said none of these things was important. Not the forms, but the massed will of the People, coming together in dancing, would invoke his Great Spirit. Thus the first Comanche sun dance, as it was prepared for and performed, was more a great socializing act than a true religious ceremony.

Many of the forms faithfully followed the customs the People had seen among the Kiowas and northern tribes. A female captive who was known to have been faithful to her captor, and thus a woman of great virtue, cut the tree for the sacred center pole of the dance compound. The pole was raised exactly according to the rituals of the Kiowas, with three false starts. A fresh-killed bison was placed upon the pole, in universal custom. The ritual preparations continued for five days, with sham hunts and battles, invoking the memory of past glories. However, the Comanches did not plan to follow the masochistic practices of other northern tribes: there was to be no hanging from the pole by thongs attached to warriors' breast tendons, no dancing with buffalo skulls dragged by cords passed through back muscles, nor dancing till exhaustion. The People were not seeking medicine visions from the dance, for Eeshatai already possessed the power vision. The ritual was to be much simplified, done without the traditional roles of the hunt police, warrior societies, or doll keepers, since the People had none of these.

Eeshatai's instinct was splendid, for all this fitted both Comanche spiritualism and cultural pragmatism.

At sundown on the fourth day of preparation, criers rode through the great assemblage of lodges, calling out every separate band to stand before their tipis. In their hundreds they began to chant their band songs. and do their special dances: Kwerhar-rehnuh from the Llano Estacado, Yampahreekuh from the Arkansas, Kuhtsoo-ehkuh, and Tahneemuh. The Pehnahterkuh were not there, however, for they had heard the talk of Eeshatai that when the dance was over, all the People would unite, fall upon the whites and annihilate them, so that the bison could return to the plains. Everything would then be again as it had been; the People would again grow numerous and powerful. The People could not fail, for the power of Eeshatai would protect them; he would lend them his own invulnerability. The Pehnahterkuh in their pitiful remnants did not believe such talk. It frightened them, for they knew better than all the others the numbers and the power of the Texans. The Pehnahterkuh chiefs took their families far away, across the Red River, where a few other stragglers joined them.

But the other bands were united as they had never been. Now, before their lodges, they merged into one great mass of dancers, moving and stamping in a growing unison, until their feet, landing as one, shook the earth itself.

The People danced for three days to the drums, rattles, and eagle-bone whistles. Their singing roared out over the prairie. The drums pounded into the night while the dancers rested to prepare for the exertions of the morrow. For three days and nights they danced. Then, Eeshatai declared that the People were one; they were ready.

He had preached that the Caddoans and Wichitas had disappeared because the warrior peoples had opposed the white men one by one, and one by one were put upon the reservations. Eeshatai invited the Kiowas, the Cheyennes, and the Arapahos to join the People. After the great sun dance had ended, he went with a large band of warriors toward the Cheyenne encampments along the Washita. The Cheyennes and the Arapahos listened to Eeshatai's prophecies. All night the warrior societies danced, while the prophet and Comanche and Cheyenne, Kiowa, and Arapaho war chiefs held council. With vast excitement, many of the warriors joined the People for this great war of extermination against the whites.

The leaders of the warriors, Quanah of the Kwerhar-rehnuh, Lone Wolf and Woman's Heart of the Kiowas, Stone Calf and White Shield of the southern Cheyennes, agreed on two matters. Quanah should be paramount war chief, and the first blow should fall upon the buffalo hunters.

The tribes rode south, into the Texas Panhandle, long lines of barbaric horsemen whose passage shook the ground. They were buoyed by an exultant faith in their new medicine. The Kwerhar-rehnuh were the core of this host, which numbered probably some seven hundred fighting men, for they alone of the southern plains bands were still powerful. But even this small alliance, moving with speed and determination, could have swept every buffalo hunter from the plains.

They came down on the old Bent fort at Adobe Walls just before dawn on June 27, 1874. The hide hunters had taken to using the abandoned buildings as a headquarters and rendezvous. Now, in early summer, there were only twenty-eight white hunters and one white woman in the camp, but the men had worked through the night repairing a roof beam. This saved them, for two men were outside when the Amerindian horde appeared on the ridges in the ghostly half-light. They gave the alarm before Quanah sent his riders into the attack.

The hunters made their living by marksmanship with the powerful Sharps buffalo guns. As the Comanches and their allies raced down upon Adobe Walls, the big rifles knocked down men and horses. Two Cheyennes and a Comanche who reached the enclosure were shot dead. Quanah's own horse was killed under him; he survived only by crawling behind a rotting bison carcass for concealment. Startled, the attackers made a characteristic but now fatal error; they split around the walls and wagons, without pressing home the charge and overwhelming the whites hand to hand.

At a distance the carbines of the Comanches were no match for the great buffalo guns in the hands of skilled marksmen. Several more warriors were killed, and the attackers drew off to the distant ridges. They charged again, but again they could not bring themselves to push the attack at close quarters, and again they were repulsed with losses.

Eeshatai sat naked in yellow war paint on his pony on a distant ridge, watching over the battle. His host could still have charged in and butchered all the hunters at any time that morning, but eighty centuries of custom and conditioning now destroyed all Eeshatai's visions and ambitions. Surprise was lost, and the war chiefs were reluctant to press the attack against serious losses. Quickly, the Amerindians slipped from elation to manic depression. Eeshatai's magic was flawed: the father of a Cheyenne warrior killed under the walls demanded of the prophet that if he were so bulletproof, why did he not go down and recover the body? Eeshatai sat immobile, and then, as if by fate, a Sharps ball knocked one of the warriors sitting beside Eeshatai from his horse, at a range of more than fifteen hundred yards.

The fragile alliance cracked with the prophet's medicine. A Cheyenne struck Eeshatai in the face with his quirt. Eeshatai blamed the Cheyennes for the disaster: one had killed a skunk the day before; this had destroyed his medicine. Ancient antipathies and suspicions boiled over as the horde withdrew in confusion. Nine warriors were dead and many more wounded, some of whom would also die. They had killed three white men behind the walls.

As the great war party retreated, the hunters hugged each other, hardly able to believe their good fortune. This had been a tiny battle; but its effect was to be one of the most decisive of any fought on the plains. The alliance between Comanche, Kiowa, Cheyenne, and Arapaho was shattered upon Adobe Walls. The Comanches saw the magic of the sun dance fail, and they would never invoke that medicine again. The People had been one, but briefly. As Eeshatai's influence collapsed, they dissolved again into their habitual separatism. Some deserted the war, returning to the reservation lands.

The war against the whites was not quite over, but now it had no plan, purpose, or cohesion. Small groups of Comanches, Cheyennes, and their allies rampaged out from Adobe Walls in all directions, carrying terror and death into five states and territories. The fear and rage of the tribes fell on travelers and ranches. Stages were stopped and stations burned; small parties of hide hunters were wiped out from Colorado to Texas. Men were staked out on the prairie; white women died with butcher knives thrust into their sexual organs. The southern plains were again caught up in the horror of a widespread Indian war, which killed 190 whites in the summer months.

The hide hunting ceased. Everywhere the whites huddled around the frontier forts and towns, clamoring for protection.

This second general uprising broke the dam of public opinion as the endemic raiding in Texas had never done. As the telegraph wires hummed with report after report of verified "atrocities," official sentiment again swung full circle. The terror and destruction destroyed the last arguments of the nineteenth-century humanitarians. Sympathy turned to exasperation and exasperation to anger. President Grant authorized the army to move immediately "to subdue all Indians who offered resistance to constituted authority." The old "peace policy" was seen as a failure; the new peace would be imposed on military terms. All restrictions were lifted from the army in the West. Any Amerindians found off their reservation were to be considered hostile, and to be pursued. If they surrendered, they were to be considered prisoners of war. If they resisted, they were to be destroyed.

The 1874 change of policy was complete and final. The government had had a "bellyful of Indians," as one official put it; the new concept was to end the autonomy of *all* the western tribes, and to force all of them onto their restricted reservations. The tribes would never again be permitted to wander off the reservations, or to make war against the whites. The southwestern raiders precipitated the change, and thus in the actions of the Comanches were caught up the fortunes and fates of all the other western peoples. The Plains Dakotas had fought with the army, but they and most of the northern tribes had never raided or killed beyond the confines of their recognized territories. Now, between 1874 and 1877, they, the Nez-Percé, and many other still autonomous peoples were to be swept up in the *revanche* launched against the southern horse Indians. There was to be a general pacification and removal. This set off the last of the great plains wars, a few brief bloody years of turmoil from the Rio Grande to the Canadian border.

These were not really "wars," although thousands of soldiers were employed. They were not declared, and the direction of the pacification was left to executive control. There was nothing new, except the spectacular western landscapes, the scope of the problem, and the fierceness of the resistance. The campaigns of the 1870s were a mopping-up process, finishing a conflict that had begun three hundred years earlier. They were an extension of the old Jacksonian policy of Amerindian removal.

The last campaigns remained more vivid in American memory not only because they were the last, but because with improved communications they received vastly more publicity. Newspaper correspondents went out with army columns (Custer characteristically took one along to the Little Big Horn, contrary to his orders), for by this era more attention was drawn to the West. It was seen as the last frontier. The reporting and recording, however, were uneven. Some operations received much attention, others none at all.

Where the army performed with the greatest efficiency and dispatch, it got the least notice and attention. Conversely, more words were to be written about Custer's last fiasco than all the other operations combined.

There was now almost no opposition to destruction of the Indian "barrier." Almost all editorial opinion throughout the nation supported government policy. What discussion there was followed the lines of placing the rights of primitives against the demands and needs of civilization. In this, or in any other self-confident era, the conclusion was foreordained. Much sympathy was expressed for the aborigines, there was the sense that an era was passing, but progress was not to be denied.

THE COMANCHES AND KIOWAS WERE ORDERED TO CONGREGATE EAST OF Cache Creek, at the Sill agency. The majority of Comanches failed to obey, staying out on the plains. The Dertsahnaw-yehkuh band, which did not want war but also refused to stay at the agency, sought neutral ground. They went to the Wichita agency, asking the agent there for protection. But under the new policy, agents could no longer provide sanctuary. The army demanded their surrender as prisoners of war; they fought, and fled back out onto the prairies. Thus by late summer, most of the Comanches were classified as hostile, and the army began its actions to subjugate them in the first of the great coordinated campaigns that involved thousands of men, converging columns, and sustained operations in the field.

Mackenzie marched from Fort Concho with the 4th Cavalry and supporting infantry, the "Southern column," about six hundred men with thirty scouts. Colonel Nelson A. Miles moved west from Fort Leavenworth toward the Arkansas. Lieutenant Colonel Davidson operated out of Sill, Buell along the Red River, and William Price's column moved into *Comancheria* from New Mexico. The Comanches and Kiowas were to be surrounded and ground down between these converging forces.

This was a military operation; the Rangers, the cowmen, the hunters, and the frontiersmen played no real part in it. The Texas Rangers, reconstituted by the first post-Reconstruction legislature in 1874, confined themselves to a defensive role. Six companies patrolled the northwest Brazos frontier, plugging the gaps between the military posts. They fought fifteen small actions in the summer of 1874. Their mission was to halt the penetration of Comanche raiders, and they did this superbly, breaking up many war parties and recovering much stolen livestock. But the Rangers left to the army the dubious glory of seeking out Quanah's Comanches in the Llano Estacado.

Mackenzie's march into the Texas Panhandle in September 1874 followed the pattern of earlier campaigns. Again it was impossible to fix and fight the Comanches in open battle. Quanah's Kwerhar-rehnuh, the hard core of Comanche resistance, shadowed his column; sometimes the cavalrymen saw the Indians circling them by moonlight. They rode out of nowhere in quick attacks, buzzing around the military bivouacs, vanishing again, as one officer said, "as if by magic." Silent arrows struck down extended pickets; the horse strings were always in peril of stampede. Mackenzie, who had forced his troopers to spend countless hours on the rifle range, placed his sharpshooters on the perimeters and flanks, and he rolled his clumsy infantry in wagons. The survival training he had initiated had toughened his black soldiers; they could endure this kind of riding and skirmishing indefinitely.

If the Comanches were more mobile and better fighters in this kind of guerrilla war, and if their repeating carbines were better weapons than the Model 1873 army single-shot carbines, which failed to extract spent cartridge cases when they grew hot from firing, the cavalry had advantages beyond its sustained purpose and discipline. The bands were now forced to carry all their women, children, and old people into the field. If they left any People on the reservation, they would be made hostages. The Comanche camps were vulnerable, and Mackenzie's strategy was to find them and to "break them up." He could resupply his forces in the field and campaign endlessly into winter. Meanwhile, continually pursued and on the run, the Comanche enemy had no time for hunting winter meat, and his bases were in constant danger.

The army had learned many years before that the only practical way it could defeat horse Indians was to search them out relentlessly, driving them across the plains until they grew hungry and demoralized, while the women tired, and the old people and infants died. If this was a war of extermination, it was a war of the tribes' choosing.

The honors went to Quanah for some weeks. Then Mackenzie forced the issue by a chain of events that never entered the official reports, but were revealed much later by his subordinates. The cavalry caught the Comanchero José Tafoya on the way to a meeting with the Indians. The colonel's actions must be measured against the fact that all Anglo-Americans in the Southwest regarded the New Mexican traders as renegades who killed white men by their gun-running to the hostiles. Mackenzie had Tafoya stretched against a wagon wheel. The Comanchero talked, revealing the general location of Quanah's hidden encampment. The main body of the bands were in the Palo Duro Canyon, a natural phenomenon of which the Americans were then unaware.

Following the Comanchero's directions, chief of scouts Lieutenant William Thompson, John Charlton, now an experienced sergeant, and a Tonkawa called Job rode out twenty-five miles from the main column. On September 27th, they came upon the lip of a vast crevasse opening in the apparently level high plateau. They crawled to the edge on hands and knees. Far below, along a stream that had cut through the earth over countless aeons, they saw hundreds of grazing ponies and a three-mile-long stand of scattered tipis. Prickly with excitement, the scouts rode back to Mackenzie, who immediately dropped his supply wagons under guard in the Tule Canyon and pushed his regiment through the night toward the Palo Duro.

The cavalry arrived at dawn. The scouts found only one trail leading to the canyon floor, a sloping passage down which the soldiers could pass only dismounted in single file, leading their horses. The enemy was in a cul-de-sac, but one that was extremely difficult to attack. Mackenzie ordered Thompson's scout detachment to go first, to spy out the passage, dispose of any sentinels, and seize a foothold on the canyon floor. Thompson, Charlton, and two dozen Tonkawa and Texan frontier scouts slipped down the trail in the gray half-light. They reached the bottom, and Beaumont's A Company of fifty troopers passed through them before the alarm was given.

Beaumont struck immediately for the Comanche horseherd. He reached it before the startled Indians, stampeding more than a thousand ponies down the canyon while yelling warriors tried to pursue on foot. Then, Mackenzie had L and H companies down and on line, and led a charge toward the tipis. But now the surprised warriors put up a splendid resistance, a covering action that allowed all the women and children to retreat down the canyon and scramble up its walls, fleeing into the surrounding plains. The slow passage of Mackenzie's regiment down the trail made it impossible for him to attack in force. Behind a hot fire, the Indians escaped, the warriors vanishing as soon as the noncombatants were clear.

Mackenzie was neither foolhardy nor vainglorious. He did not rush in among the Comanches in the rocks until his full force was assembled, and by then it was too late. When they scattered, he did not try to pursue. His men and horses had covered twenty-five miles by forced march in a few hours, and besides, he had his victory, although no one outside the army ever gave him full credit for it. He had killed only four Comanches, at the cost of several wounded, but he had captured all the Amerindian ponies, tents, and supplies. In the abandoned encampment he found tons of flour, sugar, blankets, and cured bison meat. There were also crates of new carbines and much ammunition. Mackenzie ordered everything burned. The black smoke marked the end of Quanah's hopes, as the retreating Indians saw it rise from far out on the prairie.

The captured remuda of fourteen hundred horses was a problem that Mackenzie disposed of in the only practicable way. He allowed the Tonkawa scouts to take several hundred to load the loot they filched from the camp before burning. He shot the remainder, more than a thousand, in a tremendous fusillade out on the plains. Mackenzie knew that the desperate, dehorsed warriors would make every effort to get them back as they had done in 1871, and he never forgot a lesson. There was more firing in this slaughter than at the Palo Duro Canyon fight. Then the tired, dust-grimed, and shaken soldiers rode away, leaving another funeral mound for the grieving Comanches. The thousands of horse bones lay there for many years, until an enterprising trader hauled them away for sale as fertilizer.

On the return march Charlton, who had been in the saddle for forty-eight hours, dozed and strayed. The merciless colonel snapped him alert with a snarled reprimand.

Mackenzie had destroyed Quanah and the Comanches as surely as if he had shot them with the horses. A dehorsed Plains warrior was a pitiable creature, unable to fight, unable to hunt, unable even to move across the prairie. The fleeing band, after a day or two, began to discard the few possessions the women had retrieved. When Mackenzie again took up the pursuit, the soldiers found the trail littered with abandoned Indian artifacts.

Here many of the warriors gave up. They took the long, dangerous trail back to Sill, arriving hungry and desperate, begging the agent to feed them. But Quanah and the hard core of the Kwerharrehnuh would not quit. This was their country and their life, and they would not yet abandon either to the white men. They fled deeper into the vast Llano Estacado.

Mackenzie sent his columns after them week after week, without mercy or surcease. He cut every trail, followed every scattering group, far into winter. He caught some, fighting twenty-five small actions—so small that he never bothered to report them. The Tonkawa scouts now held their last scalp dances beyond the cavalry bivouacs, shouting their victories to the autumn moon. The lords of the southern plains were no more. But the Tonkawas were no more, either; fewer than a hundred remained. In a few more years the fifty who were left would merge into the fifty-odd remaining Lipan Apaches on an Indian Territory reservation and disappear forever from the continent.

As the soldiers noted, the tribal hatreds did not vanish until the tribes themselves were gone. When, two years later, Mackenzie destroyed Dull Knife's Cheyennes in the north, he came down on a camp where the pursued warriors were celebrating a massacre of the Shoshones, whom they had stopped to raid.

Mackenzie came back to Fort Richardson in the middle of January 1875. His regiment had been in the field four months, had covered thousands of miles, and had fought two dozen actions. The Department of Texas commander believed that he had broken the Comanches so thoroughly that his talents could be used elsewhere. He was transferred to fight Cheyennes, Utes, and Apaches, and took part in the last campaigns against the Dakotas. In every campaign he served with the same efficiency, and without popularity or recognition.

The command in Texas passed to Grierson, who continued Mackenzie's policies with his own troopers of the black 10th Cavalry, and Shafter's 24th Infantry. The scouting and pursuit continued through 1875. More Comanche lodges were found and burned, more tons of meat and other supplies destroyed. To the north, Miles used the same procedures against the Cheyennes. Personally, he was one of the best friends the Plains tribes ever had; but he tried to impress upon the chiefs that unless they stopped killing and came in, there would be no mercy for them. These colonels were never Indian-haters, but they were professionals.

The Kwerhar-rehnuh and a few other small bands stayed out. The white officers knew the country now; they knew the location of all the Amerindian refuges. The bison were growing very scarce, as the hide hunting resumed, and the hostiles had few horses. By February 1875 the bands were beginning to die of hunger.

Lone Wolf and the last Kiowa warriors appeared at Fort Sill during this February, after the soldiers agreed to let them come in unmolested. One by one, all the bands except the Kwerhar-rehnuh straggled in. Some came in as families, or individuals, for even the band cohesion was cracking under mass starvation. In March, the southern Cheyennes gave up. General Pope's report read that the Cheyennes were "nearly starved to death, and in a deplorable condition." Tahbaynaneekah could not live up to his despairing boast, for he found that his wives and children could not survive on prairie dung. By April, all the bands but Quanah's had surrendered. Many Comanches died in the snows. Those who gave up were mostly those who had a strong survival urge, or who could not bear to watch their families perish.

There were now no treaties, presents, or honors. The warriors were herded into a concentration camp on Cache Creek, surrounded by fences and soldiers. Those considered most dangerous or murderous were locked in an unfinished ice house at the agency; raw meat was thrown over the walls to these prisoners once a day. All the tribesmen were disarmed. Their horses and mules were confiscated by the government. Some 7,500 head were seized. A few were given to Amerindian scouts; 5,500 were sold at auction; the rest were destroyed.

Those chiefs who had signed treaties were handled harshly. The Kiowa Set-tainte had broken parole by riding against the hide hunters; he was returned to the Texas penitentiary. This was worse than a torture death for a Plains Amerindian born on the open prairies. Set-tainte cut his wrists, but a white doctor kept him from dying. At last, he leaped from the prison roof and broke his neck. His companion Big Tree, however, was cowed by bars. He was reparoled and died on the reservation at the age of eighty, teaching in a Baptist Sunday school.

Many of the war chiefs, such as Lone Wolf, Woman's Heart, the Owl Prophet, and others, were sentenced to prison terms. A number of the Comanches, Kiowas, and Cheyennes were exiled to Florida under military guard. These measures were seen as preventive rather than punitive. After the outbreak of 1874, the army and the government were distrustful. However, the southern Plains peoples were more thoroughly broken during the hideous winter of 1874–75 than Americans believed, for the overwhelming majority of the survivors accepted the reservations apathetically. There was no need to put the chiefs in prison; most of them were soon released and, after some years, the supposed recalcitrants too were released from exile. As one Cheyenne wrote from Florida, with the help of a guard, his sons must take the white man's road, for the white men were as many as the leaves on the trees, and no one could fight them.

The diehard Kwerhar-rehnuh band lived through the winter on nuts, grubs, and rodents. They lacked horses for hunting, but they could not have hunted if they had had them. The cavalry were constantly on the plains, and the bison were vanishing. The roots of their culture had been torn up. Still, some Kwerhar-rehnuh clung to their freedom. Part of them went into the Rockies, others retreated down the Pecos River toward the Texas Big Bend country, both reverting to the skulking ways of their Shoshone ancestors. Here they might have gone on to extinction like their Apache predecessors, but the soldiers were not through with them. Sergeant Charlton and surrendered Comanches sought them out with truce flags. Charlton gave them the government's terms: the reservation, or war to the knife. He promised them that the next summer would see no survivors.

Quanah, the last and perhaps the greatest of the Comanche war chiefs, chose surrender. He gathered up all the People he could find and came into the reservation in June 1875.

The lands surrendered by Quanah's unhappy band immediately succumbed to the advancing frontier. How real the Comanche barrier had been is shown by one statistic: between 1875 and 1883 the Texas frontier advanced farther and faster than it had for forty years. The hide hunters killed the last few buffalo, while the cat-

Kwerhar-rehnuh woman, wife of Quanah Parker.
Reservation photograph, 1890s.

tlemen poured in behind them with huge herds. Charles Goodnight, at last able to move onto the rich Panhandle ranges from New Mexico, preserved a few bison on his ranch. The Canadians characteristically did more, and assured the survival of the species. Within a few months and years, the cowmen had enclosed the whole vast country; it was crossed by roads and rails, and settlement began, subjecting it to new forms of destruction. Overgrazed by hungry cattle, the endless miles of waving grasses turned into desolate stretches of arid mesquite scrub prairie. Torn by great plows, tons of rich earth were blown aloft by the strong winds, spring after spring. Each year, the wells went down deeper, tapping the stored resources of ages. The country was quickly taken and exploited by civilization, but it was still a harsh country, and man was yet but a speck upon its surface. It was possible that no matter how many migrants came or what new technologies they imported, no high order of human culture would ever sprout in the native soil of the midcontinent.

Quanah and his people surrendered unconditionally, but they were not treated harshly. Many of the colonels argued in his favor. He had killed and burned, but in the defense of his own territory. He had never sat down with any white man; therefore he had broken no promises or treaties. Even the Texans were now taking a certain pride in him. The white officers who had jurisdiction in the West respected courage as much as any Amerindian.

That respect, and his innate qualities, allowed Quanah to serve his people ably, and to make the best deals possible through successive humiliations, as the reservation was again reduced and subsidies were cut; finally, when the reservation was broken up against fervent protest, each Comanche received 160 acres of prairie soil, while the rest was opened to white settlement.

The reduction of the Comanches was complete. There were to be a few horse-stealing forays into Texas, but the wars were over. The Comanche moons rose and waned without Comanches. The surviving war chiefs abdicated; they put away their shields and war headdresses, surrendering their prestige and privileges. None of these men posed for silly pictures snapped for visiting politicans or sojourning anthropologists, got up in twentieth-century conceptions of Plains warrior dress, a melange of tribal styles with the authenticity of a drugstore Indian. If their portraits were preserved, they showed grim, naked men who stared unblinking at the camera. But in later years, beaded buckskin jackets and pseudo-Cheyenne feather bonnets became a tradition that white men expected of Comanches. They had no cultural meaning; they were distorted vestiges of a vanished culture, like the "cowboy" suits American children wore. Many years afterward, even Quanah posed thus for the camera.

The band structures cracked open. There was no longer any need for bands, since there was no more community on the white man's road or in the white man's houses. Families tended to separate. But the People felt that something was terribly lacking, and while they found no substitute for the old life of the spirit and the communion of the dance and campfire, they found some solace in peyote, which they learned from the Apaches.

There was no peyote cult before the surrender. The People had never used drugs systematically before, but now they had a desperate need for something like peyote. Unlike alcohol, peyote was not physically destructive, or even addictive. It was a hallucinogen, but unlike the war dance or the lonely vigil, its visions were gentle and stupefying, bringing euphoria instead of inciting violence. In the peyote circle the warriors could capture all that was possible to an Amerindian still yearning for his magic, and in addition to peace and relaxation, peyote created an illusion, as they sat together and joined in the experience, of a spiritual communion with each other. The People were few, beset, broken, and humiliated, but with peyote they felt less at the mercy of a world they no longer believed in, and less frightened and alone.

The peyote cult made the world more bearable. How desperate the need was is shown by the declining numbers of the tribe. In August 1875, 1,597 Comanches of all kinds were enrolled at the Cache Creek agency, with some fifty unaccounted for. One in twelve had survived the previous twenty-five years. Disease still ravaged them, especially the pure-blooded Amerindians. By 1884, there would be only 1,382 despite many births, and by 1910, only 1,171, despite the maturing of a new generation. By 1910, the pure-blood Nermernuh were disappearing; half the survivors had American or Mexican blood. The anthropologist Marcus S. Goldstein, in 1931, estimated that only ten percent of the true Nermernuh remained. There were about three thousand "Comanches" around

*Comanche mother and child, twentieth century. Baby is swaddled
in traditional buckskin carrier.*
Photograph by Edward S. Curtis.

Lawton, Oklahoma, in the middle of the twentieth century, but by then the term was racially and culturally meaningless. Very few Amerindians on the tribal rolls in the former Indian Territory were any longer "Indian," though they were not yet quite "American." They were caught between two worlds, neither of which was truly hospitable to them. Yet there was hope in the gradual assimilation, far more in the Indian Territory than in other more remote places where it had failed to take place. The descendants of Quanah Parker in the fourth generation held regular reunions with the Parker clan of Texas over the graves of Quanah, Topsannah, and Cynthia Ann, and both branches now found pride in their interwoven destiny.

To miss the meaning of this was to miss such meaning as there was in the whole Comanche tragedy. New peoples, new cultures, sprouted from the graves of the old.

NO TRANSITION COMES EASILY. WHAT WAS DEMANDED OF THE Comanches upon surrender was that they traverse eighty centuries overnight. The change was too great; many of them could not even take a single step toward it. They had been raised to the thrills of the hunt and war, and the savage freedoms of the prairies. Most of the People tried to hold on to their old world, even as they sat among its ruins.

They wanted to hunt. The four pounds of beef per week the agent gave them in hard winters (it was usually much less) never satisfied their hunger. They also needed bison hides, for most hunter-warriors detested American clothing. They wanted the garments their women sewed. And extra skins meant money, a strange new magic the Amerindians were discovering, for they could be sold to traders. A pass had to be secured before they could leave the agency, and because some hunters raided in Texas—not bloodily, but they could not resist the horses—the army officers stopped their passes.

The men besieged the new agent, P. B. Hunt. Hunt was sympathetic; he battled with the military for the passes. Finally, he arranged that the tribe could have a pass for a hunt in the fall of 1878. All could go, provided a small military escort went with them. _____

Comanche man, twentieth century.
Photograph by Edward S. Curtis.

When the time came, all the agency Comanches prepared joyously for the journey. They recalled the buffalo medicine and the buffalo dances; the old men told the young boys how it would be, and they all sighed for the taste of marrow bones. Men who had given up stirred again to new purpose, boasting how they had killed the bison in the old days, just years ago. Neither the agent nor the army acted with intentional cruelty, setting the Indians on this expedition. They believed it would be good for them.

Fifteen hundred Comanches went eagerly onto the plains to the west. The scouts were sent out, riding miles ahead. The band watched the skies for hours, but no smoke signals came. The scouts came in hungry, rode out again. They had seen no buffalo, only bones. Everywhere, the white skulls stretched across the plains in ghastly profusion. The hunters scouted every creek and stream bed, every stand of trees. They rode for days and miles. They killed a few antelope and other animals, but never enough meat to provide more than a morsel for the hungry host waiting expectantly in the tipis.

The pessimistic said there would be no buffalo, no meat, no winter robes. The issue food was running short; it was time to turn back. But the old men said no. The buffalo would come when the leaves fell, as they had always come when the leaves were driven by the strong north winds, pouring in their millions onto the southern ranges. But when the plains lay white with frost, the horizons were still empty. The women complained and the children cried. The hunters made more medicine. They prayed to the buffalo spirit, to the winds, and to their secret guardians. The north winds now howled off the roof of the world; the grass rattled throughout the night; there came a smell of snow in the air.

The time allotted for the hunting pass expired. But the officer in charge of the escort said, Let the Indians be. The white soldiers themselves watched the horizons, dimly aware of some half-understood enormity. Families began to desert the camp, trudging dispiritedly toward Cache Creek for the flour, sugar, and rice they knew awaited them. The oldest and the greatest hunter-warriors still rode the plains, searching. They saw nothing but bones, and they sat staring into the campfires.

The snow came, and the food ran out. Several of the hunters killed their ponies for meat.

The Indian agent did not understand Comanches, nor could he really feel what was happening to their souls. But hungry children troubled him. He sent emissaries, with wagons of food, out to the prairie. When these arrived, the Comanches were sitting in their tipis in a snow storm. They were starving. They accepted the food sullenly and listened to the agent's request that they come back to the reservation, where they would be cared for by the government.

The last hunt camp was broken. The tipis were struck, the bows and lances put away. Then, in a long, silent column, the Comanches left the graveyard plains, returning to the agency for the completion of their destruction.

SELECTED BIBLIOGRAPHY

MAJOR SOURCES

MSS

MSS Office of Commissioner of Indian Affairs, 1829–55. Agents' Reports. (Indian Archives.)
Texas Indian Papers, Archives.

DOCUMENTS

Commissioner of Indian Affairs. Annual Reports, 1830–75.
American State Papers. Class II, Indian Affairs. Class V, Military Affairs.
Smithsonian Miscellaneous Collection, Indian Affairs.
War of the Rebellion: Official Records of the Union and Confederate Armies. Washington, 1881–1902.

PERIODICALS

Extensive use has been made of monographs and studies published in the *American Anthropologist, Chronicles of Oklahoma, Missouri Historical Review, Southwestern Historical Quarterly, Southwestern Journal of Anthropology*, and monographs of the American Ethnological Society.

PUBLICATIONS

Atkinson, M. J. *The Texan Indians*. San Antonio, 1935.
———. *Indians of the Southwest*. San Antonio, 1958.
Bancroft, Hubert H. *History of Arizona and New Mexico*. Vol. XVII, *Works*. San Francisco, 1889.
Berlandie, Jean Louis. *The Indians of Texas in 1830*. Transl. by Patricia R. Leclercq. Washington, 1969.
Boas, Frank. *Handbook of American Indian Languages*. Washington, 1911–12.
Bolton, Herbert E. *Athanase de Mézières and the Louisiana-Texas Frontier 1768–1780*. (2 vols.) Cleveland, 1914.
———. *Texas in the Middle Eighteenth Century*. Berkeley, 1915.

555

Brown, John H. *Indian Wars and Pioneers of Texas.* Austin, 1890.

Carter, Robert G. *The Old Sergeant's Story.* New York, 1926.

———. *On the Border with Mackenzie.* Washington, 1935.

Catlin, George. *North American Indians.* (2 vols.) Edinburgh, 1926.

Cook, John R. *The Border and the Buffalo.* Topeka (Kans.), 1907.

Curtis, Edward S. *The North American Indian.* (20 vols.) Norwood (Mass.), 1930.

De Shields, J. J. *Border Wars of Texas.* Tioga (Tex.), 1912.

Dobie, J. Frank. *The Mustangs.* Boston, 1952.

Dodge, Richard I. *Our Wild Indians.* Hartford (Conn.), 1882.

Fehrenbach, T. R. *Lone Star: A History of Texas and the Texans.* New York, 1968.

———. *Fire and Blood: A History of Mexico.* New York, 1973.

Foreman, Grant. *Pioneer Days in the Early Southwest.* Cleveland, 1926.

Garretson, Martin S. *The American Bison.* New York, 1938.

Glisan, Rodney. *Journal of Army Life.* San Francisco, 1874.

Grinnell, George B. *The Story of the Indian.* London, 1896.

———. *The Fighting Cheyennes.* New York, 1915.

Gulich, Charles A. (ed.) *The Papers of Mirabeau Buonaparte Lamar.* (6 vols.) Austin, 1920–27.

Hackett, Charles W. (ed.) *Historical Documents Relating to New Mexico, Nueva Vizcaya, and Approaches Thereto, to 1773.* Washington, 1923–37.

Hodge, Frederick W. (ed.) *Handbook of American Indians North of Mexico.* (2 vols.) Washington, 1907, 1912.

Hornaday, W. T. *The Extermination of the American Bison* (Annual Report, Smithsonian Institution.) Washington, 1887.

House, E. (ed.) *A Narrative of the Captivity of Mrs. Horn and Her Two Children with That of Mrs. Harris by the Commanche Indians.* St. Louis, 1839.

Inman, Henry. *The Old Santa Fe Trail.* Topeka (Kans.), 1899.

Jenkins, John H., III. (ed.) *Recollections of Early Texas.* Austin, 1958.

Jones, Jonathan H. *A Condensed History of the Apache and Comanche Indian Tribes.* San Antonio, 1899.

Keim, Randolph de B. *Sheridan's Troopers on the Border.* Philadelphia, 1885.

Kroeber, Alfred L. *Cultural and Natural Areas of Native North America.* Berkeley, 1947.

Lee, Nelson. *Three Years Among the Commanches.* Albany, 1859.

Lehmann, Herman. *Nine Years Among the Indians (1870–79).* Austin, 1927.

Linton, Ralph. *The Study of Man.* New York, 1936.

Manypenny, George W. *Our Indian Wards.* Cincinnati, 1880.

Marcy, Randolph B. *Thirty Years of Army Life on the Border.* New York, 1866.

Mayhall, Mildred P. *Indian Wars of Texas.* Waco (Tex.), 1965.

Neighbors, Robert S. *The Naüni or Comanches of Texas* (in *Information Respecting the History, Conditions, and Prospects of the Indian Tribes of the United States,* Office of Indian Affairs). Philadelphia, 1853.

Newcomb, W. W., Jr. *The Indians of Texas.* Austin, 1961.

Nye, Wilbur S. *Carbine and Lance: The Story of Old Fort Sill.* Norman (Okla.), 1937.

Oates, Stephen B. (ed.) *Rip Ford's Texas.* Austin, 1963.

Otis, Elwell S. *The Indian Question*. New York, 1878.

Parker, John W. (ed.) *The Rachel Plummer Narrative*. Privately printed, 1926.

Richardson, Rupert N. *The Comanche Barrier to South Plains Settlement*. Glendale (Calif.), 1933.

————. *The Frontier of Northwest Texas 1846–1876*. Glendale (Calif.), 1963.

Rister, Carl C. *Border Captives*. Norman (Okla.), 1940.

Roe, Frank G. *The Indian and the Horse*. Norman (Okla.), 1955.

Smithwick, Noah. *The Evolution of a State . . .* Austin, 1900.

Tatum, Lawrie. *Our Red Brothers and the Peace Policy of President Ulysses S. Grant*. Philadelphia, 1889.

Thomas, Alfred B. *Forgotten Frontiers: A Study of the Spanish Indian Policy of Don Juan Bautista de Anza, Governor of New Mexico*. Norman (Okla.), 1932.

Twitchell, Ralph E. *Spanish Archives of New Mexico*. (2 vols.) Cedar Rapids (Iowa), 1914.

Wallace, Ernest, and Hoebel, E. Adamson. *The Comanches, Lords of the South Plains*. Norman (Okla.), 1952.

Webb, Walter P. *The Great Plains*. New York, 1931.

————. *The Texas Rangers: A Century of Frontier Defense*. Austin, 1935.

Wilbarger, J. W. *Indian Depredations in Texas*. Austin, 1889.

Wissler, Clark. *North American Indians of the Plains*. New York, 1927.

Yoakum, Henderson K. *History of Texas*. New York, 1856.

INDEX

Note: Italicized page numbers indicate illustrations.

A NOTE ABOUT THE AUTHOR

T. R. Fehrenbach was born in San Benito, Texas, in 1925. He attended public schools in Texas and California and was graduated *magna cum laude* from Princeton University in 1947. He has been a contributor to many different publications, including *Esquire, The Atlantic, The Saturday Evening Post, Analog,* and *The New Republic,* and is the author of, among other works, the best-selling *Lone Star: A History of Texas and the Texans* (1968) and *Fire and Blood* (1973), a history of Mexico. Mr. Fehrenbach and his wife live in San Antonio, Texas.

Other titles of interest

THE GREAT SIOUX UPRISING
C. M. Oehler
292 pp., 6 illus., 6 maps
80759-9 $14.95

GERONIMO
Alexander B. Adams
381 pp., 18 illus.
80394-1 $14.95

**THE LIFE OF GENERAL
ALBERT SIDNEY JOHNSTON
His Services in the Armies of the
United States, the Republic of
Texas, and the Confederate States**
Colonel William Preston Johnston
New introd. by T. Michael Parrish
807 pp., 9 illus., 9 maps
80791-2 $19.95

**THE GREAT WEST
A Treasury of Firsthand
Accounts**
Edited by Charles Neider
460 pp., 94 illus., 3 maps
80761-0 $22.95

**POCAHONTAS
The Life and the Legend**
Frances Mossiker
424 pp., 28 illus.
80699-1 $15.95

**PERSONAL MEMOIRS OF
P. H. SHERIDAN**
New introd. by Jeffry D. Wert
560 pp., 16 illus., 16 maps
80487-5 $15.95

**CRIMSONED PRAIRIE
The Indian Wars**
S. L. A. Marshall
270 pp., 20 photos
80226-0 $12.95

**THE DISCOVERY AND
CONQUEST OF MEXICO**
Bernal Díaz del Castillo
Translated by A. P. Maudslay
New introduction by
Hugh Thomas
512 pp., 33 illus., 2 maps
80697-5 $16.95

**THE ENCYCLOPEDIA OF
COLONIAL AND
REVOLUTIONARY AMERICA**
Edited by John Mack Faragher
494 pp., 126 illus. & maps
80687-8 $24.50

**GREAT DOCUMENTS IN
AMERICAN INDIAN HISTORY**
Edited by Wayne Moquin with
Charles Van Doren
New foreword by Dee Brown
458 pp., 20 illus., 5 maps
80659-2 $16.95

**ENCYCLOPEDIA OF WESTERN
LAWMEN & OUTLAWS**
Jay Robert Nash
581 pp., 530 illus.
80591-X $27.50

**FIRE AND BLOOD
A History of Mexico
Updated Edition**
T. R. Fehrenbach
687 pp., 1 map
80628-2 $18.95

**MONTCALM AND WOLFE
The French and Indian War**
Francis Parkman
Foreword by C. Vann Woodward
674 pp., 116 illus., 9 maps
80621-5 $18.95

Available at your bookstore

OR ORDER DIRECTLY FROM 1-800-386-5656

VISIT OUR WEBSITE AT WWW.PERSEUSBOOKSGROUP.COM